KING OF COMEDY

KING OF COMEDY

THE LIFE AND ART
OF JERRY LEWIS

SHAWN LEVY

ST. MARTIN'S PRESS ✿ NEW YORK

Book design by Gretchen Achilles

Library of Congress Cataloging-in-Publication Data

Levy, Shawn.
    King of comedy : the life and art of Jerry Lewis / by Shawn Levy.
  —1st ed.
       p.   cm.
    ISBN 0-312-13248-4
    1. Lewis, Jerry, 1926–.   2. Comedians—United States—Biography.
  I. Title
  PN2287.L435L47   1996
  791.43'028'092—dc20
    [B]   95-4091
                                                                          CIP

First Edition: April 1996

10   9   8   7   6   5   4   3   2   1

To my father, Jerome Sanford Levy,
who always knew it could happen

Contents

Prologue

I have never been able to develop a façade to hide behind. My emotions function on a separate wire. I can stand toe to toe with two oxes and never know I'm hurt until I'm picked up bleeding. But if a guy doesn't say good morning back, I can have a heart attack. I'm more than just a great movie star. I'm also a neurotic, temperamental imbecile.

—Jerry Lewis, 1963

For almost half a century, America has had more of Jerry Lewis than it has known what to do with. Indeed, it has had more *Jerry Lewises* than it has known what to do with.

His life has been a continuous parade of public and private faces; some the world has loved, while others have been almost universally loathed. The arc of his life and career—from live-wire life of the party to openly angry once-was—holds a dark fascination for anyone interested in America, our popular culture or the psychology of celebrity.

Few entertainers have shed so many skins in public as Jerry Lewis. The first was Jerry the Skinny Young Maniac, who bounced into the American consciousness in 1948 alongside the impeccably disengaged Dean Martin. Eight years later, after the shattering split of Martin and Lewis, emerged Jerry the Consummate Showman, singing Al Jolson songs and acting in sentimental films. With the early 1960s came Jerry the Total Filmmaker, a movie director who strove for the acclaim enjoyed by Charles Chaplin but found an attuned audience only in Europe. Presently, Jerry the Philanthropist was born, cajoling Americans into writing checks for muscular dystrophy research each Labor Day. Since the mid-

1970s, a quixotically short-tempered Jerry the Elder Statesman has become familiar, barking out his belligerent claims to greatness in movies, TV shows, and magazine interviews.

And the cadences of this evolution echo our own history. No American entertainer embodied the fate of the nation since World War II more succinctly: the giddy surplus of the postwar years; the arrogant confidence of the Fifties; the incomprehensible unraveling of the Sixties and Seventies; and our subsequent struggle to reclaim a lost mantle and place blame for the downfall. It's no coincidence that the most triumphant moment of Jerry's career—the debut of his greatest film, the mounting of a national tour in support of it, and an unprecedented wave of expectation for an innovative new TV series—came just weeks before the death of John Kennedy. Soon after, along with the dissolution of the national consensus, came the marginalization of the Court Jester of Camelot.

Jerry's reflection of the national soul has been his blessing and, in recent decades, his curse. More than any entertainer of his generation, he became a lightning rod for ridicule, the butt of quick laughs at the expense of charity telethons, French intellectuals, or physical comedy. The very thought of his voice, his comic style, or his movies provokes uncomfortable, snide laughter in many quarters.

Yet love it or hate it, Jerry's best work is the product of a completely unique comic sensibility. A gifted mimic, he studied a curious mixture of estimable predecessors, from whose work he was able to glean various tropes. Jerry's comedy evinces some of the Dadaist mania of Harpo Marx, the audience-beseeching brashness of Al Jolson, the gentle, fluent timing of Stan Laurel, the impish meekness of Charles Chaplin, the brassy childishness of Fanny Brice, and the grotesque mercuriality of the lamentably underrated Harry Ritz, whose goo-goo eyes, vocal gymnastics, and wild body language also informed much of Sid Caesar's art.

Jerry's gift, of course, was that he could allude to so many different comedic and performing styles while maintaining his air of organic ease. The young Jerry Lewis was a pyrotechnic wonder, a font of gibberish, voices, and caterwauls, a living Gumby doll, a bouncing Super Ball. He was so fast and natural that he made it look elementary, but it wasn't: Today, the undeniably agile Jim Carrey wows audiences and scoops up $20 million per film with a pale imitation of Jerry, a demeaning act with no taste, no soul, no center. Even at its crassest—and it could be crass and enobling within minutes—Jerry's comedy tried to be about the human spirit. It just happened to be the human spirit of a truly excitable boy.

It's no wonder, then, that he's among the most influential and imitated figures in the history of comedy. Many of the biggest comedy stars of the Seventies (Woody Allen, Richard Pryor, Robin Williams, Chevy Chase, Steve Martin, Andy Kaufman), Eighties (Martin Short, Eddie Murphy, Bill Murray, Pee Wee

Herman), and Nineties (Jim Carrey, Pauly Shore, Adam Sandler) can trace their comic roots directly back to the Jerry Lewis of the Forties, Fifties, and Sixties. He single-handedly created a style of humor that was half anarchy, half excruciation. Even comics who never took a pratfall in their careers owe something to the self-deprecation Jerry introduced into American show business.

It's easy to see why he was so influential. His career is absolutely unparalleled: He was one of the last, and probably the biggest, of the Borscht Belt comedians; one of the last performers to pass from the variety stage to film and television; half of the most popular two-man performing act of all time; the uncontested premier practitioner of physical comedy during most of his career; the first director who debuted in talkies to direct himself; the first Jewish comedian to direct himself; a technological innovator in the cinema; a Top Ten recording artist; the highest-paid performer in Hollywood; the highest-paid performer on network television—a catalog of feats he accomplished before turning forty. When he turned his attention to philanthropy after his entertaining career began to wane, he raised well over $1 billion. In the annals of show business, he bridges the gap in screen comedy between Charlie Chaplin and Woody Allen, on television between Milton Berle on "Texaco Star Theater" and John Belushi on "Saturday Night Live," on the stage between Al Jolson and Lenny Bruce. He met nine Presidents and performed for more than half of them. He was nominated for a Nobel Peace Prize. There is no other story remotely like it.

And yet, despite its uniqueness, Jerry's career constitutes a cultural history of American show business. One of the last performers to pass through the closing doors of burlesque comedy and Borscht Belt showmanship, Jerry would always carry traces of those bygone forms in his art; indeed, Jerry's entire career has been a version of Saturday night in a Catskills hotel, a series of variety acts strung together by an adrenalized emcee. But Jerry Lewis has never been a nostalgia-monger; his combination of slapstick comedy, traditional Jewish humor, and vaudeville brashness has always been startlingly modern. From the debut of Martin and Lewis, his was a groundbreaking act—tearing up stages and sets, breaking through the fourth wall of the TV and movie screens, skewering the conventions of show business even while dutifully emulating them.

In almost every medium at which he tried his hand—nightclubs, film, television, charity broadcasts—he has had a lasting impact. It can be put quite bluntly: American show business would simply not be the same today if Jerry Lewis had taken up another line of work.

In movies especially he was a pioneer. Many important stars of the late studio era produced some of their own works; but where John Wayne and Kirk Douglas (to name two) were only nominally producers, hiring other people to do the day-to-day work, Jerry ran his production company with obsessively minute control. Likewise, where actors such as Charles Laughton and James Cagney dilettantishly directed a film apiece in their ebbing years, Jerry started directing himself regularly in 1960, at the height of his career, reaching a position of artistic control that no one else in talking comedies had achieved besides Charles Chaplin (and that no other would until 1969, when Woody Allen took the director's chair for *Take the Money and Run* only after learning that Jerry was unavailable).

As a director, Jerry filled his works with radical experiments in sound, editing, decor, cinematography, even plotting. His movies—with their spare, modernist sets, their brightly colored furnishings and wardrobes, their brassy swing scores, their purely cinematic jokes, their aural and physical impossibilities, their meditations on multiple personality and childhood pain—constitute as coherent a body of work as that of any comedy director in history. The plots of his films have become standards: It's no exaggeration to say that almost every film comedian in his wake—from Peter Sellers to Whoopi Goldberg—has made a Jerry Lewis film.

He's even had an ineradicable impact on the worlds of science and philanthropy. Before he took the cause of muscular dystrophy as his own and worked so feverishly to make the public aware of the ravages of neuromuscular disease, telethons were occasional amusements; no one had ever heard the words "poster child" or "Jerry's kids." In addition to making an ignorant world aware of the nature and scope of muscular dystrophy, he turned televised fund-raising into a universal practice and the show-biz telethon into a global cultural institution.

Of course, there is more to the Jerry Lewis story than a list of public accomplishments. It's the story as well of a private man: the only child of small-time show people, a lonely kid who dropped out of school to follow his parents onto the stage, a lovesick teenager who proposed marriage to every girl he was sweet on, a puppy dog who convinced the heppest cat in New York to take him on as a partner, a young comic who made Hollywood his rumpus room, a budding businessman, an ambitious artist, a self-serving partner, a tyrannical boss, a mercurial husband and father, a sentimentalist, a bully, a guru, a boor. At times, this nonfictional person matches up with the various guises by which his public knew him. But just as often, the links between the man and the media image are fogged over or too repressed ever to come to light.

Jerry acknowledged all of the conflicts of his life—the gaps between Jester, Thinker, and Private Man. He, more than anyone, knew that behind the clown, the showman, the director, and the philanthropist stood another person altogether—the "real" Jerry Lewis. Always introspective, always open in discussing himself, a dabbler in psychology and an autodidact with a taste for aphorism, he relished the notion of presenting more than one persona to his public. In 1984, he posed for a photograph with half his face in clown makeup and the other half at rest in humorless stolidity; if this book attempts to decipher anything, it's that imperceptible line where the mask ends and the man begins.

Though it's sometimes hard to remember, if not believe, Jerry Lewis was the most profoundly creative comedian of his generation—and arguably one of the two or three most influential comedians born anywhere in this century. He once claimed to have been one of the ten most recognized people on the planet—and at moments during his life, that was true. Nearing his seventieth year, he made such a hit in a revival of *Damn Yankees* that he became the highest-paid actor in Broadway history, in a late-life resurgence even more miraculous than his initial ascension. As 1995 closed and he took *Yankees* on the road, he had become the Tony Bennett of physical comedy, a retro-chic act with plenty of miles left in it and a whole new audience to entertain. The only career like it in this American century, with its five-decade cycle of acmes, nadirs, rebirths, and reevaluations, is that of Richard Nixon.

Chronicling Jerry Lewis's professional life reveals just how vital his contributions to the culture have been; detailing his private life reveals the roots of some of those contributions. But by looking simultaneously at his work, his life, and the strange, thrilling spaces in between, it's also possible to contemplate the forces that drive anybody to love or hate or laugh or cry or work or suffer or scream—to see Jerry Lewis as a neglected linchpin in show business, yes, but to see him as a human being as well.

KING OF COMEDY

1.

Eight Hundred Mamas and Papas

Like many stories, this one begins with a mystery—a secret identity.

As every article, book, encyclopedia entry, press release, or other account of his life would have it, Jerry Lewis was born Joseph Levitch on March 16, 1926, at Clinton Private Hospital in Newark, New Jersey.

The 1982 autobiography *Jerry Lewis in Person* states that Danny and Rae Levitch (who used the stage name Lewis) gave their only child the name Joseph in honor of the boy's maternal grandfather, following the Ashkenazi tradition of naming a newborn child after a recently deceased relative. That boy chose the name Jerry Lewis, the book explains, when he quit school at the age of sixteen to enter show business—Lewis after his father's stage name, Jerry because he didn't want to be confused with the comic Joe E. Lewis or the heavyweight champion Joe Louis.

So for decades, the name Jerry Lewis has been presented to the public as a guise, masking the child Joseph Levitch beneath it. But the Newark, New Jersey, Bureau of Vital Statistics has no record of a Joseph Levitch, or Lewis, being born on March 16, 1926. What it does have, however, is record of one *Jerome* Levitch, born to Daniel Levitch and Rae Brodsky on that date. Although everyone knew him as Joseph or Joey when he was growing up, and although he would jokingly bill himself as Joe Levitch in cameo bits decades later, his name was properly Jerry from the day of his birth.

The matter of Jerry Lewis's real name is no earth-shattering revelation, but it does raise the slippery question of personal identity in this life of shifting guises. And it further suggests the difficulty in establishing a sure chronicle of the comedian's young life. Lewis has always depicted his childhood as a desperate, neurotic struggle with abandonment, friendlessness, deprivation, and Nazis, turning his early life into a kind of explanation of the strange course of his career. But the person upon whom the burden of that childhood fell—Joey Levitch—

was, in more than one sense, a fictional character. In effect, Jerry's recollections of his own childhood can't always be trusted; not only is their protagonist someone who never exactly existed, but like many public figures, he has given so many contradictory accounts of it that there's little that's known for sure.

The most complete tellings of Jerry's life up until now—Richard Gehman's *That Kid* (1964), Arthur Marx's *Everybody Loves Somebody Sometime (Especially Himself)* (1973), and Robert Benayoun's *Bonjour, Monsieur Lewis* (1973)—rely on a single, highly inexact source for the comic's early biography: a 1957 article in *Look* magazine that Jerry "wrote" with Bill Davidson entitled "I've Always Been Scared." As with the name Joseph Levitch, a little probing casts doubts on many of the details in that article.

Take one incident as an example. In *Look* Jerry told Davidson that the death of Sarah Rothberg, his maternal grandmother and the woman who raised him, was the most horrible episode of his young life. Sarah had been immobilized by a diabetic condition that had caused an infection in her leg. She was taken to Irvington General Hospital, just up the hill from her home, and emergency surgery was performed. From the kitchen of her empty house, a preteen Jerry could see the blue light outside the operating room—a signal used by the hospital to let people know that surgery was in progress.

Davidson records Jerry's dramatic memory of that evening: "Then, suddenly, the blue light went out. I rushed to the phone and called the hospital. I asked the operator at the hospital, 'Could you please tell me the condition of my grandmother, Mrs. Rothberg?' The operator said, 'Your grandmother just expired, sir.' I said, 'But I don't know what that means. Does it mean she's all right?' The operator asked, 'How old are you, sir?' I replied, 'I'm eleven.' She said, 'I'm sorry, son, but your grandmother just passed away.' "

Powerful stuff. But compare it with Jerry's next account of the event, the one he gave in his autobiography twenty-five years later. In that version, the blue surgery light on the third floor of the hospital has transformed into "a red light . . . above the emergency entrance." When the frightened boy called the hospital, he used not the name of her then-husband, Sam Rothberg, but rather her first married name, Brodsky. And the tragedy transpired, so he said, in the weeks following his bar mitzvah, when he would've been thirteen, not eleven.

So when *did* Sarah Rothberg die? According to another of her grandsons, Marshall Katz, it was sometime after the autumn of 1940, when Jerry was at least fourteen. Katz was overseas in the army when his grandmother died; his family didn't even tell him about her passing until he returned home after the war, so worried were they about how he might take the blow. And when did Katz enlist? "October 20, 1940," he recalled immediately when asked more than fifty years later. "I'll never forget that date."

■　■　■

Of course, there are roots to Jerry's story buried so deep that only their vague outlines are clear. Among them are his family's in the steppes of the Ukraine.

Jerry's family, like those of so many of his Jewish peers in the entertainment business, was part of the mass migration of Eastern European Jews to the United States at the end of the nineteenth century. Russia's Czar Alexander III, long annoyed by the presence of unassimilated Jews in his country, loosed his troops on their villages in 1881. The Jews took to their heels, and many of those who made it found their heels led them to America. Along with Jews from Poland, Romania, and Austria-Hungary, they teemed across the ocean for decades until a beleaguered United States finally shut the door to prevent the onslaught of immigration caused by World War I.

It was no trickle. In the forty years preceding 1880, fewer than forty-two thousand Russians were admitted to the United States; in the four decades following the pogroms of 1881, more than 3.25 million Russian immigrants sought refuge on American soil, the vast majority of them Jews. As it had to the members of British sects in the seventeenth century, America promised religious freedom and a fresh economic start to persecuted Jews. Most were peasants with little formal education and a way of life that hadn't changed appreciably in centuries. They came not in search of opportunity but out of desperation. And they flew toward the light with only the vaguest conception of the world to which they were headed.

The well-worn tales of immigrant passage—the larcenous shipping agents, the miserable, typhus-ridden boats, the anti-Semitism of Ellis Island inspectors, the shock of freedom in a nation more modern than anything they'd known—were told around tables on both sides of Jerry's family. Hannah and Morris Levitch, Jerry's paternal grandparents, arrived in the United States from Russia in 1897, a letter from a Jewish immigrant aid association in hand. Jerry's maternal grandparents, Joseph and Sarah Brodsky, had been literally chased out of their Russian village during the anti-Semitic massacres of 1903, hieing to America with their young daughters, Jean and Rose, in tow.

The two couples fit perfectly the typical immigrant mold: young, married, capable of skilled labor (the Brodskys were tailors), and seeking permanent settlement in America. Additionally, they possessed a certain level of cultural refinement. Morris Levitch, a gnomish man with a devotion to scripture, was remembered by his grandson Jerry as a vintner and by Jerry's wife, Patti, as a rabbi; Joseph Brodsky had a lifelong dream of becoming a concert pianist and eventually installed an upright Steinway in his house so his children could share his passion.

Like countless new arrivals before them, the Levitches and the Brodskys settled into Jewish neighborhoods in large eastern cities. The Levitches found a home in New York City's Lower East Side, the Brodskys in Newark's Prince

Street district. In these crowded environments, both couples flourished. The Levitches had two children: Daniel, born in 1902, and then a daughter, Gertrude. The Brodskys added two more girls: Rachel ("Rae") in 1904 and then Elizabeth, whom the family always knew as "Buhddie" (which rhymes with "goody"). Eventually, both families were able to leave the hard streets of the inner cities for the relative comforts of outlying boroughs. The Levitches moved to the Brownsville section of Brooklyn in 1904, settling at 73 Grafton Street; the Brodskys moved to Weequeeg in Newark, a district of working-class Jewish families (it would one day produce the writer Philip Roth), and later to Irvington, another Jewish neighborhood even farther removed from the railroad flats of the city.

The Brownsville of Daniel Levitch's childhood was much like the familiar Lower East Side of Manhattan: streets filled with pushcarts, trolleys, peddlers, and urchins, ethnic Jewish shops, and storefront synagogues with signs in Yiddish and English. Danny attended P.S. 156—a fact that casts some doubt on Patti Lewis's memory that Danny's father was a rabbi. Danny was certainly no scholar; by the time he was of high school age, he'd quit school entirely. He worked a string of jobs on Pitkin Avenue, Brownsville's main artery, and with neither business contacts nor scholastic ambitions, he ambled into a wide-open future.

At the very least, he knew he didn't want to follow his father's path. Morris Levitch spent his days toiling in a basement, crushing grapes to make sweet kosher wine, which he sold by the glass and jug to other Old World Jews who'd made the disorienting passage to America. In the remote obscurity of the Ukraine, Morris's was probably a noble profession; five miles from Times Square, it must have seemed to his Americanized son like oblivion.

Danny would have to look elsewhere for a horizon, and soon enough he found it. The story goes like this: One day he bought a ticket to a local vaudeville house and was thunderstruck. Danny Levitch saw his own future, and it was wearing blackface. What he'd seen was a performance by Al Jolson, and instantly he knew what he wanted to do with his life.

So many decades have passed, so many fashions in the entertainment business have bloomed and shriveled, that it might seem ludicrous to us that a hale and capable young man would find himself drawn to Jolson as a role model. But in the late 1910s Jolson was absolutely the most dynamic and successful act in the business. And he had enormous appeal for show-biz aspirants of backgrounds similar to his own.

Jolson was himself an immigrant, born Asa Yoelson in Lithuania in 1886. His father, Rabbi Moshe Reuben Yoelson, left the family for America in the late 1880s; when he'd secured a position with a congregation in Washington, D.C., he sent for them all to join him. Asa was seven when he made the grueling journey.

Like Jacob Rabinowitz, the character he played in *The Jazz Singer*, Jolson was brought up in a household that clung to Old World traditions and looked with skepticism on entertainment as a means of livelihood. But unlike Rabinowitz (who anglicized his name to Jack Robin), Jolson never attempted to tread a fine line between his father's world of piety and his own of greasepaint, chorus girls, and footlights. He was a whole-hog performer, not just a trouper but showbiz incarnate.

Once he'd become a star, the traditional bounds of the entertainment media of the day couldn't contain him. Stout and virile, with a warbling voice and a vibrant whistle, Jolson dominated every stage he took. His Broadway shows were loosely constructed, allowing him maximum leeway for comic improvisations, interpolated songs, encores of well-received numbers, even extemporaneous forays into and conversations with the audience. He would literally exhaust the crowd: taking requests, ad-libbing lyrics to popular songs to reflect the mood of the evening, teasing people who went to the bathroom. His bottomless store of energy and unmitigated desire to please his audience angered his fellow entertainers, none of whom could face a crowd after Jolson had wrung it dry for an hour.

The management of Broadway's Winter Garden Theater, home to Jolson's greatest successes, built a runway to extend the stage out into the orchestra seats to bring Jolson even closer to his audience. Penetrating the crowd on this ramp, Jolson generated an aura of excitement unlike any the business had known before. It's easy to read into Jolson's freneticism a desperation to assimilate, to join the gentile mass of the New World. Jolson's success on stage, screen, radio, and phonograph was a triumph unimaginable for the son of an Orthodox clergyman. Asa Yoelson had won over the goyim, and so long as he could caper up and down that magical riser, he could be a celebrant at his own acceptance into American society. The applause of American audiences scoured the Old World from his skin, and he emerged as a new kind of performer, a fully assimilated Jewish American Prince of Show Biz.

Jolson dazzled audiences of all ethnic compositions, but his act was especially appealing to Jews. They knew that the immigrant story—a primal upheaval early in life followed by a long quest for acceptance by a large, suspicious public—was at the core of Jolson's hunger for applause. Jolson's career became a kind of hallmark of the American Jewish experience, especially in the eyes of those who followed him to the stage. A throng of important Jewish show people emerged soon after Jolson: Eddie Cantor, Sophie Tucker, George Jessel, George Burns, Fanny Brice, the Marx Brothers, the Ritz Brothers, Jack Benny, and Milton Berle most famous among them. (Even a Lebanese Christian like Detroit's Danny Thomas, who grew up among Jews, was sucked up by Jolie's example, breaking in as a Yiddish dialect comic.) Like Jolson—and decidedly unlike their immigrant and first-generation contemporaries who forged Jewish-American intellectual or social traditions—they only wanted to make people happy.

In this light, the Eastern European Jews practically invented mainstream American entertainment. It's a remarkable accomplishment: As immigrants, as peasants, as Jews, they had a seemingly impossible triptych of hurdles to overcome in trying to win over American audiences. But they relied on resiliency, on brashness, and on traditions of music, humor, and folk culture to separate themselves from the other ethnic groups choking the grittier sections of American cities. Some of their gumption was no doubt born of the bitter difficulties of ghetto life; given the constant rebuffs show people confront early in their careers, only the thickest-skinned hopefuls are likely ever to tough it out. And as they did businessmen, boxers, and gangsters, mean tenement streets inevitably bred scrappy entertainers.

This chain of success stories has a specifically Jewish character. None of the other immigrant groups who arrived in the United States at the time—the Irish, the Italians, the Scandinavians, the Asians—produced so many entertainers. Show business was, in a way, in the blood of the Jews: The shtetl culture of Eastern European Jewry placed a high value on entertainment, and on jesters, clowns, and fools in particular. The shtetl produced a variety of archetypes that evolved into standbys of American entertainment: joking fiddlers, absentminded wise men, stumbling schlemiels. There was even a type of fool with a ritual status—the *badchen*, a cultured clown who would turn up at weddings, bar mitzvahs, and brisses, pronounce a sober benediction on the proceedings, and then spend the rest of the day entertaining guests with zany antics (a prototype of the Borscht Belt night club emcee and, later, the Labor Day telethon host). A Jewish court jester, the *badchen* provided shtetl culture with a connection to the absurd and the irrational. And the immigrants retained this sense of irony even as they neglected to bring the *badchen* with them to the New World. They never forgot the healing properties of humor, which accounts, in part, for the relative legitimacy of entertainment as a career choice in the Jewish community. Indeed, aside from the black community, which birthed an equally dazzling stream of popular entertainers in the 1930s and '40s, no other minority group has ever produced so many first-rung entertainers in so short a span of time. And Al Jolson was the master of their chosen profession.

Danny Levitch was consumed by the excitement of Jolson's act. He learned Jolson songs, he practiced Jolson-style vocals, he imitated Jolson stage mannerisms, inapt though they may have been for his athletic, eighteen-year-old physique. Adopting the stage name Danny Lewis, he began to audition for agents in their offices. The agents liked what they saw—somewhat. He got bookings not at the Winter Garden but at kiddy shows, weddings, beer garden parties. He entertained schoolchildren as they waited in line for smallpox vaccinations. He was eager to please and to keep working. Pulling in five or ten dollars a shot, he kept his head above water.

They were rollicking times—Danny dove headfirst into the world of all-night cafeterias, flimsy dressing rooms, agents' offices, bars, and of course, show women. He was a handsome young man, hearty and confident, with strong arms and a long-jawed, pleasantly equine face. He wore his hair slicked and short in the manner of the day, but there are photos where a wild forelock gives him a strikingly knavish air.

And he was something of a dude; family members vividly recall his fondness for clothes and jewelry. "I don't remember ever seeing him without a tie on," said a nephew, "even if he was just visiting my aunt's house." Danny's eye for fashion became a family joke, even popping up in one of his son's films. Watching Jerry teach an actor in *The Errand Boy* to admire another man's suit using Danny's exact mannerisms, Marshall Katz, then working for his cousin, warned him, "You're gonna get it for this!"

But despite sporting the trappings of success, Danny couldn't get enough gigs to sustain a full-time career as an entertainer. So he picked up a daytime sideline. In 1922 he began peddling sheet music for Fred Fischer, Inc., the Times Square music publisher. In the days before radio and the phonograph, the measure of a song's popularity was the number of printed copies it sold to people who wanted to play it at home. Danny would hit his route with Fischer's most recent stuff, putting it across with a combination of rakish good looks, confident salesmanship, and enthusiastic singing.

Among Danny's regular stops was an S. S. Kresge store on Market Street in Newark. To help push the sheet music, the store had hired a pianist, a young girl who could play on sight anything a customer wanted to hear. She wasn't beautiful by today's standards—she was a bit on the zaftig side, in the way men of her generation preferred—but she had a dark, voluptuous air about her, with thick, long hair and deep eyes. You get the feeling that photos don't quite convey her charm, although one, showing her on a boat deck, reveals an appealing sauciness that probably stood out in an era of imposed demureness and gentility.

As Jerry recalled it, they met cute. Danny, with his eye for the ladies, noticed the pianist immediately when he wandered into the store in the spring of 1923. He coolly selected from his sample case Fischer's 1917 hit "They Go Wild, Simply Wild Over Me" and sang it to her as she played. During the bridge, he whistled an improvisation along the edge of his business card. It was a peach of a come-on, and the pianist was swept up in it. Her name was Rachel Brodsky. She was nineteen years old.

Danny and Rachel went out for almost two years. Given Danny's line of work and his slick manner, this lengthy courtship serves as a demonstration of his honorable intentions; in fact, if family legends can be trusted, he was crazy about her. According to Jerry, Danny would call Rachel from Brooklyn, tell her that he was in Newark, and ask if she was free to see him. If the answer was yes, he'd say he needed some time to wrap up his business, then zip across two rivers to pick her up.

Eager as Danny was to get serious, Rachel wasn't so sure. Her father had died in 1922, leaving his family of girls little money. There was one precious legacy, however: a piano. Of all the sisters, Rachel had the greatest ability with the instrument, and enough gumption to do something with her talent. When she got the job at Kresge's, she was able to move out of her mother's apartment above Joseph's dress shop and rent a flat on nearby Bergen Street. She was unusually practical and worldly, an independent young woman not likely to be carried off by the first salesman who could produce a melody on a square of cardboard.

Rachel dated other men, among them Jimmy Ritz, the middle Ritz brother. Though Rachel didn't run in entertainment circles, it's possible that Danny introduced the two of them; Danny had met the Ritz Brothers when they shared the bill at the Half Moon Café in Coney Island, and Rachel might have attended one of those shows. In later years, Jimmy would never let Jerry forget his brief fling with Rachel. Jerry recalled, "He'd say to me, 'I never touched her,' and he'd tease me and say, 'You could be my kid,' or 'My illegitimate son, Jerry.' He, Harry, and Al teased the shit out of me."

Despite the competition, Danny continued to pursue Rachel with a combination of gentlemanliness and suavity. On one of their chaste afternoon outings, according to their son, he could contain himself no longer. He stole a kiss as they walked along the street—and got a smack for his trouble. In the fracas, Rachel broke her necklace, scattering the beads on the ground. Danny, abashed, apologized while helping her recover her things, then sheepishly walked her to her apartment. She must have spent the time considering her feelings for the man she'd so embarrassed, because when they arrived at her house, she abruptly announced, "I now accept the fact that we should be engaged." In January 1925 they were married.

In the Old World, Rachel and her dowry, such as it was, would have been packed off to the Levitch house in Brooklyn. But this was America, and Rachel's widowed mother commanded the young couple's loyalty. They set up house in Newark, where Rachel's older sister Rose had already married Harry Katz and begun her own family of three children: Marshall, Judy, and Natalie. Buhddie was there as well, going with Bernie Weisenthal, whom she eventually married. Jean, the eldest sister, was the only one not living in the neighborhood. She'd moved with her husband, Barney Epstein, to Brooklyn, where she remained, childless, until her nephew's success brought the Brodsky sisters and their families to California.

In Newark, Danny continued his attempt to break through in show business, with mixed success. Fortunately for him, his new hometown supported a small entertainment world of its own that was easier to crack. Adding a bit of broad comedy to his song-and-dance act, he found work as an emcee at the burlesque houses that thrived in eastern cities during the 1920s. Newark was also near the Jewish resort communities of the Catskill Mountains and the Jersey shore, where even second-rung entertainers were in demand. And when Danny's agent could get him better work, he headed across the Hudson to Manhattan, where he once shared the stage of the Irving Plaza Theater with song-and-dance man Robert Alda.

So even though Newark wasn't the big time, it offered Danny work in a viable regional vaudeville and burlesque industry, allowing him at the same time to cash in on the tremendous demand for entertainment in nearby resorts. In the summer and during the winter holidays he'd hit the hotels, with Rae joining him as a rehearsal pianist and, it would seem, chaperon. Though a newlywed, Danny was still a dashing young man; in his bearing and wardrobe there would always be a hint of the roué, and Rae more than anyone knew he could lay on the charm. She would follow him on the road as long as he was on it, even though she grew to dislike the piano so much that relatives recalled she would play at family gatherings rarely and reluctantly.

Given Rae's habit of traveling with Danny, it's likely that one of Danny's summer bookings brought Jerry into the world, that at some now-forgotten hotel engagement in the summer of 1925 Danny and Rae conceived their only child. Following this logic, the child born Jerome Levitch, the boy who became Jerry Lewis, is literally a Borscht Belt baby, who got his biological start in the mountains that years later would serve as a launching pad for his career.

When her son was still very young, Rae Lewis returned to work, taking whatever engagements her agent, Arthur Lyons, could secure for her. She played in cocktail lounges, on Newark's WOR radio station (one of the largest in the nation at the time), and on the road with her husband. Jerry, as a result, was left in the charge of Rae's sisters and mother for evenings, weekends, and even longer stretches of time.

"I was a CARE package child," Jerry said, describing his nomadic existence as the child of scrambling entertainers. "I'm sure there were people who had rougher beginnings, but as I look back I can't imagine that that's true. I'm talking about violent death, poverty, hunger, and inability to equate where I live now to why I'm going to live with an aunt Tuesday, now with my grandmother, traveling back and forth. It was devastating."

He recalled being trundled about on the road—the Catskills, small eastern cities, South Jersey shore resorts. He napped in cheap hotels and dressing rooms. He was baby-sat by hotel maids. He had no regular playmates. And most commonly, he was left with relatives while his parents raced off to engagements.

Only two or three facts about Jerry Lewis convey his character as completely as this one. The wheedling, whining, cringing, puppy-dog-on-speed-and-helium character that brought him fame; the struggling earnestness with which he dives into a song or executes a bit of soft-shoe patter on a live stage—these are hall-marks of a man conditioned to pleading for attention. As Jerry himself explained in the late 1960s: "An audience is nothing more than eight or nine hundred mamas and papas clapping their hands and saying, 'Good boy, baby.' That's all. You'll find that people who had enough 'Good boy, baby,' from their actual par-ents rarely turn to comedy."

Jerry filled his autobiography with confessions of the pain he felt when left alone by his parents. Danny and Rae left their son with Hannah and Morris Lev-itch in the fall of 1931, with Rae's mother in the fall of 1932 and the winters of 1936 and 1938, with Rae's sister Jean in Brooklyn in the summer of 1940.

Summer and winter recesses were relatively happy times. Jerry and his folks were together at resort hotels or, in one memorable instance, on a burlesque tour. But the school year was murder. Jerry lived with a constant fear that his del-icate sense of household stability would suddenly shatter. At any moment, he knew, the phone could ring and Danny could be called off to a faraway gig.

"What I felt then, as much as anything, was the difference between me and the other kids," he reflected, "the need to know what a mother and a father sur-rounded by children were all about." He would cheerfully insinuate himself into his classmate's households, arriving early in the morning to walk with them to school in hopes that he would be invited in for breakfast: "not for the food, but only because I could be around a family."

Even the other kids in the neighborhood, young as they were, recognized that something was unusual about the Lewis household. "I remember my mother explaining that Jerry's parents were traveling a lot," recalled Leon Cha-rash, a childhood playmate of Jerry's and a future member of the Muscular Dys-trophy Association's scientific advisory board. "And I remember thinking how unusual it was that his mother worked and that when he came home from school she wasn't there. Very few mothers worked in our neighborhood, even though it was the Depression."

The sight of skinny young Jerry on their doorsteps while they were trying to get their own kids off to school must have made these other women extremely suspicious of Rae and Danny. The fact that Jerry was an only child does suggest a reluctance to be burdened with family on Danny and Rae's part, but Jewish fam-ilies of the era weren't large compared with average American families. And there were obvious economic reasons. Given Danny's commitment to show biz and his resulting low income, Rae had to work. She had neither time nor, likely, inclination to fill her home with children. Furthermore, several people who knew Danny suggested that Rae went on the road with her husband to stay his wan-dering eye; a larger family would certainly have curtailed her surveillance.

Whatever the reason for their small family, it's certain that money was tight.

Danny kept sufficiently busy that the family never went on relief or suffered an eviction, and no one recalled Danny's being pressured to take up a more dependable line of work. "If that pressure came," said Marshall Katz, "it came from his family, not Rae's." But he was never a great provider. In 1929 Danny's shaky career prospects received a double blow: the Great Depression, which all but dissolved the American family's entertainment budget, and the advent of the talkies, which began inevitably to suck the vitality from the live venues that were Danny's bread and butter. Jerry always gave Danny credit for trying hard—"If he made sixty dollars, he sent forty-five to my mother." But at the same time he couldn't hide his pain when recalling his family's modest financial condition: "They were poor and couldn't help leaving me alone. But I'm supersensitive, and it killed me."

Jerry was no street urchin, but he lacked many of the little luxuries most of the kids in his working-class neighborhood had—a rocking horse, a bike, new school clothes each fall. Danny and Rae never owned their own home; they rented apartments until Jerry bought them a house in the late 1940s. The apartment where the Lewises lived throughout the '30s was the nearest thing their son ever knew to a fixed address, and when he went out on the road as a teenager, Dan and Rae relinquished even that. They moved into a hotel in Times Square, further proof that they saw themselves more as show people than parents.

Nevertheless, they did have a child, and it's worth examining how they raised him. Their frequent absences resulted not only in their son's legitimate anxieties but also in a sporadic attendance record that hampered him in his schoolwork; when he dropped out of school at sixteen, they didn't stop him. Later on in life, Danny was often noted to bear himself with coolness and even jealousy toward his son's success, and Rachel was known to be possessive of Jerry, harboring a thinly veiled antagonism toward his wife and even his children. As Patti Lewis recalled, "When Jerry's folks came to our home, they showed little affection for the boys, who were given a quick, impersonal kiss before being relegated to the background." This was a couple, it seems, that just did not care for children; more's the pity, then, that Danny and Rae *had* a child, and that they had so little apparent concern for his comfort, happiness, or security.

In Jerry's fondest recollections of his mom and dad, he is most often a spectator, watching them perform onstage or enjoy themselves among friends and family; rarely does he speak of interacting with them. There were occasions when the family did things together—Danny would take Jerry out to see vaudeville, burlesque, and legitimate performances (including the Yiddish theater) and critique the acts for his son—but Jerry's own words make it clear that he wished he could have had more to do with them. If his ambivalence toward his parents as an adult doesn't prove that—producer Perry Cross actually banned Danny from the set of Jerry's TV series in 1963 because of the funk into which the comedian would lapse after his dad's visits—then his headlong desire for a career like theirs certainly does. Not only did he crave the chance to act out his insecurity in a cathartic display, but he also felt he had to do so in the very field that drew his mom and dad away from him. When he was old enough to choose a path for himself, he turned to show business as a way of creating a family for himself.

There's a photo of four-year-old Jerry lolling in the Catskill sun with Rae and Danny. They look beatific, full of youth and vigor. But the photo takes on a more melancholy aspect when you consider how infrequent such moments were. Though Jerry wasn't an orphan, he was often made to feel like one, and in his on-again-off-again relationship with his parents can be found the origins of his thin skin, his eager manner, his quickness to tears or anger. Many people have survived worse childhoods with less obvious scars, but Jerry came out of his with these.

Among the caretakers with whom Danny and Rae left their son, none was relied on more often than Rae's mother, Sarah, a woman who'd been driven from Russia by cossacks, crossed an ocean to an alien land, raised two families, and made a home while running a dressmaking business. If anyone could handle the extra work, it was she. It's nearly certain that Dan and Rae set roots, however shallowly, in Irvington because they could rent an apartment around the corner from this always-available baby-sitter.

Sarah's children were all grown by the late 1920s; by the time of Jerry's birth, she'd been widowed and had married a second husband: Sam Rothberg, himself a widower and father of three. Rothberg was a tanner, a strong, loud man with a taste for spirits. His new wife's grandchildren called him Uncle. Like Morris Levitch, Rothberg made wine in his basement, though his was strictly for his own consumption. He was hearty. He wore a mustache. And he scared the hell out of Jerry.

Jerry remembered Rothberg as a drunken bully who commanded obedience at the dinner table and once struck Sarah in front of her children and grandchildren. Some of Sarah's other grandchildren recalled Rothberg without contempt, but Jerry spent more time under the man's roof than his cousins and probably saw more of his temper than they did. Perhaps genuinely frightened by Rothberg's ugly behavior, perhaps envious of Rothberg's proximity to his grandmother, Jerry felt a profound hostility toward his stepgrandfather, to the point where he dreamed of murdering Rothberg with a kitchen knife. Even in his most secure childhood haven, he felt besieged.

Through it all, however, Grandma Sarah remained Jerry's great love. In his autobiography he wrote in glowing terms of his maternal grandmother, "the love of my life." "I trusted her with my life, under any circumstances," he wrote of his "tenderhearted grandma, the most understanding soul you'll ever find in this vast and foolish world." The book holds no such words for the comic's parents, wives, or children. To little Jerry, Grandma Sarah was the heart of the world.

Sarah Rothberg was the perfect Eastern European Jewish grandma. Stoutly built, with a long, wide nose, she wore her hair in a heart-shaped bun. Jerry remembered her in flower print dresses; likely she made them herself. She cooked traditional Ashkenazi meals: briskets, chickens, kugels, and latkes, a thick veneer of schmaltz—chicken fat—glazing it all. She spoke accented English with liberal splashes of Yiddish, kept a kosher home, and worked hard both at her housekeeping and at her dressmaking.

Sarah's house at 63 Rutgers Street in Irvington was the nearest thing to a genuine home that Jerry ever knew. Sarah and Sam Rothberg had bought the large wood frame house across the street from Union Avenue School in the mid-1920s. Before long, the Lewises, Katzes, and Weisenthals also moved into the neighborhood, the latter two couples moving into their own houses while Rae and Danny took an apartment at 396 Union Avenue, just a block or so away.

Jerry remembered the Rutgers Street house so warmly that it was the only one of his childhood homes that he described in his autobiography. He recalled Joseph Brodsky's piano, the metal kitchen table with the chipped edge, the big Majestic radio. Jerry would spend hours listening to the radio with his grandmother, sometimes napping beneath her sewing table while she pedaled away into the night. And he hid behind the couch, weeping over the absence of his parents. Even around Grandma Sarah, he couldn't shake the feeling that his parents didn't want him.

Difficult as it must have been for him to be shunted about, he might have fared better had he been raised wholly by relatives. He enjoyed being around Danny's parents in Brooklyn, for instance. Morris and Hannah Levitch seem, like Sarah Rothberg, to have been more loving toward the boy than his own parents. Visiting their home as a five-year-old, Jerry overheard Hannah tell Rachel, "Your son will not only be just an actor—but a *great* actor." Indeed, the Levitches had no hesitation about packing their grandson off to the movies, where he might catch the same bug that drove his father into such a wayward life. In the autumn of 1931, with Dan and Rae off on the road, the Levitches sent Jerry to the Loew's Pitkin with a dime and a paper bag lunch to see Charlie Chaplin in *The Circus*.

Jerry wrote that this was his first filmgoing experience, and if it was, it's almost impossibly apt. The 1928 silent feature is, like Chaplin's later *Limelight*, a seminal essay on the nature of comic performance. Chaplin plays a bumbling handyman who's about to get fired from a circus when audiences begin paying more attention to his cloddish shenanigans on the fringes of the big top than to the main acts. The circus owner keeps him on—without telling him he's a hit. Chaplin wants to be a clown in the main ring, but he can't perform when he's prompted to act funny. Nevertheless, events conspire to make a star of him, even though he can get laughs only by overextending himself in unpredictable, spontaneous ways. It was just the sort of story Jerry himself would make again and again in his solo career decades later. As a mere five-year-old, he sat in that Brownsville theater—perhaps the very building in which his father had fallen under Jolson's sway—watching entranced and thinking to himself, "I can do it! I can be a clown."

Back home in Irvington, in the intermittent care of his mom and dad, he had few such pleasant epiphanies. More typically, Jerry remembered events like the night he flew through the streets of Irvington in a frightened frenzy at his parents' absence. He was about six or seven. Dan was on tour; Rae was playing piano in a cocktail lounge in Irvington. Sitting alone in the kitchen waiting for his mother to come home, Jerry grew more and more scared. "They don't love me," he thought. "They don't care. They never will." He bolted out into the autumn night in hopes of finding his mother.

Running up Chancellor Avenue, Irvington's main street, Jerry peered into restaurants and saloons looking for Rachel, finally coming across the crowded tavern where she was playing. He rushed in. Years later, he recalled "a garish brightness. The sound of music and raucous laughter in the near distance . . . a foul smelling rush of whiskey and beer, the tobacco smoke cutting into my lungs." (In the *Look* article, Jerry contended that the experience gave him an aversion to alcohol, but there's no evidence that he ever systematically abstained from drinking; he certainly smoked cigarettes well into his fifties and drank for at least a decade after that.)

Picture the scene from a patron's point of view: The cocktail pianist's little boy comes crying into the bar looking for his mommy. It's an appalling image. Rachel was shocked to see her son; she picked him up, said a few words to the proprietor, and hustled into the street, crying as she walked home. For his part, Jerry was still scared out of his mind. He tried to explain himself, tried to sound contrite even in his relief. His mother softened: "Her arms came around me. There was a momentary embrace and a kiss." Relief flooded over the little boy: "She loved me. They both loved me. What a wonderful feeling."

Throughout his youth, incidents like this made Jerry feel tied to an emotional pendulum. His parents didn't love him; his parents adored him. They fled him; they brought him along on exciting trips. He would always recall lying awake in bed far into the night waiting for the sounds of Rachel's heels on the linoleum, listening to the comforting sounds of jingling coins as she emptied her tip money into a jar in the kitchen. But he would also recall episodes of abandonment, loneliness, and yearning, the feeling that made him do whatever he could to receive that elusive maternal kiss.

Jerry's youth wasn't all a horror show, of course. Brightest among his memories were the times he traveled with Dan and Rae as they worked the resorts or toured the burlesque and vaudeville circuits. There was the summer of 1932, for instance, when Dan and Rae landed a plum job. At the height of the Great Depression, they got a ten-week engagement at the President Hotel in Swan Lake, New York. Doubling up at other resorts nearby, they reckoned they could take in about two thousand dollars for the season, half of which would go to room and board at the President.

It was an idyllic summer—swimming, softball, hiking, bike riding. But whatever else he did that summer, Jerry was always on hand in the hotel casino when his parents rehearsed. It was heaven. Not only could he be around Danny and Rae at their happiest, but he had a chance to see a whole variety of acts practice their routines. Jerry was exposed to a gamut of show-biz métiers, and he got the even more valuable chance to see the performers working on their bits before the show. He recalled being "enveloped in some kind of curious rapture . . . wishing all the while that one day soon I would be performing on stage just like them."

It was during this summer that Jerry's first foray on the stage took place. Danny had been performing "Brother, Can You Spare a Dime?," Yip Harburg and Jay Gorney's Depression tearjerker, and Jerry had diligently learned the song by watching his dad day after day. He urged his folks to let him sing it onstage, and they took the occasion of a benefit for the local Fireman's Association as a chance to appease him. (The notion of a Jewish resort hotel helping raise money for firefighters in a region where Jewish hotel owners were forever accused, often justly, of burning their properties for insurance money—a practice that gave birth to the phrase "Jewish lightning"—is almost too ironic as is the idea that Jerry made his performing debut during a charity event.)

For years, Jerry's official press materials gave a detailed account of this performance—Jerry stepping onstage to the surprise of his parents, the orchestra unable to play in Jerry's small-boy's key, the singing itself, full of broken and bent notes that drew laughs from the crowd, even the date: September 17, 1931. *Jerry Lewis in Person* corrects much of this misinformation, even if publicity still propagated it more than a decade after the book was published. The date, for instance: Harburg and Gorney didn't write "Brother, Can You Spare a Dime?" until 1932. And it was no spontaneous outburst of song: Rae had rehearsed Jerry and served as his accompanist. She put him to bed that night and *kvelled* over his efforts. "You didn't forget a word. Not a syllable," she said. "Good, good; keep going."

There was another memorable family trip a few years later, a trip on which Jerry underwent an even more crucial initiation. In the winter of 1937–38, Danny had been booked on a burlesque tour around the Great Lakes, and Jerry and Rae were to accompany him to Detroit during winter recess. On Christmas Day, the trio piled into a Plymouth sedan and made the drive west. When they arrived in the bitter midwest winter, they headed straight to the site of Danny's engagement, Detroit's seedy National Theater—"It ain't the Palace," Danny shrugged—and then to the Barlum Hotel, where Danny signed them all in with a magisterial flourish.

For the next week, Jerry walked around in a cloud of bliss, overwhelmed with his proximity to his parents and with his exposure to the burlesque environment. He was so excited that he couldn't rest on his cot. He'd rise early to explore the hotel, and then he'd be off to the theater to watch rehearsals, quizzing the technicians and stagehands about their jobs. At night he'd take in the show from the wings. After the evening's final performance, Rae would wait for Dan and Jerry in the lobby—giving them a convenient excuse to leave the raucous backstage environment—and the family would find a restaurant for dinner.

Jerry was in awe of his father's suave manner and stage skills, though his memories of Danny's act suggest it wasn't exactly top-flight entertainment. Jerry recalled his father introducing the chorus girls with a rendition of "A Pretty Girl Is Like a Melody," he remembered a baggy-pants comedy bit in which Danny played a German dunce, and he recalled a production number in which Danny, dressed in a ringmaster's outfit, snapped a whip at the girls, who all wore animal skins.

He also remembered feeling "gripped by a new excitement, a contagion of emotions." What he felt, of course, was the bloom of sexuality. He was almost twelve, and he was spending his nights lurking in the wings of a theater watching showgirls undress. Burlesque wasn't exactly the sort of milieu that authorities recommend for child rearing—strippers, rough-hewn stagehands, bawdy humor. And Jerry's experience was proof that a burlie house wasn't really a place for kids.

One night Danny introduced him to a stripper whose eye the kid had caught during a routine earlier in the week: "Say hello to Marlene, son." The nervous boy could barely respond, but the woman encouraged him. "Don't be shy, sweetie. I won't bite you." A night or two later, according to Jerry, she proved good to her word, taking him to her dressing room and initiating him sexually. "Whatever we did," Jerry said, "I remember it took only a minute. After that she talked to me about her little boy . . . her lips were trembling and her eyes looked awfully red." While Marlene waxed maudlin over her son, the boy whose innocence she stole slipped out of the door and went off to find his parents.

Danny was certainly wise in the ways of burlesque people. Whether or not he himself was guilty of womanizing, it's shocking to realize how instrumental he might have been in his eleven-year-old son's sexual initiation. Did he intend for Marlene to seduce Jerry? Was leading the boy to a sexual encounter his idea of being a good dad? Or did he think a sexually mature youngster would be off his hands all the sooner? If Jerry's story is accurate, Danny was either incredibly naïve or incredibly cynical; and if the incident didn't happen—if it amounts to another instance of Jerry's self-mythologizing—the story nevertheless reveals Jerry's impression of his father's world. The maternal kiss Jerry always craved, that sweet note of recognition and affection he sat up at night awaiting, now

came to him wrapped in greasepaint and lingerie. Ever after he would associate show business not only with proximity and parental attention but with his own desires and desirability as well. Only onstage could he be seen by the people whom he so desperately wanted to see him; only around show people could he find love.

Back in Irvington, the trip lingered in Jerry's mind like a glimpse of heaven. Rae went back on the road with Danny, and her son, left again in the care of Grandma Sarah and his aunts Rose and Buhddie, dragged himself reluctantly to school, where he whiled away his education in daydreams of a life on the stage. He lived for the penny postcards his parents would send, his only connection to them that winter.

Eventually, the distractions proved costly. One spring, when his fellow students as Union Avenue School were marched ceremonially to visit the classroom where they'd spend their next school year, Jerry was left behind. He'd missed too much school—and done too poorly in the part he'd attended—to be promoted. Though he was bright, he just hadn't been able to keep up. Jerry recalled this as one of the great disappointments of his life: "I thought I was a dummy, a misfit, the sorriest kid alive. I never felt more alone than just then."

It's not clear, however, what this moment actually meant to Jerry's academic career. Although he claimed in both *Look* and *Jerry Lewis in Person* to have been left back, he graduated from the eighth grade at Union Avenue School in the spring of 1940. He was fourteen, right on schedule. Given that, the only way Jerry could have repeated a grade and graduated on time would be if he had entered school a year early—to have begun first grade before his sixth birthday—and this might certainly have occurred as a result of his parents' constant search for places to leave him. Otherwise, unless the episode is a whole-cloth invention, the only other possibility is that the school left Jerry out of the class-changing ceremony as a punishment, but then let him work his way back into the proper spot in the system.

But the real impact of missing the ceremony was to change Jerry's attitude toward academics forever. While the *Look* account is frequently unreliable in its facts, its account of Jerry's reaction is vivid: "From then on, I lost all interest i school. I thought I was a dummy and I began to clown around to attract atte tion, so I wouldn't ever have to be alone like that again. If I could make peo laugh, I thought, they'd like me and let me be with them. I had to do it in defense because I felt I couldn't compete for their attention with my brains

But even if he had no knack for books, Jerry was Sarah Rothberg's grandsc Sarah Rothberg's grandsons would all be bar mitzvahed if she had any s In the fall of 1936 Jerry was enrolled in Avrom Buchom Cheldem Sc Chancellor Avenue, a storefront Hebrew school of a type common

communities throughout the area. Under the supervision of the school's Rabbi Friedman, Jerry learned the rudiments of Hebrew grammar and Jewish religious culture alongside other neighborhood boys, including Leon Charash. Leon was an able student who'd skipped a grade in public school and was thus in Jerry's class despite being a year younger. But Jerry struggled with this second language as much as with his studies at Union Avenue School. At least this learning experience would have a payoff: the bar mitzvah day itself, the day above all others on which every Jewish boy is a superstar in his own home.

Most Jewish men think back on their bar mitzvahs as golden moments. Jerry recalled his ritual initiation into manhood as "the saddest day of my life," adding, "I'll carry it with me till I die." In a by now familiar pattern, Jerry had been sent back to Irvington to continue the school year after spending most of the winter of 1938–39 on the road. March came, and with it the boy's thirteenth birthday, but Dan and Rae were still working the winter resorts around Lakewood, New Jersey. It was left to Grandma Sarah to see the boy through this key ritual in his life.

Jerry's only older male cousin, Marshall, had had a large bar mitzvah party some half-dozen years earlier; photos show a huge group of kids clowning in the summer sun. Now it was Jerry's turn to reap the attentions of his family, but instead of a brood of cousins and friends, he trundled off to synagogue with only his grandmother to support him. He made his way through the ceremony, reciting his haftarah portion and enduring the endless service in the nearly empty shul.

As Jerry recalled, Danny and Rae had called early in the day from Lakewood, saying they'd be there. Throughout the long morning, their son waited for them in vain. He dragged himself back to his grandmother's house afterward, fighting back justifiable tears. There was a reception, which stung the alienated Jerry all the more for its liveliness. Dan and Rae finally showed up, having left Lakewood hours after they said they would, accepting the congratulations of neighbors and relatives for something for which they really could take no credit. If there is any emblem of Jerry's relationship with his mother and father, this is it: the prodigal parents walking in on the party in honor of the son whom they've ignored; the sad, angry boy in the corner, at once the center of attention and a pathetically marginal character. Dan and Rae always loved parties; Jerry would grow up shy of them.

In the spring of 1940 Jerry graduated from Union Avenue School along with the other eighth graders. He always claimed this as another scarring experience, but unlike the undeniably painful memory of his bar mitzvah, it's difficult to understand why this experience should hurt. In 1984 he told *Parade* magazine how awful the day was for him: "Lewis stood up, walked over to the wall above the fireplace and took down a photograph in a black frame. . . . 'See that kid on the

far left? . . . That's me: Jerome Lewis. See, I'm the only one in the picture in mis-matched clothes. I was in hand-me-downs, and I spoiled the picture. It was hu-miliating. I look at this picture often, and I remember that on that day I decided I'd never be humiliated again.' "

Of course, he'd never been known as Jerome Lewis, but this marks the sin-gle instance of Jerry's referring to himself as Jerome in a half-century of inter-views, suggesting how jarring the memory was for him. Just as interesting, though, is Jerry's memory of the clothes. Put bluntly, judging from the original photo, he looked fine. It was no Armani suit he had on, but nor was it an Em-mett Kelly castoff. Several schoolmates were decidedly less put-together than Jerry, and he hardly marred a picture in which he appears unobtrusively on the margin. (Indeed, he had inherited Danny's reputation as a sharp dresser in his school days: "He came to school wearing spats!" remembered Leon Charash.) But this photograph captured what became a meaningful moment for Jerry. He would forever conjure up his meager wardrobe in describing his childhood mis-ery, and he seemed to make a lifelong resolution never to be embarrassed by his wardrobe again. In 1960, for instance, the Associated Press reported that he spent a hundred thousand annually on clothes, most of which were made by tailor-to-the-stars Sy DeVore—who revealed that Jerry owned eighty-eight tuxe-dos (more even than the Duke of Windsor) with solid gold buttons that them-selves cost sixty dollars per suit, and donated his old clothes to such charity cases as out-of-work actors and "an underprivileged boy with a genius IQ but only one suit to wear to college."

The other blow that Jerry suffered around this time—the death of Sarah Rothberg, which he remembered as occurring in the spring—may in fact have colored his recollection of his graduation. If any experience marked the low point in young Jerry's life, that would be it. The only person in his world whom he felt was standing behind him was gone. When her mother died, Rae was on the road with Danny. After the funeral, they took Jerry to his aunt Buhddie and uncle Bernie Weisenthal in Gloversville, New York, where Bernie had gone in search of work during the Depression, and they said good-bye at the train sta-tion. For the next few weeks, as Jerry recalled, he had trouble eating and sleep-ing. The phantom of abandonment that had always threatened his peace of mind seemed more real than ever.

2

Tummling Among the Nazis

The sense that he'd been dumped by his parents both wounded Jerry and hardened him, and he compensated with antics, attracting other kids with his audacity and recklessness. "He was a nudnik," remembered his cousin Marshall. "A real pest." He would wait on corners for buses, lift his foot to tie his shoe on their steps when they stopped for him, then walk away without getting aboard for a ride. He hung from pipes in people's kitchens, hid himself in dresser drawers, and leapt out at unsuspecting victims. He made a spectacle of himself, sledding down snowless hills, creating a stream of sparks and sailing headlong when his vehicle ground to a stop.

It made him popular, but it also drew unwanted attention to him. And in Irvington, that wasn't always a smart thing for a Jewish kid to do. Throughout his school years, in fact, Jerry became increasingly aware of a thick vein of anti-Semitism in his hometown.

It revealed itself to him whimsically enough. In the autumn of 1936 Jerry and his friends were keeping themselves busy in the playground at Union Avenue School. Suddenly, a black shadow cut across the sunny sky. A gigantic shape hovered over them, slowly drifting toward the south with a low, mechanical whirr. It was the *Hindenburg*, freshly arrived from across the Atlantic and headed toward its berth in the central New Jersey town of Lakehurst (where it would crash spectacularly the following year). The boys were predictably impressed.

They weren't aware, naturally, of the growing German threat it represented. To them it was just an exciting distraction. Their parents, however, saw something more sinister in the *Hindenburg*, and in the headlines emerging from Europe. Like other Jews across America, they knew that anti-Semitism was thriving overseas. But Irvington Jews didn't have to buy foreign newspapers, or read between the lines of relatives' letters, to understand the brutality of life under German oppression. All they had to do was leave their own homes and walk around their small city, a longtime German-American bastion.

Irvington had been founded and populated by gentile Germans many years before up-and-coming Jews made their way there. Newark had always been a German town (beer brewing was one of its chief industries), and the Germans were naturally the first to branch out into the city's environs. They ran the local businesses, they established the churches and the physical plan, and as they had in Newark proper, they built health clubs, *kureins*, with an emphasis on German gymnastic competition and Teutonic traditions of fitness and conditioning. In this relatively hermetic enclave a sense of German identity persisted, and the xenophobic impulses of the population were directed outward toward the immigrant population of Newark in general and the Jews who were infiltrating Irvington in particular.

In the previous decade, Irvington had become a popular destination for Jewish families from Newark who left the city as a sign of their upward mobility. Just southwest of Newark, across the city limits from predominantly Jewish Weequeeg, Irvington had a suburban spaciousness and prosperity that was new to the immigrant Jews of the Rothbergs' generation. Newark's Jews had traditionally lived in the city's Central Ward, primarily around Prince Street. Throughout the 1920s, though, as their economic horizons expanded, they pushed south into the developing Weequeeg area, where they bought two- and three-family homes and established a thriving religious, financial, and even political presence: Their man in city hall, Meyer Ellenstein, would eventually serve as Newark's mayor. By the 1930s the Jews represented some sixty or seventy thousand of Newark's half-million residents. Eventually, their migration out of the inner city drove them beyond Weequeeg, west into Irvington, and Jerry's family was swept along in the flow.

Although there are no accounts of anyone in Jerry's family meeting with explicit anti-Semitism in Irvington, the atmosphere was ripe for it. It was the early 1930s, and while the Jewish encroachment into their enclave was under way, the Germans of Irvington were following events in their mother country. In fact, the German-American Bund, a nationwide group designed to show support for the fascist government back home, was founded in the Irvington area under the leadership of Fritz Kuhn.

"The *kureins* used to have meetings for gymnastic competitions with some subsidy from the Hitler government for developing a militaristic organization," recalled Alan Lowenstein, a longtime leader of Newark's Jewish community. "They became quite militaristic. I don't know that they ever carried arms. I doubt it. I don't think they ever shot anybody or injured anybody. But they were part of several fringe groups of different kinds in the 1930s. You had Father

Coughlin stirring up anti-Semitism and antiliberalism, and Fritz Kuhn was attempting to build up pro-German support. It was primarily nationalistic."

The Bund was very visible in Irvington. Jerry remembered one of the organization's parades making its way down Chancellor Avenue, a hundred feet or so from his apartment: "I stood at curbside, gaping at a tangle of Stars and Stripes and the swastika, the gray-shirted bundists in Sam Browne belts trooping by with drums beating and trumpets blaring. At last I started to walk away, faster and faster, past the stores and faces along the parade route, and finally racing at breakneck speed to pull free of the sound."

This was just a little boy running away from a frightening experience, but Irvington steeled Jerry to personal threats before long: According to one classmate, he was respected around the neighborhood for refusing to rat on a gang that beat him up, and he acted out his growing boyhood frustrations in violent retaliation against anyone who confronted him. Indeed, the Jerry Lewis who so ferociously rebutted critics of his film or TV work, who disparaged disabled-rights activists who didn't like the tone of his charity work, who excoriated family members who violated house rules, who belittled employees and lashed out at people who might betray him, was the same little boy who ran frightened from that Bund parade on Chancellor Street. There was a lot of anger inside Jerry, and nothing evoked it so much as a challenge. The anti-Semites and bundists of Irvington were merely the first to bring it out.

Jerry recorded one of these reactions in his autobiography, and eyewitnesses confirm the recollection. In December 1937 Mrs. Harcourt, the Union Avenue School music teacher, was drilling the fifth-graders in Christmas carols. Partly out of a sense of personal pride, partly out of an increasingly wise-assed inability to hold his tongue, Jerry blurted out, "If you sing Hanukkah songs, I'll sing Christmas carols." Leon Charash was in the classroom, and he remembered thinking, "Who knew anything about Hanukkah songs?" Mrs. Harcourt certainly didn't. She threatened to send Jerry to the office if he didn't comply, but the boy held his ground. Sarah Betz, the school's German principal, also failed to see the humor or the ecumenism in Jerry's refusal, and after a firm tongue-lashing she sent the insolent kid back to his classroom, where he sat silently while his classmates rehearsed their noels.

Jerry probably would have liked the singing, too. And the school officials knew it. So patent was his love for performing and entertaining that, academic failings notwithstanding, he was allowed to play a pivotal role in a benefit show. Let history note that the future producer and emcee of the Muscular Dystrophy Association telethon organized his first philanthropic performance for the benefit of the Red Cross at the Rex Theater in Irvington, New Jersey, in 1938.

The show was held between halves of a matinee double feature. A few dozen kids participated. Leon Charash had a feature part—he was a straight man to

Jerry in a knockoff of a burlesque comedy skit. A trio of girls sang "Three Little Fishes," while Lillian Messinger did a takeoff on Fanny Brice's Baby Snooks.

It's intriguing that Jerry's first attempt at putting on a show included Snooks, one of the clearest antecedents in American entertainment for his own childish persona. There are direct parallels between Brice and Jerry: their ethnicity, of course, their common background in vaudeville and burlesque, their traditional show-biz career choices, even the long, intense relationships with dark, rakish gamblers—Nicky Arnstein in Brice's case, Dean Martin in Jerry's. Snooks wasn't a psychological ball of twitches like Jerry's character but rather a flat-out smartass, and she lacked the autobiographical dimension with which Jerry infused his act. But Brice was the first Jewish-American comedian to do a bit with childishness at its core. The character was enormously popular on stage, radio, and records, and the notion of an adult getting laughs with baby talk certainly made an impression on Jerry.

For that matter, so did Lillian Messinger, one of the prettiest and most physically developed girls in the school. Casting her must have reminded Jerry of the backstage world that had been his playground in Detroit. He acted just like Danny Lewis's boy, threatening to cut her number from the bill unless she allowed him a quick feel. The girl ran off and told Leon Charash about the incident. Charash approached Jerry after the rehearsal in an angry mood, and Jerry bloodied his nose for him.

The show Jerry had put together at the Rex Theater was a miniature version of the burlesque shows he'd seen his dad emcee the previous winter. That week around the burlesque performers of the National Theater had been the perfect family vacation: Danny worked, Rachel kept an eye on both her husband and her son, and Jerry got the kind of education that he really wanted, not formal schooling but a seminar in show-biz technique. "Nothing escaped my attention," Jerry recalled. "The smallest detail snapped into sharp focus, and the whole burlesque scene became a private vision. . . . I could tell why the comedy bits and production numbers had worked perfectly, and why they were screwed up. I knew it immediately. But I never said anything to the performers. Only to Dad, who would turn to my mother and say something like 'Out of the mouths of babes . . .' "

It wasn't until Jerry's early adolescence, though, that all these influences coalesced into the recognizable roots of his act. And it was in the resorts where Danny Lewis found such steady work that Jerry grew into an entertainer. Jerry is often cited as a product of the Borscht Belt hotels, but Danny was the first Lewis to exploit Newark's proximity to the Catskill Mountains of southeastern New York State. It was there, in a hotbed of hotels, campgrounds, and small pioneer towns remade into shtetls, that a thriving Jewish culture was giving birth to a thriving show-business culture. If the Jews invented American popular entertainment (and thus popular entertainment for the whole world), then the Borscht Belt was surely their laboratory.

The rise of the Catskills as a breeding ground for entertainers was directly linked to the arrival and advancement of Eastern European Jews in the New World. As the Jewish immigrants came to prosperity in America, and particularly in the New York area, opportunity arose for resort areas catering especially to them. And no vacation spot was more closely associated with Eastern European Jews and their descendants than the region of the Catskill Mountains that became known as the Borscht Belt. With its fresh air, enormous meals, and ritualistic Old World traditions, the Borscht Belt became one of the centers of Jewish American life and the most productive cradle of Jewish entertainment in history.

Jews began arriving in the upper reaches of New York State as early as 1825, but the first transplants of Jews into rural New York State that actually took root came during the migration of the late nineteenth century, when the Eastern European Jewish population of New York had achieved a greater density than the slums of Calcutta or London. Choked on the asphalt and capitalism of the city, many shtetl-born Jews looked to the farming counties of New York State for their salvation. In the Old World they'd been people of the soil, and finding the modern city overwhelming, many chose to return to the earth—even if that meant soil that had repelled earlier Jewish settlers. Throughout the late nineteenth century and well into the early twentieth, Jews became a more and more significant presence in Catskill farming communities.

But even the Jews who stayed in the city established a presence in the mountains. The first to make the trip northward were the sufferers of "worker's disease," as the tuberculosis that swept through overcrowded tenements and sweatshops was known. As early as 1890 ghetto reformers had promoted vacations in the Catskills as a means to a cure. A regimen of food, fresh air, and undemanding exercise was widely believed to combat the ill effects of tuberculosis, and a steady stream of sick city Jews left for the recuperative mountains.

Indeed, so many Jews sought cure in the Catskills that the latent anti-Semitism of longtime residents surfaced in response. Throughout the 1890s and 1900s the subtle exclusionary practices against Jews that were long the custom of hotels and boardinghouses throughout upstate New York became blatantly and even boastfully explicit. The Jews responded by buying up their own properties, building their own hotels and resorts, and claiming a stake of the healthy mountain environment as their own.

Throughout the 1910s and '20s these Jewish enclaves sprouted up wildly. Synagogues and political groups sponsored religiously and socially oriented camps. Boarders trundled their own bedding and kitchenware to rustic, barebones operations called *kuchaleyns* ("cook-alones"), tiny groups of bungalows clustered around communal kitchens and activity centers. And increasingly, as the Jews of the New York metropolitan area grew wealthy and status conscious, full-scale hotels sprang up.

The hotels began as little more than extensions of the *kuchaleyns*, with gigantic restorative meals, light regimens of exercise, and stridently encouraged socializing as their chief attractions. Eventually they expanded their seasons from the summer months, adding the Jewish holidays of early autumn, then Thanksgiving, Christmas, and New Year's Day. And they grew physically, adding ballrooms, swimming pools, gymnasia, rec rooms, tennis courts, riding facilities, and golf courses to the nature trails and small lakes they'd always offered. The Catskills holiday gradually evolved from an escape from the soul-stifling contagion of the city and the workplace to an orgiastic barrage of activity, gluttony, courtship, and of course, entertainment.

For crucial to every Catskills establishment worth the name "resort" had become two forms of entertainer: the headliner, who would appear after meals in the ballroom, and the tummler. Like his Old World ancestor, the *badchen*, the tummler was a kind of folk jester, though he had no ritual connection to any of the religious aspects of Jewish life. He was a pure prankster, a fool, a class clown for the vacationing bourgeoisie. For the Catskills hoteliers, the tummler was a kind of insurance policy against any guest's ever voicing a note of boredom. From breakfast through a slate of organized activities, through dinner, through the evening gamut of plays, shows, and pageants, the tummler was a nonstop source of fun, a comic volcano egging guests out of any sense of routine, complacency, or self-importance and insisting that they enjoy themselves regardless of what they felt like doing. On rainy days the tummler was an especially crucial part of the hotel scene, enlivening lobbies and rec rooms and otherwise distracting guests from the thought of how much they were spending to breathe the fresh mountain air that the weather had conspired to deny them.

The typical tummler was no professional entertainer, just a busboy or lifeguard with a hambone and a thick skin for embarrassment; even the smallest hotels, which couldn't afford professional entertainment, had a tummler of some sort. Indeed, tummling became the first accessible step into the entertainment business for young jokers with big dreams. Almost every Jewish entertainer who broke into music, comedy, or acting between 1925 and 1960 got a start tummling in the Catskills. Some, like Danny Kaye and Milton Berle, created the mold. Some, like Alan King, Jack Carter, and Red Buttons, exemplified it. Some, like Lenny Bruce and Mel Brooks, shattered it. And some, like Moss Hart, transcended it. But none of them ever completely shed his tummler roots.

Headline acts were something else altogether—professional entertainers, not eager clowns. They toured hotels during seasons when big-city nightclub and vaudeville business slackened. Only the largest of the region's hundreds of hotels could afford headliners, however; smaller hotels, forced by competition to hire performers of their own, booked lower-rung vaudeville and burlesque performers. And the hoteliers who couldn't afford even that would pool resources with their competitors to hire talent for a season and share it on alternating nights.

There was no mistaking that Danny Lewis was a headliner and not a tummler. Sure, he could pitch some gags, but his specialty was putting over songs with a broad, sentimental manner. He was a pro, if a small-time one, and he took only show work—no waiting tables or schlepping bags for him. He may not have played the big hotels on Saturday nights, but he could nevertheless put together a good season of steady work each summer. For a trouper like him, the mountains were a sweet gig: steady, close to home, well paying (it usually included room and meals), offering all the health benefits that drew people to the mountains, even presenting a chance to make business connections.

Jerry's childhood was dotted with trips to the mountains to be with Danny when he found steady work. The most crucial of these came during his Christmas vacation of 1938–39. Ironically, the trip wasn't to the Catskills at all: Danny had been asked to perform at the Arthur Hotel in Lakewood, New Jersey, a resort forty miles south of Newark where he'd spent some time working the previous winter. At that time, Charles and Lillian Brown, the Arthur's managers, had discovered Danny at a talent showcase after having been told by the resort's owners to hire an emcee and entertainer. "We were in this place where they had all the talent," Charlie recalled years later, "and we saw Danny perform. We liked his personality. He was suave but he was also very warm."

A few years after that first successful term with the Browns, Danny was booked for three months at the Arthur, and he called Rae telling her to round up a sax player and a drummer and prepare to move to Lakewood for the winter. He also persuaded the Browns to make a place for Jerry at the hotel, pitching the boy as a budding showman. As Lillian Brown recalled, "Danny and Rae told us that he was producing a little show at the school where he was, how he took over, produced it, acted in it, and did everything pertaining to the entire show. And they told us that the people in that school were just overwhelmed by all that talent." The Lewises and the Browns arranged for Jerry to spend his winter recess at the hotel and to attend school in Lakewood through February.

Like the Catskills, Lakewood was a Jewish resort area, drawing on the Newark and Philadelphia populations just as the Catskills hotels catered to New Yorkers. The Arthur was a modest establishment, a white stucco building with thirty-five rooms and a little ballroom, but the Browns were clever managers: In busy seasons they put guests up in spare bedrooms at local homes and fed and entertained them on their own premises. It was Jerry's first mature experience of the resort atmosphere, with the truckloads of food, the schmaltzy entertainment, and the incessant nudging of the guests into activity.

The winter Jerry spent in Lakewood, like the previous winter's trip to Detroit, was a formative experience in his life. Not only did it give him another chance to luxuriate in the aura of his parents while they were happily working—"I spent a marvelous winter there, if only to peek through those casino doors each time Dad came on stage," he recalled—but he was taken into the arms of the Brown family. The Browns had their own kids—a daughter, Lonnie, two years older than Jerry, and a son, Arthur—but they were in the hospitality business: It was their job to make people feel at home, and Jerry, it was obvious, was a child in need of attention. Charlie was especially kind to the moody boy, sensing the loneliness beneath his antic exterior. He would, Jerry remembered, "get very sentimental if he saw me brooding. In a second he would somehow know; his arm would go around my shoulder, and that was all I needed to feel good again." In later life Jerry remained exceedingly loyal to the Browns, always referring to them as Aunt and Uncle, playing engagements at their large Catskills hotel when he could have commanded much more lucrative work, and recalling his time spent among them as the most domestic experience of his life. One of the definitive ruptures between him and Dean Martin, in fact, would be instigated by his loyalty to the Brown family.

A large part of Jerry's affection for the Browns was devoted to their daughter, Lonnie. Like her parents, she sensed the despair that plagued Jerry. A shy, bookish girl, she took Jerry under her wing, becoming the closest thing he ever had to a sibling. He had a crush on her, and he followed her around the hotel and the town of Lakewood like a puppy dog. Lonnie saw how Jerry behaved around his parents, and she was sensitive to the pain her younger friend was suffering. She began to let him into her private world, an entrée that would soon have a monumental impact on his life.

There were other friends at the Arthur. The Browns had given Jerry a job as a tea boy; in the afternoons and evenings, he'd offer hotel guests cookies and tea as they lounged in the lobby. Through this experience he became friendly with Joe Unger and Norman Smithline, two waiters who sometimes participated in makeshift comedy skits with Danny. Smithline, known around the hotel as Smitty, was the headwaiter in the dining room. "He was a kind of ladies' man—a little guy with a mustache who always dressed up spiffily," recalled a busboy who worked under him. "He played the drums. And he taught Jerry how to play the drums." Jerry was surely reminded of Danny by Smitty, and the mustachioed waiter's paternalistic attention was a gift. Jerry would keep in touch with Smitty long after he'd moved on to bigger things. "Through the years, Jerry helped him out," the busboy said. "He was in an automobile accident, and Jerry paid a lot of his bills."

Smitty and Unger would take Jerry with them when they went to movies in downtown Lakewood on their nights off. One night the trio came out of a Ken Maynard western in particularly high spirits, reenacting the movie's stunts all the way back to the hotel. On the hotel porch they got an inspiration: They would liven up Jerry's tea service with a takeoff on the movie. The guests liked it. In fact, the little act became such a hit that it soon became an expected coda to the evening's more standard entertainment. The three cutups began to parody movies right after seeing them, arriving back at the hotel to an expectant audience. As Lillian Brown recalled, "They would come in and roll down the steps into the lobby. . . . And then they'd go through the whole performance they'd just seen. We used to howl." Rae accompanied the act on piano. Everyone thought it was a gas.

Except Danny. The grand spotlight Danny had always envisioned for himself had begun to dim. He had no house, he wasn't a big name, his wife had to work, his kid was moody and had problems at school. If he had ever believed he could be the toast of Broadway like Jolie, his sights were slipping lower. Now he was grateful for gigs at places like the Arthur.

But at least in his own little sphere, Danny had been able to act the Complete Entertainer—that is, until the day he turned around to find his kid killing them in the lobby in an improvised meshuggener act. People were actually leaving his own shows early so they wouldn't miss the kid. Danny grew icy. Almost everyone who met him once Jerry had become a star reported that Danny seemed jealous of his son—critical of Jerry's work and arrogant around his boy's employees, friends, and collaborators. The chip on Danny's shoulder got its start that winter in Lakewood: He was the headliner, but his kid was stealing the show with a tummler bit he was doing for free!

The boy had the knack, and he was eager to prove it to people. Jan Murray was an up-and-coming comic maybe twenty-one years old when he first met Jerry around this time. He had been playing at the President Hotel, and he ran into Danny and Rae in a drugstore there one morning. "We started to schmooze," Murray recalled, "and he says to me, 'I want you to meet my son. This kid loves you. You crack him up.'

"So he yells, 'Jerry!' and this little boy came out—he'd been in the back of the store reading the comic books or something. He came over and Danny says, 'This is Mr. Murray,' and the kid says, 'Oh, Jan Murray! Oh, boy!' Danny says, 'You know, he saw you perform last night.' And I said, 'Oh? Did you like it?' And Danny said, 'Did he like it? Show Mr. Murray how much you liked it.' And the kid did the whole act for me that I had done the night before. He remembered almost every joke I told. It was the first time I ever met him and I wanted to kill him! I said, 'I'm gonna hurt this boy—keep him away from me!'

"He had only seen the thing once, and he remembered most of it. He stood in the middle of the drugstore and did the whole damn act back in my face. He was just a natural with a great sense of humor. Even when he was doing it back to me, he added timing and inflections. He wasn't just a parrot. He really understood the nuances of comedy."

Even though he knew Jerry could pull off such a performance, Danny didn't know just how serious his son was about a career in show business. Jerry's ambitions were pricked further one February morning in 1939, when he was wandering through the Ambassador Hotel and heard music emerging from Lonnie's bedroom. He recognized a Tommy Dorsey tune, "You're a Sweetheart," with vocals by Edythe Wright. But there was another sound. He knocked on the door.

Lonnie had been singing along with Wright—she called it "practicing" her records. With the record playing behind her, she struggled earnestly to measure up to the big-band vocalist. Jerry got an inspiration: Why compete with the singer, he asked her, when you could *be* the singer?

Lonnie didn't get it, so he demonstrated. Starting the record over, he lip-synched Wright's vocal, singing the song directly to her teddy bear for comic effect. Jerry threw himself into the performance; he recalled "feeling totally alone in the pleasure of my own making." He was thrilled; he'd found a way to be the center of attention and yet lose himself in a character, to catch an audience's eye with none of the risk of self-revelation. He and Lonnie spent the rest of the afternoon trying out other records, rehearsing specific bits of business for each.

Almost all kids who grew up with recorded music have done something like this crude pantomime, and Jerry apparently wasn't aware that the act he thought he'd dreamed up was already a familiar specialty on the vaudeville circuit. The English comic Reginald Gardiner, who had made a hit on Broadway a few years earlier by imitating wallpaper, had begun doing lip-synch material in the mid-1930s, and the bit had become a comic staple. There were dozens of "record acts" or "dummy acts," as they were known in the trade, by the time Jerry and Lonnie were rehearsing Jeanette MacDonald and Nelson Eddy's "Indian Love Call" in a room off the lobby at the Arthur. But those were professional acts. These were just kids having fun.

Until the fateful night that Red Buttons turned up missing, that is. Buttons was an up-and-coming comic at the time, twenty years old or so, with a reputation at amateur nights and in resort areas. His real name was Aaron Chwatt; his stage name derived from the jackets he wore when he doubled as a bellhop. He was doing just that in Lakewood that winter, working days at the Brunswick Hotel and picking up gigs at night at other hotels.

On one particular Saturday night, when he was scheduled to appear at the Arthur, he hadn't shown up by the time the dancers he was supposed to follow were wrapping up their act. As Danny worked the phones, scrambling to find a quick replacement, Jerry and Lonnie took advantage of the moment: Gathering up their phonograph and records, they were onstage announcing their act before Danny knew what hit him. Lonnie did the Edythe Wright number, Jerry did a Jimmy Durante song, and they finished up with "Indian Love Call." To their elation, the crowd met the end of the number with a roar of applause. They were overwhelmed . . . until they saw what had happened. While they were doing their act, Buttons had arrived and was taking the stage. The ovation was *his*.

But Jerry wasn't deterred. He knew he'd connected with the crowd, and he and Lonnie did another half-dozen or so shows that winter. Jerry even went so far as to approach Danny's sad-eyed agent, Harry Cutler, and ask him to take him on. This is something like a clinical definition of moxie: the twelve-year-old son of a small-time performer pushing himself on his old man's two-bit agent in hopes of making a career of lip-synching to records. Cutler demurred—whether out of show-biz savvy or out of fear of irking Danny it's impossible to say.

At any rate, the die was cast: Jerry was going to be a performer, with Danny's help or not.

Danny and Rae began to think of Jerry's desire for a life on the stage with trepidation. They dreamed up ways to separate him from the environment that was turning his head in the professional direction they themselves had followed. In the summer of 1940, for instance, after his eighth-grade graduation, Jerry was packed off to his aunt Jean's house in Brooklyn, far from the mountains and the record players and the small, appreciative audiences.

But Dan and Rae didn't reckon on just how determined he was. Separated from the Catskills, Jerry landed a plum job: Lying about his age and calling on a family friend, he got work as an usher at the Paramount Theater on Broadway. Jerry's connection at the Paramount was Broadway Sam Roth, a ticket broker who kept a small office beside the famous theater. Roth had met Jerry at the Arthur, where he was a frequent guest; according to Lillian Brown, the older man "was crazy about him. He said he was sure Jerry was going to be famous."

For a stagestruck kid, a job at the Paramount would have been a dream come true, but Jerry managed to blow it within two weeks. Unhappy with the oversized uniform the theater manager, Bob Shapiro, had given him, Jerry griped out loud to his fellow employees one day in the locker room. Shapiro, though, was standing right behind him: "Levitch, turn in your dickey!" It was the first of a string of disappointments; Roth got Jerry jobs up and down Broadway, and the kid blew them all.

His luck was no better back in Newark, where he tried to join the top-flight theatrical program at the YMHA. The Newark Y had been modeled after Manhattan's Ninety-second Street Y, the legendary cultural bastion. And one of the key elements in its formation was the establishment of theater workshops for young people. "One of the people who was on the staff was George Kahn, who for fifty years headed the drama program," recalled Alan Lowenstein. "Moss Hart was on the staff as well. Jerry Lewis as a kid came in to be an actor in the drama department at the YMHA. But he was a hellraiser, and the legend is that he's the only one that George Kahn ever threw out of the Y."

In the fall, as a freshman at Irvington High, Jerry was in way over his head academically. The only thing he could do to distinguish himself was tummel. So famous were his antics, his distorted whoops, and his rubbery grimaces, that he became known around campus as "Id" (for "Idiot"—not a Freudian reference, however appropriate one may have been) or "Ug" (for "Ugly"). With his gratuitous clowning, he managed to ingratiate himself with the other kids even if he was struggling helplessly in his classes.

Inadvertently, Dan and Rae let Jerry get another foothold into show business in the spring of 1941, just after that first year in high school. Dan and Rae had bolted Irvington before the school year was over. This time they were off to Loch Sheldrake, a Catskill resort where the Browns had bought their own hotel, the Ambassador. Coming home from school one day, Jerry found his folks packed and ready to leave. With them was burlesque comic Lou Black, who had worked a twosome with Danny on and off over the years. Rae gave Jerry five bucks and the key to his aunt Rose's house, then left him to finish out the school year on his own.

By the time summer break rolled around, though, they'd found a way to take care of the kid. Once again, they'd pitched Jerry's skills to the Browns—it was his athleticism, this time, not his showmanship—and they'd wrangled a job for him. Rae wrote to Jerry that the Browns would pay him ten dollars a week, plus room and board, to be their athletic director. Jerry bought himself a metal whistle and caught a bus north.

The Ambassador was a much more elaborate setup than the Arthur. It had many more guest rooms, a built-in swimming pool, a rec room with a pool table and jukebox, and a huge ballroom that dwarfed the Arthur's tiny casino (there had even been an on-site barbershop before the Browns turned it into sleeping quarters for the kitchen help). The hotel was nestled in the heart of the Borscht Belt at a time when the region's influence was still ascending. The Browns had cut a great deal to get hold of the place, which would become the basis of their later fame in the resort business.

With some of their employees, though, they weren't so lucky. As an athletic director, Jerry made a great tea boy. After a few days he injured himself and politely resigned his commission. Charles Brown then offered him a chance to work as a busboy. Clearing tables would seem a step down from the relative distinction of putting old women through their calisthenics, but at least busboys got tips and a chance to schmooze the girls.

Not that Jerry had much time to cultivate his love life. He was spending time with the old gang from the Arthur—Lonnie Brown, Joe Unger, and Smitty. He was working on his record act. And he had found a new ally in his desire to make a career of himself—a schlub of a bellhop named Irving Kaye.

On the surface, Jerry's friendship with Kaye was positively cryptic. Physically, they were opposites: Where Jerry was tall, bony, boyishly handsome, and slick, Kaye was short, froggy, and rumpled. He smoked foul cigars and wore thick glasses—the guys at the Ambassador called him "Googs" for his Barney Google eyes. In a picture taken with Jerry in 1948, he could pass for the kid's aging dad; Jerry would introduce him as "my dead cousin." Due to his strange upbringing, Jerry felt comfortable with older folks perhaps even more than with people his own age. And Kaye, who had kids and a wife somewhere but seemed unconnected to anyone, must have relished the role of tutor to the bright youngster. He'd once wanted to be an actor himself—"a Jewish Barrymore," he told Jerry—but he'd drifted into comedy and would up schlepping bags. "He was slow moving," recalled one of his co-workers. "Not a Stepin Fetchit type, but he didn't seem that ambitious."

Also on the scene that summer was Lawrence Shapiro, a New York kid about a year older than Jerry whose dad knew Charlie Brown and who'd gotten a job busing tables through his connection. He got to watch Dan and Rae perform: "Rae only could play the piano in one key," he recalled, "and it was Danny's key. I didn't think Danny had a great voice. He had a strong voice but not a great one." And he got to see Jerry around his mom and dad. "He loved his parents," Shapiro observed. "That always came across. And he always seemed happy."

What made Jerry so happy, no doubt, was being close to both his parents and the parade of performers that passed through the Ambassador's ballroom. He watched Danny and Lou Black practice routines tirelessly. He watched Tillie and Jimmy Gerard—a Burns-and-Allen-style act—and a stream of solo comics: Gene Baylos, Larry Alpert, Mickey Freeman. And he saw a record act. A comedian named Sammy Birch came through the hotel doing just the kind of stuff Jerry and Lonnie had worked on the previous winter. The sight of someone presenting a polished version of his own little specialty might have crushed a kid with less gumption or less exposure to small-time show business. But Jerry took Birch's act as an encouragement. He pestered Rae to buy him a phonograph and some records, and she obliged.

As he worked on his act that summer, Jerry saw his father suffer a tremendous disappointment. Danny had gotten a chance to emcee and perform at the nearby Majestic Hotel in a showcase for an agent of the William Morris office. He and Lou Black poured hours into rehearsals for their big break, and Jerry recalled that they performed brilliantly. Of course, Jerry always recalled Danny performing brilliantly, despite his continual inability to get big dates. In later years Jerry used his clout to get his father all sorts of showcases—the Paramount Theater, television appearances, even a film role—but no one ever stepped up to make a star of Danny Lewis. That night at the Majestic was typical: The Morris agent never showed up.

Jerry, meanwhile, was preparing for his professional debut. He'd performed with Lonnie Brown at the Arthur during the winter, but now, with his own phonograph and stack of records, he had eyes for bigger things. He had worked out a variety of numbers, doing takeoffs on Danny Kaye, Frank Sinatra, Carmen

Miranda, Betty Hutton, Deanna Durbin, English comic singer Cyril Smith, and opera star Igor Gorin. And he'd managed to get a paying gig for himself performing as a pantomime soloist: He would make his debut at the Cozy Corner, a shack where hotel employees went for beers and hamburgers. One August night Jerry marched into the place with his first entourage—Lonnie Brown and Irving Kaye—and played through his stack of records. His chums in the audience, most of whom had seen him do the act countless times in the Ambassador's rec room, cheered him on, and he left the joint five dollars richer and glowing with the applause he'd received. Pointedly, Danny and Rae were not on hand.

Danny, in fact, was trying to find ways to keep Jerry out of the show racket altogether. He and Charlie Brown leaned on Kaye to get him to stop encouraging the kid. "Danny didn't want his boy to be an actor," Kaye recalled. "And Charlie said, 'Look, busboys are hard to get. Stop making an actor out of the kid.'" But Jerry wasn't really depending on Kaye's mentorship. That summer he finagled several engagements for himself at the small hotels in the area—the Waldmere, the Nemerson, the Laurel Park, Flagler's, Young's Gap. Some of these hotels had no doubt hosted Danny Lewis when he was an up-and-comer. Now they had the pleasure to present "Joey Levitch and His Hollywood Friends," as Jerry was billing his dummy act. From early morning and throughout the day, he endured the sweaty labors of a busboy. At night, with Kaye and his phonograph in tow, he was a star.

The summer ended, and Jerry returned to Irvington High without any of his Hollywood Friends. It didn't feel like a homecoming. Jerry drifted through his classes listlessly, and even Dan and Rae, whose attentions to their son's education had never been exacting, began hassling him over his poor marks, to little avail.

Jerry worked the Thanksgiving and Christmas seasons at the Ambassador. Things may not have been working out well between him and his folks; for the first time, he bunked with the help. As usual, space was at a premium during the holidays, so the Browns had Jerry, Lawrence Shapiro, and an oddball waiter share a room in the basement. "That guy smoked pot," Shapiro recalled, "and also sold it. Not to us, though. And Jerry never tried it. Neither did I." The waiter's strange behavior drew attention to him fast. "Thanksgiving he was there, and Christmas he was in jail," Shapiro remembered.

The hepcat waiter wasn't the only Ambassador employee who disappeared that winter of 1941. And Jerry's cousin Marshall Katz, who'd joined the Navy a year earlier, was among the first to learn why: He was stationed in Pearl Harbor in December 1941 and survived the Japanese attack on the Pacific fleet (Katz would fight the entire war in the Pacific, being issued a sole three-week furlough to come home to Newark and get married). The war sucked the life out of the hotel staffs all through the Catskills. The pickup musicians who accompanied

Rae—drummer Joe Kenneth Beltzer and a saxophonist—were both gone to war by spring. Increasingly, staffs were made up of kids like Jerry and Shapiro and overaged louts like Irving Kaye. Out of such historical anomalies, strange chemistries brew.

When school resumed after the New Year of 1942, with his parents performing at the Ambassador, Jerry provoked one of his teachers with a mishap involving some school equipment. By some accounts, he broke a band saw while trying to cut a board that still had a nail in it. By others, he caused a small explosion while ad-libbing a chemistry experiment (a nicer fit with the future Nutty Professor, and the version Jerry used in his autobiography). Whichever, Jerry was summoned to the principal, a Mr. Herder, of local German stock.

"Are you a wise guy?" the exasperated bureaucrat asked Jerry, and then: "Why is it that only the Jews . . . ?"

He never finished the sentence. Jerry hit him in the mouth; by day's end he'd been expelled and sent to a technical school, Irvington Vocational High. He called his parents, who voiced support but couldn't get away from their engagement at the Arthur, and he went off to learn a trade.

By March, electrical maintenance and repair had lost its allure for him. But he had a plan. He would soon be sixteen years old. He would drop out of school. He would have head shots taken. He would take his act to Broadway. On March 16, instead of dressing for school, he would put on a suit and take the train to Manhattan to find work as a professional lip-syncher.

And there was that last little change to see to. No longer would he be known as Joey Levitch, the sad, lonely boy from Irvington whose parents never had time for him. He was a professional, and he would have a professional's name: Jerry Lewis. Joey Levitch would never be heard from again. Glimpsed only in the fuzzy recollections of a man who made his living by pretending to be someone else, he became yet another persona of the mature man. Jerry he had been born, and Jerry he would remain forever.

3.

Are You for Real?

On his sixteenth birthday Jerry dressed himself up and made the round of agents, exploiting their familiarity with his dad to get a foot in their doors. He worked Times Square all day, and all day he got the classic "Call me when you're working and I'll come watch you" rebuff. "Regards to your folks," he'd hear before the door closed on him. He had quit school, he had no money, he had no prospects. He went home and called his parents with the news.

Danny and Rae weren't happy about what Jerry had done, but if it was anybody's fault, it was theirs. They had consistently shown a preference for show business over home, family, and education, they had denied themselves to their son at almost every turn, and they provided little daily guidance beyond allowing Jerry to watch them work.

"At first we wouldn't listen," Danny recalled some years later. "Then Mrs. Lewis and I realized that unless he got the idea out of his system, the desire would always be there. If Jerry was bad, she argued, he'd know it and quit."

Danny was jealous to protect his show-biz turf from his son, but he found a way to cloak his antagonism in something like paternal affection. "While I hated to have anyone in my family struggle with show business like I had, I finally gave in," he said in an article published under his byline in *TV Story* in 1952. "But I was still very much against it. So much so that neither Mrs. Lewis nor I went to see him."

Then he let an introspective note creep into his account: "The thing I regret most, I think, is that Jerry grew up too fast." Of course, this was no Tevye singing a mournful "Sunrise, Sunset" as he married off a beloved child. Danny had been as absent as a parent could be, and though his son, whom he acknowledged had "the art of natural pantomime plus perfect timing," chased after him in his desire to join him, his instinct was to shunt him away. But he told his wife he'd give it a chance, so he listened.

As Danny recalled, Jerry "had located a man who was willing to give him a chance to exhibit his 'talents,' " The man was Irving Kaye. Kaye still had some connections from his own days as a struggling comic, and he thought he might be able to get the kid work during double-feature intermissions. Jerry got his folks to agree to his scheme if Kaye would serve as chaperon, manager, and aide-de-camp: Someone, after all, had to change the records while Jerry mugged.

"I took him around and got him auditions and got him on the Loew's circuit, for fifteen and twenty dollars a night," Kaye later remembered. "He could do fifteen minutes with these records he had. Loew's had about thirty, forty theaters in the New York area, and RKO had some, and once a week these theaters, movie houses, put on a vaudeville show."

The work wasn't steady. Jerry returned to bus tables at the Ambassador in the spring of 1942, during Passover. A grocers' convention came up from Jersey after the holiday, a loud, drunken group that wasn't interested in watching a pimple-faced kid grimace to records. They brought their own entertainment: three hookers—"exotic dancers," they called them. Such was the wartime hotel business that Charlie and Lillian Brown looked the other way.

But not Jerry. He'd been after girls his own age for a while, and all he'd wound up with, as he recalled in his autobiography, was a few cases of blue balls and a sad heart. Here, though, were women who reminded him of Marlene, his courtesan from the National Theater. After the girls performed, the grocers queued up to sample their other talents, and Jerry got right in line with them.

At the last minute, though, he lost his nerve. Alone with the girl, he couldn't bring himself to perform, and he argued with her in an effort to get his money back. Businesswoman that she was, she grabbed his watch and bolted from the room, the skinny kid in pursuit. Eventually, the grocers sorted the thing out. Jerry got his watch back, but he had to fork over the dough and scram.

It must have been a relief when Irving Kaye got him some more stage work. Jerry toured Loew's theaters throughout northern Jersey on a six-week contract, with his original entourage—Kaye and Lonnie Brown—appearing at almost every show. What they saw heartened them: Audiences liked the act. "In all my years working in show business in the Catskills and other places, I've seen acts stop shows," Kaye said in flusher days, "I've seen standing ovations, but I've never seen anything like what he did."

What he did was no different from what he had been doing: lip-synching to that same pile of records he'd bought the previous summer. He had learned how to control his body better—turning scratches in the records into comic riffs, for instance. He added costumes—when he aped Igor Gorin's "Figaro" aria, he sported a fright wig and tattered overcoat in a parody of highbrow art that had all the savoir faire of a Warner Brothers cartoon. Still, skilled as it may have been, it was only a dummy act. No one would get very far with such a curious specialty.

He was getting by, though: It was wartime, and thousands of performers had been enlisted. Jerry was a kid—a kid who could do remarkable things with his body, true, but a kid nevertheless. He still wasn't eligible for the draft. And therein lay his fortune.

Of course, even a fortunate act needed a helping hand to get off the ground. The hand that reached out to help Jerry was spidery and lean.

"Right away I saw Jerry had this genius for mugging," recalled Abner J. Greshler, a Broadway agent just branching out from representing musicians to signing up comics. Jerry seemed a likely enough prospect when Greshler caught his act at the Ritz Theater in Staten Island, where the kid appeared for the princely sum of seven dollars. Greshler thought he could book Jerry on a wider circuit, burlesque houses, maybe. Jerry was delighted for the help. He had big dreams for himself, but Greshler's might have been even bigger.

Abner Greshler was born in 1910 to immigrant parents on New York City's Lower East Side. His father was a furrier who put in inhuman days in fetid, TB-infested sweatshops; Mrs. Greshler took in sewing, doing piecework in the family's fourth-floor tenement apartment, a hovel in which they used bottles as latrines and wooden planks hung between chairs as beds.

Young Abbey was asthmatic, with a frail constitution and pasty complexion, but he was a scrapper. He had to be: When his parents finally were able to afford a less disagreeable home, they moved to a railroad apartment in a mixed neighborhood, a place where Jewish kids were regularly beaten up by their Italian and Irish neighbors. Abbey was smart enough to survive in this neighborhood, trading homework for protection so that he could hold on to the pennies he earned hawking Yiddish newspapers. Across the street lived the Fischetti family, cousins of Al Capone—the toughest kids on the block, and Abbey prudently befriended them.

Abbey was a studious kid, and he began to wonder about the papers he was selling. The comics, for instance: Why, if every Jewish kid he knew spoke English except at home, were they in Yiddish? Boldly, he created a mock-up of a comics page in English and one night after he was through selling papers marched down to see Abraham Cahan, the famous publisher of the *Jewish Daily Forward*.

"What's so important to bring a boy out in the dark?" asked the imposing Cahan. The boy produced his creation, and after showing it to some co-workers, Cahan took out his wallet and handed the boy ten dollars.

"It was almost a month's rent," Greshler recalled. "And that's when I decided to go into show business."

Abbey became a kind of mascot around the paper, and Cahan took him under his wing, bringing him to concerts and plays and enrolling him in the Young People's Socialist League, one of many Jewish progressive groups in the area.

Soon afterward, with Abbey's horizons broadened, his father announced that he was moving the family to the Bronx and going into business for himself. The move liberated the family from squalor, though not from the need to hustle. To augment his paper-selling gig, Abbey added a bit of unlikely dash: He performed at vaudeville amateur nights at a nearby theater, drawn by the three-dollar first prizes.

He grew fond of the stage, but making a buck in vaudeville in the 1920s was a tough road—just ask Danny Lewis. Though only a teenager, Greshler had a keen business sense, and he began looking around for other cracks in the show-biz game that he might enter. He found one in a Chinese restaurant. On a school lunch break, he wandered into Yeong's, a huge Broadway chop suey joint catering to midtown secretaries. The place was packed, but no one was eating: The girls were dancing stag to Paul Tremain and his Band from Lonely Acres, a jitter-bug outfit hired to boost lunchtime business.

During the band's break, Greshler approached Tremain—just a kid himself, whose father was arranging his bookings.

"What do you do when you're done here?" Greshler asked.

"Nothing."

"You mean you don't play at any of the schools—the colleges, the private schools?"

"Why? Can you get us some of those gigs?"

"Sure."

Greshler ran off to find an old friend—the former bandleader Willard Alexander, who'd just been hired as a booker with a Chicago outfit called the Music Corporation of America, MCA.

"What's a 'gig'?" Greshler asked him.

Greshler ran off beating the bushes for work for the band; two weeks later, he'd lined up three bookings.

Appeasing his parents, Abbey enrolled at Morris Evening High, but he spent his days booking the band, learning how to dress like a sharpie and how to schmooze adults into forking over sums he'd only dreamed of months before—up to five thousand dollars a night. Soon enough, his name got around, and he started signing other bands. MCA even offered him a job through Willard Alexander, but Abbey liked being in business for himself. He was becoming an impresario: He bought lights, a dimmer board, risers for the band. He booked corporate parties, weddings, bar mitzvahs.

One day his mother was cleaning his room and found his Lehman Brothers investment account passbook. It recorded a balance of eleven thousand dollars. She couldn't believe the money was legitimate, and she chastised him so severely that he cried: He was, after all, still only in high school.

With his diploma in sight in the late 1920s, Abbey started looking around for ways to expand his business. One of his bandleaders, a kid named Shepard Feldman who went by the name Shep Fields, suggested Abbey try the Catskills.

Shep had grown up there; his parents had run a hotel before his father was killed in a motorcycle accident and Shep drifted down to New York to try a career in music. Abbey had done well by him; he, in turn, steered Abbey toward the mountains, where Greshler's own dad had gone long ago to recover from TB.

But the Catskills proved no Eden for Abbey: Hotel social directors were satisfied with their own rosters, and they didn't want any New York sharpies butting in. They sent him back home with his tail between his legs.

Abbey wasn't one to take rejection lightly, and he devised a scheme he thought would ingratiate him to the Catskill hotels without making them see him as a threat. He suggested that they host a string of "guest nights"—specially billed evenings when hotels would swap one another's headliners for a night. It worked. Guest nights became popular, and a few more ears bent Abbey's way. He began bringing carloads of talent up from Manhattan; the hotels footed the bill, and if they liked what they saw, they could work out a financial agreement later. Greshler was in the vanguard, bringing up Jewish comics, Broadway song artists, jazz bands, opera singers, even feature films. He became the premier booker in the area.

He was so well known, in fact, that it got a little dangerous. One day a mobster came knocking on his office door, a *shtarker* in a pinstripe suit looking for money.

"We wanna know when we're gonna get our twenty-five grand."

"What are you talking about?" Greshler asked.

"Well, we protected you."

"Protected me? I don't know what you're talking about!" But the guy wouldn't listen. Abbey would pay up or there would be ugly consequences.

It was Abbey's first contact with the underworld he knew was swirling around beneath his business, and it scared him—even more than the neighborhood toughs had, back on the Lower East Side. And it was to his boyhood neighbors he turned, explaining the situation and appealing for their help.

"I never heard another word," he later boasted.

After his Catskill business took off, Abbey devoted himself to self-improvement: Fordham Law School at night, by day the college of Abe Lastfogle. Lastfogle was a William Morris agent and a legend on Broadway. He dressed modestly, spoke softly, and had more skill at packaging shows than any ten swaggering bookers combined. Greshler had sold him acts a few times and come away almost awestruck. He was like a chess champion: When everyone else, Abbey included, was worrying about protecting his pawns, Lastfogle was mounting elaborate offensives that no one else could fathom.

Lastfogle taught Abbey to build careers, not gigs—to invest more than an act was earning in the interest of long-term return. He saw himself not as in the booking business but in "the agency business." He said it in inspiring tones. Greshler was known as a band booker and a Catskills packager, but he wanted to be in "the agency business," too. All he needed was one steady-money act, one source of income to lift him above the bookers and into the sphere of agents. And in search of that act, he was willing to go anywhere. Even Staten Island.

The question of how Greshler came to be at the Ritz Theater has been a matter of some contention. The official Lewis family version was that Greshler had heard that the kid was killing audiences and went himself to check out the rumors. Greshler, to the contrary, told people that Dan and Rae begged every agent in New York to sign their son, hanging around outside Lindy's on Broadway and coaxing Jerry into doing bits for the big shots who wandered by. Eventually, according to this version, Greshler agreed to listen to their pitch inside the deli— but only if they bought him cake and coffee.

Neither account rings true: An honest-to-God agent taking the ferry to Staten Island to watch a teenager do a dummy act? Dan and Rae spending time trying to get Jerry a leg up in the business? However it came about, though, Greshler did catch the act in Staten Island and offered to sign the kid, providing Jerry's first real entrée into the business.

Greshler didn't look like the impressive Abe Lastfogle. His skin was waxy and gray, his eyes sunken. But he was shrewd, a survivor who understood the business. Danny Lewis could see as much; he agreed to let his sixteen-year-old boy sign a standard contract.

Savvy Svengali that he was, Greshler set about reshaping Jerry's image to exploit his queer gifts to the hilt. First he addressed the look: Photos of Jerry in his teens reveal a kid with a triangular face, a mouth full of teeth, and straight, longish hair, which he usually slicked down but could wear over his eyes so as to look like an ape. He was gangly—all elbows, shoulders, and knees—and he had a touch of Danny's foppishness: In a photo taken in the Catskills in the early 1940s with his dad and some friends, Jerry sports two rings—one on his pinky— even though he's wearing simple chinos and a sweatshirt.

By the time he was working with Greshler, though, Jerry's image had been gussied up: double-breasted suits, a pompadour, even a fancy slogan: "Jerry Lewis—Satirical Impressions in Pantomimicry."

Greshler booked the kid practically the day he signed him. A burlesque house in Buffalo, the Palace, offered him $125 a week. Just the sound of it had Jerry dreaming great dreams—*the Palace*. At Rae's insistence, Irving Kaye would make the trip as well. The two boarded a train in Manhattan one September morning—Candide and Pangloss out to conquer the world, the Palace Theater beckoning like a siren.

But the siren was a trollop. Kaye knew the place but diplomatically had said nothing. The Palace was a toilet, the strippers worn-out hags, the audience just drunk and lethargic enough not to riot. Jerry was heartbroken.

He took the stage the first night and did some of his cutest bits. "Get the fuck off!" bellowed the small crowd of men with overcoats in their laps. "Bring on the babes!"

He raced back into the seedy dressing room in tears, stuffing his bags with clothes and swearing off show business, Kaye watching but saying nothing.

Another comic on that night's bill, an old-time burlesque clown, walked in on the scene.

"Are you Danny Lewis's son?" he asked.

"Yeah."

"No, you're not. You're a fraud. Danny Lewis's son would never walk away from a show."

It was Max Coleman, a friend of Danny's who'd played the National Theater during Jerry's epochal family vacation in Detroit a few winters earlier. Jerry's self-pity turned into shame. Reproved, he got a sufficient grip on himself to play the second show. It went better. He would survive.

Seeing that the Palace hadn't knocked the spirit out of him, Greshler began to coax Jerry into doing more than pantomime. While the kid was in Buffalo, Greshler booked him in Montreal and Toronto at $150 a week—ten times his usual rate. But he'd have to do more than the dummy act to earn it. If he was going to go anywhere under Greshler's hand, Jerry was going to have to open his mouth and speak onstage. He was going to have to emcee at burlesque houses, just like his old man.

This would seem a natural progression, but the prospect of appearing *as himself* daunted Jerry. There was a world of difference between the anonymity of lip-synching and the personal risk involved in emceeing a show. Jerry knew people liked him when he mugged, but nobody had ever clamored for him when he was just being Jerry. Greshler made it clear, though, that he had no choice: Either he started talking onstage, or he found another agent.

"He was a scared kid with a high squeaky voice," Greshler remembered. "He was afraid to talk, to express himself, and that was why he had been crazy to do the record act. He didn't have to speak. The record did it for him. I told him he had to talk if he wanted to make any money. I explained that if he did some emcee work as well as the record specialty I'd have a better chance of getting him jobs in clubs."

Easier said than done: This was a sixteen-year-old boy, petrified to do anything on his own. But Greshler held sway. He packed Jerry and Kaye off to the Gaiety Theater in Montreal and sat in his Radio City office waiting to hear what happened.

Jerry showed up in Montreal a nervous wreck. He made his way to the theater, stepped in front of the curtain, and introduced the acts with a robotic sense of duty. He did his specialty—the only time all night he felt himself—and escaped from the evening without messing up . . . or making much of an impression.

And what sort of emcee was he? One club owner, after enduring Lewis's petrified delivery, grabbed Greshler by the lapels and hollered, "What's with this lousy kid? Don't he tell gags or stories? You sold him to me as an emcee, not an undertaker."

Another time, Greshler brought Ed Sullivan, then a rising Broadway columnist, to watch Jerry's act. The presence of the great man in the audience couldn't have helped, but Jerry topped himself in stiffness that night. He'd always relied on the words "ladies and gentlemen" to get him through a show. Greshler counted sixty-one repeats of the phrase that night. At evening's end, according to Greshler, Sullivan turned to him and said, "He's pretty funny, but for God's sake, doesn't he know any lines other than 'ladies and gentlemen'?" Sullivan even wrote out a list of alternatives for Greshler to give to Jerry: "folks," "dear friends," and the like. Jerry diligently and mechanically added them to his arsenal. (A 1953 kinescope of a Muscular Dystrophy telethon he hosted with Dean Martin showed Jerry lapsing back into his old habit; in the course of two hours, he said "ladies and gentlemen" at least twenty times.)

Still, Greshler was slowly turning Jerry from a one-trick pony into a one-trick pony who could also introduce acts. Just as he'd promised, he got Jerry more and better work on the Loew's circuit and in large eastern cities. The audience began to enjoy the contrast between the stiff, efficient emcee and the maniacally contorted pantomimist. Jerry made the rounds of burlesque houses, presentation houses (where he performed on brief vaudeville bills before feature films), and the occasional nightclub.

The notion of this high school boy working the burlesque circuit has a quaint, bygone savor to it, but it must have been a kind of assault on Jerry's young sensibility. It was a lewd, coarse environment, and he was vulnerable to all sorts of suggestions in the air, even with Kaye as a chaperon.

Moreover, Jerry's burlesque years were central in defining his conception of show business and comedy. In significant ways, Jerry's career perpetuated many aspects of burlesque for decades beyond the medium's demise. Indeed, in later moments when his shtick seemed dated, it was often because of its dependence on the traditions of burlesque. Just as his adoption of Al Jolson's urgent, beseeching manner marked him as a Jewish American entertainer of a certain vintage, so his reliance on crude jokes, physical humor, sketch-based narratives, and broad sentimentality indicate his devotion to the entertainment world he and his father once inhabited.

Burlesque, like blackface, lingers in the collective memory under a suspicious haze, its patina of licentiousness almost as embarrassing as the racism of minstrelsy. But in its time it was a legitimate, adult-oriented alternative to the bourgeois family atmosphere of vaudeville. Where vaudeville served as the model for generations of TV variety shows, striving to offer something for everybody from cultural elitists to blue-haired old ladies to toddlers, burlesque was working-class entertainment with little in it designed to appeal to anyone but its presold masculine audience.

Throughout the 1920s and '30s, when Danny Lewis was most active on the circuit, burlesque was under fire from municipal authorities all over the country, who blamed the occurrence of sex crimes on men who'd been overstimulated by the exposure of female flesh onstage. Whenever they were threatened with censorship, the burlesque circuits responded by tempering the striptease with heavy doses of comedy, acrobatic acts, and similar specialties. Most of these acts would have preferred to work more lucrative, respectable, and steady vaudeville stages; but, like the proverbial schlemiel who cleaned up after the elephants in the circus, they couldn't bear the thought of quitting show biz.

Many acts, of course, played both. And when they were playing before wholly male, often drunken burlesque audiences, they had to deliver a more frenetic version of their repertoires. They added blue language and gestures, resorted to a more knockabout style of physical action, made their character sketches more grotesque, their ethnically or sexually oriented humor more explicitly demeaning. Where a vaudeville comedian would tell jokes and stories, maybe mix in a bit of song-and-dance patter or a few zingers at the expense of a straight man, burlesque comedians worked at a frenzied pitch of physical jousting, verbal hysteria, and outright hostility toward fellow entertainers and the audience. George Burns is an archetypical vaudevillian; Lou Costello is pure burlesque.

When Jerry got around to putting together stage shows, TV shows, and telethons (even as early as his Rex Theater benefit), he clearly had a burlesque model in mind: some singing, some dancing, plenty of bang-'em-up humor, a little cheesecake. And when he constructed his own comic persona alongside Dean Martin, he leaned toward what he'd seen on the burlesque stage: loud, almost inarticulate delivery, perilous and sometimes cruel physical humor, a taste for slapstick and sight gags over arch dialogue or situational humor, a strong central persona who played a predictable role but got laughs through the sheer force of idiosyncrasy.

In part, Jerry's emulation of burlesque helps explain why people reacted to his act so immediately when he debuted in the late 1940s. Most of his audience then had grown up on the same stuff Jerry had, and the universal affection people had for him came in part from their own nostalgia. It was like discovering as an adult the kind of candy you loved as a kid. But as that audience dwindled with age, its children—who had no firsthand knowledge of burlesque or the silent-film clowns—came to think of Jerry merely as a roistering physical comic. When their childhoods were behind them, they put Jerry behind them—a shift in public opinion from which he has never recovered. Ironically, while it was the very disappearance of burlesque comedy that made Jerry seem such a breath of fresh air after World War II, its obscurity twenty years later made him seem less vital than fossilized.

The solitude of the road weighed heavily on Jerry. He was born to loneliness, but now, with Irving Kaye sitting in as a kind of grotesque version of Grandma Sarah, with the daily reality of making his way in the world upon him, his prospects didn't seem very bright. And Kaye didn't help much. One night when Jerry was playing in Boston, Kaye sat morosely in their room at the Bradford Hotel taking stock of his life. Here he was, ward to a struggling child, changing records in the wings of burlesque houses, schlepping bags without even the prospect of a tip. As he recalled later, he looked cold and hard at Jerry's future and told him point-blank: "You'll have to change your act. Forget the lip-synch stuff, forget the records. Find yourself soon. Not twenty-two years from now—or maybe never, like me."

Jerry knew he was right. He drew up an impromptu contract giving Kaye 10 percent of all his future earnings. Kaye was heartened by the gesture, but all the same he tore the paper into shreds, certain, no doubt, that Jerry's dreams would prove to be as chimerical as his own.

A young man on the road with a desperate need for companionship surely sought more out of his nights than commiserating with the likes of Irving Kaye. Jerry was sixteen and playing near home—emceeing and doing his record act down the bill from the Louis Prima Orchestra at the Central Theater in Passaic—when a likelier distraction caught his fancy. Her name was Lily Ann Carol: brunette, twenty years old, nice to him. He would stand in the wings pantomiming as she sang; she'd let a smile sneak over her face.

Her real surname was Greco, and she was from Brooklyn. Her father and brothers would make the trip to Passaic from Williamsburg, where they worked in the shipyards, to greet her backstage after the shows. They were probably worried about her exposure to lecherous showmen, and with good reason: Jerry may have been making a big show of courting Lily Ann, getting to know dad and the brothers and making a big impression, but Prima was already exercising the bandleader's *droit du seigneur* with her, out of sight of her burly relatives.

Naïve Jerry wooed Lily Ann the only way he could—by making her laugh. She found him amusing; she encouraged him. And when she went on the road after Passaic, Jerry got that same sick feeling he used to get as a boy when Dan and Rae left. When she called him one night from Philadelphia, he was overwhelmed. He hopped a train at Penn Station and was pounding on her hotel room door at two in the morning. Seating himself on her bed—had Prima been in it that night?—he all but proposed marriage.

Naturally, Lily Ann was appalled. She managed gracefully both to rebuff his insane notion and to coax him out of her room and back to New York.

"We'll always be friends," she told him: a death sentence.

"I'm gonna run all the way to the train," he responded. "So I can get older much faster."

He was still sixteen. The train ride must have taken forever.

The summer of 1943 came, and the work came in spurts. Burlesque was dying gracelessly, shifting more and more blatantly into lasciviousness in a frantic effort to attract customers. Jerry and Kaye took a room at the Holland Hotel on Times Square, where Danny and Rae were living: an underemployed little family, with Kaye as the comic uncle.

In the fall Greshler booked Jerry into Dave Wolper's Hurricane, a Times Square nightclub decorated with a jungle motif inspired, in all likelihood, by the 1937 film of the same title: Dorothy Lamour and Jon Hall clinging to the doorways of their huts while a special-effects storm attacked their island paradise. Jerry was doing a Carmen Miranda bit by then, fruited hat and all. He must have fit right in with the fake vines. The Duke Ellington orchestra headlined for part of Jerry's run, and jazz critics Leonard Lyons and Lee Mortimer both mentioned Jerry's act in their columns when they came to see the band. But nothing came of it. The Manhattan nightclub boom was to be a postwar phenomenon. Greshler was still going to have to book Jerry as an emcee/pantomimist in out-of-town theaters. He started to string together a spring and summer tour.

But the Selective Service would have its say first. Two days after his eighteenth birthday, in March 1944, Jerry made his way to Grand Central Place in a blue suit and orange tie. He wanted to sign up, as did most young men of the day, but they wouldn't take him. Perforated eardrum, the doctor told him, and a heart murmur: 4-F, the badge of shame for a red-blooded American boy.

Jerry did the honorable thing. He signed on with the USO to do a six-week tour of hospitals and boot camps, mostly in the northeast. He added Spike Jones's "Der Führer's Face" to his repertoire and entertained kids his own age, boys who were shot up, many maimed for life. He tried to understand what sort of star he'd been born under, that not even the military wanted him. It was a strange blessing, being 4-F; he'd make a movie about it one day, *Which Way to the Front?*, but not until after he'd made five or so others playing a serviceman. In 1944, though, it felt like just another form of rejection. The USO tour ended, and he returned to the grind of emceeing and pantomime, doing the work he wanted to be doing, but still lonely, still struggling, still aimless.

That August Jerry made a triumphant return to Detroit, the scene of his youthful burlesque reveries and his sexual awakening. He wasn't playing the National or staying at the Barlum, but he was flooded with memories of his burlesque trip with his parents.

Greshler had booked him at the Downtown Theater for sixty dollars a week. He was a between-acts specialty: The show began with a road version of the "Arlene Francis Blind Date" radio game; then Jerry would step before the curtain

and do his shtick; then the Ted Fio Rito orchestra came on. The orchestra featured a twenty-three-year-old singer named Patti Palmer. She had a dark-
featured, heart-shaped face, a wide smile, chestnut eyes. Her nose was a bit flat,
her hair slightly unruly, but she could be gorgeous.

Jerry noticed her right away. Standing with his oily pompadour, in his baggy
zoot suit and rubber-soled creepers, he gave her the eye: "Hey, girlie, you should
have dinner with me tonight."

She thought he was a neighborhood wise guy and shot him down. "Are you
for real?" she snapped, breezing right by him.

Detroit was a homecoming for Patti, too. Her real name was Esther Calonico,
the daughter of Italian immigrants (actually, she had been born Pasqualina—
"little Easter"—but she begged for an anglicized name when she began to attend school). Her mother, Mary, had lived a brutally hard life in Italy as a maid
for a wealthy family, suffering beatings when her work didn't meet their standards. When she was fourteen, Giuseppe Calonico proposed marriage and flight
to America. Mary agreed, passed through Ellis Island, and found herself in a
house with linoleum floors in Cambria, Wyoming, a remote coal-mining town.

Mary Calonico had never known tenderness in her life, and the fates had
conspired to make her violent and bitter. Her husband abused her, spending his
money on booze and lashing out at her with his fists. Dragged across an ocean
and a continent to a life worse than the one she fled, Mary made her daughter
the scapegoat for her own miseries. Where most parents make their children feel
loved with the stories of their births, Mary terrorized Esther: "She said I had
weighed ten pounds and my body was covered with black hair. To top it all off,
my head was badly shaped. She was so embarrassed by the way I looked that she
felt she had delivered a monster."

When her daughter was six or seven, Mary threw a butcher knife at her husband during an argument. It wobbled menacingly in the wood of the doorjamb.
That night, Mary and her children, Esther and Joseph, left the house for good.

Patti wouldn't miss Wyoming much. She remembered weeping over that
linoleum floor on her hands and knees while her mother supervised her work.
She remembered being slapped if she held a crochet needle improperly. She remembered being chained up if she misbehaved. She remembered when her playmate, a tiny lamb, was slaughtered for the table. If Jerry Lewis thought his
childhood was something out of Dickens, Patti Palmer's was a chapter from the
Marquis de Sade. "My mother held me only once that I can remember," she said.
"When she came toward me I usually flinched because I thought she was going
to hit me. Usually I was right."

When Mary and her children finally stopped running, they were in Michigan. Mary found work in a Chrysler factory. Soon enough, her husband found

them. There was a brief reconciliation, then more fighting. Mary threw him out again, but this time he took the children.

Esther and Joseph found themselves in a string of foster homes, where life could be even more nightmarish than Wyoming. One, in St. Charles, Michigan, was a haven—a farmhouse with a garden that Esther was allowed to tend. In others, though, she was beaten and underfed. She was staying in one of the better ones when her mother, now remarried, snatched her away and sued her ex-husband for custody of the children. The judge made a Solomonic decision: The boy, Joseph, would live with his father; Esther went to Mary and her new husband, Mike Farina, in Detroit.

Mike and Mary had met at the Chrysler plant, and she had hopes for him, but he turned out to be no better a husband than the one she'd left, arguing with and hitting his wife. But at least he was kind to his stepdaughter. On their first Christmas together he bought presents and a tree. She'd never had either before. "I hugged and kissed Mike for all he had done," she remembered, "because I knew the effort had all been his. I never remember Mama putting herself out for anyone."

Throughout the ordeals of her youth, Esther had only two staffs of comfort: Catholicism, which she practiced faithfully, and music, her one worldly escape from her brutal life. Esther had always had a pleasant voice—Mike Farina used to bring her into saloons to sing atop the bar for silver dollars, and he and Mary used to force her to show her talents off at Chrysler company picnics. As she grew into adolescence, she figured she could make a little money with her singing, intending to help her mother with household expenses.

She formed a small group, Esther and Her Sailing Swing Band, and got a job playing at a Polish wedding in nearby Hamtramck. She and her musicians played for thirteen hours and each took home fifteen dollars. When she crept into her house at three in the morning, Mary was waiting for her in a rage. She didn't remember hearing anything about a job. "She started hitting me," Patti remembered; "she screamed that I had gotten the money from having sex with boys. I ran from her and huddled in a corner of our tiny kitchen. She kept coming. When I curled up enough to make it hard for her to reach me with her fists, she began kicking me furiously." Again, Mary was taking out on her daughter pain that had its origins elsewhere: Mike Farina had moved out.

More and more, music seemed to Esther the only way out of this horror show. She joined the school choir, raising the money for a dress with another gig with her band. And she took up an instrument—the accordion. Besides being a traditional Italian instrument, the accordion had the psychologically useful function of allowing her to perform an entire act on her own. Esther Calonico had never had an ally in the world. Now she'd found a way to become a singer without having to depend on a band.

After she graduated from Cass Technical High School (no one from her family came to see her get her diploma), Esther got a job at a music store and studied other instruments. She learned all the popular tunes of the day and joined an all-girl band in which she sang and played accordion and trombone. Her high school music teacher found a conservatory in Florida that agreed to take her on as a scholarship student. Mary refused. "She said all I would do was play around and get married," Patti sighed.

Stuck in Detroit, she got lucky. While working as a strolling accordionist/singer in a restaurant, she learned Dinah Shore's repertoire and style well enough to be hired by the local NBC radio affiliate WJKB as a staff singer on "Uncle Nick's Kiddies Hour." Soon she got her own fifteen-minute weekly show: "Two Pianos and Patti." She'd officially taken the stage name Patti Palmer, a name even less ethnic than Esther, aware that the change was "a drastic step in our Italian household."

And then bandleader Ted Fio Rito came through town. Fio Rito had once been a big-time musician: He'd written "Toot, Toot, Tootsie, Good-bye" (which, being a Jolson standard, was well known in the Lewis house) and had some hits with his band. He'd acquired a reputation as a star maker as well: Betty Hutton, Betty Grable, and June Haver had all passed through his band on their way to Hollywood fame. By the 1940s, though, he'd hit hard times, touring small theaters and recording for an obscure label.

Driving through Detroit in his car, Fio Rito heard "Two Pianos and Patti" and discovered a new singer for his band. He called the radio station and asked Patti to meet him at the Cadillac Hotel. She signed a contract on the spot. In August 1944 she was featured on a Fio Rito record, "Mamalu." She was going places.

She almost didn't get there. One night that summer, the band headed for a date about an hour outside Detroit in a rickety cargo truck. Returning from the gig, the musicians lined the trailer like soldiers on wooden benches. They didn't know that the taillights on their truck weren't working, though, and when another truck came barreling up behind them, they shouted to get their driver's attention. Alerted, he pulled the truck off the road, and the musicians and singers all threw themselves clear. As if God had intervened to make it so, the next day Patti met Jerry.

Jerry Lewis may have been hungry for affection, but Patti Palmer wasn't given to letting her guard down. She never, for instance, succumbed to the pressures of show business by sleeping with co-workers. "I was always rather reserved and homespun," she recalled, "in spite of my theatrical ambitions. The boys in the band knew that, and they kind of left me alone to carry my own suitcase. I guess it was the price I had to pay for not being more sexually accommodating."

It was a natural reaction, then, for Patti to take Jerry for a wolf when he leered at her that August afternoon. After seeing him perform, though, and learning that he was just a kid like her, she let him take her to dinner. Jerry asked her to Papa Joe's, a local pizza joint, and showed up late—with lipstick on his collar. While she ate, he nursed a cup of coffee (he had about five bucks in his pocket). Some naïf quality in him brought out her entire life story. If Jerry had been prone to self-pity, hearing this tale was like a bucket of water in the face. He stammered a good night and bolted, convinced she'd seen right through him.

The truth can be funny: Patti *had* seen right through him. She knew he was unreliable, that his frantic behavior covered up his pain, that he felt a bit too sorry for himself. But still she liked him. A day or two later, she found a note written on her dressing room mirror in lipstick: "Let's fill these." A pair of soap baby shoes hung beside it. Some men feel they have to marry every girl they sleep with: At eighteen, Jerry Lewis felt he had to marry each one who smiled at him.

Patti consented to see more of him. They went out with each other as often as they could. Jerry snuck around, not wanting Irving Kaye to know how serious he was. "I used to say to myself, 'Where the hell is he? Is he going for coffee and sandwiches again?' " Kaye remembered. Jerry met Mary Farina and announced, "You know, I'm going to marry your daughter, ma'am." (He wasn't bold enough, though, to tell his own parents as much: They had no idea he was serious with anyone, let alone a shiksa five years his senior.)

They were young, they were in love, and they were running afoul of Fio Rito. Patti and Jerry may have been willfully innocent in the ways of show people, but Fio Rito was frankly jaded. He'd pinned his hopes on a new singer with a good voice; he wasn't about to let some skinny kid with a dummy act derail his gravy train. He confronted Patti about her budding romance: "I suppose you were out with that Jew again?" (It's not hard to see how Fio Rito's career fizzled away in a business dominated by Jews.) His anger terrified her, and he reckoned she got the message. Besides, the band was headed for Syracuse. The pesky little Jew would be out of her life and out of his hair.

Fio Rito didn't count on the power of true love. Patti and Jerry kept in constant contact when she went back on the road and he returned to New York. And he didn't count on how life had toughened his girl singer. Threats didn't bother Patti Palmer. She told other people in the band about her predicament and sent a glossy photo and a copy of her record to Jimmy Dorsey, who'd just lost Kitty Kallen from his own band. Dorsey liked the package and hired her over the phone. Patti gave Fio Rito notice and walked, telling all the Jewish musicians in the band why she was leaving. They left as well.

Stopping in New York for a brief solo engagement at the Roseland Ballroom, Patti met Jerry to discuss their plans. She confessed to him that she hadn't known he was Jewish. "I had been brought up to fear anyone who was Jewish," she remembered, recalling how she used to run past a Jewish-owned grocery store as a girl. For his part, Jerry revealed that he hadn't told Dan and Rae about her. "I think it'll be better if I don't," he said. "They wouldn't be happy—let's leave it at that."

Patti joined the Dorsey band in Pittsburgh and suddenly saw her name on marquees. She recorded songs and played on national radio. She shared the stage with no less than Ella Fitzgerald. She was invited by Glenn Miller to sing with his band overseas. Suddenly, the girl Jerry spent his idle days mooning over was not only older than her suitor but a bigger name as well.

The Dorsey band came into New York for an extended run at the Capitol Theater, where they supported the film *Thirty Seconds Over Tokyo*. Henny Youngman was on the bill, as was the one-legged tap dancer Peg Leg Bates, and Patti and Teddy Walters sang. Jerry was working at the Glass Hat, a nightclub in the Belmont Plaza Hotel, but he attended as many of the Capitol shows as he could, inventing alibis for himself and sneaking away from the hotel where he was living with his parents and Irving Kaye.

On the night of October 2 Jerry didn't return home at all. "Jerry used to sleep a lot in those days," Kaye remembered twenty years later. "He didn't have so much on his mind then. Twelve hours at a crack, it was nothing to him. One night he went out and later I didn't see him. Towards morning he comes in and wakes me up. He says, 'Don't say nothing to *them*. I eloped today with Patti.'"

It was a Monday and the Dorsey band had the night off. Jerry and Patti headed to Greenwich, Connecticut, were married by a justice of the peace, then went back to the railroad station for lunch. Jerry, frightened to return to New York and the inevitable wrath of Danny and Rae, had a brainstorm. They would take a quick honeymoon in Lakewood, where the Arthur was open for the autumn season. Dan and Rae wouldn't welcome the newlyweds, but Charlie and Lillian Brown surely would.

Jerry and Patti spent their first night together in the hotel where he'd learned his specialty, each of them content to have found a companion in life. Neither had ever felt loved or protected in the world. Now, though they'd known each other for less than a dozen weeks, they had each other. Patti owed no one in the world anything: She had a husband, she had a future. She slept peacefully. Jerry stared at the ceiling overcome with guilt: He'd finally found someone who would stay at his side. But he also had to return to New York and face his parents.

Irving Kaye met Jerry in front of the Holland Hotel.

"You better hurry or you'll be late for the first show."

Jerry showed off his wedding band. "Is that a way to greet a friend? Where's the congratulations?"

Kaye stared down at his shoes.

"Well, say something."

"Your parents are upstairs."

"Oh, shit."

The eighteen-year-old newlywed entered the hotel like a rabbit on his way to visit wolves.

Rae attacked first. "You didn't! You didn't! How dare you! You're making me sick!"

She recalled her maternal efforts: "What did I raise you for? To run off with a Catholic?" Worse, she hit Jerry's sorest spot: "If your grandmother was alive, she'd drop dead."

Danny stood dramatically, waving his only child away: "Who needs you anyhow! Go! Get the hell out of here!"

A few days later, Patti was off on a midwest swing with the Dorsey band. Before she left, she and Jerry signed a lease on an apartment at 10 Lehigh Avenue in Newark: a walk-up flat, two and a half rooms and an eat-in kitchen, sixty-five dollars a month. (The apartment would stay in the family for years after Jerry and Patti moved to California; Dan and Rae lived there for a while, then a string of relatives enjoyed its rent-controlled comforts.)

They could afford the place on Patti's $125-a-week salary, and they would have to. Jerry was floundering, scheming and conniving just to get ten-dollar jobs in the mountains. Patti would wire money for household expenses, for train tickets so he could visit when she was playing nearby, for an allowance so Jerry could buy coffee at the drugstore and schmooze with other out-of-work comics. Jerry was spending days alone in a small north Jersey apartment waiting for word from his touring wife and feeling sorry for himself. If it wasn't for the fact that he was married, he could have been seven all over again.

Patti had an engagement in New Haven, Connecticut, that winter, and she wired Jerry money to come see her. They wandered the streets aimlessly, talking about work, Jerry's family, nothing, really. They sat in the sun on the steps of a grand-looking building at Yale.

"We're going to have a baby," Patti said.

Jerry celebrated, somewhat shell-shocked, all the way back to the station, where he boarded a train for home. He stared out the window at the chilly New England landscape. He was eighteen, estranged from his parents, underemployed, a kept man scraping by in his career. Soon he'd be a father. He would have to find a way to pull the fraying strands of his life together. He could do little about his career save keep at it. But he could try to fix his family problems. He would ask Patti to convert.

That spring they journeyed to Brooklyn to ask Morris Levitch's blessing. The bent old man scared the life out of Patti. "I lived in terror that he would find me out," she remembered. "They had never dared tell him that his favorite grandson had married a Gentile, so I had been presented to him as a good Jewish girl, and coached before each visit as to what to do."

But Morris Levitch was no rube. Jerry explained the situation to his grandfather and the old man stood and slapped a chair. "You're not fooling me," he bellowed at Patti. "I knew you were a shiksa from the first day we met!"

She sank. He wouldn't have her.

Then the old man's attitude shifted. He stared into Jerry's eyes. "Now look at my grandson," he proclaimed. "She loves him. She takes care of him. He's happy." He waved a hand around his home. "All this before God is small. Love like theirs is big."

She'd been reprieved. Patti spoke to a rabbi and made arrangements for a traditional Jewish wedding. She didn't convert, however. She clung to her Catholicism dutifully. It had served her well as a comfort in her childhood, and she would need a staff of succor in the future.

In April 1945, before the authority of a rabbi and the watchful eyes of Rae, Danny, and a small brood of aunts, uncles, and cousins, Jerry and his six-month pregnant shiksa stood under a chuppah to be married once again. Rae would forever remain cool toward her daughter-in-law. "Let's just say," recalled a relative, "that she never wanted to share her son"—especially, it was intimated, after he'd made it in the business. But her boy had found his way back home to her.

4.

The Playboy and the Putz

Anxiety, loneliness, doubt, ambition, resentment, fear.

All of these nagged at Jerry Lewis throughout the twenty-three or so hours in each day that he wasn't performing.

Dean Martin, on the other hand, couldn't give a rat's ass.

There was likely no entertainer wandering around New York in 1944 with a psyche more distinct from Jerry's. If the young pantomimist's bodily twitches and frantic yuk-it-ups were a twisted *cri de coeur*, Martin's sleepy-eyed singing and drawling stage patter were the yawn of a Roman prince who'd just eaten a huge dinner and gotten laid. Jerry stepped through life as though it were a gauntlet of burrs and thorns; Dean sauntered along as if everything were a big joke. Jerry *had* to be onstage, *had* to win the approval of the crowd; Dean couldn't believe that all those saps were paying him money to do practically nothing.

Inside Jerry Lewis, there was a little boy running desperately through the night to find his mother playing piano in a saloon. There was a boy inside Dean Martin as well, and he also headed toward a saloon: He'd heard there was a cushy job there, and he was whistling as he walked.

Nobody had chased Gaetano Crocetti and his brothers out of Italy, as the Levitches and Brodskys had been forced from Russia. The Crocettis were folk of the Italian soil—of Abruzzi, specifically, a land dotted with caves and rocky fields, a place that would kill a young man as soon as provide him a living. Young men from central Italy weren't needed as laborers in the industrial regions in the north of their own country, but U.S. factories were starved for workers of any stripe. Two of Gaetano's older brothers had passed through Ellis Island and found work in the smelters and furnaces of Steubenville, Ohio, an iron city

teeming with Italian immigrants near the West Virginia and Pennsylvania borders. In 1913 nineteen-year-old Gaetano followed.

Unlike his kinsmen, who sacrificed body and soul each day in the infernal
ironworks, Gaetano sought work less than he did freedom. He saw men emerge
from the foundry looking like survivors of a natural disaster. That wasn't for him.
He would learn a trade that had provided so many of his fellow Italian immigrants with a livelihood. He apprenticed himself to Ambrogio DiBacco, a barber
on the very block where he lived.

Gaetano had moved in with his brother Giuseppe and his family. Giuseppe
was now called Joe, and Vincenzo, the other Crocetti brother, was known around
town as Jimmy. Gaetano also anglicized his name: Ever after, he would be Guy
Crocetti, pronouncing his last name "Crow-setti" in the English fashion. Under
the tutelage of DiBacco, Guy learned the tonsorial trade—and met a suitable
young girl, Angela Barra, an orphan who lived with DiBacco and his family. Angela's father had disappeared one day when she was little, and her mother had
been committed to a psychiatric asylum. Angela had been raised by nuns in an
orphanage in Columbus, Ohio, and returned to Steubenville, where she'd been
born, to work as a seamstress.

Angela was seventeen and Guy twenty when they married in October 1914.
By June 1917 Guy had his own barbershop, and the couple had a one-year-old
boy, Guglielmo. On the seventh day of that month, Angela produced another
son. Born prematurely, the child wasn't christened until the fall: His name was
Dino.

The young Crocetti boys were raised among a large, healthy tribe of blood
relatives and friendly neighbors. Guy was a good provider, and Angela added to
the household coffers by taking in sewing jobs. The Crocettis had cars, bikes,
toys, plenty of food and wine, and lived a loud, warm family life.

Guy was easygoing, as a successful barber must be, ever lending a sympathetic ear to the miseries of his customers. But Angela had grown up under brutal circumstances, and she tried to prepare her sons for the world by instilling
some of her toughness in them. They would be men's men: cool, self-aware, re-
silient. Of the two boys, Bill, as the elder was called, had the brains, Dino the
moxie. Bill did well at school; Dino played hooky and snuck off to the alleyway
crap games that the young men of Steubenville ran in imitation of their fathers.

In fact, if anything would toughen up a boy more than the teachings of
Angela Crocetti, it was the streets of Steubenville. Like many riverfront towns
during Prohibition, the city was a hotbed of bootlegging. The immigrant population—Steubenville had huge Irish and Italian enclaves—had even less respect
for legally enforced temperance than Anglo-Americans. The city was filled with
speakeasies, illegal casinos, and brothels that served local steelworkers and their
peers from northern West Virginia and western Pennsylvania. Throughout the

region, the City of Churches, as Steubenville called itself, was known as Boys Town, or Little Chicago.

Dino knew he wasn't headed for a life in the foundries, but he wasn't following Guy into the barbershop, either. Steubenville was wide open: cigar shops fronting for gambling parlors, pool halls, strip joints. Nothing in school or Guy's shop was as attractive as those temples of learning. By the time he was in his early teens, Dino was running with a wild gang from around the neighborhood, other sons of immigrants from Italy and Greece, the future Jimmy "the Greek" Snyder—then Demetrios Synodinos—among them.

At sixteen Dino slipped out of school altogether and for good. He was tall and athletic, with dark, wavy hair and a bold Roman nose. He turned his good looks, lithe body, and quick hands into something that looked like it could realize a profit. He became a welterweight boxer: Kid Crochet.

He must have looked great on his way into the ring, with his chest bare and his handsome face held high. Inside the ring, well, that was a different story. "He was the laziest guy in the United States," recalled Emilio Julian, a bantamweight from Steubenville who saw him fight. "He didn't have too many fights. Most of them was him getting the hell out of the way from getting hit. After he got hit in the face a few times, why, he quit."

Dino never saw much money from the fight racket—ten dollars was the most he ever made for a single bout, and even that he had to split with his manager. He turned to odd jobs and finally found work in the very sort of place he'd always intended to avoid: a steel mill.

But Dino Crocetti wasn't born to work in that soul-grinding environment. Soon after returning from an abortive flight to the West Coast, Dino found work in a Steubenville gambling club. The Rex Cigar Store was the biggest joint in town: It had the most tables, the biggest variety of games. It was even the first building in the city with air-conditioning. Dino was hired by the boss, Cosmo Quattrone, to deal poker and blackjack. He was barely nineteen years old.

"He was a beautiful dealer," recalled a childhood friend. "What hands!"

The Rex was a legitimate joint: The dealers weren't asked to bilk the customers. But Dino figured out an angle of his own. They didn't use chips at the Rex, only silver dollars. Dino learned how to palm the coins and slip them into the oversized shoes he wore to work. It added five or ten dollars to his paycheck each day. One spring day Dino made the mistake of riding a carnival ride at a church fair on a break from work. His booty fell from his shoes like rain. A few days later, Cosmo walked up to his clever young dealer and said, "I hear you like to dance. I'd like to see you dance in them shoes you got on there." Somehow, Dino kept his job, but he would have to find a new angle.

Guy and Angela weren't pleased to have a gambler in the house. They were worried their baby boy was going to the bad. "My aunts said, 'Your son's gonna be a gangster,' " he remembered. " 'He's gonna die in the electric chair.' " But Dino found a way to calm his mother. He reminded her of a film they'd seen together, *The Man Who Broke the Bank at Monte Carlo* with Ronald Colman: "Remember the guy with the stick?" he asked her. "He wore the nice suit, the tie. He didn't gamble, he just worked. Well, that's me."

And it *was* him. He took to fancy clothes and fancy women. Dino and his pals ran around nights drinking cheap hooch and savoring the city's prostitutes. They had sweethearts—Dino was nominally attached to a girl named Irma DiBenedetto—but mainly they were tomcats on the prowl: out till dawn, carousing, gambling, drinking, chasing tail, golfing at sunrise, eating late suppers in Chinese restaurants while the rest of the world was waking up to bacon and eggs.

Dino was in the middle of it all, the tomcattiest of the pack, always sharply dressed, always with an eye on a skirt. "Shit," remembered Mindy Costanzo, one of the gang, "Dino used to fuck every human he could. The dealers he worked with, when they went on shift, he'd go sneak down to their apartments and fuck their wives."

It was 1938. Joey Levitch was dancing around to Danny Kaye records. Dino Crocetti was avoiding the law and his folks on the one hand, the clap, his boss, and jealous husbands on the other.

He loved it.

Even though he was always one of the boys, there was something in Dino besides his good looks and relative lack of scruples that set him apart from his chums. As they cruised the streets scamming for women and parties, Dino would sing out loud—popular songs, Italian *canzoni*, light jazz numbers. He liked to sing; he was serious about it. He had never had a moment's patience with any sort of schooling, but he sat still for singing lessons from, of all people, the mayor's wife. And he sang in clubs and taverns whenever there was an open mike and a band willing to back him.

Dino's reputation as a singer got around, and he soon found work singing and dealing cards at various clubs in eastern Ohio. He was finally approached by Ernie McKay, a bandleader from Columbus who offered to take Dino on as a full-time crooner for forty dollars a week. Though it represented a cut from even his under-the-table pay as a dealer, he took it.

McKay had made one more stipulation when he offered Dino the deal. He wanted him to sing under a different name. He remembered one of the first big Italian crooners—Nino Martini. The name sounded authentically romantic to McKay, and so Dino Crocetti made his debut in Columbus late in 1939 under the short-lived name Dino Martini.

The McKay band made its home in the State Restaurant, a Chinese joint, and it was there that Lee Ann Lee caught Dino's act. Lee was married to bandleader Sammy Watkins, who headlined in the Vogue Room, a night spot in

Cleveland's Hollenden Hotel. Watkins was a big cheese in Cleveland, but he was starting to get a bit overripe; business was falling off. He needed a new hook. In the spring of 1940 Dino sent Watkins a demo record he'd cut with McKay, and the two men met. Watkins saw in Dino the exciting presence his band was lacking, and he hired the kid to come to the big city and play to the Vogue Room's clientele of mobsters, politicians, scam artists, and blue bloods.

But there was a stipulation to this deal, too. Dino Martini sounded a touch too just-off-the-boat to Watkins (who was born Samuel Watkovitz). He wanted the name anglicized another notch: Dean Martin was what he liked, and it was as Dean Martin that Dino Crocetti sang in Cleveland in the fall of 1940.

That winter, as he performed with Watkins's band, Dean noticed a fresh-faced Irish beauty seated at a table with her father. She was Elizabeth McDonald, from Swarthmore, Pennsylvania, and she'd just been asked to leave the well-regarded girls' college in her hometown after a single semester of poor grades. Her dad, Bill, a liquor distributor, had been sent to Cleveland by his company and would soon be transferred there permanently, buying a house and moving his wife and two other daughters in with him.

Betty and Dean traded flirtatious looks for a few nights, then he finally asked her out. It must have been love. Dean had had scores of women, none of whom moved him to consider commitment. "He was a bastard," one conquest recalled, "all wine and candlelight, then a pat on the ass in the morning." But in the summer of 1942 he brought Betty McDonald to Steubenville to meet his kith and kin, and he married her in Cleveland on October 2. Nine months later, Dean was officially 4-F (he had a double hernia), he was working as a touring musician, and he was adjusting to life as a father. Stephen Craig Martin was born on June 29, 1943.

With his new family responsibilities and his growing popularity around Cleveland, Dean began pestering Watkins for more money. He was the main draw, and he knew it. Watkins drew up a new contract for sixty-five dollars a week starting in July 1943.

Within eight weeks Dean was asking for his release. Frank Sinatra had canceled a date at the Riobamba in New York, and the Music Corporation of America, whose man in Cleveland knew Dean's act well, was offering him the gig. Dean turned to Watkins for his freedom, and it was granted—in return for 10 percent of his income for the next seven years. For cutting the deal, and for all its future services, MCA horned in for another 10 percent.

On September 24, 1943, Dean Martin debuted with Charles Baum's Society Orchestra in Manhattan. With his repertoire of borrowed songs and that smooth, insouciant manner that would forever mark his performances, he made a small splash. He was getting $150 a week. As a crooner, as a hustler, as a wayward husband, he had hit the big time.

■ ■ ■

By March 1944 Dean had moved Betty to New York and another baby was born, a girl. But the marriage was foundering. Dean and Betty fought, and she constantly moved back and forth between New York and Steubenville as relations between them improved and degenerated. And though he was working, New York was more expensive than Ohio, and he often had to borrow money to keep up his family obligations and his ever-busy life. He may have become a father and a husband, but Dean was still a tomcat. His taste for partying, gambling, and the ladies, nurtured in Steubenville, had followed him east.

There was another relic of Steubenville in New York. Dick Richards, who'd managed Kid Crochet's boxing career back in Ohio, turned up looking to serve as Dean Martin's exclusive manager in his new career. Richards offered Dean two hundred dollars in exchange for a 20 percent piece of his earnings. Dean was in debt to Watkins and MCA; he owed money to bookies, store owners, friends, and acquaintances all over town; he and Betty were being served with eviction papers from the London Terrace Apartments. He took the deal.

Dean cut a lot of deals in 1944. He was being courted by Lou Perry, a Times Square agent who made nice to him by letting him sleep on his couch at the Bryant Hotel (a privilege offered a steady stream of up-and-comers, has-beens, and never-to-bes). Perry offered Dean some cash for 35 percent of his earnings. He took it. Soon after, comedian Lou Costello took an interest in Dean's career and offered to lend a hand for 20 percent. Dean took it. He was keeping busy with club dates and radio work, but he was running out of pieces of himself to sell: Between Watkins, MCA, Richards, Perry, and Costello, Dean Martin had sold away the rights to all but a nickel of every dollar he made.

That summer Dean got Richards, Perry, and Costello to broker a nose job, turning the schnozzola he'd inherited from Guy Crocetti into something a bit more presentable. He and his new nose were signed to do a fifteen-minute unsponsored radio show on WMCA in August, "Songs by Dean Martin." The musical director of that program also took an interest in Dean's future, and Dean milked it for a small payment. In exchange, he signed away 10 percent of himself: a grand total of 105 percent. He was making seventy-five dollars a week at WMCA. If he'd ever made good to his entire retinue of agents and managers, he would have been out $3.75 every time he worked.

Still, nothing bothered him. Dean Martin was one of the chosen: He slept with his friends' girls, stole from his boss, and played both ends against the middle, and nobody ever seemed to call him on any of it. His wife and children were shuttled back and forth between Guy and Angela in Steubenville, the McDonalds outside of Philadelphia, and whatever New York hotel Dean was hanging his hat in. He was chummy with everyone he knew, but no one felt like they knew him well.

Sonny King, a fledgling comic, was another of Perry's roommates-cum-clients. He and Dean would share a fold-out couch through the night and split a fifteen-cent breakfast at a Times Square automat in the morning. "Once in a while, he'd say to me, 'You're my best buddy,' " King recalled. "But in such a manner that you wouldn't believe it."

Dean wasn't a pledger; he wasn't a loyalist or a partisan or a joiner. He believed in wine, women, and song, especially insofar as his talents with the third allowed him to indulge in the first two. He wanted nothing more from the world than whatever he could take out of it without expending too much energy. He skimmed the surface of life, picking up a buck here, a broad there, singing in nightclubs and on the radio to keep the whole scam afloat. Critics who reviewed his act frequently sensed his disdain for the audience and even for his own talent. He never read them; he didn't care.

In August 1944 he was booked into the Glass Hat, the night spot in the Belmont Plaza Hotel, and if he was aware that Jerry Lewis was on the same bill, he never registered the fact to anyone around him.

If Dean Martin strode the streets of New York City in the summer of 1944 guilty of knowing all too boldly who he was, then Jerry Lewis was guilty of a lack of focus about his future and a wavering confidence in his talent.

Dean was billed around town as "The Boy with the Tall, Dark, and Handsome Voice." It was a swell slogan; Dick Richards had thought it up when Dean was still pretending to let him manage his career.

Jerry, on the other hand, had taken a more active role in promoting himself, printing up hundreds of postcards advertising his act with a subtle come-hither: "It's perpetual motion set to music when th' amusin' Jerry Lewis flashes on th' scene with his sparklin' an' laffsational antics an' tops all 'records' in rollickin' an' original pantomimicry!"

The cards featured silhouette images of Lewis performing bits of his act—seven poses in all, from Danny Kaye to Carmen Miranda to Igor Gorin. The drawings, by cartoonist Dorothy Edwards, were full of funny-page effects. And Lewis subtitled each caricature with an appropriately catchy grabber: "Enter th' mirth-maker!" "Screamlinin' th' classics!" "Platter pantopatter!" And most bizarrely, "Naive Frank Sinatra imaginational image!"

In a flush entertainment world, Abbey Greshler would have been hard pressed to sell such a bag of goods, but he had World War II on his side. People might not have been going out as often, but a huge chunk of the nation's stock of entertainers was off to war. Jerry and Dean, like other 4-Fs, were left home to man the stages, just as guys like one-armed Pete Gray and fifteen-year-old Joe Nuxhall were able to play major-league baseball. Greshler wasn't quite making Jerry a star, but there were stages clamoring for entertainers of any stripe, and the kid was kept busy enough not to holler.

After he returned to New York from meeting Patti Palmer in Detroit, Jerry was put straight to work at the Glass Hat. When he went over to the club to check it out, he discovered that his act had a new name. The billboard in the Belmont Plaza lobby bore the same old promo shot Lewis had been using— leaning toward the camera with an oily pompadour and a bucktoothed grin— but gone was the traditional billing, "Satirical Impressions in Pantomimicry," that strange, pompous locution. Now Jerry Lewis was billed as "Sotto Voce."

He had no idea what it meant. When he heard Greshler explain to him that it was a joke—"The connotation here is that you use somebody else's voice, you understand?"—he was even more confused. But what could he do? Greshler was his agent; even if he had bad taste, it wasn't as if a crowd of others was waiting to take him on.

So it was in a state of bewilderment—a professional identity crisis, in fact— that Lewis stood outside the Glass Hat when a tall, swarthy fellow in a camel-hair coat breezed past. From the curly hair to the piercing eyes to the "telltale sign of recent surgery coming down at the bridge of his nose," Lewis was awestruck by the man, who seemed descended from some allegorical painting of Cool. Even his shoes—"Pimp shoes!" Jerry recalled later, "red patent leather tops!"—didn't diminish the effect.

Jerry stood gaping as this Adonis stopped to chat with Ernie, the Belmont Plaza doorman, and then drifted into the street. Magnetically drawn after the mysterious stranger, Lewis approached Ernie himself.

"Who was that?"

"You don't know each other?"

"Nope."

"That's Dean Martin."

"He looks important."

He might also have looked familiar. When Dean had stepped out of the elevator, Jerry had been staring at the billboard in the hotel lobby, eyeing that annoying "Sotto Voce" stuff. But Dean's face was above his on the very same ad.

Jerry opened at the club soon after, emceeing and doing the record act, and the Boy with the Tall, Dark, and Handsome Voice was the headliner. There were other acts on the bill—dancers Vivian Newell and the team Cappella and Patricia, and an orchestra led by Payton Re—and no doubt they all went on to lead lives filled with pain, joy, regret, and laughter. But there was no element of fate or kismet in their sharing that stage that August. For Dean and Jerry, though, it was the conception that preceded the triumphant birth.

Both performers got nice notices in the trades for the engagement. Bill Smith of *Billboard* announced that Jerry "fills comedy job to perfection" and commented on the "poise and assuredness" of his emceeing. Smith called Dean "one of the better stylists around town." Each got a slap on the wrist, however, for transgressions of demeanor. Jerry, Smith noted, performed a hilarious Rudy Vallee bit that "was marred by some blue gestures." Dean had insulted a patron who was talking too loudly while he sang: "Hey, pallie, get your own micro-phone."

Though the engagement went well, Jerry and Dean never became more than nodding acquaintances. Jerry courted the singer, but Dean wasn't inter-ested in a record-spinning pest. Dean would later admit he found Jerry's act amusing, but Irving Kaye recalled that Jerry was positively smitten by Dean, standing in the wings, shaking his head, and repeating, "Isn't he too much?"

It would be months before they met again. Dean took off for Baltimore, where he played the Hippodrome. Jerry, coincidentally, played the same club a week later (billed, in Greshler's most surreal conceit yet, as "The Gay Imposter"). This leapfrogging pattern was repeated a few times in the next year, each man following the other in turn at some out-of-town venue. They would tell reporters in later years that they took to leaving one another notes describing their experi-ence with the locals, and while it sounded like something Jerry would do, it was completely out of character for Dean. The copious files on Martin and Lewis kept by their Hollywood producer Hal Wallis contained dozens of handwritten letters from Jerry—apologies, thank-yous, simple hellos, congratulations, and the like—and one single mark in Dean's hand: his signature on a loan agreement.

Dean was keeping busy (as any man with four managers ought) with his radio work and live engagements, and there were inquiries around town about his availability for recording dates. Jerry, however, had become a sporadically em-ployed, stay-at-home husband. He was beset by loneliness, by the pressures of family and career, by fears of failure and abandonment. It's a wonder that he could cope at all with life as a fragile teenage husband, soon-to-be father, and fledgling entertainer. If Patti hadn't kept the couple's head above water while Greshler was still struggling to launch Jerry into a real career, Jerry, like his own dad, might have had to pick up a day job. Sheet music peddling had gone the way of blacksmithing, but there were other options. Fortunately, Patti's pay-checks kept the icebox full, Greshler kept the work trickling in, and Jerry kept de-terminedly on his career track.

By March 1945, though, Patti had told Dorsey that she would have to quit the band because of her pregnancy. That change was shaping up as a turning point for Jerry. Ambitious as he was to succeed in show biz, he was confronting a cold choice: Nineteen, estranged from his family, with an expectant wife and no steady income, he could either stick it out like his folks did—struggle as a show-man all his life and raise another lonely little Lewis—or give up the business al-together.

He was playing the Glass Hat again that month, and one night after the show he was bumming down Broadway with Sonny King. Neither had any partic-ular destination in mind nor any special prospects to look forward to. Patti was on the road, and as he did when she was away, Jerry was planning to sleep in Manhattan. But he had sunk so low that he was considering joining the rotating corps of low-rung entertainers who made camp in Lou Perry's rooms at the Bryant Hotel.

Across the street, headed in the opposite direction, King recognized Perry walking along with Dean Martin. He tugged Jerry along with him to go over and say hi. Sonny and Dean talked about women. Jerry nervously stood his ground, too awestruck in Martin's presence to say a word. He recalled himself thinking: "Look at me, weighing 115 pounds—still fighting acne. Standing there in my bumpkin mackinaw jacket, T-shirt underneath and suspenders that held the pants two inches above my Flagg Brothers shoes." Jerry and Dean were the same height—a sliver over six feet each—but audiences around the world have always carried the same impression that made Jerry so silent that night: Compared with Dean, Jerry was lilliputian.

His stock in himself must have skyrocketed a few nights later, then, when he found himself in King's room at the Bryant spinning records and shooting the shit with Dean himself. They sat up till four in the morning, Dean doing most of the talking. He told tales of broads, booze, boxing, and betting, of his life on the streets of Steubenville, revealing to Lewis the gorgeous indifference that lay beneath his gorgeous exterior.

If Jerry had been in a nervous swoon around Dean before, he now fell in love. Danny Lewis had always striven to convey an air of nonchalance and suave romance to a room of ten people; Dean had so much cool that he pissed it away. Following Danny around burlie houses and Borscht Belt rec rooms was all Jerry ever wanted out of his childhood; now, following Dean as he catted and sang around New York looked like a marvelous career. Just as he'd wanted to marry every girl singer who'd paid him attention, Jerry was smitten with Dean for deigning to spend time with him. That Dean possessed so many of Danny's attributes—dark good looks, sexual confidence, a great voice—only made the attraction that much stronger.

Dean talked until he'd told Jerry his whole life story. He even became self-reflective, showing pictures of Betty and the children. Only then did he start asking Jerry about himself. He was startled to hear that Jerry was a married man with a baby on the way. They parted at dawn, Dean no doubt forgetting the encounter by the time his head hit the pillow, Jerry unable to sleep for his excitement. As the light filtered in from behind the shades, he was overjoyed at his new friendship: "I'm thinking that Dean has come along at the right time," he recalled. "I'm thinking he's going to be someone special: the big brother I never had."

Spring came and went, and with it Jerry and Patti's second wedding ceremony—the Jewish one—and the subsequent reconciliation of Danny and Rae with their boy. Greshler continued booking Jerry around the northeast as a combination emcee/specialty act—Baltimore, Montreal, D.C. And the Glass Hat evolved, luckily, into a running gig: Jerry found himself working there every few months.

Patti had quit the Dorsey band and had stopped making her five hundred dollars a month. She would never work again, even when she wasn't pregnant and her children were old enough for her to leave the house: "Jerry had to support me," she explained, "because I believe in a one-career marriage."

But Jerry could barely do the job. The couple was so broke they could afford only one maternity dress, which Patti wore until she had to throw it away. Even though his wife was well along on her pregnancy and had no family of her own nearby to look out for her, Jerry had to race off as far as Canada to make a buck.

In mid-July 1945, when the baby was due any day, Greshler landed Jerry two weeks in Baltimore at the Chanticleer (again, with no connection but kismet, Dean would follow him there on August 9). It was a mixed blessing: Jerry would produce some income—one hundred dollars a week—but he'd be hours away from home at a time when his wife would need him at a moment's notice. There really wasn't much of a choice. There'd be no money to pay the hospital and doctor bills if he didn't work. Leaving Patti in his parents' hands, he took the gig. But first he tried to show Patti that she would be in his thoughts while he was gone: He spent most of their meager savings on a spaniel puppy, which they named Mr. Chips.

When the Baltimore engagement was almost over, Patti went into labor. Rae called Jerry and he grabbed the first train he could. He arrived in Newark on July 31 and got his first look at Gary Harold Lee Lewis, who'd been born very early that morning. And with the money he'd made in Baltimore and some extra borrowed from friends, he paid the $120 hospital bill in full. Then he returned south. A few days later, Patti and Gary took a cab home alone from the hospital to an empty apartment.

After Jerry's return to Newark, the couple went out to celebrate their son's birth. Jerry was working at the Havana-Madrid, one of the Spanish-themed nightclubs then in vogue in Manhattan. (Dean Martin had always fit well into these clubs, and his upcoming performance was being advertised in the Havana-Madrid lobby that night.) Ignoring the stares of better-heeled patrons, Patti wore Jerry's latest extravagance, a squirrel jacket. She watched his act and then they went to Lindy's for a late snack of cheesecake. Seated at a rowdy table nearby was Dean. He recognized Jerry and invited the couple to join him and his friends.

"There were lots of jokes and much kibitzing going on," Patti recalled. "Dean was in charge, but Jerry played it well. I understood afterward what Jerry meant when he said, 'Dean is a worldly man . . . just too much.' "

Indeed, having grown up around Italian American workingmen herself, Patti no doubt saw a lot that was familiar in Dino Crocetti—his looks, his mien, his ability to make other men desire his company. She understood the spell under which her husband had fallen. Years later, in fact, Jerry would presume that Patti shared his attraction toward Dean. As Patti recalled: "He accused me of having an affair with Dean. I did not. We were like family. But the verbal abuse Jerry heaped on me . . . had me on my knees, crying for mercy. Now I am convinced that his accusations and tirades were a cover for his own activities. . . . Dean tried, in his own way, to offer me support, and just knowing someone else was aware of what was going on eased my pain. It also created a bond between us and helped me understand Dean's feelings."

If Patti understood Dean's feelings, it may have been, in part, because of their shared experience as show people born to Italian immigrants. Dean and Patti recognized each other across that noisy table at Lindy's. They were cut from the same cloth, however differently they wore it. Patti was demure and proper, but she had dark features and a tough, proud spine. She might have reminded Dean of his mother. There was nothing sexual between them—Dean usually went for blondes—but that Jerry was married to such a woman surely raised him a notch in Dean's eyes.

That winter Dean opened at the Havana-Madrid to the delight of its owner, Angel Lopez. Lopez expressed interest in overseeing Dean's career, and he offered Dean a thousand dollars for a piece of the action. Dean signed over 5 percent. That made 110 percent of himself that he had brokered out, and it was the straw that broke the crooner's back. In February 1946 Dean was forced to declare bankruptcy in U.S. District Court. His assets consisted of one hundred dollars in clothes, fifteen dollars in cash, and thirty-five dollars in the bank.

Jerry, on the other hand, was seeing light. During the same February in which Dean sought the protection of a court against his own financial inabilities, Greshler had Jerry playing the Glass Hat again for $110 a week, giving him enough to rent a room in town and have Patti and Gary join him. Even more exciting was his next booking: In March he would share the bill with Dean at the Havana-Madrid. Work, wife and kid, big brother: a dreamy major chord.

Lopez always booked the Havana-Madrid with a half-and-half mixture of Anglo and Hispanic acts, alternating them throughout the show. The bill for that run in March included flamenco dancers Dorita and Valero and Afro-Cuban singer Betty Reilly. Pupi Campo led the orchestra. Jerry emceed and did the record act (he'd "improved tremendously," according to *Billboard*), and Dean headlined.

Yet this was a different Dean, friskier, less aloof. Bankruptcy might have chastened him somewhat, familiarity with Jerry might have softened him somewhat, or he might have sunk into a lower slough of indifference than he'd ever inhabited before. He and Jerry joshed each other when one was offstage and the other was performing. Jerry, raised on Borscht Belt kibitzing, knew just how to swing along with this sort of banter, and before too long the two of them were regularly launching satiric salvos at each other's acts.

At the end of each night's closing show, these sorties grew into a wild, riffing jam session. Campo would stick around and try to play for Dean while Jerry ad-libbed interruptions. They did some physical stuff; Jerry even played straight for Dean, whose nonchalant way with a joke perfectly foiled Jerry's supersonic delivery. Some nights Sonny King joined in, turning the act into a hip Three Stooges.

Bill Smith of *Billboard* caught this after-hours frivolity: "Martin and Lewis do an after-piece that has all the makings of a sock act. Boys play straight for each other, deliberately step on each other's lines, mug and raise general bedlam. It's a toss-up who walks off with the biggest mitt. Lewis's double-takes, throw-aways, mugging and deliberate over-acting are sensational. Martin's slow takes, ad libs and under-acting make him an ideal fall guy. Both got stand-out results from a mob that took dynamite to wake up."

"Martin and Lewis": The phrase that would launch tens of millions of dollars had seen print for the first time.

Years later, Lewis shrugged off those wee-hours romps: "That was just bull-shitting around." But back then he must have gloried in his proximity to Dean and in their ease with one another. It was as if Danny had chosen his own son instead of Lou Black as a partner. Dean had usurped Danny's place in Jerry's eyes as an ideal, a man who with a mere gesture could possess women, audiences, and the riches of the world. But rather than eclipse Dean in some oedipal psychodrama, Jerry became his partner, a frantically engaged complement to Dean's disdainfully distant soul. Even Dean had to have been aware that they had clicked. The difference was, of course, that while he left the Havana-Madrid looking through indifferent eyes toward his next job, the episode had merely left Jerry hungry for more.

The chance for a reunion was remote, however. Right after the Havana-Madrid gig, Dean was booked into Chicago's Rio Cabana. Before he left New York, though, he made a screen test for Columbia Pictures. When the studio's autocratic boss, Harry Cohn, saw the results, his verdict was terse: "Martin may have some ability in a nightclub, but he cannot talk at all."

Jerry had more success staying on more familiar turf. He was booked back in Baltimore, opening at the Hippodrome on March 24 as part of a vaudeville show accompanying the movie *Deadline at Dawn*. *Variety* caught the debut: "Lewis is a frequent repeater here, but youthful comic has an original turn and pleasing manner of salesmanship. Mouths vocals played by off-stage recordings and makes the most of comedy panto."

He returned as well to the Gaiety Theater in Montreal that spring, to a less heartening *Variety* notice: "He's obviously a seasoned guy with plenty of know-how on selling a punchline, but this just isn't his spot."

Then it was off to D.C. and the Capitol Theater. There, as emcee, Jerry did an audience-participation piece tied into the feature film he was supporting, United Artists' *Breakfast in Hollywood*. The odd picture starred Tom Breneman, a radio journalist who did a live breakfast chat show of the same name. According to *Variety*, "Lewis does a Tom Breneman hat auction, with volunteers from the sidelines as models. Audience cooperation is along acceptable lines, with no offence to participants. . . . Bit is clever stage business and clicks."

This is obviously a different Jerry from the kid who was too nervous to open his mouth onstage just a couple of years earlier. Perhaps it was the accumulation of nearly four years of experience as an emcee in theaters and nightclubs; perhaps it was a bounce of confidence following his after-hours shtick with Dean at the Havana-Madrid. Whatever the reason, Lewis had begun, at twenty, to mature as an entertainer, able to involve an audience in a bit of spontaneous fun just as easily as he and Smitty had once drawn a crowd aping movies in the lobby of the Arthur Hotel.

Abbey Greshler had done what he'd set out to do: Jerry was now a viable emcee/specialty act on the nightclub and presentation house circuit, and he was getting work steadily. No one was going to get rich doing Tom Breneman imitations, though. Jerry and Greshler both knew that Jerry would have to develop something else, but neither of them knew just what it ought to be.

It was July, and as it did every year, a pall fell over the Manhattan nightclub scene. Everybody left the city for the Catskills or the ocean, and the entertainment followed.

Jerry hadn't played the mountains in years, but Greshler had booked him into a sweet summertime gig in Atlantic City: the 500 Club, the gem of the boardwalk. Skinny D'Amato, a legendary sharpie in the hallowed resort town, ran the joint; his partner, Irvin Wolf, booked it; and Marco Reginelli, boss of the Camden mob, owned it—though not so as you could prove it in court. The 500 Club could seat one thousand in its showroom; the illegal casino in the back had a capacity the fire marshal hadn't set a limit on.

Greshler had gotten Jerry $150 a week from Wolf to be part of a bill headlined by Jayne Manners, a former Ziegfeld girl turned singing comedienne whose affairs of the heart had made her a darling of gossip columns. There was also a singer named Jack Randall. Jerry was billed second, the old standby "Satirical Impressions in Pantomimicry" once again his billing. He did three shows a night—the last began at 4 A.M.—and he was making enough to have Patti and Gary join him by the sea, taking a room at the Princess Hotel, a block or so from the water.

By the middle of the month, though, a sour note had crept in. By one account, either Wolf or D'Amato couldn't stand Jack Randall and fired him. By another, Randall took sick and had to be replaced. Still other versions say that the act that Wolf or D'Amato or both couldn't stand was Jerry's.

Whatever the reason, all parties agree that Jerry contacted Lou Perry after recommending that Dean fill the empty singing spot. Perry recalled later on: "Lewis called me, crying that Irvin Wolf was going to cancel him, and I could do something about it." By Perry's account, Lewis begged him to sign Dean to Randall's singing spot, reminding him of the rapport he and Dean had shared at the Havana-Madrid that spring. Perry remembered that the 500 Club had long been interested in Dean, and as Dean was idle for the time being and seemed to get along with Lewis, he offered him to Wolf at a discount price—five hundred dollars a week—encouraging Wolf with the news that Dean and Jerry did some funny stuff together. A contract was drawn up and signed. Dean would debut at the 500 Club on July 25, knocking Jerry from second to third billing.

The revamped show premiered that night and, to Wolf's consternation, there was nothing much special about it. Jerry emceed, Dean and Jerry each did their bits, Jayne Manners did her act, and the show ended. Wolf, according to Jerry, got sinister: "Where's that funny shit you two were gonna do? If it ain't in the second show, you're both outta here tomorrow." (Or maybe it was D'Amato who was angry; over the years, Lewis has fingered both men for the threat.) It's clear, at least, that someone said something to someone. And no wonder: The 500 Club management must have felt they'd been sold a bill of goods; they didn't like Jerry and had only kept him on for the comedy he supposedly did with Dean. Now they wanted some comedy. It's not as likely that they would want to fire Martin, whom they'd courted for a long time, but they might have wanted both guys out on the street merely because they felt duped.

Jerry panicked—he needed the work—and he took Dean into the dressing room determined to work out an act. They had their silly stuff from the Havana-Madrid after-hours pieces to build on, and Jerry figured they could expand that into an act. As a boy he'd developed the habit of scanning the show-biz sky for examples of the best sort of comedy, and he was certainly aware of the huge success then being enjoyed by comedy twosomes: Abbott and Costello, of course, and more to the point, Hope and Crosby: a joker and a crooner.

Of course, Jerry was no Hope—it wasn't given to him to dash off one-liners or droll stories with the cool panache of a stand-up comic. So he envisioned a slight variation: the Playboy and the Putz. Dean would stand in front of the mike and ooze sex and lassitude as only he could; Jerry would dress as a busboy and do his best to ruin the mood with accidents, outbursts, and interruptions. And since Jerry really needed the gig and he himself didn't care one way or another, Dean agreed.

Here's where the story becomes ineffable: By all accounts, the first show Martin and Lewis planned and performed before a paying crowd was an earth-shattering success. Jerry, in a typical exaggeration, would repeat for decades the claim that before "literally, an audience of four," the two men did an act that "lasted over three hours." Probably it was one hundred people and an hour-long show. It doesn't matter. It wasn't so much who was there, or for how long, as what it was that they saw.

There was something inimitable and sublime about the comedy that Jerry Lewis became famous performing—the shrieks, the wild release of the id, the lack of physical and emotional control. But Martin and Lewis were just as unique, their energy sparked by the obvious conflict between them. One was a pure schlemiel in ill-fitting clothes, trying to play the drums, assaulting the microphone, dropping trays of water glasses, throwing patrons' steaks around like Frisbees. And the other was a genuine Casanova, turning even silly songs into lascivious come-ons, bouncing off of the schmuck's buffets with imperious bonhomie, utterly unflustered, never breaking into laughter, acting like it was the most natural thing in the world. It was like watching the two halves of a personality you wished you could have: insane and unrepressed on the one hand, smoothly poised and confident on the other. And serendipitously enough, they actually enhanced one another, sanding away each other's brittle edges.

The howling reaction of the 500 Club's patrons to Martin and Lewis's slapstick-and-psychology cocktail appeased Wolf (and/or D'Amato). Jerry and Dean—one relieved, the other nonplussed—walked out into the night. They stood next to each other on a pier along the boardwalk, staring out into the ocean and smoking, not saying anything, just absorbing, each in his own way, what had happened. Neither had ever heard a crowd roar like that, neither had ever felt the organic mass of the audience rise toward him and cling to him in such perfect harmony. Neither had ever gotten such a rush out of performing before. It was brilliant—magical—and they knew it.

On June 8, 1966, in the midst of an eighteen-cities-in-thirty-three-days film tour, Jerry Lewis wrote in pen on his scrupulously detailed, mimeographed itinerary, "The man that doesn't advertise may know his business, but nobody else does."

It's not the stuff of an MBA term project, nor was it something that Lewis had just realized. The clever businessman who printed all those weird postcards, and who would one day have a caricature of himself designed as a permanent logo, had an inspiration back in 1946 in Atlantic City that was intended to do for Dean and himself what the postcards had failed to do for the record act. Once they'd managed to secure their jobs at the 500 Club, Dean and Jerry began staging publicity stunts for themselves out among the crowds on the beach.

Jerry raced into the waves and pretended to drown; Dean acted the hero and swam out to rescue him. When Dean had landed Jerry and was about to administer mouth-to-mouth resuscitation in front of a good-sized crowd, Jerry broke out of his phony torpor: "I'd rather have a malted, sir!"

Dean, in unflustered rhythm, responded, "Vanilla or chocolate?" Then he eyed Jerry suspiciously: "Don't I know you?"

"I'm Jerry Lewis!"

"Well, I'm Dean Martin."

"I know that: I'm playing at the 500 Club with you!" They both bolted from the perplexed crowd, shouting out show times.

It was an old gag—no less than W. C. Fields had pulled it when he worked Atlantic City back in the town's glory days. And as luck would have it, Sophie Tucker—the Last of the Red Hot Mamas, an old-timer well familiar with such drumbeating—happened to catch one of these fake drownings. Curious about who would resurrect such material, she caught Dean and Jerry's show. She loved it.

"These two crazy kids are a combination of the Keystone Kops, the Marx Brothers, and Abbott and Costello," she told the local press. "They will leave their mark on the whole profession." This was publicity that Skinny D'Amato and Irvin Wolf couldn't have bought. Within three nights, Martin and Lewis were the hottest thing on the boardwalk. Patrons were being turned away from even the 4 A.M. show. Columnists came down from New York to get a peek at the Next Thing.

When he wasn't cooking up publicity schemes for the new act, Jerry busied himself writing material for it. He entitled his conception "Sex and Slapstick," and he outlined bits that he and Dean could do together, understanding that their appeal lay as much in their contrasting personalities as in their ability to burst into any sort of spontaneous mayhem. Gathering his thoughts at the Princess Hotel that summer, Jerry wrote the following: "Since time immemoriam, there has never been a two-act in show business that weren't two milkmen, two food operators, two electricians, two plumbers, and for the first time here we have a handsome man and a monkey."

Jerry was so delighted with his new prospects that he frankly and willingly adopted the role of the buffoon to Dean's king. He was anything but ashamed to acknowledge that standing alongside his gorgeous new partner, he looked—and acted—subhuman.

There was only one hitch in this grand conception: The handsome man and the monkey were still working for different agents. There was no way they could work together permanently as an act until they were under one managerial hand.

If Jerry had overlooked this detail, Abbey Greshler certainly hadn't. Persona non grata around Atlantic City just a week before—as the guy who'd sold Irvin Wolf the awful record act—now he arrived like a pasha to oversee his young genius in action. Smelling the fresh blood in the water, he came south to insinuate himself between Dean and Lou Perry.

Perry had been in Dean's corner a long time—he "would have gone to hell and back for Dean," Jerry said—but he had tired of the hassles involved in managing such an irresponsible and indifferent personality. Dean was pushing thirty, he was in bankruptcy, he'd pissed away his radio show, he'd cut records that went nowhere, he didn't care to be around his own wife and kids. Before he'd sent Dean down to Atlantic City, Perry had been approached by Nick Constantino, an eastern Ohio gangster who knew Dean from his blackjack-dealing days and wanted to buy Dean's contract. Perry thought about what a relief it would be to rid himself of Dean once and for all and agreed; they shook hands, but no price was set, no papers were drawn up. Dean didn't know that his days with Perry were numbered; Perry, of course, didn't know that Dean was about to become a star.

In Atlantic City, meanwhile, Greshler had begun to catch Dean's ear. He knew he had to move fast: On the strength of their Atlantic City word-of-mouth, Angel Lopez had booked Dean and Jerry into the Havana-Madrid for a September run (Dean had top billing, at $750 a week). If Greshler didn't wrest Dean away from Perry by the time the act exploded on New York, he was in danger of losing both Dean and Jerry outright. Manhattan was filled with big agents who might exploit the situation better than even Greshler could.

He went for broke. Before the Havana-Madrid engagement opened, he signed Martin and Lewis as a team at the Latin Casino in Philadelphia for six hundred dollars each. Then he had Dean sign a letter to Perry firing him as his manager. Perry immediately sought relief from the American Guild of Variety Artists, but the hearings that the AGVA held to sort out the situation were a tangled, inconclusive mess (Dean's financial history couldn't have made matters easy). Finally, Greshler offered Perry a four-thousand-dollar settlement, and Perry snatched it up. Greshler took Perry to his Radio City bank and cashed the check, to Perry's amazement. "Perry and I were in different worlds," Greshler observed.

And that was that. Dean and Jerry were united as Martin and Lewis. Perry took a belt in the nose from one of Nick Constantino's goons and began paying regular reparations. And Greshler held on tight, suspecting that he had just caught hold of the ride he'd been waiting for his whole life.

5

Gunsels, Dames, and Screen Tests

At around the time Gary Lewis was learning to speak his first words, his father was developing a verbal persona of his own. Gone were the records and the portable phonograph. From now on, Jerry Lewis would speak onstage in his own voice—or, at least, a voice of his own making. The character Lewis was to portray on and off for the next twenty years—the mewling schlemiel Lewis would come to call "The Kid" or "The Nine-Year-Old"—was born around the same time Jerry and Dean became a unified act.

It's clear, in fact, that the character developed as a reaction to Dean's extreme self-assuredness. Jerry's conception of the act was based on the opposition of personalities—"Sex and Slapstick." Dean oozed masculinity, worldliness, testosterone. Jerry aspired to all of those, but his stage persona took him in the exact opposite direction. Rather than mimic Dean, he would oppose and thus complement him, and what he hit on was a peer to Baby Snooks and Harpo Marx—not a moron, exactly, but a naïf.

Dean, too, refined his stage persona into a signature, allowing his ironic, disaffected worldview to seep out as comedy. Once a serious singer with a thinly veiled disregard—a contempt, even—for his craft and his audience, now he became a seriocomic lampoon of an Italian crooner with enough suavity and native talent to mix the roles of straight man, singer, and smart aleck without mussing his hair.

The familiar public faces of the duo were set in concrete that summer in Atlantic City: Dean the boozing, breezy, devil-may-care playboy with the soft heart; Jerry the frantic, frightened, hero-worshiping innocent with the soft heart. Though they would go on to do many things in their careers, neither ever completely escaped the guise he adopted at the 500 Club. Eventually, both men turned into self-caricatures, though not without being savvy to it: Dean parodied his public image wickedly in Billy Wilder's *Kiss Me, Stupid* and then gently on

TV for years; Jerry virtuosically tackled both the schlemiel and the sharpie in his Jekyll-and-Hyde film, *The Nutty Professor.*

Given the way the act dissolved so utterly a decade later, it's ironic how completely each performer owes the other for the character he wound up playing for the rest of his life; the team developed *as a team.* Neither man could have realized his familiar guise if it hadn't been for the guy on the other side of the mike balancing his tendencies. Without the suave, soothing influence of Martin and his singing, Jerry's hysteria would have been intolerable. Likewise, Dean's singing, while always mellifluous, tended to be too cool to pull in audiences; the adrenaline that Jerry injected into the act turned Dean's musical interludes into oases of calm. Jerry's frivolity took the lascivious edge off Martin's sexuality; Martin, with his leonine, Abruzzese, live-and-let-live air, taught the world how to love his imbecilic partner.

One crucial quality in this marriage of opposites was the terrific tension between the two; they were so different that you expected the act to explode of its contrasts at any moment. Far more than such earlier comedy duos as Laurel and Hardy, Hope and Crosby, Abbott and Costello—men cut from essentially the same cloth as one another, despite their physical differences—Martin and Lewis were presented as complete opposites, two guys you'd never figure to know each other at all if not for their being partners. There was an edge of cruelty to Dean—especially on screen, where he was always cast as a conniver who at the last minute turned good—while Jerry was more like a puppy dog that kept wagging its tail even when it was being kicked. It was a new concept in comedy, and it was widely imitated: A case can be made for their being the models for Gelsomina and Zampanò, the innocent clown and the egoistic brute of Federico Fellini's *La Strada*, as well as for the bullying Ralph Kramden and whimsical Ed Norton of "The Honeymooners," who came to television just as Martin and Lewis were at their peak.

The public, of course, assumed that each man was really like his stage character, and making the routine cohere required Martin and Lewis to play their parts with dead-on earnestness. In doing so, though, they became types. And whereas typification of this sort can make stars out of mere personalities—think of how much easier it is to imitate the distinctive Martin or Lewis than either Tony Bennett or Lenny Bruce, a better singer and a better comic respectively—it can also serve to make them tiresome. After a while, any act that goes undeveloped, unchanged, can come to seem like the work of a one-trick pony. Martin and Lewis generated an enormous amount of goodwill in their initial ten-year splash, enough to carry them at the top of the game for more than another decade, but their inability to erase their first impression (as entertainers such as Frank Sinatra and Bing Crosby had done successfully) haunted the remainder of their careers. No matter how big they became, no matter what else they did, no matter how much distance they put between each other and their shared past, they would always remain the Playboy and the Putz.

Jerry's Putz was an especially ambivalent character. A seeming mental deficient, he was acceptable, it often seemed, only by virtue of the company he kept: Chaplin, Keaton, and Danny Kaye never needed straight men, and Stan Laurel and Lou Costello certainly could've negotiated planet earth on their own. Not Jerry. He was a hopeless schmuck, but a schmuck who was nevertheless welcome in every boîte and country club in the world because his best friend was the Great Dino—a man's man *and* a ladies' man. People could accept Jerry because Jerry was acceptable to Dean.

Still, the public's reaction to Jerry was often contradictory. Those who disliked him saw his gesticulations and twitches as a revolting mockery of disability, a sophomoric brand of insult humor that belonged in a middle-school cafeteria. To others, though, they constituted a brilliant form of mimicry, an externalization of the internal and the inexpressible, a way of showing with the body what the tongue can't convey: the mood of the soul.

In each excruciating spasm and exaggerated grimace, Jerry seemed to give himself over to some inner urge civilization has taught the rest of us to suppress. Whether he was twisting his legs and biting a knuckle in a futile attempt to hide his lust from a pretty woman, curling up like a potato bug to withstand the bellowing of a tyrant whom he's crossed, or grinning insanely and kicking his heels with glee after concocting a clever new scheme, Jerry embodied—and thus expressed—what the rest of us hid.

At the moment when Jerry Lewis first appeared as the Kid, Americans had never seen a grown man behave this way before. Though they were conquerors of the world, Americans of the late 1940s were nagged by an undercurrent of anxiety that slightly curdled their sense of triumph. Jerry turned this mood inside out: As if the stress of success, global leadership, and impending nuclear holocaust made the world too much for him to bear, he seemed constantly short-circuited, giving vent to every passing sensation as if every minute might be his last. The sight of someone admitting to his own worst fears and acting out his most childish fantasies was lapped up by the public.

Jerry knew exactly why people liked his stuff. "I appeal to children who know I get paid for doing what they get slapped for," he said. "I flout dignity and authority, and there's nobody alive who doesn't want to do the same thing." But only Jerry could get away with it. The genius of his character was that it was always within and without society, a child in adult's clothing, an adult with a little boy's mind and heart.

The spastic nerd that was Jerry's stage persona was inept in every regard: as a lover, an athlete, a soldier, a worker, a son. He seemed capable of any sort of inad-

equacy, any embarrassment, any marginalizing behavior save one: Unlike his creator, who liked to indulge in touches of Yiddish onstage and often referred to
himself as a "Jewish movie star," Jerry's comic character was utterly without ethnicity. True, few Jewish comics of the era flaunted their religious roots in mainstream entertainment; but beyond that, Jerry's very position as half of a team
required he sublimate his ethnic background. Jerry's partner was highly regarded
for his way with Italian songs, and the contrast between the virile and confident
singer and his skinny-shouldered, nebbishy friend could easily have been loaded
with ugly implications had the little guy's ethnicity been allowed to surface. It
was bad enough to play a hopeless spaz; why add the burden of a still only marginally mainstream Judaism to the poor guy's frame? Even after the division of
the act, Jerry would never play an explicitly Jewish character in movies. It was for
a later generation of comics—Lenny Bruce, Mel Brooks, and Woody Allen, in
particular—to make hay of the hallmarks of Jewish identity that incited anti-
Semites during Jerry's prime.

Of course, many aspects of Jerry's new stage persona would come to the surface
only in later years, when he and Dean were making films. In the fall of 1946 there
was just a nascent nightclub act—two guys mixing song and comedy, sex and
slapstick, in a ramshackle, hellbent-for-leather stage show. They knocked over
music stands, spoiled people's dinners, squirted seltzer bottles, spilled pitchers
of water on the audience, fractured songs, harassed the help, used the entire
room—customers' tables and seats included—as their stage.

After Atlantic City, they played the Havana-Madrid, where Angel Lopez
broke with his traditional practice of alternating Latin and Anglo acts by allowing Dean and Jerry to perform back to back at the end. Dean had top billing, and
they were still doing their solo acts, but then they combined them in a finale
that was the real meat of the show.

Variety all but ignored the three Latin opening acts to write for the first time
about the wild new team that was making its New York debut: "Lewis tees off
the fun with his synchronized mugging and motions to recordings of Danny
Kaye's 'Dinah' and Cyril Smith's 'Sow Song.' Guy's got stint down to perfection.
Martin then warms up his pleasantly-smooth baritone on a group of pops. Young
crooner is greatly improved since appearance at this club last winter. He still
bounces around, jounces the mike and kids the audience but his completely relaxed manner builds up a nice intimacy with the crowd and he draws plenty of
applause."

The review was as positive as any either performer had ever received in the
trades, and it's notable that their solo work was appreciated by the writer. After
all, both were familiar faces in New York, and because little had changed in their
individual routines, the reviewer (who signed himself "Stal.") might have found
their acts disappointingly stale. Then again, his appreciation of their solo work

might have been enhanced by what followed: "Rowdy action that pulls belly-laughs starts, though, when Martin and Lewis team up to carry the last twenty minutes together. Duo goes through a bunch of zany routines, apparently following a set format but improvising most of the way along the line. The hoked-up gags, impressions, terping, etc., probably wouldn't go in the more sedate niteries, but it's sock stuff here."

The review sets the pattern for notices that Martin and Lewis received throughout their early years, celebrating while at the same time recognizing its older elements and suggesting that its appeal would be limited.

And really, there wasn't much to it: Jerry called it "Three hours of 'Did you take a bath this morning?' 'Why, is one missing?'" The secret wasn't in the substance but in the style. They had the gift of timing, each had an undeniably entertaining spark, and they were enjoying the hell out of themselves. Jerry would always credit the success of the act to the fact that "you were watching a love affair," and in retrospect, it's easy to see the truth in that. Martin and Lewis were physically relaxed with one another in a way that no other comedy team had ever been: In later years, one of their bits involved Dean's actually applying his tongue to his partner's face. Their combined talents made them into a kind of *über*star: a two-headed, eight-limbed, singing, miming, Don Juaning, clowning, dancing, joke-spritzing variety act, spinning three shows a night off a few simple premises: the sergeant and the recruit, the maître d' and the busboy, the handsome man and the monkey.

Even within these simple confines, their energy and magnetism were indescribable. Everyone who saw them in person agreed that they were hilarious, but almost no one could rationally explain what was so funny. Reviewers constantly resorted to a kind of critical head scratching—something along the lines of *Variety*'s "probably wouldn't go in the more sedate niteries." It was the ultimate "you had to be there."

"People couldn't tell you when they left the Copa what the fuck Martin and Lewis did," Jerry recalled. "They knew one was a singer and one was a monkey. That's it. People used to sit in Lindy's and say, 'They tore the fuckin' joint apart.' 'What did they do?' 'Uh . . . uh . . . you gotta see it.' No one ever said what we did. No one could ever write what we did. They could try it, and good writers on *The New York Times* attempted it, and Dean and I used to sit and get hysterical. Laughing hysterically because they're trying to be uppity and up-scale: 'Of course, the straight man, who would come on after the comic, would do a gag or two, and he would sing some songs. . . .' Well, Dean and I would say, 'They don't fucking get it. They just don't get it.' And we would laugh hysterically. We were putting on the whole fucking world."

The sophomoric Martin and Lewis high jinks, at once hip and inane, captured the moment of the postwar years exactly: As America rose to global dominance, Martin and Lewis provided a kind of nervous escape hatch, a temporary flight from the American sense of responsibility. They acted out the urge to piss on the boardroom table that returning GIs turned businessmen repressed for the good of their families and their nation. There was nothing dangerously subversive in their act—it was still, after all, an age of relative consensus, before Elvis, before Jack Kerouac, even before Brando. But Dean and Jerry were instantly gobbled up by audiences that felt increasingly, if unconsciously, at sea amid the trappings of progress, wealth, and success.

Abbey Greshler, for his part, felt no existential burden at all. In the winter of 1946–47 he was overseeing bookings for a wildly hot act—he even had Jerry and Dean's lives insured, lest some calamity rob him of his new sinecure. By the end of the Havana-Madrid engagement, Lou Perry took Jerry aside to tell him he was no longer representing Dean. In October the gig Greshler had presumptuously booked at the Latin Casino found Jerry and Dean billed in unison for the first time: Martin and Lewis. (The billing order, which custom has made sound so natural, was arrived at, according to Jerry, when Dean announced they should be billed alphabetically: "*D* comes before *J*.")

In Philadelphia that fall, Jerry ordered matching two-hundred-dollar tuxes for the duo, despite Dean's protests that the material was far too expensive for their knockabout style. Jerry, seeing that the very luxury of the suits would set off the slapstick nicely, not only ordered the tuxes over Dean's objections but had a second set made as well.

He also contributed another sartorial touch to the act, which he felt was crucial to its success. Since both men stood just over six feet tall, and since both were slender and freshfaced, Lewis hit upon height as the dimension to exploit in distinguishing and enhancing their images. To exaggerate the physical differences between himself and Dean—to make the Putz look less prepossessing than the Playboy—Jerry had fractions of an inch shaved off the soles of his shoes and fractions added to the soles of Dean's.

"When we used to read 'the little guy,' " Jerry said, "Dean used to pound the table and say, 'They don't even know we're the same fuckin' size, those idiots!' I said, 'Leave them alone, Dean. We're making a fortune. Let them write "the little guy."' He said, 'But don't they watch?' "

The effect was subtle—Jerry would intensify it by performing in a crouch and peering up at Dean like a little kid—but it made a slight physical variance seem like a deep psychological rift. A half-inch here, a quarter-inch there, a hunch of the shoulders, and Jerry's worship for Dean was writ physically into their posture. Dean would always refer to Jerry as "the boy," both in and out of character, and while Martin was indeed almost a decade older than his partner, the term referred as much to a maturity gap in their characters as anything else.

Jerry *was* still a boy, though, and even though he had a little family of his own and a swiftly rising career, he had a boy's problems. In addition to nightclub owners and booking agents throughout the northeast, all of whom were mad to showcase his act, Jerry was being courted by Danny and Rae—who, though still working, were now finding plenty of time in their schedules to see their son perform. They may have balked at his getting into the business, but now that he was becoming a success they were determined to keep close tabs on him.

Danny called Jerry one morning during the Latin Casino run to announce that he and Rae would be making the trip down to Philly to catch that night's dinner show. Waking Jerry up, Danny tried to mask his embarrassed resentment over having to request tickets to his son's hot new act. Jerry sensed his dad's discomfort, but, as any twenty-year-old would, he blamed himself for the awkward situation: "In some incomprehensible way I felt guilty," he later recalled, "as if everything I had become only made his life more painful, much harder to bear."

If coming with hat in hand to request a ringside table at the Latin Casino stuck in Danny Lewis's craw, he must have choked outright the following January, when Dean and Jerry were booked at the Loew's State Theater in Manhattan at fifteen hundred dollars per week in support of *The Jolson Story*, the film of his hero's life. With their five or six shows a day, Martin and Lewis were as big a hit as the film, which finished third in the year's box-office derby. Jerry even began working Jolson material into the act. This wasn't irony: This was fate spitting in Danny Lewis's eye. The engagement was a smash. *Variety* wrote appreciatively of the "fresh, clean, youthful appearance of the pair" and once again seemed at a loss to describe just what it was that was so funny: "All they do cannot be detailed, but virtually every bit of it is good for solid laughs." Whatever it was they had, it was infectious. The Loew's chain picked up both of its options to book Dean and Jerry again later that year at an additional $250 a week.

Part of the furor at the State was created by the scores of servicemen with whom Greshler had seeded the audience. He gave them each two bits and some quick lessons in applauding and laughing on cue. The idea of spiking the crowd had come from George Evans, the publicist Greshler had hired to promote the act. Evans was a stone legend in public-relations circles at the relatively tender age of forty-five—the Irving Thalberg of flack. Thin and quiet, with wire-rimmed glasses perched on his slender nose and with dark, thinning hair, he looked more like a college administrator or small businessman than a behind-the-scenes show-business genius. But he was universally regarded as just that. Over the years, he'd pitched such acts as the Glenn Miller Orchestra, Lena Horne, and Duke Ellington, and he was the publicist for the Copacabana, the ne plus ultra of sophisticated nightclubs.

Evans had made himself immortal in his trade a half-dozen years earlier, when he turned Frank Sinatra into a star: He planted bobby-soxers in the audience whenever the singer performed, arranged to have ambulances parked out front to rush swooning girls to the hospital, and supplied ushers with smelling salts and ammonia to help revive the victims of the Voice's charms. The press reported all of the resultant commotion—real and imagined—as news, never questioning Evans's role in creating the hubbub. Even more valuably, perhaps, Evans was an expert at extricating his clients from messy situations of their own personal manufacture. Sinatra's marital misadventures were widely joked to have cost Evans his hairline, and while Dean and Jerry weren't quite big enough yet to give their publicist ulcers, they were working on it.

With the act in increasing demand, Greshler was approached by the Copacabana with an offer of $750 a week. Though the club was universally regarded as the premier night spot in the country, Greshler was frankly insulted that its bookers would offer his boys less than half of what they were making elsewhere. He turned the deal down. Dean and Jerry were aghast, as was Evans, and the duo discussed dismissing Greshler, but the tough-minded agent succeeded in persuading them that the club would be after them again—and for more money. Besides, he was booking them into such lucrative dates that they couldn't say no.

Martin and Lewis premiered in Chicago in May 1947, playing the Rio Cabana for a month at $1,750 a week. The date was just another in a series of their successes that spring and summer—the Stanley Theater in Camden, New Jersey, the Earl Theater in Philadelphia, return engagements at Loew's State and the 500 Club. But it marked one minor sea change: During their stay in Chicago, Dino Crocetti, the barber's son from Steubenville, applied scissors to his partner's greasy pompadour, cutting it into a juvenile buzz. (By some accounts, Jerry fell asleep in a barber's chair and Dean slipped the haircutter a few bucks to do the deed.) Jerry didn't exactly love the effect at first, but he realized how crucially it affected the act. Gone forever was Jerry's unlikely attempt to resemble a gigolo. He would be a crewcut-and-brilliantine guy evermore.

The hair: It developed as yet another means of differentiating him from Dean, making one look more the Casanova and the other more a chimp. But along with the notorious screech of "Hey, Laaaa-dy!," it has become Jerry's permanent trademark. Jerry's haircut is as much a physical signature as Bob Hope's nose, Groucho's mustache, or Buster Keaton's deadpan. And it is an almost irresistible butt of humor: Johnny Carson ("If you'd ever take that shoe polish out of your hair, you'd be a nice-looking boy"), David Letterman ("The big Labor Day weekend is coming up, which means that sometime soon Jerry Lewis will apply the first ritual coating of shellac to his head"), and scores of lesser comics can no more ignore Lewis's haircut than they can political sex scandals or airline food.

It was a near-crewcut in the early years, adding an additional patina of boyishness to Jerry's already youthful looks. After Martin and Lewis, it became a bit more elaborate: razor-fine along the temples, longer (and greased down) on top and over the edges of the crown, tapered in back—a modified D.A. Jerry was said to cut it himself, but he also went to elaborate lengths to get just the look he wanted when the occasion demanded it. Thirty-five years before Bill Clinton's notorious Los Angeles airport haircut, Lewis flew his California barber to New York at the cost of five hundred dollars so his hair would look perfect during his epochal run at the Palace Theater. It was always jet black, suspiciously so as Lewis hit middle age. Lit up with spotlights onstage or in movies, it could look like an ebony skullcap—a grotesque approximation of the black widow's peak of greasepaint sported by the Pierrot figure in the commedia dell'arte.

Lewis explained his coiffure simply: "I kept my hair long and it's very, very fine. I can't stand stuff in my eyes, so I used that shit to keep my hair out of the way." And he could see, in retrospect, how awful the original, tall pompadour looked on him: "I got some pictures where I look like Anthony Quinn's cunt," he admitted, bizarrely. But the practicality of the hairdo is less telling than its persistence. Where Jerry's hair once bespoke childlikeness and then represented a kind of cleancut hipness à la Harold Teen or Elvis-just-out-of-the-army, it has evolved into a mark of age, a symbol of a man at once out of touch and defiant about it.

As Lewis approached seventy, he knew as much—"You know what a joy it is for me never to use that shit?" he said—and with his hair relaxed for a day of lolling about the house or yacht, he would let his temples appear frankly gray, with tinges of auburn about his head. Onstage, however, he still went to some lengths to style his hair in the old manner, as determined to maintain that element of his character as he was to keep telling Polish jokes and singing Jolson songs.

In the fall of 1947 Greshler booked Martin and Lewis into the Riviera, one of the most fabulous steps on the nightclub circuit, a gigantic north Jersey dinner theater with a glass roof that revealed the night sky and the Manhattan cityscape across the Hudson. Dean and Jerry were making $2,250 a week—the Riviera, the gem of the Bergen mob's string of gambling parlors and nightclubs, could afford it—but they'd begun to chafe a bit at Greshler's management and even at each other. Each accused the other of trying to upstage him, and each was probably right. The act was so loosely put together, such a helter-skelter toyboxful of bits, that upstaging was a matter of course.

At first they took it in stride. "I remember once Jerry was onstage doing something by himself," Dean recalled later. "I went back to the dressing room and got my suitcase, walked through the club and across the stage, and at the edge turned and said to him, 'When you're through, kid, lock up.' " But now they were sniping about each other to Greshler. The agent got so annoyed with the bickering that he approached the powerful William Morris Agency and offered to sell the act to them outright for $17,500 (more than quadruple what he'd paid Perry for Dean alone a year before). Morris said no.

So Greshler saddled up his frisky ponies and rode to Chicago, where an even bigger gig awaited them at the Chez Paree, the swank nitery that was to the land of Capone what the Riviera was to Fort Lee, New Jersey. It was a long, extremely lucrative gig—nearly thirty thousand dollars for Martin and Lewis as a team for some twelve weeks of work. And like that Christmas vacation Jerry had taken with Danny and Rae in Detroit a decade earlier, this winter-long hiatus in Chicago would mark a passage into a newer, more mature phase in his life.

Living in a Chicago hotel with Dean, surrounded each night by mobsters in tuxedos offering him drinks and showgirls in sequined costumes offering other favors, Jerry would begin to turn from the nervous kid who had palled around with Irving Kaye and Lonnie Brown into a slick, jaded young man. In imitation of his partner and idol, Jerry began to hang out with tough guys and cheat on his wife. If he was going to act like a baby while he was onstage, he would be the most macho of men when he got off it.

Jerry almost didn't survive his initial look at this new life. He was onstage at the Chez Paree, bleeding the crowd for laughs, and some guy at a front table was not only not laughing but sitting with his back to the show altogether, talking to a friend.

Jerry wouldn't have it. He reached down from the stage and grabbed the man by the shoulder.

"Hey, pal, the show is up here!"

The man stared him down cold. "If you don't move away, right now, I'll blow your fuckin' head off!"

Jerry looked at the guy's white-on-white tie and shirt, remembered that he was in Chicago, and felt a cold chill on his neck. He finished the show and summoned up the courage to go over and apologize.

"Sir, there's no excuse for stupidity, but I'm young, I'm trying to do what I think is good on the stage, and I got carried away, and what I did was rude and disrespectful, and I'm really very sorry."

"After I tell you I'm gonna blow your fuckin' head off," the man responded, "you got the guts to come over here. You're all right."

He extended a hand. "My name is Charlie Fischetti."

Jerry had never heard of him, but he was Al Capone's cousin, Trigger-Happy Fischetti, who ran Chicago from his ringside Chez Paree table.

Fischetti was Jerry's first mobster, but he wouldn't be his last. Over the years, Jerry would be voluntarily candid with journalists about the gang lords he'd known. He was more apt, in fact, to drop the names Fischetti, Genovese, and Siegel than those of presidents or monarchs he'd met. Told the FBI wouldn't release its file on him without his permission, he responded, "There's a lot of blacked-out stuff. Especially stuff pertaining to John Kennedy—all of that is struck—Marilyn Monroe, my friendship with [Sam] Giancana . . ." He bragged about the value of his marker, how on trips to Italy strangers would greet him as "an American man who my family said is okay," how at various times in his troubled economic history connected men would appear with suitcases of money (which he refused), how he'd been able to get—and sometimes get out of having to play—gigs ("you just have to know what calls to make"), how the Fischettis supported his charity work: "There's never been a telethon where I don't get very, very heavy-duty checks from that family, every year."

It's no great secret that there were intimate ties between show biz and the mob throughout the century, from New Orleans honky-tonks through the founding of Las Vegas to the celebrities who showed up at John Gotti's trials to offer their support. In the late 1940s hoods ran the most prestigious night spots in nearly every American city, and every entertainer who regularly performed before live audiences came to know a veritable Who's Who of underworld figures. But even those show people who actively sought the companionship, sponsorship, and confidence of gangsters have been more discreet about their connections to the mob than Lewis. Frank Sinatra, for a pointed instance, always threatened to sue writers who focused on the darker side of his social life, and continually denied any connection to mafiosi even when everyone from the Justice Department to Garry Trudeau could prove otherwise. Lewis, on the contrary, spent the 1980s and '90s bragging about his familiarity with gangsters to *Penthouse, Vanity Fair, Esquire,* a journalist writing a book about Dean Martin, and his own biographer.

Why all the ruckus? Obviously, Jerry Lewis knew mobsters. But just as clearly, he was never an intimate of theirs in anything other than a social sense. He never, like Sinatra, entered into business ventures that bore the spoor of mob money. He was never forced to testify about organized crime before an investigatory body.

He was, however, able to call upon a gangster when he found himself in threatening straits. In January 1961, he stood to be named (along with such others as Dean, Sinatra, John Kennedy, and Sammy Davis, Jr.) in a divorce suit being filed by a Southern California restaurateur against his starlet wife, who wanted to collect on her soon-to-be-ex-husband's estate. Jerry, according to Judith Campbell, who was working for him at the time, "ranted and raved. He would be ruined, his wife Patti would divorce him, his audience would desert him, his friends would hold him in contempt." He asked for advice—"How can I stop it? Do you have any idea at all? Do you know anyone who could help?"—and Campbell put him in touch with her boyfriend, Giancana, who convinced the private eye who'd gathered a file against Jerry to quash the evidence.

But the only time Lewis's name ever came up publicly vis-à-vis a gangster was during Mickey Cohen's 1961 trial on tax evasion, when Cohen called Lewis as a witness to verify his destitute financial condition. "I loaned Mr. Cohen five thousand dollars in 1957," Lewis told the court. "It was a personal loan. There was no interest. He was having financial difficulties." Magnanimously, Lewis declared that he never asked for the money back. Another time, according to Lewis, Cohen had approached him with a moneymaking scheme: a film bio of himself that Jerry would produce. "I thought it would make a good picture," Jerry said, "and Mr. Cohen thought Robert Mitchum should play the role." Although the Hollywood trade papers linked Lewis to the project, it never went beyond the discussion stage, Lewis claimed, because "it was not in keeping with the levity of Jerry Lewis productions."*

The extent of Lewis's mob connections would have been a matter of little certainty or concern if he hadn't talked about it so much. And its reality was less intriguing than his insistent reference to it. Like many show-biz and sports figures, he wore his familiarity with gangsters as a pinky ring, and he insisted on wagging it under people's noses. As he shed the juvenile persona of his early career in the 1970s and '80s, as his body thickened, his reflexes slowed, and his voice achieved a naturally rich baritone, he found himself playing roles that called upon his familiarity with mob types: a garment district tycoon under pressure from actual mafiosi on TV; a crime boss trying to revenge himself on a former colleague (named Dino!) in the film *Cookie*.

There were grace notes in these performances that indicated a familiarity with the culture—a way of chewing the insides of his cheeks and cocking his head as he listens to news he doesn't want to hear, an aura of imminent explosiveness suggested by his barrel chest. But then again, as he aged he projected these same qualities in person. It was as if he had cast himself as a don in his own life, and an exiled one at that: Prospero with a suntan and a three-stroke handicap. His habit of dropping mobsters' names seemed a way of insinuating that the decline of his career was based on some dark, noble mystery, some manly secret that very few others could appreciate. As if to exculpate his many years of acting like an infantile chimp, of wheedling sympathy out of reluctant audiences, he spun a cocoon of seeming menace about himself, and his references to the shady characters who dotted his life were part of that self-mythology.

Jerry's fetish for gangsters might simply have meant that his new situation was turning him to the bad. Gangsters had always been drawn to Dean, who diplomatically but definitively rebuffed them. Jerry, however, was more easily flattered by such attentions, and quicker to accept and boast about them.

And it wasn't the only symptom of change in his character. The desperately lovesick lad who practically proposed to Patti Palmer the night they met was just three years later straying from his marital vows with impudent regularity. Dean had never taken the slightest pains to conceal his infidelities, but Jerry was still college age, still writhing under his parents' thumbs. He surely required some encouragement—if only by example—to carry on. While there are implications that Danny's example offered that encouragement, Dean, like Danny's evil twin,

---

*Stepping off the witness stand after being cross-examined by a district attorney, Jerry strangely quipped to reporters, "Now I know how Eichmann feels."

practically led Jerry by the hand into a variety of practices: gambling, drinking, women. In Chicago, with his wife and baby hundreds of miles away in their little Newark apartment, Jerry felt the license to rove. George Evans counseled him and Dean to be more discreet, but he wasn't heard. They were merely exercising the same sexual rights that every big-time entertainer before them had enjoyed.

Unbeknownst to them, however, their shenanigans had gotten out of hand. According to Greshler, Dean and Jerry "went out with the wrong girls"—gangsters' molls. "That was a no-no," he said. Though he had sent the team to Chicago in the care of his assistant, Freddie Fields, Greshler made a trip west himself to clean up the mess.

"I got them out of Chicago about two steps ahead of Dean getting killed," he recalled. "I did it with the help of Sidney Korshak. He's a very dear man, but some people say he's the mob's attorney. I never asked him that. You learn not to ask."

Indeed, so many years around the business had inured Greshler to a certain kind of rough customer. "I know every underworld character in the world," he said late in his life, "but I never had any problems with them. They kidnapped my kid once, but outside of that, it was quiet."

Just as he could gloss over a story like that, Greshler didn't tell Jerry and Dean how close they'd come in Chicago to not being able to apologize for what they'd done. He didn't want to worry them: As he'd predicted, the Copa had called back with more money, and Dean and Jerry would open there after they returned from Chicago. There was enough on their shoulders already.

When they got back to New York, Dean and Jerry made a movie—a home movie, actually, in eight-millimeter color. They walked around Times Square in windbreakers, smoking cigarettes, looking like typical Manhattan sharpies of the era. The movie was shot beneath the marquee of the Loew's Capitol, where Greshler had booked them at twenty-five hundred dollars a week. Universal Pictures' trendy new film *The Naked City*, a strange mix of murder mystery and pseudo-documentary American neorealism, was the feature, and Tex Beneke's orchestra had top billing. The combination of their high jinks and Mark Hellinger's hardboiled crime story wasn't quite as natural as the pairing with *The Jolson Story* had been—business was good and the reviews generally positive, but it was no sensation. In the home movie they walk unrecognized down Broadway: They had yet to make a significant splash in the big city.

Indeed, at that moment, just prior to their debut at the Copa, their private lives were more dynamic than their stage ones. Dean made a grand gesture in the role of family man, leasing a ten-room apartment on Riverside Drive so that he, Betty, and the kids (now three in number) could finally live together. Jerry, on the other hand, moved into a hotel by himself, leaving Patti and Gary in Newark. It wasn't their first separation—during these skyrocketing days, according to

Patti, Jerry had "on many occasions . . . decided not to come home at all"—but it was a serious one, a genuine marital crisis.

Patti was a thousand miles from her family and living with her baby amid Jerry's less-than-supportive relatives. She was devastated, but she'd grown up with worse. She determined to persevere. Hard as the estrangement was on Patti, it couldn't have been easy on Jerry, even if he was the one who instigated it. "Jerry used to tell me that every person is really two people," she recalled. "He certainly was—the husband and father who was solicitous one day and vindictive the next." He must have fought with himself over what he'd done, his romantic and selfish sides battling within.

If the solicitous Jerry was ever going to reemerge, it would be against the protests of his parents. Danny and Rae were thrilled by the fame and fortune their son had come into. Now, to top it off, he was free of the meddling shiksa who'd stolen him away. "His parents were elated," said Patti, "for now they would have their son all to themselves. They lingered backstage and milked the parent role for all it was worth." It was a bitter experience of rejection, even for a woman who'd spent her whole life prior to meeting Jerry in a series of sour familial relationships. "I was hurt, not 'playing' hurt," Patti remembered. "His folks worked hard to undermine my place. Their attitude—our son is finally back!— should not have surprised me. I had never been the little Jewish mama with real Jewish roots. To them I was Patti the interloper, the Italian outsider."

The couple were sufficiently reconciled, however, that Patti was there for the Copacabana opening on April 8, 1948. The pressures of the gig may have sent Jerry back into his wife's arms, or it may have been a genuine urge to be a good husband and father. Jerry always smarted from his lonely childhood, and he wanted a large family to help him keep his fears of abandonment at bay. Moreover, his hero, Dean, was able to combine a life of constant womanizing with a growing brood of kids at home. It looked to Jerry like a fair approximation of the perfect life; he'd certainly grown up himself in an atmosphere of intermittent family unity. He and Patti would simply have to reach an accommodation.

Besides, part of the reason they'd separated was surely the anxiety Jerry felt prior to the engagement at the Copa. Failure there would erase the previous two years of good fortune. Greshler had ensured that it would be a lucrative gig. He'd originally sought three thousand dollars a week, though when club owners Monte Proser and Jules Podell balked, he settled for twenty-five hundred for two weeks—with a ringside table and an open bar tab thrown in for himself. Jerry was impressed at the way Greshler had overcome the reluctance of Proser and Podell (who fronted for the real owner, mob kingpin Frank Costello) to book such a wild act in their high-toned nightclub. But Greshler knew New York crowds well enough to guess that they would go for his boys. "Brazenness, cunning, mental toughness, willpower—those were his weapons," Jerry said admiringly of his agent, and he and Dean were set to reap the benefits of Greshler's persistence.

They weren't at the top of the bill—Broadway and Hollywood song star Vivian Blaine (later to gain fame as Adelaide in the original production of *Guys and Dolls*) had that slot—but they had most definitely arrived.

They rehearsed for the premiere more than they had ever bothered in their lives. Jerry, in particular, was on edge. "I keep thinking we ought to be better prepared," he told Dean. "This is the *Copa*."

Dean, unperturbed as ever, tried to relax his partner, but a few days later, Jerry had some news. "I hired a writer. I paid him one thousand dollars. Don't worry—it'll come out of my half." The writer, Danny Shapiro, the first gag man they'd ever used in a career made up of bits borrowed and stolen, delivered a sheaf of routines to Jerry, one-liners and all. Just as nervous as he'd been a few years earlier when he was breaking in as an emcee, Jerry pored over the material.

"He was studyin' those lines just before our opening," Dean recalled later. "I looked at him. I knew he didn't wanna do 'em. I said, 'Jer, you don't want to read those lines, do you?' He said, 'No.' I said, 'Tear 'em up.' " Jerry did, filled with the nerve that Dean exuded.

The day of the premiere, Jerry raced into Manhattan to Saks Fifth Avenue to buy a new mink for Patti, presenting it to her at Lehigh Avenue, where she was giving Gary a bath. They made their way into town and met Danny and Rae, Mary Farina, Betty Martin, Abbey Greshler, and the other friends and relatives who were assembling for the show.

Jerry was nearly sick with stage fright, but he found his dressing room, got into his tux (in the old show-biz tradition he followed throughout his career, he dressed completely in his stage clothes save his pants, which he donned only at the last minute to avoid creasing them). He paced backstage in his dress shirt and underwear, trying to work out what he would do and coming up blank. Just outside the door, the World-Famous Copa Girls, the club's dancers, made their way to the stage to perform their own act. He could hear the sounds of the Nat Brandwynne orchestra, the applause, the shuffling of the chorus line back to their dressing room.

The big moment came. He and Dean hit the stage on a wave of sheer guts, flying by the seats of their pants. Jerry walked up to the mike. Scanning the room he saw Walter Winchell, Milton Berle, and Billy Rose, none of whom, he knew, were there to see him. He saw his wife, his parents, and a few other familiar faces.

When he spoke, it came out straight: "My father always said, 'When you play the Copa, son, you'll be playing to the cream of show business.' "

He peered quizzically over the mike, then shifted into Yiddish inflection: "*Dis is krim?*"

It was just the opening salvo they needed. Dean sang "San Fernando Valley," "Oh, Marie," "Rock-a-Bye Your Baby" and a few others. Jerry stuck prop buck teeth in his mouth, knocked over busboys' trays, and ran through the club like a ricocheting bullet. It was the same act they'd been doing for nearly two years, but it had been propelled into glorious hyperdrive by the sheer thrill of the setting. The Copa, as Greshler had suspected, was the perfect presentation room for the act—sophisticated, yes, but not stuffy.

They'd been told they could do twenty-five minutes—and Podell had been known to yank acts who overstayed their time limit. After fifty minutes, and with the crowd hollering for more, they left the stage exhausted: They had to conserve energy for the second show, after all, and they had nearly run out of stuff.

The room was on fire. In her dressing room, Vivian Blaine must have felt like she was awaiting execution. She was the headliner, the local girl who'd gone west to sign with Twentieth Century–Fox and returned in triumph. But listening to Martin and Lewis absolutely slay her audience, she knew the night would be a disaster for her. She gamely made her way to the stage, sang a few songs to a crowd that barely acknowledged that she was in the room, and cut her act short.

Jerry and Dean were entertaining their guests backstage, still high on the buzz of the reception they'd gotten, when they noticed a look of concern on Greshler's face.

"We have to be in Proser's office as soon as the crowd clears out," he told them.

They were sure they had done well, but now they got a sick feeling: Had they stayed on too long? Had they been too wild?

They made their way sheepishly to the office.

"I'd be a damned fool if I did nothing about this show," Proser told them. "It's coming off all wrong."

Greshler leapt to his clients' defense: "Where the hell did they go wrong?"

"It's not them I'm talking about," Proser said.

It was Vivian Blaine. Once word of the show hit the streets, he knew he wouldn't be able to keep her in the headline spot. She'd have to switch billing with Martin and Lewis.

Jerry couldn't believe what he was hearing. "I tore my gaze from Proser and glanced at Dean," he later recalled. "He had a pipe stuck in his mouth, sucking it noisily and doing Eddie Cantor bits with his eyes."

Proser broke the news to Blaine, who quit outright rather than suffer the humiliation of having the bill upended on her. And just as he'd imagined, the papers went crazy for Martin and Lewis.

"Here's a case of two being better than one," wrote *Variety*. "They work in yeoman fashion and permit one another enough latitude for individual scintillation. It's only after each makes impact on his own that whatever stepping on one another's laughs and lines occur. And then it doesn't matter."

Nothing mattered. The two weeks got extended through the summer—more than a dozen weeks in all, at five thousand dollars per. Greshler negotiated for a suite of rooms in the hotel above the club, a place for Dean and Jerry to crash between shows, to hide out with girls and do whatever they might want to do in private. Privacy was at a premium now: The two guys who'd been signed as a second act were absolutely the hottest thing in town.

Take as proof the deal Greshler got for them *during* that first run at the Copa. The gigantic Roxy Theater, the Broadway motion picture palace, reopened that spring with renovations that included an ice rink on which its chorus girls performed before films. To herald the changes, the Roxy hired Dean and Jerry to do one show a night along with the skaters and a suitably overblown piece of cinematic hokum, *Give My Regards to Broadway*, which starred Dan Dailey in a story about an attempt to revive vaudeville. Racing from the Copa after the supper show to the rink at the Roxy and then back to the Copa for the midnight performance, Martin and Lewis pulled in an additional ten thousand dollars a week. Over twenty-one exhausting days in that incredible summer of 1948, each man earned $22,500.

Success had a funny way of spilling off Dean and Jerry like water. Everyone around them benefited. Spendthrift Jerry walked into the Dunhill store on Fifth Avenue and bought a few dozen engraved gold lighters for friends. He rented a humidor full of Cuban cigars for Irving Kaye, whose taste for rancid stogies had always been a joking point between them. (As proof of his ambivalence about his marriage, though, he and Patti continued to live in their rent-controlled apartment, the monthly cost of which represented less than one percent of Jerry's weekly salary.)

Danny Lewis might have gone apoplectic over his son's rise but for Greshler's ability to get him some premium bookings as well. Folks were eager to get any piece of Dean and Jerry, even if it meant going to see Jerry's father sing. In June Danny played a fifteen-minute stand at the Latin Casino in Philadelphia and was reviewed by *Variety*: "Success can be retroactive. Skyrocketing of young Jerry Lewis (Martin and) is carrying special premiums for his not-so-old-man, Danny Lewis. After years on the borscht circuit and moderate stage success, Lewis, Sr., is getting his chance for a bid at top niteries. . . . Lewis has a voice so much like Al Jolson's that it might easily be palmed off as same, if you weren't looking. However, he does it straight, wisely eschewing those worn-thin imitations of Jolie's mannerisms."

It was no rave, but Danny didn't mind. He still honestly believed he was going places, and by Greshler's graces, he returned to New York to play the Glass Hat and Loew's State (conscious, no doubt, that his son had beat him to the punch in each). He no doubt would have resented the hand-me-down quality of his success more if he weren't so confident that he deserved it.

Back at the Copa, Jerry was coasting along on his own brilliant streak, though not without hitting the same sorts of bumps he'd stumbled over in the past. Screwing around at the bar one night between shows, he got on the nerves of a particularly brutish customer.

"Why don't you knock off that shit and be quiet?" the bruiser growled.

Jerry was stunned for a moment. "I figured he was either kidding or too drunk to appreciate who I was," he recalled. "So I threw him a stock line. 'That's what happens when cousins get married!' "

Dean, standing nearby, cringed. The bartender looked at his shoes.

The man stuck a finger in Jerry's face. "That's not funny, you stupid son of a bitch. If you open your mouth once more, it'll be without teeth."

Dean stepped in to make peace. "My partner is a little young," he said. "He didn't mean any harm." He grabbed Jerry's arm. "Now, Jer, just say to the man that you're sorry and it won't happen again."

Frozen still, memories of Charlie Fischetti in his head, Jerry did as he was told.

The man addressed Dean this time. "You keep the little bastard away from me. Tell him he's lucky I've got a sense of humor."

They mumbled thank-yous and yes-sirs and walked away. Dean pushed Jerry into a corner. "For your information, schmuck, that was Albert Anastasia."

Even Jerry recognized the name of the Lord High Executioner of Murder, Incorporated. Despite the sick feeling in his stomach, he played the second show that night: "I couldn't see them in the darkness, but I swear I could feel Anastasia's cold steel eyes hitting me like bullets through the performance."

Mobsters weren't the only big shots keeping company with Dean and Jerry at the Copa. Through their New York offices, the Hollywood movie studios had heard wondrous tales of the sensational new act. Dean had had some flirtatious encounters with the movies in the past—his failed screen test for Harry Cohn and a few passing inquiries from MGM musical producer Joe Pasternak—but Hollywood had always turned up its nose at him. Now, though, the studios smelled a moneymaker, and a few producers were making the trip east to catch Martin and Lewis in New York.

First among the crowd was Hal Wallis, the veteran Warner Brothers production chief who'd overseen such classic films as *Casablanca, Jezebel, Little Caesar, I Am a Fugitive from a Chain Gang,* and *Yankee Doodle Dandy.* Wallis had left Warner Brothers in 1944 and formed an independent production company with Joseph Hazen, a former staff lawyer at the studio who, like Wallis, had bristled under the yoke of Harry and Jack Warner. The company they formed, Wallis-Hazen, had been courted by various studios when it was begun, finally striking a long-term distribution deal with Paramount Pictures. It was a small company, true, but it was still young enough to have its pocketbook open.

Wallis was quite a catch for Paramount. He was one of the more assured showmen of his time—he'd been the publicist on Jolson's *The Jazz Singer*, back in 1927—and he had a knack for discovering and cultivating fresh young talent. Within a few years of his arrival at Paramount, he signed Kirk Douglas, Burt Lancaster, Anna Magnani, Lizabeth Scott, and Charlton Heston.

As his résumé indicates, comedy wasn't Wallis's métier. Still, hot was hot, and when he found himself in New York in the spring of 1948, he checked out the act at the Copa: "Nightclub comedy is not my favorite form of entertainment, and I expected very little as they came out onto the stage. They were strangely ill matched. Dean, tall and very handsome, didn't look like a comedian, and Jerry, equipped with a mouthful of oversized false teeth and a chimpanzee-like hairpiece, seemed grotesque. But even before they began their act, the audience was screaming with laughter. Never before or since have I seen an audience react as this one did. The team (I am not given to superlatives) was an outright sensation."

Wallis came backstage after the show to meet Dean and Jerry and to announce that he wanted to sign them to a film contract. Greshler played his hand as cool as he could, telling Wallis that he'd arranged for a date in Los Angeles later that summer and that they could talk again at that time. Dean and Jerry would have bent over backward at the first Hollywood offer that came along, but Greshler wanted to see what price he could fetch on the open market.

Jerry's notion of a big future had always involved performing at a first-rank vaudeville house. His horizon had never surpassed the corner of Broadway and Forty-seventh Street, just beneath the marquee at the Palace. Now it reached all the way to Hollywood, and he could hardly believe it.

There was nothing firm waiting for him and Dean in L.A. besides a nightclub date, but that didn't dampen the excitement a bit. Their smash at the Copa had created a buzz that carried them forward more quickly than they'd ever dreamed. The world held no limits that summer. Whatever they did, wherever they went, they were kings.

At around this time, Jan Murray met Jerry again. They had shared the bill on a club date a few years earlier—Murray was the headliner, there was a girl singer, and Jerry opened with the record act. Murray had thought Jerry was terrifically funny, and when Martin and Lewis started to hit it big, he recognized Jerry as the opening act from a few years earlier. One night, when Martin and Lewis had become so famous that they required a police escort to go out to dinner in Times Square, Murray was eating in Lindy's when Jerry and Dean arrived with full entourage.

"He passed my table," Murray remembered, "and he pointed at me and he started screaming in that high voice: 'There he is! There's my idol!' I thought he was putting me down. I got so mad, I could've killed him, really. 'Cause I thought he was making fun of me, an older comic or something—even though I was only a few years older. I just felt he was ridiculing me because of his attitude, with the high voice and all that. So he went to his table, and there were people standing around it so that he wouldn't be disturbed. I got up to go to the men's room, and I stopped at his table, and I said, 'You know, you're a very successful young punk. I found that very embarrassing.' And he looked at me, and he almost had tears in his eyes, and he says to me, 'Jan, what are you talking about? I was so thrilled when I saw you sitting there. Don't you remember me?' And I said, 'I don't know. Are you the guy who did a club date with me once?' He says, 'Yeah, but don't you remember past that?' I said no. He says, 'I met you when I was nine or ten years old in the drugstore of the President Hotel and I did your act for you.' And the whole thing came back to me, and I said, 'Oh, my God . . .' And he says, 'You're the first comedian I saw, and I imitated you.' I apologized and I gave him a hug and he invited me to sit down with him and Dean. He told everyone the story: 'The first time I met him he wanted to kill me!'"

Murray had already been in the business over a decade, but he had never seen anything like the way audiences took to Martin and Lewis. "Boy oh boy, they were the sensation of America!" he recalled. "I can't begin to describe what a hit they were or how popular they were. It was tantamount to an Elvis or the Beatles. They were like the hottest thing in the country."

It was only natural that they would bring their act to television, and even their quick six-minute debut on the infant medium had an epic dimension. It was Sunday, June 20, 1948, and they spent the morning rehearsing for an appearance on a sort of vaudeville show for television, a mix of singing, dancing, comedy, interviews, and walk-ons to be hosted by the gnomish Broadway gossip columnist Ed Sullivan. The show was called "Toast of the Town," and it premiered that night.

Abbey Greshler had always had an eye for novelties, and he thought TV variety shows were a good idea, a way of shunting all the touring vaudeville and burlesque acts onto a new circuit without anything like the production costs of film. Sullivan and his coproducer, Marlo Lewis, approached Greshler with an offer of more than half of their talent budget for just a few minutes of Dean and Jerry. Greshler said yes—to two hundred dollars. The other guests—Rodgers and Hammerstein, dancer Kathryn Lee, concert pianist Eugene List, a New York City fireman who'd recently made headlines, and boxing referee Ruby Goldstein, who'd just worked the Joe Louis–Jersey Joe Walcott bout—split the remaining $175. Also on hand were the June Taylor Dancers (billed as the Toastettes) and the Ray Bloch orchestra.

The show aired on six CBS stations at 9 P.M., playing in New York opposite a political interview program on NBC and two obscure movies on local stations. Such was Sullivan's relatively obscure stature at the time, and such was the freakishness of televised vaudeville, that none of the New York papers bothered to review the broadcast. *Variety* saw it and liked it, though. "Tops were Dean

Martin and Jerry Lewis," wrote their old friend "Stal.," even though he slapped the hand of CBS for letting them "give out with some blue material, okay for their nitery work but certainly not for tele."

Another hot young comedy duo had been slated to appear on that first "Toast of the Town," the witty New York cabaret favorites Jim Kirkwood and Lee Goodman. Sullivan had apprehensions that the team's allusive, topical humor might be a bit too sophisticated for the mix he was trying to achieve, but he liked them so much that he didn't let them know about his concerns—or, for that matter, which other acts he'd booked.

"We got to the theater about nine-thirty on that Sunday morning," recalled Kirkwood (who went on to write *P.S. Your Cat Is Dead* and *A Chorus Line*), "and we walked in and there were Dean and Jerry rehearsing. They weren't just good, they were socko. I said, 'Jesus, Lee, are *they* on the show, too?' I knew we were dead."

Nevertheless, Kirkwood and Goodman rehearsed their act—to a silent auditorium. Sullivan and his team huddled in the corner. Someone suggested that Kirkwood and Goodman go with their most physical bit—they wore kitchen strainers for fencing masks and did a comic sabre dance to "Night and Day"—and so they rehearsed that one a few more times.

Finally, they were presented with a Hobson's choice. They were welcome to stay and appear on the show, but only if they could cut their bit to three minutes. "Ed feels that Dean and Jerry are pretty strong," they were told. "No shit," Kirkwood replied, and he and Goodman, like Vivian Blaine before them, walked.

From the Sullivan show, Dean and Jerry returned to Atlantic City for their third engagement at the 500 Club. They played two weeks to jammed houses and returned to New York on August 2 for another TV appearance. The next week, they headed west toward their destiny.

Greshler had known New York would go for Dean and Jerry's high-voltage act; Hollywood, though, was another thing—a company town with a decidedly less urbane sensibility. Sure, there had been interest from the studios, but they took a look at anything that had a patina of heat about it. Word of Martin and Lewis had already drifted west—Hal Wallis's appearance at the Copa was proof of that—and George Evans's West Coast man, Jack Keller, was fanning the incipient flame. But the team's momentum was a fragile thing to maintain, and Greshler had a lot riding on it. In the right setting, he knew, he could generate a bidding war for Martin and Lewis's services. He was hoping he could put together a West Coast showcase as natural for the act as the Copa had proven, a venue with the combination of prestige and ease that Frank Costello's New York nightclub had afforded Dean and Jerry.

Slapsie Maxie's Café, in a then-fashionable section of Wilshire Boulevard's Miracle Mile, was the nearest thing Los Angeles had to the Copa in 1948. Maxie

Rosenbloom, a former pro boxer who'd been dubbed "Slapsie Maxie" by Damon Runyon himself and had become a familiar cameo actor in roles calling for tough yeggs or punch-drunk types, took over the former Wilshire Bowl in 1947, fronting for clothiers Sy and Charlie DeVore and gangster Mickey Cohen, who kept an office in back.

Greshler had negotiated a plump contract with the club: four thousand dollars a week (high by L.A. standards) and three first-class train fares for him and the boys. (Like Betty Martin, who was expecting a baby, Patti stayed back east.) Mickey Cohen would later take credit for fronting Rosenbloom and the DeVores the cash to close the deal. Along with Irving Kaye, who was now on Jerry's payroll as a road manager, Dean, Jerry, and Greshler arrived in California on August 9, the very night they were to open at the club.

They rode as far as Pasadena, getting off there, as did all the famous stars, to avoid the crush of the press at L.A.'s Union Station. Not that L.A. was panting for their arrival; they were just two nightclub comics from back east, not film royalty. Unless George Evans had done some big preselling of the act, nobody would come to greet their train no matter where it stopped.

Charlie DeVore was planning to be there on behalf of Slapsie Maxie's. But Evans, who operated almost exclusively out of New York, told Dean and Jerry that his West Coast man, Keller, would be handling the big arrival. They didn't know who to look for, but Greshler assured them, "Just look for a dynamo." They prepared for their big arrival. Dean sported a thick-striped suit, and both of them wore gaudy painted shoes.

Sure enough, when they disembarked, a small knot of pressmen and photographers came toward them, led by a potbellied, unshaven, bleary-eyed bear of a man in a rumpled suit.

"I had a hangover," Keller later admitted.

He approached Dean and Jerry and bowed. "Jack Keller. At your service."

Jerry nudged Dean.

"Some dynamo," he whispered.

Keller turned to the newspeople, who seemed to be under his express direction. "Okay, boys, here they are—Lewis and Clark!"

Silence.

He shot a puzzled glance at Dean and Jerry, then snapped back to the reporters. "No, it has to be Stanley and Livingstone . . . Leopold and Loeb . . ."

The reporters broke up. The suspiciously haggard press agent turned out to be just the master Evans promised. Keller's "cynical masculinity," as Jerry called it, perfectly suited Martin and Lewis. Where Evans was all shrewd calculation and quiet brilliance, Keller was chumming-with-the-press, three-shot lunches, and afternoons on the golf course. "He handles the press," wrote Richard Gehman, who dedicated his book on Jerry to Keller, "without the press having the slightest notion that it is being manipulated." A former door-to-door sales-man, pool hustler, small-time con artist, and golf pro, Keller was nobody's yes man, but he capitalized on his self-effacing charm and friendly relationships with reporters to smooth over any contretemps into which his clients stumbled. Eventually, he would work solely for Martin and Lewis, then for Jerry after the split, orchestrating promotional campaigns and product tie-ins for Lewis's film and TV projects as a full-time member of Lewis's production staff.

Whether it was Keller's doing or the workings of the Hollywood grapevine, the opening night at Slapsie Maxie's was a riot of eager activity. Greshler must have been dizzy with anticipation as he watched a veritable round table of Holly-wood royalty—Crawford, Bogart, Gable, and their ilk—squeezed into tables or shut out altogether. Hal Wallis was in attendance, as well as the heads of several other studios, Louis B. Mayer among them. Everyone had come to see the hit act. And Dean and Jerry lived up to their renown.

They opened the show straight—an increasingly rare occurrence—with Dean singing. But then Jerry made his entrance, and along with the house or-chestra, led by New Jersey transplant Dick Stabile, they tore the joint apart. It was exactly what Hollywood clubgoers had heard about from friends back east, and it was a smash. "They topped every word of their advance build-up," wrote Alan Fischler in *Billboard*. In *Variety*, "Kap." agreed, saying that "high-priced screen talent was draped all over the place laughing incessantly."

"I've seen nightclub engagements by the best in the business," recalled Jack Keller years later, "and I never saw anything like that. That room must've seated nine hundred. There was a bar at one end, and there were terraces around the floor. I saw hundreds standing up on the bar so they could see the stage. You couldn't move in that joint. 'You wanna make a reservation? We can take you seven weeks from today.'"

Within a week, Martin and Lewis had been seen by every studio head in town, and the famous faces who couldn't get a seat at their shows would have made an impressive portrait collection. It was a publicist's dream. An agent's dream, too. Greshler's feeding frenzy was about to begin.

Wallis believed he had dibs on the act. Backstage at the Copa, he had told Jerry, "I assure you, we're going to make a movie together." But he would have to outbid at least two other studios for Martin and Lewis's services. Universal was offering a deal of thirty thousand dollars per picture, but they demanded control over the team's outside work, a concession Greshler would not make. Dean and Jerry were shocked that their agent would turn down such a sum, but he assured them they'd get more.

MGM, represented by producer Joe Pasternak, who'd once passed on Dean as a solo, offered forty thousand dollars per picture, but he too demanded approval over other appearances. Again Greshler balked, again Dean and Jerry registered their frustration, and when Pasternak countered with an offer for Dean alone, it seemed possible that the act might split up altogether.

But Greshler had left his trump card—Wallis—for last. He held several meetings with Joe Hazen, Wallis's partner, and they arranged for a screen test for Dean and Jerry. It almost backfired.

"I felt a shockwave of disappointment," recalled Wallis of his reaction to the footage. "The charisma that live audiences responded to so enthusiastically disappeared in the transition to film. On the screen, nothing happened."

Wallis asked for another test. It too was a flop. And then he understood what had been going wrong: "They were doing things written for them," he realized, "playing characters."

He had them submit to yet another test, but this time in their stage personae. "I thought those burlesque routines would be too extreme for movie audiences," he remembered, "but I was wrong. The moment Dean and Jerry did their act exactly as they had done it on the stage, they were fantastic. They burned up the screen. Everybody in the projection room was in stitches."

Having hooked Wallis, Greshler was still stringing along MGM. At the same time, he was playing a couple of networks against each other for a TV deal. After a lifetime of knocking on doors, Greshler now had everybody lined up at his— and it could get exciting, even scary. Joe Pasternak actually threatened him, approaching his table one night at Slapsie Maxie's and announcing, in front of Dean and Jerry, "If you take the Wallis deal, you'll never make a picture."

Jerry, meanwhile, insisted that Greshler visit Louis B. Mayer with him and hear him out. Mayer—who, according to Wallis, had initially dismissed the team, saying, "The guinea's not bad, but what do I do with the monkey?"—told them he'd match Wallis's offer dollar for dollar, but insisted on approval over all outside work. The legendary movie magnate, at that time the most highly paid man in America, took them on a personal tour of the studio. And Mayer had done his homework: As they walked through the lot, he asked Greshler how his sister Rose was and if his father was still in the fur business. Greshler, who prided himself on always being better prepared for negotiations than the other guy, was stunned.

Mayer's sentimentality—he had a large painting of his mother in his office—held an enormous appeal for Jerry. Although later in life he would declare that "my first love was Paramount," he was flattered by the great man's attentions. He urged Greshler to sign with MGM. But Greshler liked the idea of working with an independent—Wallis's little company would want the team only for a dozen or so weeks a year—and he held firm. So firm, in fact, that he snapped. After meeting with Mayer, Greshler had a nervous collapse and was admitted to a hospital.

Within a few days, however, he had recovered sufficiently to close some business. On August 20, 1948, he signed Dean and Jerry to a recording contract with Capitol Records with a guarantee of eight releases a year. And a few days later he signed the deal with Wallis and Hazen: five years, two pictures per, with fifty thousand dollars for the first, sixty thousand dollars for the next, and so on to a cumulative ceiling of $1.25 million. They could make one outside picture per year, and they had control over their own stage, TV, and radio work. Wallis allowed them approval over their first film, an enormous concession to make to new talent in the studio era. The only limit on them was that they couldn't do outside work during the shooting of Wallis's films.

The fine print didn't matter too much, though. They were made. They'd been in Hollywood less than two weeks, and they had signed a contract for more money in a year than either of their fathers had made in a lifetime. They made plans to bring their families out west and buy huge Hollywood homes.

But first there were some wild oats to sow. Dean had been carrying on an affair with MGM star June Allyson practically since he got off the train, and it wasn't long before Jerry took up with her friend Gloria DeHaven. The daughter of a show-biz family, DeHaven had, like Jerry, grown up following her parents around on the vaudeville circuit. Her father, Carter DeHaven, had directed several silent films and had even served as assistant director to Charlie Chaplin on *Modern Times*, in which Gloria made her screen debut at age eleven. At MGM Gloria was featured—often alongside Allyson—in light comedies and musicals, usually playing a daft, oversexed ingenue. But it wasn't her résumé Jerry was interested in. The four of them were married—Allyson to Dick Powell, DeHaven to John Payne—but they carried on so shamelessly that George Evans had to get Hedda Hopper to sit them down and scold them.

There were other girls, too. "Shit, yeah, we started knockin' 'em off," Jerry would boast later on. "In truth, I fucked more than he did; but it was always like they wanted to burp me." It was a refrain Jerry repeated frequently over the years, and it revealed unintentionally just what sort of impression he carried of himself. The women who passed through his life are cast by his words as mothers, not sex partners. Lewis offered the "burp me" line as a way of undercutting his boasts of sexual conquest—presumably, the women who slept with Dean didn't have baby burping on their minds—but instead it reveals his shaky self-image, showing just how strongly his promiscuity was a compensation for his childhood feelings of inadequacy. It would be cheap Freudianism to suggest that he slept around because his mother hadn't shown him sufficient love, but he was the one who repeatedly conflated extramarital sex with the care and feeding of an infant.

Patti had recognized early on that Jerry would be on the road without her and fall prey to temptation. "I know you're human," she'd said. "I know you'll meet lots of girls who want to be friendly when you're away. I just ask you not to do anything that would make people feel sorry for me." The product of a brutally broken home, Patti was determined to keep her family together even if it meant some discomfort. She could handle domestic blows, she felt, but not public humiliation.

In discussing his marriage during the 1950s and '60s, Lewis would contend that Patti's dignified request had "fixed" him and kept him on the straight and narrow. But after his 1980 divorce, Lewis would admit to a lifetime of infidelity. "A couple of times I was as discreet as a fucking bull taking a piss in your living room," he said in 1984. He would brag that he was "no different from anyone else in Hollywood, except I was a little busier." A few years later, he declared that John Kennedy—whom he and Dean had met in Chicago in November 1950, when the future President was still a fresh-faced congressman—was "one of the great cunt men of all time. Except for me."

This kind of stuff was shocking, especially coming from the mouth of someone who made his living making children laugh and who claimed to have quit the film business in the 1970s because of its turn away from family movies. Indeed, like his obsessive references to the mob, Jerry's sexual boasting seems rooted in a desire to erase the impression of sexless prepubescence created by his onstage behavior. After years of acting like a childish clown, he seemed to want the world to know for certain that his sex life was not only normal but superior.

In 1948, though, the availability of willing women seemed like just another contractual perk of success. Sex and money: They even sang about it. Before they headed back east in September to an engagement at the Latin Casino in Philadelphia, Dean and Jerry stopped at Capitol's Hollywood recording studios to cut their first single for the label, a pair of novelty tunes—"The Money Song" and "That Certain Party"—about the two things they suddenly found themselves swimming in: dough and broads.

As in their early film appearances, Martin and Lewis seem under wraps on these recordings. Dean begins each record singing straight, with Jerry joining—never interrupting—in various stages of accelerated frenzy. Some "comic" touches were added technologically; on "That Certain Party" Jerry's voice gets speeded up into an insane babble (prompting Dean to ask, "What are you doing—singing in shorthand?"). Between the two sides, Jerry does half a dozen voices: British, baby talk, operatic, a Jimmy Durante growl, fake Japanese, fake German, a bit of Yiddish. Dean mainly sings straight, though he does a kind of Rudy Vallee on "That Certain Party" and some fake Spanish and real Italian on "The Money Song."

They weren't very funny records—in fact, they made a better showcase for Dean's dry wit and deft timing than for Jerry's incessant aping, the strength of which was at least as visual as aural. Capitol hawked the single with fake dollar bills called "Martin-Lewis Mazuma" ("200 Fins Worth of Laughs," "50 Double Saw Giggles," and "10 C Note Guffaws"), and they may have even chosen the wrong song as the A-side. "That Certain Party" had been written for a vaudeville act in the 1920s, and technological tinkering aside, it had an air of live performance to it. The melody isn't very elaborate, and the lyric, a repetitive question-and-answer variation on "Billy Boy," was extremely flexible. Then again, "The Money Song" hadn't been recorded before—for a few months it became a Martin and Lewis signature tune—and its herky-jerky cha-cha beat led to a chorus that was an especially appropriate motto for the singers' lives at the moment they recorded it: "Funny, funny, funny what money can do."

Dean and Jerry went east to fulfill a club date in Philadelphia, where their wives and children were waiting for them. On weekends they slipped off to New York to tape a TV show and to spend their time with Allyson and DeHaven, who'd followed them.

Lewis recalled George Evans's appalled reaction to this comportment: "He had fuckin' migraines, the way we carried on. We went arm in arm down Fifth Avenue. Two married men with the biggest stars in Hollywood."

Jerry seemed to have the sense—borne, perhaps, of insecurity—to see his affair with DeHaven as the crazy fling it was. "What we were doing was playing our little fucking fantasyland," he confessed. "I never had fifty bucks in my pocket at one time; now I'm walking around with thirty-five hundred in hundred-dollar bills, and I got a starlet on my arm. It's fantasyland."

He was also smart—or scared—enough to be discreet, keeping well away from DeHaven when Patti joined him in New York. But Dean had no concern for such niceties, and he flaunted Allyson in Patti's face. Word got back to Betty, who was stuck in Philly with her four children, her increasingly antisocial liquor habit, and a nagging case of pleurisy. The news didn't help her mood.

Perhaps Patti had her own suspicions about Jerry, but she kept them to herself, just as she'd learned to bury her anxieties as a girl. In a way, Dean's flagrancy was a blessing. Any apprehensions Jerry and Patti had about their new life—any self-doubts on Jerry's part or rumors Patti might have heard—paled in comparison to the unraveling of Dean and Betty's marriage. Even Jerry felt sorry for Dean's overburdened, ailing wife. But he was riding a magic carpet, and he wasn't going to upset it in midflight by getting preachy with his big brother. Besides, he was having far too much fun.

Funny what money can do.

6

The Importance of Being Seymour

Built on a few wooded acres in the heart of Beverly Hills, 1100 Tower Road was a Spanish-style stucco house with the requisite Hollywood swimming pool, seventeen rooms, and bathrooms with sunken tubs. It had been built for Maria Montez, the Dominican sex symbol from the early 1940s whose career had waned when she lost her battle with her waistline. Still, because Hollywood landmarks are so few and so fleeting, the "Maria Montez House," as it was always known, remained a regular stopping point on tours of stars' homes long after its original owner herself had been forgotten.

The house rented for fifteen hundred dollars a month when Jerry signed a lease for it in late 1948. Back in Newark, the rent-controlled Lehigh Avenue flat passed on to Dan and Rae, who would also keep quarters in their son's new home. Other relatives would make their way west—Rae's sisters and their families—drawn in the wake of the sad, pesky kid who had miraculously made good.

The Lewises' happy ménage contrasted sharply with the state of affairs at the Martin house. Dean rented a smaller though similarly luxurious home in Bel Air. His parents, who had moved to California a few years earlier, helped him prepare it for Betty and the children. But the strains on the Martin marriage had followed them west. Even the proud tour Dean gave Betty of their new home couldn't drive the demons from their relationship.

While his boys were buying furniture and setting up house, Abbey Greshler was keeping busy arranging guest appearances on television, negotiating with NBC for a Martin and Lewis radio program, and preparing for their first film. Hal Wallis had decided the team would appear in a film version of the popular "My Friend Irma" radio show, to which he'd recently bought screen rights. The series, created by writer Cy Howard and developed along with writer-director Parke Levy, was a situation comedy about a daffy working girl (Marie Wilson, as Irma), her commonsensical roommate and best friend, Jane, and their misadventures in life and love in postwar Manhattan. On the radio, Wilson wasn't hampered by her rather plain looks and delighted people with her dumb misapprehensions and foolish assumptions. It was enormously popular.

Wallis, whose lifelong claims to highbrow standards are punctured by his choice to make a film of "Irma," had planned the movie as a low-budget programmer, a half-million-dollar investment that would either sink without doing much damage or succeed and make him a pat fortune. Plans for the film were already underway when somebody had the idea that Irma and Jane would make perfect matches for Jerry and Dean—a pair of nitwits and a pair of sharpies. It was an ideal method of introducing Martin and Lewis to movie audiences: *My Friend Irma* was effectively presold, and surely the same people who went for Wilson's dumb blonde act would go for Jerry; if the picture flopped, on the other hand, it would do little damage to Martin and Lewis's future, since it wouldn't really have been their film. Wallis figured that Dean would be easy enough to fit into the role of Jane's boyfriend—they merely had to rewrite the script to make him an aspiring singer—but for Jerry's talents there was no such obvious use. The radio series did have another male lead—Irma's con-artist boyfriend, Al— and Jerry got it into his head that he could fill the role.

As Wallis recalled it, Lewis was "desperate to play Al" and "fancied himself a handsome leading man." Jerry had never actually acted before, and while Wallis might not have been certain of how to use him, he was damned sure he wasn't going to hand a meaty role over to him just like that. Wallis asked George Marshall, the director he'd chosen for the project, to test Lewis in the part. And when the test was screened, everyone agreed Jerry couldn't do the job.

There were more tests—nine, by one account—and acting lessons, all to no avail. Wallis remained sure that he wanted Martin and Lewis to debut in the film together, but he was equally sure that he'd have to cast a different Al. He asked Cy Howard to create a new character, a sidekick for Dean with plenty of physical business and verbal foolishness cut from the cloth of Lewis's stage persona. In a backhanded gesture, Howard named the character Seymour—his own given name, a name he loathed.

Lewis was livid when he saw the script. Dean, he felt, was being allowed to play a real character, but he was just being asked to act the monkey. He requested a meeting in Wallis's office to lobby for the role of his choice. Wallis arranged for both screenwriter Howard and director Marshall to be there to back him up. "Cy pointed out that he hadn't a hope in hell of having audiences accept him as Al," Wallis remembered. But "Jerry said it was Al or nothing, and that he would never play Seymour."

In retrospect, it's an interesting battle for Lewis to have fought. He was, after all, to play Seymour, or roles like it, throughout the flush of his career. Yet he began that era refusing to make a film in exactly the guise that had already brought him fame. He would never again shun the character so fully, though he

would spend years trying to find nuances in it—primarily a level of pathos he aspired to after studying Chaplin and Stan Laurel. Still, this moment of hesitation
reveals just how ambivalent Lewis was about his public face. As he gained
greater control over his career, he would increasingly refer to his character in the
third person—"The Kid," "The Boy," "The Nine-Year-Old," "The Idiot"—and
would reveal in public a sober, sententious demeanor that didn't so much erase
the infantile-imbecile image as weirdly underscore it. Whenever Lewis came out
of the closet as a Man of Passion, Intellect, and Thought, it became obvious to
people that his famous moron guise was calculated, and the sight of him out of
character was received, more and more over the years, as an affront. This might
explain why he was only sporadically popular on television, where he indulged a
greater variety of personae than on screen; indeed, it wasn't until he began doing
his muscular dystrophy telethons in 1965 that the public swallowed him in the
role of a grown-up. By then, of course, his film career was effectively over, and it
was too late for him to re-create himself for the screen.

Maybe Jerry was canny enough to know all of this in 1948. Or maybe Wallis
was right: He was just vain. The conference with Wallis, Marshall, and Howard
lasted into the night. Jerry stood firm: He would play Al or refuse to do the picture altogether. Finally, Wallis revealed his trump card. Don't play Seymour, he
told Jerry. Dean would make the picture as a single, and Wallis would continue
to look for vehicles for Martin and Lewis as a team. It was a low blow, hitting
Jerry in the softest spot he had—his feelings of inadequacy next to Dean—and
he caved. Sulking, Jerry swallowed the situation and resigned himself to life as
Seymour.

In 1994, when he produced an autobiographical television documentary
that touched on these events, Lewis tried to erase all memory of them: "I went
to Wallis and I said, 'Why do you take Dean and I out of the Copacabana, bring
us to California to put us in movies, and change what you saw that you like that
you're paying all this money for?' He said, 'Well, if you can come up with something better than that test, go ahead.' And we wrote what now is traditionally
known as the first Martin and Lewis stand-up comedy sketch in a film." The account completely elided Jerry's battle to play Al, his rejection of the role of Seymour, and Wallis's threat that he either play a character derived from his stage
persona or get bumped off the film. Either Jerry really didn't remember any of it,
or he chose in the 1990s—with Wallis, Howard, and Marshall dead and Dean regally indifferent—to become his own historian, turning the near derailing of his
young career into another example of his infallible creativity.

In the interim between casting and the actual shoot, Greshler had Dean and
Jerry booked on a Bob Hope television special and then a four-week run at the
Beachcomber Club in Miami. They would make a solid twelve thousand dollars
a week between them—enough to bring Dick Stabile and his band back east,

anointing them, in the process, as their official orchestra. They would open two nights before Christmas and ride in the New Year's Day 1949 parade as part of the Orange Bowl festivities. In late January, just before they went before the cameras, they would come home to Los Angeles for another engagement at Slapsie Maxie's.

Since they would be apart during the holidays, the two families celebrated together before Dean and Jerry headed east, having an early Christmas dinner at the Martins' new house with Guy and Angela Crocetti and all the kids. It was a picture-perfect moment—and it was likely the last meal they all ate together.

Whatever indulgences Miami promised for the traveling stag party that Martin and Lewis had become, there was no way that Dean could have been prepared for what happened there. On New Year's Eve, when he and Jerry were performing at the Beachcomber, he glanced over at a table where the Orange Bowl queen and her court were enjoying themselves. Dean locked eyes with a gorgeous blonde, one of the queen's ladies-in-waiting, a twenty-one-year-old Floridian named Jeanne Biegger. Dean was thirty-one, married, with four children. He fell in love.

When Dean had married Betty, he'd been a rough kid from the wrong side of the tracks. He was just starting an unlikely singing career and was as liable to fall back into bad company as he was to make something legitimate of himself. He had a big nose and a sackful of debts. Betty was bright, cute, cool. They were suited to each other.

But by 1948 Betty had become an angry, lonely alcoholic, dragged down by the kids and the difficulties of marriage to a philanderer. She and Dean had grown impossibly far apart. Where he once seemed the social climber for daring to ask her out, she now seemed a forlorn tether holding back an ever-rising balloon.

Jeanne Biegger, though, was another matter entirely. She was fresh faced and healthy and pert, a professional model and a relative innocent. She caught Dean's eye at just the right time. Naturally, she fell for him—"The most beautiful broads went crazy for Dean," Jerry remembered. But that he fell for her reveals a more emotional Dean than is commonly supposed, a man who wanted to share his good fortune but was unable—largely through his own faults, to be sure—to do so with the woman he'd married. He wanted a mate, even if nothing in his character suggested that he had any regard for such conventions. By the time he and Jerry returned to California, he was already planning his new life.

Jerry watched what was happening with extremely mixed emotions. He was happy his partner was in love—even jealous, perhaps. But he wasn't so eager to split up his own home. He was still only twenty-two, for starters, and he still wanted a large family. For her part, Patti was less stricken by circumstances than Betty, and she was more willing to endure adversity for the sake of domestic harmony. If Dean's marital strife was a warning to Jerry about the dangers of going too far in the direction he'd been heading, he could rationalize the situation to make it distinct from his own: "People fall out of love," he later said of the Martins' failed marriage. "I think Dean just fell out of love."

While Betty looked on, Dean brazenly planned to bring Jeanne west. By early February, while Dean and Jerry were in the midst of another engagement at Slapsie Maxie's, Jeanne, who still didn't know that Dean was married, arrived in Los Angeles and was stashed away in Dick Stabile's house. On February 9 Dean rented a small place in West Hollywood. Five days later, Betty filed a suit seeking three thousand dollars a month (or one-third of Dean's income, whichever was greater) in support. The next week, just as production was about to start on *My Friend Irma*, the story of Dean's high jinks with Jeanne broke in the gossip columns. It wasn't exactly the splash Hal Wallis was hoping for.

At the time that Martin and Lewis were stepping onto sound stages at Paramount to film their first scenes, they were unknown to the vast American public—a cult act, really. They had appeared on television a half-dozen or so times, their single of "The Money Song" and "That Certain Party" had fizzled on the sales charts (Capitol wouldn't cut another record with them as a team until 1954), they had yet to make a splash on radio or indeed anywhere but nightclubs. They had a long-term contract with Wallis, but so did lots of promising young performers.

In fact, being signed with Wallis wasn't a guarantee of anything but frequent work in low-budget films. Wallis had made a specialty of scouting fresh talent and securing it for a long run: He kept Kirk Douglas, Burt Lancaster, Charlton Heston, and the rest working in low-budget pictures until they made names for themselves, then loaned them out at handsome fees to other producers who made more prestigious (and expensive) films. The value of Wallis's contracts with his players thus increased without his having to raise their salaries or even, when they were working for him, the budgets of their films.

He had learned the technique from David O. Selznick, who'd been the model independent producer when Wallis was still on staff at Warner Brothers. But Selznick specialized in prestige films and could spend years working on a single project. Wallis averaged more than three films a year from 1945, when he joined Paramount, until 1960, when his contract with Jerry Lewis was finally satisfied. He specialized in melodrama, thrillers, action films, and, as years went on, lowbrow comedy. A few of his Paramount films were of genuinely high quality— if not great films, then certainly the sort of stuff the Motion Picture Academy beat its breast over: *The Rose Tattoo; Come Back, Little Sheba; The Rainmaker; Gunfight at the O.K. Corral*. But for the most part he made pap; as soon as he lost Martin and Lewis as a team, for example, he signed Elvis Presley for the infamous string of dreadful films that turned the singer's career into a sad joke.

And if he was a miserly boss—Shirley MacLaine would later refer to her tenure with Wallis as her "slave days"—he was also a stickler about details of his performers' lives, even in those parts of their careers over which he had no say. Wallis's files were filled with angry memos ripped off to Greshler or Martin and Lewis's TV and radio producers about routines they'd performed that too closely resembled material in their films for him, about someone's failure to announce an upcoming film as "a Hal Wallis production" (he went crazy whenever anyone referred to one of his pictures as "a Paramount film"), about the pair's use of material he felt wasn't up to standard, about their overexposing themselves in other media.

When Jerry began working for Wallis, he was overwhelmed with respect and admiration. He sent letters from the road just for the hell of it; Wallis kept dozens of notes in Jerry's hand. In November 1948, while Dean and Jerry were in Las Vegas, Jerry wrote a note to Wallis on Flamingo Hotel stationery just to say hello, signing it "Child Star." Jerry would personally thank Wallis for birthday gifts, for presents sent to Patti when babies were born, for Christmas presents, for congratulatory telegrams received when he and Dean began new pictures or TV seasons or nightclub runs. Wallis was, if nothing else, an old-school gentleman, and Jerry was flattered by his attentions.

But even while maintaining this veneer of civility, Jerry was to grow increasingly antagonistic toward Wallis. "I had great respect for him till I saw him cut comedy," he recalled. "Wallis didn't know how to make fucking comedy. He was a butcher. He cut anywhere. He was a complete butcher. If the film got released, I was in complete shock. Even in my beginning, when I didn't understand what film was.

"He was a great filmmaker when you come to *Casablanca, Fugitive from a Chain Gang, Emile Zola*. He made great movies. That kind of editing is not difficult to know. You just follow the fucking well-written script. . . . But he was a fucking tyrant. I used to say to Dean, 'The only problem with Hal Wallis is when he needs to confer with humans.' He was a heartless, cold cocksucker, and there was no such thing as morality. . . . I mean, if he could beat you for thirty dollars, he'd fuck your dog. I was very grateful to him, his putting me in the picture business. But that's where it stopped."

In one sense, Jerry was absolutely right to bristle under Wallis's thumb. Not only did Wallis lack any inherent feel for comedy, but he always rebuffed Jerry's advice about how to write or shoot or cut comic scenes, haughtily reminding Lewis which of them had more experience making movies: "I know you feel very keenly about your work and you have had a great deal of experience with this type of material you do," he wrote Jerry once, "but in transferring this to motion pictures you must blend the two mediums in order to get the most out of it for the screen." Much of the dullness in Martin and Lewis films was largely the effect of Wallis's touch; once he realized how profitable the team was, Wallis made sure Martin and Lewis's films stayed on a narrow track.

Ed Simmons ran into the problem a few years later when he and Norman Lear, at the time Dean and Jerry's head TV writers, were hired by Wallis to rewrite *Scared Stiff.* "We had always liked Dean," Simmons recalled, "'cause Dean was very funny, and we felt he wasn't given a chance to do things in pictures. . . . So we kept writing and putting in scenes for Dean, and Hal Wallis kept sending them back. And we were writing right behind the picture. So finally he called us up to the office and said, 'Why do you keep sending me this stuff?' And we said, 'Because Dean is funny. And he should be doing this stuff, this is a good scene for him.' And he said, 'Fellows, look. A Martin and Lewis picture costs a half-million, and it's guaranteed to make three million with a simple formula: Jerry's an idiot, Dean is a straight leading man who sings a couple of songs and gets the girl. That's it, don't fuck with it, go back to the typewriter.'"

During the filming of *My Friend Irma*, which began on February 22, 1949, Jerry alternately stewed in his frustration at Wallis and ran, frankly, amok. He posted a plaque outside his dressing room that read MONSTER'S LAIR and spent expensive hours in practical jokes and generally berserk behavior. He would pour water on people, props, and sets, cut colleagues' neckties or ignite their handkerchiefs, destroy journalists' notes and clothing, acting even off camera like the schlemiel from the Martin and Lewis stage act. While Dean was an amenable professional when it came to his film acting, he participated in the shenanigans, too. It made for nice publicity pieces—the zany eastern comics whose high jinks on the set mirrored their professional hilarity—but Wallis was all about business, and he was rarely amused.

"One day, they came into my office and asked if I would like a shoeshine," Wallis recalled. "I declined, but they pretended they hadn't heard and began rubbing large quantities of black shoe polish into my brown shoes." Another time, according to Wallis, "Jerry played a trick on me that Errol Flynn once played on Jack Warner. He fell into my office covered in bloody bandages, wheezing in pain. Horrified, I ran to call a doctor. When I returned, Jerry, neatly dressed in a suit and tie, was sitting in my chair smoking an outsized cigar, feet on my new blotting pad." Wallis didn't mention laughing at either incident.

But the rushes that came from the set assuaged the stodgy producer. Despite his grudging acceptance of the role of Seymour, Lewis was brilliant. The picture, which was meant as a showcase for the "Irma" radio cast, was absolutely usurped by Dean and Jerry. George Marshall, the quintessential hack director (with over four hundred films—eighty-eight of them features—to his name), had just the indifferent touch to let the team run off with the film. Marshall was known as a director of comedies: Under contract to Paramount and Fox before that, he'd worked with many top-notch comedians—Laurel and Hardy, Will Rogers, the Ritz Brothers, W. C. Fields, Bob Hope, and Bing Crosby. He may not have been a funny man himself, but he knew enough to stand back and let the comics be funny, and it was this reputation that got him hired for *Irma*.

As the film came together, it became clear that Wallis had what he wanted, even if he had almost nothing to do with getting it that way; "He had lightning in a bottle, and he knew it," Jerry reflected. One bit in particular delighted the producer endlessly, a routine in which Jerry's hand had turned into a claw at the end of his arm because he'd squeezed too many oranges. "I laughed aloud every time I watched this scene," Wallis remembered.

But he wasn't uniformly delighted with his new discoveries. On March 23, just a month into production on the film, he sent Martin and Lewis each an angry telegram, chastising them for a benefit appearance they'd made at the Coconut Grove nightclub earlier in the week "without first obtaining my consent."

Although Wallis always remained punctiliously vigilant about the way his players spent their time off the lot, Abbey Greshler persuaded him to allow Dean and Jerry to do a radio show for NBC. The contract, signed in December 1948, called for two thousand dollars per week during development and twenty-five hundred per week when the show was on the air. The network had put together a demo recording of the team at the time they'd signed them, and it aired to little notice before Christmas.

Indeed, listening to a surviving recording of that broadcast, it's fairly obvious that Dean and Jerry barely made an effort to prepare for it. They played characters called Dean and Jerry, hot young comedians who were just about to start a new NBC radio show. They had an agent named Abbey and rising reputations: "He's the talent. He's the one the critics rave about. He's the one the people love," says Dean when a fan denigrates Jerry. Lucille Ball was their guest, singing "The Money Song" with them, and Jerry ended the show by stepping out of character to thank the audience and make a plea for the March of Dimes—his first recorded charity pitch. The live studio audience loved it, and NBC decided to turn it into a series.

The debut of "The Martin and Lewis Show" was widely heralded, preceded in early April by an appearance of the team on Bob Hope's hugely popular radio show (Hope, in return, guested on Dean and Jerry's debut). "The Martin and Lewis Show" premiered at six-thirty the following Sunday. By seven o'clock Wallis was on the warpath.

"I was quite disturbed last night," he wrote Greshler the next morning, claiming that a routine from *My Friend Irma* had been used "almost word for word" on the program. He saw such matters no so much as plagiarism but as a threat to his investment: "If millions of people hear the radio show and then catch the motion picture a few months later and hear the same jokes, the picture is going to suffer."

The NBC show did, in fact, include a routine from *My Friend Irma* almost verbatim—and it stood out in sheer quality from the rest of the listless material.

As in the pilot program, Dean and Jerry were rising stars who shared an apartment—with one bedroom—and the services of a maid, played by comedienne Florence MacMichael. Over the ensuing weeks, NBC secured a lot of high-powered talent to guest on the show—William Bendix, Jimmy Durante, Dick Powell, Henry Fonda—but the ratings foundered and the network had trouble finding a sponsor.

Capitol Records could have told NBC why: The nation still hadn't *seen* Dean and Jerry, and without a visual dimension, their act was a bunch of old jokes and corny bits, however hysterically pitched. Reviewing the team's radio debut, "Rose.," in *Variety*, said that "potentially, the boys have got it, but bridging the gap from a nitery visual assist into a strictly audio medium still remains a big 'but.'" Two weeks later, *Newsweek* chronicled NBC's efforts in launching the show but concluded that "the freshness of the Martin-Lewis humor, so evident on the nightclub floor, was—on the air—a sometime thing." A month later, *Time* concurred: "Radio cannot show the half of what Martin & Lewis have; they must be seen, on television or in a nightclub."

If they were going to take off outside nightclubs, *My Friend Irma* would have to be the vehicle.

Betty Martin filed for divorce late in March 1949, Dean agreeing to a sixty-thousand-dollar settlement and three thousand dollars a month for her and the children. It would be several months before the break was final—Betty had to establish residency in Nevada first—but Dean was free.

On April 9 he and Jerry appeared on a benefit Milton Berle hosted on NBC-TV for the Damon Runyon Memorial Fund, a charity founded by Walter Winchell two years earlier in honor of the legendary writer, who died of throat cancer in December 1946. A few days after Runyon's death, Winchell had ended his radio show by asking America to chip in whatever it could to fight the disease. He wound up raising thousands—so much, in fact, that he didn't know what to do with it. He considered donating it all to the American Cancer Society until he discovered that the organization didn't contribute 100 percent of its proceeds to research. He established the Damon Runyon Memorial Fund as a completely research-oriented body: Literally nothing was spent on expenses, which were paid for by the Walter Winchell Foundation, an independently operated and financed entity.

To help raise money for his charity, Winchell employed all his wiles as a power broker in the world of show business. And borrowing a page from legendary fund-raiser Basil O'Connor's successful March of Dimes campaign, he organized star-studded marathon shows to wheedle money out of typical Americans. O'Connor had used radio and the stage to help raise money for polio, but Winchell had his eyes on the new medium: He would raise money on television.

In the spring of 1949 he arranged with NBC to run a TV fund-raiser for the

Runyon Fund. He cajoled Milton Berle, the new medium's biggest star, to host the show, and filled it with all the talent he could muster, including Martin and Lewis. To publicize the program, NBC had coined the term *telethon*. The sixteen-hour show was broadcast on fifteen stations and wound up raising $1.1 million (a Berle radio-thon on a single station the previous year had managed to garner only a hundred thousand dollars). Berle would do annual telethons for the next several years, to nearly unanimous acclaim from colleagues and critics alike.

Jerry harbored strongly mixed feelings toward Berle, whose career had become a yardstick against which other comics measured their success. In addition to his rising fame as "Mr. Television," Berle was widely acknowledged to be the reigning verbal comic—a status Jerry may have envied, given his dependence on physical shtick. Jerry had once idolized Berle, according to Irving Kaye, who recalled Jerry sitting in a Boston hotel room and announcing, "I'll be as big as he is." But he'd also been humiliated by Berle one night when he was still emceeing. Berle had walked into the club and Jerry launched a few jibes at him from the stage. "Milton tore him to pieces," Kaye remembered. Jerry did too. So when the whole world praised Berle for his good efforts on behalf of the Runyon Fund, Jerry couldn't help noticing with a bit of jealousy.

My Friend Irma finished shooting on April 12, and Dean and Jerry headed back east to open at the Copa a week later. Wallis finished cutting the film that summer, and on August 8 he showed it to the trade press at the Ritz Theater in Los Angeles. As he'd anticipated, the results were extremely positive. Crediting the "comedy know-how" of George Marshall, "Brog." of *Variety* described Martin and Lewis as "a team that has decided film possibilities if backed with the right material and used properly." Jerry, the review said, "will rate loud guffaws for his mugging." Dean, however, it noted, "needs to tone down nitery mannerisms for films." *The Hollywood Reporter* paid a bit less attention to Dean and Jerry in its review, asserting that their "tomfoolery . . . is just as effective on the screen as on the night club platform." Jerry was praised as "a comic whose sense of the ridiculous is simply sublime," while Dean, again somewhat backhandedly, "sings a lot and clicks with every number." The review cited Marshall's skill—he "pulls laugh after laugh right out of the air and socks them across with his customary ease"— and made the shrewd observation that "Hal Wallis knows gold dust when he sees it."

The fact is, *My Friend Irma* was an extremely deft debut for the team, giving them just the right amount of exposure and presenting them in patterns they would follow for the rest of their screen careers, both together and apart. It wears well even four decades later, especially when compared with comedies of the era by Bob Hope, Danny Kaye, Red Skelton, and Abbott and Costello.

Marshall did indeed keep a brisk pace, helped along by the competence of his cast and by the deft scripting of Howard and Levy. Although the film is named after Marie Wilson's character, it's Jane Stacy, Irma's practical roommate (Diana Lynn), who carries the bulk of the plot. Soon after she is hired as secretary to a millionaire stockbroker (Don DeFore), she meets Steve Laird (Dean), a clerk at an orange juice stand who possesses a golden voice. Steve has been recruited by Al (John Lund), who hopes to be rescued from unemployment by working as his manager. As Steve and the rich guy compete for Jane's affections, Jane swivels between them. Meanwhile, Seymour (Jerry), Steve's partner and friend, tries to get Al to promote *his* career. There are some farcical crossings of plot wires, and it all resolves rather patly and quickly.

The point, though, isn't so much the story as the texture of the characters. Wilson is agreeably insipid, pulling off malaprops with deadpan eagerness. As Al, Lund is all bluff, swagger, and corn. His dialogue is like something out of Damon Runyon, all his sentences clipped to achieve a staccato, side-of-the-mouth rhythm. The subsequent aura of low-rent larceny and cheap romance is certainly more convincing than anything Jerry could have projected.

Not that Jerry need take a back seat to anyone. Although most of the screen time belongs to Wilson, Lynn, and Lund, Jerry overwhelms the picture with three or four set pieces. The orange juice scene that so delighted Wallis, a scene as a manic parking valet, a hilarious interlude in which Lund convinces Seymour he's got a future as a dramatic actor, and a brief re-creation of the Martin and Lewis stage act is all Jerry needs to set the picture into orbit. Wearing a surprisingly long haircut and dressed in a boyish, belted sports coat with a little bib of a tie, he seems more Jewish than in later films, barely disguising the Yiddish roots of his verbal humor. He constantly ends sentences on a lilting up note, turning simple words like "yet" and "already" into surreal questions. He's so nimble and assured that you almost forget he's only twenty-two years old, but his wiry physique, softly cleft chin, sunken cheeks, and pronounced mouth have the thinness of youth.

Dean, too, looks young, even at thirty-one. His face is smooth and fleshy, and his hair is cut close above the ears. As a performer, he's cool and assured in his singing scenes, and he deflects Jerry smoothly in their scenes together, even getting a few solid laughs of his own. He's asked to do a lot of straight acting—as lover, rival, and careerist—and he acquits himself competently: a natural on screen.

The highlight comes when Dean and Jerry perform together at a café. The scene is so genuinely funny that Marshall had trouble getting it shot: You can actually hear the giggles of cast and crew members in the background—an unintentional laugh track—and various extras visibly struggle to keep their laughter under control. Dean and Jerry do some verbal sparring (including the scene Wallis recognized in their radio program), and then perform "Donkey Serenade," a south-of-the-border novelty number that was a staple of their nightclub dates.

It's a showstopper: Jerry imitates castanets by clucking his tongue in his mouth, Dean sings a syllable-choked lyric, Jerry starts mugging and contorting without missing a beat, and they end by yodeling together and stopping on a dime. It's the oldest record of their stage act anywhere, and it's thrilling. Imagine it wilder, more ribald, and simply longer, and you get a sense of just how intoxicating they must have been.

Patti Lewis found the dissolution of the Martin marriage unnerving. She and Betty were never really close—"She was an interesting woman and a casual friend," Patti recalled a bit coolly years later—but the example that Dean was setting for his adoring young partner worried her.

When she caught Dean with June Allyson, Patti was explicit about her discomfort with his behavior, which affronted her not only as a wife but as a Catholic. "Forget it," Jerry told her. "It's nothing. Anyway, Dean's personal life is his own affair. It has nothing to do with you and me."

Patti informed Jerry that she would cease contact with Dean if he carried through with his divorce, and Jerry, in turn, threatened *her*: "If you turn your back on him, you're gonna hurt me, because Dean's my friend. Do you understand what that means?" They'd separated only a year earlier. Patti knew vividly what he meant. Mechanically, she caved in: "I'll do my best, if that's what you want."

Patti had nothing personal against Dean, her *paisano*, Jerry's "other wife." But, she said, "because of my background and because I always felt like an underdog, I really hurt for Betty."

When Dean married Jeanne on September 1, 1949, at the Beverly Hills mansion of Herman Hover, proprietor of the Sunset Strip nightclub Ciro's, Jerry stood as his best man, even though he'd advised against the marriage. "What the fuck are you rushing for?" he'd asked. Patti was there as well, out of spousal obligation, "though somewhat reluctantly," as Jerry recalled, "still smarting from the hurt she felt for Betty."

Jerry found himself drawing away from his increasingly gloomy spouse. It wasn't so much about Dean and Jeanne. There was another unresolved problem eating away at the Lewis marriage, something more unsettling than Dean's divorce, or the coolness of Danny and Rae toward their daughter-in-law, or Jerry's philandering: Patti and Jerry wanted a big family, but Gary had turned four, and no new children were forthcoming.

"God, did we want kids," Jerry said. "But after our firstborn, Patti was told by a number of doctors that she couldn't have any more. It was horrible. Neither of us accepted it."

They were so desperate that Patti submitted to a series of exploratory operations in hopes of detecting and correcting the problem. Patti was obviously a willing subject, hoping, no doubt, that she could strengthen and secure her marriage by increasing the size of the family. "In my heart," she said years later, "I will always believe that Jerry came back to me because I provided some stability in the home." Children would fill her days—Jerry frowned on her doing anything outside the house, even playing golf, and she herself had expressly chosen the role of homemaker—and they would also, she hoped, reawaken Jerry's increasingly absent conscience and keep him home more, too. By late 1949, however, none of the operations had been successful, and the couple began looking into adoption.

Whether Patti was able to fill the nursery on Tower Drive or not, Jerry had taken up other hobbies besides women to keep his energy channeled. His exposure to the intricacies of the Paramount lot during the previous year had ignited a yen to learn all about moviemaking. He had, after all, spent his year at vocational school studying electrical maintenance and repair. He was drawn to the cameras, the lights, the sound equipment, the makeup and miniature departments at Paramount, just as he had been intrigued by the backstage apparatus of the National Theater in Detroit when he was a boy.

Along with his new interest in filmmaking, Jerry developed a fetish for cameras and tape recorders. He spent hours combing camera shops, and filled a room of his house with photographic and sound equipment. In late 1949 he opened a camera store of his own on Vine Street in Hollywood, right next door to the fabled Brown Derby restaurant. The Jerry Lewis Camera Exchange was housed in a tiny space, maybe five hundred square feet; its marquee sported a huge photo of Jerry in one of his *My Friend Irma* costumes. The counters, shelves, and other furnishings had been built by Joe Stabile, bandleader Dick's younger brother, who had some experience in carpentry. To run the store, Jerry sent to New Jersey for his cousin Marshall Katz, who'd studied photography on the GI Bill.

Opening night was orchestrated by Jack Keller as a Hollywood extravaganza, with klieg lights and celebrity guests and radio mikes. George Jessel pronounced the store officially open, cracking a prop champagne bottle over Jerry's head. And Dean showed up in a choreographed surprise, wearing a tuxedo and a chef's toque and pushing a hot dog cart up the street with a sign that read "Film Developed Free."

"You gonna buck my business like this?" Jerry asked.

"You wouldn't go halfies with me," Dean shot back.

Cameraman Ralph Staub recorded the event for his "Screen Snapshots" newsreel series, which were distributed by Columbia Pictures. Dean and Jerry were becoming news.

But the shop didn't fare all that well. "It was too small," Katz recalled. "There was barely enough room for all the equipment and for me." After a year or so, it closed, a money-losing fancy that its owner had grown bored with. (Katz, who'd been brought out to California expressly to run the place, was given a job in Paramount's international distribution office.)

Collecting had become more and more Jerry's style. He'd begun amassing guns, for instance, and enjoyed firing them in the wooded property of the Tower Road house along with his neighbor, Danny Kaye. He'd even taken to sleeping with a gun beneath his pillow, though this was less a sign of materialism than of his innate insecurity. He'd become a notorious clotheshorse, inaugurating a life-long indulgence in expensive suits, golf clothes, and tuxedos, an absurd habit of throwing socks away after wearing them only once, a love of jewelry.

And, like many rags-to-riches comics before him, he was becoming famous for his gifts: inscribed gold watches, gold I.D. bracelets, gold lighters and ciga-rette cases, clothing, cash, you name it. Old friends and family members got jobs; new friends hung around the house and got fed. The kid who'd never had two nickels to rub together was supporting a burgeoning retinue.

Watches, especially, were his hallmark: "Watches by the pound," Jack Keller recalled. "If you said good morning to him, he'd buy you a watch. One of the funniest lines Dean ever got off was one day when he and I were walking up Vine Street and along came a guy with a great big turnip watch. Dean said, 'Must be a friend of Jerry's.'"

Of course, no one, not even Patti and Gary, received more of Jerry's munifi-cent bounty than his parents. For her birthday in 1949 Rae Lewis got a diamond ring and (naturally) a watch. The next February, on their twenty-fifth anniver-sary, Danny and Rae received a check for twenty-five thousand dollars from their son—five good years' pay for a Catskills trouper.

They loved the gifts—they came to expect them—but they never bright-ened their son's day without also adding a level of guilt as well. "I brought you into the world," Jerry recalled Rae reminding him. "I took from my mouth to give you. I went without clothes. So why don't you call?" It sounds like a comedy routine about a nagging Jewish mother, but no one was laughing. No doubt Rae had sacrificed by working through the Depression, but she'd also denied herself to her boy for years. The guilt she ladled on him now that he had succeeded was like calling in a marker she'd laid out nothing to earn. And Danny was increas-ingly open with his resentment, criticizing Jerry's performances and telling peo-ple he'd make a better partner for his son than Dean.

Patti had certainly suffered worse treatment at the hands of her parents, but she felt no urge to mend the breaches between them and herself. Jerry, on the other hand, still craved parental affection, even as a married man with a child of his own and a thriving career. Patti knew how much it hurt her husband to en-dure his parents' slights, how vulnerable he was to any note of rejection. "I will always admire Jerry for his loyalty to his parents," she reflected, "even in the rough times and in spite of their controlling natures." His home life increasingly a source of unhappiness and discomfort, Jerry began to devote himself to his career. Fortunately for him, that had become pure clover.

Dean and Jerry had visited Las Vegas on a gambling trip before their families had moved out west. Now, in September 1949, Greshler had booked them there at the Flamingo Hotel at $15,000 for a week. Jeanne Martin came along—the gig was practically her honeymoon—but Patti stayed in Los Angeles. Jerry loved Vegas, "the most joyful city in the world," as he called it. And left to his own devices there, he went ballistic, spending all of his offstage time in the casinos. Within seven days of arriving there to earn $7,500 a week, he was in debt for well over $100,000 (sometimes he said $137,000, sometimes $187,000; at any rate, it was a lot). "I love to gamble," Lewis recalled, "and at that time, at the ripe old age of twenty-three, I knew about as much about gambling as I do about root canal." He was called into the hotel's office by one of the crew that inherited the Flamingo after the murder of its founder, Bugsy Siegel—either Gus Greenbaum or Moe Sedway; in different versions of the story he has remembered each.

"What right do you have to run up a marker of $187,000?" Jerry remembered being asked.

"What right do *you* have in letting a twenty-three-year-old schmuck who's only getting $700 [sic] a week from you run up a tab of $187,000?" he remembered responding. "Doesn't that make you a fucking idiot?"

"You're a brisky kid," came the reply. "How do you wanna pay it?"

By one of Jerry's versions of the story, a phone call to the Flamingo's New York owners followed; by another, he simply stated his preferred course of action. In either case, the result was the same: He was to pay it as he got it, as he could pay it, but he was to pay it all. And he was no longer permitted to try his luck in the casino. (His luck outside the casino was a sight better than within: It took him less than two years, by one of his accounts—just under three by another—to pay the debt off.)

After Vegas, Jerry returned home and grew restless. On the success of the previews of *My Friend Irma*, Wallis had begun developing a sequel that would feature Martin and Lewis more prominently, now that it was clear that their act worked on screen as well as on stage. Plans had been made for a New York premiere of *Irma* at the Paramount Theater—the very palace from which Jerry had been bounced as an usher less than a decade earlier; Dean and Jerry would play six brief shows a day in support of the film along with Dick Stabile's band, earning nine thousand dollars a week while drumming up business for their own film. But Jerry was antsy, and he headed east alone in advance of the September 28 opening.

■　■　■

The trade screening of *My Friend Irma* in Los Angeles had told the film industry that Martin and Lewis had arrived. The film's New York debut, topped with the team's personal appearance at the Paramount, told the world. Audiences mobbed to see it; attendance at the Paramount was so high that Greshler managed to wheedle bonuses out of parsimonious theater manager Bob Weitman. Critics, while not quite mad for the picture, generally praised it, slight comedy that it was. But for Martin and Lewis—especially Jerry—there was nothing but wide-eyed enthusiasm. "Frankenstein-faced Lewis all but steals win, place and show money in this comedy sweepstakes," wrote the *Los Angeles Examiner.* "There just hasn't been anything like him ever on land, sea or celluloid."

Bosley Crowther, fusty voice of *The New York Times*, proclaimed that "the swift eccentricity of his movements, the harrowing features of his face and the squeak of his vocal protestations . . . have flair. His idiocy constitutes the burlesque of an idiot, which is something else again. He's the funniest thing in it. Indeed, he's the only thing in it that we can expressly propose for seeing the picture."

As welcome as these notices were, though, each was accompanied by a swipe at Dean, who, according to the *Examiner*, would "undoubtedly be more at home on the screen with added experience," though "he shouldn't oughta listen to any more Bing Crosby records." Crowther, crueler still, called Dean Jerry's "collar ad partner."

When the *Los Angeles Daily News* had run promotional photos for the film—six in all—the previous month, only one image of either Dean or Jerry was shown, such was the status of the "My Friend Irma" radio show and the anonymity of Martin and Lewis. The caption to that sole photo had misidentified Jerry as Dean. No one would ever make that mistake again. But the reason wasn't only that they'd become famous. It was also, in part, that the public had taken a shine to Jerry.

It was a strange trick of fate. Dean had rescued Jerry from life as a pantomimist and emcee, had given him class and a voice and an identity. Now, in the eye of the public, Dean was just a sideshow to his little partner. For the first time, he'd been pegged as the straight man, and he began to have heaped about his feet the indignities to which straight men have always been subject. Jerry, more than anyone, understood Dean's comic gift, his impeccable timing and rhythm, the way the play of their personalities created something bigger than either of them. But the public wasn't as analytical about comedy as he was, and it gravitated toward the monkey at the organ grinder's expense. *My Friend Irma* was a big hit—Wallis would recall that it earned $5 million, probably an exaggeration, but generally indicative of the film's success—and Jerry was cited by the press and the public alike as the reason. It was the first inkling of the way the act was to be viewed as their fame spread, but in their rise from obscurity, not even Dean himself seemed to mind the slight.

■ ■ ■

Now that they would never again be unknown, Dean and Jerry found themselves playing to audience expectations. They still, of course, had plenty to show new audiences from their impressive bags of stage tricks, but they also had to do what was expected of them—namely, go wild. At times they overdid it, or, rather, they seemed like they were overdoing it to critics who didn't realize that the very essence of the act was the constant defying of limits. Dean and Jerry supported Irma at the Paramount, for instance, Variety chided them for "double entendres" and "nance stuff," referring to the crude homosexual innuendoes and effeminate minces that Jerry had lifted—as had many comics—from Harry Ritz.

Still, no matter how unpredictable they got, no matter how outré, they were hot, and while movies were a natural for them, television, the scorching-hot new medium, was even better suited to their act. Unencumbered by silly plots and theatrical costars, they could just do a few minutes—cleaned up, naturally—of their stage act, the very thing that had made them such a sensation.

Greshler had been flirting with TV offers for some time, and he was close to hooking NBC to a variety show deal. For the time being, Dean and Jerry kept raising their profile on TV with guest spots, and while they were still in New York promoting Irma they appeared on "Texaco Star Theater," the most popular show yet on the fledgling medium. The host was Milton Berle—despite feeling burned by him, Jerry still respected his place in the business—and he was as exacting a boss as they'd ever had. Berle conducted rehearsals for his show with a referee's whistle hanging from his neck, assigning every act a precise time allotment and demanding strict obedience.

Martin and Lewis's reputation for cutting up, stretching their routine, and thumbing their noses at authority had preceded them, and although there'd been no trouble when they'd performed on "Texaco Star Theater" a year earlier (with then-host Morey Amsterdam), Berle was anxious that they be on best behavior when they appeared live on his show.

"We have a timed show here, boys," he admonished them. "You must stick to eight minutes. Not ten. Not nine. I'm talking about eight minutes on the nose. You got it?"

"Sure, Milton," Jerry said.

"Good. No ad-libbing."

They nodded their comprehension.

"No extra shtick."

"We got it, Milton," Dean reassured him. "Eight minutes."

No sooner agreed than forgotten. Once on the air, they went bonkers. If Berle did a joke, Dean or Jerry ad-libbed a topper; if Berle mugged or did a double-take, Dean or Jerry undercut it with an even more exaggerated physical bit. Berle tried to introduce another act; Dean cut him off with "I'm not finished talking!" Berle tried to cut to a live commercial; Jerry leapt up in front of the camera, stuck his face in the lens, and shouted, "Milton Berle: big deal!" At one point, when the script called for Martin and Lewis to strip Berle of his pants, they nearly yanked his undershorts as well.

The zanies had taken over the most professional of shows; Berle's trashing of Jerry before a tiny nightclub audience had been revenged in front of the entire nation. Jerry was thrilled, letting everyone know just what he thought of the humiliated Berle—"I like Milton, but I don't like the way he treats other performers"—and bragging to the Associated Press, in an astonishingly adult voice, that he'd let King of Television off easy: "I've taken him on three times and cut him to ribbons. But I would never do that before a TV audience. I wouldn't let them see me get nasty."

Dean and Jerry were even becoming moguls. In December, while playing the Chez Paree in Chicago, they bought the screen rights to a military farce by James Allardice that was in the midst of a brief stage run there. *At War with the Army* would be the first film made under their own York Productions banner, the first of the outside projects Greshler had insisted on as part of their Paramount contract. To Dean and Jerry, it promised yet another nice payday—even nicer, they figured, since they would be their own bosses. To Greshler, though, *At War with the Army* was the advent of a lifelong dream. He wouldn't be a mere agent but a producer. The pasty boy who'd slept on a drafty board was becoming a player.

Greshler had sought funding for Martin and Lewis's production venture from a number of sources. He'd had a meeting with Howard Hughes, a bizarre encounter in which he was forbidden to shake the other principal's hand and was left alone for long stretches of time while Hughes made phone calls to verify his accounts of Dean and Jerry's financial dealings. But the money for York finally came from another playboy millionaire, Texas oilman and sometime mob associate Ray Ryan. Ryan had been at the Flamingo that fall when Dean and Jerry were performing, and he had been sufficiently taken with them that he was willing to back Greshler's business plan.

With Ryan's money behind it, York was formed with Dean, Jerry, and Greshler each owning a third of the stock and Greshler installed as president and executive producer. Operating on a classic independent production model not unlike that of Wallis-Hazen, York would buy properties, hire talent and crews, lease equipment and facilities, and auction off distribution rights to the finished product to a major studio. Greshler would draw a producer's fee in addition to his 10 percent as agent to the stars (an arrangement that would eventually be declared illegal as an instance of someone selling something to himself and charging both sides a fee for the service). Dean and Jerry, meanwhile, delighted to be self-employed, were persuaded to take their cut out of the back end; they were guaranteed 97 percent of the film's gross. Nowadays, everyone who reads the entertainment pages of a newspaper knows that even the most profitable films can be disguised as money losers by wily accountants; but back then . . .

"Greshler had this gift," Jerry remembered, "a captivating and thrilling way of presenting things." He was their agent; they had no reason to suspect him. But he'd "neglected to tell us the difference between net and gross profits, among other things." By the time the film was completed, Dean and Jerry would hold a very different opinion of the man who'd orchestrated their rise.

Another man had helped create the act: George Evans, tireless champion of hot (and often incorrigible) talent. On January 26, 1950, after an argument with a journalist about Frank Sinatra's dalliance with Ava Gardner, Evans, forty-eight, dropped dead of a heart attack. His lieutenants, Bud Granoff and Jack Keller, divvied up the talent he'd been promoting. Keller, the West Coast man, got Dean and Jerry, who were increasingly considered a Hollywood property.

That same month, Patti and Jerry Lewis took into their home a baby boy, Ronald Stephen, whom they hoped to adopt. After six months, if all went well, they could petition the court for full adoptive custody. Their family growing, through whatever means they had at their disposal, they began to think about buying a house of their own.

A few days after Evans's funeral, which they weren't able to attend, Dean and Jerry began the filming of *My Friend Irma Goes West* at Paramount. All of the key principals from the previous film—Marie Wilson, Diana Lynn, John Lund—were on hand, and a new Hal Wallis discovery, a French ingenue named Corinne Calvet (after whom the producer crudely lusted), had been added. To direct the new Cy Howard/Parke Levy script, Wallis hired Hal Walker, a quickie artist who made the prolific George Marshall seem a fastidious aesthete.

The night before the film began shooting, NBC suspended "The Martin and Lewis Show" on the radio: Even though they were quickly becoming familiar to a national audience, their appeal still didn't carry over into a nonvisual medium. The canceled show was the only blemish on their résumés, however, and, with Wallis building his new picture around them and not the eponymous Irma, they didn't miss the radio business very much.

And indeed, at Wallis's behest, *My Friend Irma Goes West* was a Martin and Lewis picture. Where the team was an added comic attraction in the first film, in the second they were the impetus of the plot. The title refers to a train ride the five principals take to Hollywood to help Steve (Dean) establish himself in a career there. Where the previous film's romantic plot concerned the competition for Diana Lynn's Jane, the new film's romantic roundelays spun around Dean, who, while still engaged to Jane, was pursued by French actress Yvonne Yvonne (Calvet). Where Jerry had been given a few brief comedy sketches in his debut, the second film gave him plenty of extended opportunities to run amok, several brief asides, and a partner who could match him in his puerile antics: Pierre, Yvonne's chimpanzee companion.

Having a chimp as an escort (and, by the script's fatuous innuendoes, lover) was a horrible embarrassment to Calvet, who considered herself a serious actress and had accepted the role under duress. Wallis, pawing her every time he got her alone, had promised Calvet that he'd promote the career of her husband, actor John Bromfield, if she played along with him in her roles and in the boudoir. While she fended off the latter proposition, the former was out of her control: Wallis held her contract and a loan on her house. She swallowed her pride, prepared for the role, and met Dean, Jerry, and Pierre.

"I found Dean friendly, a man of the world, self-assured and quiet," Calvet recalled in her autobiography. "Lewis was exactly the opposite, nervous and trying to override his shyness by flattering and entertaining everyone around him. He seemed to be afraid of silence, to feel compelled to fill the empty spaces. I was sensitive to his great anxiety, his wanting to be liked by everyone."

During the shoot, Pierre began to harass Calvet even more crudely than Wallis had, smacking his lips at her, fondling himself in her presence, practically masturbating whenever she was nearby. She mentioned the matter confidentially to the chimp's trainer, who asked her if she was having her period. She was; the chimp, she was told, was merely responding to it as a signal of fertility. He'd calm down when her cycle was over.

Jerry's behavior was, however, less easily handled. Aping Pierre, he hounded his costar. "Lewis couldn't resist the urge to imitate the chimp and turned into a human monkey, harassing me without restraint," Calvet wrote. "Controlling my mounting hysteria, I could do nothing but pretend to be a good sport about it." The film's finale, in which Yvonne Yvonne fell for Seymour and ended up in a romantic clinch with him, loomed before her like a nightmare.

Calvet wasn't the only person Jerry managed to offend during the production. Early into the shoot, he returned home from a day's work and wrote a sober apology to Hal Wallis for "the very silly way I acted yesterday," promising to "respect your decisions" in the future. Here Jerry was, not yet twenty-four years old, a week into his second film, having to apologize for questioning the judgment of a man who'd been in the movie business before he was born. Whatever Jerry had thrown his fit about, Wallis accepted his apology in a letter written two days later, acknowledging Jerry's enthusiasm and concluding, "I am sure that a rational discussion of any points of difference in the future can eliminate any need for off-stage 'scenes.'"

The film wrapped in mid-March. A month later, Martin and Lewis opened at Ciro's, Herman Hover's ritzy Sunset Strip club; Wallis sent flowers and telegrams to wish them luck. Two weeks later, they were off to New York. There was another Berle show to appear on—bruised ego or no, Uncle Miltie knew a ratings grabber when he saw one—and there was a legal proceeding to attend: a hearing of the American Guild of Variety Artists in the matter of Martin and Lewis's failure to play at the Latin Casino in Philadelphia the previous autumn.

The mix-up was all Greshler's fault. With his love of bidding wars, he'd verbally committed to both the Chez Paree in Chicago and the Latin Casino for the same couple of weeks, and then opted for the more lucrative (and mob-tied) Chicago date. The Latin Casino's owner, Harry Steinman, filed a protest with the AGVA asking for damages from Martin and Lewis; they, in turn, filed a grievance against Greshler for obliging them to an engagement without their consent. The AGVA committee found for Dean and Jerry and released them from any obligation to pay Steinman, noting, in their decision, that Greshler had "embarrassed and inconvenienced the team and jeopardized their careers."

In fact, Greshler really was jeopardizing their livelihoods. Although they were commanding the highest prices possible for their live work, had a lucrative film contract, and got top fees for their television appearances, Dean and Jerry were living from hand to mouth—in the poshest of circumstances, true, but eking by nevertheless. With so much of his money obligated to Betty and the kids, and with specters from his past threatening lawsuits over all those percentages of himself he'd signed away, Dean was so cash poor that his new car was repossessed. Jerry, though not as beleaguered as Dean, had tax problems. "We thought Greshler was paying our taxes," he confided to a friend. "Greshler had led us to believe he was. So we went on spending money like we were making a fortune."

It looked swell, but it was a dicey existence. "There I was," Jerry recalled, "driving around in a Cadillac, living in a movie star's home, and sometimes I didn't have enough money to pay the grocery bills."

Only clever little Abner Greshler was making a killing off the act—though he never comported himself in such a way so you'd guess. And Martin and Lewis were so hot that whenever they squeaked to him about money he could sign them to something new and silence them with contracts swimming in zeroes.

The latest sop he threw them was a television deal with NBC. The contract, which Greshler had signed with NBC programming executive Norman Blackburn, had originally called for Dean and Jerry to host a series of ten shows for a total of ninety-five thousand dollars. The shows would be part of an omnibus of variety programs sponsored by Colgate-Palmolive-Peet and hosted on rotating weeks by Abbott and Costello, Eddie Cantor, Donald O'Connor, and Martin and Lewis. After the AGVA flare-up, feeling in hot water with his guys, Greshler had renegotiated to $25,000 per appearance and extended it to a five-year deal, neglecting to tell his clients that, in addition to his straight agent's commission, he had dipped his beak for a healthy side fee. Greshler stood to collect $350 from NBC every week the show aired—no matter who the host was. They called him a "special consultant," even though he was merely being rewarded for delivering

Dean and Jerry. In the show-business milieu of 1950, after all, you couldn't get much more special than that.

Proof came in the form of trade press reviews of *My Friend Irma Goes West*, which once again hailed the comedy duo while describing the film as barely professional. After a June 26 preview in Las Vegas, *Variety* called it "a slapstick melange of gags and situations plentifully supplied with raucous laughs," and announced that Jerry "grooves the guffaws in sock fashion." When the picture finally opened in August, newspaper and magazine reviewers followed suit, praising Jerry and somehow making space to recall that Dean was also present. *Newsweek* liked Jerry, but dismissed the picture as "malarky." *The New York Times* chimed in, calling the film "a nondescript affair," and reported the reaction the film elicited from the crowd at the Paramount: "During the first ten minutes of this helter-skelter comedy we missed most of Jerry Lewis's witty remarks, for every time he opened his mouth the audience went into hysterics. There were a lot of young, high squeaking voices bouncing off the rafters, but while the small fry may have been most responsive they did not account for all the merry sounds."

As backhanded as they may have sounded, the critics were actually being kind. If over the years Jerry would come to deplore Wallis's fostership of his movie career, *My Friend Irma Goes West* alone offered plenty of fodder for his gripes. It's archetypical sequel dreck, no more deft or professional than a Blondie movie or a made-for-TV comedy feature. The first half-hour of the film, for instance, alternates between two almost static set-ups: Dean and Jerry performing on television and Diana Lynn and Marie Wilson watching them in their boardinghouse apartment. The continuity is inept and abrupt, the dubbing of action sequences frankly amateurish. What was vivid and light in the previous film is forced and ponderous in the sequel: Lynn isn't wry or pert but shrill and spiky, Lund not knavish and appealing but crude. Marie Wilson gets a few genuine moments out of the mess, though even the best of those are the reactions of others to her doltishness.

Jerry would forever remain certain that Wallis doted on Martin and Lewis films at the expense of more prestigious projects. "He put all that stuff on the back burner when it came to us. We made him a fucking bloody fortune. Ooooh, boy oh boy." But it's hard to imagine that Wallis was paying much attention while this stinker was being birthed (indeed, he was busy planning a third film in the series, the never-to-be-realized *My Friend Irma Goes Abroad*, which he commissioned from Howard and Levy two days after the trade press screening of *Irma Goes West*).

If the film's content is worth remarking at all, it's because it contains another batch of early footage of Dean and Jerry, still not top-billed but obviously the main attraction. Dean is shunted off to the side—the trailer for the film advertised Jerry as "the hot new Western star"—but he's allowed a song that would evolve into one of his first big hits, "I'll Always Love You," a delicate ballad with a Latin underbeat.

Jerry, on the other hand, is everywhere. He romps with a monkey, he does comic double-talk (in an adult's voice), he sulks in a long series of comic asides, he repeats his famous orange-squeezing routine from the first film (with a very funny fake crying bit thrown in), he sings three times, he takes pratfalls, he does fake American Indian dialect, he wrestles with gangsters. Wallis later accused Jerry of "trying to push Dino into the background," but it's obvious that in these early days Jerry was encouraged—by his writers, his director, and his producer— to take center stage.

Seymour's eagerness to be in show business had been a skeleton of a gag in the first *Irma*, but in the sequel it's insisted on again and again, almost as though Howard and Levy planted Lewis's real-life store of bald ambition into the script as an act of sabotage. Seymour is like Lucy Ricardo to Steve's Ricky, constantly scheming up ways of breaking into the act, and forever fumbling his chance. Twice Seymour interrupts Steve's performances, stopping the film, in effect, to allow for bits lifted from the Martin and Lewis stage show: Jerry conducting the band, calling a square dance, and interpolating nonsense verses into songs while Dean sings blithely along as if protected by a force field of cool.

The film ends in an apotheosis of Seymour's deluded self-confidence. Yvonne Yvonne inexplicably persuades her producer to hire Seymour, not Steve, as her leading man in her next film (a funhouse-mirror image of Calvet's actual career situation). Awakened from a nap to this news, Seymour turns into a parody of an arriviste movie star. It's like watching Jerry's ego escape his body and walk around the set unchecked.

"I always knew I was a great actor," he declares. Segueing into a mock upper-crust British tone, he addresses Steve: "Here, my boy. I shan't forget you. Here. You shall be my stand-in, press my clothes, and do various small things around the studio."

The next line is delivered with no accent at all; in fact, it's barely acted. Seymour addresses the entire cast with only thinly veiled superiority: "Yes. You shall all benefit."

He then grabs Calvet, and in a smoldering Charles Boyer voice he continues, "And you, my French beauty. I shall love you and kiss you, love you and kiss you, love you and kiss you. . . ."

Bending her backward into a full clinch, he looks up at Dean and asks in his little-Jewish-boy voice, "For this you get paid?"

Everything

In their quest to keep from spending their careers subject to the indifferent proctorship of Hal Wallis, Dean and Jerry began shooting *At War with the Army* on July 5, 1950, at the Motion Picture Center, a Hollywood backlot-for-hire. Although they'd made the mistake of choosing Hal Walker to direct the picture, they would be the stars of the film themselves, and, even more crucially, they would be their own bosses.

The idea that actors might produce and release their own films would have been thought lunacy just a few years earlier, but the studio system was wobbly, and the chinks in its foundation allowed all manner of strange mutations to emerge.

The studios had formerly been omnipotent: They owned the talent, they produced the films, they acted as their own distribution arms, and in almost every case, they owned showcase theaters throughout the country. It was a perfect vertical monopoly. In 1948, though, the U.S. Supreme Court had ordered the studios to divest themselves of their theater chains, thereby breaking their monopoly on the distribution of their own products and opening up bidding wars on the most desirable films. Paradoxically, while such auctions created the potential for large sums to pour into studio coffers, the situation actually cut the number of films the studios made: They curtailed production of the bottom-of-the-bill movies with which they had kept their own theaters filled, concentrating instead on potential blockbusters.

As production philosophies changed, so did the tradition of the contract player. It was less profitable than ever to hold large stables of actors under contract, while the handful of reliably bankable stars increased enormously in value. Name actors were now able to auction off their services on a per-film basis, commanding enormous salaries, getting deals to produce and even direct, and setting up their own companies to make movies and then sell them to the studios for distribution. No less an icon of the American status quo than James Stewart was the herald of this metamorphosis, jumping in 1950 from the hallowed MGM lot to Universal-International Studios in exchange for a rich package that included funds for his own production company and percentages of his films' profits. Lew Wasserman of MCA, who engineered Stewart's deal, surfed the industry's volatile surface more adeptly than anyone, and the most ambitious and sought-after talent in the business began to swim in his wake—leaving behind the old-timers, the schmoozers, the men who had created the agenting business—of whom Abbey Greshler was an exemplar.

In a sense, Greshler had been paving the path for his own downfall. Though he was only in his late thirties, he still had a prewar mentality. He had been brought up with vaudeville and broke into the business booking big bands. He bore himself like an old man; he thought of Dean and Jerry as kids. Nevertheless, he was savvy enough to know that the business was transforming beneath his feet, and in response he had hired some younger guys to help him fathom the changes.

One of these was Freddie Fields, kid brother to Abbey's old client Shep. Freddie had done a bit of agenting during the war booking the Coast Guard band, so Greshler was persuaded to take him on as a gofer. By days, Fields ran Greshler's errands; by nights, he hit the clubs in Greenwich Village and the Upper East Side scouting talent. He had a touch—he found both Kaye Ballard and Imogene Coca for Greshler—and he grew itchy for more responsibility. But Greshler's was basically a one-man operation; Fields was doing a good job, but there was nowhere to promote him. Greshler didn't want to expand his office with new agents—"My father once had a partner who screwed him silly," he would say—and Fields understandably began to seek other pastures.

No pasture seemed more fertile than MCA. Freddie's brother Shep had a friend there—another young vet named David Begelman—and Freddie heard stories of the agency's "team" philosophy, with the entire firm working in concert to further a client's interests. It sounded swell, and he put himself in a position to be courted into the field.

When Dean and Jerry were playing at the Paramount in support of *My Friend Irma*, Fields came backstage and found Greshler. MCA's Sonny Werblin had offered him a job. It was the same hundred dollars per week that Greshler was paying him, but it had real potential for an ambitious young man.

"What should I do?" he asked Greshler.

"You gotta take it. It's a good opportunity. I want you to have what's good for you."

Fields, overwhelmed by his boss's magnanimity, began to cry. Greshler embraced him. "You're my son," he said. "I want you to be happy and have . . ." Then Greshler started to cry, too.

Fields composed himself and returned home, intending to finish a few projects at Greshler's office before moving to MCA. The next day, when he arrived at work, he found Greshler had changed the locks on the office doors.

Greshler had feelings for the kid, all right, but he wasn't about to kill his business over them. He knew MCA couldn't have hired Fields just because he was a promising young agent; he understood that MCA must have thought it would be a good move to have someone on staff who was close to Martin and Lewis. Still, he didn't reckon on just how quickly MCA would act on its new access.

In June 1950, when Dean and Jerry were once again playing at the Copa, Fields came backstage to schmooze with the pair—and, no doubt, to sniff out how they were getting along with Greshler. He listened sympathetically when they started griping about their money problems, and then he began his pitch. He told them about Lew Wasserman's organization at MCA, how safe he felt there, how powerful. "You guys have gotta meet Wasserman," he told them.

They said it sounded great, but they were headed west the next day. To make the meeting happen, Fields would have to call Wasserman at home and wake him up—not necessarily the best way for a junior agent to get the boss to notice him. Fields steeled himself and made the call. Wasserman grumbled that he'd be willing to sit down with Dean and Jerry.

At the meeting the next morning at MCA's New York office, Wasserman, Fields recalled, was brilliant. He sat behind his Queen Anne desk and never once bad-mouthed Greshler. He didn't even mention him. He just talked about how much he esteemed Martin and Lewis as an act, about what he saw for their future, about how much MCA would like to be a part of it. When they parted, he told them, "I'll have Herman Citron, our top man in California, pick you up at the train, and I'll be out in a few days." It was a classic Wasserman touch—having the biggest man in the office serve as a chauffeur—and it had its intended effect. Dean and Jerry undoubtedly rode west over the next few days scheming up ways to leave Greshler for MCA.

What followed was complex, expensive, and ugly, even though Jerry remembered it very simply: "He was stealing from us," he said. "I don't wanna talk about it. It's not worth anything."

But Martin and Lewis's separation from Abbey Greshler was a byzantine affair, costing everyone involved years of annoying legal entanglement and dashing any chance that *At War with the Army* might have had of being a good movie. Through July and August, while they were filming the picture that was to mark their creative emancipation from Wallis, they were embroiled in a series of legal maneuvers that had to have hurt their work.

The entanglement began when they returned from New York and visited MCA's California offices with copies of their NBC contract for Lew Wasserman's perusal. One look at the document told Wasserman that Martin and

Lewis were his. He read the papers gravely and then looked at them in wonder across his antique desk. "How could you have signed this?"

"With a pen," said Dean.

"What's wrong?" Jerry wanted to know.

"You've been hoodwinked, boys," Wasserman bluntly responded. "NBC's got you for peanuts."

They had thought twenty-five thousand a show was a tidy sum, not realizing that they were in a position to get much more. Wasserman told them that if they left Greshler and signed with MCA, he would reopen the NBC deal and get them what they were really worth. As an added inducement, he offered them a forty-thousand-dollar signing bonus.

It sounded swell, but Dean and Jerry had signed a new three-year contract with Greshler only the previous August. If they were going to fire him, they would have to make a case out of it. On July 6, 1950, the day after production began on *At War*, Dean and Jerry sent Greshler a letter telling him that they had "sufficient cause" to "terminate and cancel all agreements . . . between us," and concluding, "You are no longer to represent us or to act in our behalf in any capacity whatever."

They also wrote "a quick note" to Wallis to inform him that "Abner Greshler is no longer acting as our agent or manager," and that "MCA will handle all our business" (the copy in Wallis's Martin and Lewis legal papers was the only paper in that vast collection sent by Dean).

On Sunday, July 9, Greshler tracked down Wallis's partner, Joe Hazen, at a hotel and told him he'd heard that Dean and Jerry were promised that MCA would "straighten out that stupid contract they have with Wallis-Hazen." Hazen had had some prickly dealings with MCA in the past—he'd been forced to renegotiate his deal with Barbara Stanwyck after she'd signed on with the agency—and he immediately made a call to Jules Stein, MCA's semiretired founder.

After lunch on Monday, Hazen went to Stein's office to get his assurances that Martin and Lewis's film contract would stand. Stein told him he knew none of the details of the contract, and he summoned Wasserman and Taft Schreiber, the two sharks to whom he'd passed on day-to-day operation of the agency, to hear Hazen out.

Hazen told all three agents "that I wanted assurance that we would not be treated rough or worked over and that the boys would go ahead with the contract," and the MCA men agreed.

"You have a contract," Stein told him, "so you have nothing to worry about." And for the time being, he and his hatchetmen were good to their word.

Meanwhile, Martin and Lewis brought action against Greshler and his wife for fraudulent business practices. Filing a complaint with the Screen Actors Guild, they identified a fictitious company through which they alleged the Greshlers had diverted 10 percent of Martin and Lewis's income—beyond the usual agent's 10 percent—as a charge for business management, which was presumably what Greshler was paid for. Greshler's wife, Violet, they claimed, was the recipient of these additional funds, which totaled more than thirty-nine thousand dollars. Beyond restitution, the complaint sought to have Greshler disciplined by the Guild.

Now that Dean and Jerry were turning on him, Greshler wouldn't be as readily tolerated around town. But he wasn't through yet. He was still scrappy Abner Greshler from the Lower East Side, and it would take more than MCA to scare him off. While Dean and Jerry told anyone who asked what a crook Greshler was, Greshler was suing them and their new agents for $1 million, accusing Dean and Jerry of breach of contract and MCA of "luring away" the act. It was a "steal," he told the press, and he would get MCA "for its pants."

Greshler started launching his own public attacks on Dean and Jerry. He told reporters about their gambling habits—"The golf sharpies are just waiting for them"—and about how they couldn't handle their money: "Several months ago they were in debt to me for $40,000 in cash—not commissions or fees—but in cash money put out in personal loans. Recently they needed money. I negotiated a deal with NBC wherein they get a loan of $75,000 cash in return for which they agreed that all their radio appearances over the next three years would be on NBC."

In fact, they'd been borrowing money all over the place. Jerry had borrowed $3,000 from Wallis in April 1949, another $10,000 three months later, and $5,000 in February 1950. Dean had borrowed $12,500 over the same span. There were reports that they'd asked for advances and even cash loans from club owners. Martin and Lewis had been a moneymaking machine, it turned out, for everyone except Martin and Lewis. "Plenty of pockets were getting filled," Jerry remembered, "but there was a big mysterious hole in our own."

MCA, however, had the clout to plug that hole for good. Upon signing Dean and Jerry, Wasserman called Norman Blackburn at NBC and told him to forget all about the deal he'd made with Greshler. At Wasserman's prompt, Blackburn flew out to Los Angeles with an NBC staff lawyer to find out how, with the Colgate series set to air in less than two months, he could keep the deal afloat. Wasserman assured him that the deal was quite viable—but at much, much more money. Say, $150,000 a show.

Blackburn was sickened, but he kept his cool. His lawyer, however, couldn't contain himself: "We stand absolutely firm!" he exclaimed. Blackburn dragged him out of Wasserman's office and into a handy conference room.

"We can make them stick to the contract," he told him, "but you know what will happen? Right before we go on the air, Jerry'll come down with a stomachache, and Dean'll have laryngitis, and we'll be stuck with sixty minutes of airtime with nothing to put on the tube."

"But they'd be lying," the lawyer said.

"It doesn't matter," Blackburn responded. "You can't prove they're not sick unless you send them to the Mayo Brothers. Believe me, I know what I'm talking about. I've been in show business a lot longer than you."

And with that, he went back to Wasserman and cut a new deal: $100,000 for the first show, $150,000 for each of the next four, and another round of renegotiations after that. Wasserman phoned Dean and Jerry with the news—proof positive of how much they'd been missing with Greshler.

To their regret, however, they came to learn that Greshler was no small-timer when it came to taking care of himself. As the months wore on, they couldn't get him to cooperate in their suit against him, not even to submit to subpoenas demanding that he sit for a deposition or turn over documents. They were satisfied, for instance, that the money had been siphoned away, but they had no way to prove it. And while he was evading them on one front, Greshler was, in the interim, filing grievances against them with the American Guild of Variety Artists for commissions on money they were collecting while their litigation against him was still pending. He was, after all, still contractually their agent.

It all proved too time consuming and, in the face of the money MCA was bringing in for them, too bothersome. They chose to settle with Greshler and kill his suit. Not only would they be forced to fulfill their three-year deal with him (signing over to him 10 percent of everything they made, including the newly renegotiated NBC deal), but they also paid him a sum (never confirmed in public) estimated at $2 million in cash, plus a Brentwood mansion with formal gardens and a swimming pool. Greshler might not have been in the driver's seat anymore, but he made damned sure all memory of the railroad apartment where he was raised would be expunged as payback.

"I was not Lou Perry," Greshler boasted years after the settlement. "They ended up fighting with Abbey Greshler, and that's a whole different thing." Maybe so, but just as sure as he'd bought out Perry, Greshler was now on the outside. He would represent other acts over the years—Tony Randall, Jack Klugman, David Janssen, Cloris Leachman, Vince Edwards. And he would gain a reputation as an old-school character around Hollywood: Both Francis Ford Coppola and Martin Scorsese would consider him for small roles in their films (*The Godfather, Part II* and *The King of Comedy*, respectively). But he would never again command the business the way he did when he had Martin and Lewis under contract. Like all the managers Dean had signed with and sloughed off over the years, he'd have to watch Martin and Lewis's star ascend from the paying seats.

Television was their last frontier. Even though it had movie men like Hal Wallis worrying holes through their stomachs, television was becoming the miraculous cash cow of show business. And along with the realization that Dean and Jerry were becoming the biggest thing in movies came the suspicion that they would also be a natural for TV.

Norman Blackburn and the MCA crew spent the summer of 1950 assembling a creative team for the Martin and Lewis leg of "The Colgate Comedy Hour," and they brought the principals together for a skull session in August. Making the trip out west for the meeting would be the producer Blackburn had hired, Ernest Glucksman, a lumpy, well-dressed man born in Vienna in 1902—an unlikely regent, at first blush, to the Princes of Mirth. But Glucksman's background was unique: He had roots in both the Borscht Belt, where he'd run summer stock theaters and done stints as a social director, and in early television, where he'd worked on "Your Show of Shows" with Sid Caesar and "The Phil Silvers Arrow Show." The combination made him a serendipitous find.

The show would be broadcast from New York, where NBC had refurbished the Park Theater off Columbus Circle, and broadcast live to the eastern states only (the West Coast was fed by kinescope on a one-week delay). To flesh out the operation, Glucksman had hired verteran director Kingman Moore and a kid stage manager named Bud Yorkin. As writers, he hired Ed Simmons and Norman Lear, a pair of former baby-photo salesmen whose work Jerry had admired on a recent TV broadcast. As Lear recalled, "We were writing for Jack Haley's 'Ford Star Review,' and we did a sketch called 'Blind Date' that Jerry saw and thought, 'I've got to get those writers.'. . . It was the first or second show for Haley and the first television we'd ever done. We were replacement writers." (They'd actually been extraordinarily lucky, having signed with MCA agent David Susskind just around the same time Dean and Jerry left Greshler for the agency: "We wrote something that somebody from MCA saw Danny Thomas do in California, and four days later we were in New York writing this show, and eight days later MCA says, 'Jerry Lewis wants to talk to you,'" Lear recalled.)

Even though he'd assembled a crack creative team, Glucksman still hadn't met his stars when he arrived at MCA's Beverly Hills office for the big meeting. "I felt awful," Glucksman recalled more than a decade later. "I had been up all night on the plane, my pants were baggy, I was unshaven, I felt like Willy Loman." He slunk into the austere MCA conference room, where a bunch of Lew Wasserman's immaculate minions sat stolidly, and waited for Dean and Jerry to arrive. He'd never forget their entrance.

"This was Hurricane Bertha within the confines of a small room," he said. "I tell you—the goings on, with the inkwells, with the pencils, with the cutting off neckties, fooling around with the agents, kissing them." In the commotion, Glucksman felt his attention drawn to one of the pair in particular. "I don't know how it happened," he recalled, "what with the two of them changing positions every minute or two, I just happened to gravitate toward Jerry."

Glucksman managed to find enough quiet in the mêlée to ask Jerry if they could meet privately to discuss plans for the show, but Jerry told him he was tak-

ing Patti to Hawaii the next day for their first real vacation. So Glucksman asked
if he could come by the house that evening, and Jerry agreed.

When Glucksman rang the bell that night, the door was opened by Irving
Kaye. Glucksman had bumped around the mountains and Broadway for nearly
as long as Kaye had, and he recognized the old bellhop immediately: "What the
hell are you doing here?"

At that moment, Danny Lewis stepped into the foyer to see who had arrived, and it happened again: "Danny, what are *you* doing here?"

It was Old Home Week: Glucksman had auditioned Danny and Rae for a
Catskills theater once, but the gig hadn't materialized. If the producer had felt
drawn to his young star at MCA, now he understood why—he and Jerry were cut
from the same cloth, regardless of their age difference.

But where Glucksman saw a familiar face, Danny saw an opening: Of all the
people now running his son's hot career, here was one who would appreciate *his*
talent. He took Glucksman aside and started promoting himself: "I'm a great comedian, too. Why don't you have the writers write a spot for me on the show?
You know, Ernie, if it wasn't for me, Jerry wouldn't have the talent he has today."
Glucksman diplomatically danced around all of this, afraid to alienate his new
boss's father. When Jerry finally rescued him and took him into his study to talk,
he was relieved. Now it would just be him and the kid, whom he recognized as
just another tummler. What he saw when they were alone, however, shocked
him.

"He was to the point, he was businesslike, he showed me that he had every
bit of information about every appearance he had ever made, every bill he had
ever played on, carefully documented and bound," Glucksman remembered.
"He was big business. He was organized."

Sobered by his host's change in demeanor, Glucksman listened intently as
Lewis explained how he wanted the show to be presented. "When you talk to
the writers," Jerry announced, "I want you to be sure to remind them that Dean
and I are *two* comics, not a comic and a straight man."

Glucksman left that night thoroughly impressed with the gravity of his
young star. He knew, though, that he'd never have the same opportunity to par-
ley with Dean. When he'd left MCA that afternoon, he'd approached Dean in
the parking lot and suggested that they have lunch together so they could get familiar with one another. "Nobody gets to know me closely," Dean cut him off.
"Not even my wife."

True enough, but there was another reason Dean didn't need to see to his
business affairs. Jerry, like a doting hen, attended to every detail of their careers
and zealously protected his idol. It was a happy coincidence of temperaments.
"My hero was my partner," he recalled. "And his best friend in the world was this
kid that was helping him make a fortune."

Dean wanted freedom, comfortable working conditions, and the pleasures of golf, women, and money. And he had a full-fledged singing career to maintain, with recording sessions and even occasional solo TV appearances. For his part, Jerry was anxious not to let any aspect of their careers escape his scrutiny and approval. Even amid the splendors of his success, with new riches and opportunities being thrown at him each day, he still felt as though it could all evaporate at any moment, and he spent enormous amounts of energy on the details of his career.

As far as Dean was concerned, the kid could knock himself out. "He got in no one's way," Jerry remembered, "which was perfect, because the way he would have gotten into would've been mine." Jerry frankly admitted in later years just how badly he wanted the career that he was so busily developing: "I had an all-consuming desire to be in the movies. I used Dean and us and what we had and geared for that."

They'd worked it so that Dean could have his leisure and Jerry would do all of their business work. "He was not a great businessman," Jerry said later. "That's why he loved that I took it and handled it. And we had a great relationship. He played golf, I stayed in the office. I used to say to him, 'We'll never get anything done if we're both playing golf. And we *certainly* won't get anything done if we're both in the office.' He said, 'I love what you're doing, pal. Love what you're doing.' I took his fucking money to the bank in the beginning. You wanna talk about trust? But that was a long time ago." (Best friends or not, Dean or MCA or someone else thought better of the arrangement: Hal Wallis began issuing the team separate checks in December 1950.)

Jerry's workaholism eventually became a standing joke among his employees and those who observed him in the industry. He gained a reputation as a nit-picker who'd worry more about the colors of his crew members' shirts and on the gifts he distributed to employees than, it often seemed, about such niceties as scripts. Ed Simmons saw Jerry's vaunted multifaceted approach to filmmaking and show business in general as a destructive symptom of his anxieties: "I think he's frightened. I think he was frightened all these years, which is why he would not let himself grow. I think a lot of the things he did as a director—or, as George Jessel says, 'director, set designer, choreographer, grave digger, door-to-door sales-man'—was evading Jerry the Comic."

Jerry's need for order and completeness may not have alienated his peers, but it certainly belied a desperately shaky self-image and lack of confidence. Dean, after all, the most self-assured man alive, could sign away 110 percent of himself and not bat an eye. Jerry, on the other hand, had to shore up his surroundings with objects, secure his working life with projects, and control his career and his personal life with a devotion to minutiae that wound up, to some degree, costing him the thing he held most dear—his relationship with Dean.

But that would be another, darker day. In August 1950, on the beach in Hawaii, with his third film in the can, his fourth and fifth films in preproduction, a new TV series in the works, and a new son in the family (Ronald Stephen was formally adopted on July 20), Jerry was a twenty-four-year-old prince. He liked to call himself "Child Star"—he even had custom shirts hand-embroidered with the moniker—and at that shining moment in his young life he was absolutely right.

Dean and Jerry were getting too big for traditional comedy venues. In September 1950 they played the Connecticut State Fair in Hartford and appeared as part of the Harvest Moon Ball Finals at Madison Square Garden. The following Sunday night, the seventeenth, they hosted their first installment of "The Colgate Comedy Hour." There were guests—starlet Marilyn Maxwell and Leonard Barr, Dean's uncle, who did a wacky dance routine in nightclubs—but the show was really nothing more than a nonstop hour of Dean and Jerry doing skits. Lear and Simmons provided their new bosses with three sketches: a slice-of-backstage-life bit, a satire of the film industry's anxieties about television, and a send-up of the ballad "Frankie and Johnny," with Dean singing the tune while Jerry and Maxwell lampooned the lyrics with a full-scale enactment.

The reviews were uniformly positive, none more so than Jack Gould's piece in *The New York Times*. He called Dean and Jerry "a pair of mad zanies of the first rank" and their appearance "sixty minutes of slapstick and horseplay that for the most part were swell nonsense."

That was the first paragraph. What followed, however, was unsettling: "It is the Lewis half of the partnership who is the works. . . . He was a one-man Hellza-poppin' who clowned his way through everything and everybody." After assessing Jerry's talent for two more paragraphs, Gould shrugged Dean off as "a competent straight man" with "a baritone voice that should not offend either the Crosby or Como fans." He finished his review by declaring that Jerry "should have more support on future programs."

Just like the reviews of *My Friend Irma*, Gould's review went out of its way to note that it was Jerry who made the pair a hit. Jerry always bent over backward—during his partnership with Dean and afterward—to correct this impression, declaring that "Dean was born funny," or reassuring his partner after performances, telling him, "You did it again," or, "Thank God we got what we got." The detached Dean was no doubt as flattered by Jerry's reassurances as he was flustered by the critics' judgments—which is to say, not at all. He sauntered along, taking the good as coolly as the bad. Jerry admitted that he wouldn't have been nearly so easygoing: "If the tables were turned, I don't know that I could've handled it." But to Dean, it was still a sweet racket. There was simply too much money to worry about which one the schmucks in the audience thought was the Golden Boy.

Gould's assessment of Dean wasn't the only unusual bit of fallout from that first Colgate show. The nation's movie theater owners and film producers were outraged by the skit that mocked the picture people's grudge against TV. The exhibitors and the Hollywood studios were fighting the onslaught of television with a "Movies Are Better Than Ever" publicity campaign, and Dean and Jerry's writers put together a savage parody of their efforts. In the skit, Dean and Marilyn Maxwell played the proprietor and ticket seller at a deserted movie theater: She performed a striptease to attract customers; he led away an usher who'd gone stir crazy from isolation. When Jerry wandered by, he was shanghaied into buying a seat. Once inside, Jerry was overcome by the echoes in the empty auditorium, and Dean bopped him over the head for mentioning the word *television.*

Harmless enough stuff, but to an industry at war, it was like an act of sabotage. The very day the skit aired, the *Motion Picture Herald* had declared Dean and Jerry the "Stars of Tomorrow" in its annual exhibitor's poll, the first team and the first comics ever so honored. Unable to reach Dean and Jerry, who'd left New York for a string of club dates, enraged exhibitors began assailing Hal Wallis's office with telegrams and letters of protest. Wallis already hated their being on television: Not only did it overexpose them, he felt, but they would be subject to what he considered inferior writing and direction, thus jeopardizing their pull at the box office. Now that one of their TV appearances had caused a small fire to ignite in his lap, he demanded they correct the situation. Dean and Jerry took out ads in *Variety* and the *Hollywood Reporter* to apologize for the flap, and even gave a free performance in Pittsburgh for a convention of Allied Theater owners by way of apology. Jerry typed out a personal note to Wallis from Pittsburgh ("Dean joins me in sending fondest regards," he assured his boss) and signed it "MOVIES ARE BETTER THAN EVER."

After Pittsburgh came Steubenville and Dean Martin Day, a weekend-long celebration of the local scalawag made good. Jeanne Martin came east for the festivities, her first visit to Dean's birthplace. She and Jerry met all of the characters Dean had told them he'd grown up with. There was a parade; there were reunions, keys to the city, formal banquets. Sentimental Jerry loved the idea of the prodigal's return. Dean? "He loathed the whole thing," his wife recalled, only enjoying the chance he seized to escape to the golf course with some old friends.

Jerry found contentment in his own ways, big spending among them. In October he and Patti paid sixty-five thousand dollars for their first real home, a twelve-room, five-and-a-half-bath ranch-style house on Amalfi Drive in tony Pacific Palisades. Size aside, it didn't look much like a movie star's house—compared with the Spanish stucco gaudiness of the Montez home, its brick façade was modest—but it was handsomely appointed within, with pine-paneled dens and plenty of storage rooms for Jerry's troves of goodies. The backyard was expansive, a large garden where Jerry and Patti would build an outbuilding for entertaining. There was a vacant lot next door, which Jerry later bought and converted into a baseball field for his sons and their friends. For two rootless children grown up, it was like living in a dream.

At work, though, Jerry and Hal Walker had something less than a dream on their hands. *At War with the Army* was cheaply made, and it looked it. Piecing it together, they were reluctant to show it around—even to Hal Wallis, who angrily demanded a screening. They wouldn't, in fact, be ready to preview the picture until December 7, when they would already be in production on their next Wallis film.

That's My Boy, as Wallis's new picture was called, would be a departure from the *Irma* films, a seriocomic story with Dean and Jerry playing real roles, not just thinly veiled incarnations of their stage selves. The script Wallis had commissioned from Cy Howard concerned a legendary all-American running back, Jarring Jack Jackson, and his Milquetoast of a son, Junior.

That's My Boy was filmed on a tight schedule—seven weeks total, including time off for the Christmas holidays. It would have to be. Wallis had yet another film for Martin and Lewis set to begin filming in mid-February, and there were still club and TV appearances to satisfy. When Dean and Jerry asked for time off from the shoot for these other obligations, Wallis would hear none of it. He had a firm commitment to two films a year from this gold mine of a team, including exclusive use of their time during film production, and he didn't give a damn what anyone had promised NBC or the Chez Paree. In November NBC had offered Wallis-Hazen several hundred thousand dollars of advertising in exchange for access to Dean and Jerry once every four weeks, even when they were making a film; Joe Hazen had flat-out rebuffed them, citing the time the team would need for rehearsal and travel (as well as "the risk of their flying").

In fact, their movie bosses never ceased griping to Dean and Jerry about their TV work. On November 14, after their second Colgate show, Hazen wrote Jerry an absurdly long memo complaining about their material. Coming from a partner to the producer of *My Friend Irma Goes West*, it's remarkable reading. Hazen declared of the overall production, "This sort of thing is all right for a couple of broken-down has-been vaudevillians; it is certainly not worthy of Martin and Lewis."

He had specifics in mind: "I think the frightful slapstick ending of the show, where you pour water over Dean while he is singing 'Singin' in the Rain,' and Dean throws water over you, is a far cry from any kind of creative performance which requires your unique kind of talent and ability." In conclusion, he advised Jerry that "anyone could do that sort of thing but there are few, if any, performers who can do the things which single out Martin and Lewis as a unique comedy team."

Aside from the intriguing detail that the memo was addressed to Jerry alone—Dean's indifference was apparently well established—Hazen's comments demonstrate how difficult it was for Wallis-Hazen, or Hollywood as a whole, to absorb the frantic comedy that Martin and Lewis represented. Live audiences positively shrieked at the material on the Colgate shows. And the "Singin' in the Rain" bit Hazen found so off-putting is still funny forty years later. Martin and Lewis on TV were brilliantly anarchic, teetering on the edge of improvisation while never straying too far from written structures.

In contrast, Willis and Hazen wanted to make predictable types out of Dean and Jerry, to cut and paste them into various pat situations. They'd be a cool sailor and a nebbishy sailor, a cool paratrooper and a nebbishy paratrooper, a cool guy and a nebbish investigating a haunting, a cool guy and a nebbish in a circus—whatever. Dean and Jerry were gifted enough to submit to a variety of yokes, but in their purest form—on a nighclub stage or, in a slightly sanitized version, on the Colgate show—they approached the Marx Brothers in their rebellion against sense, propriety, and authority.

Indeed, so offhand and spontaneous was their live comedy that Martin and Lewis were never able to reproduce it on screen. Hollywood signed them for what was unique about them and then declawed them, turning them into a version of everyone else. This was par for the course during the studio era: When vaudevillians like W. C. Fields and the Marx Brothers broke into movies in the 1930s, producers didn't know how to corral their talents and let them run wild, but by the 1940s, those comedy pioneers had been tamed and screen comedy was pretty much domesticated. The verbal comedy of situation all but eclipsed the physical comedy of personality. Rather than let stage and radio comics break up film narratives to do their usual stuff on screen, Hollywood developed a handful of comic formulas into which any comedians could be stuffed. There was little important difference between, say, a Danny Kaye film, a Bob Hope film, and a Red Skelton film. Each clown had his own métier, of course—Kaye was a highbrow klutz, Hope a roué, Skelton a doofus—but the basic stories were interchangeable.

Ditto for the comedy teams: As exemplified by the *Road* films of Hope and Crosby—which settled into a pattern immediatley upon proving successful—the comic-fish-out-of-water formula was merely expanded to include a duo in the place of the solo clown. When Martin and Lewis hit Hollywood, the traditional comedy pattern wasn't altered to exploit their talents for onstage mayhem. Dean and Jerry were simply squeezed into the mold. As a result, all but a handful of their films are disappointingly tame, even in the comic moments, while their TV material, which was much looser and more broadly written, reveals something of the excitement that entranced their first audiences.

On December 7, 1950, *At War with the Army* was screened for the trade press. Lewis and Walker had patched together what they had—cloudy sound, murky photography, and all—and come up with a picture almost devoid of life. But no one seemed to notice. "Lewis is so funny," wrote *Variety*, "the customer is likely to lose track not only of the plot but of the strong contributions of costar Dean Martin." While congratulating Jerry for "the guffaws that greet his every appearance," the reviewer noticed Dean only as the guy who "teams handsomely with Miss [Polly] Bergen." *The Hollywood Reporter*, while recognizing the quickie picture for what it was—"the show appears to be put together with string and cardboard"—found Dean and Jerry more an integrated act: "They are on screen constantly—mugging, singing, making jokes and disporting themselves exactly as one should expect."

The film opened in late January 1951 in New York at the Paramount, to withering reviews in the mainstream press. "The farces are growing more depressing, just as are the wars," noted *The New York Times*. *Time* derided Dean and Jerry's "ragtag of nightclub bits and pieces." And Phillip K. Scheuer of the *Los Angeles Times* savaged the production—"a kind of timeless vacuum through which men in uniform drift rather than advance"—and had harsh words for both Jerry ("It is a little embarrassing to have to laugh at him") and Dean ("We do not care one way or the other what happens to him, but nothing much does").

The reviews were unfortunately apt. More than four decades later, *At War with the Army* remains a depressingly lifeless, unfunny, muddled piece of busywork. Somewhere deep inside of it is an attempt at a farce—characters wander in and out of an orderly room and keep missing one another in a moron's approximation of Feydeau—but the surface is so ugly and spotty that it defies deeper analysis. It is the only Martin and Lewis film to have fallen into the public domain, and as a result all circulating prints are of horrid quality—grainy, overly contrasted, and even torn, with sound as from under a layer of topsoil. Once again, although the miniature plot revolves around Dean's love life, it's Jerry's film: He gets a production number as an intro ("The Navy Gets the Gravy but the Army Gets the Beans"), he's allowed to dress in drag and pantomime a kind of Marlene Dietrich imitation, he struggles on an obstacle course, he hits the jackpot with a balky-for-everyone-else soda machine (a Harpo Marx-ist joke that may have been Jerry's own creation, as it predates the many technology gags of his later films). There's a brief re-creation of some Martin and Lewis stage business, none of it funny: a fancy-feet dance number, an imitation (without satire) of the finale of *Going My Way*, with Dean in the Bing Crosby role and Jerry as Barry Fitzgerald. For the most part, though, it's third-rank military japery on the level of a "Gomer Pyle" episode. That the film was successful enough to spawn a pair of subsequent Martin and Lewis service comedies is geniunely astonishing.

At this remove, though, a few lines in the film bear so obviously on the lives of its stars that it seems impossible that they'd merely been carried over from the original play without a wink—or a grimace. There's the moment when Jerry, playing a character whose wife has just had a baby, is denied a pass by Dean and shouts, "If my wife forgets what I look like, you'll be responsible!" Surely, wayward husband Jerry understood that the line applied to him and Dean as much as it did Private Corwin and Sergeant Pucinelli. Likewise the line he speaks when Corwin tries to remind Pucinelli of their pre-army friendship: "We were just like brother and sister." Nothing out-weirds an earlier line, though, for revealing Jerry's habits of mind or as an inside joke about how difficult the production was: "The first thing I'm gonna do if I get overseas is surrender. A concentration camp's gotta be better than this!" A Holocaust joke coming from a Jewish comedian in 1950: It's not just embarrassing to have to laugh at this stuff—it's downright degrading.

Despite its flaws, *At War with the Army* grossed more than ten times the four hundred thousand dollars that York had invested in it, a return more stunning than that of either *Irma* film and proof positive of the public's attraction to Dean and Jerry. The stars of the film, though, would never see a dime of the fortune they'd gleaned from their adoring public. In August 1951 Screen Associates, the corporation that Ray Ryan and his fellow investors had set up to fund *At War with the Army* and a projected skein of additional Martin and Lewis films, filed suit against the comedians, York Pictures, and Hal Wallis. Screen Associates claimed that Dean and Jerry had signed a seven-picture deal in April 1950, and that Paramount and MCA had succeeded in coercing the pair to ignore the obligation. The fact that the contract had been brokered by Greshler didn't lessen the eagerness of Ryan and his partners to get another moneymaker like *At War with the Army* in the can. They pressed and pressed until Dean and Jerry forked over their majority interest in the film, just to wash their hands of the matter.

"Legally, the Screen Associates contract was no good and probably wouldn't hold up in court," recalled MCA agent Herman Citron, the former policeman who'd taken over Dean and Jerry's business affairs when they signed with the agency. "But I figured the only clean way I could get them out of it was for them to give up their interests in *At War with the Army* and walk away"—which is what they did, writing off their first independent film as an exorbitantly expensive lesson and waiting until November 1952 before they even considered doing another.

Not that they needed the work. In fact, Dean and Jerry were running themselves ragged. They finished filming *That's My Boy* on January 10, 1951, then went to New York to do a Colgate hour. They returned to Hollywood to begin work on *The Stooge*, which went before the cameras from mid-February through late March. In April they were in Chicago at the Chez Paree, where they did yet another Colgate show live before heading to New York and the Copa.

Patti caught up with them in Chicago and went on with them to New York so she and Jerry could stand as matron of honor and best man at the wedding of Tony Curtis and Janet Leigh that June in Connecticut. As he had when Dean married Jeanne, Jerry tried to talk Curtis out of it, telling him right in front of his fiancée what damage he was liable to do to his career. (Curtis was astonished and told Jerry off on the spot; Jerry later called Leigh to apologize, explaining that Curtis's agent had put him up to it.) Although they were an hour late and almost wound up missing the service, Jerry showed up in *Life* magazine bussing the bride in a full Valentino clinch.

Curtis and Leigh were part of the coterie that had begun hanging around the house on Amalfi Drive. The gang also included Jerry Gershwin (son of George); John Barrymore, Jr.; actor-writer Danny Arnold; comic Larry Storch; actors Jeff Chandler and Mona Freeman; Jerry's personal physician, Dr. Marvin Levy; and various hangers-on, sycophants, and freeloaders. Patti hated having the crowd in her house at all hours—she was often called on to serve dinner to as many as a score of guests on short notice—and even with a butler and maid (Sam and Carrie, a middle-aged, married black couple), she found it difficult to cope. She was genuinely fond of Curtis and Leigh, though (Bernard Schwartz and Jeanette Helen Morrison, as they'd been born), who were an apt match for the Lewises: young, handsome show people from divergent ethnic backgrounds getting their first taste of Hollywood fame.

"We played games," Leigh recalled of those halcyon nights on Amalfi Drive. "Or we'd go to a movie. But we all loved to play games." They played parlor games like charades (imagine a young Jerry Lewis in a game of charades!) and Categories, a game in which players choose a five-letter word and five categories and try to fill in a grid by listing words or phrases appropriate to the categories and beginning with the letters in the word. Leigh recalled one such game. "The category was 'ways of death' and the five-letter word was *tulip*, and for *u* Jerry wrote, 'Up the ass a bullet.'"

They were young and happy and rich and famous and they knew they were at the beginning of the lives of immortals. Still, no one could have anticipated what happened next. In July 1951 Dean and Jerry were booked into the Paramount Theater in support of *Dear Brat*, a pale third entry in a dying string of Paramount comedies about a family cursed with a mischievous teenage girl (played by Jerry's pal Mona Freeman, already twenty when the series began six years earlier). The Paramount was the nation's premier presentation house, a picture palace that had survived the demise of vaudeville with its prestige intact. It was a big moneymaker, able to seat 3,650 for a combined live show and film presentation. Like other large Broadway houses, the Paramount was usually programmed so that weaker movies would be accompanied by the most magnetic stage acts— hence the combination of *Dear Brat* and Dean and Jerry. They would play six shows a day (seven on Saturday) for a guaranteed paycheck of $50,000 a week, plus 50 percent of all weekly receipts above $100,000. The top ticket price was $1.50, the average less than a dollar. Nobody had ever come close to the box-office record that Benny Goodman had set at the Paramount five years earlier playing in support of the Hope and Crosby hit *Road to Utopia:* $135,000 in a week. Martin and Lewis shattered it. After two weeks, nearly 300,000 people had come to see their eighty-six shows, bringing the gross to $289,500, half of which was theirs. More than 22,000 people a day came to see them; the lines formed outside the theater as early as 6:00 A.M.

And earning more than seventy thousand dollars a week was their least impressive feat. They created virtual gridlock around Broadway and Forty-fourth Street. In order to empty the auditorium and sell more tickets—after considering cutting off food and drink to its patrons (who got wise and started smuggling in provisions)—management promised the audience that Dean and Jerry would perform impromptu shows for them from the window of their dressing room. There were some eighty-odd free performances in all. Thousands of fans filled the streets to catch a glimpse of their heroes, who mugged and waved and smiled and threw glossy photos of themselves to the masses below. Dean played the trumpet, they sang, they tossed bow ties and shirts and hats and handkerchiefs down to the street, Jerry waved a shotgun (he had three on hand) and dared the screaming teenage girls below to come and get him. There had been nothing like it since Sinatra, and there'd be nothing like it again until Elvis or the Beatles. "Little girls were practically having orgasms every time Dean and Jerry opened their mouths," recalled Norman Taurog, their latest film director, who'd come east to catch the show. (In the middle of this mayhem, little Ronnie fell and broke his leg back in California. Patti, who had traveled east with Jerry, flew home to see to him; Jerry couldn't leave, but he had a phone put next to Ronnie's hospital bed and monitored the boy's condition constantly.)

Not even the guardians of official culture could ignore the hubbub. *The New Yorker* deigned to make the trip across town to see what all the noise was about, and its "Talk of the Town" writer was predictably droll and condescending, taking careful note of Jerry's ways with money (grabbing four fives for a twenty from Paramount Theater publicist Jack McInerney, he commented on the thickness of the man's bankroll; later, he asked aloud for no apparent reason, "How do you make a check out for eight people?"). Dean and Jerry, the piece noted, "seem to have a frenzied following not only among the Copacabana set but among the Howard Johnson set."

It wasn't just a New York thing, either. After the Paramount, they hit Chicago and Detroit, to similarly incendiary receptions. *Life* put them on its cover that August—a brilliantly blurred jumping-and-mugging shot by photographer Phillippe Halsman. Inside, there was less text than image. The message was clear: Whatever the cost, you had to *see* them.

Just a few years earlier, Jerry and Dean had been part of a *Parade* magazine publicity stunt in nearby Columbus Circle: Jerry dressed down, Dean put on the dog, and each went up to strangers and tried to bum some change. The results

were unspectacular (Dean, for the record, did better), but the stunt worked because nobody on the street knew who they were. As in that home movie taken in
Times Square in 1948, they were invisible to the public.

Now that public was wild for them. The films, of course, had all been smash
hits, but television gave them the real bounce. There was a difference between
being showcased in *My Friend Irma* and going berserk in people's living rooms.
The box office had been solid, though only *At War with the Army* had thus far
been Top Ten caliber (*That's My Boy*, which hadn't opened yet, would outearn
it). But on TV they were indomitable: Slotted opposite Ed Sullivan's ratings
powerhouse "Toast of the Town," the show they'd helped launch back in 1948,
they were cleaning up, pulling in almost half of the national audience some
nights. NBC had renegotiated its deal with MCA to guarantee Martin and Lewis
a $1 million annual minimum for a slate of six to eight shows. Only Milton
Berle, who worked every week and whose show was higher in the ratings, was
paid more. But Martin and Lewis were worth every penny: The public couldn't
get enough of them, be it live, or TV, or in the movies.

Who else, after all, was there? Berle, Red Skelton, Jack Benny, Sid Caesar,
Jackie Gleason, Lucille Ball were all exclusively TV people by 1951. Abbott and
Costello were waning at the box office. The Marx Brothers and Laurel and Hardy
were virtually finished. And on stage? Forget it. Nobody commanded the same
money. For the next few years, they were absolutely tops in every single thing
they did. Even radio, where they'd laid their only egg, wanted them back, this
time with sponsors: Chesterfield and Anacin. "The Martin and Lewis Show" on
radio was just another moneymaking perquisite of their thrilling rise. It was so
awesome, in fact, that Jerry collapsed from sheer exhaustion. They were in
Chicago on August 2 when it happened, and they had to cancel a Minneapolis
appearance that would have earned them another fifty thousand dollars.

That's My Boy opened that week. Archer Winston of the *New York Post*, for
one, went nuts for it, calling it "fine gold" and "mature moviemaking." Though
he found the conclusion sentimental, he thought the remainder "brilliantly expressed in hilarious comedy" and concluded by sighing, "We can never count on
many pictures like 'That's My Boy.'"

It's no classic, but it's certainly a welcome rebound from Dean and Jerry's
previous two films—in part because Wallis for the first time truly built the script
around them. *That's My Boy* gave Jerry a chance to act like a human being, for a
change; there's barely a trace of the Kid anywhere in his performance, and in his
scenes with Eddie Mayehoff and with a psychiatrist (John McIntire, pleasantly
seedy) he's positively touching.

It must have been easy for him to relate to his part; when Jerry says, "I can't
follow in Dad's footsteps. His shoes are too big, and I'm uncomfortable in
them," he's expressing an emotion he knows firsthand. Of course, the real Jerry
Lewis chose not only to put on his father's shoes but to stomp over his father

with them. Nevertheless, Junior Jackson embodied a kind of fear that nagged at the actor who played him.

That's My Boy also has in its favor the rich black-and-white photography of Lee Garmes, the inventive cinematographer; even under the direction of Hal Walker, Garmes achieves such nice effects as flashes of light off Junior's thick eyeglasses and the rustling shadows of leaves covering his face as he endures his father's browbeatings. But, like *My Friend Irma Goes West*, this is another film laden with sloppy bits: Jerry, playing a high school senior and college freshman, wears a wedding ring in some scenes, and he appears in some sequences with braces on his teeth and in others braceless. Still, the generally thoughtful subject matter, the concentration on story at the expense of block comedy sequences, and the inspired casting of Eddie Mayehoff (he would go on to reprise his role in a spin-off TV series) lift the film above the ranks of mediocre productions Wallis had generally assigned Dean and Jerry to make.

That's My Boy would have been a terrific building block for further films for the team, films that allowed for drama and pathos along with the antics, but Wallis didn't see the team as actors. To him they were clowns, and he wasn't interested in making *Pagliacci*. He sunk them into the most formulaic pictures he could devise. In September they went to work on *Sailor Beware* (known around the studio until the Screen Associates suit had been filed as "At Sea with the Navy"), and four months later they began work on *Jumping Jacks*, a paratrooper comedy ("Aloft with the Air Force"?). Wallis had done so well making by-the-numbers fare with Martin and Lewis that he had begun collecting art: impressionist paintings, Remington bronzes. Dean and Jerry were still scrambling to pay the back taxes Greshler hadn't bothered with, but Greshler was driving a Rolls Royce, and Wallis was amassing a notable hoard of works that would one day be doled out to museums on both coasts and in Europe.

Even Danny Lewis was getting fat. When *That's My Boy* opened at the Paramount that August, Jerry was able to pull strings and get him booked as the headliner in support of the film. It was a corny bit of novelty programming that demonstrated just how unnecessary a live show was with a Martin and Lewis film on the bill. Dean and Jerry's old friend "Stal." at *Variety* reviewed Danny's show: "Lewis père is trading too much on his son's rep. Where once he made his own way with a voice resembling but not matching that of Al Jolson, he's doing the Jolie bit now only as an opener. Then he lets the audience in on his true identity and rides it into the ground from there." It wasn't a great review, but no one cared: The film did monster business, outgrossing even *At War with the Army*, and Danny played to full houses, as he felt was his due.

And there was one last beneficiary of Dean and Jerry's supernova, one last focus for Lewis's energy and hunger for attention. Their "Colgate Comedy Hour" stage manager, Bud Yorkin, approached Jerry one afternoon at rehearsal and

asked a favor. Yorkin's sister had a young son who'd been stricken with a debili-
tating disease, muscular dystrophy, and was dying from it. Doctors could do
nothing to save the boy, but Yorkin asked Jerry if he would be willing to take a
minute or so at the end of an upcoming show and make an announcement about
the newly founded Muscular Dystrophy Association, asking viewers to send
whatever money they could to help the group sponsor the necessary research.
Jerry made the appeal, and money rolled in, proof of both Martin and Lewis's
popularity and the American public's receptivity to celebrity-endorsed charities.
The end-of-the-show MDA spots became a staple on the Colgate shows: Even
when guest acts had to be cut because the show was running over its time allotment, Jerry would briefly step out of character just before the closing credits and
make his pitch, using his natural voice for the first time all evening.

Jerry became more and more involved with the MDA. He met Paul Cohen, a
dystrophy sufferer who founded the organization, and various doctors who were
pioneering neuromuscular research. In imitation of the March of Dimes and its
fight against polio, the MDA was telling people that it was merely a matter of
money before the disease would be vanquished. Jerry took to the task of fund-
raising with characteristic zeal—the MDA, at Yorkin's suggestion, had been but-
tering him up with honorific titles and plaques—and he and Dean made plans
to host a telethon that would put the infant organization on the charity map.

The telethon wasn't actually a muscular dystrophy event, but rather a fund-
raiser for the construction of the New York Cardiac Hospital. As hosts and chief
attractions, though, Martin and Lewis were permitted to earmark a percentage
of the total pledges toward a charity of their choosing, namely, the MDA. Ernie
Glucksman was tabbed as producer, and all of the personnel and facilities of
WNBT, NBC's New York flagship station, were at the telethon's disposal for the
March 15 show.

Production coordinator Bud Granoff assembled a stunning roster of show
talent to fill out the sixteen-and-a-half-hour broadcast: Jackie Gleason, Phil Silvers, Henny Youngman, Yul Brynner, Nat "King" Cole, Mel Tormé, Perry Como,
Cab Calloway, Gene Krupa, Sarah Vaughan, Harry Belafonte, Sid Caesar, Ella
Fitzgerald, Milton Berle, and dozens of others. Frank Sinatra worked with them
for the first time, and such ghosts from their pasts as Shep Fields, Sonny King,
and Vivian Blaine were on hand. They did a nostalgic section with Dean's uncle
Leonard Barr and Danny Lewis dropping in; Danny brought Jerry, who would
turn twenty-five the next day, a birthday cake. The big finale featured Eddie
Fisher, just out of the army and still in uniform, and an astonishing burst of energy from the hosts, who Charlestoned, squirted the crew with seltzer bottles,
and cavorted with the band.

When the take was tallied, they had raised nearly $1.15 million from
243,000 donors in the New York area alone. Jerry recalled that $68,000 went to

the MDA (roughly 5 percent of the total donated). But almost as monumental as the money was the impression that Dean and he made on the public with their unprecedented performance.

The New York Times canonized them: "They gave an astonishing demonstration of patience, understanding and personal dignity," wrote Jack Gould. "Aside from being capital performers, Martin and Lewis are very genuine human beings." *Variety* went much further: "By any kind of reckoning," wrote Leonard Traube, perhaps himself exhausted by the broadcast,

> it was one of the greatest show biz shows in TV history. . . . It compared favorably with the outstanding public affairs telecasts of our time—the Kefauver Committee hearings, the United Nations Security Council visualers or the Jap Peace Treaty Ceremonies.
>
> While smashing over for a great cause, it gave trade and public a new view of the comics. They not only worked themselves silly, staying on screen virtually all the way and taking time out only for a change of garb and maybe a fast cuppa coff, but emerged as guys with considerable personality quite divorced from their "in character" zaniness. The tally added up to a parade in which the word colossal seemed a little pale even as liberally applied in many of the industry's facets.

There it was, in black and white: They were as big as the end of World War II.

And they knew it, as an eyewitness remembered. Richard Grudens was a studio page working at NBC's studio 6B, home to Berle's "Texaco Star Theater" (and later to Johnny Carson's "Tonight Show"). He, like all his colleagues, had volunteered to work on the telethon, and he'd been assigned to check the performers in as they came and went. He also had the responsibility to keep everyone out of Berle's private bathroom, which was located behind the studios. Nobody, not even Dean and Jerry, had permission to use the facilities, and Grudens, who'd witnessed Berle's horrible temper on many occasions, was loath to cross his boss. He directed people to an elevator some hundred feet away and to the toilets on the floors above or below.

Informed that Berle wouldn't let anyone use his bathroom, "Jerry was furious," Grudens said, "and demanded I find someone who could authorize his use of the facilities. Jerry's father and Jerry and I tried to release the keys to Jerry, but no one would dare permit it. He ranted and raved that Berle had no right and he would sue him." Jerry and Danny berated the teenage page for what seemed to him like the length of the telethon, finally relenting and going up to the seventh floor to see to their needs. Once again Berle had bested Jerry, and someone, even if it was just a volunteer kid, was going to have to take the heat.

8

Home Movies

How big had the Martin and Lewis snowball become?

So big they could blow off the Copa. In December 1947 they'd been so desperate to play the club that they almost fired Greshler for holding out for more money. In May 1952 they just plain didn't show up for a four-week engagement at the very spot that had launched them. They'd been slated to make six thousand dollars a week—Jerry had drawn a ten-thousand-dollar advance on his share—and they were willing to pay management a total of thirty-four thousand dollars out of their own pockets just to make peace. But the Copa wanted *them,* not their money: There was a lot more than thirty-four grand to be made with Dean and Jerry onstage for a month.

They were so big that Ralph Staub's innocuous newsreel footage of the opening of Jerry's camera shop—along with a few minutes of Dean and Jerry at the black-tie opening of Barney's Beanery, the West Hollywood night spot later frequented by the likes of Jim Morrison—was touted by Columbia as a Martin and Lewis featurette ("Fame's *Funniest* Pair," read the ads), causing Hal Wallis and the attorneys at York Pictures to threaten legal action. Wallis clipped an ad for the newsreel from the trade papers and attached it to an angry memo he wrote to Joe Hazen: "This is a good example of how these parasites move in on our people [and] sell their shorts on the strength of their names."

They were so big that they had logos, like a corporation. Many people would grow familiar with the stylized pen-and-ink drawing of Jerry with his eyes closed and mouth opened pelican-fashion. An artifact of the Martin and Lewis days, it was an icon Jerry used to identify himself as a commercial commodity, well into the 1990s; he used it on his stationery, on glassware in his home, and even on the welcome mat of his yacht. Dean's cartoon likeness, which he abandoned when the act split up, showed him with his face cocked jauntily and his lips puckered in full croon. The caricatures were so much a part of the act that the team had gold cuff links designed out of them—one head per cuff link—and gave them away to crew members and other employees.

They were so big that a few of Jerry's "Colgate Comedy Hour" stock phrases had caught on in the popular parlance. There was "Don't lick it!," which he would whine whenever Dean or a bit actor appropriated his lollipop or ice-cream cone. There was "Melvin?," probably Dean's most famous ad-lib; Jerry's character would frequently bear this unfortunately nerdy name, and he would be greeted by Dean with a skeptical repetition of it whenever he introduced himself. It became a running gag, with everyone on the stage repeating it in a chain reaction. Once, after Jerry said his name, Dean blew a whistle and an entire military-style line of extras marched onstage, executed a brief drill routine, and turned to the camera to ask "Melvin?" And there was "I like it! I like it!," Jerry's excited reaction to anything insane or pleasurable he did (eating a thermometer, for instance).*

They were so big that they had a national fan club—the Jerredeannes, based in Brooklyn and composed primarily of bobby-soxers. Hal Wallis was sent a membership form, but he declined to enlist.

In fact, they were so big that they spawned imitators. In November 1950 a sixteen-year-old kid named Sammy Petrillo appeared on one of their Colgate shows in a cameo bit as Jerry's baby son. Petrillo was perfect for the gag role. Not only was he a gangly, bone-faced, crew cut–sporting double for Jerry, but he'd grown up in a small-time show-business family: His mom had been a photographic double for Alice Faye, and his dad was a Borscht Belt comic and hoofer. He'd caught Milton Berle's eye by sneaking into a "Texaco Star Theater" rehearsal and doing his amazing imitation of Jerry. Berle, no doubt hoping to needle Jerry, referred the kid to the Colgate people.

Like Jerry, Petrillo was a natural mimic, and he had expertly learned the older comic's moves, voices, and postures. His voice was a bit wheezier than Jerry's in one part of its range, a bit more nasal in another, and his physical imitation, while perfect in its various poses, lacked Jerry's effortless, mercurial fluency. Watching Jerry was like watching a fire or a waterfall, something that changed

---

*This last phrase became so popular that Jerry recorded it as a song. Capitol Records, finding that Martin and Lewis novelty discs were harder to sell than Dean Martin solo material, allowed Jerry to cut a string of novelty records in his stage voice. The earliest of these was released in 1949 under the billing "Jerry Lewis (Child Star)." During 1951–52, Jerry cut more than a dozen sides: kiddie songs, sound effects–based tunes, and novelty numbers written around catchphrases from the act. Some of the results were quite entertaining. "I'm a Little Busybody" is a remarkably engineered novelty in which Jerry sings hundreds of syllables without a breath to a melody cribbed from Paganini; Jerry appears to babble for ninety seconds at a time without inhaling. The records never made any impact on the *Billboard* charts, but Jerry showed up at the studio for seven dates during his two-year flirtation with the music business. (Dean, in twice as many dates, cut three times the number of sides Jerry did, with far more commercial success. It's hard not to see Jerry's attempt to become a latter-day Spike Jones as an effort to keep up with his singing partner on yet another front.)

aspect instantly and without any obvious conscious effort; Petrillo seemed more like he was scanning a crib sheet and adopting postures he'd memorized. It was the difference between a jazz musician creating an improvisation and a devotee of that musician memorizing and then replicating those same passages; the passion, the spontaneous wit, and the genius were drained from the structure, even if the shape was identical.

Still, Petrillo's ability was notable. Reviewing his appearance with Dean and Jerry, *Variety* wrote that he was "an amazing double for Lewis, both visually and vocally." The kid was a hit—too much, in fact, for his own good. A few days later, Sammy recalled, he got a call from one of Jerry's secretaries and was told, "He's angry because you got a good write-up with him." As far as Sammy could see, however, Jerry didn't *seem* upset; in fact, he helped Sammy sign with MCA and discussed various propositions with him, asking him to steer clear of TV in the meantime.

So Sammy stayed put, and even though he was signed to the most powerful talent agency in the business and sponsored, apparently, by the hottest comic, he got no work. Jack O'Brian, entertainment columnist for the *New York Journal American*, wondered out loud about Sammy's inactivity, and he raised suspicions in the Petrillo house when he wrote that he hoped Jerry had nothing to do with it. "My dad and I realized," Petrillo recalled, "he's keeping me back on a shelf because he doesn't want me to work."

Because he was only sixteen, Petrillo was able to break his contract with MCA, and he soon found himself on television with some frequency. He did another Colgate show—this one with Eddie Cantor—and an assortment of variety, comedy, and quiz shows. For a brief while he teamed as a live act with George De Witt, a singing star from the "Name That Tune" series, and they played such familiar Martin and Lewis venues as the Paramount, the Copa, and Las Vegas, where they finally split. By 1952 Petrillo was living in California and doing one-shot appearances in nightclubs. He found a new mentor—comedian Joe E. Ross, the excitable "Oooh! Oooh!" guy, who would later become well known on "Car 54, Where Are You?" And he met up with a new partner, a sometime singing actor named Duke Mitchell.

Like Dean, Mitchell was the son of Italian immigrants (he'd been born Dominick Mitchell, an anglicized version of Micelli) and had grown up fond of westerns. Like Dean, he'd married young and moved away from home—from Brooklyn to Florida—in pursuit of a singing career. Also like Dean, he was nearly a decade older than the rubbery young comic with whom he found himself teamed. Mitchell had even worked with Dean, playing a tiny role alongside him as Jerry's corner man during the comic boxing sequence in *Sailor Beware* (Mitchell's counterpart in the opposing corner was played by an unknown young actor named James Dean, in his film debut).

It's not exactly an uncanny set of coincidences, but Mitchell and Petrillo exploited it fully in developing their act. Mitchell sang pop standards and trendy new songs in a vigorous tenor; Petrillo yukked it up like a child alternately frightened and emboldened, making a shambles of the clubs where they appeared and forever seeking approval from his cool older partner. Mitchell and Petrillo even had caricatures of themselves drawn up in imitation of Dean and Jerry's logo.

Developing a reputation as a poor fan's Martin and Lewis, Mitchell and Petrillo played around Los Angeles in small clubs that couldn't possibly afford the real thing. Naturally, there was a ready market in the business for just such an act, and Maurice Duke, who was managing the team, began looking for somebody to build a film around them. He found his angel in poverty-row producer Jack Broder, who had gone from rereleasing Universal horror classics to making low-budget features like *Bride of the Gorilla*. Broder must have been fond of primates: The script he finally approved for Mitchell and Petrillo's film debut centered around experiments to evolve a chimp into a gorilla and then into a man. To boost the box office, Broder signed a marketable name for the picture and then used it in the title: In the spring of 1952, plans were set to film the mellifluously dubbed opus, *Bela Lugosi Meets a Brooklyn Gorilla*. (At the time Broder signed him, of course, Lugosi was also considering offers from Edward Wood Jr.)

The success of Mitchell and Petrillo hadn't gone unremarked in Dean and Jerry's camp. As early as the previous December, the easily perturbed Hal Wallis was wondering aloud to Joe Hazen whether he could simply put Mitchell and Petrillo out of business: "Jerry told me today that they are also beginning to appear on television; that some people have spoken to him about their shows and were under the impression that they are watching a not very good Martin and Lewis show. . . . I think something should be done about it if possible."

Three weeks later, Wallis sounded out legal advice from Dean and Jerry's lawyer about whether or not Mitchell and Petrillo could be stomped out. He began by quoting an item he'd read that morning in *The Hollywood Reporter*: "Duke Mitchell and Sammy Petrillo, the two kids being sued by Martin and Lewis because they look and act so much like Martin and Lewis, inked with Maurice Duke for four indie pix. Says Maurice, 'Look, I could hit Sammy with a truck and he'd STILL look like Jerry Lewis!'" An incensed Wallis declared, "This is obviously an attempt to capitalize on Martin and Lewis, and I think you should put Mitchell, Petrillo and Maurice Duke on notice at this time before they get too far into their plans to make a picture."

The report Wallis clipped was correct about Martin and Lewis's annoyance with Mitchell and Petrillo's act, but the older team hadn't gone so far as to sue. Nevertheless, the buzz around town cast Dean and Jerry as the heavies. There they were, an apparently lighthearted duo who'd enjoyed all the success they could possibly imagine, yet they seemed intent on sabotaging the careers of a couple of less able, less in-demand young guys whose big crime was putting on a mimic act that any kid could see through. *Life* did a story on the flap; *Quick* magazine put both teams on its cover; entertainment columnists all over the country kept bringing the skirmish up, thanks largely to Jack Broder's own publicity machine. The ruckus was backfiring on Dean and Jerry: Joe Ross told Wallis about a columnist who told him "that if Martin and Lewis want to stop these two impersonators, the columnist would say that Berle and others should stop Martin and Lewis."

Although Mitchell and Petrillo welcomed their newfound fame, they were serious enough about their careers to want recognition for their work, and not just for their resemblance to a more famous duo. Sammy, no doubt recalling the way Jerry had undercut him in New York, wanted to eliminate any dependence on Martin and Lewis altogether. "We were gonna dye my hair blond," he recalled. "We even talked about wearing glasses and all kinds of things not to look like the guy, 'cause they figured I was physically funny anyway." They took pains to tell the world they didn't mean to rip off Martin and Lewis. "Sammy looks like Jerry—it's an act of God," Duke Mitchell told reporters. "But I should be on the other end of a lawsuit. I should be suing Dean Martin because he went out and got a nose job to look like me!" When they got wind of Wallis's and Jerry's efforts to put an end to their film career, however, they didn't feel they needed to play nice anymore. "He's not gonna threaten me," Petrillo recalled thinking when he heard rumors that Jerry was mulling legal action. "Nobody's gonna threaten me! We went ahead and did it."

Boasting a fifty-thousand-dollar budget, *Bela Lugosi Meets a Brooklyn Gorilla* was shot that May in nine days. It was directed by William Beaudine, by most accounts the single most prolific director of feature subjects ever to work in Hollywood. Beaudine kept busy by refraining from being picky: His résumé is padded with Bowery Boys films, sex education documentaries, and religious propaganda. In 1952, when he was conceiving of a cinematic idiom in which to express the comic personalities of Mitchell and Petrillo, he directed at least six other films.

As Broder made plans to release his picture, Jerry tried to keep Mitchell and Petrillo's feet to the fire. He spoke with Louella Parsons about his resentment at being imitated: "I met Sammy when he was just a punk kid of sixteen and we had him on one of our television shows as a gag. He looked like me and so he went and hired a partner and had him cut his hair just like Dean's. You can't create something and have people swipe it right out from under your nose without doing something about it."

Although Jerry was making all the noise, Wallis was taking decisive action. He forced Jack Broder and Maurice Duke to screen their film for him, and the sight of this bastard offspring of his own quickie productions made him angrier than ever. His lawyers wrote to Dean and Jerry's counsel to spell out the urgency of the problem. Fearing a situation wherein theaters would advertise Mitchell and Petrillo as a "Poor Man's Martin and Lewis," and correctly surmising that

Broder would be happy with profits that Wallis-Hazen would consider modest, they actually suggested that a court be asked to view all of Martin and Lewis's films and the Mitchell and Petrillo film in order to see how obviously the latter pair had infringed upon the former's material.

Wallis, however, was shouting in a wilderness. He prevailed on MCA, York, and Dean and Jerry's lawyers to join him in his struggle to suffocate *Bela Lugosi Meets a Brooklyn Gorilla*, only to be met with indifference. The negative backlash in the entertainment press would be too risky, thought the Martin and Lewis camp. They proposed that Wallis file suit first; they'd follow, they said, by joining the suit a few weeks later. After an hour of arguing on deaf ears, Wallis resigned himself to letting the matter drop: "We did not want to be made the 'fall guys' in this matter. . . . If Martin and Lewis's advisors were not concerned or did not want to take direct action . . . we would let the matter rest, since they had the greater stake in the situation."

The Mitchell and Petrillo affair found Jerry and Wallis pooling their interests at an ironic time. During the months in which Jerry was fuming at Sammy Petrillo's effrontery and Wallis was worrying about some small-time producer bleeding his hottest property for profits, the two were barely on speaking terms.

Wallis, naturally, had never stopped acting the gentleman with Jerry in all the expected ways. For his twenty-fifth birthday the previous spring, Jerry received a shirt and substantial gift certificate from his producer, and he expressed his gratitude appropriately in a brief, sweet-sounding letter.

But there was an astonishing gap between the dozens of polite and boyish notes Jerry wrote to Wallis over the years and the feelings he later admitted to harboring toward the producer. It was a characteristic ambivalence: Alongside the anger he allowed himself to generate toward authority figures, Jerry always seemed cowed and impressed by them, and he would go out of his way to flatter important people in just the way he wished himself to be flattered by others. Jerry was still prone, though, to lose his temper with anyone around him, even his boss. In November, between the productions of *Sailor Beware* and *Jumping Jacks*, he once again had to write an apologetic note to Wallis about his behavior, promising never to act inappropriately again. Again Wallis accepted the apology, and again he was magnanimous, prevailing upon Paramount to provide Dean and Jerry with brand-new dressing rooms of their own on the lot.

A few months later, Wallis suffered another slight. Seven times in one day he phoned Jerry (who was performing in San Francisco), and seven times he was told that Jerry couldn't take his call. When late that afternoon he heard from Herman Citron that *he* had talked to Jerry earlier in the day, Wallis angrily wrote and filed an account of the entire episode, though he made no explicit mention of his annoyance to either Jerry or Citron.

But the worst was yet to come. Martin and Lewis, supported by the mighty

MCA machine, were preparing to push Wallis's patience to the limit. Their wounds from the Greshler and Screen Associates suits fully healed, they began to think about making another York picture, and they approached Wallis-Hazen in search of funding. Wallis played grand pooh-bah with them, saying he'd put up the money for the film only if he could produce it and control the distribution—if, in effect, it was his film. They demurred.

Wallis didn't really care who produced their annually allotted outside picture, since he had them for two films a year. They'd been before his cameras three times in 1951, making *The Stooge* (which had been finished for almost a year but hadn't yet been released), *Sailor Beware*, and *Jumping Jacks*. And he had them in preproduction on another film, this one a remake of Bob Hope's 1940 comedy *The Ghost Breakers*. Nightclub owners and NBC executives had to tread carefully around Martin and Lewis and MCA, but Wallis could afford to play hardball with them. He tried to be evenhanded—he gave York a percentage of *Jumping Jacks* when it became clear that legal entanglements would prevent Dean and Jerry from making a film of their own in 1951—but he made sure they knew who was in the driver's seat. This was not the sort of balance of power to which Lew Wasserman and his legions were accustomed. While Dean and Jerry were on a four-city club tour in February and March 1952, MCA hatched a strategy that would remind Hal Wallis just who was boss.

According to their contract for the new film, signed January 4, 1952 (when they were still in production on *Jumping Jacks*), Martin and Lewis were to report to Paramount on March 24 to begin rehearsals. They never showed. The next day, Wallis got a thirty-inch telegram from them that called the script "degrading, offensive, insulting and an indication of the indifference with which you have viewed our futures, both as artists and persons." They stated in no uncertain terms their unwillingness to continue working with Wallis in the manner that had become standard: "We do not propose to burn out the candle so to speak to make inferior pictures so that you can capitalize on our current popularity without regard to the future." And they ended by accusing the producer of "subjugating our artistic and personal integrity to your greed."

This was the act of mutiny Wallis had been anticipating ever since Dean and Jerry signed with MCA. He knew they were trying to get more money from him, maybe even to back out of one of their two-a-year pictures. They had taken great care to complain only about being asked to act in a remake, but they had a remake in release at the very moment they were complaining: *Sailor Beware*, the fourth version of material that had originally appeared in 1930. In his reply telegram, Wallis made it clear that he understood what was really happening: "We are shocked by both the substance of your telegram and the intemperate language in which it is expressed. Such a telegram so expressed raises questions in our minds as to your own good faith and the real purpose of such a communication." Wallis couldn't really prove that Dean and Jerry were looking for money

or freedom and not just artistically higher material, but he served them legal notice to appear on March 26, and then he began to look into what was really happening.

He discovered, in part, that there actually *was* an orchestrated cabal against
him. MCA, while claiming to represent Martin and Lewis, refused to make any
deals, explaining that their contract with the team required that Dean and Jerry
explicitly approve all negotiated agreements. Dean had disappeared to Palm
Springs; he and Jeannie had rented a vacation house, a sure sign to Wallis that
the holdout had been conceived well in advance of Martin and Lewis's receipt of
the script.

In the face of such premeditated stonewalling, Wallis fought pettiness with
pettiness. He withdrew an application he'd made in Jerry's name to the prestigious, all-Jewish Hillsdale Country Club, stopping the six-hundred-dollar company check he'd used to pay the application fee. He canceled an order he'd put
through to the Paramount construction department for seven hundred dollars'
worth of furniture for Dean and Jeannie. He instructed W. F. Combs, the chief
of the Paramount police force, to monitor Martin and Lewis's arrivals and departures from the lot and to notify the Wallis-Hazen office in secret whenever the
two stars came or went.

In early April, when Jerry was in Phoenix to play golf, Cy Howard bumped
into Dean on the Paramount lot and mentioned that Wallis was going to be in
Phoenix as well. Dean responded, "Gee, he'll see Jerry there and Jerry isn't supposed to talk to him." Wallis did, in fact, run into Jerry, and the two spent an uneasy afternoon together. As Wallis later recalled in his files, Jerry was deluged
with messages from Lew Wasserman, who tried to reach him at the drugstore,
the golf shop, and other places at the hotel. "I would put two and two together,"
Wallis wrote, "and assume that Wasserman learned of my trip and was phoning
Jerry to coach him."

Soon enough, Wallis-Hazen began the hard negotiating with MCA—learning, as they'd supposed all along, that it wasn't the principle of the thing that
was at stake but the money. They would have to cut a new deal or run into a similar buzzsaw on every future picture.

The holdout was followed avidly by the entertainment press. Louella Parsons assured her readers that the rift would be healed but that Dean and Jerry
would never make *Scared Stiff,* as the project-in-limbo had come to be called.
Variety reported that "the delay in settling the contract hassle is costing Martin
and Lewis an easy half-million, they figure, because one-nighters and the [Lon-
don] Palladium have to wait."

The estrangement was hard on Jerry. He was capable of despising Wallis, but
he was just as easily flattered into adoring him. At times, such as when they'd
made *That's My Boy,* he'd felt like a surrogate son to the producer, and parent-
starved as he was, he was genuinely unhappy with MCA's strict orders to keep

away from Wallis. On May 12 Jerry violated the counsel of his lawyers and agents and called the producer at home. Wallis wasn't there, but that didn't stop Jerry from baring his soul to the producer's wife, former Keystone comedienne Louise Fazenda, whose account of the conversation Wallis shared in a memo to Joe Hazen. Confessing to his boss's wife that he felt that he himself "was a business-man and that Mr. Wallis was a businessman," Jerry hoped that "they could sit down and discuss their problems." He acknowledged that only agents and lawyers were profiting from the holdout. He went on to claim that Martin and Lewis "wanted to do all of their pictures with Mr. Wallis, including their outside pictures," even if that meant only doing a single picture each year. He knew that Wallis wasn't talking to him for legal reasons, and he admitted that he was call-ing "without the knowledge of his agents or attorneys." Then he went on to claim that "he was very fond of Mr. Wallis, that he 'loved the guy' and hoped the situation could be straightened out." Fazenda listened patiently, then told Jerry that she knew little of what he was talking about but shared his desire to see the matter resolved amicably.

A week later, they were. The Hollywood trade papers carried reports of Dean and Jerry's new contract with Wallis-Hazen, a seven-year pact at $1 million an-nually (up from about $125,000), with an obligation for a single picture each year and the freedom to do anything they wished to on their own. Soon after-ward, they went to work on *Scared Stiff*, under the direction of George Marshall (who had directed the original Bob Hope picture on which the film was based); they marked the occasion by sending Wallis a telegram welcoming him to their new picture. And they began plans for a film of their own, the first since *At War with the Army*. The new picture was going to have a golf theme—Dean had long loved the game, and Jerry had picked it up in imitation of him and of Jack Keller—and Jerry would take an active hand in writing it.

Jerry's contribution to the script of the new York film (officially written by Danny Arnold and Edmund Hartman) wasn't his first foray into behind-the-camera filmmaking. For a year or so he'd been writing, directing, and editing short feature films at his house. Since arriving in Hollywood, he'd gleaned a lot of practical knowledge during the long pauses between shots on the Paramount lot, and he'd purchased all the cameras, lights, and sound and editing equip-ment necessary to make his own sixteen-millimeter films.

He had only fooled around with his equipment: Jan Murray remembered having to stand for a screen test when he visited the house. "He'd put you up there with the lights and camera," he remembered. "And he'd talk to you: 'All right, Mr. Murray, you're up for this part, and we'd like to ask you a few ques-tions. . . .' And then he would tease you and heckle you and force you to do com-edy. He had screen tests of everybody. Often when we came to his house for dinner we'd sit and watch these screen tests, and we'd scream."

But Jerry got more serious with his filmmaking knowledge and toys when Tony Curtis started beefing to him about the sort of roles he was getting at Universal. "Tell you what," Jerry told him. "I'll write a funny part for you and we'll make a movie right here."

Jerry put together a parody of Paramount's sophisticated 1950 hit *Sunset Boulevard*. Ladling a good deal of his idiosyncratic humor into the film, he called it *Fairfax Avenue*, transforming the elegance implicit in the title of the Billy Wilder classic into a reference to the middle-class Jewish neighborhood around the Los Angeles Farmer's Market. Calling on the famous faces who frequented his house on the weekends—Curtis (in the lead as screenwriter-gigolo Yakov Popowitz), Janet Leigh (in a takeoff of the Gloria Swanson role), Jeff Chandler, John Barrymore, Jr., Shelley Winters, and others—Jerry (playing the Erich von Stroheim role himself) set about creating the first of what would become a string of Gar-Ron Productions. (In the grand tradition of Jewish garment center firms, the fictitious company was named after the Lewises' sons, Gary and Ronnie.)

Among the less-famous contributors to these productions was Don McGuire, an aspiring actor and screenwriter who hung around the Lewis household hoping to be discovered. As McGuire later recalled, the first Gar-Ron production was *How to Smuggle a Hernia Across the Border*, a bawdy farce in which Jerry, with whom he co-wrote the script, played at least two showy roles: an effeminate army recruiting officer and a near-naked American Indian. (Jerry never bothered to list this film when he reminisced about his Gar-Ron pictures, but a 1951 puff piece on his home moviemaking mentioned it, as well as hinting unbelievably that such stars as Gregory Peck, Bing Crosby, and Lana Turner had appeared in it.)

Whichever picture came first, Jerry was delighted with the results. The people who were making them with him enjoyed themselves as well, Janet Leigh recalled: "A lot of us would gather there and make these funny movies. And we would then all go and have dinner, and we would go back and continue our shoot the next day. They were funny and quite wonderful. We just had great fun doing it."

Jerry started taking the whole thing seriously, investing significant amounts of time and money in his avowedly offhand productions. *Watch on the Lime*, a spoof of Lillian Hellman's *Watch on the Rhine*, came next. He wrote several more treatments—*A Streetcar Named Repulsive*, *Come Back, Little Shiksa*, *The Re-Enforcer* (a send-up of the Humphrey Bogart drama *The Enforcer*)—and collaborated with McGuire and Danny Arnold in developing scripts from them. He upgraded his equipment and outfitted the summer house in his backyard into a full-scale theater—the Gar-Ron Playhouse. He paid prime rates to have a laboratory process his film overnight. He even coerced Dean into joining in, casting him as tough guy Joe Lasagna in *The Re-Enforcer* (key lines: "Send up-a da broads" and "Make-a look-a like-a an accident") and as Doc Delaney in *Come Back, Little Shiksa*.

The enterprise evolved quickly from a lark into a full-scale project. On some weekends Patti had fifty or more people around the house ("She had to be greatly relieved when Jerry was working during the week," observed Leigh). Such hangers-on as Irving Kaye, Jerry Gershwin, and Dr. Marvin Levy turned up in small roles, as did Jack Keller. *Life* ran four pages of pictures about the making of *The Re-Enforcer*, with Hal Wallis visiting the set and posing for gag pictures as Jerry's assistant.

Gar-Ron films were premiered in catered, black-tie parties at the Lewis house, for which, oddly, Hollywood turned out: the Wallises, Darryl Zanuck, columnist Sidney Skolsky, Ronald Reagan and new wife, Nancy Davis. Jerry hired klieg lights, doormen, a red carpet. He commissioned a film crew to record the event newsreel-style. He designed an Oscar-inspired statuette, "The Jerry Lewis Award," to present to his stars. He even printed up elaborate opening-night programs. The one for *Come Back, Little Shiksa* included lengthy mock biographies of the film's stars ("DINO CROCETTI . . . a graduate of the well known BLACK HAND PLAYERS for the Mafia Theater Guild in Sicily, a well known summer resort approximately 7364 miles east of Ossining, New York") and culminated in this description of its principal creators, Jerry and Danny Arnold:

> OUR PRODUCER
>   JOSEPH LEVITCH—a Jew
> OUR DIRECTOR
>   ARNOLD ROTHMAN—another Jew
>   (There are many known varieties.)

That the Gar-Ron films, which have circulated only in brief snippets, were larks can't be denied: Not even Jerry has ever claimed they were anything more than elaborate party jokes. "They were like a sophomore play," recalled Norman Lear. "You had to be in the group to laugh. They were not very good. They all laughed. Nobody else did." The clips that have circulated are dark and grainy, like most old sixteen-millimeter footage, and the sound is tinny and remote. The shots are painfully tight: Within the confines of his house, Jerry was practically on top of the people he was filming. Specific moments of the source-material films are re-created *Mad* magazine–style, with key bits of dialogue and action twisted into punchlines and slapstick. *Fairfax Avenue*, for instance, replicates a scene from *Sunset Boulevard* in which retired actress Norma Desmond calls Joe Gillis's screenwriting partner to reveal that Gillis is a gigolo; in Jerry's version, Leigh makes an anonymous phone call to offer the bombshell "Yakov Popowitz eats ham." But even with all of these limitations, it's clear to both Jerry and the people who made the Gar-Ron films with him that this was his first real taste of directing. As Janet Leigh recalled, "I'm sure that Jerry started his apprenticeship with those movies."

Jerry was also aware that he had another motive in making these little movies: "The things I did while in the company of my buddies were artfully planned so as to win over their loyalty and affection." For what were the Gar-Ron weekends other than an effort to convert his house into a Catskills hotel, complete with a pool, a softball diamond, a garden playhouse, and a tummler prodding the guests into becoming part of the show?

Besides, he couldn't stand being out of the spotlight, even at home on his days off. In the words of his friend and frequent fellow performer Steve Lawrence, "Jerry is a total show-business animal." An old show-biz joke was revived in his honor: When Jerry Lewis opens the refrigerator and the light goes on, he does twenty minutes.

Take, for instance, his habit of showing up at other entertainers' shows and taking the stage with them. By December 1952 the American Guild of Variety Artists had reprimanded and fined him at least four times for performing for free at AGVA-endorsed night spots. *Variety*, writing about one of these hand slappings, referred to Jerry's "penchant for putting on cuffo, impromptu performances in niteries." The AGVA went so far as to put Jerry on probation, threatening him with suspension from performing in nightclubs or theaters with Dean should he get caught performing for free again.

For all that, he was certainly encouraged in his hunger for affection: He and Dean made a cameo appearance in *Road to Bali* that winter, popping up in a dream sequence—necking, even!—in order to return a (contractually agreed) favor Hope and Crosby had done them earlier by appearing in a similar cameo in *Scared Stiff.**

He even showed up on Broadway. In June 1952 producer Joshua Logan mounted *Wish You Were Here*, a romantic musical comedy set at a Catskills hotel and based on a 1937 play called *Having Wonderful Time*. That fall, Jerry attended a matinee performance and went backstage during the intermission to meet the cast and crew. He importuned Logan to let him say a few words to the audience. The producer proved agreeable and took the stage before the curtain rose, announcing, "There's a member of the audience who is very enthusiastic about our show. He'd like to tell you that the second act is about to begin." Jerry came out to a roaring ovation to declare, "This is the story of my life in the Catskills. I want the second act to begin in a hurry so I can see what's gonna happen to me."

Jerry's desire to stay busily in the limelight had costs for him at home. The production of Gar-Ron pictures wound down soon after the premiere of *Come Back,*

---

*It's telling, by the way, that Hope and Crosby never actually appeared on screen with Dean and Jerry. In June 1952 Hope and Crosby hosted a U.S. Olympic team telethon on NBC and had Martin and Lewis as guests; Dean and Jerry came out so full of piss, vinegar, and anarchic energy that they literally drove Hope and Crosby off the stage—Hope in a joking, confident fashion, Crosby quite literally, out of fear, Jerry later learned, that these insane upstarts would strip him of his toupee.

Little Shiksa, in part because Jerry was increasingly able to vent his creative impulses on the real films that York was now making. He could replace the friends and hangers-on at home with a staff of real employees at work.

But Patti had grown more distant from her husband through the commotion he orchestrated at home on weekends. As Janet Leigh had surmised, Patti was happy to be rid of the ruckus surrounding Jerry's home movies. She had been forced to deal with the burden of Jerry's psychological need for guests by working to entertain, clean (despite two full-time servants, she did a great deal of her own housework), and see to the children.

"I had tried to be a composite of Patti Palmer the entertainer; Esther the mother and caretaker; and Jerry's grandmother, Sarah, who had nurtured him when his parents could not," she recalled. "I assumed the responsibility for the boys and our home. I was lover, nurse, and friend, fulfiller of Jerry's wishes and, often, the bridge over troubled waters."

But Jerry didn't always reciprocate her solicitous manner. He could be syrupy and sentimental, composing elaborate paeans to her for her eyes only ("Just 'Cause I Love Her," he entitled one that ran nearly fifteen hundred words; in another, he described her as "the first human being that has ever cared about me or for me") and smothering her in gifts of jewelry, perfume, and clothes. By the same token, he could cut her off cold. "When we had a crisis, or if I were ill, Jerry coped by distancing himself from the problem," Patti said. "He simply ignored any unpleasantness."

Jerry's remoteness from Patti might have arisen out of guilt over his hot-and-cold, loyal-and-indifferent behavior. Even when he was steely toward her, he couldn't stop seeking her approval and affection. As Ernie Glucksman recalled, "No matter where he was, or how many girls he was fooling around with on the road, he'd always be phoning Patti—sometimes fifty times a day." Patti was aware of what was going on, but she'd been raised to suffer in silence. Her usual reaction to his behavior was to act so much the ideal wife that even wanton Jerry would be made to feel guilty. (As for the kids, the man who made his living acting like a wild child, who was famous for playing outrageously with his food at formal dinner parties, sent Gary and Ronnie to Black Foxe Military School and provided ample, stern discipline at home: "I give them what they need," he told a reporter, "a spanking with love." Only one Lewis would be allowed to misbehave.)

To help insulate herself against her mercurial husband, Patti returned to one of the sources of comfort that had sustained her through her brutal childhood. She had never fully converted to Judaism, but she had observed Jewish holidays for Jerry's sake and had agreed to let Gary have a ritual circumcision. By 1952, however, she had begun practicing Catholicism again, attending Mass and getting Jerry's permission to break the strict rules he'd forced on her concerning their home: "No crucifixes in the house, no New Testament." She also brought her mother, Mary Calonico, to live with her, giving her an ally in her increasingly isolated situation.

Jerry was glad that his mother-in-law moved in with them. She was "a big comfort to Patti," he recalled. "Just her being there helped to smooth over some very sticky problems of my own." Besides, he'd taken on a burden that would make it harder than ever for him to work on his marriage: He'd finally convinced Danny and Rae to move out to California. Danny, having turned fifty, had swallowed his pride sufficiently to let Jerry buy airplane tickets and arrange to move his and Rae's furniture to an apartment in Beverly Hills. Until their things arrived, Jerry's parents stayed at his house, in an atmosphere weighted with all of their mutual resentments.

Finally, Danny broke. "We're gonna go back to the mountains."

Jerry lost it. "Well, if *that's* what you want, let's say good-bye," he barked. "However, before you leave, you should know I just spent nine thousand dollars to give your goddamn furniture a vacation!"

Somehow this incident was swept under the rug, and Jerry set about looking for a car for his dad as a birthday gift, a custom-built Cadillac. He drove it over to his parents's apartment, wrapped it in a giant red ribbon and bow, and called up for them to look out the window. Danny took in the sight of his new car for a moment and then asked, in earnest, "How come it's not a convertible?"

Danny and Rae had grown spoiled by their son's munificence. Ed Simmons recalled Rae's reaction to one of Jerry's gifts: "They'd had a picture taken, he and Dean, a wonderful color picture. One of the best pictures they ever had taken, a keynote picture. His mother was in Chicago with us. And he had the picture framed and autographed it to her, and he had it behind his back. He says, 'Mom, I've got something here for you.' She says, 'What is it? What did you get for me?' He gives her the picture, and she says, 'Oh.' He says, 'What's the matter?' She says, 'I thought it was a mink coat or something.' They were small-time people, two-bit people. They weren't anything remotely resembling a Jewish mother and father. It was one of the saddest moments I've ever seen for Jerry."

Jerry was defenseless in the face of such behavior. Every time he tried to please them, it seemed, he was rebuffed. And when he had to deliver bad news— he took a trip by himself to their apartment to tell them that Patti had begun practicing Catholicism again—he felt, in his own words, "like a soldier coming home after losing the war."

It's no wonder that, with his parents sniping at his every overture and his wife shrinking from his every excess, Jerry surrounded himself with yes-men. The people who spent time with Jerry because they genuinely liked being with him and Patti were gradually outnumbered by socially ambitious acquaintances and career-minded friends. "You know what it started to get a little bit like?" said Janet Leigh. "It started to get—and we kind of felt this—almost like the ones who were around got to thinking about 'Who's closest?' and 'Who can get the biggest present?' And it got almost to be like 'Who could outdo the other?' And that took away from what the essence of our association and feelings were. So Tony and I kind of pulled back a little bit. This was Jerry's group. It got so that it was not this fun nucleus but it was 'Who could buy their way to being the closest?,' which was not our cup of tea."

Leigh's talk of gifts isn't metaphoric. Jerry was, of course, an inveterate gift giver, if not always a considerate one. He was constantly expressing his gratitude toward employees and colleagues with elaborate presents engraved with his and Dean's names or cartoon likenesses. "Jerry was still continuing to do things like that long after it was really seriously a joke," recalled Norman Lear. "He gave Ernest Glucksman a floor model television set that had a brass plaque on the top that said 'Love, Dean and Jerry.' So the guy, in order to have it in his home, had to let the world know it was a gift."

"Like a lot of comics," Simmons remembered, "he indulged in a lot of the passing of the gold. A gold lighter, a gold pen, a gold one of these, a gold one of these. And it would say, 'Thanks, Dean and Jerry.' You'd say, 'Thanks a lot, Jerry,' and he'd say, 'Don't thank Dean yet, I haven't told him.'"

However gaudy or surreptitious, the gifts were Jerry's heartfelt way of showing affection and appreciation, on the one hand, and seeking those same things, on the other. As Jan Murray recalled, "You would leave his office like a quiz show winner. You had a clock and a fountain pen and a watch, all with his logo on it. I'd have my arms full like I just answered four questions correctly. I used to kid him and say, 'What about spending money? What am I supposed to do the rest of the week?' He'd heap things on you."

The rub of the thing was that he came to expect gifts in return from his friends and associates, even encouraging them with loud expressions of gratitude that evolved into still more acts of ostentatious generosity on his part. People invited up to Amalfi Drive for dinner or a weekend of softball and moviemaking began to bring their host gifts as a matter of course. The gift giving even became part of the postdinner entertainment, with guests retiring to the playhouse to watch their host unwrap his goodies like a five-year-old at a birthday party.

For those who were currying favor with Jerry, the gifts were a way of demonstrating their fealty; for others, especially Jerry's employees, the expectation was an expensive burden. Among the most resentful were Norman Lear and Ed Simmons, who were among the few staff members who could actually afford to regale Jerry with costly tokens. "We got sick and tired," Simmons recalled. "It wasn't that we didn't want to buy gifts, it was that it just didn't matter. He would get these gifts that somebody went out and spent three, four, six hundred dollars on, and he'd just throw them aside like they were trash. It was just ridiculous." (Another employee of later years recalled Jerry receiving a bust of himself as a gift and then refusing to let it be put in his limo with him; a cab had to be summoned to carry the statuette to Jerry's house.) One evening Simmons and Lear made fun of the entire enterprise by disappearing just before the gifts were opened and pretending to hang themselves by their neckties from a tree in Jerry's backyard, apparently despondent over forgetting to bring a present. "We ruined the neckties but saved ourselves a grand," Simmons boasted.

Another time, anticipating the need to bring a gift but angry that it was required of them, they came up with the perfect idea: The one thing that they could think of giving Jerry that no one else had was a live human being—gift wrapped, of course. The gag might have remained a dream had not a short, beefy repairman turned up in their office that afternoon to fix a window. He was an old Frenchman who spoke only broken English, but when they asked him if he wanted to make twenty-five dollars that night helping out with a joke, he understood enough to agree. They had a box built for him to crouch in, and they told him he'd have to wait in the car through dinner and then climb in the box and get wrapped and carried into the playhouse.

As the twenty or so dinner guests retired to the playhouse to open gifts, Lear and Simmons went out to wrap the old man. When they put him in the box, they had another brainstorm: They offered to give him another five dollars if he could keep from smiling through the gag. Telling him to "act deadpan," they wrapped him and carried him into the party.

"Hey, look at Simmons and Lear—they got him a television set!" yelled someone from the back of the room. The two writers carried the large box over to the coffee table, where Jerry sat amid the debris of dozens of expensive gifts—watches, radios, cameras—for which he truly had no need. Eagerly, he stood to open the huge package. When he opened it, he saw an old man hunched over with his eyes shut and his mouth tightly pursed, trying desperately to keep from laughing and looking for all the world like . . .

"A cadaver!" Dr. Marvin Levy shouted.

"Everybody was shocked," recalled Lear. "Patti screamed." He and Simmons coaxed the man out of his pose. But there was no way of dispelling the pall that had fallen over the room.

"Everybody else, on behalf of Jerry, all the sycophants, were shocked that we could do such a thing," Lear remembered. "The only people laughing were Hal Wallis and Louise Fazenda. And [Wallis] roared; he loved it. He understood it and could afford, in his relationship with Jerry, to laugh at it. But they were the only ones."

As Simmons said, Wallis saw the joke beneath the joke: "The key line of the story is that it wasn't just a joke-joke, it was 'Jerry, we're giving you something: your very own human being.' But the room had a hundred people that were his own human beings, that he owned and that revolved in his orbit."

9.

The Stooge Turns

This was only a twenty-six-year-old young man, recall, albeit one who had shot to the top of his profession without serving any significant apprenticeship. He left his parents' house at sixteen, was married at eighteen, became a father at nineteen, found a partner at twenty, and woke up on his twenty-second birthday well on his way to becoming rich and famous. By twenty-six he'd made eight movies, he was costar of the most watched and anticipated program on television, he was on a popular radio show, he was doing endorsements for Chesterfield cigarettes and Van Heusen shirts, he'd cut records, he was writing a feature film. He was supporting his wife and sons, his parents, various relatives who'd traveled west in his wake, and an assorted collection of acquaintances and friends. For all intents and purposes, he was the Sun King at the center of his world.

And his partner, at thirty-five, had an equally impressive list of accomplishments to his name. No one had ever quite pulled off this sort of triumph before them, and it would be left to the next generation of entertainment gods—the rock stars—to replicate the sort of success and fame that Dean and Jerry enjoyed. They were multimedia events in and of themselves—movie stars, TV stars, stars of radio and nightclubs—and they controlled their own destinies.

Jerry had never felt like he belonged; he had always assumed, because of the treatment he'd received from Danny and Rae, that no one liked him. Now the world was throwing itself at his feet. Not coincidentally, he became a monster of temper around the house and, increasingly, at work. He developed a reputation for spouting off angrily whenever his will was opposed; witness his chronic set-tos with Hal Wallis. But nowhere did his volatility surface more than at the TV studio. Unfettered by the nagging Wallis, Jerry comported himself like a tyrant, with all of the hot-and-cold running capriciousness the word implies. Employees whose birthdays (and whose children's and spouses' birthdays) never passed without opulent attention from Jerry were subject to withering dressings-down when they failed to satisfy some unforeseen expectation.

Only one person was spared Jerry's volatility, and that, of course, was Dean. All the success and money and toadyism he enjoyed still hadn't diluted Jerry's worship for his partner. Jerry liked to feel he was the only person permitted within Dean's private force field. He even fought with Jeanne Martin over her husband. "She and I had a couple of little fracases," he recalled, "only because I was so protective of him. If she said something like, 'Well, he's not all that attentive,' I would get very protective and I would lean on her a little, and then she would tell him that I got fresh with her. Those little things happened. But I cared a great deal for her, more so than she knew, because she gave him so much pleasure."

Dean's marriage to Jeannie was considerably more stable than his first marriage, but it was still a bumpy relationship. They'd had their first child together in November 1951: Dean Paul Martin, Jr. (Dean had taken Paul as his middle name when he'd been confirmed in Steubenville). But they were prone to angry little separations, spats during which Jerry always took Dean's side, in hopes, perhaps, of bolstering his position as his partner's closest friend. Whenever he got wind of an estrangement at the Martin household, Jerry would offer Dean a bedroom at Amalfi Drive. Wisely, Dean usually chose to stay at a hotel instead. But once, according to Jack Keller, Dean accepted Jerry's offer. "I happened to drop by Jerry's house," Keller recalled, "and found him tidying up everywhere, emptying ashtrays, behaving like a servant. I said, 'What the hell's going on?' He said, 'Dean's coming.' He was as excited as a teenager."

As much as Jerry yearned for Dean's companionship, he didn't like having to compete with him for public attention. Norman Lear recalled that Jerry used to go to great lengths to draw attention from Dean during the "Colgate Comedy Hour" rehearsals. "Jerry, who was supposed to be the funny one, couldn't stand it if Dean got any laughs. Dean could be insanely funny with a line. Any morning that Dean would come in and start being funny with the lines or do funny things, Jerry would wind up in a corner on the floor someplace with a bellyache. And a doctor would have to come. This was always true. Whenever Dean was very funny, strange physical things happened to Jerry. Sometimes he would go to the extreme of calling Marvin Levy, who was his doctor at the time, to fly in from California to treat him." (Shirley MacLaine recalled seeing this same behavior pattern when she worked with Dean and Jerry in 1955.) Others recall Jerry ripping off Dean's jokes, taking lines Dean had ad-libbed at rehearsal and spouting them on the air as if they were his own.

Dean never specifically signaled that he didn't appreciate his partner's behavior; that wasn't his style. But he had his own sly ways of letting people know he was aware of how controlling and excessive Jerry was. Simmons recalled how annoyed Dean became when Jerry had Danny appear on the Colgate show singing from his Jolson songbook: "Danny was on, and he was rehearsing, and I was standing in the back with Dean. Dean was smoking and looking at Danny with such disgust. This was still a major show, remember, although Dean put his uncle on it once, Leonard Barr. And Dean flicked his cigarette to the ground and said, 'That's it. Next show I'll put my mother on. She'll make a dress.'"

In a similar vein, Dean saw how grand Jerry's comic ambitions had become, and he was perfectly willing to call him on them. According to Simmons, "When we were on the set of *Scared Stiff*, there was one scene where Jerry has been a stowaway on a boat and has been in a steamer trunk for a few days. And it's a regular comedy situation: The trunk is opened and he gets out. Has to be funny. I'm standing watching them shoot, and again, I'm standing with Dean. Jerry gets out and it looked like he was bucking for an Academy Award: He was showing pain, he was showing ache, he was showing crippled, he was showing everything but funny. He got out of this thing and it just wasn't funny. He was a good enough actor: You felt for this guy who was stuck in this thing. But the audience wasn't gonna laugh at this. And I turned to Dean and said, 'What is he doing?' and he says, 'Chaplin shit.' And he rubs out his cigarette with his shoe and walks away."

By all accounts, however, the two partners remained genuinely friendly throughout these, their glory days. If Jerry alternated between outright idol worship and petty jealousy of Dean, it wasn't the only hot-and-cold relationship in his life; if Dean acted cool and cynical toward his younger partner, what else was new? They kept making movies together, they kept doing TV and live gigs. They were each grossing more than $1.5 million a year: They could forgive one another's foibles.

When *Scared Stiff* wrapped, Dean went on vacation to Las Vegas and got a chance to perform solo, filling in for an ailing Kay Starr at the Flamingo. Soon after, they were off to Chicago and another engagement at the Chez Paree.

Their commitments were starting to pile up unmanageably. The starting date for *The Caddy* kept getting pushed back by Paul Jones, whom York had hired to supervise production. That, in turn, was pushing back Wallis's next Martin and Lewis project, *Money from Home*, which, in typically market-driven good taste, Wallis had decided would be shot in 3-D. There were still the monthly Colgate shows, though they had allowed the superfluous radio shows to fall by the wayside. There were live dates waiting at year's end: the Texas State Fair, a string of club dates back east, including a ten-day commitment that it turned out they absolutely couldn't refuse.

Somehow in the mountains of verbal promises to show up they had neglected an obligation to play some date somewhere. The particulars really didn't matter; what mattered was that the club they'd somehow forgotten was owned by mobsters, and they simply had to make good on their marker. That, however, would mean further indulgences of time from Wallis, and the producer was loath to hand them anything more than they were already getting. In August Jerry called Wallis from Chicago and asked for more time between the end of *The Caddy*, projected to finish shooting in early January, and the start of *Money from Home*, which Wallis had hoped to take before the cameras in mid-February. Wallis protested and followed up with calls to Y. Frank Freeman, Paramount's chief of production, and Herman Citron at MCA.

With Freeman, Wallis was deferential, accepting the gentlemanly former banker's word that the new film would start when he wished it to. With Citron, however, he was less guarded, as his phone transcripts (he'd begun recording his phone calls during Dean and Jerry's holdout) revealed. In particular, he was frustrated by Jerry's insinuation that he and Dean would be in some physical peril if they didn't show up: "I just had a call at noon from Jerry in Chicago—one of those again where he said, 'We're obligated to play a nightclub.'. . . It's the same story we got last year . . . what these fellows were going to do if they didn't perform."

After complaining about how this might affect his own plans, Wallis spoke about the biggest irritant in the whole episode: If he didn't get Martin and Lewis in front of his cameras early enough in the year, he'd have to forgo his annual art-buying trip to Europe in order to finish the picture: "I'm going to be duplicating my last couple of years where I'm sitting here all summer, and I just don't want to do it." Citron was all sympathy: "I don't blame you." But he had no reason to bend his clients to Wallis's will. Dean and Jerry took their time on the road— that fall they earned three hundred thousand dollars in a month of personal appearances—and they didn't start work on *The Caddy* until late November. Wallis and his 3-D masterpiece would simply have to wait.

For Sammy Petrillo and Duke Mitchell, however, time was of the essence. Jack Broder had to release *Bela Lugosi Meets a Brooklyn Gorilla* as quickly as possible, not only to capitalize on Martin and Lewis's success, but also to avoid litigation. In September the picture premiered to universal indifference. *Variety* correctly predicted "a quick demise" for the film. Broder could secure only limited distribution for the picture, even after marketing it under such clever titles as *The Boys from Brooklyn* and *The Brooklyn Gorilla*.

Why Brooklyn should figure at all in the title is just one of many unexplained mysteries about the dreadful film. And for all Wallis's fears, there was only a single reference to Dean and Jerry in the thing: Mitchell and Petrillo, having fallen out of an airplane, are rescued by an island tribe whose chief attempts to ascertain their identities by examining their clothing. He finds an issue of *Variety* and puts it aside, and then he notices a label sewn into a jacket: "Mervyn Fine Tailoring."

"I think one of them is named Mervyn," he announces, beginning a chain reaction of puzzled rejoinders: "Mervyn?" "Mervyn?" "Mervyn?" Hearing this chorus, Mitchell and Petrillo sit bolt upright in their sickbeds.

"Who said that?" asks Duke.

"Which one of you is Mervyn?" asks a native girl.

"Aw, lady, you got us mixed up with two other guys," answers Sammy.

Sammy is cruder and less winsome than Jerry, with a knobbier face and a more grating voice. He has aspects of Jerry's shtick down cold—physical stuff like the way he skips or crouches in fear or puts a hand on his belly and leans forward in mock dignity—but he's just an imitator. There is no comic invention in his persona, which is stolen whole cloth from Jerry, or in his block comedy routines, which would come off poorly no matter who tried them. He even—Italian boy from the Bronx!—indulges in Yiddishisms.

Still, he deserves his role at the center of the picture, if only because his partner is so phenomenally untalented. Duke Mitchell lacks Dean's looks, charm, voice, manner, acting ability, comic instincts, even his height: Though he's supposed to be the tall, dark, and handsome one, his partner has a few obvious inches on him. When Bela Lugosi finally turns him into a gorilla out of romantic jealousy, it's a welcome change.

And when Sammy takes a bullet to the heart trying to protect his gorillafied partner from being hurt (at a preview screening, Jerry allegedly shouted, "Thank God!"), it's impossible to imagine that the film could get more surreally awful. Yet it does, turning out to be a *Wizard of Oz*–style nightmare: Sammy wakes up backstage at the Jungle Hut in Passaic, New Jersey, where he and Duke are about to go onstage. He's been having a dream. Petrillo gets one last chance to mug before he and his partner arrive onstage ("Those two fireballs of fun," shouts an unseen emcee) and launch into a wan knockoff of Dean and Jerry's act: Duke sings careeningly, Sammy pretends to conduct the band.

Fade out. End of picture. End of career. Whether Jerry conspired to squelch the team is unclear. Sammy Petrillo bitterly recalled being thrown off a Colgate hour at the last minute; the episode was hosted by Abbott and Costello, and Lou Costello allegedly told Sammy that Jerry had pulled the plug on them. Neither Sammy nor his partner blamed Dean for their downslide. "He don't want no trouble," Mitchell told reporters. "He used to tell Jerry, 'Leave the kids alone, let 'em make a buck.' I'm sure Dean never, *never*, bum-rapped us once." But they didn't blame themselves, either, despite the silence that greeted their awful film. They pursued their chimerical career as though something other than their resemblance to a famous act had called it into being, finally breaking up after Dean and Jerry split.

In 1982, a year after Mitchell's death, Sammy Petrillo made a final, inadvertent TV appearance. Amid a montage of clips introducing a "Today Show" segment about Jerry and his autobiography, audiences caught a brief glimpse of what looked like a young Jerry mugging with Eddie Cantor. "That wasn't me," Jerry told Bryant Gumbel. "It was Sammy Petrillo, a kid that I found walking on Fifty-third Street here in New York, and I brought him out to Hollywood to work on a sketch with Dean and I, and then he worked with Eddie Cantor two weeks later." Jerry explained that he'd never worked with Cantor, then joked, "Not only that, but I was never that good-looking." When, a few days later, David Letterman's office contacted Sammy and asked him if he'd come and surprise Jerry, who'd be making an appearance on "Late Night," he refused.

Mitchell and Petrillo weren't the only team whose stars rose along with Dean and Jerry's. Norman Lear and Ed Simmons were increasingly recognized around the industry as writers of talent and wit. Reviews of "Colgate Comedy Hour" episodes routinely cited their contributions: "Their wild imaginings have raised M&L to the peerage of their particular type of comedy," wrote *Variety* in a typical notice. Dean and Jerry had themselves acknowledged as much in the spring of 1951, when they bought a full-page ad in *Variety* announcing to the world how grateful they were to their writers, showering them in superlatives and brilliant absolutes.

But as Jerry came increasingly to cast himself as the font of all of Martin and Lewis's inspiration, he grew prickly toward anyone who might vie with him for credit, and no one more so than Simmons and Lear. Not only were they not cut from the typical sycophant mold, after all, but they were creative people, people who supplied Jerry with the stuff that made him so popular and wealthy, people who had the ability to sit down with nothing and stand up later with a finished product.

Jerry had long been vocal about not needing writers—he was said to have snapped at Billy Rose during his first Copa appearance when the impresario suggested he and Dean should commission a written act—and he wasn't very comfortable with having to buy scripts for his TV and radio work. Late in life, Jerry spoke of himself as a writer first and foremost—"I began as a writer and that's been the secret of much of my success: what I've been able to get down on the paper."

But during the 1950s, though he took (and undoubtedly deserved) credit in interviews for much of the material he and Dean performed, he had never received a writing credit for a film or a TV show. He ascribed it to modesty, telling interviewers that he wanted his work accepted on its own merits and not just on the strength of his signature. He also said that he refused to take credit for his behind-the-camera contributions to the team's work so as not to overwhelm Dean in the act (a qualm that didn't, however, stop him from adding a credit to *Money from Home*—"Special Material in Song Numbers Staged by Jerry Lewis"—even though the material was just his old record act pulled out of the hope chest for the occasion).

Ed Simmons had a simpler explanation for Jerry's lack of writing credits: "Jerry couldn't sit down and write like a writing-type person." To be fair, with all of his other creative and family commitments, he was probably too busy to write his once-a-month television show, but as Simmons recalled, he was also an un-willing collaborator: "Jerry never met with us. We'd have to go chase after him and pin him down. We pretty much had free rein."

Simmons and Lear, along with "Colgate Comedy Hour" director Bud Yorkin, exploited the fact that Dean and Jerry were too busy to supervise the TV scripts. They devised a routine whereby Dean and Jerry would have scripts pre-sented to them at rehearsals, when it was too late to make major changes: Sets and costumes had already been designed, supporting cast members hired, tim-ings worked out. They had, in effect, taken pains to Jerry-proof the show.

This sort of precaution was more and more necessary, given Jerry's stature in the business. Not since Shirley Temple had someone so young had so many en-tertainment executives jumping through hoops. Jerry was revealing a spoiled-rock-star temperament at a time when Elvis Presley was still in school. You can see it in the way he boiled over at Wallis, in his imperious attitude toward Sim-mons's and Lear's work, in his ambition: He wanted to play the London Palla-dium, to direct films—in short, to be another Chaplin. He incorporated a Chaplin routine into *Jumping Jacks* (cavorting along with Dean, who also sported a derby, bamboo cane, and square mustache for the bit), and he wrote about his screen hero in publicity materials released with *That's My Boy.*

He referred to Junior Jackson as "a pathetic figure very reminiscent of the character made famous by Charlie Chaplin and others of his era." The reason for this approach, Jerry claimed, was that "at heart I really belong to the old school which believed that screen comedy is essentially a combination of situation, sad-ness and gracious humility." He was careful to point out that he had "no inten-tion of imitating Chaplin or any of the other great humorists of his day," knowing full well that "imitators never get anywhere." Indeed, he was convinced that too many modern comedians aped previous artists. He declared that he hoped only "to capture the same warm, sympathetic quality which Chaplin and a few others had."

Regardless of whether Jerry wrote this manifesto himself or Jack Keller threw it together at his request, several elements in it reveal Jerry's self-image clearly. Chaplin (and his thrice-unspecified peers) was still alive as Jerry was writing this—working, in fact, on *Limelight,* his late masterpiece about the nature of humor, sentiment, and comic performance (the film also featured Buster Keaton, whom Jerry never named). Jerry, however, writes as if he alone among living comics was capable of bringing a long-lost Chaplinesque mixture of slap-stick and pathos to the screen.

Furthermore, Jerry's identification of his comic persona (even as it is muted in *That's My Boy* and *The Stooge*) with Chaplin's is brazen at best. Taking into account the films Jerry had made or was planning to make, his relatively limited contributions to his own films (Chaplin, under the aegis of Mack Sennett, as hands-on a producer as Wallis, was allowed to direct almost from the start), and the fact that he worked in talkies and with a partner, it's difficult to fathom how, in his mid-twenties, he felt comfortable linking himself to Chaplin—while in the same breath decrying comics who imitated other acts!

"Chaplin shit" aside, the most telling aspect of the brief manifesto is Jerry's confession that he "really belong[ed] to the old school." It's a gesture that runs contrary to the typical vein of self-promoting press materials, especially materials concerning hot young comedy acts. Rather than posit himself as a ground-breaking modern performer or one of the first multimedia stars—both of which he was—Jerry chose to legitimate himself with a backward glance toward a universally recognized master. In reality, the strength of his comic persona was its aptness for the postwar era. By acting like a little boy in 1952, he was exactly in tune with the Baby Boom, and his audience identified with him as a peer. But Jerry could only accept legitimacy in the terms of an earlier culture, one in which such values as "sadness and gracious humility" still held currency. That in his private life he tried as much as possible to comport himself like an up-to-date adult only further revealed the split he felt between himself and the world around him. Even though he was adored, highly compensated, and kowtowed before, he felt as if the only time in which he wanted to be loved—his child-hood—had passed him by.

There was enough child still in Jerry, however, for Dean to buy him a motor scooter as a gift (making Jerry a kind of Sal Mineo to his partner's James Dean). Jerry kept the little bike on the Paramount lot and scooted around raising a rumpus throughout the time *The Caddy* was in production. In January 1953 he cracked the thing up and was admitted to Cedars of Lebanon for knee surgery (Louella Parsons incorrectly reported that a previous injury to the same knee had kept Jerry out of the army). The injury set back shooting on the film for several weeks, and it pushed Wallis's new picture back as well.

Wallis had *The Stooge* out at the time, though, after sitting on it for well over a year. Though the film had ceased production in March 1951 and had been intended as a follow-up to *That's My Boy*, it sat on the shelf for nineteen months before Wallis finally previewed it for the trade press. The delay, highly out of character for an efficient businessman like Wallis, had nothing to do with the work of Dean and Jerry or their director, Norman Taurog. It was due, strangely enough, to the script by Fred Finklehoff (who'd written *At War with the Army*) and Martin Rackin. *The Stooge* was an uncomfortably bald look at the relationship between an egoistic singing comic and his moronic, underappreciated sidekick, based on the reminiscences of former professional stooge Sid Silvers, who'd worked from the audience as part of accordionist Phil Baker's act in the 1920s. Though in some ways the relationship between the central characters was exactly the reverse of Dean and Jerry's, the disparities in their stage personae and even their physical appearances were the jumping-off point for the film, and the cruelty implicit in the portraits made even the imperious Wallis ill at ease.

Taurog was yet another in the string of journeyman directors with whom Wallis entrusted Martin and Lewis, but he developed a rapport with the team that none of his predecessors had; after *The Stooge*, and until they split up, he directed every York film Martin and Lewis produced. Taurog, like George Marshall and Hal Walker, was another Hollywood lifer, having acted for Thomas Ince at fourteen and directed Larry Semon comedies at Vitagraph at twenty. As a director, he'd worked with W. C. Fields, Mickey Rooney, Bing Crosby, and other comedy and light romance stars. By the time he signed on with Wallis and Martin and Lewis, Taurog was seen as a sort of B+/A− director, capable of turning out a minor classic like *Boys Town* but generally commissioned with light, often quasi-musical fare.

The Stooge, as it appeared under his signature, had many of the familiar contours of a Taurog picture—gentle comedy, the occasional song—but little of what audiences had come to expect from Martin and Lewis. This, and not some dark intimation that the film presaged real conflict within the team, was probably what caused Wallis to hold it from release for nearly two years. But on its release, *Variety* read into the film a possible expansion of the Martin and Lewis audience, which, like the audiences of randy teen comedies in the 1980s, was presumed to be largely young and male: "The change of pace, mixing as it does schmaltzy sentiment into the fun, will make a favorable impression on those, particularly the femmes, who heretofore have not wholeheartedly accepted the team's uninhibited antics."

Bosley Crowther of *The New York Times*, who followed Martin and Lewis's rise with less concern for the box office than for the human condition as the team seemed to represent it, was also surprised by the film. "Students of the exotic and the brazenly bizarre are likely to find the display more intriguing than will the addicts of straight belly-laughs," he reasoned in a generally positive review, while adding that "the going gets rather sticky and unfunny toward the end. This is not only oddly depressing; it is perilous to one's simple faith in man."

A heavy moral to draw from a movie starring a couple of jesters, but in fact, the film, set in the 1930s, is barely a comedy. Dean's Bill Miller is a thorough heel, an egoist driven to further his career at the expense of friendship, marriage, and simple decency. When he breaks with his old partner and flounders as a single, his agent (a pleasantly subdued Eddie Mayehoff) suggests he get a stooge—a shill planted in the audience, off whom he can bounce jokes and song introductions. Enter Teddy Rogers (Jerry), nearly twenty minutes into the film. Teddy immediately becomes Miller's slavish devotee—performing with him, mending his clothes, feeding him, sending loving telegrams back home, covering for him when he gets drunk. But he's more than just a stooge—he's such a natural comic that he becomes the real center of the act, even though Miller won't even grant him billing. When everyone around Miller criticizes him for his selfishness, he fires Teddy, then flops again, then confesses his dependency to an audience at the Palace Theater, and then they reunite: sob, sniff, curtain.

The Stooge offers an interesting contrast to *That's My Boy*, in which Jerry's meekness was sympathetic and Dean's boorishness rooted in more humane motives. The presence of the overbearing father in that film was a problem for Dean and Jerry to overcome together; here, the villainy comes from one of the characters we ought to be rooting for most, and all of the secondary players—Mayehoff, Polly Bergen as Dean's wife, Marion Marshall as Jerry's unfortunately named sweetheart, Frecklehead—spend the whole film castigating Dean for his behavior. Wallis was right to be nervous about the picture; Dean has a meaty role and sings a lot of swell old songs, but he's an outright creep.

The most interesting motif in the film, and one that became a theme throughout Jerry's work, is the notion that an untrained, unrehearsed neophyte can somehow perform before a live audience and score a hit merely on the basis of having a funny personality and a sincere heart. (This alone may account for the fact that decades later Jerry would declare *The Stooge* his favorite Martin and Lewis film.) Teddy Rogers doesn't even know he's supposed to be part of the act, but he steals it with his purity of spirit—just like the character Chaplin played in *The Circus*, who had no idea the audience was enjoying his unintentionally funny antics. It's a philosophy of comedy that helped Jerry reconcile life and art throughout his career—his comedy, the argument ran, came from some genuine store of humanity within him that superseded anything untoward he might do off stage. But it's a dubious theory, and it's shakily presented in the film: When in the finale Teddy is reunited with Bill Miller, he performs a completely polished act—in drag and without his usual high-pitched whine. It's a funny bit, actually. Dean sings straight and Jerry responds to each line of the song with ironic undercuts, innuendoes, and bad puns; it's probably cribbed from their nightclub work. But it just doesn't fit in with the rest of the picture: How did this schnook get so smooth all of a sudden?

Wallis, of course, didn't worry about whether his Martin and Lewis films achieved overall harmony; he just wanted them to make money. To that end, he spent the early part of 1953 helping arrange for Dean and Jerry's first overseas trip. A lifelong Anglophile, Wallis had encouraged Jerry's enthusiasm to play the London Palladium, and he had been writing for several years to Val Parnell, the Palladium's manager, suggesting he book the act. Not only did Wallis feel Dean and Jerry would do very well before English audiences, but he also believed that their appearing there—where "The Colgate Comedy Hour" had never aired—

would boost their United Kingdom box-office performance, which he monitored very closely. (The previous June he'd acknowledged to Paramount's U.K. office, which had just reported to him that *Sailor Beware* was a hit, that he knew "it was going to be a matter of education and an uphill fight.") Wallis and Jerry had wanted to undertake the Palladium trip at least a year before, but the *Scared Stiff* holdout had interfered. Finally, however, plans were made for Dean and Jerry to play outside the United States for the first time that June, just after *Money from Home* wrapped.

They traveled first class on the brand-new *Queen Elizabeth* (Elizabeth II had been crowned just the previous year), along with a full entourage including musicians, writers, a road manager, an accountant, and a few more hangers-on (the tickets cost thirty-two thousand dollars all told). Patti, Gary, and Ronnie made the trip with Jerry; Dean, though reconciled with Jeanne, went stag. They arrived in London on about June 10 and spent a few days sight-seeing and playing the classic Scottish golf courses. Jerry bought English suits and shirts for himself; Dean, who had won twelve thousand dollars in the ship casino on the way over, carried on a brief affair with actress Pier Angeli, whisking her away from his fellow Wallis wage slave Kirk Douglas, who was shooting Vincente Minnelli's *The Story of Three Loves* (another loan-out project) with the actress.

On June 15 they hit Glasgow along with Patti; Gary and Ronnie stayed in London with a nanny. In Scotland a small knot of adoring fans waited for Martin and Lewis's arrival—bobby-soxers chanted their names outside their hotel—and they gave a few interviews. Jerry assumed a remarkable gravity in these talks, taking time not only to bare his soul to the Scottish press but to take several pointed swipes at Wallis, the very man behind the overseas trip. In interviews in London and Glasgow, Wallis was repeatedly castigated by both comics as a poisonous influence on their careers. While Dean nodded vigorously in agreement, Jerry lambasted their producer before a string of reporters: "We keep telling him that it's far better to make $20 million over ten years than $8 over two. You can even keep more of it in the end. But that man can't see it. I suppose he's afraid one of us will break a leg or something. We were the Number One box-office attraction last year—but we won't stay that way if we do the same thing all the time. We've got three more films to make for that man. Then we'll be our own bosses."

All of these tirades were reported to Wallis in Hollywood, prompting him to send an angry telegram to Jerry at the Savoy Hotel stating, among other things, that "I have devoted twenty-five years of my life building up and achieving an enviable reputation and standing in the motion picture world and I cannot stand by silently and see you distort facts and unwittingly harm it."

But Wallis wasn't the only focal point of Jerry's strange introspection.

Maybe it was being overseas that caused him to speak as if at a distance from himself. Maybe he was a little drunk—he was never much for booze, but the British interviews were generally held during cocktail parties he and Dean threw for the press, and at least one quoted him as asking for "another one of those stale drinks." Whatever the reason, he reflected on his fame ("Success is still so new I enjoy every minute of it. Every night I pray everything will stay all right and every morning I wake up thinking I'm a lucky fella") and on his unusual partnership, hinting, even, that Dean didn't provide everything he wanted from a friend: "I'm Jewish with a theatrical background and I have to show my emotions. Dean is Italian from a tough steel town in Ohio where it's supposed to be sissy to show what you feel. So he covers it up and pretends never to be serious or nervous."

Dean, watching the spectacle, kidded to a reporter, "The boy's sick. He's having an off day." But something about the trip had struck a deep chord in Jerry. After a warm reception for their June 15 performance at the Glasgow Empire, he returned to London to prepare for the June 22 debut of Martin and Lewis at the Palladium (at seven thousand pounds for the week) in the same kind of reverently subdued mood that caught hold of him before they debuted at the Copa. "Over in Hollywood they seem to think of the Palladium as a turning point," he told a reporter. "Sort of a steppingstone to the big time."

Such a perspective may seem odd coming from a performer as popular as Jerry, but it speaks to his conception of show business as he inherited it from his father: Television was no big deal; movies weren't the real thing; the great live stages—the Palace in New York, the Palladium in London—were where the true legends made their marks. He was the most popular comedian in the United States, but he approached the stage of the hallowed London variety house that night with trepidation.

For once, his anxiety was well founded. Following a standard roster of opening acts—a chorus line, an impressionist, a knife thrower, a juggler, a couple of dancers, a British stand-up comic—Dean and Jerry did their act as they had always done to killing success back home: mugging, singing, spritzing, yukking it up with the band. They were received, according to about half of the newspaper critics on the scene, with the fits of laughter they were used to hearing at home. But as their act wound down, Jerry approached the microphone out of character, much as he did at the end of each "Colgate Comedy Hour," to offer a word of thanks.

"When we return . . ." he began.

"Never come again!" came a shout from the balcony.

Jerry stopped dead and looked up into the audience in disbelief.

"Go home, Martin and Lewis!" rang out another cry. And shouts of "Rubbish" and "A disgrace to variety" were also recorded. A torrent of boos began to rain out of the stalls, though observers couldn't agree later whether they were meant for Dean and Jerry or for the people who'd heckled them. Whichever it was, the two comics ran for the safety of their dressing room without attempting another word of gratitude.

Backstage, after agreeing that they should forgo an encore, Val Parnell assured them that they had done fine. The political atmosphere in London, he told them, was ripe with anti-Americanism. There was a great deal of sympathy among the British public for Ethel and Julius Rosenberg, who had recently been executed, and there was a lingering bitterness in the air following the visit to London of another pair of American clowns—Roy Cohn and G. David Schine, staff lawyers to Senator Joseph McCarthy. Parnell tried to calm his stars by assuring them that the reception that had so shocked them was in fact part of an orchestrated cabal. (Several weeks would pass before *Variety* would run a story proving that Parnell was right: The ringleaders of the heckling mob were "two young men who read *The Daily Worker*" and who had similarly disrupted an April Palladium performance by, of all people, Vivian Blaine.)

But Jerry couldn't be persuaded out of feeling betrayed by the audience. "We are human beings," he told a reporter, "and therefore we are hurt." It was the most stinging reception he'd been accorded since the days when he was a nervous, stammering emcee. And what hurt at least as much as the incident was the way it was covered by the press. All but ignoring the appreciative welcome the act had received from the vast majority of the house throughout the performance, the London papers concentrated on the booing, assuming it was the crowd's reaction to the show: "For twenty years, Jerry Lewis, the monkey-faced American comedian, has dreamed of playing at the Palladium," wrote the *News Chronicle*. "And last night, when he topped the bill there with his partner Dean Martin, he was booed." "A Tragedy for Two Comics," was the headline in the *Daily Mirror*. Several reviewers who made hay of the evening's strange denouement assumed that the commotion was a reaction to the content of Martin and Lewis's act, and they took it upon themselves to impute their own opinions of the act to the audience. "Theirs is the humor of village idiocy," wrote the *Mirror*, "with straws in its hair—witless and very embarrassing."

That the whole incident was politically motivated (Jerry, by his own confession, knew absolutely nothing of politics), and that much of the booing was probably meant for the hecklers themselves, didn't matter. Whatever pain the incident had inflicted on him was only worsened by the press coverage. For the remainder of the engagement, Jerry performed politely and within strict limits, never once taking an encore regardless of the reception.

When he and Dean arrived in Paris after a tour of U.S. military bases in France, they went tooth-and-nail after the British press. Speaking at lunch with Art Buchwald of the *International Herald Tribune* at the Hôtel George V, they took no care to hide their resentment. "I'm never going back to England," said

Dean (in a passage presumably sanitized for print), "on account of the British press stinks. And you can tell them I said so. The British press are a bunch of two-faced people. They tell you how much they like you to your face and what great admirers they are of yours, and then the next day you read in the paper that you stink."

Jerry ordered a lunch of "a nice roasted English reporter garnished with lots of French fried potatoes" and then complained that "they called me a gargoyle. One of the reviewers said he wasn't sure but someday he'd succumb to my ape-like qualities. Warped minds, that's all they have."

Dean, who was to return home directly after the Paris stopover, was aware of the gravity of his remarks, asking Buchwald when the story would run: "I just wanted to know when the war would start." Russell Holman of Paramount's European offices wrote directly to Jerry to caution him about any more such comments, but nobody got in touch with Dean. He sailed back to New York on the *Liberté* along with David Niven, who committed the faux pas of announcing to reporters that Dean and Jerry were courageous and accurate in their attack on the British press. Back in New York, Dean carried on with his criticism, citing the murmurs of approval he'd heard from others in Hollywood for his frank assessment of the British writers. Hal Wallis was aghast that one of his biggest stars was persistently and willfully alienating the press in one of his biggest markets. When he tried to silence Dean, the singer complained that Wallis's quickie productions were turning him and Jerry into a second-rank comedy team: "Wallis would like to put us in anything, like the way Abbott and Costello make pictures."

The American papers reacted to the episode by calling Dean and Jerry crybabies; the *San Francisco Chronicle* even ran an editorial chastising them for their petulant refusal to accept negative press. Walter Winchell chided them for "a Major Bubu: You never publicize the raps." Hedda Hopper offered advice: "The boys should have taken the reviews and made an amusing sketch about them for their TV show."

Jerry missed the whole ruckus. He and Patti toured France and Italy until mid-August. They were spotted by paparazzi on the Via Veneto and touring the Roman Forum, looking for all the world like a happy, handsome young couple. After Jerry and Patti returned to the States, Jerry and Dean played several engagements in New York, including another profitable turn at the Paramount, and then returned west to make the next York film. Eighteen months after boycotting *Scared Stiff* because it was based on an earlier film, he and Dean were producing a new version of the classic Ben Hecht screwball comedy *Nothing Sacred* (which just the year before had been transformed into an unsuccessful Broadway musical). Called *Living It Up*, it was the first of York's final trilogy of films; they would all be remakes.

■ ■ ■

The only absolutely new material being prepared for Martin and Lewis was the stuff that Simmons and Lear were writing for "The Colgate Comedy Hour," whether Dean and Jerry appreciated their contribution or not. They would, of course, tell journalists that they were funny on their own, and even Simmons agreed. "Dean and Jerry *were* funny," he said, "and they had a good relationship, but the stuff was written. That's not to say they didn't add. But we felt shitty when they'd say they didn't need writers."

Jerry was certainly not the first comedian to declare himself to be born whole cloth a comic genius, but with his phenomenal success, he began to believe it himself, and he grew testy with collaborators. As Lear recalled, "Something happens to some comedians—not just this comedian, but something happens to some funny people. They develop a kind of popish aura. Comedy is a religion, and they are the pope of that religion. And as a consequence they begin to know everything. So they become producers and directors and mavens on every subject. And that was developing in Jerry along with the rift with Dean. He knew everything that was best for Dean as well as himself."

Jerry's proprietary attitude was probably strongest toward his television work because TV was the medium in which he had the most power: When making films, he was answerable to Hal Wallis or the Paramount executives who oversaw York films; when performing live, he took pains to tread carefully around Dean and the mob-backed nightclub owners they worked for. But Dean didn't give a damn about how their TV shows were put together, and no one at NBC felt powerful enough to rein in Jerry, a legitimate movie star who deigned to appear on their network.

So Jerry didn't take advice from his writers and chums, Simmons and Lear. And both men felt it hurt his career as a comic. "He never understood the essences of Jerry Lewis," mused Lear. "He never understood what was best about him. So he accented some of the things that were most irritating. He hasn't welcomed collaboration in his life. He stopped doing that early in our career together. He would pay no attention. He just didn't require it."

Simmons, too, spoke of a great fondness for the comic gifts he'd seen in Jerry when they first knew each other, and he also felt that Jerry's increasingly imperious attitude wound up hurting his art as well as his business. "He had stopped taking advice very, very early," he reflected. "He had stopped taking advice a year into their success as a team." But Simmons saw a different reason for Jerry's eventual fortunes: "Jerry once was very funny. It isn't that Jerry changed. It's that he should've changed but didn't. Because he at sixty-six or sixty-seven years old is still the Kid. And he was the Kid through all these movies even when he wasn't the Kid. And he did not grow. When he was twenty-two years old, there was no funnier person in this world. But with each year that went on you got less from the same things. Now, you watch the progression in the 'Colgate Comedy Hours,' both in the time I was there and then after that, you see him getting older but still playing the baby. So suddenly it becomes like Harry Langdon. And Jerry did not grow, in my estimation. His nightclub act is the same. He does talk shows and they kid him about the sounds he made. Everybody who does an impersonation of Jerry Lewis does Jerry from the Fifties."

Simmons and Lear were on the scene to witness Jerry's transition from Brilliant Kid Comic to Serious Businessman Comic. When they first joined Martin and Lewis as writers, it was like joining a rock band. The four of them were all about the same age, all live wires, all full of themselves and their amazing success. "When we started to work together, it was like a fraternity house," Lear remembered. "We played pranks, they played pranks; and it was just great fun. And Jerry was absolutely a genius." Jerry would have Simmons and Lear stay at his house when they were in California, and he would come into their bedroom and start pillow fights or serve them breakfast.

Even Dean was playful with them, though not without a certain edge. "Because of the street fighting he'd done growing up, Dean knew every nerve center in everybody's body," said Simmons. "And they were both reasonably sadistic. Well, once I'm standing watching a rehearsal, and I had this fucking excruciating pain, and I had no idea who did it. I turned around and I swung—it could've been a secretary—and I hit Dean in the arm. I could've hit fifty blows, but whatever it was, I hit the right place, and his arm went absolutely dead. Dean looked at me and said, 'Boy, you're pretty strong for a writer.' I said, 'Let that be a lesson to you. Remember one thing: Don't ever fuck with Big Ed.'"

For their part, the writers were taken with their bosses and imitated them in starstruck fashion: "We never knew what loafers were until we saw them wearing loafers, so we got loafers," Simmons remembered. "Brylcreem was the other thing, all the Brylcreem in their hair. Things like that. And the cologne. Jerry used to use Aphrodisia and Dean would use Woodhue. I think they used to get the stuff by the case, or it was given to them, or whatever. And they would *use* it. Two showers, two bottles. So we decided we were gonna get cologne. Well, I was closer to Dean, so I got Woodhue, and Norman got Aphrodisia. They were appearing at the Chez Paree, and we were gonna go to the Chez Paree. We're putting on cologne, and we figure we'll do it the way they do it: It isn't just a touch of cologne, so we pour it on our necks and our faces and down in the crotch. In the cab, I say, 'Jesus Christ, something's going on!' And Norman says, 'Me too.' We burned our balls off! We go back to the hotel, we call the doctor, and for days, wherever we walked, we'd leave a little trail of dandruff. It was dead skin falling off us."

The charmed relationship that Simmons and Lear shared with Dean and Jerry soured, eventually, over money and over the question of who the truly creative parties to the Colgate show were. In November 1953 the hot young writers were awarded by the hot young comics with a new contract, a seven-year deal at $10,400 a show. It was the most money anyone had ever paid for writers in the brief history of the medium, and as such, it was news. *Variety* and *Billboard* wrote stories revealing details of the contract, and *TV Guide* published an editorial lauding the fact that television writers were now receiving their financial due. "We blew a lot of smoke up our respective asses at that time," Simmons recalled.

But just as he stole Dean's one-liners, Jerry couldn't abide this sort of thing: Only one person in the operation would be renowned for generating brilliant ideas, and it would be him. In what Ernie Glucksman took to be a practical joke or a passing whim, Jerry picked up the telephone one day and fired Simmons and Lear. Even though they were producing brilliant material for him. Even though he had just signed a long-term contract with them for all that money.

Simmons and Lear promptly sicced lawyers on Martin and Lewis, and they won their point: They would be paid $10,400 for every full-length script they submitted; they were still the principal writers of the show. For the next few months, they diligently prepared their material and submitted scripts to Martin and Lewis at the appointed time. And Jerry took each one of those scripts and tossed it into the trash without a glance. Simmons and Lear got paid, but the scripts Dean and Jerry performed were written by a new team assembled from among Jerry's friends: Danny Arnold, Harry Crane, and Arthur Phillips. The unusual (and, for Dean and Jerry, costly) flap made headlines in the trade papers, though Jerry insisted publicly that he and his writers got along fine.

The entire 1953–54 season went that way, until Simmons and Lear finally couldn't bring themselves to submit another script that would never be aired. They moved on to less hostile pastures when the season ended, taking up writing for George Gobel, a comic as distinct from Jerry in both on- and offstage demeanor as there was. At the end of that same season, Dean and Jerry's "Colgate" director, Bud Yorkin, also moved on to the Gobel show, just as weary of Jerry's ways.

The Caddy debuted that fall. It's one of their sloppier films, part quasi-autobiographical biopic, part Dean-and-Jerry domestic comedy (Dean the wayward partner, Jerry the wifely loyal pal), part silly sports film. It opens as Joe Anthony (Dean) and Harvey Miller (Jerry), a hot young act, are enjoying a monumental run at the Paramount Theater (actual footage of their own Times Square hysteria was included, fleshed out with tame re-creations). While they perform a lively stage number, "What Wouldcha Do Without Me?," Dean's just-offa-da-boat pop (Joseph Calleia) tells a reporter how Joe and Harvey teamed up.

Harvey is yet another browbeaten son, the offspring of a champion golfer. Yet unlike the man who plays him, Harvey is afraid of crowds—the film's freshest gag shows a golf ball staring up at him like a giant eye—and he quits competing in tournaments. His fiancée's wayward brother, Joe, is himself a good golfer without any phobias. Harvey eggs Joe into tournaments, serving him as caddy, tutor, manservant, surrogate mother, and Jiminy Cricket. Joe wins a club championship, then enters a pro tournament, but Harvey is too disruptive and they're run off the course. Luckily, a corpulent man who's been laughing hysterically at Harvey's antics turns out to be a theatrical agent who signs them to a lucrative show-biz contract.

Though the script doesn't bear Jerry's name, his signature is all over it. He reprises from *That's My Boy* the theme of the squelched son who finds a hero in a paternalistic peer just as Dean was a Danny whom Jerry could live with. He allows himself a full-blown production number, "The Gay Continental," in which he cavorts around a pool in a simulation of Groucho Marx doing a Noel Coward song. Inaugurating a lifelong habit of casting his sports heroes in his films, he filled the picture with great golfers—Ben Hogan, Julius Boros, Byron Nelson, Sam Snead. And through Paul Jones, the nominal producer of the York films, he hired the Paramount crew with whom he and Dean had made almost every one of their pictures: cinematographer Daniel Fapp, costume designer Edith Head, art director Hal Pereira, editor Warren Low, optical effects man Farciot Edouart.

It's one of the first films in which Jerry explicitly assumes a female role vis-à-vis Dean, cleaning and cooking for him when they play in tournaments away from home, sharing a bed with him (a joke used in almost all of their films together), fretting over him like a mother hen, dressing as a señorita opposite Dean's matador in a makeshift Spanish musical number. The final Jerryesque touch is its weirdly postmodern ending, in which the "real" Dean and Jerry follow Harvey and Joe at the Paramount and get mixed up backstage with Harvey and Joe's girls. After Donna Reed and Barbara Bates are whisked away by Joe and Harvey, "Dean" wonders aloud, "How lucky can two guys get?" and "Jerry" unctuously pats both himself and his partner on the back, responding, "Yeah, we got it real bad, ain't we Dean?" Frame-breaking devices of this sort would be trotted out at the end of some of their other York films, and they became a hallmark of Jerry's work when he came to direct himself years later.

As *The New York Times* noted in its review of *The Caddy*—and in ignorance of the extent to which Jerry had a hand in creating the film—there were fewer and fewer chances for Dean to stand alone. "Mr. Martin, for his pretty singing and his romancing, rates the usual nod," wrote a prophetic Bosley Crowther, "but Mr. Lewis is slowly taking over. Just give him a couple of more years."

It's ironic, given this, that the single most memorable thing about *The Caddy* was a song that Dean performed in it, a novelty tune written for the picture by Dean's *paisano*, Harry Warren (born Salvatore Guaragna). Warren had been selected by Jerry to write songs for Dean, but he didn't like working for Jerry. Late in life he told an interviewer, "I watch his telethon just to see if he's as crass as he used to be. He was a pain in the ass." He did, however, enjoy Dean's company and was happy to write expressly for him. Dean didn't care for the song's ridiculous lyrics at first, and he allowed Jerry to take a chorus of it with

him when it was presented in the film. But there was something undeniably
catchy in the melody, and corny or not, the lyrics had a definite hook, starting
with the opening couplet:

> *When the moon hits your eye*
> *Like a big pizza pie . . .*

"That's Amore" became Dean's breakthrough hit, rising to Number Two on the
charts and remaining on the Hit Parade for nearly five months. It was a long-
overdue success for Dean—a bit of limelight he didn't have to share with his
partner.

Dean and Jerry did a second Muscular Dystrophy telethon late that November,
as different a program from the previous one as could be imagined. Rather than
accept phoned-in pledges, the telethon called upon the services of U.S. postal
carriers, who had agreed to sacrifice their Thanksgiving holidays by making their
routes to collect MDA envelopes they'd delivered with the mail earlier that
month. Rather than running on NBC's New York affiliate, the show was broadcast nationwide by ABC, the puny third network that had nothing to lose by airing a charity show in prime time. Instead of sixteen hours, the show ran merely
two. Those two little hours were made to seem like an entire day, however, by the
show's somnabulant structure, its lack of top-flight guests, and by Jerry's endless, sober-toned repetitions of "ladies and gentlemen," the deadly refrain he'd
resurrected from his emceeing days. The desperate lifelessness of the enterprise
was captured in its attempt to simulate a real telethon: After a mere half-hour,
Dean and Jerry undid their ties and opened their shirt collars. Hard work, all that
entertaining.

The telethon had come in the midst of the production of the current York
picture, *Living It Up*, in which they had cast their old friend Janet Leigh. It was a
bowdlerized version of *Nothing Sacred*, the classic 1937 screwball comedy about
a cynical reporter who hears about a dying small-town girl whose last wish is to
visit New York. He plans a series of sensational articles around the girl, even
after he discovers that her diagnosis was mistaken and she's not fatally sick at all.
Jerry was cast in Carole Lombard's role as the girl, Leigh in Fredric March's role
as the reporter, and Dean was given the beefed-up role of Jerry's doctor and co-
conspirator. It marked the first time Jerry was cast in a role previously played by a
woman, and it underscored some of the obvious disparities between him and
Dean as personalities: Virile, handsome Dean monopolized the team's masculinity; Jerry had long played the spoiled, frightened kid in response, but now
he and his writers had found another way for him to pair off with Dean's profound maleness. (Having Jerry play a woman was a rather clever switch, in a
sense, for having him play a Jew, the inevitable sexist and even homoerotic tones

Rae, Danny, and Jerry, August 5, 1930.

Right Grandma Sarah Rothberg with her daughter Elizabeth ("Buhddie").

Below left Rae Brodsky.

Below right Rae and Danny—perhaps before their marriage (Danny has no wedding ring).

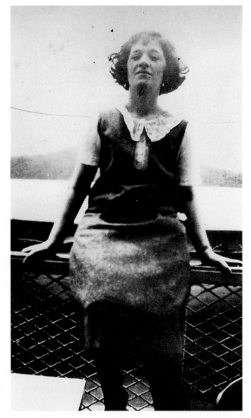

Above Performing the record act at Grossinger's—as skinny as the mike stand.

Left Pre-Greshler: The cryptic record-act promo card.

JERRY LEWIS
SATIRICAL IMPRESSIONS
IN PANTOMIMICRY

JAMES KOLL

Post-Greshler: Sleek, sophisticated, and incomprehensibly billed.

Above Three Brodsky sisters (Rae, Rose, and Buhddie, left to right) flank Bernie Weisbaum, with Jerry, Patti, Gary, Stephen Weisbaum, and Marcia Weisbaum (seated).

Below Danny and Jerry in a rare frisky mood, late 1940s.

The playboy and the putz.

Dean pitches woo with Vivian Blaine to Jerry's bemusement, 1947.

Above Hal Wallis, one of his Oscars behind him, signs Martin and Lewis, a sinecure that will win him no prizes.

Below Hometown boy makes good, 1948.

Above Making the scene in Hollywood, late 1940s.

Below The boy mogul shows off one of his dozens of scrapbooks, 1950.

Right Irving Kaye on the Paramount lot.

Below Getting into red-face makeup for *My Friend Irma Goes West*, 1949.

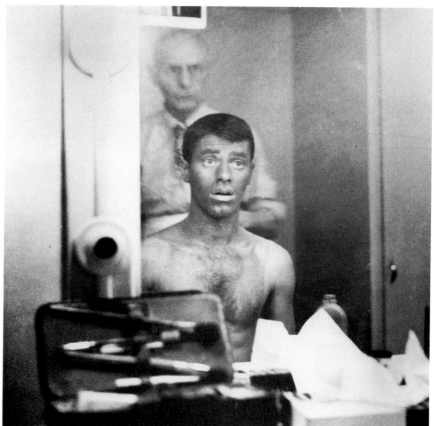

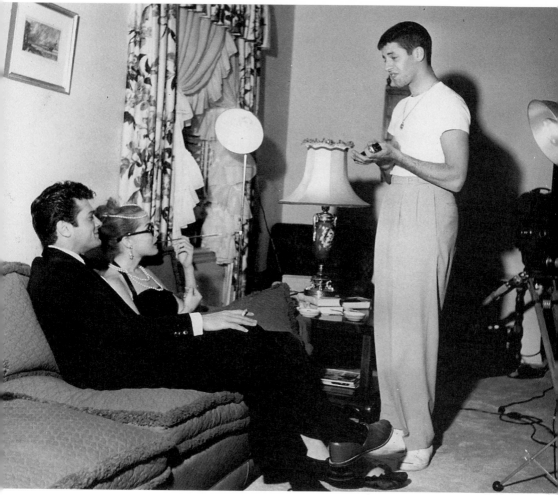

Directing Tony Curtis and Janet Leigh in the Gar-Ron film *Fairfax Avenue*.

Archive Photos

Right Jerry and Dean with Patti and Jeanne.

Below An early Martin and Lewis fund-raising effort.

HELP FIGHT MUSCULAR DYSTROPHY

Archive Photos

At the London Palladium, 1953, with bandleader Dick Stabile saving Jerry from Dean (note the Martin and Lewis caricatures on the music stands).

As Jerricho the Wonder Clown in *Three Ring Circus*

Left Posing for the United
Press the day after he held
a burglar at bay, April
1957.

Below Sonny Boys: With
Danny and Gary on NBC,
1957.

Mr. Smooth, early 1960s.

being less disturbing to Jerry than hints of anti-Semitism.) There had been a touch of this in *The Caddy*, where Jerry followed Dean around like a wife or maid, but *Living It Up* took that hint to an extreme, rewriting a romantic comedy as a story for two men.

Leigh recalled that the atmosphere on the set was akin to the mood that prevailed when she was making the Gar-Ron pictures. "They clowned around and such," she remembered, "but that was part of their charm, and they executed it very well. So it was great fun, but it was still very professional." She was aware, however, that they didn't seem to see much of each other away from the set. "There wasn't a lot of socializing with the two families," she said. "At that point, we knew Jerry better than we knew Dean. Dean and Jeannie came to the premieres and everything. We knew them and liked them. It wasn't like there was a problem. It's just that he sort of had his group and Jerry had his group and all of that. I don't know why they didn't socialize. Maybe they felt that when they were on the road together they saw enough of each other and when they were home they should sort of have their own lives."

It had, in fact, been a conscious decision. Jerry had heard from no less an authoritative source than vaudeville comics Chick Johnson and Ole Olsen that the wives ought to be kept apart from each other, to prevent jealousy and other hazards. As for Dean and Jerry, they would be successful as long as they had each other.

Right?

10.

The Wonder Clown

Of the sixteen Martin and Lewis films, only one has a legend surrounding its making—*Three Ring Circus*, their 1954 job for Hal Wallis. Every account of the production has presented it as a classic "troubled shoot," the sort of catastrophe that would today be fodder for syndicated tabloid TV shows, though not a drop of resentful ink about it was spilled in the late days of the studio era. Years after the film was made, stories circulated about Dean and Jerry feuding openly, about Jerry trying to control the direction, writing, casting, and even the music for the film, about breaches of contract, legal maneuverings, and personal rudenesses. The moneymaking show-biz beast Martin-and-Lewis was beginning its lengthy, ugly dissolution, and everyone in its vicinity was caught in the whirlpool.

What had happened?

For one thing, the two fame-starved up-and-comers who'd palled around Broadway and teamed up in Atlantic City had new ambitions that didn't necessarily coincide. Jerry's desire to make people laugh had become a desire to create. He had a yen to participate in filmmaking on a greater scale than his backyard movies afforded. And he was deliberately trying to institute a shift in his persona, to transform from a zany clown to a sentimental clown. He had, in effect, matured, and he sought to express that maturity in ways that weren't necessarily compatible with the mode of expression he'd developed alongside Dean.

As for Dean, he'd had his first important solo success—"That's Amore," which sold more than two million copies and had even been nominated for an Academy Award. Having triumphed in one more medium than his sidekick, he imagined a more languid pace for himself than the frantic one Jerry sought to maintain. He wasn't as eager to be forever in the spotlight or to be sharking after the next paycheck, especially when MCA was doing so well by them. He was wearying of Jerry's shtick and his aesthetic pretensions, his "Chaplin shit." And he was tired of the oversights and insults that came with being partner to a live-wire comic.

There had been an incident during the making of *Living It Up*, a brush-up that Jack Keller later recalled as their first falling-out. A Paramount publicist had arranged for *Look* to do a photo story about a wild dance sequence featuring Jerry and Sheree North, and the piece almost entirely omitted Dean: Even the photograph the magazine had taken of the two of them together had been published with Dean cropped out. Dean blamed Keller—who claimed to have been sick when the story was arranged—correctly suspecting that the press agent's loyalties lay more with Jerry than with him. But he knew the real source of the problem. As Jerry recalled later, "He took a very heavy load for ten years. He was the straight man. There were times they never even mentioned his fucking name in a review. Everybody talked about the kid or the monkey or the funny guy. How long do you think I could've taken that? *I* wouldn't have made ten years."

Jerry had always been susceptible to the flattery of a coterie, but now the relatively self-contained Dean was beginning to listen to people in bars, casinos, and golf course clubhouses who were urging him to forge a career of his own. Jerry would attribute these whisperings to people wishing to revenge themselves on him: "He had outside factions telling him that he's nothing. He had all these poison-droppers . . . these shit stirrers." But Dean was more ambitious than he let on. He figured he could be a sympathetic actor, too, if he was only given half the chance. He knew, though, that he'd never get that chance if his partner, who was forever taking more control of the act, kept the sweet roles for himself.

Frustrated by his increasingly marginal role in the partnership and in the films he made, Dean was the first one to bridle at the script Wallis had commissioned for *Three Ring Circus*.

The legend goes something like this: Dean and Jerry wait until the day before shooting is to begin in Phoenix to announce their displeasure with the script. They have Wallis in a bind, with the entire Clyde Beatty Circus on his payroll and a clock ticking off the very expensive minutes they have to make the picture. They tell Wallis they don't like the episodic nature of the story, in which each man has about ten minutes alone before they come together at the circus. Wallis, in an indignant fit, picks up a copy of the script, rips out the first twenty or so pages, announces, "Now you've met!" and orders them to report to Phoenix immediately.

Wallis, of all people, was responsible for the propagation of this myth—he told the story to Arthur Marx in 1973 and repeated it in his own autobiography seven years later. But he certainly knew just how wrong the account was. Wallis's file of memos, telephone and conference transcripts, telegrams, and letters concerning the production of *Three Ring Circus* was as thick as a small city's phone book. In some instances, dozens of pages of material were devoted to the intrigues and negotiations of a single day. He was put through such merry hell for so long on the film, it's no wonder that he dreamed up and stood by a pat little story about its production. The actual events were too detailed, and probably too painful, to recall.

The picture was originally called *Big Top*; like the very first film Jerry said he saw, Chaplin's *The Circus*, it was a tale of love, deceit, and redemption among circus performers. The script was written by Jerry's old friend Don McGuire after Wallis had seen *Meet Danny Wilson*, the Frank Sinatra picture of McGuire's first produced script. Wallis had called McGuire into his office and, aware of the writer's friendship with Jerry, asked if he had any ideas for a Martin and Lewis picture. McGuire answered immediately: "GIs can study lion taming under the GI Bill of Rights!" The stolid Wallis, laughing out loud at the notion of Jerry learning to tame lions, sent McGuire off to write it up.

When he got wind of the project, Jerry counseled McGuire against having Wallis as a boss. "Why do you want to work for that schmuck?" he asked. "We're not gonna work for the old bastard anymore. We're not gonna show up." McGuire told Wallis about this threat, and Wallis told him to relax. The whole thing had already been worked out with Herman Citron the previous November. Wallis had a firm start-up date set, and not even MCA could shake it loose. Not only wouldn't Dean and Jerry get paid if they threw a wrench into the proceedings, but they couldn't do their own film for York or fulfill their obligations to NBC until they'd done the work they owed him. He had them but good, and on the very first business day of 1954 he sent them legally binding start-up notices demanding that they report to work on the film on February 8.

By mid-January, however, Jerry and Herman Citron were making noise about Wallis's choice of director for the film. Wallis had tried to hire any number of important directors for the film—Billy Wilder, Vincente Minnelli, Frank Capra, Nicholas Ray, Howard Hawks, and William Wyler among many names on an ambitious A-list, with Norman Taurog and George Marshall held over from the list of old reliables—but all of them had either refused to do the film or were rejected by the Martin and Lewis camp. He finally settled on Joseph Pevney, the director of *Meet Danny Wilson*. Though Pevney was yet another working-stiff director, he was, unlike the other hack directors Wallis had hired, of Dean and Jerry's generation (born in 1920) and had a background similar to theirs: He'd sung and danced in vaudeville, in nightclubs, and on Broadway from his early teens through his mid-twenties. Recently, Jerry had sent Pevney a note expressing admiration for his comedies, even asking to work with him as an assistant. Nevertheless, when Citron got wind that Pevney was Wallis's choice for the next Martin and Lewis film, he announced, "They still don't think he is a good comedy director, and I am going on record to tell you that you are in trouble."

The trouble, however, would be over the script and not the director. Visiting

Dean and Jerry at the Plaza Hotel during an engagement at the Copacabana, Wallis pleaded with his stars individually to let him have the script revised according to everyone's best interests. Jerry originally balked at sitting down with Wallis, saying that he'd recently had a meeting with agents Citron and Lew Wasserman and attorney Joe Ross, who had "beat his brains out" and told him "in the future he was not to discuss business." But Wallis had two advantages that MCA's brass couldn't trump: He was present in New York while they sat scheming in Los Angeles, and he could call upon his off-and-on pseudopaternal bond with Jerry to gain leverage with him.

Dean and Jerry opened at the Copa on January 21, with Wallis, Joe Hazen, and their wives watching from a ringside table (Jerry introduced them to the crowd). Afterward, the two couples went to the stars' suite at an adjoining hotel to congratulate them. Wallis used the opportunity to invite Jerry to lunch at 21. As he recalled in a memo, "Jerry got very nostalgic about our being there and recalled that we had discovered them there a few years ago, etc. We spoke about the luncheon date the next day, and I asked Dean if he wanted to join us, and Jerry kiddingly said to Dean, 'You better let me go with him alone. I can get more out of him.'"

At that lunch, Jerry listened as Wallis walked him through the script, which was then undergoing revision. Jerry made various suggestions for improvements, writing them out on a waiter's notepad, and Wallis held on to these. Jerry asked Wallis if he could sit in when the picture was cut, and Wallis agreed. After nearly three hours they parted, with Jerry telling Wallis "he was very enthusiastic and was even going to talk to his TV writers, some of whom were with him, to work up additional ideas and pieces of business." Wallis spent the next few days looking into other properties he might acquire for Dean and Jerry—*The Pajama Game* and *Guys and Dolls* among them—and then returned to Los Angeles convinced he could get to work on the picture.

Back home, he ran into an MCA buzzsaw: Citron was complaining loudly about the script on Jerry's behalf, just days after Wallis and Jerry had agreed to work together to repair it. Feeling betrayed and used, Wallis accused MCA of bad faith: "I made it very clear to Citron that whenever I was with Jerry, usually out of the city and away from the influence of members of the MCA organization, I had no problems with him and had a fine working arrangement, but that as soon as they involved themselves in it I then had difficulties."

He was blaming the agents, but really he should have blamed the client. Jerry simply didn't have the gumption to rebuff Wallis personally: He was willing to hold out on him, sabotage his schedules and budgets, and have his agents and lawyers attack the producer like pit bulls, but face-to-face he was chummy and compliant. Wallis rightly took this as hypocrisy and was frank with Citron about how annoyed he was: "This is a goddamn good script, and this boy who has been in the business for three years isn't going to tell me that this is a lousy script! I've been in it twenty-five years, and I've made some goddamn good pictures, and I'm not going to be upset because he says it's a lousy script!"

As the start-up date for the film approached, Dean began to make *his* objections known through Lew Wasserman. Whereas Jerry was mostly concerned with rewriting the comic elements in the script, Dean felt that his character was too much of a heel and that he and Jerry spent too much of the picture apart from one another. Wallis tried to quell this storm on a couple of accounts: that the script was being rewritten per Jerry's suggestions and that Dean's character wasn't essentially different from the one he'd played in recent Martin and Lewis films (including *The Caddy* and *Living It Up*—both York films). Again he seemed to have won his point, and he awaited the start of production of his $2 million project with nervously bated breath.

Come the big day, neither Dean nor Jerry showed. Citron and the Martin and Lewis brain trust put the case to the producer: Dean was upset with the script, even though it incorporated changes suggested by him and Jerry; Jerry wouldn't do a film his partner wouldn't do. Wallis had eighty-five people and a fifteen-car circus train waiting in Phoenix. He hit the roof: "I don't like having a gun held to my head forcing me to meet Martin and Lewis's requirements!"

It became a battle of nerves, and Wallis became more jittery as the meter ran. He agreed to a script revision meeting, provided Dean and Jerry would show up for wardrobe and color tests the next day. At 8 P.M. Wallis, McGuire, Pevney, Citron, Wallis's assistant Paul Nathan, and Dean and Jerry's TV writers, Arthur Phillips and Harry Crane, all met in Wallis's office. Phillips was particularly eager, offering advice in nearly every instance in which Wallis wanted to cut or alter something McGuire had written. McGuire played along respectfully, occasionally defending his script. After several hours, Pevney and the three writers retired to work into the night and meet with Dean and Jerry the next day to find out what changes would fly.

McGuire was so humiliated by the process that he asked out loud if *any* part of the script was still safe, but he was assured that the problem was not so much his material as the deteriorating relationship of the stars. "Jerry's problem is Dean," Citron told him. "If he loses Dean for a while, it takes him a long time to get him back. . . . Hal knows it better than anybody."

Once again, when they were due at the studio the next morning, Dean and Jerry failed to report. At noon they appeared in Wallis's office with Citron, Crane and Phillips, Wallis's lawyer Jack Saper, and Judge John B. Millikan, a friend of Wallis's. At this conference—the site of Wallis's apocryphal tearing-up of the script?—Jerry confessed that he had nurtured the script along with only his own interests in mind. He had accepted the script thus far because his character (who, unique among his roles thus far, was named Jerry) became a clown and was the center of a cloyingly sentimental finale. Now he admitted to seeing only his side of things: "I am enough of a ham that when you told me this business with the elephants and the other sequences that I could only see what wonderful things I could do, and when reading the script I overlooked the point concerning Dean and I being together." Dean was less subtle: As Wallis recalled in a memo written immediately after the meeting, "He said that he doesn't want to play a cheat, and doesn't know what he is doing in the picture, that Huntz Hall could play the part."

After scolding both of his stars for their "belligerent attitude," Wallis brokered a compromise. They would do their wardrobe, color, and vocal tests, and Jerry would work with Crane and Phillips on the script. They all shook hands.

Dean refused to have anything to do with the revision of the script, telling Citron that he was "laying his confidence" in Jerry and their writers. After another long night, the rewrite was completed to Jerry's satisfaction. Wallis then met with Dean, who announced that "this was exactly what he wanted, that he was enthusiastic and ready to start the picture." When Wallis asked him why he hadn't voiced his displeasure with the original script sooner and saved everybody all of the hassle, Dean answered, "You know I never have much to say. I let Jerry do the talking." And he and his spokesman/partner went off to Phoenix and fought like longtime rivals.

As Jerry remembered it in his autobiography, "During the filming, Dean kept blowing his top at me and everyone else, saying he was fed up to the ears playing a stooge. It got pretty hairy. There were days when I thought Dean would ditch the whole package. It almost happened. One morning he arrived an hour late on the set and stared daggers at me. 'Anytime you want to call it quits, just let me know.'"

The tension between the two stars was only part of the trouble on an absurdly off-kilter set. Dean and Jerry had announced to Pevney that they wouldn't do an iota more than what was required of them; Jerry actually refused to say, "Thank you, sir," at the end of a scene because it wasn't in the script. Another time, Dean showed up at three in the afternoon, did one scene, and left, saying, "That's all you're gonna get from me." Costar Zsa Zsa Gabor wouldn't stay with the rest of the key members of the cast and crew at the plush Arizona Biltmore, putting herself up at a nearby dude ranch—not to keep out of the way of Dean and Jerry's fighting, but to facilitate a private liaison with her boyfriend, international playboy Porfirio Rubirosa, who showed up with his own airplane and a small knot of reporters. Composer Walter Scharf, upon reviewing rushes, noticed that "Dean was *always* in the background. Jerry was *always* in the foreground." When he told Wallis about it, he counseled the producer that "I had no doubt whatever that Dean wouldn't take much more of it." Wallis replied, "As long as they don't kill each other, I'll be happy."

To Kathleen Freeman, a comedienne with a small role in the picture, the friction between the stars was ominously palpable. "It was difficult," she recalled. "It's always tough when you're around people that aren't getting along very well. That's not a happy state of affairs. The crew were friends of mine, so it wasn't so terrible on me. They would come over and say, 'The boys are having trouble,' so that I wouldn't think I had done something incorrect. Which was very dear of them to do. And the minute I heard that, I just relaxed and let whatever was going to happen happen. I figured, 'Well, there's nothing I can do to help 'em.' Their troubles were so large, they weren't paying attention to anyone else."

Wallis was well aware of Dean's rising animosity toward his partner. One morning he ran into Jerry outside the Biltmore as the comedian was unloading film and cameras from the trunk of his car. After some opening pleasantries, Wallis recalled, Jerry "went into a long discourse on how serious things had become between him and Dean, that he had just had a quarrel on the set, that the situation between them was becoming impossible, that he had been fighting it as long as he could, that he was going up to phone his attorney, Joe Ross, to see what could be done about it, etc." Wallis asked if he could be of any help, but Jerry told him that "the quarrel was not about me, that it went deeper than that and that he was at the end of his rope, hadn't been sleeping, had been worrying, etc."

Finally, Jerry's spirit was broken. He called Joe Pevney later that day to say that "they were coming in the following morning and that they were going to pitch in and do a good job." Then he called Wallis to say "that he had had a long talk with Dean that they were now straightened out and that everything was going to be fine."

When the Phoenix location work was done and the crew returned to Los Angeles to finish the picture, Dean and Jerry were called in to MCA's offices for a reconciliation. Lew Wasserman and Joe Ross laid out their commitments to Wallis, to NBC, to various club owners, and to companies whose products they endorsed. In effect, they were told, there was too much money riding on them for anyone to allow their spat to harm the act. They would have to find a way to work amicably together. They agreed to behave better.

The filming continued without incident in L.A., but Wallis was out forty thousand dollars in reshooting costs for the scenes Dean and Jerry had ruined. Just as he had when they held out on *Scared Stiff*, he suspected that the problems he'd had with Martin and Lewis had actually been an attempt by the comics to wrest even more control over their films from him, and he gathered evidence to make his case to Joe Hazen. He cited all of Dean and Jerry's instances of truculence and refusals to cooperate; he recalled bumping into Dean at the hotel bar and hearing him complain: "Jerry and I agree that we are going to do certain things, and then he crosses me up." And he recalled another heartfelt talk with Jerry at the orphanage where the film's finale was shot: "Jerry went into great detail about his personal relationship with Dean, his feelings about him, his thinking that it would be best for him to go on alone in his career, the fact that NBC had flown someone out from New York to discuss television shows with him if the team broke up, etc. He then told me that Dean was burned up at him in Phoenix because he had spoken to me and because he had decided to pitch in and go to work. When Dean confronted him with this, according to Jerry, Jerry said, 'Sure, I switched. I found out that I was doing the wrong thing and that *we had been badly advised*, and when you learn a thing like this, you don't keep doing wrong—you try to correct it.'"

Once again, Wallis sensed the black hand of MCA behind the sabotage, but he finally had his film in the can, and he figured the hell with it. The picture was guaranteed box office, and he was able to wrap it in time to take his summer art-collecting trip to Europe. He could drown his sorrows in acquisition.

During this period of friction with his adored partner, Jerry had nowhere to turn with his sorrow and aggravation but to his family. Rather than seeking advice or a shoulder to cry on, though, he used them as an outlet for his anger. He expressed his frustration with Dean in hostility toward Patti. "It really got me," he recalled. "I had a double whammy because I was taking it all out on her." Patti couldn't stand it, and she actually packed and left. "We had, I think, a one-week separation," Jerry said.

Patti recalled the problem differently, saying that she left home not because of Jerry's difficulties with Dean but because of the way he had turned their home into a clubhouse for fawning hangers-on. "I've been sitting around for ten years waiting for you to grow up," she snapped, "and I've waited long enough!" Complaining about his retinue of "yes-men and hungry actors," she remembered, "I was fed up. I picked up the kids and went to Lake Arrowhead to get away. He came running after me. I never intended leaving, I just wanted to scare him. That's the closest I ever came. I walked off the job for two days."

Patti's action came near the holidays, and Jerry couldn't, of course, stand the thought of being left alone: It was too much like his parents' constant departures in his boyhood. His bond with Dean eroding, he panicked at the thought that his marriage, one of the very few relationships in his life that had nothing to do with business, might crumble. He even began drinking a little. Some of his retinue tried to convince him he'd be better off single, but that advice only drove him back toward his family. "It shook Jerry when I left," Patti said, "and finally he learned who his true friends were and he understood why I left. He learned he couldn't buy friendship." "I made an ass out of myself," Jerry admitted after it was all over.

Patti was still trying to find a way to deal with the stress on her marriage when she received another jolt. In April 1954 she and her brother, Joseph, who was living in Southern California with his family, lost their mother. Mary Calonico had been a source of stability in the Lewis household—she had actually taught Jerry to crochet!—and Jerry took her passing hard. Solace came from an unlikely source: Jeannie and Dean made themselves available to Patti and Jerry throughout the wake and funeral and the period of grieving just after. After the graveside ceremony, family members and friends met up at the house on Amalfi Drive, and Dean and Jerry went off into a room together for a talk. When they emerged, it seemed that their relationship had been patched up. Dean eventually recanted his criticisms of *Three Ring Circus*—he had recently told a magazine that "there was no sense in me being in that picture at all"—and the pair were able to see through the slate of commitments ahead of them. Patti, deprived of her own partner by Jerry's tendency to favor his relationship with Dean over his marriage, briefly saw a therapist to work through her grief.

That summer Dean and Jerry took what was for them a long break from filming—seven months—and they worked on smaller projects: Colgate shows, their first recordings as a team since "The Money Song," live appearances in Los Angeles, New York, and Atlantic City, where they premiered *Living It Up* as the capstone to Martin-Lewis Day (a bench along the boardwalk was fitted with a plaque commemorating the genesis of the act on the site).

As usual, the trade reviews were somewhat kinder than those in the mainstream press. *Variety*, which almost never balked at anything they did, recognized Martin and Lewis vehicles as the purely commercial projects that they were, and called the picture "94 minutes of film fun that has been expertly packaged for customer enjoyment." *The New York Times*, inexplicably calling the film Dean and Jerry's sixth (it was their eleventh), seemed to wish that the source material had been left untouched and said cryptically that the comics "behave like the blandest of cliff-dwellers."

By August they were back at home, planning the next York project—a remake of *The Major and the Minor*, the picture with which Billy Wilder debuted as a director in 1942. In that film, Ginger Rogers played a down-on-her-luck showgirl who disguised herself as a kid to get a discount train fare back home; she wound up spending time at a girls' school and falling for a naïve serviceman (Ray Milland). In writer Sidney Sheldon's remake, titled *You're Never Too Young*, Jerry, forced to pass himself off as a kid after witnessing a crime, would hide in a boarding school to save his skin. Once again, Jerry was cast in a role originally played by a woman; the tendency obviously didn't bother him, since York was making the film.

That month they were due to play two weeks at Ciro's. Jerry had initiated the deal, assuring Herman Hover, the club's proprietor, that he could book Martin and Lewis at a dirt-cheap price; he told MCA that Hover, his close personal friend, was to be given special consideration, and the engagement was booked for August 19. At the very last minute, though, Jerry called in sick, leaving Hover with no act to present to an audience that had paid fifty dollars a pop as a cover. Dean went gallantly onstage, and a variety of other performers helped fill the hole beside the singer: Alan King, Ethel Merman, Tony Martin (Martin and Martin, they billed themselves). On August 30 Jerry took an ad in *The Hollywood Reporter* claiming that a high fever had prevented him from attending his own opening and thanking his partner, "who showed everyone what a true showman looks like." (Years later, Hover remembered spitefully, "Between the two, everybody liked Dean, and practically nobody liked Jerry.")

In October they went to Lake Arrowhead to film *You're Never Too Young*. Diana Lynn, who as a teenager had appeared in the original, was in the cast; she had metamorphosed into a stage actress since the *My Friend Irma* pictures, though she did appear as Ronald Reagan's love interest in *Bedtime for Bonzo*. Norman Taurog was once again directing, and such pros as Nina Foch and Raymond Burr had been cast in key roles. It was a quiet shoot, especially compared with the nightmare they'd just been through. Jerry had a bout with the flu, and he was hit on the head with a water ski while filming the climactic chase scene (Dean, according to press accounts, rescued him from the water). The animosities between the pair still bubbled under the surface, though: When Taurog took Dean aside one day to chastise him for reporting late to the set, the actor bristled, "Why the hell should I come in on time? There's not a damn thing for me to do." But Dean would never show his emotions to a whole crew, and he had no intimates to speak of; only those close to Jerry knew how angry Dean had grown. To them, he expressed his hostility with iciness: "You'd pass him and you'd get a freeze," recalled Irving Kaye.

Despite the crumbling relations between its stars, despite the turmoil on the set, *Three Ring Circus* opened on Christmas Day to some of the best reviews of their film career, most of them heaping praise on Jerry. John L. Scott in the *Los Angeles Times* wrote that Jerry's "subdued" performance was his best since *That's My Boy*. *The Hollywood Reporter*'s Jack Moffitt went further, invoking the name of Chaplin and saying that Jerry "has learned to blend pathos with his slapstick, until he has begun to show the potentialities that can make a great actor and a great star."

The reviewers were right to focus on Jerry: He'd stolen the picture, not only performing brilliantly (in his clown sequences, at the very least) but almost smothering Dean out of it. It's nearly an hour before Dean gets to sing his first song, which the writers had contrived to have him croon to a menagerie of spooning animals. He never, in fact, gets to sing to a woman, though he's intimate with two in the film. And he's a heel, just as he'd complained—installing gambling tables on the circus midway to help business and shunning a benefit the rest of the performers agree to appear in.

Jerry, on the other hand, is everywhere. Five times he gets to don clown makeup—thick white lips, a five-o'clock shadow, bulbous red nose, and heavy eyebrows—and cavort, sometimes in set pieces and once, with genuine inspiration, alone in a circus tent while dreaming of glory. He does block comedy bits with elephants, lions, a bearded lady (Elsa Lanchester, vivid and vital amid Pevney's uninspired cast of real circus players), a dunk tank, a tightrope, a human cannonball routine. It's like a one-man show, save that every now and again Jerry turns to Dean and declares eternal palhood. The only times the partners seem to be together come when they bump into one another on the midway and ask each other questions. If this is the way the script read after Jerry and the writers regrouped to do a better job of integrating Dean, one can only imagine with suspicion the earlier drafts.

Jerry's performance is uneven—he slips out of character during several speeches—but at least in clown makeup, he achieves a consistent personage. "Jerricho the Wonder Clown"—as Jerry's character is known in his clown guise (and as the film was renamed when it was briefly rereleased in the late 1960s)—is a nice, concise emblem for his creator. He joins up with the other clowns when one of their ranks falls ill and, to the resentment of the drunken star of the troop, Puffo (Gene Sheldon), steals the crowd's affection and applause. Where Jerry Hotchkiss botches everything he attempts, to the dismay of all those around him, Jerricho's inadvertent mishaps amuse everyone—another instance of Jerry's theory that the performance of a sincere amateur can be more affecting than the work of a seasoned but heartless pro.

The Dean-and-Jerry conflict comes to an uncomfortable head in the finale, in which the circus plays a benefit at an orphanage. Dean doesn't want to spare any time from the circus's busy travel schedule to do the date, and Jerry is heartbroken that his pal could be so cold. When Dean insists that Jerry simply doesn't understand business, Jerry retorts, "That's the story of your life. Nobody ever understood you. But I understand you now. . . . You ain't nice anymore." (It's impossible to ignore the sensation that you're watching documentary footage of the feuding partners and not a fictional scene.) He goes off with the other performers to play the benefit, greedy Dean be damned.

At the orphanage, Jerry's capers have the kids in the palm of his hand—all, that is, except for one crippled girl in the front row whose face never registers anything but deep sorrow. Jerry sits beside the girl and violates the clown's canon by speaking aloud and all but begging her to laugh or smile, to no avail. It's all too much for good-hearted Jerricho; he sheds a crocodile tear. This simply slays the despondent child: "Look, he's crying! The clown's crying," she guffaws, suddenly, sharply, unrealistically. All those assembled applaud this metamorphosis, and Jerry returns to the ring to the congratulations of his peers. Still, he's wan: His best pal isn't here to share the moment. Suddenly, to the strains of "Hey, Punchinello," Dean drives onto the scene in a car filled with clowns (had these people also shunned the benefit until now?). The partners link arms and sing together to the enthralled audience of children.

Peace, goodwill, and fortune were theirs once again.

■ ■ ■

At around this time, with his relationship with his hero-partner at an ebb, Jerry discovered a new father figure for himself, a new colleague who truly appreciated his art. Frank Tashlin was a bearish man—six-foot-three, about 220 pounds— with a blue-collar aspect: cropped hair, bristly mustache, black, no-nonsense eye-glass frames. "He has the air," wrote Peter Bogdanovich after meeting him in 1961, "of a person with an infinite amount of patience who is duped by nothing."

Throughout his life, Tashlin cheekily sabotaged attempts to establish his bi-ography, but his career was unique enough for journalists to refer to it whenever they wrote about him. He was, by his own unverified claim, born in 1913 in Weehawken, New Jersey (site today of the western mouth of the Lincoln Tunnel, five miles or so from Irvington). An only child, he claimed to have had a troubled relationship with his father, who moved the family to Astoria, Queens, during Tashlin's school years. Sometime in his midteens he dropped out of school to work, and held a variety of low-wage jobs—among them a tenure as office boy at Max and Dave Fleisher's Out of the Inkwell Studios. Tashlin was a gifted drafts-man—his cartoons and drawings had appeared in school publications—and in 1930 he landed a job as an artist with Van Buren Studios, which produced the "Aesop's Film Fables" animated series.

He became something of a local celebrity; newspapers ran articles about the gifted boy cartoonist. In 1933 he caught the eye of Leon Schlesinger, a Warner Brothers animation producer. At Schlesinger's prompting, Tashlin moved out to Los Angeles and spent several months working on "Looney Tunes" and "Merry Melodies" shorts. At the same time, he began publishing a comic strip in the *Los Angeles Times*; he eventually left Warner Brothers when he and Schlesinger quarreled over the amount of time he was putting in on this outside project.

Tashlin had always had an eye for dynamic, quirky humor, and he moved from Warner Brothers to a job at the venerable house of slapstick, Hal Roach Studios, where he wrote gags for low-budget comedies for a few months. Throughout the remainder of the 1930s and early '40s, he put in stints at a string of Hollywood animation studios, working for Ub Iwerks, Screen Gems, Colum-bia, and Disney; he even passed two more brief tenures with Schlesinger. By the mid-1940s, though, Tashlin was burnt out on cartoons. He was no longer a kid phenom who dazzled the press with his precocity, but a thirty-year-old vagabond animator who had trouble keeping a job. Harkening back to his Hal Roach days, he began seeking work in live-action films. He made contributions to dozens of films at a number of studios in the next few years, and did a lot of script doctor-ing and gag writing for such comedians as Bob Hope, Red Skelton, and the Marx Brothers; he is said to have written gags for Harpo Marx in A *Night in Casablanca*, including a famous bit involving a collapsing wall.

Tashlin was finally asked to write whole screenplays, and in 1951 he was al-lowed to direct Hope in a few sequences of Paramount's *The Lemon Drop Kid*. It was a successful debut, and Tashlin was soon directing comedies at RKO and Paramount: *Son of Paleface* with Hope, *Marry Me Again* with Robert Cummings and Marie ("Irma") Wilson, *Susan Slept Here* with Dick Powell and Debbie Reynolds. He became known for his way with musical numbers and for outrageous gags that were clearly reminiscent of his work as a cartoonist and animator: Hope sharing a bed with a horse in *Son of Paleface*, an Oscar statuette narrating the action in the Hollywood-themed *Susan Slept Here*.

It was this last film that drew Hal Wallis's eye to Tashlin. He had been developing a script for Dean and Jerry that would cash in on the current national mania for violent comic books and the call for censorship that accompanied the craze. The film was based on a story called "Rock-a-Bye Baby" by Norman Lessing and Michael Davidson, and Wallis had Herbert Baker and Hal Kantor, two old Paramount comedy hands, working on revisions. Don McGuire spent a few weeks with the script as well, and then Tashlin got a crack at it, but Wallis wasn't sure about making the project Dean and Jerry's next film.

His opinion was swayed, however, by Tashlin's enthusiasm for the material. Tashlin "is absolutely overboard" on the film, Paul Nathan told Wallis. "It is right down his alley, and he promises you he can get one hell of a picture for Martin and Lewis." Nathan supervised Tashlin's script, and a month later he wrote to Wallis to say, "The more I see of him and his work the more I think that it's going to be our next picture." Casting began in January 1955, and the film, retitled *Artists and Models*, began shooting toward the end of February.

In January, while playing at the Sands, Jerry got a horrible shock. His cousin Judy, the thirty-year-old daughter of Rose and Harry Katz, was murdered on the streets of Irvington. She was mugged on her way home from the grocery store on a Friday evening; her attacker beat her over the head with a pipe or tire iron, and she died almost immediately of head injuries. Jerry offered a ten-thousand-dollar reward for anyone who could help authorities arrest and convict the killer, and he flew back to New Jersey for the funeral, arranging for family members in California to return home as well.

The mere possibility that the big hometown movie star was coming to Irvington brought crowds out to the synagogue where the funeral was held. "I almost couldn't get in myself," recalled Judy's brother, Marshall Katz. Jerry had to return to work in Vegas immediately, but he did whatever he could to help assuage his relatives' grief. "I brought her mother and her father and her sister and her brother and my mom and dad all out to the Sands to try to help them forget," he remembered. "And they had a wonderful two-week vacation. I made sure they had a great time. But it was tough. It was tough."

Jerry had remembered Judy affectionately from childhood as someone who'd always had a kind word for him when he'd been dumped on her family's doorstep by Danny and Rae. "She was such a fan. She was so supportive. She believed that everything that I did as a kid was perfect," he said. "The family thought I was a fucking lunatic and that I should have a keeper. But Judy was always saying, 'Jerry, you've got something going within you.' And I'd try things out for her, I'd audition for her. I was always in Judy's room. She was really my best friend. She didn't treat me like the rest of the family did. The family treated me like the fucking village idiot."

Jerry kept raising the reward he offered to help catch the man who'd killed Judy, but nothing ever came of it. The horror of the crime would stay with him over the years: "I've had fantasies of this young Slavic-looking guy coming up to me and saying, 'I never liked you, I never liked your work, I never liked anything about you, and I want you to know that I killed your cousin Judy.' I have fantasies about that." It was an exceedingly odd combination of empathy for his lost cousin and selfish focus on his career, but it was sincere. He would reflect on the loss in genuinely heartfelt terms: "When a human being has touched your soul or is part of something that's important in your life, that's tough, boy."

Jerry returned to Hollywood with Dean in February to begin work on *Artists and Models*. At the outset, at least, Wallis was spared the nightmares that had beset him on *Three Ring Circus*. Much of the credit for this relative calm was due to Tashlin, who immediately hit it off with Jerry. It was a perfect combination of temperaments: the manic comic and the stolid cartoonist. Jerry became an instrument Tashlin could deploy to bring outrageous conceits to life. He used Jerry's physicality—the gangly limbs, the elastic face, the sound-effects voice—to wring out the sort of gags he could have constructed previously only with animation cels. Tashlin furthermore showed good managerial judgment in allowing Jerry to consult with him about the mechanics of filmmaking, giving the aspiring director a sense that he was more a collaborator than a mere actor. Their budding rapport was a counterpoint to the undercurrent of animosity between Jerry and Dean, though the partners behaved civilly together throughout the shoot.

There were some bumps in the production. Jerry protested about a dance number he was asked to perform with Shirley MacLaine, insisting that some ideas of his be incorporated into Charlie O'Curran's choreography. As Nathan told Wallis, "He has some cute bits of business, but it really doesn't change the number at all. He just wanted to have something to say." Tashlin, for his part, was having trouble with Dorothy Malone, who had been cast opposite Dean. Wallis didn't care for the way his director was shooting his female lead—he objected specifically to a scene in which she wore dark glasses—and he asked Nathan to investigate the matter. Tashlin had an explanation: He said he was trying to hide "the big bags she was showing under her eyes." But the problem, according to Nathan, ran deeper: "He feels this girl hasn't an ounce of sex, and he is trying to build some up for her in cuteness."

More seriously, Jerry and Wallis butted heads toward the middle of the production. Early on, things were pleasant enough. Jerry wrote Wallis one of his sweetie-pie letters asking for a print of *Money from Home* for his private film collection, ending it, "Don't you think this would make a wonderful gift to such a wonderful Jew as I? THE HAPPY MONSTER."

Jerry got his film, and he and Dean had behaved so well that they got permission from Wallis to fly to New York during production to be fêted at the Friars Golden Jubilee Dinner at the Waldorf-Astoria. But within a few weeks, Jerry and Wallis were fighting openly on the set. It was hardly their first set-to, but Jerry was feeling increasingly powerful as a filmmaker in his own right, and he wasn't as willing as he used to be to write apologies to the boss. "We got into a really heavy argument," he recalled. "I can't remember what the argument was, but I wouldn't back down, and he wouldn't back down. And everybody in his own office told him that I was 100 percent right. And we were dealing with something that had to do with a morality issue. . . . I wrote him a letter that night, 'cause the issue hung. I hadn't won the point yet. I wrote him a letter, and whatever I said in the letter was a restatement of my position. But in the end of the letter, I wrote, 'P.S., Please don't confuse my gratitude with my principles.' I told him, 'You're an immoral prick. You're pushing human beings around.'"

There was another flare-up soon after; Jerry went AWOL halfway through a day's work because of Wallis's imperious attitude toward the crew: "I left the set because he yelled at a fucking hairdresser in such a manner. I never heard a human being treated like that. I left the fucking set. I knew I was gonna cost him money. They couldn't find me for three hours. I went to a fucking café somewhere on Melrose and just sat there and had coffee just to fuck him for three hours' worth of money. The joy in my heart!"

The disappearance was typical of a larger pattern of uncooperative behavior on Jerry's part. He left the set for hours on end—even when Dean stayed nearby practicing his golf swing and joking with crew members—and did what he could to make Wallis's life difficult in little ways. His rebellion had its intended effect. When Herman Citron called Wallis late in the shoot to try to get Dean and Jerry some rehearsal time for a Colgate broadcast, the producer couldn't believe his ears. He spilled his heart to the agent, telling him just how taxing Jerry had become. "There was one day they waited on the set—they turned the lights off . . . they sat there for an hour and a half while he was having a meeting about his record business with Mannie Sachs in his dressing room," he revealed, adding that no one could get the star to cooperate: "They sent down for him . . . they sent the assistant . . . Tashlin went down . . . everybody. And he says: 'I'll be there when I get through.'"

Wallis was more than weary with this sort of behavior. "This is not new," he said. "I—what the hell—I gave it up. I told you. I wasn't going to eat myself up on this picture and that's maybe why—I thought I had told you about it. But this has been going on all through the picture. . . . I would say that he is responsible, at least, for four to five days being behind schedule." But when Citron indicated that he'd bring Wallis's concerns up with Jerry, the producer balked: "Don't tell him we're complaining . . . tell him that if he wants to do his TV show and wants to get time off he's got to be on the job."

The exchange revealed how subtly power had shifted away from Wallis and the film studios in general toward Citron and the talent agencies, of which MCA was the most potent. Wallis took great pains not to offend Citron—or even Jerry, for that matter—and the agent merely heard the producer's complaints with cursory interest; he would do nothing to lessen his clients' interests, nor did he have to. For his part, Wallis had been put through such hell on *Three Ring Circus* that he was loath to indicate anything more than mild displeasure to the Martin and Lewis camp, and he was even willing to suspend his production for a few days at a time to keep the peace. Patience paid off in the long run: The film wrapped at the start of May, only a few days behind schedule.

Dean and Jerry did a "Colgate Comedy Hour" the following week. Their next York film—*Pardners*, a remake of the Bing Crosby–Martha Raye western *Rhythm on the Range*—was scheduled for an autumn-winter shoot and was being rewritten by Sidney Sheldon. On May 9 Dean and Jerry boarded the Golden State Limited at Union Station for a seventeen-day, fourteen-city club date tour. For two weeks they traveled together as they had in the old days—no kids, no wives, no bitterness, no suspicions: Kansas City, Omaha, Des Moines, Toledo, Philly, the Boston Garden, Chicago Stadium.

It was another big moneymaking spree, and it was the last such trip they would take.

11

The Other Shoe

There'd been Dean Martin Day in Steubenville, and there'd been Martin-Lewis Day in Atlantic City, but there'd never been a Jerry Lewis Day—in part because there was really no hometown for Jerry to return to, in part because wherever they went, wherever they performed, Jerry turned the world into his playpen, the calendar into a series of Jerry Lewis Days. Nevertheless, when Uncle Charlie Brown called from the Catskills and offered to host a gala premiere of *You're Never Too Young* at his hotel, Jerry's first reaction was to leap at it. He would be offered a chance to play the local-boy-made-good in the one place he truly felt nostalgic for, the Borscht Belt. Brown's Hotel would pick up the whole bill—transportation, rooms, meals, booze, entertainment, a newly constructed Martin and Lewis Playhouse in which to hold the premiere. But aside from what York and Paramount would save on promotional expenses, the offer conjured an irresistible image in Jerry's mind: "the sight of me returning home as a sort of hometown hero, the big international celebrity and King Shit of the Catskills."

Jerry was still reeling from this vision of himself a few days later when he broached the idea at a meeting with Wallis, Paul Jones, Norman Taurog, and Jack Keller. The assembled mavens were delighted at the prospect of so much free publicity. It was a go.

Only one person hadn't signed on to Jerry's big homecoming: his partner.

The day after the meeting, Jerry approached Dean and described the plan. Dean seethed. "You should have consulted me first," he said.

"I'm consulting you now."

Dean let out a resigned breath. "Actually, Jerry, I really don't care where we hold it."

Given Dean's characteristic indifference to matters of business and protocol, Jerry had no reason to believe this was anything but a yes, so plans for the elaborate event went into motion. They would do "The Colgate Comedy Hour" show on June 5, 1955, then leave by rail for New York two days later. After a night in Manhattan, they would drive up to the Catskills for the Friday night premiere, reprising their old Atlantic City act—two solos followed by the team.

The night before their scheduled departure, Dean's bodyguard-procurer Mack "Killer" Gray, a former boxing manager who had worked as George Raft's factotum for twenty years, approached Jerry with astonishing news: "Your partner isn't making the trip."

Jerry, still vulnerable to anything resembling a slight from Dean, assumed it was a joke. "Are you putting me on?"

The coffin-faced Gray was hardly joking. "I'm relaying this straight from Dean's mouth. He said he's tired. He's going to take Jeanne on a vacation to Hawaii. What else can I tell you?"

It was the most vivid indication yet of Dean's animosity, and Dean handled it like a Machiavellian CEO, waiting until the last minute, when no appeal could be heard, and then sending a henchman to do the job. The very notion of people fawning over Jerry, or even himself, rubbed Dean the wrong way. He was lacking in sentiment almost to the same degree that Jerry was overloaded with it. "The main difference between them," recalled a friend, "was that Dean couldn't show the love and respect for other people that Jerry could, and that worried Jerry. And it must have worried Dean, too. In Jerry's case the worry came out warm; in Dean's it came out cold."

Furthermore, Dean was beginning to show his resentment at Jerry's increasingly authoritarian approach to material for the team. Dean had always ceded business decisions to his partner out of a genuine lack of interest, but time commitments were another thing entirely. For Dean to be dragged up to the Catskills as if by order would be the ultimate sign of the monkey leading the organ grinder around by the leash. And since he truly didn't care where or how the premiere of *You're Never Too Young* was held, he flouted his indifference by heading west while Jerry and the others went east. It was a hell of an insult: A man allegedly too tired to go to the Catskills was instead going three thousand miles in the opposite direction.

Dean had some business to take care of in Los Angeles before he went to Hawaii, though. He met with Herman Citron to discuss solo work on TV. Then he spoke about it with columnist Earl Wilson: "I want a little TV show of my own, where I can sing more than two songs in an hour. I'm about ten years older than the boy. He wants to direct. He loves work. So maybe he can direct and I can sing." On the matter of the junket, he cut deeper: "Outside of back east, who knows about the Catskills?"

Jerry was devastated. He now had three miserable days of train travel ahead of him, three days to simmer in tight quarters with a family to whom he couldn't express his hurt or anger, three days to prepare to face a battery of reporters and photographers who would lick their chops at the whiff of bad blood between the boys. He and his family were photographed in Los Angeles boarding the train; when they arrived at Penn Station on June 9, a hoard of ravenous writers met them. All Jerry could manage was "no comment." The next day, he drove north to Brown's past scores of embarrassing billboards promoting the gala weekend with Martin and Lewis. As the car turned into the driveway and he caught sight of Charlie and Lillian Brown standing in wait for their bubbelah, Jerry grasped Patti's hand in childlike panic: "Momma, what am I going to tell them?"

He did what he had always done when he felt hurt, confused, or betrayed: He retreated into his shtick, making it through the disaster by playing the nutty kid to the hilt—dressing as a bellhop, a busboy, a waiter, yukking it up with guests and press alike, acting as if no real-life worries could dent his naïve armor. He dedicated the playhouse, introduced the film, did his best to seem carefree. Backstage, though, he agonized to bandleader Herb Sherry: "Herb, I'm going downstairs to announce that this film is the last time Martin and Lewis will ever appear together."

The weekend was capped with a gala Saturday-night performance featuring Alan King, various dance orchestras, Patti (singing "He's Funny That Way" to her husband), and Dean and Jerry's old pal Sonny King doing a brief twosome with Jerry that harkened back to their salad days (and suggested to some in the audience that Jerry was auditioning a new partner).

Finally, Jerry cracked. As the show ended very late that night, he spoke frankly to the press, literally crying tears of confusion and frustration. "Maybe I'm using the wrong words," he said to the hushed room, "but I don't know the right ones. Maybe the lawyers wouldn't want me to say anything at all. But you've been wonderful. You know we have a cross to bear up here, and I want to thank you all for saving me embarrassment by not asking questions I couldn't answer. I want you to know I appreciate your wonderful cooperation during this weekend."

The well-oiled audience of reporters and Catskills loyalists were deeply moved by the star's open emotionalism: Jerry's words "brought down the house with one of the most sustained mittings ever heard on a nitery floor," observed *Variety*'s Hy Hollinger. Another reporter noted in *Screen Life* that Jerry's "deeply sympathetic and grateful audience rose and honored him with a standing ovation for ten ear-splitting minutes, with most of us surreptitiously wiping away our own tears."

But after the emotion had passed, the reporters were left pondering Jerry's words. *Lawyers?* The bad blood had spilled into the open. The press, even *Newsweek* and *The New York Times*, made hay of it: The most popular act in the nation was having a public spat. And there was more to their sensational reports than even the scandalmongers could have known: After the Brown's Hotel disaster, Martin and Lewis didn't speak to one another for two months.

When Jerry returned to California from the Catskills, he went immediately to Lew Wasserman's office at MCA and asked him to begin to unravel the act. Wasserman wasn't eager to put an end to a cash cow that was bringing MCA millions a year. He tried to broker a truce between the boys.

"What about Dean?" he asked, stalling for time.

"We don't talk to each other," Jerry told him. "Just get me out of my commitments, and I'll be happy." Demanding that Wasserman inform both Dean and Paramount of his decision to sever the act, Jerry went home to await the fallout.

For his part, Dean once again turned to the press to air his grievances. "To me, this isn't a love affair," he told a reporter. "This is big business. I think it's ridiculous for the boy to brush aside such beautiful contracts." Once again, "the boy." If Jerry could invoke lawyers and agents, Dean could pull the rank of maturity: Who in the country wouldn't believe that Jerry wasn't acting like a petulant child if his keeper and best pal said so?

A peace summit was finally held in the office of Paramount vice president Y. Frank Freeman, the first Dean and Jerry had seen of each other since before the Catskills junket. In the presence of Freeman, Wasserman, Wallis, and their attorney, Joe Ross, the pair had their future laid out before them: Wallis still had them under contract and wanted more films out of them, NBC was expecting more episodes of "The Colgate Comedy Hour," etc., etc. It was a reprise of the previous year's sit-down: No one gave a damn how they got along. Their signatures were on the contracts, and the people who held those contracts wanted satisfaction. They'd have to find some way to carry on, period.

An unhappy ceasefire was reached. Jack Keller put a shine on the alleged reconciliation for the press. The boys were no longer feuding. The Colgate show and the next York film—entitled, ironically, *Pardners*—would proceed as planned. The news actually made headlines.

Jerry, though, was a wreck. The public may have been happy that the feud was only temporary, but Jerry, who'd been Dean's partner for his entire adult life, was left to confront the fact that his partnership, the act that was based on the friendship of two unlikely buddies, was a sham, a lie to both the public and himself. "In order to maintain the Martin-Lewis relationship," he reflected years later, "I went through a ten-year period of lies. The whole situation was against my nature, but I didn't know that. When you're between the ages of twenty and thirty, you think that whatever you're doing is right. But between the ages of twenty and thirty is a period that men in medicine have finally found a title for. It's called *stupid*."

Dean, who had just turned thirty-eight, was thick-skinned enough to fake anything: Insufferable as Jerry may have become, he was good for business. A split career—some solo stuff and an occasional Martin and Lewis gig—wouldn't have been onerous to him. Jerry, however, comported himself as the soul of sincerity. The idea of clowning with somebody he couldn't get along with made him feel like a bad person. Financially, he was still tied to Dean; emotionally, though, he began to cut himself off from his hero-partner and cauterize the wound that had been opened by Dean's coolness.

For the first time in their years together, Jerry didn't rebound from one of Dean's slights like a happy puppy willing to let all bygones slide. He brooded: "I didn't help fix it. I could've fixed it. But I knew it was over. What was I gonna fix? You gonna give aspirin to a cancer patient? That was it. Period. I knew it was over."

Years later, he compared it to a divorce: "If you go home tonight and find your wife in bed with a man, are you gonna say, 'Well, I think I understand'? Are you gonna be rational? What do you think will happen to you? What do you think? Have you ever thought about that? You think you're gonna be able to turn the other cheek and be a wonderful human being? 'Well, it's for the children'? Bullshit. God willing, it doesn't happen to you, but what do you think you're gonna do? Everything you think you're gonna do, you're not gonna go near what you think. 'Cause until the time happens, you haven't the faintest idea where your head's gonna be.

"Well, we're talking about the same thing. This relationship was very strong. When you scar a relationship, you're never gonna have it right again. Let's assume that you forgive your wife. Whatta you think you've got? You've got staying up at night waiting for the other fucking shoe to fall. So that's the scar on a relationship. Once a relationship is scarred, everything you do is a façade. All the cheer and the happiness and the giggling is bullshit. You can only do that without scars. Then it's real. So I knew in my gut this could not be retrieved."

As he dazedly confronted his ruptured career, Jerry had some sources of consolation at home. He and Patti had conceived another child after nine exploratory operations. "The doctor agreed to always cut across the same incision," Jerry revealed. "And because of a small video camera, the problem was detected, and the doctor said we'd have another child within a year." The baby was due in late winter. And Danny Lewis was giving his son career advice that, for the first time, wasn't self-promoting or resentful. As Jerry recalled, Danny was among the first to counsel him to split up the act while it was still a success. "'You hit the galaxy,'" Jerry recalled Danny's telling him, "'and you gotta know that a shooting star doesn't stay in place.' He says, 'You've been the greatest shooting star in the history of show business. Recognize that it tails off. But don't wait until it's gone out of the sky and then you decide, "Well, let's do something." Uh-uh. You gotta do it while the crest is there.'

"My dad said, 'What's the worst thing for you in boxing?' And the worst thing for me has always been to watch a guy get knocked through the ropes. It's such a fucking indignity. How did Joe Louis wind up? He went that one fight too many, and he got knocked through the fucking ropes. This great icon, this great champion of champions, went one fight too many."

But what *was* one fight too many for Martin and Lewis? Dean seemed satisfied with a primitive form of partnership—civil interactions during rehearsals and performances. Jerry needed the combined thrill of mass adulation and mutual affection. It was over as far as he was concerned; there were still commitments, and there was all that money to make, but he had ideas he wanted to realize, and he was increasingly willing to see them through on his own.

Hal Wallis didn't care if Dean and Jerry spat blood at each other off the set, as long as they showed up on time and knew their lines. *Artists and Models* looked like yet another hit, and he was keeping the pipeline filled with potential projects for the team, whose services he still had under contract through 1959. His immediate needs were being met by "Route 66," a script being reworked by Tashlin from an original story by Erna Lazarus. (Wallis had originally purchased it years earlier as a vehicle for Shirley Booth and Humphrey Bogart.)

Wallis had other projects in mind as well. He had tried to get the rights to *The Pajama Game*, the hit Broadway musical about a labor dispute at a garment factory, but he had been told by the producers of the play that "they did not regard Martin and Lewis as any plus factor in the situation and that, as a matter of fact, there seemed to be considerable reservation as to whether or not they would be willing to sell the property if Martin and Lewis were to appear in it." He tried to get the rights to *Teahouse of the August Moon*, but producer Dore Schary (like Jerry, a son of Jewish Newark) was "not interested in having Martin and Lewis in it—period." He even considered a summer stock production that Bette Davis had discovered on vacation in Maine—*Fore and Aft*, a musical farce set among pirates—but passed on it after Paul Nathan told him "It reminds me of *Abbott and Costello Meet Captain Kidd*, which, unfortunately, I just happened to see."

As he made his plans, Wallis bore in mind the friction between his two stars, and with a premonition of the team's possible demise, he decided the 1957 Martin and Lewis vehicle should be *The Martin and Lewis Story*. Paul Nathan registered the title and began compiling notes on the lives of the boys. It was a cynically astute move: Since Jerry's public breakdown at Brown's Hotel, news about the team had been more and more frequent in the press. Their Colgate scripts even made joking reference to their troubles—when Dean repeatedly dunked Jerry in a tank of water during a parody of a quiz show, the half-drowned comic shouted, "Haven't you read the papers? The feud's over!" Wallis recognized they had become a subject for scandalmongering in the way Hollywood figures with far more outrageous personal lives had long been, and he figured he could lure people into theaters with a biographical film that promised personal revelations with a veneer of happy collegiality.

But in fact, the pair was far from collegial. Though they were staying together to make money, they still had massive financial problems stemming, years after the fact, from their split with Abbey Greshler. During rehearsals for *Artists and Models* they had taken advances against their salaries from Wallis: $5,000 for Dean, $15,000 for Jerry. And in the summer of 1955, they found themselves in a jam with the IRS. The government had come looking for $650,000, and there was no way they could get that sort of money out of Wallis. Jerry turned to Paramount production chief Y. Frank Freeman. Freeman didn't ask for details; he wrote out a check against his personal bank account and handed it over to Jerry, who promised to pay it back in sixty days. In September, a few hours early, Jerry returned the money to Freeman. The transaction had taken place without Dean's knowledge or, for that matter, his interest. It was literally business as usual.

Later that autumn, though, Freeman asked a favor. He would be chairing a benefit for underprivileged children on November 10 at the Shrine Auditorium, and he wanted to know if Dean and Jerry would be willing to perform. Jerry said yes, once again neglecting to get his partner's approval in advance. As the day of the show approached, Jerry reminded Dean several times of their obligation and of how Freeman had bailed them out so generously just two months earlier. Dean seemed to agree at all times: "For Chrissakes, Jerry, I know how important this is. You got it." On the afternoon of the tenth, however, Jerry couldn't find him. He sent Dean a note reminding him of the appointment, and he sent copies to Jeanne Martin, Mack Gray, and the Lakeside Country Club. Jerry showed up at the Shrine on time and, when it became clear that Dean wasn't going to turn up, did twenty solo minutes, apologized for his partner's absence, and left the stage as quickly as he could. It was like the finale of *Three Ring Circus*, only in real life and without "Hey, Punchinello."

Freeman, ever the gentleman, let Jerry off the hook, but Jerry had once again been stabbed in the heart by his partner. He confronted Dean, who absolutely brushed him off: "Nobody told me there was going to be a benefit." If Jerry was going to make commitments without consulting him, then Dean was going to treat those commitments the same way he had his marriage vows or the friendships of men whose wives he'd screwed on the sly in Steubenville. He was through acting as if he cared. And it certainly meant nothing to him if Jerry got hurt by his actions. If Jerry had declared the partnership dead in his own mind, Dean acted like it had never even existed. Jerry liked to brag about how he could shut his heart against people, but he was underprepared to win a battle of cold shoulders against Dean.

Dean and Jerry shot *Pardners* that winter in Phoenix and Hollywood. It was an honest-to-God Western, with songs by Jimmy Van Heusen and Sammy Cahn. There was a big show-stopping finale—the two stars linked arms and sang together, "You and me, we'll be the greatest pardners, buddies, and pals!" The film, with Norman Taurog directing again, became the most expensive York production yet: Bad weather in Phoenix washed out many costly days, and Jerry demanded shooting time for elaborate scenes of his antics—including a square dance sequence and a scene in which he tore up a trail camp, neither of which made the final cut. When it was all over, it was a $2.6 million picture, which meant whatever profit it might see wouldn't be very impressive. The fact was, though they had freedom when working for York, Martin and Lewis did better financially working for Wallis.

That December, after Colgate-Palmolive decided it no longer wanted to sponsor "The Colgate Comedy Hour," NBC offered Dean and Jerry $7.5 million a year for the next five years for a minimum of four shows annually—a sign of the series' continuing popularity. When *Artists and Models* opened that Christmas season, however, it got hammered in both the trades and the mainstream press. With at least two films a year since 1949, Martin and Lewis had worn their critics past the point of acceptance, to weariness and even anger. "Almost anybody might have written at least as good a script," wrote Bosley Crowther in *The New York Times*; even kid-gloved *Variety* carped that the film "overdoes specialty situation material almost to the point of no laugh return."

The pity of these notices is that Tashlin's is easily the best direction Dean and Jerry ever had, and the film is, in the main, one of the best they ever made—certainly one of the most vivid and memorable. The very opening credits are startling—curvy, live models (Tashlin can't resist randy focus on the female figure, even if he jokes about it) pose beside easels while Dean sings the title song—and the initial sequence is drenched in wild colors: Dean and Jerry, two billboard painters, spill buckets of yellow and red on their bosses below. The whole film is charged with visual energy that no other Martin and Lewis film remotely approaches. Tashlin surrounds his stars with an amazing number of American cultural signifiers—advertising, television, astrology, the military, comic books, bohemians, wholesome youth groups, the Cold War, cosmetics, espionage, "The Honeymooners," *Rear Window, An American in Paris*—turning the whole of civilized modernity into a kind of dream world with Martin and Lewis at its center.

This time out, Dean and Jerry are Rick and Eugene, childhood buddies from "Steubendale" (the Paramount censors wouldn't let them use Steubenville, since the script refers to Dean's having to leave home to avoid a couple of shotgun weddings) who have come to Greenwich Village to become, respectively, a painter and a children's book writer. They can't hold on to jobs or girls, and to make matters worse, Eugene is addicted to violent, blood-and-guts comic books—then all the rage in real life—and is given to shouting out the lurid contents of his nightmares. All of this comes together when Rick gets a job drawing comic books and uses Eugene's outbursts to provide his narratives.

The picture is brimming with outrageous gags to match Jerry's excesses. Tashlin's roots in animation—and his ear for the American vernacular—are evident in a scene involving a neighbor lady Jerry inadvertently awakens with his middle-of-the-night yowling. Dean doesn't even believe the woman exists outside of Jerry's feverish dreams—"You're flippin' your butch," he tells him—and he peeks out the door to calm his buddy's nerves. We hear a smashing sound and a splash, and Dean reenters the apartment with a hot water bottle busted around his head like a cheap straw hat. In typical Tashlin fashion, it's a joke that could only happen in just this impossible way.

Tashlin also has fun with his supporting players; as if to catch up with Jerry, everyone becomes a caricature—even Dean crosses his eyes in exaggerated comic frustration—and the effect is to make Jerry look normal and believable.

Of course, there are the usual limits to Jerry's ability to inhabit a character. There's the ever-present jewelry—a wedding band on the left hand, an onyx pinky ring on the right. And, perhaps as an outward sign of his anguish over the troubles with Dean, he's puffy in the belly and face; the absurdly gaunt marionette of a few years earlier, pushing thirty, is carrying an extra twenty or thirty pounds. Still, Tashlin alone of his directors has the sensibility to put his mugging to the service of the story and not the actor's ego. Jerry gets to overdo it, but always at an appropriate moment—imitating an already exaggerated Eddie Mayehoff, enduring a pummeling at the hands of Shirley MacLaine, succumbing to the effects of knockout drops—and Tashlin's camera never lingers too long. He seems in tune with the world around him, although he does confess to a TV panel investigating the influence of comic books that "I'm a little retarded." Most surprisingly, cast opposite the similarly limber, frantic MacLaine, he shows a touch of comic leading man. They made a promising pair (Wallis knew as much, but MacLaine was pregnant when he cast his next—and last—Martin and Lewis film, and the two never performed together again).

Just as he makes Jerry seem possible, Tashlin pulls off a clever and jam-packed final act, including a Dean and Jerry duet and an inventive free-for-all fight (suits of armor are thrown at the villains and appear to walk down the stairs). In the final frames, Tashlin magically transforms the costumes of Dean, Jerry, MacLaine, and Dorothy Malone into wedding attire; though it's a physically impossible transformation, it's handled in fluent rhythm and has a kind of poetic truth. *Artists and Models* is a Martin and Lewis film all right, but it contains the seeds of more than just high jinks, and it remains the capstone of their work together.

Ignoring, as usual, the critics and their carping, Wallis liked Tashlin's work (and the box office for the film) enough to let him develop the Erna Lazarus screenplay, but he hadn't yet settled on it for certain. Jerry, however, was wildly keen on Tashlin and his script. Paul Nathan reported to Wallis that Jerry asked, "Please don't break us up with Tashlin," and then said "he would kiss my fanny" for a chance to do "Route 66," which Tashlin had described to him.

The script still roughly followed Lazarus's original story, but Shirley Booth and Humphrey Bogart would never have entered anyone's mind had they read Tashlin's version first. Rather than following a down-on-her-luck ex-chorus girl and a con man as they made their way west, Tashlin's revised script was about a con man (guess who?) and a starstruck dope (guess who?) making their way to Hollywood in a car they each won half of (one honestly, one crookedly) in a raffle. Lazarus objected to the revisions on several grounds, even threatening a lawsuit. The final script, though largely rewritten, would bear her name alone as a result—such was the prestige of a Hal Wallis production that she was willing to fight for credit even though the work wasn't, for the most part, hers.

On Washington's Birthday, February 22, 1956, Patti gave birth to Scott Anthony Lewis—eight pounds, thirteen ounces—at St. John's Hospital in Santa Monica. She was helped through the delivery, her first in twelve years, by Dr. Blake Watson. Jerry had been hoping for a girl—"We've got several thousand dollars worth of girl's clothes and not a thing for a boy," he told the press—but he was actually very proud. He was just shy of his thirtieth birthday. Years later, he would refer to Scotty as "his first son as a man."

The new daddy was feeling his oats. He had been asked to host the Emmy Awards broadcast by the Academy of Television Arts and Sciences, but when the nominations were announced and he and Dean were ignored, he was livid. He called ATAS president Don De Vore and chewed him out while a startled *New York Post* reporter sat nearby and listened. What good, after all, was power if the whole world didn't know you could wield it?

Hal Wallis finally decided to shoot Tashlin's revision of "Route 66." Retitling it *Hollywood or Bust*, he scheduled production for April 15, with preproduction duties for the stars to begin on March 7. Normally, there would only be a week between preproduction and the actual shoot, but Dean and Jerry had asked Wallis for two weeks' leave to play Las Vegas (they were booked into the Sands, where their old pal Jack Entratter had come out west from the Copa to run things). Reluctantly, knowing how hard it was to hold them to commitments without letting other engagements intervene, Wallis agreed to the unusual arrangement. Predictably, he lived to regret it. Dean and Jerry never showed for wardrobe tests on March 7—as Wallis wrote to Joe Hazen, "this despite the agreement on which the ink is not yet dry."

The next day, after calls from their lawyer, the stars appeared. Jerry called Wallis to apologize, but the producer had reached his absolute limit with them. He wrote to his partner: "This is the way it usually works out. We finally get what we are entitled to after calling agents, lawyers, finding the boys wherever they may be, and going through a torturous hell every time."

He felt he had only three options left to him: (1) Cut a deal with Paramount to allow the studio to make the remaining Martin and Lewis films, leaving himself with some sort of stake in them, (2) sell the contract outright to another producer or studio, or (3) shut down the picture at the next sign of intransigence from Martin and Lewis and let his lawyers fight it out. He concluded the letter with a heartfelt gesture: "The fact remains that there isn't enough money in the world that makes it attractive enough for me to go through the torture of making these pictures. There is no personal satisfaction and too much wear and tear on my constitution is involved in making these things. I don't want to make any more Martin and Lewis pictures."

The poor, exhausted man: How could he know that the worst was yet to come?

Erna Lazarus was the first to get wind of it. She was standing on the sound stage near the start of the shoot. Jerry, who made a point of becoming friendly with the crew on all of his films, was talking with a grip. "This is nothing against you or to do with you," he confided, "but I intend to make it as difficult as possible for everyone connected with this picture." Jerry was going to revenge himself on Dean and perhaps also on Wallis, and he didn't care who got sucked into the mêlée (he might have done as much on *Pardners,* which went into production just after Dean's no-show at the Shrine, but that was a York picture, and Jerry considered those projects his personal creations). Even Frank Tashlin, Jerry's new mentor, wouldn't be spared; Jerry became a spiteful, one-man guerrilla campaign against the picture, against Wallis, and against Martin and Lewis.

Wallis had put Paul Nathan in charge of the day-to-day operations of the picture, and Nathan's memos from the set provide a vivid account of Jerry's insubordination. There was the Battle of the Dog, for instance. Jerry's traveling companion in the film was a Great Dane named Mr. Bascom, around whom several comic set pieces (and even a romantic plot line) had been written. Jerry, however, decided to make an issue over the dog's presence in the film; even if it required an extensive rewrite, he wanted the dog out. Tashlin, who'd written the dog into the script to begin with, naturally objected. As Nathan told Wallis just three days into the picture, "Jerry is violent about the dog and about Tashlin, and Frank thinks we must do something to keep the peace. . . . I can't believe the dog can be this much of a threat to Jerry's throne." Tashlin had chosen his own strategy for dealing with the stars: "Frank told me he is going to stay out of the middle of this project—come what may. He is going to shoot the script exactly as it is, without any temperament from anybody."

Jerry finally lost the fight—Mr. Bascom was, in fact, one of the more memorable things in the completed picture—but there were other occasions to needle his colleagues. Just a few days after the scrap over the dog, Slapsie Maxie Rosenbloom had a bit part in the picture, and Jerry prolonged the former prizefighter's work on the film by ad-libbing obscenities during every take and persistently engaging in a mocking imitation of a punch-drunk pug. Rosenbloom had the maturity to ignore Jerry's cry for attention, but Nathan realized Jerry wouldn't stop unless something was done.

"We have a major problem and I promised myself to keep calm on this picture, but I think this has to be ironed out immediately," he wrote to Wallis. "When you see the new dailies on *Hollywood or Bust* you will realize that Jerry Lewis is not playing the part and is really terrible." He reported that assistant director Buddy Coleman and Tashlin himself claimed that Jerry didn't know the lines and kept the crew working on the scene endlessly. Tashlin, in fact, had reported that at least one actor—Rosenbloom—would've been off the payroll already if Jerry had cooperated. Instead, however, Jerry had made life hell for everyone, stalking the set and muttering, according to Tashlin, "'That scene is shit.'" Nathan concluded by laying the worst case out for his boss: "Tashlin apparently has no control over this fellow. I hate to take such a gloomy attitude, but unless we straighten it out right now, the whole picture is going to end up as nothing."

Despite warnings from all around him, however, Jerry continued to sabotage the production. One scene took place in front of a movie theater; Jerry's character was to list all of the theaters he regularly attended, but Jerry insisted on changing all the theater names—a minor matter, except that Paramount's legal department had already cleared all the names in advance with any theater owners whose businesses happened to share the names in the script. Jerry's ad-lib, which he changed from take to take, forced the legal department to repeat the laborious process all over again. As Nathan told Wallis, "It is a pain in the ass for everyone concerned." He added that Bob Richman, the man in charge of obtaining clearances for the studio, "who never has anything to say, said this scene sounded like an insane man reading, and he can't believe anybody could ever lose a character the way Jerry did." (Eventually, the material was simply cut from the picture.)

The whole series of obnoxious disruptions had been aimed at Dean, but Dean had already stopped caring about what Jerry did, and it was the innocent bystanders—the cast, the crew, Tashlin, Wallis, and Nathan—who suffered most from Jerry's behavior. Finally, Tashlin had seen enough. One day midway through the shoot, he got the impression that Jerry was about to launch into another disruptive fit. He stamped it out immediately.

"I want you off the set," he announced.

Jerry thought it was a joke: "Ho ho."

"I mean it, Jerry—off! You're a discourteous, obnoxious prick."

The entire sound stage watched as Jerry flushed with shame. He tried to apologize. "Hey, Tish, whoa—calm down. Where did you get the right . . . ?"

"Jerry, as director of this picture, I order you to leave. Go. Get your ass out of here and don't come back."

No one had spoken to him so roughly in years. He slunk out of the studio and went home. Later that night he called Tashlin and apologized in earnest, promising not to disrupt the production any further. Tashlin patiently agreed to let him return to the set the next morning.

As they said good night, Jerry added a final note of gratitude: "Tish . . . thanks."

"For what?"

"I don't know, maybe for saving my life."

There was a dose of melodrama in that statement, but there was some truth in it as well. Tashlin had managed to get Jerry to turn his behavior around—though he confessed to Nathan that "it has not been easy or fun for him, and at the end of the day he is so beat he can't stand it."

Jerry's anger toward his partner and his circumstances still festered within him. Not that he said as much to Dean; in fact, according to Jerry, the two didn't speak a civil word to each other apart from their dialogue throughout the production of the film. It was an intolerable working environment, but Jerry was determined not to crack: "We're good actors, we're good performers, he's a good director, we're professional people. It's that simple. You're paid a lot of fucking money to show up every day. It's very simple. You just do it." But the pain of the production was so great it never left him. "I'll never see it," he said of the film decades later, the hurtful memories still quick to leap to his mind.

On Wednesday, May 18, 1956, he emceed a Screen Actors Guild testimonial dinner for Jean Hersholt, the quintessential Hollywood philanthropist. According to Louella Parsons, who was in attendance, "Jerry covered himself with glory" that night. Even though he was out of character, she said, "he was never funnier or better." But when he got home that night, he felt terrible: nauseated, dizzy, with a gripping sensation in his chest. Patti took one look at him and was shocked: "I'm calling Dr. Levy."

She rushed him over to the doctor's office, where it became increasingly clear that he had had a heart attack or something very close to one. Levy immediately sent for an ambulance to take Jerry to Cedar-Sinai Hospital, where he ran a series of cardiac tests. It hadn't been as bad as it looked—a murmur or a flutter rather than something more severe—but it was clearly a signal that Jerry was endangering himself with his anger. Levy ordered Jerry to stay in the hospital for a few days of tests and relaxation. And he had some advice for him: As Jerry recalled, Levy said, "'I'm gonna write you a prescription: Do a single.' He says, 'You're gonna die.' He says, 'This is just your warning, but you're gonna die.' He saw the emotional stress. I mean, it showed up on the instruments, in my blood workup."

He lay in the hospital contemplating the inevitable: The only thing he had left of his partnership with Dean was bile. He would have to sever the relationship and start a new career.

Danny Lewis came to visit his son in the hospital. He found him inside a plastic tent, attached to wires and machines and intravenous tubes.

"What happened to you?"

Jerry was so happy to see his father that his eyes clouded with tears. "Nothing," he said. "I'm taking a vacation."

Danny came closer as if to share an intimacy. Instead, he delivered an accusation: "Do you know what you're doing to your mother?"

Appropriately, Jerry turned away from the stinging question. He feigned sleep—he was weak enough for the ruse to work. Danny left, and neither he nor Rae visited the hospital again before Jerry was released on May 21.

Soon afterward, still at work on *Hollywood or Bust,* Jerry summoned up the courage to talk to his partner and see if he could heal the breach between them. He tiptoed over to where Dean was biding his time between setups and said, "You know, it's a hell of a thing. All I can think of is that what we do is not very important. Any two guys could've done it. But even the best of them wouldn't have had what made us as big as we are."

Dean stared at him. "Yeah? What is it?"

"Well, I think it's the love we still have for one another."

Dean didn't buy it for a minute. He thought for a moment, studying his shoes, then looked up and delivered the *baccia di morte:* "You can talk about love all you want. To me, you're nothing but a dollar sign."

It was each man at his worst: Jerry mawkish and pompous and begging for affection; Dean callous and dismissive and curt. It pushed Jerry over the limit. He went home and told Patti he was quitting the act, that no one would talk him out of it. She more than anyone knew the psychological and physical burden the strain had put on him: He'd been visiting a psychiatrist sporadically for the past year. She said nothing. She was probably relieved.

There were loose ends still: Don McGuire had written a new screenplay for them, a buddy story based on Jerry's fascination with the myth of Damon and Pythias, the classic best buddies. Jerry would forever compare his and Dean's relationship to the bond shared by the two warriors who exchanged places in prison so that one might go free. Various people in his circle—Jack Keller, Ernie Glucksman, McGuire—claimed over the years to have told Jerry the story first. Now he had come up with a parody of a juvenile delinquent picture, in which he would play a nebbishy street kid named Sidney Pythias who is accidentally mistaken for a hood, and Dean would be Mike Damon, a cop who befriends Sidney in hopes of reforming him. Dean was disgusted at the thought of appearing on screen in a police uniform, and told Jerry as much. That ended *that* collaboration.

There was a press conference promoting *Pardners* on June 15 at a ranch near Newhall. Jerry, Keller, and all the Paramount people were there, along with more than two hundred members of the press. Dean called in sick, two hours late. Just a week earlier, he had celebrated his birthday with his wife and some friends at a swank restaurant and hadn't thought to invite Jerry and Patti. He didn't care enough to put an end to the partnership, but he wouldn't lift a finger to hide his disgust with it, either.

Jerry took his case to Wasserman, Wallis, Freeman, the people at NBC, and all the lawyers. He wanted out: Renegotiate the contracts; to hell with the money; out. It hit the press on June 18: Martin and Lewis were through. "This break sounds so final," wrote Louella Parsons, "that I have to believe what both Dean and Jerry tell me."

The divorce of Martin and Lewis was more than a financial matter, although it was in fact a monumental financial matter. There were several substantial contracts to reckon with: Wallis, York, NBC, endorsements. The public showed no signs of tiring of the act, despite all of Wallis's fears that they would overexpose themselves: They hadn't had a Top Ten box-office hit since 1952 (when both *Sailor Beware* and *Jumping Jacks* had achieved that distinction), but their films and TV broadcasts were reliably popular and profitable. Nevertheless, the money the pair could anticipate earning wasn't that important to Jerry: Everyone around him assured him he would do well without Dean. It was honestly for him a matter of principle and comfort. Whatever it cost—at various times he estimated the unrealized earning potential of Martin and Lewis to be between $20 million and $41 million—he was dissolving the act.

"I was heartbroken," Jerry recalled. "I knew it was over. There was no question about that. I knew we were teetering on it being over. And that was killing me. This was my baby I was watching die. You mustn't forget that. It wasn't just two men. It was my baby. I breathed life into it. I put thirty-two hours a day into it."

Part of the heartbreak was rooted in uncertainty: Once they had split, what would happen? The kid who'd met Dean Martin on a Broadway corner, and clowned with him at the Havana-Madrid, and teamed up with him in Atlantic City, hadn't before that moment had an ounce of appreciable commercial success. With his partner, he had quite literally conquered the entertainment world. But would anyone want him alone? They hadn't, after all, before Dean. "It's pretty tough riding the crest of the wave and figure you're gonna drown in four days," Jerry recalled. "It's terrible. Who knows if the audience was gonna accept me by myself?"

And there was another worry, one that gave the lie to the affection he still harbored in a hidden corner of his heart: "Who knows if the audience is gonna accept *him* by himself? The most important thing that happened was that he did well. Because my doctor said to me, 'Your biggest problem has got nothing to do with you. You've got all the talent in the world. They're not gonna take your talent away. Your problem is if he fails. If he fails, you'll go under.' And he was right. If he failed, I *would* go under. Because of my love for him and my feelings for what we had. I knew in my heart I was gonna be okay. I was more concerned with his doing well—because I broke it up, I was responsible for it ending. And you carry a heavy load with that kind of guilt."

Financial arrangements were worked out. Paramount released Dean and Jerry from their agreement to produce films as a team through York. Wallis, with greed and spite and no small modicum of revenge, only gave them leave for a single film each; if they wanted to continue to make films separately, they would have to pay him $1.5 million for the three films they owed him plus a percentage of their profits from the last two films they'd made for him. NBC also played hardball: The $7.5 million they were to get annually as a pair was cut down to $5 million; for that sum, York would produce thirty-four one-hour specials, seventeen with each man as a solo, over the span of the next five years. And *The Delicate Delinquent*, as McGuire's Damon-and-Pythias screenplay had come to be called, would be produced for York, with another actor in the cop role, by Jerry himself.

There were some dates left to fulfill—ten days in Atlantic City to premiere *Pardners*, a Muscular Dystrophy telethon at Carnegie Hall, two weeks at the Copa. Coincidentally, the Copa engagement would span the last week of July—exactly ten years after their first show together at the 500 Club. It would make a perfect swan song. Jerry proposed the plan to Dean: "I said, 'Let's finish it. Let's make the Copa our last thing together, and let's go out with fucking dignity while we're still on top, while we're still making all the money in the world.' And he agreed. It was his chance to finally get his feet wet and do what he wanted to do career-wise, stand on his own without the fucking monkey. And I had a chance to stretch."

Though they'd agreed on a graceful conclusion to their partnership, they sniped at each other in the press. Dean announced that Jerry wanted to direct, telling Louella Parsons, "I do not feel he is capable of directing me." And he expressed frustrations with the limits of the act: "As long as I do Martin and Lewis pictures, the formula is always the same—for eight reels, I'm the heel, then at the last minute I'm a right guy. I want to do something more than that."

Jerry was much franker and more openly bitter, saying that Dean was the one holding him back, both in his career and in his personal maturation: "I'm tired of being restricted. I don't want to work twelve weeks and sit around for forty. He wants to work for twelve weeks and play golf for forty. . . . I'm not a happy man unless I can perform and entertain and make people happy. I feel like a completely frustrated cripple when I'm not allowed to do it. The time comes when you look in the mirror and say to yourself, 'All right, be a man.' So it's time I became a man. . . . They [NBC and Paramount] know that [Dean] doesn't want to work. All he wants to do is sit around a pool and play golf. I don't want to sit around a pool that I may not continue to own if I don't work. . . . I can't be a part of his wrongdoing." The golf was a particularly sore point. When columnist Louis Sobol came to Paramount and asked Jerry where Dean was, he got a pointed response: "Oh, he's a pretty busy man. He's out trying to cut down his golf score."

At the end of June they flew east—separately—to wrap it all up. They appeared live on "Today" from the 500 Club and could barely stand to look at one another. Then they went north to play their final string of shows wearing happy faces.

Jerry was being eaten up inside, and he suspected that Dean was too: "Dean had his own personal pain," he reflected. "He had to work through that. He had the same thing I did. He just was able to work through it differently." His pain didn't diminish the vigor of his performance; during their first week at the Copa, he fractured two toes on Jerry's left foot during a rowdy gag. "It was purely an accident," Jerry told the press when they asked how it happened.

The last show of the last night had been sold out weeks in advance. The crowd was as stellar as any they'd ever played to: Jack Benny, Eddie Cantor, Jackie Gleason, Sammy Davis Jr., Milton Berle.

"It was one of the most electrifying evenings in the history of show business," recalled Steve Lawrence. "They were always magnificent performers together, but this night, because of what was involved, was a highly charged, emotional evening for them and the audience. I don't think there was a civilian in the room. Everyone was either in show business or around it: performers, writers, producers, columnists. There was a reason for their being there."

They hit the stage from their respective dressing rooms, and Jerry shot a look at his soon-to-be-ex-partner: "His face was a mask," he remembered. "He would play it cool even if it killed him." They did a long set, well over an hour, and climaxed with the title song of *Pardners*, which would open the next day: "You and me, we'll be the greatest partners, buddies, and pals!" They hugged. Then they ran off the stage, each to his own dressing room, forswearing any encores.

Jerry lay on his bed practically hallucinating. He called Patti in tears. He worked up the nerve to call Dean.

"Hey, pallie," he heard. "How're ya holdin' up?"

"I don't know yet," he lied. "I just want to say . . . we've had some good times, Paul." (He often used his partner's middle name as a sign of closeness.)

"There'll be more."

"Yeah . . . well . . . take care of yourself, that's all. . . ."

"You too, pardner."

They said good-bye.

■   ■   ■

A quarter-century later, Jerry sat down to write his autobiography. For the opening pages he chose to write not about his birth or his stage debut or his wedding day or the births of his sons or his first day as a movie actor or his first day as a director. He wrote about the moment in the dark in a hotel room above the Copa, the moment he lost his brother, his hero, his partner. The person he loved more than anyone else in the world—more even than his parents, his wife, or his children—was gone from his life, and he never fully recovered.

12.

One-Man Show

It was as if he were an athlete: He was thirty years old, and it looked like his career was behind him. "There was only a foreboding sense of failure," he recalled, "of my life emptying away and becoming an absolute blank." He returned home in confusion and no small panic. What was he going to do? He had a pair of films lined up—*The Delicate Delinquent* and a solo project for Hal Wallis—but there was nothing else in front of him, not even a direction. "You ever see a guy scared to death?" he wondered to an interviewer a few years later when asked how he'd felt. "I mean, so it's in his bones, they shiver under the skin? That's how I felt."

He had had his flirtations with psychiatry in the preceding year. Some colleagues recalled him talking about seeing an analyst, but he forever claimed that he had a single visit to Dr. Henry Luster, a Beverly Hills psychiatrist. "I think it would be a mistake if you were to undergo analysis," Jerry recalled Luster telling him. "Your pain might leave, but it's also quite possible that you won't have a reason to be funny anymore." Nevertheless, whether he was under regular therapy or not, Jerry was certainly interested in the process: "I'm about ready to hang up my shingle," he told a reporter soon after the breakup. "I know pain. I know when someone's hurt."

And he had developed a way to understand the pain he felt. "My doctor gave me a book to read that told about how if a puppy had only known one master and that master left him, the puppy would die because his heart would stop," he revealed. "Don't you believe that could happen to a human being too?"

Poor puppy: He sat around the house, moping, festering. Patti couldn't stand it, but it wasn't like it had been a few years before, when she left him. This time, she knew, the thing to do was to go away together—someplace he liked, someplace where he wouldn't sulk.

Along with Jack and Emma Keller, they went to Las Vegas to unwind. "We went to shows, gambled a little, slept in the sun, everything," recalled Keller.

"The Super Jew even got to go and do some shopping. It was just dandy-wandy. Everything postponed. Everything cool." Jerry actually began to calm down. Four days at the Sands restored him, prepared him to return home and speak with his managers and associates and figure out what to do next.

He was packing for home when the phone rang. It was Sid Luft, Judy Garland's husband. Garland was in Vegas, playing the Frontier Hotel; Jerry and his party had been to see the show. Now Luft was telling Jerry that Garland had awakened that morning with a horribly sore throat. He wanted to know if Jerry would bail her out by performing in her stead. Jerry balked at first, but eventually he let Luft talk him into it. A baptism by fire. The last time he'd played a real single was at the 500 Club just before he begged Lou Perry to let Dean join him in Atlantic City. Now he would walk in front of a thousand or so people who had paid to see one of the great all-around performers of the era and . . . do what? It might have been tantamount to professional suicide: an impromptu single just thirteen days after dissolving the twosome that had been his public identity. He didn't even have a tuxedo with him. Patti ironed his dark blue suit; he borrowed a pair of black socks from Keller—they were too small and scrunched his toes— and rode nervously over to the Frontier. Do or die.

Garland was waiting for him backstage, crying in her dressing room and assuring him that the crowd would be on his side. He wanted to believe it; he was afraid that there were people who blamed him for the split with Dean. He sucked it up and headed for the stage as the orchestra played "Over the Rainbow" and an all-male chorus line sang "Miss Judy Garland!" There was an audible gasp of surprise when he hit the lights. He walked tentatively to the mike with a shy grin and asked, "I don't look much like Judy, do I?" The sound of laughter from the auditorium encouraged him, and he wound up doing almost an hour: pantomime to the orchestra, jokes, voices, physical bits, some singing. He wasn't, of course, known as a singer, though he could put a song over in a showy, old-fashioned sort of way; nevertheless, for him to sing onstage and sing earnestly was to act as though he'd subsumed Dean's contribution to the act. He'd dissolved Martin and Lewis into Lewis, and despite the hubris of the gesture, the audience was buying it. They *liked* him.

When he'd exhausted his repertoire, he turned to Garland, whom he'd asked to sit beside him during the performance so the crowd would believe that she couldn't perform, and asked her how she closed the show. She told him that her usual finale was "Rock-a-Bye Your Baby with a Dixie Melody." It was too perfect: an old Jolson tune. It was as if his whole life, the decade with Dean included, had been leading him to that stage, that crowd, that song. He recalled all of his father's throaty imitations of Jolson and dove into the number greedily, even dropping to one knee in a classic Jolson pose. The audience cheered wildly, and he left the stage reborn: He was a solo. He could do it all. Alone.

■   ■   ■

He had told the world that he broke up with Dean because he wanted to work, and when he got back to Los Angeles he tried to live up to his word. Paramount had agreed to let him produce *The Delicate Delinquent*, but he couldn't get Frank Tashlin to direct it. As part of the fallout from the horror show of *Hollywood or Bust*, Tashlin had squirmed out of his contract with Hal Wallis. Too bad for Wallis: The final Martin and Lewis film, released half a year after the act's demise, would be one of their more cinematically stylish efforts, if somewhat painful to watch.

The trade press was at sea in writing about the film, not really sure what to make of the spectacle of the sundered team still yukking it up on screen. The film was like the light from a star finally reaching the earth years after the star itself had imploded. "The boys are certainly quitting while they are way ahead," wrote James Powers in *The Hollywood Reporter*, while *Variety* mused that "with all the wordage about the M&L divorce, it seems odd at this point in the interlocutory period to find them still a team."

But in fact, though they spend almost the whole film on screen together, they are barely a team. Where they used to smile warmly and genuinely at one another in their early films, they pull their lips into tight little grimaces throughout this one. Where Dean had previously lost his patience with Jerry without ever quite losing the fraternal tone in his voice, in this film he lets ferocious, convincing bitterness come through. At a few points, he seems on the verge of physical violence, or at least ready to flick a cigarette at his partner.

Indeed, it's hard to see through the conditions under which the film was made to the film itself. You notice that Jerry is even fleshier than he'd been the previous year; turning sideways to the camera during a bullfighting sequence, he reveals a small paunch and meaty fanny completely at odds with the prototype of Jerry the Animated Scarecrow. Dean has a tight-eyed glower on his face much of the time, and when he raises a hammer in mock anger at Jerry's inability to fix a car, it seems possible that an atrocity is about to occur.

It isn't nearly as vivacious a film as *Artists and Models*, and lord knows Tashlin had all he could handle just getting it shot without worrying about stylistic flourishes. In part, he's hampered by the fact that his protagonists are on the road all the film long (an idiot's Sal Paradise and Dean Moriarty); as they decide who's going to drive or wonder where they'll get the money for gas, there's very little opportunity for Tashlin to skewer his favorite American sacred cows.

The pervasive dreariness of *Hollywood or Bust* is summed up in a moment near the end, when Dean and Jerry, having lost all their money at Hollywood Park, wander through an empty Hollywood Bowl looking for a place to spend the night. They are shown at first from the last row of the cavernous amphitheater, a pair of insects walking through a seashell. Their voices echo amid the empty seats. They lay their heads on the conductor's podium—one man on each side, not bunked down together as in so many of their earlier films—and drift off to sleep. Tashlin may not have known for certain (or, for that matter, cared) that the team was dissolving, but he found a perfect cinematic metaphor for the dissolution.

Now, though, Tashlin was over at Twentieth Century–Fox, directing the two films that would cement his reputation as a major comedy director: *The Girl Can't Help It*, with Jayne Mansfield and Tom Ewell, and *Will Success Spoil Rock Hunter?* with Mansfield and Tony Randall. (Though Ewell and Randall, both lanky and clean-cut, looked like Jerry, they were subtle comic presences, and Tashlin deployed them the same way he had Dean; it was Mansfield, in her unlikely physical contours, who served him as Jerry had—as a vehicle for cartoonish gags.)

Jerry himself had been instrumental in liberating Tashlin from Wallis's reign. Tashlin despised the producer as early as *Artists and Models*, but he was locked into a multifilm deal with him and could see no way out of it save a drastic one: "I have to find a way to get the fuck out of it," he told Jerry, "or I'll kill him and then I'll die." Jerry suggested a simpler course of action: "You're in the editing stage now, where you're gonna hand the picture over to Wallis. The minute you see the first run-through of his cut, write him a letter and tell him you think he's a fucking butcher, that he doesn't know how to cut, that he doesn't have the faintest idea about editing and has no sense of humor. And you'll be out of your contract the day the letter is received."

Tashlin didn't believe it could be so simple, but it was. He bided his time and sent the inflammatory telegram. Wallis exploded. Tashlin was free.

But his departure from Paramount left Jerry without his preferred director for his first solo project. He turned to an unlikely corner for someone he could trust: Don McGuire, who'd written the screenplay for *The Delicate Delinquent* with Jerry, had just premiered his first film as a director—*Johnny Concho*, a Frank Sinatra Western. Jerry hired him. Rather than go with an experienced hand on his first film as a solo performer and a full-fledged producer, he felt more comfortable with a former yes-man, someone he could control without argument.

There was another bit of business to take care of before filming on *The Delicate Delinquent* began. Jerry couldn't forget the rush he'd felt singing "Rock-a-Bye Your Baby" in Vegas. He approached Capitol Records, where he'd cut all those novelty songs a few years earlier, and asked if they'd be interested in recording him singing standards straight. They brushed him off. So he hired arranger-conductor Buddy Bregman, rented a recording studio, and went in and cut a few sides anyway. On August 21, 1956, he stepped into the same Capitol recording studio where he and Dean had cut "The Money Song" eight years earlier and recorded four songs—"Rock-a-Bye," "I'm Sitting on Top of the World," "Come Rain or Come Shine," and "Back in Your Own Backyard." The first two were plain and simple Jolson tunes, and Jerry sang them in the barrel-toned tenor that he'd grown up hearing from Danny. He joked with his musicians and engineers—cutting up on the third take of "Rock-a-Bye," he announced, "I'm laughin', but I'm payin' for the date!"—but he didn't require more than a half-dozen stabs at any of the songs.

He took the completed demos to Capitol but was again rebuffed, so he began to shop them around. Decca Records was interested enough to ask him to flesh out the material into an entire LP worth of songs. In September, when *The Delicate Delinquent* was shooting, he cut eight more songs in a single day. There were more Jolson tunes—"Mammy" and "When the Red Red Robin"— and a couple of Judy Garland numbers—"Get Happy" and "Birth of the Blues." There was also the pointedly chosen "By Myself," an Arthur Schwartz–Howard Deitz composition written originally for Fred Astaire but adopted by Jerry as a signature number in the days after Dean; he sang it in *The Delicate Delinquent*, its lyrics transparently appropriate to his new life:

> *I'll face the unknown,*
> *I'll build a world of my own . . .*

Decca was delighted with the results, and within six weeks they had an album entitled *Jerry Lewis Just Sings* and a single of "Rock-a-Bye" out on the street.

The craziest thing happened: The record hit. Within three weeks, "Rock-a-Bye" was Number Ten on the *Billboard* charts; it stayed in the Top Forty for fifteen weeks, selling 1.4 million copies. The album, which sold a quarter-million copies, rose as high as Number Three on the LP charts and came to be known among industry wags as "Music to Get Even with Dean Martin By." It was only partly a joke: Dean had never had a hit album in his career, and only two among his many singles—"That's Amore" and "Memories Are Made of This"—had sold as many copies as "Rock-a-Bye." Hearing Jerry on the radio, watching "Rock-a-Bye" climb up the charts where he hadn't had a hit in over a year, he must have felt as though he'd been slipped some bad liquor.*

The Delicate Delinquent cost $487,000 and was shot on a skintight five-week schedule in black-and-white—Jerry's first black-and-white film since *The Caddy*. Darren McGavin filled the role Dean had spurned, a Paramount starlet named

---

*In the coming years, Jerry was to absorb Dean's stage persona into his own more totally than anyone but he would realize. On stage and TV he made a staple of doing his old pantomime shtick to a recording of Mario Lanza singing "Be My Love." Lanza was a contemporary of Martin and Lewis—he made his first film in 1949, the same year as *My Friend Irma*. But Jerry's appropriation of "Be My Love" was a deliberate lampoon of an Italian tenor. It was no accident: Jerry was probably guided toward Lanza's material by Jack Keller, who had been Lanza's publicist. Lanza represented the theatrical, florid aspect of Dean's stage persona, and in satirizing him, Jerry was undoubtedly mocking one of his former partner's very few pretensions toward art.

Martha Hyer (who a decade later would marry a widowed Hal Wallis) played the female lead, and lots of young actors who specialized in juvenile delinquent types were on hand—Frank Gorshin, Richard Bakalyan, Joseph Corey. In some ways, it was like one of the Gar-Ron films: Jerry's record producer Buddy Bregman did the music, his old Broadway pal Milton Frome had a part, Don McGuire himself played a bit role, and the script had a cop named Levitch working alongside McGavin in the precinct house. (Bandleader Dick Stabile, who had every reason to consider himself one of the gang, felt insulted by Bregman's presence and sued Jerry for $92,500 for breach of oral contract to hire him for the picture; the suit was settled when Jerry—uncharacteristically—forgave Stabile the affront of the suit and agreed to use him on other projects.)

It was a good thing it took only five weeks to make the film, because Jerry seemed determined to do everything in show business at the same time. He did literally dozens of charity benefits that year—most for the Muscular Dystrophy Association, but several for the Motion Picture Permanent Charities, of which he'd been annual campaign chairman, and Cedar-Sinai Hospital, for which he'd raised three hundred thousand dollars in recent months and to whose board of directors he'd been named. He spent time planning the first of his programs for NBC, scheduled to air in January 1957. And he was getting ready for his most audacious move yet: In November 1956 he announced plans to play a four-week run at the RKO Palace on Broadway. He wouldn't be happy just to make the world forget Dean Martin; he wanted it to forget Jolson, too.

Although he had a hit record, his activities hadn't really been very public; he'd granted no interviews and made only the sole live appearance in Vegas. In November he emerged back into the limelight. He came to New York and sat in for Edward R. Murrow as host of "Person to Person." In a single day he appeared on "What's My Line" and "The Steve Allen Show." And he began speaking to the press again, for the first time since he'd split from Dean.

For all his talk decades later about Martin and Lewis being "a love affair," for all the nostalgic warmth with which he spoke about his old partner, the Jerry Lewis of 1956 sounded as nasty as a spurned lover. "I've never been happier in my life," he declared to reporters at the Essex House in New York that November. "For the first time in ten years, I am rid of a cancer."

There was more. He gave an extensive interview to Bill Davidson of *Look*, a full, autobiographical as-told-to cover story bearing the professional name "I've Always Been Scared." It ran nine pages, with nearly a dozen photos. "All my life," it began, "I've been afraid of being alone." Jerry, with the advice and assistance of Jack Keller, had decided to present himself to the world in a new light. Gone was the madcap monkey, Dino's little partner, the irrepressible imp. In his place was a thoughtful, insecure, ambitious, and humble man. He bared his soul, discussed his fears, his pains, his dreams.

And while he was being so honest about himself, he saw no reason not to be equally honest about Dean. He spoke about his former partner's coolness ("he was never as warm and outgoing as I hoped he'd be"); he announced that Dean favored vulgar comedy ("Dean wanted wild, crazy noise without rhyme or reason"), he blamed Jeanne for disrupting the rapport he had with Dean ("Dean divorced Betty and married his second wife, Jeanne, and suddenly our families weren't friendly anymore"), and he accused Dean of professional jealousy: "I'm sure he felt I was writing the material to build myself up. I'm sure I did things to irritate Dean, but in this matter, my hands are clean. As producer Hal Wallis and others know, I leaned over backwards to give Dean more to do at my own expense."

The article wouldn't appear until February, but it was hot stuff. Hollywood columnist Sidney Skolsky got an advance copy and asked Dean what he thought. Dean insisted that he'd been a gentleman throughout their split: "Jerry has been shooting his mouth off . . . but I decided not to say a word, not to answer him. I thought we broke up an act, a partnership, not a friendship. But this is different. Jerry talks about Jeanne and that's going too far. . . . I don't want to hurt Jerry. No one can hurt him more than he's hurting himself." Of course, that didn't mean he couldn't try. He got in a dig that cut deeper than he could have known: "The two worst things that happened to Jerry were taking a good picture with a Brownie and reading a book about Chaplin."

This sort of thing made for wonderful gossip in Hollywood restaurants and in trashy magazines, but Dean looked to be on the losing end of it: Here was Jerry with a hit record and commitments all over the place for TV work, movies, and live dates. What was Dean doing? Next to nothing. He had no live dates lined up, he hadn't begun to make plans to fulfill his obligations to NBC. Not even Paramount wanted to touch him. Joe Pasternak at MGM had been hot to work with Dean for more than a decade; Y. Frank Freeman decided to loan Dean out to him for a picture, an awful musical romance about a hotel manager in Italy entitled *Ten Thousand Bedrooms*.

As far as the public could tell, Dean seemed to be keeping busy mostly by lashing out at Jerry: "Jerry was jealous of Jeanne. . . . He was happy when Jeanne and I split up. . . . I respect other wives. I could talk about Patti and Jerry knows it, but I won't." He turned up—drunk, apparently—on a live TV broadcast and denigrated his former partner's comedic ambitions. *New York Post* columnist Harriet Van Horne wrote, "I'm willing to bet that the first shattered atom split more sedately than Martin and Lewis." Jerry, who liked to bind and frame all the press clippings about him that he could retrieve, began to collect material for a leather-bound book he labeled "Dean Shoots His Mouth Off."

Always solicitous of writers, Jerry was able to make hay of Dean's vengeful spree, revealing to reporters just how much of Martin and Lewis's success was due to his own hard work and talent: "I've written, directed, and produced a great part of our shows. Why didn't I get a credit? Why didn't the picture say codirected by Jerry Lewis? Why didn't a television show say written by Jerry Lewis? To begin with, this was my doing. I knew I never had a chance to get the credit because I knew about Dean's subconscious resentment of the fact that I got most of the team's publicity. How could I go on from this point? How could I possibly let people know that I also was the writer, the director, that I coordinated it, produced it, and was the businessman of the act? Well, how much can you overload on one side? So I never approached Dean about what in my heart had always hurt me."

See? people said. *Jerry was nice to Dean all along.* He was the little guy, the creative one, the easily hurt one, the one who protected the other. Dean, who that spring bought out of York and cut the last financial links between them, took stock of his situation and realized how ugly he looked compared with his soulful ex-partner. He gave a conciliatory interview to *TV Guide*'s Dan Jenkins in hopes of ending the months of hostility. "I'm getting a little tired of being the heavy in this thing," he said. "I get the reports. Jerry has stripped his house of every picture of me, all my records he used to have on the wall. Now isn't that pretty silly? I've got pictures of him all over this house. My kids have got Jerry's clown pictures in their rooms. Why shouldn't they?"

But by then Dean—and even Martin and Lewis—seemed like old news. Back in December Jerry had debuted as a solo in a full-fledged revue at the Sands in Vegas, pulling in twenty-five thousand dollars a week for a three-week run. The act, Jerry said, cost seventy thousand dollars to assemble: Nick Castle did the choreography, Buddy Bregman conducted an orchestra featuring Lou Brown on piano, Georgine Darcy (the curvy "Miss Torso" from Alfred Hitchcock's *Rear Window*) was a comic foil, and a seven-man chorus line was billed as the Aristocrats. The opening night was overlong and shaky; the next night he cut the show in half, to just under an hour, and got much better notices right away.

"Jerry Lewis emerges as a major entertainer in his own right," crowed Philip K. Scheuer of *The Los Angeles Times* upon seeing the revised show. *Variety* was slightly less enthusiastic—"Lewis, while good right now, is not sock"—no doubt because reviewer "Scho." was incensed by the lewdness in the act: "He's not only doing a panz, but doing it overly broad and too often. It goes beyond the laugh stage; it gets to the shock point."

Jerry finished up in Vegas in time to return home for Christmas, then hit the Chez Paree in Chicago for two weeks and moved on to New York for ten days of rehearsal for his NBC solo spot. Sponsored by RCA and Oldsmobile, "The Jerry Lewis Show" aired on January 19, 1957, with guests Jan Murray, Woody Herman, and the Aristocrats. Jerry had chosen to do the show live from New York because he preferred the spontaneity and appreciative animation of eastern audiences to the blasé Hollywood crowds who, he said, had grown jaded from seeing too many movie stars on the streets and attending the tapings of several shows in a single day.

For the most part, it was a one-man show ("I'm a ham and I admit it," Jerry told columnist Hal Humphrey). He sang and did some pantomime, and he performed in pathos-heavy vignettes he'd written with Harry Crane and Artie Phillips. Critics were underwhelmed. "Jose." in *Variety* said, "He has the germ of an idea of what he wants to do in the solo comedy line, but at the moment seems without the means of articulating the character he wants to create." "At no time was he as funny as in the old days," wrote Ben Gross in the New York *Daily News*. And Jack O'Brian in the *Journal American* was downright nasty: "He needs Dean Martin badly. Very, very badly. . . . It was a program almost entirely empty of fresh material or techniques, even taste. . . . There was no speed, none of the reckless impertinence of early Dean-Jerry performances which counterbalanced the vulgarity. . . . There was no vitality, no evidence of what is called 'class,' too many slips into the lowest taste . . . a perfectly dull performance."

Jerry heard these negative reviews. "A lot of those guys will lay lilies on my grave and make long speeches about what a great guy I was," he told columnist Barry Gray. "I wish they had some consideration for the living and would give me a whiff of the flowers now." But the ratings were acceptably gaudy, and he was too busy to stew over bad press. He did a week at the Fontainebleau Hotel in Miami and another week at the Sands, where he had recently signed a five-year agreement with Jack Entratter. Finally, he returned to New York to prepare for the Palace.

Jerry's breakneck pace, his apparent thirst to show everyone he could stand on his own two feet without the crutch of a partner, was the subject of a great deal of talk on Broadway and in Hollywood. A friend spoke to *TV Guide* on the condition he remain anonymous: "Whether he knows it or not—and I think he knows it—Jerry has dedicated himself to become the great institutional American entertainer. The pattern is there—heading up charity drives, doing benefits at the drop of a hat and, consciously or unconsciously, pouring his heart into the old Al Jolson songs. It's pure and simple ego drive."

The anonymous friend was right: Jerry *was* doing it all to prove something to the world. He was free now to follow his ambitions: He was going to be the Ultimate Showman, the King of Entertainment. "For twenty years I wanted to play the Palace," he told the press. "I asked Dean to play it with me. It didn't mean so much to him and he said no." People thought Dean Martin had helped him get to where he was? He would show them his old partner had done nothing but hold him back.

The past decade hadn't been particularly kind to the Palace, thought it was still held to be the nation's premier vaudeville theater. What talking movies and radio hadn't wiped out, television decimated. Variety shows like Ed Sullivan's and "The Colgate Comedy Hour" were bringing top- and bottom-of-the-bill vaudeville acts into American homes with a wider distribution than any of the old touring circuits ever offered—and for free. Still, the allure of vaudeville as the grandest of all show-biz formats—and the glamour of Broadway's crown jewel—hadn't entirely diminished. True, the Palace had turned into just another presentation house in recent years, hosting a combination of new movie releases and smallish live acts. But RKO president Sol A. Schwartz trumped up a "vaudeville revival" in 1956, luring big-name performers into his theater for exclusive multiweek presentations. He'd had Danny Kaye in for a successful engagement, and then Judy Garland did an astonishing fifteen record-breaking weeks; a grateful Schwartz renamed the dressing room after her. Jerry popped up in the audience late in Garland's run, bringing the singer a cup of tea onstage and dueting with her on "Rock-a-Bye." Now the theater would be his.

Broadway showhounds were predictably leery about Jerry's chances: "If some of the TV reviewers made him mad, wait till he runs head-on into the drama critics," a cynic at Lindy's told Dorothy Kilgallen. The consensus was that Jerry was talented enough and certainly had the drive, but that he still hadn't arrived at just the right formula for a solo act. Nevertheless, when advance tickets for the four weeks of ten shows a week went on sale, Jerry grossed an unprecedented ninety thousand dollars, with a top ticket price of six dollars.

The format was the same one Schwartz had used for Kaye and Garland: half variety acts, half headliner. The first part of the bill consisted of the Wiere Brothers (a knockabout comic trio), dancers Chiquita and Johnson, sketch comics Charlotte Arren and Johnny Broderick, the Seven Ashtons (a family of young comics from Australia), and a twenty-five-year-old singer named Eydie Gorme, whom Jerry had selected to close the opening set.

"I was doing 'The Steve Allen Show,'" Gorme remembered. "I had a minor record deal at Coral Records, and I made a record called 'Too Close for Comfort.' And it came to my attention around that time that Jerry Lewis was in California running around to deejays and promoting my record. We had met Jerry, but we weren't that friendly at the time. But he just went crazy over the way I sang and my record. And he asked me to come and be on the show at the Palace. And my agency and manager at the time said, 'No, no, you're not ready for anything like this. You're just a kid, blah, blah, blah.' And I wanted to do it very, very badly. And frankly speaking, my agency said, 'If you do this, we won't represent you any longer, because we don't think you're ready.' I said, 'Well, if I think I'm ready, and Jerry Lewis thinks I'm ready, then I'm ready.'"

On opening night, February 7, Jerry paced backstage with the jitters. He'd flown his barber in from California at the cost of five hundred dollars. His parents were in town, as was Patti, who was pregnant again. The audience was spiked with famous faces: Joan Crawford, Marilyn Monroe, Phil Silvers, Nanette Fabray, Jack Carter, Lou Costello, Robert Merrill.

"Jerry was an enormous star at the time," according to Gorme, "and of course, everyone was coming to see him fall on his rear end. As a result, the place was jammed. I was so nervous I was dead."

The first half of the show went over well, Gorme especially. Then came an intermission, and then Jerry's moment. He was introduced by the Aristocrats and walked onstage to an ovation. When the applause died off, he made a gesture toward the chorus line and announced, "I used to do a double but I cut it down to eight." The audience liked the line, and Jerry launched into a ninety-minute act. He imitated Elvis Presley and Jolson. He did dialect comedy, including a Japanese routine with protruding rubber buckteeth and soda-bottle eyeglasses. He did a comic dance lesson routine. He conducted the band in herky-jerky fashion. He put on a wild fright wig and attacked a typewriter with his fingertips to a classical score. He sang ("Rock-a-Bye," of course, and "By Myself," and "Rolling Along"), he danced, he told jokes. He made his way out into the audience to lead a group sing (shades of a Catskills campfire) of "Shine on Harvest Moon," even egging Joan Crawford into singing along. And when he saw a man in one of the stage-side balcony boxes not singing, he got a ladder and climbed up to coerce him as well.*

By the time it was over, his body and his repertoire were exhausted. The audience, which had been in the theater for nearly two and a half hours, shuffled out abuzz. He hadn't fallen on his ass after all. It was clear to everyone that Jerry had shed Dean forever. He could apparently do anything he wanted to do. Although some of the bits he did that night would be mainstays of his act for the rest of his career, that night he was fresh, protean, and electric—an unqualified success.

Variety crowed loudest. Editor Abel Green himself reviewed the show and filled his notice with superlatives: "Ninety minutes of Jerry Lewis, with his great versatility, makes this Palace excursion very worthwhile. That Lewis had first-night jitters is incidental, because despite the somewhat uphill struggle, it cannot be denied that he has nothing but talent and is as potent a comic as there is to be found. . . . *Vaudeville is not dead!* . . . Uneven or not, there is no gainsaying Lewis' boffola sum total. . . . This is a special type of prowess. . . . Like Sammy Davis, Jr.'s electrifying 'discovery' by theater customers . . . so too is Lewis a revelation in person . . . a one-man talent of great versatility."

Other notices weren't as wildly complimentary, but they were, in the main, much better than the reviews he'd gotten two weeks before on TV. Pointedly, the negative reviews concentrated more on Jerry's material than his actual performance. People may have been drawn to the theater to see if Jerry would lay an

---

*This community-sing bit became a staple of his act for a few years; when comedian Hal March was at one of his shows, Jerry tried to coax him into singing, but March refused, saying, "You wanted to do a single, so do a single!"

egg, but once they'd seen him perform, they were won over by his sheer desire to please. As Lewis Funke wrote in *The New York Times*, "Not to be entirely with Mr. Lewis last night amounted to something not unlike heresy."

The best notices, though, went to Gorme. "I had just made a record called 'Guess Who I Saw Today' that was also going very well," she remembered, "and I did that and 'Bye Bye Blackbird' and 'I'm Always Chasing Rainbows.' Well, to make a long story short, I was a smash. I was on in the first half of the show, and Jerry always said to me, 'What did I do? What did I do? I came to Broadway to make a big splash for myself, and you took all the headlines!' Of course, I certainly never intended to do that; it just worked out that way. With the exception of *Variety*—and I'll never forgive them for that—the headlines in the other seven papers were 'A Star Is Born,' and it was me."

The engagement was a resounding financial success. The Palace did $61,500 the first week and nearly $275,000 for the entire four-week run. Schwartz would have let Jerry play forever. On the last night of the gig, he came onstage to present Jerry with a silver plaque engraved with the façade of the theater. Steve Allen appeared with Jerry that night also, handing Jerry a gold record of "Rock-a-Bye," which had sold more in his version than in Jolson's.

Back in California the next week, he found himself living a bad dream. He had conquered the Palace, he had a hit record, he had produced a movie—and he was starring in *The Sad Sack*, a military comedy produced by Hal Wallis, directed by George Marshall and based on the comic strip by George Baker. It might as well have been *At War with the Army II*. He had tried to get out of it, sending signals to Wallis as early as September that he didn't want to do another service picture, having his doctor impress upon the producer that he needed his rest, asking Herman Citron to find a way out of the picture for him. In November he told a reporter the movie "should be shot at the Menninger clinic."

Wallis took all of these protests in stride; he'd heard it all before, and worse, and he knew that he would get his way. He was so confident that he even had start-up notices sent to both Jerry and Dean—they still owed him pictures as a team, and until a divine hand wrote words to the contrary on the hallowed gates of the Paramount lot, he expected to get them. As for Jerry's antipathy toward service comedies, he'd not only included police academy scenes in *The Delicate Delinquent* similar to scenes from his service films with Dean, but there was reassuring news from Paul Nathan. Ed Beloin and Nate Monaster, the authors of the *Sad Sack* script, had lunched recently with Jerry, who had told them point-blank that he wouldn't make another service picture. In pleading their case, the writers told Jerry that they were shaping their script along the lines of *No Time for Sergeants*, the popular Broadway Army comedy, to which Jerry responded, "I tried so hard to buy that and Lew Wasserman missed it by ten minutes!"

Jerry lost his battle and on March 18 began shooting the film. David Wayne had been cast in the role that Wallis had originally intended for Dean, Phyllis Kirk played the female lead (for which Eydie Gorme, without knowing it, had been considered on the strength of her Palace success). By the end of May, the picture was in the can and Wallis could go buy paintings.

On April 21 Jerry got a bizarre jolt of the sort that only celebrities can appreciate. According to the UPI report filed the next day, Jerry told police that a "wild-eyed stranger" had rung the doorbell of his home and shoved a piece of paper into his hand that said something about wanting to kill people. Patti and the boys were watching television in the next room. Jerry slammed the door, set off a silent burglar alarm, and ran to his desk for his .38 revolver. He spotted the intruder in the backyard and, dressed only in a T-shirt and jeans, chased him down and held him at gunpoint until the police arrived. The man was identified by police as a "frustrated musician" with "a yen for giving Hollywood stars the heebie jeebies." He was booked on suspicion of burglary, and Jerry went inside to calm himself and his family.

He had behaved bravely; most people in his situation would have locked the doors, called the police, and cowered with their loved ones, waiting for help and giving the intruder a chance to escape. But as the years passed, he must have come to feel as though he hadn't been brave enough. Retelling the story decades later, he rewrote it, making himself less a gutsy Everyman than a righteous James Bond. The intruder "was, unfortunately, a black man," Jerry began. "I say unfortunately because today that's what it always is. He was crawling into a window that had not been locked before we went to bed. And if it hadn't been locked, then the alarm system shouldn't have been secure. But the alarm system was secure, so why check windows? There was a defect.

"Patti says to me, 'I hear something in the kitchen.' Now, in the kitchen is an entry through a huge bay window. This man was exactly twelve feet from my children, because that was the children's quarters. I had a .357 Magnum in my drawer, and I put a robe on—thought I'd look like a gentleman. I walked in with the .357 Magnum, and he's straddling the window just getting his head under. I put the barrel of it on his forehead and I said, 'If you know nothing about guns, my friend, let me tell you what will happen to your head if you make another move, moreover, if you even talk. Don't even talk, or I'll blow your fucking head all over this community.'

"I know now why I didn't want him to talk. 'Cause I was handling it so well, I didn't want to get rattled. The phone was no more than one-half a step from where I was standing. Called the police, they came and got him . . . they took him away. Whatever happened to him, God knows."

The discrepancies between the account he gave the night of the incident and the version he concocted later were reminiscent of his boasting about his Mafia ties or the women who'd "burped" him or all the money he'd gambled away. He simply didn't trust the realities of a remarkable situation to impress his audience, and in altering facts to fit his self-image, he turned his version of events into a hyperbolic joke: the bathrobe, the Dirty Harry dialogue.

Only when he spoke about how he felt after the police left did his retrospective account seem to coincide with the actual events of that long-ago night: "I fell apart. I was so cool that that's why I said, 'Don't even talk.' I didn't want the sound of 'Oh, mister, please don't' or any of that shit to throw me. I was like fuckin' Terminator 4 until I put the gun back in the drawer. Then you could hear the house tremble.

"It's an amazing thing—if somebody came near your house, and your wife and children were in jeopardy, you wouldn't believe what would come over you. You wouldn't believe, first of all, what your capabilities are. It's frightening. I cocked that son of a bitch, and it would not have taken a microsecond to just blow his fucking head off. Knowing what I had in my hand, you don't have to do it twice. Just one time. *Bam!* And the thought of that is what gets you crazy, that you are that confident to kill a human being."

This frightened, uncertain man was far more plausible than the suave superhero he'd just described, but Jerry didn't like to present himself in this light when it came to manly pursuits. The irony is that in altering the events to make himself seem more heroic, he wound up looking more helpless. At least when he confessed to fear or uncertainty, he seemed like a real person. When he put forth his revised version of his behavior, he seemed less like a he-man than like a caricature of one. It would have been a great comic role if he had played it in a movie instead of living it.

A second NBC special in June was Jerry's last of the season. As a novelty—and yet another way of laying claim to a show-business heritage that transcended Martin and Lewis—he brought Danny and Gary on with him. Danny played the big star throughout rehearsals. He'd recently made his film debut as a nightclub owner in *Short Cut to Hell*, a remake of *This Gun for Hire* directed by James Cagney. Now he took credit for Jerry's singing success. "His Jolson-type songs, you know, are what I used to do," he told UPI. "When you hear us you can't tell us apart." He added, "I'm proud to be Jerry's father, but when people introduce me as his father, well, I'd like them to know my name." Gary, only eleven, was the only one who seemed unspoiled by show business. "I'm going to be just like my dad," he exulted. "Dad has taught me how to get the right notes when I sing. We're going to be dressed exactly alike in the show—tuxedos!"

Jerry orchestrated a cutesy routine around the Three Generations of Lewises: He sat on Danny's knee while Danny sang "Sonny Boy," then Gary got on *his* knee while *he* sang it. The show was more structured than the first—the guest stars included Dan Rowan and Dick Martin and Eydie Gorme (when, at the last minute, Jerry cut a big production number built around her, she remembered that "I almost killed him. I'm not kidding. I really almost killed him."). But even with all of that, the critics didn't buy it. "A pitiful reminder of Milton Berle's early TV shows," wrote Jack O'Brian in the *Journal American*, "except Uncle Miltie did them better." "Even more embarrassing than the first one," said the *Herald Tribune*'s John Crosby.

Although Dean hadn't matched Jerry's exposure on stage and television, he beat him to the punch in the movies. Unfortunately, he made his solo debut in the execrable *Ten Thousand Bedrooms*, and was lambasted: "Mr. Martin is a fellow with little humor and a modicum of charm," wrote Bosley Crowther in *The New York Times*. Asked about his former partner's career woes, Jerry said, "I wouldn't clap my hands if I heard he was doing bad. But I don't know whether I'll see his picture."

Jerry's first solo outing, *The Delicate Delinquent*, fared considerably better when it opened in June after previewing for the trade in Palm Springs. *Variety* claimed the film was "neither fish nor fowl," identifying it as "slapstick blended with pathos and some straight melodrama tossed in" and calling it "overlong" at a mere one hundred minutes. *The Los Angeles Times* was frankly puzzled by the film's mixture of tones and genres: "The spectator may find himself confused, to say the least." But *Newsweek*, which, like most major weekly and monthly outlets, had long ago stopped reviewing Martin and Lewis films regularly, called it "nicely mixed-up."

It is, in fact, a transitional film, and its varied tones and dependence on a variety of genres only proves its intermediate status. It's another schnook-makes-good story: A nebbishy apprentice janitor (Jerry) is mistaken for a young hoodlum by the cops, and a do-good patrolman (Darren McGavin) decides to take him under his wing and reform him. Jerry resists McGavin's help at first, but pretty soon he wants not only to reform but to join the police force . . . and, incredibly, he makes it (though not, of course, without the usual complications).

Juvenile delinquency was a genuinely pressing social issue at the time, and McGuire's touch with it is, figuratively and literally, extremely dark. Shot almost entirely in small apartments or offices and on darkened backlot streets, the film is frequently played as straight dialogue with no underscoring. Chief among these are moments when Jerry and McGavin talk about Jerry's self-conception, conversations that Jerry called upon his relationship with his beloved grandmother Sarah Rothberg to help write: "What am I? That's a very good question. But the answer ain't very nice. I'll tell you what I am. I'm a nowhere. And that's the worst kind of somethin' there is. . . . When I was a boy, I was jerky. And now, now I'm a man, and I'm empty." With its dingy atmosphere, its jazz-tinged score, and its overemotional script full of elided final *g*s, the film is like a minor work of American neorealism, a forgotten cousin of *On the Waterfront* or *Marty*.

But of course, it's a Jerry Lewis movie, so there are the usual capers. The film's one unforgettable comic scene occurs when Jerry comes across a theremin owned by an eccentric scientist neighbor. The idea of such a gifted physical comic interacting with a musical device that is activated by the movement of human bodies in front of it is truly inspired, and Jerry's approach to the thing— an evolution from wariness to confidence to abandon—is primally satisfying, like watching a chimpanzee figure out a mirror.

On the other hand, being a Jerry Lewis movie, it's a little sloppy. Again, Jerry is unable to stay wholly in character: His voice shifts not in comic ways but in a way that reveals the actor behind the fictional character. Sidney Pythias is surprisingly capable of sober, considered thought, and when he indulges in it, his voices takes on a gravity and self-import utterly at odds with the rest of his behavior. Moreover, he's wearing the inevitable wedding band and pinky ring, and he's got a picture of Patti, Gary, and Ronnie Lewis in his basement flat—so he's obviously not as much of a nobody as he appears.

But the strangest thing about it, really, was that it was neither a Martin and Lewis movie nor a buddy movie but—who would ever have believed it?—a Jerry Lewis movie. And the public loved it. Jerry had produced—and carried—a hit.

The cynics and savants had been right: Dean was in serious trouble, but Jerry's talents and popularity knew no bounds. He went out to promote the film that summer, making personal appearances in twenty-six cities. He took the opportunity to make a tour of his past, as if touching all the spots he had played with Dean or as a struggling pantomimist would erase it. He played the 500 Club. He showed up at Brown's Hotel and renamed the Martin and Lewis Playhouse; it would henceforth be the Jerry Lewis Playhouse. He went to Buffalo and visited the Palace Theater, where he'd debuted in front of that ugly burlesque crowd sixteen years earlier. He was fêted at Ebbets Field and given a silver-bound Jewish Bible by the American-Israeli Cultural Foundation.

In Toronto the unremitting workload finally broke him down. In a single day he managed to alienate the Canadian Broadcasting Company, a prominent radio talk host, and the city's mayor. Along with his eighteen-member entourage, he kept the mayor waiting for twenty minutes to deliver a proclamation in his honor. At the CBC studios, he barged into a serious news interview program shouting, "Where's the corpse?" At the Imperial Theater, where *Delinquent* was playing, he found fault with the stage and microphone arrangements. "Instead of controlling his temper, as a nice guy would," reported CKEY radio announcer Stuart Kenney, who was at the theater, "he cursed the stagehands and unleashed oaths left and right." Kenney was to have Jerry as a guest on the air later that day, but refused after witnessing his tantrum. A few days later, Dorothy Kilgallen reported that "those who know Jerry well say he's been extremely tense lately."

Patti was among them. As Jerry became more and more of a show-biz Superman outside of the house, she found him increasingly tyrannical with her. "The disruptive strain of his personality emerged at home, where he remained more director than husband and father," she recalled. "I feared his temper and was not assertive enough to do battle. I just kept trying to hold everything together."

In August complications from her pregnancy caused her doctor to confine her to bed. Jerry came home from his tour. She made it through the episode well enough for him to return back east in September and play the Town and Country nightclub in Brooklyn. On October 9, 1957, another son was born. "I don't think Katherine is going to fit," Jerry joked with the press when they asked the baby's name. He'd wanted a girl again; instead, he'd gotten Christopher Joseph. Jerry bragged that he was "even with Crosby"—Bing Crosby had four boys—but he made no mention of his ex-partner's seven kids.

He was back on NBC that fall with a newly negotiated contract: twenty-five shows over five years for $7.5 million. He had heard the negative reviews loud and clear, but the money and the ratings convinced him he shouldn't do anything new or different. He was thin-skinned enough, however, to attack his critics. With the exception of the angry, rowdy interview he and Dean had given Art Buchwald that day in Paris, in which they'd insulted the entire British press with giddy insouciance, he had always kept quiet about critics. And why not? In the past, the critics may have jeered, but they'd almost always preferred him over Dean. The things they said about him as a solo on TV got his goat, however. He'd never been talked or written about this way since becoming a star, and he didn't feel he had to take it.

Rather than attack the critics as people, Jerry explained that he had a bigger aim in mind with his work. "I've had my brains handed to me," he reflected that autumn. "I got a going-over after my last television show—but the public wrote me two hundred thousand letters of thanks, an unprecedented thing. . . . I know I can do ingenious things that would get rave notices. But I've put them all away in favor of amusing the public." He was a man of the people—hundreds of thousands of them. To hell with the critics.

He might have done well, actually, to heed the advice of at least some of them, if for no other reason than that some of the words he found so hurtful were remarkably insightful. Harriet Van Horne reviewed his first show of the new season in the *World Telegram* with some of the most apt analysis of Jerry that has ever seen print: "In his field of comedy, which happens to be both narrow and rutted, Mr. Lewis stands as a sort of witless genius. His jests aren't even memorable, let alone quotable. He's the only performer I know who can be both endearing and disgusting in the space of two minutes. You applaud the high artistry of his pantomime. But you flinch from the soulless vulgarity of his spastic twitches and low-class leers."

Van Horne wrote with great appreciation of the best parts of Jerry's act: his empathetic powers, his rubberiness, his ability to reveal—apparently—the content of his soul through the contortions of his body: "If Mr. Lewis practices the comedy of insult, he insults only himself. He is tortured and mocked, swindled and scorned. His occasional look of horror is a mute and terrible comment on the world around him. At such moments, he is not only endearing, he is fascinating."

Van Horne enjoyed that night's show; she especially preferred it to Jerry's shows of the previous spring, which failed, she felt, because of his "anxiety to crash through the home screen as a personality." On the new program, to the contrary, "we had Mr. Lewis the buffoon, the patsy. Much more lovable, this character, than Lewis the veteran showman, great and infallible and only thirty."

Jerry read this stuff and liked it—for a few years, his official publicity biography quoted the phrase "witless genius" as though it were unmistakably a term of praise. He couldn't have helped noticing, then, Van Horne's lack of enthusiasm for his efforts to establish himself as an all-around entertainer. It wasn't, after all, as though she was alone in her impression: "Jose." of *Variety*, reviewing the same broadcast, spoke of his "sticking to his dream of being a one-man cavalcade of show-biz," and also noted that Jerry stood panting at one point during the show and "should take it easier."

Fat chance. By the time the NBC show aired, he was at work at Paramount again, on another Jerry Lewis Production, with Frank Tashlin directing and collaborating with him on the script. The film would take advantage of the publicity Jerry had gotten for his hit record and for the new babies in his family. It would be called *Rock-a-Bye Baby* and feature Jerry as a hapless small-town schnook whose lifetime love has gone off to become a famous actress. When her agent decides that the triplets she's borne will hurt her career, she dumps them back home on Jerry and her sister, whose crush on Jerry is unrequited. Now a successful producer, Jerry cast both Danny and Gary in the film—the elder Lewis in a cameo as a furniture store owner, the younger as Jerry's younger self, sharing a ballad with his father in a fantasy sequence.

Jerry was delighted with the chance to work with Tashlin one on one. During the shoot he managed to break Wallis's will and renegotiate their deal for future Martin and Lewis films. (Reminded, prior to this development, of his obligation to do more pictures with Dean, Jerry responded to reporter Joe Hyams, "The only thing I have to do is die.") Wallis had been owed three Martin and Lewis pictures when the pair split; now he would get three films from each man independently. Jerry had already delivered *The Sad Sack*; he would have to do two more pictures with Wallis, and the first one wouldn't begin shooting for a year. With that in mind, Jerry and Tashlin began writing yet another script, one they could produce before Jerry reported to Wallis. So what if he did three pictures in a year: The public was still buying tickets, wasn't it?

In the middle of the production of *Rock-a-Bye Baby*, Jerry took time off to go back to New York and do an MDA telethon, a nineteen-hour shot studded with guests: Milton Berle, Tony Bennett, Dizzy Gillespie, Jan Murray, Sarah Vaughn, Steve Allen—dozens of them. The show raised $702,000—better than the half-million that he and Dean had raised for MDA the year before, but a hundred thousand dollars less than Dean had managed to wring out of the public in support of the City of Hope a few months earlier. Many in the business had suspected that neither Dean nor Jerry would ever do another MDA event, so intimately linked was the charity organization with them as a pair. But Jerry had never stopped pitching for the MDA on his TV programs, he'd never stopped doing benefit performances for them across the country, and he'd never stopped inventing new ways to combine his passion for showmanship with his increasing devotion to charitable works.

There was Little Boy Blue, for instance. Jerry got a call at Paramount one day in 1957 from a nurse in Middleboro, Massachusetts, telling him about an eight-year-old dystrophic boy at the Lakeville State Sanitarium, where she worked. The boy was known in court and hospital records only as "Francis X" because his father was serving a prison term for murdering his mother six months earlier. His birthday was just a few days off, and the nurse wanted to know if Jerry could do anything to lift the dying boy's spirits. Jerry got the inspiration to do a private show for him and beam it into the hospital in Middleboro. "I went to [NBC president] Bob Sarnoff," Jerry remembered. "I said, 'Bob, I'm gonna ask you for a six-hundred-thousand-dollar favor.' I explained it to him. He said, 'You want to go co-ax from Burbank to somewhere in Massachusetts?' I said, 'I wanna hear you say no to me.' He said, 'You are not someone that I think I can say no to.'"

With only a few days of planning, Jerry got a slew of entertainers to agree to appear with him: George Gobel, Eddie Fisher, Eddie Cantor, Tennessee Ernie Ford, Dinah Shore, cowboy actors Hugh O'Brien and James Arness, the Mouseketeers, even Danny and Gary Lewis. Jerry opened the ninety-minute broadcast by singing "There's No Francis Like Our Francis" to the astonished child. "The only people that saw the show were the few nurses and Little Boy Blue," Jerry remembered. "And we put that fucker together in forty-eight hours. And there it was, in that one room, for an hour and a half. His own special." Newspapers the next day carried a heartbreaking photo of a wheelchair-bound, bathrobed child wearing a Lone Ranger mask (to protect his anonymity) and cutting into a birthday cake.

The Little Boy Blue episode was the sort of grand, full-hearted gesture Jerry couldn't resist, a moment in which a star descended from his celestial heights to touch the heart of a pathetically neglected child. Jerry identified strongly with sick children, whose condition seemed to remind him of his own childhood. At the time of the Little Boy Blue broadcast, he and Tashlin were writing a script evoking similar emotions. It was a strange combination of service comedy and show-biz story: Jerry would play a struggling magician on a tour of American military bases in Japan, in a sentimental plot cribbed from the classic Chaplin weepie *The Kid.*

The Geisha Boy, as it came to be known, is structured less in a point-

counterpoint fashion, with each episode featuring Jerry and his plot line balanced by one focused on a contrasting plot line, than in a block-by-block fashion, with chunks of material utterly unrelated to the plot being dispersed
throughout the story as comic relief. Its straightforward narrative borders on
melodrama, but it incorporates material wholly independent of the narrative
throughout: a Los Angeles Dodgers exhibition game in Tokyo, a montage of
botched performances at military posts, subplots concerning the jealousy of a
hulking Japanese first baseman and the vanity of an American movie actress.
The formula allowed both star and director to indulge in his specialty. Jerry
could break away from the story to sing, do impressions, cavort in block comedy
scenes; Tashlin could stop the plot at any moment for a gag.

It became a working formula, the basis of the four films Jerry and Tashlin
were to make together between 1958 and 1964 and the germ of the movies Jerry
hoped to direct on his own. Tashlin, Jerry later claimed, let him "codirect" *Rock-
a-Bye Baby* and *The Geisha Boy*. (The films do, in fact, bear more resemblance to
Jerry's self-directed films of the 1960s than to *Artists and Models* and *Hollywood
or Bust*, but it's hard to say whether this is because Jerry Lewis produced them or
because of some stylistic influence he exerted on Tashlin.) In fact, directing was
the logical next step. He had already, in a sense, equaled Jolson, the greatest Jewish stage entertainer—the singing, the Palace, the charity work. But until he directed, the greatest screen comic, Chaplin, was on a plateau beyond his grasp.

By January 1958 Jerry had produced two films. *The Delicate Delinquent* was a
global smash hit, on its way to earning nearly $6 million, and there was no reason
Rock-a-Bye Baby shouldn't equal its success. "Around the lot here they call me
the hero producer," he told Joe Hyams. "A businessman is a big operation here.
You don't put an idiot in charge of a million dollars."

He validated his new status as a mogul with something more than just a new
nickname. Big-time producers didn't live in ranch-style houses in Pacific Palisades. Leaving behind the Gar-Ron Playhouse and the baseball field they'd built
on the empty lot next door, he and Patti bought a mansion on St. Cloud Road in
Bel Air. Sitting on two acres in the middle of one of the poshest neighborhoods
in the country, it was a two-story brick colonial with thirty-plus rooms, a dozen
bathrooms, three kitchens, a swimming pool, tennis courts, a huge garage, and
servants' quarters. It had been on the market for $450,000, but Jerry and Patti
were able to get it for $350,000, in part because they knew the former owner, a
man who'd died just the year before and whose widow was happy to sell the
house to someone her husband had liked. His name: Louis B. Mayer. Jerry was
sobered by stepping into the shoes of the onetime most powerful man in the
business. "I think I've grown up," he explained to Louella Parsons. "The home is
going to be an inspiration to me."

With the new house (to which he was adding projection and sound facilities and some other personal luxuries) not scheduled to be ready until May, he traveled. A musicians' strike against the studios forced him and composer Walter Scharf to score *Rock-a-Bye Baby* in Mexico City. In April he returned to London to play the Palladium again, not as one-half of the show-biz equivalent of Roy Cohn and David Schine, but as a showman extraordinaire, an heir to the grand tradition of Sir Harry Lauder. The royal family was in attendance. Jerry remembered the reception he and Dean had been accorded and puttered backstage nervously. Just as he dressed to hit the stage, Jack Keller gave him a pep talk: "Go out there and do the best you can with the shit you got." He played an hour and got the same sort of reaction he had at the Palace: The audiences loved it, and the critics admired his showmanship, if not his material or persona.

Making films that made money all over the world, playing before enthusiastic crowds at the great theaters of New York and London—it was no wonder he began to treat television with disdain. He fulfilled his obligation to NBC, but the network was increasingly unhappy with the results. The reviews were tolerant at best; more than film critics and far more than audiences, TV critics had wearied of his singing, his hogging of the spotlight, his seemingly bottomless desire to prove his versatility. Oldsmobile, his sole sponsor, was making noises about leaving. Jerry tried to spice the show by performing it live in Las Vegas and from an auditorium at UCLA, but NBC refused to pay the additional cost of transmitting the feeds for these broadcasts in color; he had to make up the difference himself. He could afford it—Paramount bought out his interest in York for an estimated $2 million that spring—but it gave the program the air of a vanity product, an indulgence like the Gar-Ron films but without the spirit of spontaneous group fun.

That summer, he toured the country in support of *Rock-a-Bye Baby*, playing concert dates in large outdoor theaters. He was one of the most in-demand live acts in the country, earning an average of forty thousand dollars a week for personal appearances. When he played at the Starlight Theater in Kansas City, he spent twenty-five hundred dollars of his own money to build a runway from the stage across the orchestra pit and into the audience—yet another touch of Jolie. He played the huge Greek Theater in Los Angeles for a week of sold-out shows. Even before a massive crowd sitting outdoors on a summer evening, he demanded complete attention—to a fault. On opening night, after he sang his traditional closer, "Dormi," the stage darkened and members of the audience began to head for the exits. Jerry returned to the stage to take some extra bows and, he said later, to give credit to Lou Brown and the orchestra for their work. Seeing so many people on their way out, he shouted into the mike for everyone to get back in their seats. When he didn't get full compliance, he got testy, swinging the microphone like a lariat. He claimed it was all in jest—some in the crowd had laughed—but Joe Schoenfeld of *Variety* wasn't impressed with his explanation, chiding him for his sharp words and adding, "Surely Lewis is aware of the fact that audiences generally do not walk out on good shows."

Gary Lewis turned thirteen that summer, a signal event in the life of any Jewish boy, as, indeed, it had been for Jerry. But where Jerry's thirteenth birthday was marked by a painful bar mitzvah that his parents failed to attend, Gary's was marked by a phantom bar mitzvah staged to convince Danny and Rae that their grandsons were practicing Judaism. In fact, Gary had been attending catechism classes and was confirmed in the Catholic church, as all of his brothers would eventually be. According to Gary's younger brother Joseph, however, Dan and Rae would accept their grandson's confirmation only if he was also bar mitzvahed. "Neither of my parents wanted this," Joseph explained, "so dad, being the photographic whiz he is, shot photos of my brother dressed for bar mitzvah, in a yarmulke and holding a Torah, and showed them to his parents. They went to their graves thinking Gary had been bar mitzvahed."

Jerry was capable of anything, it seemed, even creating events that didn't happen. Not coincidentally, he increasingly thought of himself as more than just a comedian or stage performer or movie star. He had come to consider himself a spokesperson for the world of show business, granting portentous interviews about the state of the film industry. He spoke disparagingly about filmmakers whose movies tackled social issues. "Selfish stupid men who don't know anything about entertainment and call themselves producers are ruining a great industry by not giving a damn about the public's needs," he told *The New York Times* from the set of *The Geisha Boy*. "They're making movies just to impress themselves, so they can exchange messages telling each other how great and arty they are."

At least as far as public pronouncements about his career were concerned, he was adopting an anti-intellectualism that validated his financial success while nullifying the barbs of critics. "I have often been asked to play a heavy dramatic role," he told *The Los Angeles Examiner*. "It would be a change of pace, but I don't feel any need to change. There are five thousand actors who could do a dramatic role better than I could, but not many have my knack for making people laugh."

But rather than see himself as a humble showman of the people, he actually had come to see himself as a heavyweight player in the film business, not just a clown but a major producer and even a visionary. He spent part of the summer working on a treatise, "Observations of a New Motion Picture Producer by Jerry Lewis," a dozen or so pages of his thoughts on the industry and what it could do to improve itself. In July he sent Hal Wallis a copy of it, which the producer filed away. It began in appropriately humble fashion, apologizing to "the producers whom I served as an *actor*, for some of the headaches and/or heartaches I gave them," a reference that had to have rankled Wallis, the *only* producer aside from himself for whom Jerry had ever worked.

The bulk of the idiosyncratically composed tract consisted of Jerry's pre-scriptions for the industry. Some of these were familiar middle-brow bromides, such as his call for happy endings; some were impracticable business proposals, such as cutting ticket prices or letting theater managers select the films they run; and some were just strange, such as his call for less frequent publicity for movie stars: "There has been too much exposure of stars in pedestrian atmosphere (as cooks in their own homes, in unflattering dungarees, etc.). The public needs idols around whom they build their own illusions." (In 1951 he'd been pho-tographed for *Movie Stars Parade* magazine sitting in his kitchen, poring over the *Betty Crocker Cookbook* with his maid, Carrie, and wearing dungarees, so he must have known what he was talking about.)

When he spoke about the public's need for idols, he was, in a strange way, revealing his own needs. Ever building inside him was the need to prove him-self—to the parents who ignored him, to the partner who deserted him, to the world that had jeered at him when he was a kid. Show business had always seemed to him to be the way to win unqualified approval from others. For a long time it had been enough to be a bigger hit than Danny. For the last eighteen months, it was crucial to be bigger than Martin and Lewis or Dean as a solo act. He had done all that and more. He was a movie star first, but the public loved him regardless of the format: They paid steep prices to see him perform live, they donated money to benefits and telethons he hosted, they bought his records. Only his NBC show, which he performed almost with his eyes closed, wasn't a tremendous hit—at least not with the critics. He could legitimately claim to be the biggest star in the business. He was making money hand over fist, living in Louis B. Mayer's house, commanding respect as a film producer, siring a new son each year. He was even starting to buy into a string of nightclubs and dinner theaters around the country so that he could be his own boss when he was on the road. He didn't have to take crap from anyone. Anyone.

The TV critics got theirs. On KTLA in Los Angeles in October he called them all "caustic, rude, unkind, and sinister," adding that "they're burying the business they're paid by." He could see only the basest of motives for writing a negative review of a TV show: "If a reviewer writes a performer is a nice guy, he may be approached at the golf club the next day and told he's a sissy." Two nights later, his first NBC show of the season aired. He got hammered. Sid Bakal talked about the show's "unprepared look" (it consisted, in fact, of bits lifted from his summer stage show and a takeoff on material in *The Sad Sack*). Jack O'Brian decried "Lewis' apparent permanent addiction to bad taste." John Crosby wrote, "Humility becomes him not at all and I frankly prefer Lewis when he's calling us critics names. He seems more himself."

That really was what it was all about: Film audiences saw a character com-pletely distinct from the man; live audiences witnessed a protracted, exhausting, emotional outpouring of old-fashioned show business, and they had to cheer at the resolution and enthusiasm, if not the talent; but on TV, in their living rooms, people saw something else—the naked man, whom they didn't necessarily prefer to the roles he played. Without the sheer magnetism with which he could put over his material in person, his routines looked wan and old. The coolness of the medium sapped his act of its appeal. People who couldn't get enough of the insane character he played on screen, who found themselves genuinely moved by his onstage charisma and versatility, looked at their televisions and saw nothing but a man performing old songs, skits, and one-liners. Other comics did great on TV: Berle, Gleason, Sid Caesar. Playing themselves or a string of diverse characters, they turned the medium warm by acting as if they belonged in your house. Jerry, lacking on the one hand the time and budget to organize and compose that film afforded him, and on the other the ability to feed off the crowd's attention and affection that he felt onstage, never adjusted to the medium. His efforts to burst through and hug the crowd, which worked for him so well when he was on a stage or enlarged on a movie screen, looking scattershot and desperate on a tiny TV set.

Oldsmobile was willing to back just one more show with him that season, and when Oldsmobile left, NBC couldn't find a replacement. They pulled the plug. Five shows were canceled in all, giving Jerry some needed time off, his first professional come-uppance, and—because he had an ironclad pay-or-play contract with the network—five hundred thousand dollars.

His health was, in fact, shaky. On October 30, 1958, Patti had him rushed to the hospital when he woke up in the night convulsed in stomach pains. He was diagnosed with a perforated ulcer, and his doctors were concerned about his heart as well. They flew in Paul Dudley White, President Eisenhower's Boston-based cardiologist, to take a look at him. White told him to slow down. The holes in his stomach and the flutters of his heart were the result of the stress he was placing on his body. He spent two weeks in the hospital; the diagnosis—overwork.

Dick Stabile offered a second opinion. He blamed it all on Dean. In July the two old partners had bumped into one another at a movie preview party at the Coconut Grove nightclub. In October Jerry had been performing on Eddie Fisher's TV show when Dean, coaxed by Bing Crosby, surprised him on the air, bursting through the curtain as Jerry was about to break into a tune, and shouting, "Don't sing! Just don't sing!" But then he'd blasted Jerry in the papers again, complaining that Jerry was hogging too much credit for the creation of the Muscular Dystrophy Association and bragging that "I'm doing four times better financially than when I was with Jerry. I'm a much happier man since the break. I can do what I want. I have more time with my family. I love working for myself. If something goes good, I know it's me; if something is bad, I don't have to wonder who's at fault."

About most of this, Dean was right, but it was absurd for him to lay dibs on the MDA's success. Martin and Lewis's charity work had always been undertaken at Jerry's instigation. One intimate of the team's recalled just how unconcerned with the MDA Dean had been: "One time we were on the train going from New York to Los Angeles. They brought the Muscular Dystrophy posters in to take pictures on the stop there, and some children. Dean refused to let them take pictures of him. He took his golf club in his hand and walked about twenty-five yards away and started swinging the club while Jerry posed. That hurt Jerry. It hurt him very much. Dean did a lot of things like that."

According to Stabile, even two years after their split, stuff like this broke Jerry's heart. "'I'm sick,'" Stabile recalled him saying. "'I can't work. This time if Dean wants a feud, he'll go it alone. I pray to God I'll never say a word against him, even in my defense.'" The bandleader knew the two men well: "There's no other man alive who can hurt Jerry as Dean can, and of this I believe Dean is well aware. I was present when they broke up. Jerry cried for three solid hours. Dean? One tear in his left eye."

Jerry may not have had the stomach for a feud before his hospital stay, but he found a way to one-up his old partner before long. In December Dean was set to appear on Eddie Fisher's Christmas show. Part of his appearance fee was to be paid with the installation of a new electric kitchen in his house, a $7,500 model like the one Fisher and Debbie Reynolds had in their home. The deal was signed, but when the estimate for installing the kitchen came in $4,000 higher, Fisher's people balked at the added expense. Dean then threatened to play Dinah Shore's show instead, and when the Fisher office told him they'd pay him $20,000 to appear, he raised his price to $25,000. Two weeks before the show was to air, negotiations broke off and Dean's appearance was scrubbed. At the last minute, however, Jerry stepped in and agreed to do the show—for free.

The press had a ball with it, especially when the business about the new kitchen was revealed. Dean felt insulted by Jerry and said so. "Jerry's playing the grandstand martyr," he told *The Los Angeles Times*. "It's not good for show business performers to work for nothing. But then Jerry never did anything good for the business anyhow. He just wanted to make me look bad." He succeeded. Dean spent the holiday depicted as a show-biz Scrooge, Jerry as a munificent Tiny Tim. "I'm not mad at anyone," he purred. "Remember, it takes two to make a feud. I'm not a party to any disagreements. I just went on to help Eddie. I hope everyone has a Merry Christmas."

Hal Wallis got his two remaining films from Jerry in succession: *Don't Give Up the Ship* and *Visit to a Small Planet*, both directed by Norman Taurog between October and July. That was that. Wallis had come to New York and found Jerry in a nightclub, had fought with Jerry when he wanted to appear on screen as something other than the character he had created for himself, had taught Jerry the business by examples both positive and negative, and now they were through with each other. Jerry had acted the grateful jester for a long time, and then the surrogate son, but he eventually evolved into a condescending, insubordinate saboteur. Still, he could never let go of a human connection easily if somewhere in his heart he once held it dear. When *Visit*, which was based on a Gore Vidal stage play, wrapped, Jerry presented Wallis with an engraved silver plaque to thank the producer for all he had done for him. He called a stop to the day's work, according to *Variety*'s Army Archerd, to make a ceremony of it. After "telling Wallis how much he loved him, etc.," Jerry handed over the gift. Once again, Jerry felt the pathos of the moment more than did his parting colleague. According to Archerd, "There were tears in Lewis' eyes. None in Wallis'."

Jerry had another disastrous outing on TV that spring—not on a show of his own, but on the Academy Awards broadcast. He had hosted Oscar shows in 1956 and 1957 without incident and to no small credit. His dignity had impressed people—yet another facet of a personality that they thought they'd known simply as Dean's wacky partner—and his ability with an ad-lib stood him in good stead in a role often taken previously by Bob Hope. People in the industry welcomed his ability to comport himself with maturity and good taste.

But this year was different. At first there were no signs of trouble. Dean was there to present the Best Song award along with Sophia Loren. Indeed, he'd made a comeback of sorts, shocking the world with his actorly, career-saving performance in *The Young Lions*. (On location in France shooting the film with Marlon Brando and Montgomery Clift, Dean broke up the cast and crew by embracing a toothless village-idiot sort who was watching the shoot with the greeting, "Jerry! How long you been in Paris?") Jacques Tati, the brilliant French comic actor and director, took the Foreign Film prize for his film *Mon oncle* and castigated the Academy for its failure to recognize the contributions of the great American film comedians to the medium: "I am not the uncle but the nephew. I respect Hollywood."

For the finale, screenwriter-producer Jerry Wald, who'd produced the broadcast, had all of the evening's winners and presenters come out onto risers and sing "There's No Business Like Show Business" with Mitzi Gaynor leading them. As the remarkable choir—including James Cagney, Bette Davis, Elizabeth Taylor, Doris Day, Rock Hudson, John Wayne, Irene Dunne, Janet Leigh, Cary Grant, Maurice Chevalier, and scores more—made it through the third chorus of the song, Jerry was signaled by Wald from the wings that there was still another twenty minutes to go in the scheduled broadcast. The show had gone off *too* well—with none of the usual delays or long-winded speeches.

Jerry had to improvise. "Another twenty times!" he shouted to the singers.

Conductor Lionel Newman and his orchestra kept playing, and the singers continued. Several stars paired off and began dancing. When Dean waltzed by the podium where the winners' statuettes were on display, he grabbed one for himself. Jerry ad-libbed, "And they said that Dean and I wouldn't be on the same stage again!" "He needs me," Dean shot back.

It got worse. The singers began to disperse. Audience members filed out of the Pantages Theater. Jerry returned to the podium. "We would like to sing three hundred choruses," he announced. "We're showing Three Stooges shorts to cheer up the losers. We'll have a test pattern for the next hour and twenty minutes." He grabbed a baton from Newman and began conducting: "We may get a bar mitzvah out of this!" Before long, he'd picked up a trumpet and started to play off-key. NBC finally broke in with some archive material—a sports film about competitive pistol shooting—and the messy thing was over.

Somebody had screwed up royally. A TV show celebrating the film industry, produced by the best creative talents of the entertainment capital of the world, had dissolved into a chaotic free-for-all. Years later, Jerry recalled that he had seen the whole thing coming and had warned Wald about it to no avail: "He didn't believe me. I said, that afternoon, 'I've got my musicians in here, let me rehearse a couple of things, I have a feeling you're short.' He said, 'We're long, not short.' We were twenty-four minutes short. He was a fucking moron, anyhow. See, I try not to be negative about anybody, but when it's an out-and-out moron and there's no other word to take its place, you've got to say it." By one other account, confusion developed between Jerry and director Alan Handley about whether winners should keep their acceptance speeches brief. Handley had made allowances for long speeches, but in his absence during that day's rehearsal, Jerry told people to be quick, and as a result, the show ran short.

The press didn't care about any of this retrospective finger-pointing. They'd all seen Jerry's antics before, and now they saw him turning the finale of the Academy Awards into what looked like another ego-driven display of wackiness. They all assumed the mistake was his fault, and they all blamed him. Dorothy Kilgallen was particularly incensed, referring to him as "an egg-laying comedian" and deriding his "ghastly evening shirt" and "grisly accent." In the future, Jerry would serve briefly on the Academy's board of governors, and he would lobby with success to have the Academy present Stan Laurel with an honorary award for life achievement in 1960, but he would never appear on an Oscar night telecast again.

He may not have had sufficient glamour or high-brow cachet to be in the Academy clique, and it may have hurt him inside, but there were balms for that. In May 1958 producer Jerry Lewis complained to the *Motion Picture Herald* that the reckless bidding for the services of stars by the studios was drawing money out of the industry and preventing the development of new talent. In June actor

Jerry Lewis signed a record-breaking contract with Paramount Pictures—$10 million for fourteen films over seven years, "the largest price ever paid for acting talent in movie history," according to the studio. Only John Wayne and Marlon Brando among male stars commanded similar per-film fees, and they didn't work as their own bosses. He would own half of the films outright, and the other half would be owned by a combined interest of Jerry Lewis Productions and Paramount, which would distribute them all.

The deal was seen around the industry as a signal from new production chief Jack Karp that Paramount, which had lost many stars to studios with more willingness to open their wallets, would be more aggressive in signing talent (an industry joke had held that a dead man—the late Cecil B. DeMille, whose movies were still making money—was the studio's hottest talent). To those who expressed astonishment at Paramount's willingness to spend so much for Jerry Lewis's services, the studio had a simple answer: The first twenty-one films in which he appeared had grossed more than $400 million worldwide.

Paramount wasn't signing a crazy comic with a dark side; they weren't signing a mere pretender to the thrones of Al Jolson and Charlie Chaplin; they were signing a franchise.

13.

Today You Are a Man

In 1921 Samson Raphaelson, a first-generation American Jew born on the Lower East Side and educated at the University of Illinois, published a short story in *Everybody's Magazine* about a cantor's son who spurns a religious vocation in order to become a singer of popular songs. Entitled "Day of Atonement," the story was immediately recognized by members of the Jewish show-business community as a fitting emblem of their experience of assimilation into gentile society through the medium of mass entertainment. One cantor's son in particular—Al Jolson—felt an intense attraction to the material, bringing it to the attention of a variety of movie people as a possible vehicle for himself (D. W. Griffith, the director of *The Birth of a Nation*, dismissed the story as "racial"). When Jolson finally met Raphaelson at a nightclub and told him of his enthusiasm, the author developed a proprietary attitude toward "Day of Atonement" and short-circuited Jolson's plans by adapting it himself into a stage play.

Raphaelson's dramatic version of his story premiered on Broadway in 1925, with George Jessel—not, pointedly, Jolson—in the lead role; in this new incarnation, it was called *The Jazz Singer*. Although reviewers didn't care much for the production—*The New York Times* wrote that it was "so written that even the slowest of wits can understand it"—the play ran for a full season of thirty-eight weeks, after which both Jessel and the story were bought up by Warner Brothers.

Warner was literally the only studio in Hollywood willing to touch such explicitly Semitic material. Whereas the Jews who ran the other film studios erased any trace of their ethnicity from their movies, Harry Warner was a champion of various social issues and made films that addressed matters of race, tolerance, and bigotry. He felt that a story about Jewish assimilation would help others understand his people, and he was eager to make a major film of Raphaelson's play. To that end, he and his brothers, Jack and Sam, decided to use *The Jazz Singer* as the occasion to introduce synchronized sound on screen. Furthermore, they instructed screenwriter Alfred A. Cohn to turn the story—which, after all, was about a singer—into a musical. For this reason (and perhaps because Jessel's Yiddish humor smelled too strongly of the ghetto for even their tastes), the Warners cast Jolson as Jacob Rabinowitz, the starstruck Jewish boy who changes his name to Jack Robin and makes a hit in the gentile show world, only to return to his late father's synagogue to conduct a Kol Nidre service in his honor.

The screen version of *The Jazz Singer* debuted on October 6, 1927 (the day after the sudden death of Sam Warner, who oversaw the technical innovations in the film), and it became an instant classic, revolutionizing practically every entertainment medium. Competing studios scrambled to develop their own sound systems. Talent scouts scoured Broadway and the vaudeville and burlesque circuits for actors with resonant voices. Dialogue writers were suddenly in urgent demand. Radio became a new venue for advertising films and film stars. But above all, Jolson, already a legend in the ranks of show professionals, became a god. To aspire, as young Danny Lewis had, to sing and dance and thrill a crowd the way Jolson did was one kind of conceit; to see oneself as a star of groundbreaking movies that encapsulated the immigration experience of one's family and race was an aspiration of quite another order. *The Jazz Singer* was a genuine milestone of show-business history, an Everest for entertainers who aspired to Jolson's mantle.

By 1959—and in the wake of an ill-fated '50s remake starring Danny Thomas—everyone in Hollywood considered *The Jazz Singer* moldy and sacrosanct at once. Astonishment and wicked anticipatory glee therefore greeted the news that Jerry Lewis would appear in a made-for-TV version of it. In Jerry's hands, the story would be about a young man who forsakes his father's traditional religious life to become not a crooner but a clown. "Rudolph the Red-Nosed Cantor" was the disparaging nickname foisted onto the project by Hollywood snickerers, who saw in it irrefutable proof of the baldness of Jerry's ambition to usurp every important spot in the traditional show-business hierarchy. "This is something that has been bugging Jerry for some time," wrote Cecil Smith of *The Los Angeles Times*. "He is a man who runs with such ferocity that he makes Sammy Glick seem like a cigar store Indian—he continually sets up goals to prove himself; he must prove things over and over and over again. He is always saying that he has no interest in what critics write about him—'the day you entertain the critic, you lose the audience.' But he says it too often, so this must bug him too."

Smith was right about Jerry's hubris, but he didn't quite glimpse little Joey Levitch standing behind the project and straining to show the world that he belonged in it. In fact, *The Jazz Singer* was one of Jerry's most personal and heartfelt undertakings. He changed the name of the protagonist from Jack to Joey and further christened Joey's sympathetic mother Sarah, after his beloved maternal grandmother. And while he atavistically retained the title of the project even though there was no jazz singing in it, he could have written from personal experience the story of the son eclipsing the father and then sentimentally capitulating to him.

Jerry admitted as much to Hal Humphrey of *The Los Angeles Mirror News*, harkening back to one of his deepest pains to explain the genesis of the project: "When I was thirteen, my parents couldn't afford my bar mitzvah. Dad was on the road making twenty dollars a week in burlesque and I was living with my grandmother. I had to accept a charity bar mitzvah from the synagogue. You can't imagine how badly my family felt about this. So *The Jazz Singer*, with its relationship between a Jewish father and his son, is kind of close to me."

Nevertheless, it was ironic material to work with. Danny had virtually retired, after all, and had long resigned himself to Jerry's career choices. He lived primarily off of his son's largesse, though he still reserved for himself the right to criticize Jerry's material and colleagues. His bitter grumblings about his failed career, however, were hardly analagous to Cantor Rabinowitz's pious grief over his son's departure from religious traditions. For Jerry's part, while he felt a filial bond with his father and sentimentally bragged about Danny's show-biz prowess, his hero worship for Danny had died, and he found himself increasingly uncomfortable in his presence.

Still, he hoped to craft *The Jazz Singer* into an autobiographical project—by his own description, the bar mitzvah he never had. NBC didn't quite see it the same way, trying to rein Jerry in as much as possible from creating a statement of his artistic maturity. For one thing, the network limited the show to an hour— thirty minutes shorter than Jolson's version—and insisted against Jerry's objections that it be taped rather than broadcast live. This particularly irked the star. "I need the charge I get from a live audience," he complained to Humphrey. "It's the only real way to find out anymore if people really like you."

The Jazz Singer was broadcast in color on October 13, 1959, as an installment of the "Ford Startime" series of specials and made-for-TV movies. Ralph Nelson directed the show under the supervision of producer Ernie Glucksman (the two had collaborated on the teleplay). Yiddish stage legend Molly Picon appeared as Jerry's mother, Eduard Franz played Cantor Rabinowitz (reprising his role from the Danny Thomas film), and Anna Maria Alberghetti, the twenty-three-year-old Italian-born contralto who'd played opposite Dean Martin in *Ten Thousand Bedrooms*, was cast as Jerry's sweetheart.

The critics were only slightly kinder after the broadcast than they had been beforehand. "Lewis," wrote "Jose." in *Variety*, "is hardly the figure to swing between the double masks of comedy and tragedy with any degree of ease, and there were times when the demands of the role were just too much for him. . . . The spectacle of Lewis singing 'Kol Nidre' [the final prayer of Yom Kippur, the holiest of Jewish holidays] in blackface just about twenty-four hours after the

Day of Atonement just didn't sit right along ecclesiastical lines, and looked like a dramatic gimmick of a bygone era."

It wasn't a flop on the scale of Neil Diamond's laughable 1980 version of *The Jazz Singer*, but it was hardly proof to the world of its star's dramatic talents. Some weeks later, asked about his recurrent bad luck on television, Jerry sneered to the *New York Post*, "TV is a joke."

He was lucky enough, anyhow, not to have to depend on a medium he couldn't get the hang of to make his living. He was, as he liked to say, "a Jewish movie star," and people were still happy to see him on stage and the big screen. He had been selected 1959's Star of the Year by the people who knew from stars: the Theater Owners of America. He did Paramount producer Norman Panama a favor by making a cameo appearance in his film of the Broadway musical *Li'l Abner* as Itchy McCrabby, gangling noisily out of the crowd to take a gander at Stupefyin' Jones (Julie Newmar), then adopting a grotesque, stock-still pose at the sight of her pulchritude. During the late summer and autumn he toured the southwest at a string of supermarket openings, gala one-shots that filled his wallet and kept him in front of live audiences. He spent even more time on the road doing personal appearances shilling *Don't Give Up the Ship*, a heroic task considering that it was a Hal Wallis film.

On October 17 Patti gave birth yet again, to Anthony Joseph, named after her patron saint. "With all the babies we've been having," Jerry told reporters at St. John's Hospital in Santa Monica, "maybe I ought to go downstairs and open a charge account." He now had five sons to carry on his name.

Two days later he went before the cameras in the fourth Jerry Lewis production, *Cinderfella*, Frank Tashlin's gender-reversed reworking of the fairy tale. It would be a full-scale musical, a glossy production with big sets, a budget approaching $2 million, a soundtrack recording, and a Christmas release. Such high-profile performers as Dame Judith Anderson and Ed Wynn (the only important comedian ever to play a major part in one of Jerry's films) filled key roles. Jerry's plans were grand enough to induce him to ask Grace Kelly, three years retired to regal family life, if she would appear in the film. Confiding that he had "something of utmost importance" to discuss that could benefit the princess, her husband, and all of Monaco, he wired her in July requesting an audience either by telephone or in person and declaring his readiness to "fly to Monaco immediately pending your answer." (In mid-August Herman Citron told Jerry that he'd finally heard from Kelly's former agent Jay Kanter, who said that the princess "tried to reach you, but was told you had gone away for two weeks." So much for being at the princess's beck and call.)

The production ran into little speed bumps like that all along. The folks at Disney, angry at the resemblance of the film's title to their 1950 animated movie, threatened to take action against Paramount unless Jerry's film was more clearly distinguished from theirs; a logo was designed in which the *f* in *Cinder-fella* was printed in an elongated red typeface, and the protest was squelched. Early in the production, costar Erin O'Brien found herself on the wrong side of her producer and was fired (the first of several young actresses whom Jerry would dismiss early in his films); she was replaced by Anna Maria Alberghetti, but not until Jerry agreed to play the Palmer House in Chicago to compensate for pulling Alberghetti from an engagement there in order to make his film.

Then, on November 18, disaster: Jerry collapsed on the set after attempting several consecutive takes of a frantic run-up an enormous flight of stairs. "I was eating at the restaurant across the street from Paramount," recalled Jerry's cousin Marshall Katz, who'd been working in Jerry's offices since *The Delicate Delinquent*, "and I got a call that Jerry had collapsed, so I ran across the street and I ran up those stairs myself. And that was a huge staircase."

Frank Tashlin also ran up the stairs, and he later confessed his helplessness in a memo to Paramount publicity director Jack Karp, saying "It is unfortunate but I am completely ineffectual when exposed to another's illness. . . . If Mr. Lewis had been in real serious trouble I would have been of absolutely no help."

Tashlin credited a studio policeman, Fritz Hawkes, with cool-headed action. Hawkes called an ambulance, and Jerry was taken to his dressing room; when it was determined that he was merely out of breath and not suffering a heart attack, he was given oxygen. The workaholic producer-star was back on the set that afternoon, and three days later he hosted an MDA telethon from the Ziegfeld Theater in New York—"The Jerry Lewis 1959 Thanksgiving Party"—with his doctor, Marvin Levy, watching anxiously from the wings.

He simply couldn't stay out of the limelight. "Money can't really give you anywhere near the comfort of being embraced by a mob," he told a reporter. "A mob wanting to touch you and hug you, that embrace is far more warm than a deposit at the bank." Take television, for instance. Not since he was booed off the stage of the Palace Theater in Buffalo had he been so summarily rebuffed as a professional. And yet he was always lured back to the most popular of media, the tool by which he believed he could reach the largest conceivable audience. In January 1960 NBC found another sponsor for his occasional shows, Timex, and he was back on the air with a newly philosophical attitude about his enemies in the press. "The critic has a psychological problem right off when he realizes he *must* review," he mused to a writer from *The New York Herald Tribune*. "Well, conditions are not always right for objective reviewing. If I'm a critic and I have a headache, the guy cutting up on TV is more irritating than entertaining to me. Maybe I had a fight with the wife. Or the kids are acting up. So many elements enter into a reviewer's attitude toward a show. The thing I take offense at is when a critic will write, 'Jerry Lewis is not my cup of tea.' This is not criticism. This is an expression of the critic's personal taste. It's completely unfair to the performer. But what am I saying? I promised to quit fighting the critics."

But he couldn't stand any note of rejection. When the three Timex shows were, inevitably, slammed in the press ("a study in disorganization"; "Lewis, listening to inner voices, should settle down to hear the voices of others"; and "a disaster . . . a fiasco," wrote three different *Variety* reviewers about them), he once again blamed the messenger for the bad news. Driving along Sunset Boulevard in a new convertible, wearing a black leather jacket, corduroy slacks, and cowboy boots, and racing off to the christening of dancer-choreographer Bobby Van's child (to whom he had been named godfather), he once again sounded off spitefully to a reporter: "I can write the reviews for my show before we ever go on. . . . The critic who belts my show does me a favor. They create a bond between myself and the fans I know are watching. I don't need a critic. I know when I've done a good show or a bad one. Don't tell me when I've made a flop, just let me crawl into a corner and lick my wounds. You tell me how to entertain 240 critics instead of 40 million people. It's impossible to entertain them both and I prefer to please the people."

But he was finally feeling the burns under his skin, and later in the year he and NBC decided to scuttle the Timex show for the 1960–61 season. He had bigger fish to fry.

As Jerry always told the story, Barney Balaban, Y. Frank Freeman's successor as head of production of Paramount, approached him in January 1960 with the request that *Cinderfella*, which had not yet been edited, be completed for distribution in July. Each year since 1954, the studio had released a Jerry Lewis (or Martin and Lewis) picture during the summer months and another one at Christmas. The schedule for this year, however, called for the Wallis production of *Visit to a Small Planet* to be released in April and *Cinderfella* to premiere in December. And since the first film didn't quite seem like summer entertainment, with its droll political satire and Gore Vidal dialogue, Balaban was eager to get a lighter version of his star into theaters while the kids were out of school.

Jerry could have acceded to Balaban's request easily; he did, after all, owe Paramount two films a year. But he didn't want to tinker with his elaborate plans for *Cinderfella*. He had, after all, learned how to promote a film at Wallis's feet (even working himself into a lather when early publicity referred to it as "Paramount's *Cinderfella*" and not "A Jerry Lewis Production"). He told Balaban he'd give him *another* Jerry Lewis movie for the summer. In fact, he'd *direct* a Jerry Lewis movie for him.

Balaban was a money man with a taste for old-style showmanship. An immigrant grocer's son from Chicago, he'd entered the picture business as a theater owner in 1908 after his mother pointed out to him that moviegoers paid their money *before* they got the product. He was a sober businessman who had parlayed a single theater into the national Balaban and Katz chain. Yet he had built fancifully exotic movie palaces in the glorious old style: the Valencia, the Oriental, the Tivoli, the Riviera. In 1936, when Paramount was in trouble, he was re-cruited to come in and reorganize it, and he'd climbed the corporate ladder steadily ever since. So while he could appreciate the commercial potential in Jerry's idea, he was shrewd enough to refuse to finance it.

But Jerry was a step ahead of him. He was a man with a hundred-thousand-dollar-per-year personal clothing bill; he'd pay for the movie himself. He'd done it before in his own backyard, after all. Balaban would be allowed to share distri-bution rights to the film without taking any financial risk whatsoever. He gave Jerry the green light: *So where was the script?*

By Jerry's account, there *was* no script. He flew to a nightclub engagement at the Fontainebleau Hotel in Miami that night and had an epiphany: He would make the movie there, a movie about a bellboy, done all in pantomime. If he could convince owner Ben Novak to let him use the hotel as a set, he'd save a fortune in production costs, he'd be out of eyeshot of Paramount executives, and he'd get to work in his favorite of all environments: a Jewish resort hotel.

This last element of the plan appealed to him most of all. Whereas the backyard parties that served as breeding ground for his Gar-Ron films merely simulated the conditions of a Catskills hotel, a big Miami hotel in the winter-time *was* a Catskills hotel, just one that had flown south for the winter. The same northeastern Jews who vacationed in the mountains in the summer were now able to travel by plane to Miami in the winter; the trip by air from New York took about as much time as a drive to Loch Sheldrake. And where the traditional audiences went, the traditional entertainers followed. The Miami Beach strip was lousy with old Catskill acts—acrobats, lounge singers, comics, and danc-ers—and Jerry knew they'd all be thrilled to have walk-on parts. He could pull the whole film off for about a million bucks. Novak was amenable, and Jerry set to work.

"I wrote the script," he recalled in his autobiography, "stayed up eight days and eight nights. Not one wink of sleep. I turned out 165 pages like some kind of drugged madman, alternately writing and hallucinating scene after scene." On January 30 his engagement at the Fontainebleau ended. On February 8 *The Bell-boy* went before the cameras. Twenty-six days later it was wrapped, and it opened in July, just as Balaban had insisted.

The funny thing about this improbable story is that it's true. Written drafts of some of the material were as much as four years old, but the "silly farce by Jerry Lewis," as an early version called it, was essentially conceived, written, shot, and released in about six months; no papers in the copious Jerry Lewis Produc-tions files on the film are dated before January 1960. Jack Keller confirmed al-most every aspect of Jerry's story in a conversation with Peter Bogdanovich: "I'm sitting here in Hollywood resting, when I get a call from Jerry. He says to me, 'Jake, you better come down here right away, we're starting a picture on Mon-day.' I said, 'Where *are* you?' He says, 'I'm in Florida.' I say, 'What picture? We ain't got no picture!' 'We do now,' he says. 'The trucks are already on their way.' I asked him, 'Who's gonna be in it?' He says, 'What's the difference? We'll cast it from Celebrity Service.' Every scene was written the night before he shot it—for whomever was in town."

As impressive as the pace of the production was, though, the novelty of it was even greater. It was unusual enough for a popular movie comedian to write and direct a film in 1960—no comic who'd debuted in talkies had ever done it. That Jerry did it, and did it under conditions like those of a (well-financed) independent film, is mind-boggling.

Part of the reason he succeeded was that he was willing to abuse his body to produce work. His history of collapses and ulcers and cardiac emergencies was directly related to his tendency to overwork himself. He fueled himself with tobacco, four packs a day at times, with a bowl of cigarettes on his desk that he insisted his secretaries keep filled. "Don't tell anybody I told you," he was quoted as saying, "but that's the secret of all my pep. It's my corpuscles fighting off the nicotine. Very combustible."

During the shooting of the film, Dr. Marvin Levy was flown in (at the expense of the production) to consult with Jerry for a week. The discussions were more than just medical. As Patti recalled, "A friend confided that Jerry had our family doctor fly to Florida to discuss some of his problems and answer questions about the ramifications of his someday leaving me." Miami—his first extended trip away from home with neither his wife nor his ex-partner to observe him—apparently agreed with him. Patti and the boys did come east for part of the production—four-year-old Scotty had a birthday party on the set—but for the most part Jerry was left to his own devices.

As an expression of his feelings of independence, he flaunted his freedom from Paramount. He'd learned from watching Tashlin's dealings with producers and executives just how suffocating the studio could be to a director of outlandish tastes. If he had tried to make the film in Hollywood, he would be scrutinized every day. And since he was making what amounted to an experimental film—a series of comic vignettes—he would have been fought at every move.

He knew, for instance, that his very working method would be criticized, for he had begun employing a radical new technology, the sort of thing that only an autodidact and gadget-lover could bring to so institutionalized a medium. One thing that Jerry had always liked about television was the use of closed-circuit monitors to cut rehearsal time; a director watching a scene on a monitor could see the broadcast just as it would look on the air and give immediate feedback to the actors and technicians. Jerry's idea for filming *The Bellboy* was to mount a small video camera beneath the regular film camera and connect it to a closed-circuit monitor. Whatever the big camera saw, more or less, the little camera would show him. He couldn't tape anything, but he could see and do a lot more than ever before. He could use the monitor to help actors see what they were doing, to reduce the amount of conference time he spent with the director of photography, even to direct scenes that he himself was in, watching the monitor right up until the moment he made his entrance or the camera panned to his mark.

Today, every movie director in the world uses some version of this "video assist," as Jerry dubbed it, but in 1960 Jerry was the first. And he was convinced that his experiment was a wild success, writing to Paramount technician Russ Brown: "It is an absolute blessing. . . . I feel like I have had the experience of 10 pictures under my belt rather than but one."

The studio sent Bruce Denney, supervisor of its technical departments, to Miami to observe the shoot and file a detailed report on the experiment. He wrote nineteen detailed pages crowing about the myriad ways in which Jerry and his crew benefited from use of the system and itemizing the very few technological hitches in it that had to be corrected. But Paramount wasn't convinced, and for the next few years, Jerry was the only director on the lot permitted to use a closed-circuit monitor or videotape system on his set. By the time the industry caught on, however, there were so many variations on the idea that Jerry couldn't even get a patent on it.

On the day he sat in the director's chair for the first time, Jerry got a well-wishing telegram from Paramount's chairman of the board, Adolph Zukor, and another from his agent, Herman Citron. Addressing his client as "Boychick," he congratulated him bar mitzvah–style: "Today you are a man." The new director put himself and his crew through twenty-one different shots and setups, some requiring as many as seven takes. The film was still being written and cast as it was being shot. Some performers whom Jerry had hoped might appear in cameos bowed out; others invited themselves to be in the picture. Most of them were familiar names from the Catskills—stars like Milton Berle and Henny Youngman, troupers like Joey Adams, Jack Durant, Sonny Sands, and Sammy Shore, even old family friends like Jimmy and Tillie Gerard (Danny and Rae weren't invited to appear; nor was Lenny Bruce, who was in Miami during the shoot and hung around with Jerry for a while). Along with Bill Richmond, a writer he'd met a few years earlier, Jerry wrote block comedy scenes for his inept, mute character, called Rutherford in early drafts of the script but known as Stanley in the completed film. The original script was far too long; it would have made a three-hour film, easily. Nevertheless, he shot as much of it as he could, to give himself that much more to choose from during editing.

The pace was grueling; Jerry had to wrap shooting by early March so he could fulfill an engagement at the Sands in Vegas. Most days were as busy as that first one, and the crew even put in two Sundays. When he finished, he went home for a week and then was off to Vegas with an overabundance of footage to cut into a film.

In Vegas, Jerry was literally too tired to take the stage. But a coincidence of booking at the hotel would make it impossible for him to cancel gracefully: Of all acts to have preceded him at the Sands, Dean Martin had just closed on Saturday night. Jerry had, in fact, caught his ex-partner's closing set. "It was the first time I had seen him work alone since we split and I was surprised and delighted," he said a few months later. At the end of the show, Dean introduced Jerry to the crowd and brought him on stage, where they mugged a bit and sang a comic duet of "Come Back to Me."

"We strained trying to remember what we used to do, and for fifteen minutes there wasn't a dry eye in the house, including ours," Jerry recalled. "It was a beautifully emotional thing, with two people who cared for each other for very many years, and then, because of their own insecurities, led the world to believe that they didn't care anymore. You just don't turn off caring. Your subconscious lets you think you do. Of course, this doesn't mean we're going to team up again—Dean is doing just great, he doesn't need anybody to help him, and I'm doing fairly well, too. I still maintain that our problems never really stemmed from the two of us but from the fringe. Because if I were ever in trouble, the first one in line, you could bet, would be Dean. And vice versa."

He made the severed relationship sound more secure than either of their marriages, and he was probably right. On the following Wednesday, when he was too fatigued to fulfill his obligation to the hotel, Dean stepped in to play the date in his stead.

In April, while he was playing yet another live engagement, this time at the Moulin Rouge nightclub in Hollywood (his writing partner, Bill Richmond, sat in as a drummer), he finished cutting *The Bellboy* into a sixty-five-minute film. Two weeks later, it was previewed to military personnel and their families at March Air Force Base, near San Bernadino, and Camp Pendleton, near San Diego. The servicemen could be a harsh audience—"I predict that it will go over worse than 'The Geisha Boy,' " wrote one marine who fancied himself a canny movie executive—but Jerry found fault with the film himself: "Re-Edit!!" read a note he scribbled during the second screening. "Stay on the Kid!" On May 23, several scenes were reshot at Paramount; thinking ahead, Jerry had had a crewmember swipe some Fontainebleau wallpaper so he could match the other shots from three thousand miles away. By June 1, the film was completed.

The Bellboy wound up costing $1.34 million of Jerry's own money—less than Wallis had spent on *Three Ring Circus* six years before—and much of that was spent on material he didn't use: Sequences involving Henny Youngman and Corrine Calvet (her career at such an ebb that she was willing to forget Jerry's abusive antics of ten years earlier) didn't make the final seventy-two-minute cut. Included in the budget was a bill for $16,325.02 from the Fontainebleau (which Jerry's accountants whittled down to a payment of $5,495.28), a $768 bill for

gifts of liquor to the crew on closing day, and an untallied bill for forty-eight bottles of Arpège perfume to female hotel staffers. Jerry paid himself $50,000 for
the script and another $150,000 for his own services as producer, director, and
star.

The money didn't come out of his personal bank account, of course, but was
routed through the companies he'd set up after signing his big contract with
Paramount—a web of corporate entities that included the Jerry Lewis Pictures
Corporation; Patti Enterprises, Inc.; Jerry Lewis Enterprises, Inc.; and the Gar-
Ron Pictures Corporation, all under the banner of Jerry Lewis Productions, Inc.
His business card listed them all. Under the terms of the contract, Paramount
gave him $2 million up front for each of the seven pictures he would produce;
given the quickness and tightness with which he'd shot *The Bellboy*, he was better than a half-million ahead before the film even opened. Successes like that
convinced him he could do business for himself without the advice of his agents
at MCA. He insisted that publicity materials for the picture not be run past the
agency because "MCA has a habit of knocking these things out." He was
adamantly his own boss.

He was also a thinker. He had begun assembling a book of quotations,
apothegms, maxims, moral tales, and wisdom, a kind of Victorian miscellany
along the lines of Elbert Hubbard's *Scrap Book*. He called it his "creed book,"
and he filled it with familiar aphorisms like the one he shared that summer with
columnist Sheila Graham: "There are only three things in life that are real. God,
human folly, and laughter. Since the first two pass our comprehension, we must
do what we can with the third." He began a lifelong habit of dropping names like
Hemingway, Saroyan, Tacitus, or "someone far brighter than I," sounding like
the archetypical dropout trying to pass as an intellectual, even though he
claimed a year or so earlier that he'd read only one book in his life. Still, in show-
business circles, the gleaning of even trite bits of popular philosophy into a volume *was* a form of intellectualism, and it was yet another way for him to prove
he wasn't the dope that his persona made him seem. He considered the creed
book to be a legitimate work: He had copies bound and gave them to family
members and close friends.

Among his newest friends was Stan Laurel. Jerry had been introduced to the
great comedian by Dick Van Dyke, who had looked up the comedy legend after
hearing that he was living in modest seclusion with the aftereffects of a stroke.
On a Sunday morning Jerry drove to Santa Monica to pay Laurel a visit. He had
always admired Laurel as a graceful comic who perfectly combined the physical
with the verbal to achieve a blend of humor and pathos. But now that he met
the man, he was even more impressed with what they had in common: sons of
small-time showmen, halves of famous comedy teams that paired them with
men who were their temperamental opposites.

Jerry showed Laurel his script for *The Bellboy*, which had already wrapped but was still being edited. He listened to the older man discourse on life and comedy. After a second visit, Jerry offered Laurel a job as a consultant with Jerry Lewis Productions at a salary of $150,000 a year. Laurel demurred, indicating to Jerry that he considered the generous offer to be mere charity. Jerry insisted that Laurel could be of great value to him, but the older man wouldn't hear it. He was embarrassed by his mild debilities and, unlike his young devotee, he was constrained by modesty from thrusting himself before the public.

By June Paramount was so satisfied with the feeling they got from *The Bellboy* that they encouraged Jerry to put another film into production. He already had a story in mind—it was known as "The Girls' Boy"—and all he needed was some help in getting it written.

Jerry hadn't received a writing credit for anything before *The Bellboy*, although he'd been collaborating with his writers for years. He was, in fact, used to writing along with a team. Since he had two films to finish before the year was out—*Cinderfella* still hadn't been previewed—he decided to hire another writer for the new project. He chose Mel Brooks.

They were a natural match. Brooks, born Melvin Kaminsky in Brooklyn three months after Jerry was born in Newark, had also begun performing in the Catskills as a teenager, playing drums and doing impressions. Unlike Jerry, he had served in World War II as a combat engineer. Though he'd had aspirations to become a star, choosing as his stage name an abbreviated form of his mother's maiden name, Brookman, he had better luck breaking into show business as a television writer, finding work with Sid Caesar on 1949's "Admiral Broadway Review" and remaining a part of the legendary writing team (along with Carl Reiner, Neil Simon, and Woody Allen, among others) on "Your Show of Shows" (1950–54), "Caesar's Hour" (1954–57), and "Sid Caesar Invites You" (1958). In 1960 he was still well regarded as a writer and a kind of comic's comic—not quite as popular with audiences as with those in the business. Jerry's offer of three thousand dollars a week for about four months of work was, for such a cult performer, a great opportunity. (Bill Richmond, by contrast, was paid five thousand dollars total for the same period.) The deal was consummated on June 15 with a telegram from Brooks's new boss: "Here's to a wonderful relationship."

Before they could begin work together, however, Jerry rushed off to New York for a quick publicity tour in support of *The Bellboy*. There would be no several-city caravan for the film. Paramount wasn't even showing it to the trade press until the night before it opened, a strategy designed to protect the curious experiment from the hostility that Jerry and the distribution office feared the critics would direct toward it. That he had written, directed, produced, and starred in the film was the target of enough hostile humor around Hollywood already; why let his enemies vent their scorn on a little comedy? He did at least ten newspaper interviews that week, and appeared on a half-dozen or more TV and radio programs. On June 23 he sat all day for illustrator Norman Rockwell, who painted the poster art for *Cinderfella*. Arrangements were made with the Loew's theater chain for Jerry to return on July 20 and 21 and put in more than twenty personal appearances before showings of the film (when it was suggested to him in a memo that he show up in a bellboy's uniform, he scribbled "Forget it!" across the page).

The press was intrigued by Jerry's one-man approach to filmmaking, but when they began comparing him to Charlie Chaplin, Jerry wisely downplayed the resemblances without dismissing them outright. Indeed, he found some small advantage in the comparison: In recent years, Chaplin's politics had made him anathema, and having been asked about his professed master, Jerry chose to distance himself from him. "To compare me to Chaplin is ludicrous in a sense. Chaplin was a real master. I'd have to work fifty years to begin to touch what he did. But we work differently. I don't impose my thinking as a person on an audience. I don't think comedy has room for a political approach."

He hedged less when he described the joys of hard work and being his own boss. "When you do so many jobs on a picture, it sometimes means a twenty-one-hour day, but it's a wonderful thing for you—physically, mentally, and spiritually. What's the advantage? Well, look at it this way: You're not as careful with your cigarette ashes in another guy's office as you are in your own home. Nobody will work quite as hard for you as you will for yourself."

On July 5, 1960, the Hollywood press was finally allowed to see what *The Bellboy* looked like. They hated it. "Minor league screen comedy," wrote "Tube." in *Variety*, "the victim of its energetic star's limited creative equipment." *The Hollywood Reporter* was even less kind: "It is the least entertaining motion picture in which Lewis has ever appeared, and, objectively considered, is a shameful waste of a major comic talent." The next day, the film opened to somewhat more receptive reviews in daily newspapers. "He has kept his energetic demeanor in reasonable check," observed Eugene Arthur in *The New York Times*, though John L. Scott of *The Los Angeles Times* noted, in a generally positive review, that "if director Lewis hadn't allowed star Lewis to 'mug' quite so much, the results would have been much funnier." There was a positive rave in *The Rochester Daily Democrat-Chronicle* (Jerry kept a copy of the review in his files on the film). Critic Stephen Hammer, calling the film a "masterpiece," astutely remarked that "he doesn't sing, dance, wisecrack or upstage anybody, as he has so many times before. Instead he concentrates on the areas in which he is superb: Ideas and pantomime."

The Bellboy was shot in black-and-white, there was no story to speak of, and the lead character could not talk; for a Hollywood film released in 1960, it was virtually avant-garde. To answer Paramount's baffled reaction to the film, Jerry added an introduction in which a phony film producer, "Jack Emulsion," explained to the audience that they were about to see "a film based on fun. And it's just a little bit different . . . a visual diary of a few weeks in the life of a real nut."

What followed was a series of some forty-odd vignettes and set pieces, all but two or three of which centered on Stanley, a mute klutz of a bellboy, and all but two or three of which took place in the Fontainebleau. Some of the gags were right out of Frank Tashlin's valise of cartoonishly impossible stunts: Stanley gives a dieting woman a box of chocolates and she balloons in an instant; Stanley fills an empty auditorium with perfectly orderly rows of chairs in sixty seconds; a man gets a polka-dot suntan after Stanley lays a mesh cloth over his face; Stanley takes a flash photo of the night sky and turns 3:00 A.M. into broad daylight. Many of them were old-style burlesque and Borscht Belt routines, but there are also a few gags that only Jerry could have conceived, bits that could have worked only in a film: Stanley's brilliant 'conducting' of a nonexistent orchestra, his theft of a commercial airliner, his inability to find a place to sit and eat his lunch when an entire cafeteria suddenly fills with diners, his inadvertent destruction of a sculpture in an art show.

Yet there was an entirely personal, even autobiographical dimension to the whole film—notably in the long passage in which the Fontainebleau hosts the big movie star Jerry Lewis, who is holding a special preview of his new film at the hotel. The star (billed as played by "Joe Levitch") arrives in a limousine escorted by a cadre of motorcycle cops. He is accompanied by an entourage of twenty-seven sycophants, all of whom emerge from the limo before him. His handlers brush off his clothing so much they rumple him; when he starts to smoke, so many lighters snap open in front of his face that his cigarette is crushed; when he tells the hotel manager he isn't feeling well because of a death in the family, the entourage breaks out in phony laughter. It's a tart portrait of the life of a celebrity, an acknowledgment of the empty spaces that exist between identities of public man, movie character, and private man. This theme is further doubled by the brief appearance of Milton Berle in the film as both himself and a bellboy, and by the appearance of an unnamed character played by Bill Richmond, a simulacrum of Stan Laurel who wanders through the film pulling off utterly surreal gags in an explicit homage to one of *The Bellboy*'s most direct influences.

At least two of the film's gags were taken right out of Jerry's life. In one, Stanley runs off and fetches a steamer trunk with great difficulty, only to find out that the bell captain wanted not the trunk but the hat box on top of it; the gag was a take-off on the solicitude of Jerry's second son, Ronnie, who was so eager to please his father that he would rush from the room to fulfill a request of Jerry's before it had been made explicit; according to Patti, "It upset Jerry very, very much." And the beating Stanley suffers at the hands of an older couple, played by Danny and Rae's old friends Jimmy and Tillie Gerard, was certainly an emblem of Jerry's own relationship with his parents; though the husband and wife are screaming viciously at each other about which of them spends more money, they marshall their forces to squelch any hint of interference from the outside, however benignly it was intended.

Much of *The Bellboy* is hackneyed and must certainly have seemed that way when the film debuted. Yet Jerry's characterization is vivid and fresh—Stanley is chipper and eager, whistling along while he works his destructive magic (Paramount wanted to hire professional whistler Muzzy Marcellino to dub the film, but Jerry did his own whistling). He's not a believable fictional character—any bellboy this inept would surely be fired—but rather an emblem for a class of low-profile bunglers and hapless nothings; his only ambition seems to be the desire to eat his lunch in peace. There's no sentimental veneer to the character—unlike the sad clown Jerry often played, Stanley rebounds instantly from every slight or incident of ill will that befalls him.

In the finale Stanley reveals the most certain sign yet of his universality. He finds himself sitting at the head of a table while the other bellboys voice dissent with the management of the hotel. Stanley keeps making gestures as if he wants to say something, and he's in the middle of one such bit of pantomime when the manager walks in on the cabal and accuses him of leading it. Asked if he can't speak in his own defense, Stanley shocks everyone in the room by doing just that: "I suspect I can talk as well as any other man," he responds, adding that he'd never spoken before because "nobody ever asked." With that, he walks insouciantly out of the film while a narrator delivers the moral: "You'll never know the other guy's story unless you ask."

It's not much of a philosophical insight, but it's as apt a way as any to end an arbitrary assemblage of comic set pieces. *The Bellboy* may lack the heartrending pathos of *City Lights* or the sophisticated polish of *Artists and Models*, but it is a debut film shot under conditions much more harried and uncertain than just about any Hollywood feature; indeed, in the breakneck pace of its production, it mirrored more the low-budget efforts of the silent clowns or such Hal Roach Studio artists as Laurel and Hardy than any film Jerry had ever worked on before. It's an experimental film—and a successful one. Jerry demonstrates mastery of camera placement, editing, and comic timing, and the thing swims along so fluently that you're left wanting more; the notion that almost as much material was left out of the film as included makes one wish he would release a collection of the unused footage. Forget the Gar-Ron films or Jerry's claims that he codirected his late-1950s movies with Tashlin. *The Bellboy* is his debut as a director, and it's as accomplished a first film as any comic director ever made.

Jerry was such a surefire box office attraction that it almost didn't matter that *The Bellboy* was such an original film; the public flocked to see him no matter what he appeared in (as Hal Wallis had learned, to his good fortune, time and again). In Los Angeles *The Bellboy* grossed $200,000 in its first week and

$118,000 in its second; in New York it grossed $106,000 in its first two days on twenty-one screens (at an average ticket price of about seventy-five cents, that meant that 141,000 New Yorkers saw the film within forty-eight hours of its premiere). One week after the film opened, Jerry got his second telegram of the year from the aged Adolph Zukor: Addressing him as "Sonny," he remarked of the *Bellboy* grosses, "They are phenomenal and so are you."

The picture was enormously profitable. Jerry would sometimes claim it had earned $10 million; while it didn't do all that business only at home or only in its first year of release, it was a big, big hit, earning about $5 million during its initial run. And, as he remembered with glee in his autobiography, "I had no partners!" Paramount got a flat distribution fee from Jerry Lewis Productions. The leftovers belonged to Jerry.

Whether Hollywood would let him enjoy them was another matter. Jerry hadn't earned a reputation as a breezy, friendly guy over his dozen years in the business, and the sight of him attempting something as ambitious as *The Bellboy* rankled both the press and his peers. "There was a period where I was gonna quit, just quit," he remembered years later. "I was getting depressed—right after *The Bellboy*—because the talk in town was 'Jerry wrote, produced, acted, and directed and probably painted the sets.' And I'm thinking to myself, 'What's my fucking crime? Who have I injured? What pain have I imposed on someone?' And I'm walking down the Paramount street, and I walked right by Billy Wilder—he's coming this way, and I walked right by him. And I looked at him, but I must've looked through him. And he said, 'Jerry, what the hell is the matter, you walk right by me like you don't even wanna bother. We're not friends anymore?' I said, 'Oh, I'm sorry Billy, I'm just so goddamn depressed. The little squibs in *Variety* and *The [Hollywood] Reporter* and the newspaper people with that "Jerry Lewis has to direct himself and write and produce . . ."'" He said, 'Listen, if you quit, they beat you. The only reason that they're talking is that they can't do it. And the thing they hate more than anything is that you're doing it and you're showing them they can't.' He said, 'I don't give a fuck because they say that I write and direct. I don't give a shit what they say. I do what I do good. Now get back in your fucking office and keep doing what you're doing.' I'll never forget him for that. Because that town can do that to you."

When *The Bellboy* opened, however, Jerry seemed less bent on quitting the business than on absorbing it entirely. The very day the public got to see the film for the first time, its creator was muddling through the first of several weekly script conferences for "The Girls' Boy" with Mel Brooks and Bill Richmond. In order to ensure that no inspiration be lost, Jerry recorded the meetings and had the tapes transcribed. The transcripts reveal that although he had hired—at great expense—one of the top comic writers in the business, Jerry was an unwilling collaborator. From Jerry's initial draft, Brooks and Richmond worked out many revisions and new ideas, but Jerry systematically shot them down or used them as springboards to ideas he was comfortable calling his own.

At that first meeting, for example, Jerry became rattled when he realized just how much of his original material the two writers had reshaped, and told them he was too busy for the meeting to continue. Richmond asked, "You haven't got time to listen to a story concept we have?" Jerry, defensively, shot back, "Why, do you want to change everything?" Brooks tried to explain what he and Richmond had done: "No, we're aiding and abetting," to which Jerry retorted, "Don't lie!"

The following week, the writers were better prepared to deal with their balky colleague, having spoken about their ideas with other people on the lot. "I brought up the nursery with Ernie [Glucksman]," said Brooks, "and he didn't agree with me. I thought it was very funny. But George Abbott—" Jerry cut him off: "Everyone who's heard it has thought it was funny and we're never gonna know until I photograph it."

Like *The Bellboy*, the new film was shaping up as a series of gags. And as he had in his first film, Jerry was hoping to build this one more in the editing room than in the script, so he was willing to spend the time and money to shoot sequences that might not make the final cut. In a way, it almost didn't matter to him that the writers had improved or altered or remade scenes. He would shoot all of the material he had. He wasn't using Brooks and Richmond as collaborators or even, really, as screenwriters; he was using them as gag men. And he could be brusquely dismissive: "We have a pretty good idea here," Richmond told him one day. "Would you like to hear it?" "No," Jerry told him. "Put it on paper."

It got to the point where Jerry was appropriating his writers' ideas as soon as they voiced them: "It's a funny joke, but let me take it"; "I've done the poor room joke a hundred times. But you've given me an idea." He finally began using them as an audience, launching into long free-association screeds about what character names were funny or what sorts of wacky poems the main character (who, he'd decided, should be a serious writer) would compose. Before long, it became obvious to Brooks and Richmond that this wasn't an active writing collaboration. They continued, nominally, to work on the script, but they also started looking for other ways to spend their time.

Another new employee was on Jerry's payroll at around this time. Judith Campbell, mistress to both Sam Giancana and John Kennedy, had met Jerry in New York the previous fall, and he'd tried to woo her immediately, calling her several times for dates and finally inducing her to go out with him by dangling an invitation to meet Sophie Tucker. (When Jerry introduced Campbell to the grand old lady as his secretary, Tucker saw right through the ruse and gave him a withering look.)

Campbell wasn't at all impressed with Jerry's come-on. He liked to use big words, she noticed, and he liked to touch, "experimenting, always trying to see how far he could go." But she found him perfectly resistible. "He quickly goes overboard," she said. "You expect him to start speaking French. Although he is very serious about his flirting, from a woman's viewpoint it is funnier than his pratfalls."

Whether or not it was part of his courtship ritual, Jerry expressed an interest in Campbell's artwork (she was a painter), and told her that his new film might offer him a chance to avail himself of her "proclivities." He never, however, could explain to her just what he wanted her to do. He spoke of an illustrated book commemorating the making of the film, but it never materialized. All Campbell wound up doing was reporting to an office with her name over the door and pestering her boss to pay her the one hundred dollars a week she'd been promised.

Campbell found Jerry's inability to focus infuriating. While speaking with her about her project, he'd dictate unrelated memos ("In the course of a day," she recalled, "he dictated more interoffice memos than any corporation president"), talked about musical arrangements for the film, and generally comported himself like a hyperactive child. "His attention span where others were concerned was severely limited," she remembered. "He concentrates best when he is listening to himself. He may have been listening to himself talking to someone, listening to a record of himself, reading something he had written, or listening to someone reading it to him, listening to someone compliment him or discuss him or his movies. He would listen to you on other subjects, but better make it quick if you don't want to get caught talking to yourself."

She wasn't the only employee who was uneasy working around him. As Brooks and Richmond knew, the offices of Jerry Lewis Productions were a place where nobody but Jerry could really relax and get to work. The large, oak-paneled rooms were covered floor to ceiling, in Victorian fashion, with photos of Jerry and his family and friends, stills from his films, plaques and certificates he'd received from various charities and film groups, an autographed photo of John Kennedy, the gold record from "Rock-a-Bye Your Baby." There were framed cartoons of Jerry, printed slogans and mottoes ("The funny bone has no time for statistics"), fake record jackets (*Adolph Sings Songs for Passover, Jerry Lewis Sings the Songs from "Ben Hur"*), and pictures of his yacht and his dog, Mr. Chips (the spaniel he'd bought Patti when she was pregnant with Gary and for which he'd recently bought a fifteen-thousand-dollar hearing aid). Tables beside Jerry's large, wide desk were choked with electronic gizmos, camera equipment, typewriters, and telephones (employees suspected that a nearby dictaphone was surreptitiously used to record conversations). On his desk he kept a large bowl of Kool cigarettes and another large bowl of sharpened pencils; if either was appreciably less than full, he could blow his stack. He had cartons of trinkets personalized with his caricature logo: pens, rulers, cigarette lighters, stationery (including pads he kept in the bathroom bearing the slogan "JL Doodling on the Throne"). He had a solid gold Nikon camera with a diamond viewfinder, a gold-plated golf club. Outside the building he kept parked a personalized golf cart on which he whooshed around the Paramount lot (one time, seeing Dean walking along toward him, he ducked between two sound stages to avoid saying hello).

Jerry would arrive at the office sometimes as early as 4 A.M. to prepare for the work on the set, and he would be so busy throughout the day that he would eat and get his hair cut at his desk. Often he didn't leave for home until after midnight, or simply crashed on one of his modernistic office couches. Most of his employees took their cue from his grueling pace—but not Keller, who was never impressed with Jerry's displays of workaholism. "Jack wasn't affected by that," recalled one employee. "I had just got out there and I was worried about my job, and we'd be talking and Jack would stand up and say, 'One o'clock! I'm gonna go for lunch. Come with me!' Jerry would be sitting there, and Ernie, and they'd say, 'We're working in this meeting!' And Jack'd say, 'I don't give a fuck about this meeting. Let's go have a drink and get some lunch.' So I'd go with him. We'd have an hour-and-a-half lunch, lots of booze, and then go back. Ernie and all the rest of them were very proud that they ate lunch in. In all the time I was there, Jack never ate lunch in. And he talked to Jerry like he didn't give a shit. And Jerry respected him. I don't think Jerry respected Ernie because Ernie was such a yes-man. Jerry really was in awe of Jack."

But Jerry was, of course, also really in awe of Jerry. Among the duties he had thrust upon his cousin Marshall Katz, who served as an assistant to the producer on Jerry Lewis films, was the responsibility for staff photography. Dick Cavett, who was to enter Jerry's orbit in a few years, recalled that "he had a photographer whose job was to be there when he awoke, I think, and stay until he began snoring. And he photographed him all day, with a bag the size of a mailman's pouch of film. All day, every day: Jerry drinks water from fountain, Jerry attends meeting. The archive must be voluminous." Another employee, Art Zigouras, himself a shutterbug, recalled with envy that "he'd go out and shoot twenty-eight rolls of thirty-five millimeter and have them blown up and everything." Katz had a photographic lab built in a warehouse that Jerry had rented to store all his personal and business memorabilia, and Jerry would impose upon the Paramount photo lab for special rush jobs or color prints when he wanted them.

In August 1960 Patti finally got her husband to take a vacation, though even then he found a way to connect it to business. They took all five boys and went to Hawaii, where they stayed at Sheraton's Royal Hawaiian at Waikiki. Jack Keller, whose duties now included negotiating corporate tie-ins with Jerry Lewis Productions projects, had managed to get the hotel to print and send one hundred thousand postcards advertising *The Bellboy* (and, of course, the Royal Hawaiian) to former customers of the chain's hotels. Charlie and Lillian Brown, who, like other Catskill hoteliers, were watching their old vacation customers fly off to Florida, Las Vegas, California, and even Hawaii, had tried to get Jerry to host a premiere of *Cinderfella* at their hotel. More desperately, they wanted a mention in the script of *The Bellboy*, just so the audience wouldn't forget which hotel *really* meant something to him. Both efforts had failed; even if its sons were conquering the world, the traditional Catskill hotel was dying.

Cinderfella was previewed later that month, but Jerry let Frank Tashlin worry about that one. *The Ladies' Man*, which his next film had come to be called (after such names as "The Girls' Club," "The Bashful Boyfriend," and "Wonder Boy" had been rejected), was taking up all of his time. It dealt with the misadventures of a character known only as "The Kid," who, although loathing women after being rejected by his high school sweetheart, accidentally winds up working as a handyman in a boardinghouse full of beautiful single girls. It was a variation of the root idea of *The Bellboy*—a yutz on the loose in an orderly environment—but there was a distinctly psychological touch to it. The character had an emotional history; the orderly environment was a kind of dreamscape; there was even a story, albeit skeletal and fantastic.

With the large grosses earned by *The Bellboy*, Paramount was convinced that he knew what he was doing, so they footed some of the bill for the new movie. He was thus able to indulge his unusual ideas about filmmaking just a bit more. What he envisioned this time was truly revolutionary—a gigantic indoor set in the shape of a life-size, four-story cutaway dollhouse, complete with working elevator, fully constructed on three of its four sides so he could film anywhere around it. Using a huge crane, he could put a camera, a microphone, and lights into whichever room of the house he chose, or he could move back and capture the action in various places in the house as it occurred simultaneously. For the dozens of actresses who'd populate this gargantuan construction, he would build dressing rooms right on the set. To pull it off at Paramount, he'd need to use the combined space of two adjacent sound stages with the wall between them knocked out.

It was an outrageous request: a Christmas list, really. No one believed he could do it, much less get Paramount to pay for it. Estimates ranged over five hundred thousand dollars to build and furnish the set. Jerry admitted it would be expensive, but he argued that the cost of construction would be offset by the amount of time and money he would save working in its unique prefab contours. Furthermore, he would pay for the set over time because it could be dismantled and reassembled or rearranged. Besides, not only was he a ruthlessly efficient producer—he signed off on every conceivable expense and oversaw every aspect of production down to the most minute and technical detail—but he also had the confidence of Zukor and Balaban. Each and every one of his twenty-three pictures for the studio had grossed at least $3 million. So if he could bring this one in at the right price, he had their blessing to go ahead and do it.

Whether it could be done at all was the next problem. The same studio technical staff that had refused to adopt his closed-circuit system was now telling him that what he wanted to do couldn't be done; you couldn't move lights and boom mikes willy-nilly around so huge a set. Again, Jerry brought to the situation a perspective that could have belonged to no one else. He wouldn't try to light the set from the outside; he would light each room from its own ceiling. He wouldn't try to mike the whole set at once; each room would have its own sound system, an innovation that would serve to reduce the time the camera crew spent making sure they didn't inadvertently photograph the boom mike or its shadow. One by one, the objections fell before his vision and persistence.

The autumn was a festival of electronic tinkering for him. The set, which he designed with Artie Schmidt, his editor and assistant, was under construction; the steelworkers who built it to its 25,000-square-foot, 36-foot high magnificence (working weekend shifts at his insistence), erected a flag over the finished frame, as per their custom. He shopped around for the largest movie camera crane in existence, for the most precise and compact microphones and recorders, for upgrades to the closed-circuit system. He was inventing something entirely new, part resort hotel, part TV studio, part burlesque stage, part film set.

While that was going on at work, he spent a hundred thousand dollars on a radio station and connected his house to it by means of a cable link. Another hundred thousand went for a satellite studio in his home, which allowed him to join the broadcast of KJPL (as he renamed the station after himself and his wife) whenever he wanted, just as if he were there live. He did it often, interrupting announcer Del Moore to introduce houseguests such as Pat Boone (doing Elvis impressions) or simply butting in with shtick. He had the airwaves of Los Angeles at his fingertips around the clock; he'd taken the art of attention-getting to staggering heights.

In October he finally marshalled all the clout and money he'd accrued to launch yet another attack on his bête noire, television: He produced and directed a pilot episode of a situation comedy about a group of female naval reservists called "Permanent Waves." (Imagine a distaff "McHale's Navy," though that successful series didn't appear until 1962.) None of the three major networks bit at the pilot; NBC executives might have lost interest when they learned that Jerry would be making a guest appearance on "The Ed Sullivan Show" in November, the first time since "The Colgate Comedy Hour" premiered that he would perform on a rival network. The ten thousand dollars he would be paid for his eight-minute segment was forty times what he and Dean had split on Sullivan's first show a dozen years earlier.

That same month, he fired Mel Brooks, who had never quite adopted the obsequious tone Jerry preferred from his employees. Take the simple matter of the working day, for instance. Like a philistine studio boss of the old school—the sort who felt his writers were loafing if he walked past their offices and didn't hear their typewriters humming—Jerry insisted that Brooks and Bill Richmond put in a full nine-to-five day, reprimanding them in a tart memo. Richmond apparently kowtowed appropriately, but Brooks, a legendary straggler, bridled. On September 27 he submitted notes on the latest draft of the script and got written instructions from Jerry about how to revise his revisions. Three days later, when his work was due, Brooks was hurrying off to catch a plane to New York. He called Jerry to let him know he could only see him early in the day, but the two never met. He stayed out of the office for several days, and when he returned, he was caught talking on the phone for an hour and a half with Carl Reiner, planning what would become the famous Two-Thousand-Year-Old Man album. That was the last straw. Jerry fired him the next day and told his accountant to dock Brooks's pay for the days he had spent in New York.

Brooks got under Jerry's skin one last time, however, when his agent protested to the Writers Guild that the final script credit for the film neglected to name him (*The Ladies' Man* was credited to Jerry and Richmond). When Ernie Glucksman broke the news to Jerry, he hit the roof: "He never wrote *word one* of this screenplay . . . he was hired to do so and had to be paid off because of not delivering any material whatever." (Brooks, in fact, didn't get credit on the final film.)

Judith Campbell also didn't make it to the end of the film. She had spurned all of Jerry's advances, and he had never really figured out why he'd hired her. He was cutting down his staff overhead anyway, so he decided to fire her.

But how do you fire the girlfriend of the Chicago don, the man who just a month or so earlier saved your good name from being dragged into divorce court?

It was another thing that Jerry never figured out.

At first, he tried a back-door maneuver. While he was off in Phoenix, he had a bookkeeper tell Campbell that she was being let go because the staff of Jerry Lewis Productions was being trimmed. She called Jerry and he told her that the bookkeeper was mistaken, that the staff reductions didn't include her.

A month or so later, however, when Campbell accompanied Jerry and the rest of his entourage to Vegas, he tried to cut her off again. Campbell was drinking at the bar of the Sands with Jerry's secretary when Jerry and Patti walked past, utterly ignoring the two women. A moment later, the secretary was paged and excused herself. When she returned, she was visibly upset.

"I was just given instructions not to talk to you," she told Campbell. "You tell me what's going on."

Hurt by this news, Campbell returned to her room and called Giancana. "Get out of there," he told her. "You don't need that crap. Come on up to Chicago."

When she arrived at O'Hare, she found her boyfriend in an unusually agitated state. "Do you want your job [with Jerry] back?" he asked.

She was so frightened by his demeanor that she chose to deflate his anger rather than give it a focus. "I don't think so," she answered. "I'd rather forget the whole thing."

Giancana wasn't satisfied. "All you have to do if you want your job back is say the word. If you want more money, you'll get more money."

She assured him that money wasn't the issue, but he still simmered. As soon as they got to their hotel, Giancana put in a call to Vegas and within minutes had Jerry on the phone.

When Giancana asked why Campbell had been cut off, Jerry blamed Patti, explaining that she was jealous of Campbell. Giancana wouldn't have it: "Listen here, you son of a bitch, I don't give a damn about your stupid wife. All Judy has to do is give me the okay and she's got her job back. Do you understand me?"

Jerry was reduced to groveling, pleading his case to Giancana. The mob boss held the phone out for Campbell to hear. "He sounded like he had gone into his spastic routine," she recalled. "I could just picture him, jumping around and per-spiring, scared out of his wits."

Giancana ended the phone call with a final reminder. "You better thank God she doesn't want your stinking job back," he sneered, "because she'd have it back and with a big raise in pay. Stop sniveling and thank your lucky stars that this lady wants nothing more from you."

While Jerry sweated in Vegas, Campbell glowed with satisfaction in Chicago. "I felt Jerry had it coming," she said. She considered him a manic nightmare of emotional highs and lows: "He could make a problem out of just absolutely nothing, and carry on like he was demented, cry like a baby, then snap right out of it, laugh and joke."

Campbell had begun to see a therapist at around the time she began work-ing for Jerry, and her new boss's fits had made her feel positively healthy. She felt especially good when she compared herself with other employees. "Most of the people working closely with Jerry were caught in a love-hate situation," she re-flected. "They were kept in a state of chronic anxiety. I think many ended up ei-ther with a psychiatrist or an ulcer, or perhaps both."

She had always hated the way he flagellated people around him, recalling how Jerry couldn't stand to lose pickup basketball games on the Paramount lot or have his performance in them criticized. "He abused people every day—and got away with it," she said. "Now he was getting it back from someone he feared, someone he had no control over."*

Given the potential technical difficulties, the actual production of *The Ladies' Man* turned out to be a wonder of cooperative professionalism. Following on the

---

*Some months later, according to Campbell, her other boyfriend, John F. Kennedy, needled Jerry about the incident. When the comedian visited the White House, the President greeted him with "Hi, Jerry, how's Judy? Have you seen her lately?" Jerry was quietly infuriated that Kennedy was less interested in him than in Campbell.

heels of the premiere of *Cinderfella* (which opened in Chicago, with Jerry arriving at the city's Harvest Moon Ball in a horse-drawn coach), the $3.4 million undertaking was news in and of itself. Jerry held a PR event at which he revealed the mammoth set and its high-tech accoutrements to a startled trade press. He showed them a time-lapse film of the thirty-nine-day construction of the boardinghouse and then lifted a curtain to reveal the thing itself, with thirty-six actresses from his seventy-seven-member cast wandering through it like bees in a human-scale hive. He told them about his miking and lighting and closed-circuit systems. They'd never seen anything like it. William Perlberg, a fellow producer on the Paramount lot, stopped in for a gander and walked off amazed: "If this works as well as I think it will, it is the most revolutionary development in films since sound." Reports of the set ran in papers around the country; *Life* published a two-page color photo of Jerry sitting atop his huge crane (labeled "Jerry's Toy") in front of his audacious dream house.

When filming actually began, Jerry did his best to instill a familial, partylike atmosphere, once again replicating the vacation mood that had characterized the Gar-Ron films, the set of *The Bellboy*, and his Catskills adolescence. "This is NOT a closed set!" announced a sign on the front door of Stage 15; another, dwarfing all the rest, pronounced the set the "Jerry Lewis Comedy Stage" (with the *e* in his first name reversed as if in a child's hand). A Jerry Lewis Productions logo—with a Janus face that bore Jerry's countenance in both its sad and mischievous guises—made up another component of the gaudily decorated set door, along with the new JLP motto, "Films for Fun," which was also printed on stationery and the covers of scripts. (Work shirts were printed for crew members with the logo emblazoned on the breast.) A set of bleachers had been erected on the sound stage so that anyone who so wished could watch the proceedings (in later years, Jerry claimed that a frequent visitor was young Francis Ford Coppola, who lived nearby and who would one day make a film, *One from the Heart*, with technological elements strikingly similar to those in *The Ladies' Man*).

Jerry had made it a long-standing matter of principle that he knew the names of all the members of his crew—more important than ever, now that he was directing. Everyone was greeted by name; crew members' birthdays were lavishly celebrated; crew members' spouses' and children's brithdays were celebrated. No touch was too small to command his attention. "He couldn't stand the sight of paper cups or foam cups for coffee," reported his cousin and assistant Marshall Katz. "So he made everybody a mug with their name painted on it and the name of the movie. And every morning you would get to work and there were all the cups hanging on hooks all cleaned for you." His fastidiousness became a running joke: "What do *I* do?" replied a bemused production assistant when asked by a reporter what his job was. "All that's really left for me to do is make peanut butter sandwiches and sweep up."

Jerry's omnipresence touched large matters, as well. Kathleen Freeman, the veteran character actress who'd played bit parts in *Three Ring Circus* and *Artists and Models* and who'd been cast in the ill-fated "Permanent Waves," had third billing in *The Ladies' Man* and found herself dazzled by her boss and costar. "He is the only man I ever worked with, around, or for in Hollywood that if he were to call me to do something, I'd do it," she said. "There was never any discussion about billing, salary, or anything. I'd say, 'If you want me, I'll come.' I don't think he got that from a hell of a lot of people. I told my agent, 'Whatever he says is fine with me.' He did a very dear thing on *Ladies' Man*. It's common if there's [a guarantee of] x number of weeks of employment to take less [per week]. . . . So I did. And he dragged me into his trailer one day and said, 'How dare you do that?' and he gave me a raise retroactively. It was only a couple of hundred dollars, no big deal, but it was the symbol of the thing that was extraordinary."

He couldn't offer such generous salary deals for the more than three dozen young actresses he'd hired to populate his vision, but they were lavished with gifts. Eventually, according to Freeman, they came like spoiled children to expect them: "He loved to give gifts. In fact, the front hall closet of his home was filled with wrapped gifts, ready to give. I used to go to dinner, and you never left without a watch or a lighter or some damn thing. And not ten-cent things. On *Ladies' Man* he used to come in every morning, and he'd have something for everyone. A ruler advertising the picture, or whatever. And he'd fling things—he loves to throw and catch stuff. Anyway, first two weeks of the shoot he was doing that. One day he threw little pearl bracelets to every girl. And two and a half weeks went on; every day he walked in the door with presents. Some were rulers and some were pencils, but there were also pearl bracelets. It was insane. And he marches onto the set, feeling real chipper, and this girl, who shall remain nameless, is standing there. And he had built all the dressing rooms on the sound stage so he didn't have to go running around to find people. And this girl stands there and she puts her hand out, and she goes, 'So what's for today, Jerry?' And I just happened to be right there. And this guy's face went like somebody smacked him. He turned around and went back to his dressing room. Crushed. I knocked at the door: 'Lemme in, it's Katie!' We talked a lot about it, and he told me some very personal feelings. But it was just like somebody went *whap!* That's the way his face was. And I thought to myself, 'You dumb broad.'"

In fact, despite all the trappings of a big family enterprise, there were a few little spats. For instance, not everybody was welcome on the set. Art Zigouras had arrived in Hollywood from New York to shoot a public service announcement with Jerry for the Muscular Dystrophy Association. But when he chose to spend his days watching the impressive production, he found himself asked to leave: "I was watching the shooting of this film, and I was really intrigued by it. I'm watching and watching, and one of the guys comes over and says, 'Ernie Glucksman wants to see you in his office.' So I went in. Ernie was the biggest con man, the sweetest kind of shyster. And he calls me in and says, 'Artie, you're

doing this for dystrophy and you're doing this on Paramount's time, and the guys
from Paramount are a little annoyed with you standing around and watching, so
they asked me to tell you that you aren't allowed on the set any longer.' And I'm
thinking, 'What did I do? Jesus, I was just standing there looking.' And I was really nervous because my boss was there, and he was a real bastard, and I thought
if he heard I was kicked off the set of a Jerry Lewis film—which nobody ever
was—I'm gonna be in big trouble.

"So we shot the PSA and I returned to New York and it never became an
issue. And soon Jerry came to town to meet key volunteers—we had a big meeting every year with them, and this was like a public relations meeting and Jerry
would speak and do shtick. So Jerry comes in and here was [MDA founder] Dr.
Paul Cohen and some other people, and instead of getting over to them, Jerry
comes over to me, and he's like, 'Hey Artie, how've you been? Good to see you.' I
couldn't believe it, because he ignored all these other people. And Jack Keller
told me later that it was because it was Jerry who had me thrown off the set because he couldn't stand my looking at him knowing he had to do this PSA later
in the day and it was making him nervous, and rather than be up front with me,
he told Ernie to get me off the set. And Ernie, being a devious guy, invented the
whole story about Paramount."

An even more serious problem developed between Jerry and cinematographer Haskell Boggs, who'd shot *The Bellboy, The Delicate Delinquent, Rock-a-Bye
Baby*, and *The Geisha Boy*. Jerry's ideas about what he wanted to do on the film
were ironclad, and in mid-December Boggs, like Mel Brooks before him, found
himself fired when he and his director suffered "differences of opinion on how
The Ladies' Man should be shot," according to *Variety*.

Still, for the most part, Jerry ran the set like an antic despot. Beside him at
all times he kept a big Harpo Marx–style horn, which he would honk if a scene
didn't work out to his satisfaction. If a crew member's attention wandered, Jerry
would chase after the offender with a long paddle labeled "The Not Listening
Stick." He played catch with his crew, he tossed lit cigarettes at them from atop
his crane, he dressed up as an Indian and did shtick for them, he blew up inflat-
able clowns and performed bits for them. Peter Bogdanovich, then a twenty-one-
year-old film critic, came by to report on the set for *Esquire* and dubbed it Jerry's
"make-believe kingdom."

Indeed, so collegial and spontaneous was the atmosphere that one of the
troupe of actresses, twenty-four-year-old Daria Massey, actually chose to hold
her wedding on the set and have Jerry film it for possible use in the picture. It
was a publicity stunt, of course, dreamed up in part by Jack Keller, but Jerry was
all sobriety and munificence about it. He stood as best man to the groom, and he
paid for a Las Vegas honeymoon for the newlyweds. (He wasn't crazy enough,
apparently, to use the footage in the finished film.)

Such antics wound up driving the budget for *The Ladies' Man* way over the original estimates. The final bill, as calculated just before the film was released, was more than $3.4 million—almost triple what *The Bellboy* had cost. It might have been worse, but because he had the loyalty of the crew, he was actually able to save money. In *The Total Film-Maker*, the book-length treatise on moviemaking compiled in 1971 from recordings of his seminars at the University of Southern California, he told how his crew pitched in for Jerry the director to the benefit of Jerry the producer: "I had to wrap up a sequence or it would have cost an additional hundred thousand. The crew knocked off at eight o'clock, went to dinner, and then came back to work until three in the morning to finish it. Two days passed before the unit manager told me that the 116 technicians had all punched out at eight o'clock, and had dinner on their own time. They contributed the time between nine o'clock and three the next morning. Had they stayed on the overtime clock, it would have cost something around fifty thousand dollars."

He was happy about such savings, of course, but note that it was days before he even wondered about what things cost. If the opulent set didn't cripple the budget, if weddings and daily gifts and an inveterate gagster in the director's chair didn't bankrupt the production, then Jerry's sheer fastidiousness behind the camera might. As Freeman recalled, he could rehearse a scene ceaselessly until he achieved on film what he saw in his head: "He was more than lavish about the whole thing. He was in seventh heaven. He had this idea with Walter Scharf of having all the women in this building come down to breakfast. I was Katie the housekeeper, and the end goal was the breakfast room, where it looked like we were serving everybody. So he had this design idea of people waking up to rhythm. It was really groovy, and the finished product is lovely. And I think he had visions of doing it in one, and with that kind of choreography, forget it. But he had these visions. And we started working with three girls from this room and six from that, boom, bing. And in the hall, bingity bong. He was getting monstrously frustrated, because you'd rehearse it again and one girl would be late in catching up to the rhythm and he'd be, 'Enough, enough! That's not gonna work!' He got down off the crane at one point and shouted, 'All right! All right! We're gonna get spontaneity if it takes all night!' And then he kind of laid back and said, 'Oh,' and he broke up."

On February 21, 1961, the filming finally ended, fourteen days behind schedule. Jerry was exhausted. The previous fifteen months might well have killed him. He had produced, starred in, and supervised the release of three films, two of which he had also written, directed, and edited. He had gone on three publicity tours. He had done four one-hour TV shows and produced and directed a pilot. He had played live dates of at least a week each in Miami, Las Vegas, Chicago, and Hollywood. He had created a new way to film movies, overseen construction of the largest set in Hollywood, bought and operated a radio station, begun to compile a book, reunited briefly with his ex-partner, and taken his family of six on an extended vacation in Hawaii.

Now, in February, Ernie Glucksman persuaded Jerry to reorganize the hierarchy of Jerry Lewis Productions. Glucksman rose from associate producer to producer, while sometime film editor Artie Schmidt rose from assistant to the producer to associate producer. They told everyone that it was to take the strain of daily cares off Jerry's shoulders, but it was really just a cosmetic change; Jerry hardly ever left the office, arriving as early as 5 A.M. and staying very often until two the next morning. Nothing was being done without his say-so.

Cinderfella had opened at Christmas time, just as Jerry had insisted, but it hadn't generated either the receipts or the accolades he had anticipated. In retrospect, it seems as if he was bucking for Academy Awards by releasing a big-budget musical with a prestigious supporting cast at the end of the year. But for all its accoutrements and despite the contributions of the mischievous Frank Tashlin as both writer and director, *Cinderfella* was bloated and stodgy. "Either one goes with Lewis all the way or has reservations," wrote *Variety*, "which in this case could be considerable. . . . The pace engineered by Tashlin is uncomfortably deliberate for a comedy." Howard Thompson of *The New York Times*, having been handed the responsibility to cover Jerry's films by Bosley Crowther, who couldn't abide them, called the film "one of the dullest comedies of the season—make that the year," and came to the conclusion that Jerry had "become fascinated with the very sound of his own breathing. . . . We'll bet good money that even the kids will be bored stiff." People came to the theaters, but not in droves; it didn't lose money, but it was no hit.

The Ladies' Man, with its enormous scale, stood a chance of running into similar problems, but the gag-after-gag structure kept it from becoming too monstrous. Jerry spent the early spring cutting it, and it previewed in Modesto in mid-April. At the same time, he and Bill Richmond began concocting material for another film (though Jerry would receive the sole writing credit). Rather than ask Paramount to build him another fantasy set, he would use the back lot itself as his set for a movie about an inept studio gofer. There would be more of a story than ever this time; a corporate intrigue would form a backdrop to the inevitable string of gags. Plans went ahead for a July shoot, and Paramount executives began to wonder when the Jerry-as-Chaplin experiment would end and they could get their profit-generating star into another comfortably familiar moneymaking film.

Other groups hoped to use him for moneymaking as well. The Democratic National Committee asked him to play a one-hundred-dollar-per-plate birthday dinner at the White House in May. Five thousand people saw him perform in fealty to his handsome young king. The contact between Jerry and JFK had been sporadic since their days in Chicago together a decade earlier. And the rift between Jerry and Dean didn't help matters. The members of Sinatra's Rat Pack—who had shot their own gilded resort-town homage, *Ocean's Eleven*, at the very same time Jerry was shooting *The Bellboy*—despised Jerry for all of the friction between him and his former partner, whom Frank Sinatra had personally recruited into his clique. Peter Lawford, liaison between the JFK White House and the Rat Pack, worked hard to keep a wedge between Jerry and the President, and the DNC fund-raiser was one of the few times that Lewis and Kennedy met during the days of their mutual ascendancy. A photo taken of them mingling at the event shows the comedian smiling with profound warmth at the President.

When *The Ladies' Man* opened in July, it got some of the best trade notices Jerry's work had received in years. "Lewis is trying to broaden his now set characterization and let it mature," wrote James Powers in the *Hollywood Reporter*, adding that "'Ladies' Man' will probably be one of the most successful Lewis pictures." *Variety*'s "Tube." used the film as the occasion to crown Jerry as the film industry's premier comic: "He is Hollywood's clown prince, the only true clown now operating in the Coast film capital." There was a sentence in the *Variety* notice that might have given Jerry some pause, however, if he'd thought about it. According to the convention whereby film reviewers in the trade papers tried to predict the box-office potential of a film, "Tube." wrote, "He's the king of the lucrative Little League legions, a funnyman whom parents are willing to entrust with the chore of keeping their charges entertained." In other words, the comic who'd begun his career in a nightclub twosome that was often chastised for a slightly blue tone was becoming a children's entertainer. And while children's movies stood to make a lot of money—Jerry liked to point out that children came to movies with parents or in packs—children's acts were treated as minor specialties by the studio in budgeting and distribution decisions; the kiddie movie was a kind of ghetto.

Jerry wasn't bothered by such intimations, however. As he had with *The Bellboy*, he hit New York for a two-day publicity binge for *The Ladies' Man*, putting on twenty-eight twenty-minute shows (complete with four-piece combo) at RKO theaters and appearing on three national television shows. (Although he made the rounds of the city in an air-conditioned bus, he had a telephone-equipped limousine following his caravan the whole time that kept him in constant touch with home, where Scotty was having his tonsils out.) He was like a monarch touring his domain, extending his appearance by organizing drill routines with Boy Scouts and other kids outside theaters, accepting gifts and even food from fans (not that he needed their sandwiches—his bus was stocked with box lunches from the Four Seasons, his and Patti's favorite New York restaurant), joining in a sandlot baseball game, darting from the bus as it passed through Coney Island to scoop up some Nathan's hot dogs. Of course, he loved it.

The Ladies' Man was indeed a film to be proud of. As experimental in form as *The Bellboy*, it's a riot of color, sound, and motion, as lush a meditation on the means of the cinema as any of Frank Tashlin's films—or even, in the views of some of its later critics, Federico Fellini's. It many ways, it resembles *The Bellboy* in shape: a series of gags about a clod set loose in a staid environment. It differs crucially, however, in its attempt to create a psychology for its main character: Stanley was just Everyputz, but here a prologue of several minutes and a series of confessional speeches illuminate the interior life of Herbert H. Heebert, Jerry's character.

Herbert, a small-town college valedictorian ("I'm very glad that you choose me," he blurts out at his graduation), swears off women forever after he finds his sweetheart kissing a football star. Despite the blubbering protests of his mother (a hideously over-made-up Jerry), he leaves home. Arriving in Hollywood, he quickly finds a job as a caretaker in a large house; unbeknownst to him, though, it's filled with young women. The skittish misogynist is now surrounded by dozens of available girls (and two older, motherly women—housekeeper Katie and housemistress Miss Welenmellon). It's not a film about the fear of women; on the contrary, given Jerry's off-camera predilections, it's more about life amid a surplus of them, the thinly veiled autobiography of a man half-schmuck, half-satyr.

As in *The Bellboy*, a series of comic riffs ensues, with the merest cobweb of a story line holding it together—Herbert encourages an ugly duckling in her career, while she encourages the other girls to express their appreciation for him. The girls represent a collection of types—vamp, beatnik, method actor, man-eater—although none receives any more considered treatment than did the hotel guests in *The Bellboy*. There are the trademark sight gags—a butterfly collection comes to life, the lipstick on a portrait smears, a ferocious-sounding beast turns out to be a puppy dog. And there are longer gags that demonstrate real artistry: an encounter between Herbert and a surly gangster (Jerry's great stock actor Buddy Lester) whose hat, hairdo, and suit the incompetent houseboy ruins; a fantasia in the forbidden bedroom of Miss Cartilage, a stark white set that mutates in size (so as to include Harry James and his orchestra) and takes Circean hold of Herbert's limited senses.

Ironically, given the high-tech conditions of the production, one of the weakest sequences involves the airing of a live television show from the house (the den mother is a former opera star whose munificence with the girls is considered news). Otherwise, from the very opening shot—a pan down the main street of Herbert's hometown—*The Ladies' Man* fluently orchestrates motion and light, often in ways that have nothing to do with the story or even the jokes. It's a virtuosic performance by Jerry the director in only his second film.

But Jerry the performer leaves a gaping hole in the center of the film that no amount of technical wizardry can fill. Jerry never for a moment looks the part of a juvenile; his body is thick (he has love handles and a potbelly), and he looks like he's grown out of his clothes. People keep calling him "kid," but it's a thin masquerade; he keeps yelling "Maaaaaaa!" when he's afraid, but it sounds more like a generic squeal than the voice of someone who's recently left his mother's home. His voice won't find a consistent characterization; at times it's deep or swishy or Jewish or plain. Herbert isn't the Kid, but he isn't anyone else, either. Jerry invents an idiosyncratic physical bit for him—his eyeglasses are forever misapplied on his face—but he doesn't create a character. In the middle of a thrilling, exotic film, the central role is woefully underrealized.

Jerry's inability to achieve a true characterization in *The Ladies' Man* was the jumping-off point of a savage attack on the film—not a review, but an opinion column by "Li'l Abner" cartoonist Al Capp in the *Los Angeles Mirror*. Capp related his experience in accidentally wandering in to see *The Ladies' Man*. After about twenty minutes of the film, he felt he could no longer endure the sight of "the most uninventive modern comic" and left the theater: "Not simply because I was bored. It was something more painful: I felt it had been somehow indecent of me to peek at a grown man making an embarrassing, unentertaining fool of himself. We all do now and then—privately. But what made this exhibition something to write about was that Jerry Lewis was doing it in public on a screen a mile long, in full color, and charging money."

Capp analyzed Jerry's career, and in particular, the way Dean's presence had tempered Jerry's shtick into something palatable: "Under the glare of Martin's disapproval, Lewis restrained himself enough to become wildly, almost tastefully funny." Without a partner, Capp argued, Jerry "got rid of that priceless ingredient in all creativity—constructive disapproval." He concluded with a coup de grâce: "When creativity is permitted to erupt unchecked, and its excesses remain undisapproved of, it can become unintelligible and unbearable. It can become *Ladies' Man*."

Jerry couldn't stand to be told that things he envisioned for his films couldn't be achieved technically; he couldn't stand to be watched by anyone he felt might be second-guessing him; but to be blindsided like this on the opinion page of a major newspaper left him sputteringly mad. He underlined various sentences in Capp's column and composed, on his own typewriter, a furious reply of several pages to the cartoonist.

Confessing that he felt "compelled to write and, if nothing else, feel better that I did," he savagely attacked Capp's motives: "Can it be the inability to display your talent minus the cartoon strip? Or is there any talent at all, without your little friends from Catpatch?" He concluded by attacking Capp's own creative work: "You see, Al, when creativity is permitted to erupt unchecked, and unedited, and it's [sic] excesses remain undisapproved of, it can become unintelligible and unbearable. . . . It can become Li'l Abner . . . (and I at least saw more than one episode)."

Even this furious raspberry didn't assuage Jerry's sense of outrage. As soon as he finished venting his spleen on Capp, he wrote a little parable about a stallion that can't be tamed and that, in its liberty, evokes the jealousy of the broken, corralled horses. It concluded, "All the horses in that distant corral hate that stallion causing all the trouble . . . but they sure would love *getting all that attention*, and had they the opportunity to start all over . . . you can bet, they couldn't get a rope, a saddle, or anything on them either."

There could be no doubt that the bold stallion was none other than Jerry himself, attention-craving nonconformist par excellence, subject of the jealousies of the rest of the world, a man utterly beyond the control of nay-sayers, managers, or moral authorities.

It was this self-image that led him to try to secure a popular novel that he wanted to direct and star in for the screen. *The Catcher in the Rye* had been published to universal critical acclaim and enthusiastic public reception by J. D. Salinger in 1951, but Jerry seemed to have first become aware of it in the early 1960s. "*Time* magazine did a profile of Salinger," recalled Art Zigouras. "Jerry had read the profile and sent out people to get copies of *Catcher in the Rye*. I don't know if he read it or not, but a few weeks later he wanted to play Holden Caulfield. I didn't say a word, but Jack Keller said, 'Jerry thinks that he's the Jewish Holden Caulfield.'"

Even though he was in his mid-thirties and had never attempted anything besides "The Jazz Singer" that remotely resembled real drama, Jerry was telling people that he was the perfect choice to play Salinger's alienated teenaged antihero. "You never saw a more Holden Caulfield guy than you're sittin' with right now," he informed Peter Bogdanovich. "If a person ain't genuine, I know it. I can spot a dirty, lying, phony rat. I can smell 'em." He tried to approach Salinger through his agent, but the representative of the notoriously reclusive author didn't even respond to his queries. Salinger wouldn't even let not-for-profit groups like the Yale Drama School produce adaptations of his works; he certainly wasn't letting Jerry Lewis get his mitts on them.

But Jerry had other ways of approaching the problem, according to Zigouras. "He found out later that Salinger's sister was a buyer for one of the department stores in New York, and he wrote to her to influence Salinger to go ahead with it. He said, 'Don't worry. I'll get him.'" He apparently did find the sister. "Salinger's sister told me she used to call him 'Sonny,'" he revealed to Bogdanovich. "That's what my grandmother used to call me. It's frightening." He never did succeed in wheedling the rights to the novel from Salinger, but even in the late 1970s he was discussing the possibility with dreamy enthusiasm. "Salinger's sister told me if anyone would get it from him it would be me," he told an interviewer. "I'm still trying. He's nuts also. And that's the only reason that he's entertaining talking to me—because he likes nuts."

■ ■ ■

If he was worried that he might spread himself too thin, he didn't show it. Starting in late July, he shot *The Errand Boy*, which wrapped on September 1, 1961, five days ahead of schedule, at a budget of $1.79 million. There were few problems or personality conflicts (though Jerry did chew out veteran comic Fritz Feld when the sixty-two-year-old man couldn't reproduce his dance steps exactly), and there were no mountains of technology to scale. The company files on the film are dotted with carbon copies of telegrams of thanks and congratulations from Jerry to the cast and crew. The speedy completion of the film was due, in part, to the diligence of the director and his employees: They shot past 11 P.M. several times and wrapped up work at 1:20 A.M. on the last day of shooting.

Still, the thing went so smoothly that he could take a night off to team up with Bobby Darin on the pregame show of an Angels-Yankee broadcast. He was a big baseball fan—his *Errand Boy* cast notes include a handwritten account of a discussion he had with cameo player Leo Durocher about which games the Dodgers needed to win to secure the pennant—but when he showed up with Darin, reporters didn't care so much about his ability as a sports prognosticator as about the whiff in the air of a possible new partnership. He'd always been asked the same questions whenever he showed up to perform with a singer, so he knew how to brush them off. And he shared a secret about himself and Dean with UPI's Rick DuBrow: "You know what a team like that is? It's two guys scared to death who need each other. That's all it is. It's pretty cozy to see someone up there. It's murder up there alone. Try it."

14.

The Jewish Bataan Death March

From the time he broke up with Dean through the early 1960s, Jerry's involvement in the Muscular Dystrophy Association had been limited, if highly visible. He did telethons and short broadcasts for the organization; he made public service films that were shown in theaters and on television; he lent his name to fund-raising activities, but not on a regular basis and not always on the most accommodating of terms. The organization found itself in a strange double bind with him: On one hand, he had for all intents and purposes built the organization by adopting it as his personal cause; on the other, he seemed to want to keep some distance between himself and an organization that, in the minds of many, had been synonymous with Martin and Lewis. Furthermore, key personnel at Jerry Lewis Productions, Ernie Glucksman and Jack Keller among them, had a hard enough job keeping him focused on his responsibilities to Paramount, nightclubs, and NBC; they participated in his MDA activities but somewhat grudgingly, seeing in the charity a kind of rival family of co-workers for their boss.

There were little conflicts between MDA and Jerry and his own production company. Art Zigouras, one of MDA's key creative personnel, had to deal with Jerry and JLP often, and he found that being caught in the shoals between two sensitive groups didn't allow him too much say in his own work. At the time he was asked to leave the set of *The Ladies' Man*, he'd been sent to California to film a public service spot with Jerry that was also partially a promo for the film. "He got up on the crane," Zigouras recalled, "and he had a microphone—this is Jerry, the great technical guy—and he showed the set and all this, but he was turned away from the microphone, and we couldn't use it. But Jerry was very touchy about doing things for dystrophy. So we couldn't go back and tell him it wasn't any good. We just sort of put it aside and said, 'Oh, yeah, we can use it, Jerry, it's great, blah, blah.' And then Paramount, since he did it on their time, sent us a bill for like ten thousand dollars, since it was their crew and such, and we paid the bill, which was way more than we would've paid for anyone else to do it."

At other times, Jerry's sheer ego kept him from being as helpful as he might have been to the organization. "Jerry's involvement with dystrophy was a mixed bag as far as I could tell," said Zigouras. "He was so bloody busy doing these other things. Once we did—on kinescope—a show from the Roosevelt Hotel in Los Angeles with all these stars coming on and thanking people for supporting muscular dystrophy. I coproduced it with Ernie, and Jerry always had the final say-so. It was called 'High Hopes,' and it was done at the Coconut Grove at the Ambassador Hotel. We had Donald O'Connor, Richard Boone, and many others, and the audience was filled with minor celebrities. We wrote material for Jerry—I had written some stuff, Ernie had hired some writers—geared to dystrophy's needs at the time, which was more public education than financing. Jerry came in and just threw it out. Egotistically: 'No, no, tell me what you want me to say and I'll do my own stuff.' And we were leery of that—we being the dystrophy people—because Jerry had a tendency to fuck things up. He would start out to say something and get so convoluted that it never became clear. But he was top man: He was making films, he had all this money, he was hot, he was arrogant, he was egocentric, and he was a son of a bitch, and he just tore us apart. So we went up to do the show, and he ad-libbed, and we had to edit around him. And it was editing on kinescope, which wasn't as easy as it is now. So we learned our lesson. The second show, we went to him and said, 'Do what you want.' So the script said something like, 'Jerry does shtick with Donald O'Connor,' or 'Jerry does bit for MDA'—there was nothing written. And the director was going out of his mind, because he didn't trust Jerry to come through with it. And Jerry came through. A lot of times he fucked up the lines, but that time he came through."

At various times, the organization may even have considered going on without Jerry altogether. Zigouras was one of those most vehemently in favor of such a move, and not only for professional reasons. Having spent a fair amount of time around Jerry in his Paramount offices, he knew enough about the comedian's private life to become afraid of what the chance of scandal might mean to MDA. "I got a lot of surprises when I was first out there," he recalled. "I was really surprised to find that Jerry had been fooling around so much and having all these affairs. I'd come back to New York and I'd keep saying, 'Let's not put all our eggs on Jerry, because if any of this ever comes out, we're killed, we're dead.' "

Jerry did very little to hide his womanizing from the people around him, as Zigouras remembered: "Jerry was very friendly with me. We'd sit around and talk. He said to me once, 'You know, Art, if you go out with a woman and you get laid, it's because she likes you. If I go out and get laid, I don't know if it's because I'm Jerry Lewis or not.' "

But it was an era when the peccadilloes of movie stars, politicians, and athletes weren't discussed in public except in the most outrageous and unforgivable cases. Jerry was thus at liberty to cheat not only on Patti but on women with whom he engaged in relationships outside his marriage. "He had a secretary [with whom] he was having an affair," said Zigouras. "One time I was there, and there was a young girl who'd come over to audition for one of the films he was doing. We were in the Paramount offices, and on the lot he also had a dressing room, which was this huge beautiful place. Jerry was there with this young girl, and he had said to [his secretary], 'I want you to wait till I finish.' And [the secretary] was there, and it's getting to be nine-thirty, ten, ten-thirty, eleven o'clock, and she starts crying, 'That son of a bitch, he's doing this deliberately to me.' And finally Jack [Keller] says, 'All right, that's it, let's get out of here.' "

Keller, in fact, was in part responsible for Jerry's bold-faced behavior. More than anyone in the comedian's life, he was able to argue with him effectively, but he was also a press agent, a man whose job it was to camouflage the private man with a public screen. He may not have approved personally of Jerry's doings, and he may have been the only one with the audacity to tell Jerry when he was wrong, but he had learned his trade at the feet of George Evans, and he went along with whatever his employer did or asked him to do. Likewise, the MDA hierarchy ignored Jerry's philandering because of his worth to the organization as a spokesman and fund-raiser. He was, indeed, top man, and the people at MDA were grateful for whatever he was willing to do for them.

In November 1961, with no films of his own in the production pipeline and his first Paramount project in more than two years scheduled to roll in just a few weeks, he hosted an MDA telethon in New York. It was a big deal to the charity, which was forever insisting to him, against his own judgment, that telethons were the best possible fund-raising technique, but for Jerry it was just an engagement between nightclub runs in Philadelphia and Las Vegas. (During the Vegas date, he appeared for free on columnist Ralph Pearl's TV show and acted the crazy kid—ignoring questions, tearing up the script, destroying the set. When Pearl wrote angrily about his behavior, Jerry went on the show of rival columnist Jack Kogan and denounced him.)

At the time he was appearing in Las Vegas, he should have been on a sound stage at Paramount filming *It's Only Money*, a Frank Tashlin–directed comedy about a TV repairman who inherits a fortune without knowing it. But when shooting on that film was scheduled to start on December 13, he refused to show up for work, declaring the studio had breached his contract; *Variety* speculated that his qualms were strictly financial. For the next week, Jerry's office traded barbs in the Hollywood trade press with York Productions (the corporation persisted as a wholly owned subsidiary of Paramount even though Jerry and Dean had been bought out years before). On December 16, while teeing up at the Bel Air Country Club, Jerry was served with a subpoena to appear in Los Angeles County Superior Court, where York was seeking to enjoin him from working anywhere else until he fulfilled his obligations. In retaliation, Jerry sued York for breach of contract and subpoenaed every key member of the crew of *It's Only Money*, effectively crippling preproduction work on the film.

The holdout and the subsequent legal mêlée were resolved to everyone's satisfaction by February 1962: Jerry would make *It's Only Money*, after which he would be permitted to supervise all of his films, whether Jerry Lewis Productions or Paramount was the producing entity. For his loyalty and combativeness throughout the siege, Ernie Glucksman, who'd been associate-producing Jerry's movies on a film-by-film basis, was awarded by his boss with a new five-year contract that assured his position as producer on all JLP films throughout the tenure of the deal.

Before production on the delayed film began, Jerry did a few weeks at the Sands and spent some time in Hollywood preparing for a new commercial venture. In conjunction with restaurateur Maury Samuels, he opened a Sunset Strip restaurant called, creatively enough, Jerry Lewis's. Some years earlier, Samuels had gone into business with Dean Martin—just a few blocks down the Strip, in fact. That restaurant, Dino's Lodge, was immensely popular, serving home-style Italian food and grilled entrées in a wood-paneled atmosphere meant to replicate the great roué's den. It was such a temple of hipness that the producers of the hit TV series "77 Sunset Strip" chose it as the backdrop for their program, shooting the title sequence in front of the place and having teen heartthrob Edd "Kookie" Byrnes play one of its parking valets. Dean himself didn't visit the place much, but the restaurant wasn't about him so much as his image (indeed, after he'd sold out his percentage, he sued the owners to have his name and likeness removed from signage, menus, and advertising—and lost, so abstract had his connection to the place been all along).

Jerry Lewis's was a different sort of operation altogether. Like everything else its owner had a piece of, it was an extremely hands-on enterprise. If Jerry was in town, he was a good bet to be at the restaurant, table-hopping and schmoozing like a Borscht Belt hotelier. In contrast to the understated masculinity of Dino's Lodge, Jerry Lewis's was a study in gaudy textures—dark walnut paneling, silver-and-purple highlights, heavy drapes, huge chandeliers, deep banquettes, and plush armchairs. The two massive sets of double doors that led into the place bore silver handles in the shapes of *J*s and *L*s. The gigantic menus (ten-by-twenty inches closed) were covered in black velvet and embossed with a grandiose silver *JL* logo on the front. The china was black-and-white, the maître d' (Luigi, hired away from Dino's Lodge in a none-too-subtle tweak) wore tails, and the waiters and busboys wore double-breasted maroon uniforms. The menu featured French-inspired gourmet dishes such as caviar and roast pheasant. "The restaurant reflects Jerry's thoughts on what he would like to be," Jack Keller told a reporter whom he treated to a tour and a free meal.

Not everybody was taken in by the atmosphere of Jerry Lewis's. Each elegant touch was undercut by a vulgar one: In the largest of the three dining rooms, a long curved window revealed Los Angeles beneath the Hollywood hills, but the same room sported a large framed stained-glass composition of Jerry as a hobo clown; the middle-sized dining room was dominated by a cockleshell-shaped chandelier towed by six cupids attached to the ceiling (the third dining room was private, with its own entrance). A reporter noted that the place "would make the Medici feel at home." But it didn't have the same impact on customers. *Variety* sent somebody to the February 16 opening and that reporter was most impressed with the lax service and long waits he endured, noting that "quite a few of the standees tired of waiting and left." Eventually, Jerry's own attention wandered away from the restaurant and it closed down, another whim that couldn't outlast his initial enthusiasm.

The delays in shooting *It's Only Money*, which wrapped at the end of April 1962, had ensured that it would be the first summer since 1949 that Paramount didn't have a Jerry Lewis picture to distribute. *The Errand Boy* had opened to strong reviews the previous December. *Variety* flat-out declared it "one of the best and funniest Jerry Lewis pictures to come along," while the far more resistant *New York Times* admitted that the film opened with "a screamingly funny half-hour."

In crucial ways, *The Errand Boy* is simply the third version of his now-settled formula: a series of episodes in which Jerry runs amok in a staid environment— this time, a movie studio. After having been hired on as a spy for a tyrannical studio boss, Jerry (as Morty Tashman) goes from job to job, set to set, trying to remain anonymous but making a conspicuous mess of everything. The film includes many jokes tailored to the Hollywood setting—Morty accidentally redubs a musical, he stumbles onto sets and is trampled, he fails to distinguish acting from life and walks into scenes, ruining them. There's plenty of typical Lewis stuff there (Morty, like many of Jerry's other characters, is always interrupted in his lunch, and works of art come to life and nearly kill him), as well as some routines that are woefully old and, in their protracted versions, painful to watch.

The most typically Lewisian thing about the film is the meager plotline that develops in the closing minutes. Morty may be the world's worst industrial spy, but he is naturally funny. As in *The Stooge* and *Three Ring Circus*, an idiot who can do nothing right is recognized for his genuineness and honesty and becomes a hit. In the finale, Morty Tashman is a big movie star (his breakthrough film is entitled *It Could Happen to You*) giving lessons in how to get ahead in Hollywood to an inept sign painter—played by Jerry as an even bigger dope than Morty. If it's meant to be an allegory of Jerry's own rise in the business, it's dishonest and glib. But it's a fully realized version of his philosophy, based on themes in Chaplin's *The Circus*, that comedy has to come from the heart. Delivering such a message in a film with elaborate production sequences and a cast of hundreds (in many ways, it's the most opulent film Jerry ever directed) doesn't seem to rattle Jerry at all.

The audience certainly didn't mind the incongruity. The sight of Jerry disrupting the operation of a movie studio delighted them and kept them buying tickets. The lack of an immediate follow-up was therefore all the more disappointing to Paramount.

Jerry, on the other hand, was hardly wanting for ways to fill his time. He had a new film of his own in development—an updated version of *Dr. Jekyll and Mr. Hyde* he was writing with Bill Richmond—but it wasn't scheduled to begin production until late fall. He began investigating new television venues for himself, and he told Vernon Scott of UPI that he'd been offered $35 million to do a Jack Paar–style late-night show for eighteen months. (Paar had recently left "The Tonight Show," and there was much speculation in the trade press about how the late-night talk-show scene would shake out when young emcee Johnny Carson took the program over that fall.)

A movie studio might not have been afraid of the notion of tossing tens of millions at Jerry Lewis. ("What do I think of him?" responded an incredulous Barney Balaban to a reporter who asked about Paramount's top comedy star. "Look at the money he's made the studio during the last five years. If he wants to burn it down, I've got a match.") But TV network officials hooted at the figures Jerry was mentioning. "All we'd have to do is sell the network to pay him that much," one told Scott. Nevertheless, despite all of his flops on the small screen, rumors of a big TV deal continued to swirl around him.

He did an hour on ABC that spring and got paid $250,000 for his trouble. It was, in effect, a one-man show, with Jerry spoofing the twist, TV doctor shows, kabuki, folksingers, and crazes in teen culture. He sang "Mammy." The critics were appalled: "Can a show advertised as a big time special be as bad as this one?" asked a critic with *The New York Herald Tribune*. "I don't suppose a worse show has ever been put on television."

Nevertheless, NBC—memories of those wildly successful "Colgate Comedy Hour" days still warm in its corporate heart—wanted him back, and in a unique spot: During the interregnum between Paar and Carson, various guest hosts were being used to keep "The Tonight Show" in the public eye. Jerry would be given two weeks in June. The network would have one of the biggest film stars in the world for an exclusive fortnight, while Jerry would have entrée to American living rooms for the same span of time, which would surely settle once and for all the question of whether or not he was talk-show host material.

The results were spectacular. NBC had hired a prestigious roster of talent to fill in on the show during its six-month revamping, Groucho Marx, Art Linkletter, Donald O'Connor, Joey Bishop, Hugh Downs, and Mort Sahl among them, but Jerry's ratings were absolutely the highest. For two weeks he ruled the airwaves as he had at no time since he and Dean were together. Part of the appeal was that he had no respect for the familiar "Tonight Show" formats, making a shambles of guests, advertisers, the band, and the audience. But it was also that he was in a role he never filled previously: He was ringmaster rather than main attraction, and his interjections, asides, and idiosyncrasies were the spice of the program and not the meat. For the first time since "The Colgate Comedy Hour," the TV audience unequivocally loved him.

Even the critics appreciated what he did to the already tired contours of the late-night talk show formula. Longtime Lewis watcher Harriet Van Horne wrote yet another canny critique of him in *The New York World Telegram:* "Mr. Lewis, as we who read *Photoplay* under the hairdrier well know, is a Pagliacci . . . a grave and thoughtful man who must periodically cut short his musings on the decline of Western culture to cross his eyes, wail like a banshee and regale the ground-lings with his version of the shaking palsy. . . . Once you've accepted this strange dichotomy in Mr. Lewis you find yourself sympathizing with it. A man's reach should exceed his grasp and—well, his does. As some critic remarked of the poet Southey, 'His pretensions jostle one another.' In Mr. Lewis' case, the jostling is frequently abrasive. And this, too, is a compelling, quirky business to watch. Mr. Lewis is a man who loves big words, who makes offhand allusions to his riches and grandeurs and who sometimes seems embarrassed by his distinct gifts for low comedy. He will give us a turn that is wildly, outrageously funny—then look acutely annoyed. It's as if the Student Prince were to be caught cheating at cards. . . . Mr. Lewis may not think so from the above but I find him fasci-nating."

Jerry knew that his "Tonight Show" run had helped alter his public face, telling a journalist that his two weeks on the show proved "that I can communi-cate with people and that I can step out of character and not be some kind of wild chihuahua all the time." He reflected further on his newly mature image: "Once I was a terrible liar. Maybe I'm growing up. Mayby I've stopped hating myself."

Despite this self-analytic breakthrough, his success on "The Tonight Show" wasn't the most exciting thing that happened to him and Patti during their two weeks in New York. They had decided to take what they called a "second honey-moon" in the city, and following Jerry's usual custom, they had booked a suite at the Essex House on Central Park West. It was to be a major vacation, apparently; they brought along a valet, a dresser, a secretary, and their best clothes and jew-elry.

On Tuesday night, June 26, 1962, while they were at RCA studios in Rocke-feller Center taping a show, burglars used a celluloid strip to enter the suite, emptied Jerry's jewel box of everything but his upper plate, slashed open Patti's suitcase (which was in another bedroom—not her husband's), and made off with everything they found.

It was a real-live jewel heist—quick and precise. The perpetrators had left behind two valuable watches, a chinchilla coat, Jerry's traveling camera kit, and the tip he'd left on the dresser for the maid. They took all of Jerry's treasures, even an onyx pinky ring Patti had given him back when she was still touring and he was courting her. Patti lost twenty-five pieces, including a ruby bracelet, three diamond-and-sapphire bracelets, and a lavish necklace-bracelet set. The total haul was estimated at $195,000. "But you can't measure what it was worth in heart value," Jerry said, adding, "maybe three and a half million."

It was the Essex House's third such burglary in recent weeks, and one of three with celebrity victims in New York during that same span of time—Rosalind Russell had been taken for $70,000 at the Plaza, Errol Flynn's widow for $15,000 at the Pierre. But Jerry lost a literal fortune right from under the eyes of a huge television audience.

He was devastated: "They did a beautiful job, an unbelievable job," he told the press. "They hit everything." He tried to stress the emotional impact of the experience, explaining that he most missed that old pinky ring and a watch Patti had given him when he opened in London with Dean in 1952. "It's been my good luck charm," he said, though, of course, London had been a disaster. But he couldn't lose sight of the money he'd lost, big by even his standards: "I'd pay two hundred grand for three shots at his face, whoever did this," he said. "Just to punch him against the wall."

"You can punch me for a hundred grand," cracked a reporter.

He didn't like the joke. "I can't be whimsical or irresponsible about a tragedy like this. Patti's heart is broken. She's a very emotional Italian woman who takes these things seriously. She's acting calm to protect me, but her heart is broken. And I don't know how I'm going to fix it."

The FBI was called in, dozens of cops showed up (he did shtick for them: "I can never get more than ten or twelve people around me and not consider it an audience"), and the story broke big in the papers. But it had been a real professional job; the FBI had nothing. The stuff was gone. It was, of course, insured back in California, but it was all a memory. And truly, it was the sentimental loss that bothered him.

Years later, Jerry recalled how he had reacted to that sense of loss in the extremely public forum that his visit to New York had afforded him: "I went on the air the next night and I said, 'I know about heists because I know about the people that do that, and I'm not proudly proclaiming that I know them as friends, but I do know their modus operandi. So therefore, I'm not really concerned with the three hundred fifty or four hundred thousand dollars' [sic] worth of jewelry, but there was a ring that my wife gave me.' And I described it. I said, 'I doubt that that ring could possibly cost more than sixty dollars, because she bought it for me in 1943 [sic]. So if any of you guys before you fence all this stuff run across that ring'—and I'm looking right in the camera on 'The Tonight Show'—I said, 'you have my marker for the rest of your life if I could get that one ring back.' "

He offered a five-thousand-dollar, no-questions-asked reward right there on

TV. A few nights later, somebody showed up at the "Tonight Show" taping to give Jerry a ring like the one he'd described. Jack Keller got wind of it and called the cops. Three squad cars and four detectives showed up, but it was a false alarm—it was just a fan who wanted to make sure that Jerry had some kind of ring like the one he'd lost. But then, as Jerry recalled, "Two weeks passed, I finished 'The Tonight Show' in New York, I went home, and I had an appointment at Paramount at seven-thirty in the morning. I get in my car and it's sitting on the seat of my car in an envelope." TV audiences really *had* learned to love him after all.

Back at Paramount that summer, he worked his usual day-and-night schedule on his new film. It was unlike anything he'd tried until now. Not only was it fully scripted as a linear narrative (as opposed to a series of jokes hung off a slight frame), but it called for him to play two complete roles, the Jekyll and Hyde of the story. It had been almost a year since *The Errand Boy* had wrapped, and the pace of preparation on the new film was infinitely more deliberate than usual. There had been intimations of his doing a version of Jekyll and Hyde for at least two years, and even earlier than that he'd investigated the matter of remaking a property that was in the public domain. So this was hardly a headlong rush like *The Bellboy* or even the partially spontaneous *Ladies' Man*.

He dedicated himself to the picture, eventually dubbed *The Nutty Professor*, right up through the start of the shoot—no TV, no nightclubs. As was his wont, he oversaw every single aspect of the production, from the logistics of filming exterior sequences on the Arizona State University campus in Tempe to the casting of key players. And, as was his wont, if he didn't get his way, he could get furious.

MDA's Art Zigouras was talking with Ernie Glucksman in his Paramount office one day when Jerry got some bad news about the film: "Ernie's office was connected to Jerry's office by a door that was behind a bookcase. It was like a secret door, and it opened with a kind of pneumatic hiss; evidently, Jerry had some sort of secret control. And I didn't know this. So we're in there talking about some thing for dystrophy, and the door—*shoooosh*—opens up. Jerry storms in, furious at Ernie, and just chewed him out the way you would chew out some minor servant who'd left a watermelon peel on the table, even though Ernie was a producer in his own right. It seems Jerry had asked for John Williams, the British actor, to play the dean of the school in *The Nutty Professor*, and it got back to Jerry without getting through Ernie that John Williams would not be in this movie, that he didn't think much of Jerry, that he didn't think Jerry was a good director, that he wouldn't bother with this piece of trash. Well, of course, if you told Jerry that the script was trash he'd start yelling. And he thought that somehow Ernie had fucked it up: 'You're supposed to be my producer and you didn't get John Williams and you screwed it all up.' Ernie turned white. He was about sixty-five, sixty-six. And I never felt more sympathy for him than at that moment. And Jerry stormed out and the door went *shoooop* and Ernie turned around and chuckled and said, 'Well, now, let's get on with our business.'"

The part of the college dean went to Del Moore, the announcer for Jerry's homemade radio station. Other parts went to other old friends—Kathleen Freeman, Buddy Lester, Milton Frome, and Larry Storch (a longtime Lewis hanger-on whose role wound up being cut). Some new faces were hired: a comic named Henry Gibson, a gigantic young actor named Richard Kiel.

As his leading lady, Jerry cast a twenty-six-year-old starlet named Estelle Egglestone. She was born in Hot Coffee, Mississippi, and was married, became a mother, and got divorced while still in her teens. She fought a court battle to keep her husband from taking her baby away, she attended Memphis State University (where she acted the Marilyn Monroe role in a production of *Bus Stop*), and she posed as one of Playboy's most popular centerfolds. She had broken into movies in 1959 when Frank Tashlin cast her in Twentieth Century–Fox's *Say One for Me*. Critic David Thomson likened her life to a Preston Sturges scenario, adding that it was "perhaps more than Sturges could've handled." Maybe Al Capp would have been a more appropriate point of reference. After all, Egglestone and Jerry first met on the set of *Li'l Abner*, in which she stole several scenes in the role of Appassionata von Climax under her *nom de scene*: Stella Stevens.

Stevens was the era's sexy blond bombshell par excellence, a voluptuous young woman with an adorable and naïve air that simultaneously undercut and heightened her allure. Jerry was absolutely bowled over by her. Three weeks into the production, he stayed late at the office to write what could only be described as a mash note to her. "I was completely inspired last night," he told her. "You are the reason men can't live without the pride and thrill of direction. . . . Perhaps one day you too will know the feeling." He must have realized how far overboard he'd fallen, admitting, "This is not the kind of a letter I would want to dictate."*

The film had begun shooting on October 9, 1962, and the set wasn't run in the familiar everybody's-welcome fashion. Although he hosted diplomatic contingents from Morocco and the Ivory Coast and a group of children from the Los Angeles County Juvenile Court, Jerry closed the set to all outsiders when he was in makeup for the "Hyde" personality. (He did, however, take a Saturday away from the set to go over to MGM, where Stanley Kramer was shooting the mammoth slapstick film *It's a Mad, Mad, Mad, Mad World*, and contribute a cameo as a speed-crazy driver who crosses several lanes of traffic to run down Spencer Tracy's hat.)

---

*Compare this note with the angry memo he dictated to the cast and crew just a week earlier when he discovered that a football pool had been circulating on the set: "I will not stand for any of my staff gambling on the set of our production. *You should know better!*"

Another time, he virtually shut down the set for two hours so he could spout off to a *Variety* reporter about the ills he thought were plaguing the film industry. He especially decried the tendency toward adults-only films, which he said were stifling the industry by alienating patrons early in their lives and turning them into inveterate TV-watchers. "I have to hire a projectionist for fifty dollars to show *Babes in Toyland* at home to my kids on Saturday afternoons," he said. "I'm certainly not going to let them go to a theater and see a Lesbian [sic] concept."

He saw himself as the last sane man in an increasingly insane business: "We let The Twist come out and then made movies from it. The Twist should have come from the movies. We created degradation by latching on to a motion picture subject that comes from a degraded form just because it is lucrative. It is degrading to take our talent and apply it to this just because of the greed of some people. To put a dame in a film because of her measurements is not substantial enough to make product—there just mustn't be that kind of greed."

Never once passing to think that anything of what he had said might have had any reflection on his own work, he went on to detail all of the tie-ins Jack Keller had arranged for *The Nutty Professor*—Planter's Nuts, Willys Jeeps, Vic Tanny Fitness Centers, North American Van Lines—and then put his false teeth in his mouth and went off to film his curvy Playmate of the Month leading lady.

In November the shoot moved to Tempe for three days of exteriors and establishing shots. Jerry kept regally above the throng of students who milled about the set—he literally rode a crane over their heads—but occasionally alit to entertain himself. Scott Townsend, then a student at ASU, recalled that Jerry dismounted the crane, "got in his Lincoln Continental, and drove all of fifty feet across the street to one of the athletic fields. He took his golf clubs out of the car, and he proceeded to hit about fifty brand-new golf balls out into the field. Of course, there was a huge crowd watching, and there was a smaller crowd that were trying to get the golf balls that he hit for souvenirs. After fifteen minutes or so of hitting golf balls, he got back in his Lincoln and drove the fifty feet back across the street."*

On the last night in Tempe, Jerry put on a full-scale performance in Goodwin Stadium on the ASU campus. It was the same material he'd done in Vegas the previous winter, with jokes about Phil Harris, Richard Nixon, the Edsel, Arabs, folksingers, and the movie *Exodus*. He did cane tricks and golf and hat routines. He lit an audience member's handkerchief on fire and then replaced the immolated object with a monogrammed hanky of his own (a perennial Lewis

---

*The golf balls were custom jobs, with the omnipresent Jerry Lewis logo on them. A few years later, filming on a beach, he hit cartons of them into the ocean; crew members returned afterward with scuba gear to collect them.

bit). He sang "I'm in the Mood for Love," "What Kind of Fool Am I?," and an Al Jolson medley, and he talked about his family. He was memorialized with a bronze caricature in the student union, and he enjoyed his trip to college so much that when it came time to preview the film he lobbied to do so in Phoenix (Ernie Glucksman, however, convinced him that the audience there would already be predisposed to like the picture, and Jerry wound up not only forgoing a Phoenix preview but skipping the town altogether on his promotional tour for the movie).

The Nutty Professor wrapped on December 18, 1962, five days behind schedule and $380,000 over budget. Of the $1.892 million final cost, $80,000 went to Jerry as director, producer, writer, and star, a relatively modest sum but altogether superfluous in another light.

On November 27, along with various ABC executives, Jerry had announced that he had signed a deal for a new series. Both the money and the show were unusual. Jerry would be the host and star of a two-hour live variety/talk show set to air on Saturday nights opposite "Gunsmoke" and "The NBC Saturday Night Movie." For a schedule of forty shows each season, he would receive $8 million— $50,000 a show. It was a five-year deal, with a $40 million ceiling. As he had just three years earlier with Paramount, Jerry Lewis had signed the biggest contract in the history of the medium; he was now the highest-paid star in movies *and* TV.

Word had been circulating for some time that NBC and CBS had been trying to sign him to a similar deal, based on the strength of his two weeks on "The Tonight Show" that spring. But he had pushed for concessions that those networks simply wouldn't allow him: 100 percent creative control, a premium time slot, an absolutely live broadcast. ABC didn't give him the whole house—they didn't include any series pilots from Jerry's production company in the deal— but they had given him his own set of keys.

ABC president Leonard Goldenson agreed to Jerry's terms in large part because his network's generally weak standing made such risks necessary. Moreover, he had flown out to Paramount to meet with Jerry and Ernie Glucksman and been impressed with the comedian's energy and vision.

As for Jerry, he finally felt as though he had the medium that had so long frustrated him by the throat: "I'll be in complete control," he announced. "It'll be something I've never done before. It'll be what people want—strictly entertainment. No song-and-dance stuff. No working under pressure with people who are frightened."

He elaborated on this last comment, an obvious jibe at the NBC executives who had heretofore overseen his TV career: "I was tired of being governed by a lot of frightened people who don't have the courage of their convictions. I walked away from frightened people in a frightened medium years ago. Now they're getting some guts."

But as to what he was going to do during eighty hours of live TV each season, he sounded a little unsure: "I'm going to play it loose. I'll be what I'm with. I suppose I'll have guests. If they're hostile, I'll be hostile. If they're warm, I'll be warm. If they're zany, I'll be zany."

After Christmas, he took the reels of *The Nutty Professor* with him to Lake Tahoe, where he played three weeks at Harrah's. Along with him he brought his editing team—Artie Schmidt, John Woodcock, and Rusty Wiles—and Glucksman. Not only did they have the release of one film to handle, but they were set to begin production on another in the spring—a Paramount production called *Who's Minding the Store?* to be directed by Frank Tashlin—and now a major TV series scheduled to premiere in nine months.

For some reason, the TV series seemed to matter least of all to Jerry. The deal itself seemed to satisfy him somehow. And of all the people in his coterie, only Jack Keller had the nerve and the standing to tell him that the TV series was too big, that his priorities were backward, that the movies ought to have been someone else's concern, and that he should have been concentrating on the show. Art Zigouras recalled that "the only person who said to him, 'Don't do it' was Jack Keller. 'It's not your thing,' and all. And Jerry was fuming at him. Jack and I used to go out and drink and he'd say, 'It's no good, he's gonna fuck up, it's not his thing.' And I remember him saying, 'Jerry just thinks he can make a funny face and do a funny bit and he'll get by, but you can't do that on ABC television any longer.' He would tell Jerry that, and he and Jerry would have these real arguments."

But Keller was getting a bit long in the tooth. He had begun to groom a protégé, a young publicist named Jim Flood, and he had been balking at another of Jerry's schemes. For the launch of *The Nutty Professor,* Jerry wanted to go on a national tour with a band and a full retinue. He would open the picture in each town with live performances at a number of theaters, do TV and radio and press conferences, and greet his audience one by one, as it were. He would visit twenty-five cities in forty-four days, doing about two dozen twenty-minute shows in each town. Jerry reckoned it would boost the gross for the picture by about $1 million and drum up an audience for the TV series. Keller reckoned it might kill him. He tried to talk him out of it: "What's to be gained?" he'd asked. "The picture's going to make money whether you do it or not." But Jerry wouldn't change his mind. So Keller set about planning the tour, coordinating it, and eventually going along on it. In typical sardonic fashion, he dubbed it "The Jewish Bataan Death March."

The spring of 1963 saw three previews of *The Nutty Professor*—one in Jamaica, Queens, was filled with old friends of Jerry's from Times Square and the MDA— and the start of filming on *Who's Minding the Store?* When that film wrapped at the end of May, Jerry had a week to rev up for the *Nutty Professor* promo tour.

It was an enormous undertaking, with several buses and limousines, a five-piece combo under the hand of longtime Lewis bandleader Lou Brown, and a retinue that included Keller, Glucksman, Bill Richmond, a secretary, dresser Dick Jarrod, stage manager Hal Bell, ABC producer Perry Cross, some Paramount distribution people, personal photographer William Woodfield, and a rotating crop of hangers-on. Even more grandly, Jerry allowed Richard Gehman, a freelance journalist who'd written a story about him in *The American Spectator* the previous year, to accompany him for twenty-four-hour stretches as part of a book-length chronicle of the tour and its star's life. He was Johnson traveling the provinces with his own Boswell.

Jerry had a massive loose-leaf binder prepared for him, with each day's itinerary mapped out in painstaking detail down to the name of every reporter he would meet. Shopping trips to camera stores were noted; dinners with friends were scheduled. The outside of the sixty-six-page binder read:

Jerry Lewis
Personal Appearance Tour
for
"the NUTTY professor"

Under that he wrote in pen:

and
Jerry Lewis Show
ABC TV
AND
for the future!

Just packing for the thing was a logistical nightmare. Jerry was used to traveling with so much stuff that he took two cars along when he went down to his yacht for a weekend. For the *Nutty Professor* promo tour, Jarrod was in charge of the following: ten tuxedos with matching shirts; six sports coats designed by Jerry along with matching trousers; six store-bought sports coat–and–trouser ensembles; ten pairs each of white yachting sneakers and black leather loafers; a gross of pairs of white socks; four dozen pairs of black socks; thirty-six sweatshirts; twelve pairs of twill yachting slacks; ninety pairs of broadcloth shorts monogrammed with Jerry's caricature; a half-dozen baseball mitts and a dozen hardballs; a set of golf clubs; a suitcase of Indian nuts; a suitcase of Pep-O-Mint Lifesavers; a suitcase filled with cigarettes, mouthwash, caffeine pills, aspirin, soap, and assorted toiletries; a suitcase of recording equipment; four suitcases of cameras, lenses, film, and photographic equipment; an oxygen tank; three electric typewriters; a carton filled with Jerry's self-published book *Instruction Book for Being a Person*; a box of specially printed "Think Pink" stickers; a scrapbook entitled "The Mad World of Jerry Lewis"; a portable phonograph; and a box of Count Basie LPs. (In part, the opulence fed his sense of having been deprived as a child, but the multiple changes of clothes were necessary because Jerry fetishistically refused to wear any pair of socks twice and gave away all of his suits as soon as they needed to be cleaned; similarly, he would insist on beginning each day with a newly opened, full pack of cigarettes.)

The tour began in Houston on June 4. He held court with reporters at the Sheraton-Lincoln Hotel and set about charming them immediately: "I say this respectfully, and I love you, but I couldn't care less what you say." But they were saying nice things about him: He was another Chaplin, right? Nope. Unlike Jerry, Chaplin had gone to the bad: "He was wonderful when he wore the baggy pants, but somewhere he went wrong. He forgot his roots."

He dashed off to Dallas, Fort Worth, San Francisco, Des Moines, Omaha, Denver, Kansas City. In St. Louis he told reporters at the Chase-Park Plaza Hotel that he was too busy to get home for Father's Day. He had taken two days to fly back to Los Angeles for Gary's high school graduation, though, so it wasn't as if he didn't love his children. Patti was pregnant again. The other kids were great. He attributed the success of his marriage to them: "We've been married nineteen years. When you think about it, that's what it's all about. You know it; I know it. But we tend to overlook it. It's like apologizing to a stranger for bumping into him. You'll spend more time apologizing to a stranger than you will telling your kids how much you love them. You know, our house without a baby is nothing. We're here to reproduce the best possible citizens. They are our children until they're grown, then they hand in their resignation and you wish them well and send them on their way with your love. We call them 'rental babies.' The little ones take their places. We're going to have children just as long as we can, and then we're going to start adopting them. My wife and I are buying a seventeen-acre ranch. We're going to call it 'Love State' and keep it fenced, and kids will get everything there, including love. Everyone should have their own little place like that."

He rode off to Cincinnati, Philadelphia (he appeared on "American Bandstand"), and Washington, D.C., where he coincidentally ran into an MDA publicity event, much to the chagrin of its organizers, who included Art Zigouras. "I was working very closely with Patty Duke," Zigouras recalled. "Her show was on the air at the time, and her manager was a guy named John Ross. We had twin poster children, and we were trying to get them in to see President Kennedy. We tried that with all the poster children, and we couldn't ever do it. Well, John Ross and I went out for a drink once, and I told him we couldn't get in to see the President, and we wanted to get some publicity with him. And he says, 'Why didn't you come to me sooner?'—Peter Lawford produced 'The Patty Duke Show'—and he said, 'I'll talk to Peter,' and a few days later we were invited to the White House.

"It was the same time that Jerry was doing the promo tour for *The Nutty Professor*, and he just happened to be scheduled to be in Washington, D.C., on the day we were going to the White House. And Jack Keller is calling me saying, 'Why isn't Jerry in on this deal? What the fuck is this?' Well, we couldn't do anything about it because it's Peter Lawford and the Rat Pack. And there's no love lost between Jerry and the Rat Pack. So Jerry is fuming and furious and screaming."

On the day of the visit, Zigouras arrived at the White House aware of having alienated MDA's highest-profile supporter but convinced that getting the President in on the campaign was worth the risk. "This is before the assassination," he recalled, "and before we were so aware of security and so forth. I wasn't supposed to go in there, but when it came for our turn to go in there, I grabbed a wheelchair because I wanted to see the President. And I go in from the waiting room, the family goes in, and I turn around, and there's Jerry. There's Jerry! Jack Kennedy looks over at him and says, 'What the hell are you doing here?' He's ribbing him. And Jerry says, 'I'm on a tour and these are my kids, blah, blah, blah.' The whole thing went very well and we filmed it. I never heard any repercussions back from the Peter Lawford camp, but Jerry was not supposed to be there. . . . We did put together a PSA to be released in November, with the kids looking through their album and saying, 'And here's when we went to see President Kennedy, and he was so nice.' We used wire service footage, and we sent the thing out, and soon after that he was assassinated. And the stations said they couldn't play it because it would look like we were cashing in."

Having crashed a party at the White House, Jerry and his buses moved on to Atlanta, New Orleans, Jacksonville, and then north to Detroit, where Richard Gehman met up with them to begin his chronicle.

Detroit was, of course, something of a homecoming for Jerry: He visited the National Theater and the Barlum Hotel—scenes of that long-ago winter vacation with Danny and Rae—and some of the sites he visited with Patti when they first met. But there was little misty-eyed reminiscing. They'd all been on the road for three brutal weeks, and they were fed up. Keller was, as he'd known he would be, exhausted. "This is the last one of these for Your Old Father," he proclaimed. "After this I wouldn't go out on tour with the Pope."

Jerry was showing signs of stress as well—chain-smoking Kools and skipping nights out on the town with the boys to spend quiet time in his hotel suite with his secretary. One night, a bug flew into his ear while he was on stage, and he had to be rushed to an emergency room afterward.

He finally lost his temper when the string of theater appearances was converted, without his approval, to a string of *drive-in* theater appearances. He disappeared out from under the noses of his retinue for almost an entire day, and he was still depressed when he made his way back to the hotel, offering no explanation for his absence and threatening to scuttle the rest of his commitments in Detroit and take off for Montreal, the next stop.

As Jerry sulked, the others in the suite tiptoed around him. Then he remembered that the *Detroit Free Press* had published a negative review of *The Nutty Professor* that morning. "Send him a Candygram," Jerry barked. "'DEAR JOE,' or whatever his name is, 'THANK YOU VERY MUCH AND I PROMISE TO DO BETTER NEXT TIME. MOST SINCERELY, JERRY LEWIS.'" He stormed into his bedroom and slammed the door.

Keller did as he was told: Jerry had him send telegrams all the time. Several a day went off to Patti and the boys (on top of multiple daily phone calls), others went out as gags. Indeed, pleasant thoughts of the Lewis family were among the few bright spots left in the ordeal for those around the star. The three drive-in appearances were canceled lest Jerry go mad, and they set off for the airport and Montreal, an escort of motorcycle cops with sirens paving their way.

"The Mood," as the Lewis entourage had come to refer to their boss's ever-fluctuating demeanor, was brighter when they woke up in Montreal. As he had when he first arrived in Detroit, he reminisced about gigs he had played there as a young pantomimist and emcee: The Normandie Roof nightclub at the Mount Royal Hotel, the Gaiety Theater. He could turn any sort of appearance into a dewy-eyed homecoming if he wanted to.

Even better was the reception he got from the journalists in the city, who not only liked *The Nutty Professor* better than their counterparts in the States but asked questions of Jerry as a fellow intellectual, seeking his opinions on matters of state and morality. "Boy!" he announced to his retinue at the end of a press conference. "Did I enjoy that! What an audience! Those are perceptive, articulate people out there. If this is the kind of reaction I'm gonna get up here, I'll stay over for a couple more days and dump some cities off the States schedule. Wow!"

He really did respond well to journalists when he felt they were on his side. Indeed, with the passing of old-style Hollywood journalism—a glib combination of authorized studio publicity and tepid lifestyle reporting—he was finding it more and more interesting to deal with the press. There were new-style journalists out there, people like Richard Gehman and Peter Bogdanovich who wrote lengthy, psychologically focused profiles of their subjects. Jerry granted these writers total access to his life, his home, his office. He spoke frankly with them about his fears, his passions, his biases. It was as if he was psychoanalyzing himself in their work, using the printed page as a mirror on which he could test his moods and attitudes and see how he looked to other people. He had long been fascinated with psychotherapy, and in the absence of an analyst of his own, he turned the press into his confessor.

Back in the States, however, he ran into more of the hostile, insensitive questioning that drove him crazy. In Buffalo, a reporter actually asked him, "Are you in town for a picture, Mr. Lewis?" Jerry angrily wrote the question down on his itinerary. His treatment at the hands of the press so agitated him that he canceled two stage shows and three interviews.

The tour ground on: Rochester, Toronto, Boston. He took a few days off and flew home. Then came Chicago, where he began to lose his cool altogether. He was fed up with exhibitors who wanted more and more from him when he appeared in their theaters but did nothing to accommodate him. He decried their "greed" and barked, "I'm through playing toilets!," making headlines in local papers as well as *Variety*. Hotel employees who wandered into his presence were subjected to rude treatment, reporters who failed to attend a late-Friday-afternoon press conference (a time when many of them were under deadline for their Sunday editions) were castigated to those colleagues of theirs who did attend the function, and some absentees, including influential columnist Herb Lyon, received vitriolic telegrams.

Even the entourage took its cuffs—"I'm surrounded by such stupid people!" he shouted to one of his party within earshot of reporters. "Get out of here! I'm sick and tired of looking at your worthless face." When he saw he had an audience of journalists for this outburst, he hugged the man and patted his head, proclaiming, "I love this guy. He's been with me for years, just like most of my staff. We're fantastically loyal to each other. They love me, and I love them." In the pages of his itinerary, he wrote in a large, angry hand "Greed greed!! GREED!," as disgusted with himself as with anyone around him.

When the tour finally rolled into New York for its final four days (including an unofficial homecoming in Newark), everyone was relieved. They'd been on the road for seven weeks and had been to eighteen states and two Canadian provinces, putting in something like 770 appearances in theaters, on radio and TV, and before the press. It was an inhuman routine, and it was no wonder Jerry had begun fighting outright with reporters, hotel desk clerks, and his own employees toward the end of it. Keller wasn't literally right—the trip hadn't killed Jerry—but he was in a state of near-collapse. He was visibly rattled, not like a man who'd been busting his back but like a man on drugs. "He's like a machine," said a member of his entourage. "He doesn't eat. He doesn't drink [alcohol]. If he drank, he'd be dead. He lives on pills and vitamin shots and the only way he unwinds is by sitting around talking to people. He never goes to bed." And yet, despite his never-ceasing chatter and despite the presence of his soon-to-be TV producer on the trip with him, he had done very little preparation for his new ABC series, which was a mere nine weeks off.

But he had, just as he'd predicted, raised the grosses of *The Nutty Professor*. It set records everywhere for the opening of a Jerry Lewis film, even in places where he hadn't taken the tour. Actually, grosses in those cities indicated that the tour might not have even been necessary. In Los Angeles, for instance, where he hadn't done much publicity, the picture did $52,000 in its first two days—just slightly better than *The Bellboy*, but more than half as much again what *The Ladies' Man* or *The Errand Boy* had earned, and quadruple the two-day figures for *Cinderfella*. The first week there constituted the best opening of any Jerry Lewis picture ever. Other cities reported similar successes. And Jerry monitored them assiduously: In his papers he had a three-inch-thick report from the Paramount distribution office reporting the proceeds earned by *The Nutty Professor* for each day of its first two weeks in every theater in the country where it was playing; the document was filled with notes, observations, and questions in his hand.

Such attention to the minutiae of his business was typical for Jerry, but in the case of *The Nutty Professor* the punctiliousness was justified. Simply put, the film was his one undeniable, ineradicable masterpiece, the one piece of work that even his critical antagonists would concede had true merit. Upon its initial release, the film got moderately positive views in *Variety* and *The Hollywood Reporter*, but word of its quality or Jerry's sheer universal impact that summer drew other, unlikelier reviewers to it. In *The New Yorker*, which didn't bother to review most of his films, physician and theatrical director Jonathan Miller, slumming as a critic, wrote, "This is a very funny movie, with some brilliant visual gags and a stunning parody by Lewis of a Hollywood Rat Pack cad." *The New York Times* agreed, calling it "his most painless romp in some time and probably the most curiously imaginative one of his screen career . . . less of a showcase for a clown than the revelation (and not for the first time) of a superb actor."

At three decades' remove, even these glowing notices seem modest. *The Nutty Professor* is so far superior to Jerry's other films that it's almost inexplicable. It's clear how he built toward it in his first three efforts as a director, but it's utterly unique from them. Most of the traditional Lewis themes and gags are absent, the plot is carefully constructed (there is only one free-floating gag in the whole picture, and it's not a bad one at that), even Jerry's performance is completely realized, not only in each of his two characters but in the delicate moments when each of his two personae begins to peek through the other. It's astonishing that the man who had just made *The Errand Boy* had anything to do with the film. With one stroke, he went from faux silent gagster to masterful orchestrator of pathos and wit. Disappointingly, he would never come close to this apex again; his next film would attempt a full-scale narrative, but with far less success, and the remainder of his career as a director would be spent in clumsy hybrids of episodic comedy and structured storytelling. But for 107 minutes of film in that summer of 1963, he was an indisputable master of his art.

Although *The Nutty Professor* is clearly derived from Robert Louis Stevenson's tale of Dr. Jekyll and Mr. Hyde, there's a sublime twist on the familiar escape-of-the-inner-monster theme. Whereas Jekyll accidentally unleashes his inner demon, Julius Kelp—a Milquetoast chemist who has fallen unrequitedly in love with one of his female students (Stella Stevens, as Stella Purdy)—deliberately hopes to find an artificial means of altering his body into something more assertive and desirable. He winds up unleashing Buddy Love, a depraved, alcoholic libertine who wears absurdly stylized clothes, retaliates to threats or sarcasm with violence, and has the confidence to sing to an audience. The transformation is one from insecure little man (Kelp is stuffed in a small closet by an angry student and sees himself in a flashback as a baby with bifocals) to exceedingly confident big man, from private worrywart to public peacock, from Joey Levitch to Jerry Lewis.

At the time of the film's release, a handful of viewers theorized a connection between Buddy Love and Dean Martin. In France, where the film was known as *Docteur Jerry et Monsieur Love*, critic Robert Benayoun saw the film as the acme of Jerry's long obsession with doppelgangers and doubling, themes that were the principals of cohesion of Martin and Lewis as an act. It's easy to see the despicable Love as a rap at Dean, but it's also facile and biographically unlikely. The film was written in 1962, more than a half-decade since the team's acrimonious split and two years after Dean's selfless performance in Jerry's stead in Las Vegas. Relations between the two were nonexistent, but there was no cloud of animus, either. Decades later, even before he began publicly pronouncing that he'd always loved his former partner, Jerry swore that the character wasn't based on Dean.

And in fact very little about Buddy Love is like Dean. The traditional Dean Martin character may have been a small-time conniver, a cad with the ladies, a singer, and an occasional tippler, but he didn't do any of it with the headstrong, ugly purposefulness of Buddy Love. Dean romanced women; Buddy commands them to heel. Dean worked angles with a material purpose in mind; Buddy manipulates people for the sheer pleasure of seeing them do his bidding. They both sang, but in Dean's case singing was usually a means by which his character hoped to make his way in the world or to express his feelings for a girl; Buddy sings because it's a surefire way of getting attention, period. Dean worked with a partner; Buddy Love is a solo (albeit one with a partner/alter ego tucked away inside of him). Dean was courtly, if a roué; Buddy pulls up to a romantic spot, hands his girl a handkerchief, and sneers, "Take this, wipe the lipstick off, slide over here next to me, and let's get started." Dean was a boxer; Buddy punches like a sissy. And Dean was never a dandy; Love comes on like a degenerate Little Lord Fauntleroy in tight-fitting suits with loud patterns. In fact, looking at Buddy Love's thick eyebrows, apparently mascaraed eyelashes, plump lips, and dripping-with-grease hair, one notes more of a resemblance to Tony Curtis than to Dean.

So if Buddy Love isn't Dean, who is he? Well, Jerry Lewis, obviously. The cigarettes, the tyrannical outbursts, the overdone wardrobe, the fondness for brassy big-band swing, the hipster's lingo, and the unctuous manner with the ladies were all attributes of Jerry's private personality. Indeed, insofar as the "real" man he conveyed to his audience on TV shows, on nightclub stages, and in the press was itself a role, Buddy Love was very nearly that character: loud, arrogant, abrasive, abusive, and conceited. Only once before, when playing the character Jerry Lewis in *The Bellboy*, and not for another two decades, when he played a caustic legend of show business in *The King of Comedy*, would Jerry offer such a dark—and unmistakable—portrait of his off-camera self.

Julius Kelp, the pathetic soul from within whom Love emerged, on the other hand, was nearer to the persona Jerry presented in movies—the well-meaning bungler, the Kid grown up and invested with a Ph.D.—and nearer, in certain regards, to Jerry's own view of his deep-down inner self. Jerry saw himself as a bright man with strong empathetic feelings who suffered slights in childhood and desperately wanted to be loved. Like Kelp, he transformed himself into a performer to receive affection and attention; like Kelp, he suffered nagging doubts about whether the public loved the real man or the mask. *The Nutty Professor* is, in effect, a confessional about Jerry's neurotic compulsion to perform and the perils of succeeding in the public arena. It's not explicitly a show-business story—Buddy Love, for all his swagger, is not a professional performer, just some guy who shows up at a bar and sings—but it's Jerry's most meaningful statement about the heart of the entertainer: Kelp's climactic confession takes place, after all, on a stage.

For all that, though, it's still a hilarious and adeptly poised comedy. Kelp, the only completely realized character Jerry was able to create after the Kid, is a wonder: articulate and stammering, intelligent and utterly naïve, with a chipmunk's voice and teeth and a tweed wardrobe from the set of an Agatha Christie mystery, bullied but unvanquished, a zealous explorer of scientific puzzles, a hopeless klutz trying desperately to walk a tightrope of decorum and respectability. He blows up classrooms, he wrecks gymnasia, he myopically hurls his bowling ball at people instead of pins. Yet he's utterly charming, all the same. Unlike the Kid, Kelp never wheedles for our affection; his speech is affected but never attention-grabbing; he tells terrible jokes and then, still reaching for a connection to his unamused audience, tries to explain them; standing on the sidelines of a prom, he is transported by the sound of the Les Brown band and dances with delighted abandon by himself.

Until this film, Jerry had been a one-trick pony as an actor: The Kid was the sole undeniable manifestation of his comic genius, and none of his attempts to play sympathetic, mature characters felt like real performances. With Kelp, traces of whose personality had popped through in his comic riffs as early as his days with Dean, he created a second full-bodied characterization. Like James Joyce answering the charge that Stephen Dedalus was his only living, breathing character, Jerry created of Kelp a Leopold Bloom: a bucktoothed, greasy-banged chemistry professor who simply wants the world to treat him like a man.

The creation of Kelp (and the revelation of his own inner Buddy Love) was only half of Jerry's achievement with *The Nutty Professor*. Among Jerry Lewis films, it has no peer in technique, professionalism, or sheer judicious choice-making. Shot in warm but vivid color, expertly paced and edited (there's no support in the film for the traditional charge that he lingered too lovingly on his own antics), and filled with comic set pieces that explicitly furthered the plot and characterization, it's rivaled only by Jerry's best work with Frank Tashlin as an artistic achievement. There are moments of marvelous cinematic invention— the point-of-view shot of the newly emergent Buddy Love walking from a haber-dashery into the Purple Pit nightclub (a shot ironically echoed by the famous Steadycam shot into the Copacabana in Martin Scorsese's *Goodfellas*); a hilari-ously composed sequence showing Kelp's reactions to sounds as he suffers a brutish hangover; the devolution of Love into Kelp in the final confessional scene. Kelp's first transformation into Love is filmed as a horror movie sequence, with dark lighting, a discordant score, makeup far more monstrous than Buddy himself, crashing laboratory equipment. It's the longest piece of drama Jerry ever shot, and it works splendidly.

There are also the inevitable clumsinesses in the film—notably the shots of Stella reacting to Kelp or Love by looking into the camera, the uncomfortable fantasy in which Kelp imagines Stella dressed in a variety of come-hither outfits. But the very fact that these less masterful moments revolve around the object of Kelp's desire oddly justifies them: He can't control himself in the best of cases; around a girl who arouses him, he's completely lost.

Inevitably, as in most of Jerry's films, there's a drive toward a homilistic fi-nale. At a prom both Kelp and Love are expected to attend, the professor makes an appearance and then hurriedly prepares his potion. The hastily blended solu-tion proves inadequate however, and soon Love is turning slowly into Kelp—who reveals, after putting his glasses on in a genuinely heart-touching moment, what the experience of being two different people has taught him: "You might as well like yourself. Just think about all the time you're going to have to spend with you." It's an ironic message, coming from such a fragmentary figure as Jerry Lewis, but to hear Julius Kelp espouse it is to take it as truth. Of all the sympa-thetic endings Jerry ever attempted, this is the most successful.

Part of the reason it's so easy to take is that it's undercut by an ironic coda. Kelp's father has discovered his son's formula, turned himself from a henpecked wimp into a dominating swinger, and begun marketing the elixir as Kelp's Cool Tonic (with the slogan "Be Somebody, Be Anybody"); he interrupts one of his son's lectures with a sales pitch. Stella, who has proposed marriage to Kelp, es-corts her fiancé through a mob of students who want to buy the formula for themselves. The audience is meant to be charmed by her affection . . . and then sees that she has made off with two bottles of the elixir for herself—a kind of marital aid, the revelation of which causes her to turn and wink toward the camera. There's no reason, she seems to be saying, for the sexually vibrant Buddy Love to disappear from Kelp's (or her) life forever.

More has been written about *The Nutty Professor* than about any other film Jerry ever made, for these and any number of worthy reasons. And the man who made it, a thirty-seven-year-old Jewish American prince of show business, was the highest-paid actor in movies, the highest-paid performer on television, one of the highest-paid live acts in the world, an accomplished producer, an innovative cinematic technician, the author of two self-published books, a restaurateur, a radio station owner, a philanthropist, the father of five boys.

Julius Kelp looked in the mirror and saw a nonentity. Buddy Love looked in the mirror and fell in love. When Jerry looked in the mirror in the summer of 1963, he saw the King of Comedy. Jolson, Chaplin, Dino, Berle: Nobody had ever been where he was.

He had done everything he had ever dreamed he could do—and he was certain that there was more to come.

15.

Lawrence of Bel Air

Among the members of the Lewis organization, there were a few pet catch-phrases. There was "I want my nana," a kind of whining cry that could indicate infantile weariness or self-pity or anxiety. There was "Hey, Eddie!," a variation on the "Hey, lady!" screech mimics took as Jerry's signature. And there was "pussy-cat," perhaps the most frequently invoked of them all.

"He's a pussycat," Jerry or one of his chums might say of some favored person. "Isn't that a pussycat?" might express appreciation of, say, a new car or a fortuitous turn of events. It was a term of unqualified praise, and it had no bounds of gender, shape, or aspect: Patti Lewis was a pussycat, according to Jerry, but so too was Jack Keller.

The biggest pussycat of all, though, was the *Pussycat* itself, a forty-one-foot cabin cruiser loaded with the electronic gizmos its captain loved—things like closed-circuit cameras that photographed the fore and aft views from atop a mast, for instance. It was Jerry's first big boat—Joe Stabile had introduced him to speedboating a year or so earlier—and he kept it moored in San Diego. He and Patti and the boys would board it on weekends for short cruises to Mexico or Catalina. (He sailed as often with a crew as without, which may not have been a good idea; according to Judith Campbell, "There were stories about his yacht and how the operators of various marinas would shudder when they saw Jerry at the wheel because Jerry thought he was an expert skipper and the result was an endless string of disasters.") It was a private world beyond the private worlds over which he already held domain, a recreational outlet, a means of escape, a platform from which to entertain guests, a den.

It was to the *Pussycat* that Jerry repaired after the draining *Nutty Professor* tour. He needed the recuperative sunlight and fresh air, he wanted some time away from the Paramount offices and the corps of colleagues with whom he'd just passed two hellish months on the road, and he had some projects to work on that required concentrated thought. He had the ABC show to plan, of course, and there was a new script in the works, the story of a bellboy who finds himself transformed into a comedy star by some cynical Hollywood operators. He was calling it "The Schnook," and he had a January start-up date in mind. It was a lot of work for a man allegedly resting up from an arduous routine, but as he'd told Richard Gehman, "I get nervous when I got nothin' to do. The happiest I am is when I press myself."

If that's true, then he must have been delighted that summer. Not only was he embarking on a two-hours-a-week, live, prime-time series, but he had purchased, with his own money, a huge Hollywood theater in which to mount the show. The El Capitan on Vine Street, one-half block north of Hollywood Boulevard, had opened in 1926 as Hollywood's first major legitimate theater. In 1942 Cecil B. DeMille briefly converted the theater to a motion picture palace, but it reverted to live shows that same year. In 1950 NBC bought the theater and converted it into a TV studio. Over the years, the El Capitan had hosted broadcasts by Eddie Cantor, Frank Sinatra, Tennessee Ernie Ford, and Martin and Lewis, who performed several "Colgate Comedy Hour" shows there.

Now it was to be known as the Jerry Lewis Theater, and it had been completely gutted and rebuilt as a state-of-the-art TV studio. The very wiring and plumbing had been replaced. Eight hundred new gold-upholstered seats were installed. There was a new gold curtain on the stage, new plush red carpeting on the aisles, 350 speakers in the auditorium, and a gigantic closed-circuit monitor suspended above the stage so the audience could see the show exactly as it was broadcast. A walnut-paneled control room had been built, complete with a wireless communications link to the stage and a paging system connecting it to all twenty dressing rooms. The desk at which Jerry would sit when talking to guests was equipped with a control panel that allowed him to override the director and choose shots while the show was in progress; at a cost of thirty thousand dollars, it was designed to be broken down and taken anywhere in the world on location. The theater was air-conditioned, there was an outdoor rehearsal stage on the second floor, the marquee held three thousand lightbulbs. A logo of Jerry's face was set in the cement on the sidewalk out front, his initials were set in tile in the floor of his dressing room john, and the star on his dressing room door was a six-pointed Mogen David. A box had been built just above the stage from which Jerry's personal guests could watch the show. It was a $1 million reconstruction job, and Jerry oversaw every detail down to choosing the material for the ushers' shirts.

He had grandiose plans for the show itself, but he seemed unable to articulate them fully or even to explain how all of his divergent notions would gel. For instance, he boasted of attracting such potential guests as Cardinal Spellman, Winston Churchill, Queen Elizabeth, Jimmy Hoffa, and Helen Keller, but he also insisted that the show would always be live and spontaneous: Even the most prestigious guests would have to agree to appear live with the host; he didn't even want to meet them in advance. In part this was Jerry's version of confidence in the medium, in part it was a concession to his sense that the show would work best if it were improvised within loose parameters. "If we find Jerry clicking in a certain groove on a specific show, he'll have full latitude to stay with it as long as he wants," Ernie Glucksman told reporters at a September 11 press conference. "You can't fail when you're a tall, good-looking Jewish movie star," Jerry chirped when asked if he felt at all daunted by the undertaking.

But the whole thing was incredibly audacious, from the economic daring of ABC executives to the cheeky confidence of the star. It was billed as a break-through experiment in television, and it was. But it was something else as well, however, something more personal. With the elaborate, customized theater, the live audience, the shifting guest roster, and the box seats just off the stage, it had all the trappings, once again, of Casino Night in a Catskills Hotel. Just as he had with the Gar-Ron Playhouse and the productions of *The Bellboy* and *The Ladies' Man*, Jerry took a major new step in his career by harkening back to the favorite show-biz model of his youth. Even though he was the highest-paid film and TV star in the world, his idea of security was to surround himself with em-ployees who were like family and perform a spontaneous show for a pampered crowd, and now he was going to get to do it on a scale no one else had ever at-tempted.

ABC was growing suspicious about Jerry's plans for the show, however. "Lewis was very full of himself," recalled ABC president Leonard Goldenson, "and he wouldn't tell us what the show's format was. He kept giving us double-talk and double-talk and double-talk, insisting he would take the country by storm." Whenever programming director Tom Moore tried to pin Jerry down, Jerry would appeal to Goldenson; "Lewis regarded me as a gofer," Moore recalled. Still and all, the network—in for a penny, in for a pound—threw a good-luck banquet for him at the Beverly Hilton Hotel. The place was choked with stars, network and studio executives, and sponsors; Peter Bogdanovich found himself seated at a table with Joan Crawford and George Gillette, the shaving products magnate. The Los Angeles contingent of the Brodsky family were all present, as were Danny and Rae. As was his habit of late, Danny wasted no time in letting Jerry know what was bugging him about the evening. This time it was the seating plan. "Do you know that we're sitting alone with strangers?" he asked his son. "The least you could've done was put us in with some of your crowd." Rae stepped in to forestall an argument, but Jerry was deflated.

It was typical of their dealings of late. Danny would show up at the office or on a set, so duded-up that one new employee took him for "a slimy mafioso guy," and Jerry would immediately shrivel into a depression.

Bogdanovich witnessed this exchange between the two of them in 1962 on the set of *It's Only Money*, when Danny came by to tell Jerry he'd been booked for "The Ed Sullivan Show":

"So how you been, Jerry?"

"All right."

"Everything all right?"

"Yeah, everything's swell."

"That's good. Watch me on the show."

"Yeah, Dad."

"So everything's okay, huh?"

"Sure."

"Well, I'll see you."

"Yeah, Dad."

Danny never sat down, while Jerry slumped in his chair the whole time and concentrated on sipping a malted; Danny left as quickly as he'd arrived.

Dick Cavett, whom Jerry had hired away from "The Tonight Show" as a writer for the ABC show, recalled that "every time his father came into the studio, he went into a funk that ruined that night's show. They imprisoned him or something on opening night. I remember [producer] Perry Cross practically had sentries out: 'If you see Danny Lewis coming, slap him in irons.'"

Danny had realized long ago that he would never get the sort of acclaim he felt was coming to him, just as he'd realized he could never hope to compete with his son's success. He'd faced up to these realities by withdrawing, shrinking back from his ambitions. He was in his sixties, but he seemed much older to his son, who'd once idolized him as a giant in show business. Jerry no longer felt like boosting his father's career; he was embarrassed by his very presence. As he remembered later, "I got angry at this hero of mine. He settled. He lost his drive. He had no desire to be anything other than what he was, a big fish in a small pond." If he saw in his father's diminishment a presage of his own fate, he couldn't say. But he knew his father made him uncomfortable, and the people around him respected his moods enough to keep Danny at bay.

The uncertainty that reigned during the genesis of "The Jerry Lewis Show" was palpable, and to make matters worse, the media had drummed up an anticipatory murmur about the program throughout the land. *The Nutty Professor* was still packing theaters in which Jerry had just recently appeared. People were hungry for news about his new project. But even the press was baffled about what the show would be like. "'What are you going to do for two hours?' was the national cliché," Cavett recalled.

The writing staff, which consisted of Jerry, Cavett, Bill Richmond, and Bob Howard, felt they had to confront questions like these head-on in the debut show. As Cavett remembered, "We wanted to play off the pretensions that were around the whole thing: everyone in tuxedos and 'Tonight this man embarks upon the greatest adventure in the history of television,' and so on and so forth. I had this idea that I thought deflated all that, and Jerry loved it too. It was that he'd be discovered on the corner of Hollywood and Vine, half a block from the studio, live, and he'd put out his cigarette—he smoked on camera in those days—and a voice-over says, 'This man is about to embark on, etc.' And we follow him walking toward his studio as the voice-over says, 'You are part tonight of one of the most daring experiments in the history of television . . . a legendary comedian and so on . . . and this theater has been rebuilt . . .' And you'd see Jerry Lewis's face in the pavement out front and the marquee of the Jerry Lewis Theater. 'And now, ladies and gentlemen,' and a drumroll, and Jerry straightens his tux and goes to open the door and can't get in. And I thought he would play it just right, he would underplay it; he'd try the first door and it would be locked and it would be embarrassing, and he'd move to the next one and finally realize that he really cannot get in, that the locks have gone or something. And he thought this was a brilliant idea, he could see himself doing it, and he got up in the office and showed just how he'd play it, and everybody said, 'Cavett, you'll get a raise, this is great,' and all the other writers were jealous. But then he came out and sang 'When You're Smiling' instead. That's sort of a paradigm for what happened to ideas on that show."

The debut of "The Jerry Lewis Show" was one of the most highly anticipated TV events in the medium's history. Jerry preceded it with an appearance on "The Danny Kaye Show," but otherwise he focused on the task before him. It was yet another grueling schedule. Watching his boss put in twenty-hour days, Jack Keller remarked to Edward Linn, "He digs agony. He'd be the happiest S.O.B. in the world if somebody would only crucify him."

As the September 21, 1963, premiere approached, work on the theater still hadn't been completed and the very format of the show hadn't yet been settled. Nevertheless, the guests had been booked; along with regulars Mort Sahl, Kay Stevens, Jack Jones, and announcer Del Moore, the opening-night roster consisted of the Harry James Orchestra and, curiously, editor and critic Clifton Fadiman. The sponsors had been lined up as well; the two hours would be paid for through the combined efforts of Nytol, Heinz, L&M cigarettes, Dial, Aquanet, Vista floor cleaner, Brylcreem, Dodge, United States Plywood, Gold Medal flour, and Polaroid. (Jerry, who had been given final control over whose money he'd take, had turned down an underarm deodorant ad, saying, "I cringe at some of the things that are projected into the home.") Whether the theater, the script, or the star were ready, the show would definitely go on.

The big night found Jerry in an uncharacteristically jittery mood. The day before, stories about the series had run on the front pages of the The Hollywood Reporter and Variety, which also ran eighteen pages of paid congratulatory ads from such people as Charles and Lillian Brown, ABC executives, sponsors, and assorted employees and friends. Jerry had tried to make a joke of his butterflies, sending a memo to a secretary asking her to remind him that he had two things to do that day: get a haircut and go to the theater.

When he got there, he encountered a riot of activity: The press was outside en masse covering the premiere, workmen were putting finishing touches on the building, a full house of eight hundred were led to their seats by ushers sporting THINK PINK buttons (a reference to Patti's pregnancy; the couple was hoping for a girl), and a crew of more than 170 technicians and cameramen in tuxedos buzzed about the stage, wings, and control room. ("It would take me two hours to tell you what a tuxedo will do for a cameraman," Jerry responded when asked about his crew's attire. "If nothing more, it'll dress up his ability. He'll be a little more'n a cameraman. All of a sudden he'll be delivering a little more'n I might get ordinarily.")

So many friends and celebrities had wanted to attend the premiere that Jerry spent forty-two-thousand dollars on a separate reception at the Beverly Hilton Hotel, a black-tie affair with cocktails, a closed-circuit broadcast of the East Coast feed of the show, and a sit-down dinner. As a gift to those lucky enough to get tickets to the theater, the on-air sponsors joined yet more sponsors in providing a pack of product samples: Pepto-Bismol, Brylcreem, Max Factor bath oil, Heinz catsup, Ballantine's beer, Metrecal, a stuffed Green Giant doll, soap, toothpaste, hair spray, and more.

Jerry was up in his dressing room frantic with nerves. Although the room had been furnished just that afternoon, one of the lightbulbs around the mirror was out: It was an old superstition of Jerry's to leave one bulb dim. Jerry allowed Richard Gehman in to see him, and they wouldn't let the writer leave before the show began: "Don't go, Beard," he said, using his nickname for his biographer. "Stay and talk to me." He disappeared into the bathroom to shave one more time. Then he shouted wildly—"Don't leave me!"—and then he whined: "I want my nana."

Lou Brown stopped in to try and settle him down. Ernie Glucksman came by, as did Marshall Katz and director John Dorsey. Jerry brushed them all off—though he did give Dorsey a shot list he'd thrown together, since his desk wasn't yet ready to allow him to choose shots from the set. He was smoking; he was groaning; he gulped down a glass of brandy. Finally, six-thirty came (the show aired live at nine-thirty in the east), and he could submerge his anxiety in performance.

When it was all over, he wished he had never left his little sanctuary. The two hours passed like an eternity. The show drew a huge audience—it ran opposite reruns of "Gunsmoke" and "Have Gun, Will Travel"—and those viewers witnessed one of the greatest fiascos in television history. Decades later it would remain the stuff of legend, but that night it was sheer torture for the star, for his employees, and for the network.

After being introduced by Del Moore (who jokingly announced him as "Jerry Lucas, I mean Levin, Lewin . . ."), Jerry emerged to be engulfed by a swarm of tuxedo-clad crewmen with cameras, microphones, and lights. He shooed them off and broke into "When You're Smiling," with lyrics specially written for the occasion. As soon as he finished the number, he became aware of the first technical snafu of the evening. The giant monitor above the stage was out, preventing people in the far reaches of the theater from seeing the show. "That's live," he said mockingly. "P-tooey!"

An extremely self-conscious and even defensive monologue followed, with many references to the problems of filling two hours (he actually announced how long each of the evening's segments would last, commercials included), many direct addresses to Leonard Goldenson, several jokes about his being a persecuted Jew (he called himself "Lawrence of Bel Air"), and repeated references to such inside matters as the union waivers that were secured for the show. It was as if there were no monologue, as if he were flailing around for something to talk about and the only thing appropriate was the show itself.

They made a big deal of the unveiling of the set and the pricey desk, though it wasn't significantly different from the traditional talk show stage. He finally sat down with Del Moore and did an ad for L&M cigarettes, totally improvised and providing the first fresh laugh of the evening: Holding up the pack, he shrugged, "Here it is. You wanna smoke it? That's your business." (But then he tempered the joke by opening the pack, lighting a cigarette and making a great show of how much he enjoyed it.)

Ernie Glucksman had cooked up some surprises for him—though, as controlling boss par excellence, Jerry didn't like such gimmicks. Robert Stack walked out in a tuxedo to wish him luck. Jimmy Durante popped out. A phone rang, and Johnny Carson was on the other end, watching from home in New York and saying how much he was enjoying it. He said he had a scout in the audience taking notes for "The Tonight Show" (which he'd been hosting for about a year), and the cameras panned to find Steve Allen scribbling in a pad. Allen came on stage to join the very strange group and make a plea for network ecumenism (though the next week he would savagely parody Jerry's botched debut on his own syndicated show). Jerry seemed genuinely taken aback by these cameo bits—none of these men, after all, was a close friend or in any way associated with his career. He sat there unable to muster any snappy banter or do much of anything besides look swept away—a man drowning on live TV.

More technical screwups followed. The control booth lost contact with the cameras, so the director couldn't order specific shots. Not that it mattered all that much: The cameras themselves had lost the red lights that let the performers know when they were on. Throughout the evening, people read dialogue into cameras that weren't filming them, or action would be covered from cameras halfway across the theater. "It's okay, it's live," Jerry kept saying, but even he knew it was a train wreck, finally blurting out, "Watch next week on tape!"

Nearly forty-five minutes into the show, the first talent was introduced—Jack Jones. Fair enough, but then Jerry followed his house singer by singing a song of his own. He introduced Patti, Rae, and his "Jewish Boys' Town" in the stageside box, then he sang "Think Pink," a hokey novelty number about the Lewises' family situation. It was dreadful, but no more so than every other scripted bit on the program. There was a gag about a Jerry Lewis look-alike contest; Jerry introduced a huge blond surfer type as the winner. There was a sketch to which all the actors but Jerry were given a script, and he had to improvise and figure out the situation while they played it (when he discovered the sexy actress he'd been coming on to was playing his mother, he hugged her and muttered, "I want my nana.") Mort Sahl performed a typically sardonic topical monologue, the Harry James Orchestra played, and Jerry conducted Lou Brown's band briefly, injecting some much needed life into the proceedings.

Watching from the wings, Jack Keller muttered sadly, "He thought he had trouble in those Detroit drive-ins." Finally, it wound to a welcome close. (Despite having two hours of airtime, they hadn't made space for Fadiman and wound up bumping him. "I remember him fuming backstage in his tuxedo," said Dick Cavett. "They couldn't squeeze him in. I think he walked.") Jerry sang "Make Somebody Happy" and stepped quickly off the stage.

The upstairs dressing room was funereal. Jerry was too embarrassed and depressed even to chew people out. "It almost all was ABC's responsibility?" he asked Glucksman sheepishly. "We'll move in our own engineering crew on Monday and get all the bugs worked out." Glucksman, numb, just nodded.

Sycophants and hangers-on lied through their teeth to him: "Good show, Jer." "A gas."

An ABC censor stood meekly in the corner waiting to deliver the news that Sahl's joke comparing Alabama to Nazi Germany was out of bounds. Jerry took pity on the poor messenger: "Don't be unhappy, Ed. I'm the one who lies in the corner and dies." (A few days later, ABC's Tom Moore would tell Jerry that the network felt there were too many references to Jewishness in the show, and Jerry took it less well, sensing an anti-Semitic dimension to the criticism.) He gathered himself together and, resisting Patti's suggestion that they just go home and go to bed, headed into the night toward his expensive party at the Beverly Hilton.

The critics were as flabbergasted by the disaster as the star. The broadcast was so far beneath their expectations that they were kinder than they might have been out of sheer confusion. The notice in *Variety* on Monday morning, while certainly negative, actually understated the show's failures:

It's conceivable, now that the premiere nervousness with the attendant bugs and kinks are in the past, the Jerry Lewis Saturday night two-hour marathon on ABC-TV might settle down to some form of respectable entertainment. It better had. . . . It's truly amazing that so much could have gone awry. What was billed as "an informal two hours of fun, entertainment, discussion and interviews in a spontaneous atmosphere" came off as disjointed, disorganized, tasteless. . . . The responsibility was Lewis' to fill the void and the lapses. On his getaway show, whether from nervousness or distraction, he just didn't fill the bill.

Cleveland Amory, writing in *TV Guide*, announced that "the show runs two mortal hours, and the very idea of five years of them, as presently constituted, is an appalling thought."

The second week's guests were to be Ruby Keeler and Bobby Rydell. Long hours were spent in seeing to technical problems and giving the show a more coherent feel. But it didn't matter. The entire nation had watched him take the steepest nosedive of his career. The ratings plummeted.

On week three, Mort Sahl made a crack about John Kennedy, Sam Giancana, and Frank Sinatra that aired to the East Coast but was squelched on the West by ABC censors; Jerry ripped off an indignant telegram to Leonard Goldenson.

Week four featured Sammy Davis, Jr., in the show's first genuinely lively interlude. "There was great spontaneous by-play," recalled Dick Cavett. "Everything the show might've been was apparent." Sammy did nearly forty-five minutes solo and with Jerry (they did a bit to "Me and My Shadow" with Jerry tailing Sammy move-for-move). The critics finally had nice things to say: "The show seemed to have a cohesiveness previously lacking," wrote *Variety*.

But by then even Jerry had lost interest. The show was a bomb, and the whole world knew it. He began disappearing altogether during the week. "Perry Cross, the producer, would pull clumps of his hair out," recalled Cavett, "because Lewis would do the show and then go on to his boat and be incommunicado up to the day before the next show, if you can imagine." To Jack Keller, Jerry was explicit. Sitting in his dressing room before the sixth episode, he told his old friend, "Get me off this show."

He had forgotten about the obligation even as he was fulfilling it, spending his time working on his new film script and suddenly announcing a November nightclub engagement in Las Vegas without telling Cross. Speculation that the show had failed because he had arrogantly assumed he could pull it off just by showing up was now universally taken as truth.

The staff adopted a gallows humor about their plight. As Cavett remembered, "Once I made Mort Sahl actually laugh hilariously. We were walking across the street from the theater, where there was a foot-long hot dog place.

And I said to Mort, 'Take a look at the marquee.' And it said, 'THE JERRY LEWIS "LIVE" SHOW'—with 'live' in quotes. And I said to him, 'If you went up there and rearranged the letters, it would be 'THE JERRY LEWIS "VILE" SHOW.' I also pointed out that in the thousands of dollars' worth of stationery and on the marquee and everywhere, they had the illiterate use of quotation marks, with 'live' in quotes, which meant that it was *not* live. Jerry grasped this immediately and had it all reprinted."

It wasn't his only extravagance, even in the face of the utter failure of the series. "One of my great losses is that I used to have transcripts of all those shows," said Cavett. "Each of us was provided with one. Jerry had them made to make it easier for historians. I gave one to Woody Allen one time. We have a running joke about a Comedy Black Museum—like Scotland Yard's Black Museum—and what things should be put in there. . . . And some of these transcripts belonged. Of course, parts of them were utterly unintelligible: 'Well, Del-sy, what about *ya, ya, ya . . .*' And then it would say, 'Jerry makes funny sound with mouth.' And, 'But here's another thing,' then, 'dot dot dot Jerry makes funny gestures.' And then conversation that would've kept S. J. Perelman rolling on the floor."

Leonard Goldenson certainly wasn't laughing. His expensive bid for a big-time variety show had turned into a public humiliation. ABC's contract with Jerry had called for a minimum of thirteen shows, and by mid-November, the network announced that the thirteenth installment of the program would be the final one. Tom Moore delivered the news to Jerry, who held a grudge against him for years after.*

The final broadcast of the show, delayed a week by the Kennedy assassination, would come on December 21. ABC bought out Jerry's contract and even took the theater off his hands. He walked away with a $2 million handshake, but he was stung. Critics dissected the failure even before the show was off the air. "He boasted to the press that he would by his sheer personal magnetism produce guest stars never before seen in entertainment programs," remembered Tom Mackin of *The Newark Evening News.* "He mentioned Winston Churchill and Cardinal Spellman. He settled for Jimmy Durante and Peggy Lee. It is sad to see a TV series depart. So many hopes, dreams and fortunes go with it. But in Lewis' case, it is easy to hold back the tears."

On the penultimate show, he asked a priest in the audience to administer the last rites to the program. He joked with guests Frank Gorshin and Jack E. Leonard about being unemployed. His self-pity disgusted the critics. "For his final show," wrote Hal Humphrey in *The Los Angeles Mirror News,* "Jerry should

---

*On "The Tonight Show" in the late 1960s Jerry scathingly imitated Moore's criticisms of his Jewish humor, only to learn afterward that Moore's son was a writer on Johnny Carson's staff; humbled, Jerry returned to "The Tonight Show" studios two weeks later to apologize to the young man personally.

keep his mouth shut about what happened and who did what to whom, and show his audience he is a trouper."

But the finale was as morose and awful as could be imagined. Jerry acted punch-drunk and made lewd gestures through a rendition of "I'm in the Mood for Love." Sammy Davis, Jr., returned for the purpose of squaring off with his host in a duel of seltzer bottles. Jerry told the audience that ABC and the sponsors had forced him to compromise his vision for the program, that television was still an infantile medium: "I don't like to do like I'm supposed to do," he said in a self-revealing monologue. "There are rules and regulations. Some I did not adhere to, and for this I am sorry. . . . The important thing is to play the game the ways it's to be played. . . . There's no debating the power of a TV rating. I wish I knew that in advance."

Toward the end of the show, he produced a smiling hand puppet of himself and sang to it. For the first time on television, he performed a song he had just a few years earlier incorporated into his live act, a song that had premiered without words in a film score of 1936. The lyrics, which Jerry sang straight, were written by John Turner and Geoffrey Parsons:

> Smile, though your heart is aching.
> Smile, even though it's breaking.

But it was the composer who most interested Jerry when he chose the song. The film in which the melody premiered was *Modern Times*, written, directed, starring, and scored by Charlie Chaplin. In the midst of his most miserable beating, Jerry once again emulated his boyhood hero.

Dick Cavett reached even further back for a point of reference for the failure of the show. He had, after all, read "Ozymandias"—and Thomas à Kempis, for that matter—and he was put in mind of both when he left Hollywood for New York: "On the last day, I went to the bank to withdraw my savings, rounded the corner of Hollywood and Vine to take a last look at the theater Jerry had done over in his image, and was just in time to see a giant pulley lowering the 'Jerry Lewis Theater' sign to the street. On the sidewalk in front of the theater a workman was chiseling away the caricature of Jerry's face that had been embedded in the pseudomarble pavement. He was up to the eye when I walked up. For the benefit of the unseen camera I muttered, 'Sic transit gloria mundi.'"

ABC, far less philosophical, immediately converted Jerry's theater and time slot to more profitable uses. The marquee soon read "The Hollywood Palace," the name of the series that the network ran successfully on Saturday nights for the next six years with a new guest host every week—Dean Martin prominent among them.

■ ■ ■

The ABC debacle was crushing enough, but then Jerry got kicked when he was down: A Los Angeles County Superior Court ruled that he had to defend himself against a civil suit brought against him by a novice screenwriter named Lor-Ann Land, who contended that *The Nutty Professor* was derived in part from her unproduced screenplay "Treat Me Beat." Land had met Jerry in Blum's Soda Fountain in 1962. He'd been sitting at the counter, and she sat beside him and announced that she'd written a script with him in mind. He asked to see it, she claimed, and she sent it to his office. A year later, she learned that *The Nutty Professor* was in production and, feeling it resembled her work, sued him for $1.5 million for plagiarism.

Jerry had been talking about a film like *The Nutty Professor* since at least November 1959, so Land's claim that he'd stolen her ideas wasn't likely. And after a year of litigation, the superior court ruled that he hadn't, in fact, plagiarized her material. But he *had*, according to the court, potentially entered into a contractual obligation with her by asking to see her script, and the court ordered further hearings to determine the nature and value of that agreement. According to Judge Macklin Fleming, "Producers who discuss plots with would-be script writers, even at cocktail parties or soda fountains, do so at their own peril. The contractual relationship between the parties can only be untangled by a resolution of the conversations, promises, events and disclosures which took place at Blum's."

In addition to having to prove he hadn't established a contract with Land, Jerry also found himself—along with his various companies and Paramount Pictures—the target of a $1 million slander and libel suit filed by the screenwriter. The whole thing was tawdry and insulting; he wasn't even allowed to enjoy his best work. He had his lawyers settle the suits out of court.

Sixteen days after the final installment of "The Jerry Lewis Show," Jerry began production on his fifth film as director and star. Known now as *The Patsy*, it was a kind of show-business *Pygmalion*, with Jerry as a clumsy bellboy who wanders into a hotel suite where the vipers who once ran the career of a popular comedian are wondering what they'll do now that their gravy train has died. They decide to make a star out of the bellboy—they know all the tricks of the Hollywood trade—and the film chronicles their efforts to reshape and launch him as a comedian. As written by Jerry and Bill Richmond, it was a cynical, caustic story of Hollywood careerism, made all the more credible by the casting of veteran actors as Stanley's new "friends": John Carradine, Everett Sloane, Keenan Wynn, Phil Harris, and in his final screen role, Peter Lorre. Buddy Love revealed a dark side to Jerry's character, but the film in which he appeared wasn't itself dark humored. *The Patsy*, on the other hand, from the title to the situation to a lengthy stream of tearing-the-mask-off-Hollywood jokes, was the acidulous vision of a man who was weary of his work, his public, and maybe even his station in life. It's easy to see in its basic shape a parable about how the lighthearted goof of *The Bellboy* was poisoned by the toadies who convinced him to do two hours a week of live television. In retrospect, *The Patsy* seems a calculated good-bye to the life of sycophants and the star-making apparatus on which he had thrived.

On January 7, 1964, Patti gave Jerry another baby, and this, too, proved a disappointment. Despite all the thinking pink, it was a boy—Joseph Christopher. Two days later, Jerry made contact with an adoption agency in hopes of getting a daughter that summer. "She and our new son will grow up together," he told the Associated Press. "By next Christmas I'll have a kid for every day of the week." (Despite his optimism, the adoption never went through.)

On the day of Joseph's baptism, Jerry typed up a kind of meditation on the child's birth and placed it beside a photo of himself holding the baby. It's a completely strange document, a poem, really—the original is enjambed and indented like an ode. Assuming his infant son's voice, Jerry consoled himself for his own lost childhood and seemed to declare that his own parents' neglect of him was a qualification for fatherhood. In effect, he turned the baptism of his child into a celebration of his own neuroses. The document ended with its infant voice declaring, "I can't help but feel a little sorry for you, Dad, 'cause I think you would have loved it too."

Patti was touched by the note and saved it, though she had little reason to sympathize with Jerry's hurt feelings about life. He had been awful to her through the course of the past year. "Although I was thrilled with the prospect of having another baby," she recalled years later, "I also had the feeling of being an inconvenience to my husband. During this pregnancy, more than any other, Jerry developed a black belt in sarcasm."

But she, too, saw the root of their marital problems in the dysfunctions they'd suffered as children: "Our marriage contained precious few role models of genuine love. We had received no training in the give and take a marriage requires. We possessed no understanding of what stardom does to Hollywood families, and we had only had glimpses of the value of abiding faith."

Patti was being charitable to her husband to lump herself in with him. Despite having been raised in a brutal environment, she was the nurturer in her household, always trying to improve herself and mend rifts between herself and Jerry. She had chosen to be docile with her husband, and he had taken that as a license to take advantage of her. Although he spent the bulk of his time at the studio, on the road, or with other women, Jerry dominated Patti thoroughly, discouraging her from doing anything about the gray hairs she began to acquire in her twenties or leaving the house during the day and thereby being out of reach of his neurotic barrages of phone calls, telegrams, and flowers.

In part, Patti saw her husband's mix of volatility and neediness as a manifestation of his poor self-esteem. In part, though, she recognized in it his distaste for competing with their brood of boys for her attention and affection: "I felt his jealousy of the time and love I lavished on the boys. He was not predisposed to share me that much, and I had trouble knowing when to draw the line. At times, Jerry seemed unreasonable, but now I understand it a little better. As one of my 'boys,' he needed a portion of child love along with adult love." The difference, of course, was that her sons never used her as an outlet for their frustrations as Jerry did, nor did they flagrantly abuse their relationship with her as he did with his affairs. She had been ill used as a child, and she had married a man who treated her in like manner.

If Patti had to suffer through her pregnancy and marriage, at least she was doing so in genuine splendor. There would never be more money in the Lewis family coffers than there was in that winter of 1964, and everyone who stepped into the palatial Bel Air manse was overwhelmed with the opulence they saw there.

Pulling into the driveway, visitors came across as many as two dozen cars, all belonging to Jerry (Jack Keller once accompanied his boss on a trip to an automobile dealership where he purchased—and paid cash for—four Lincoln Continentals). Peter Bogdanovich visited once and was sent home with one of Jerry's cars: "He didn't even want to see me driving this rotten '51 Ford I had. He was sick of seeing it come into his driveway. He said it made his driveway look like shit. So he said, 'Take one of my cars, I got a lot of them. Take one of them, I don't care. I don't want to see you driving in here with this garbage, this piece of shit.' So he gave us a Mustang for about a year."

With Jerry as its owner, the doorway of Louis B. Mayer's one-time mansion was marked with a mezuzah and a golden plaque that read: OUR HOUSE IS OPEN TO SUNSHINE, FRIENDS, GUESTS AND GOD. Friends and guests were led into a paneled living room furnished with low couches and crammed with memorabilia of the Lewises' family life and Jerry's career. Like many movie people, Jerry had the script of each of the films in which he appeared bound in leather, and those volumes occupied several shelves. But he also had books made out of clippings that represented various live engagements or TV projects or interviews or other ancillary activities connected to his career. And as for family matters, the dozens of titles on display included "Our Son Chris Is Four Years Young, Oct. 9, 1961," "Honolulu, Second Honeymoon, 1950," "Jerry Plays with Sam Snead, Bel Air Country Club," "Jerry's 36th at Jerry Lewis Restaurant, March 16, 1962," and "Paramount Executive Party at Our House, July 3, 1959."

On the wall opposite this library of personal volumes was a glass-enclosed case choked with plaques, certificates, engraved trophies, and the like—the booty from Jerry's tireless years of charitable efforts. It also contained a baseball autographed by Babe Ruth and three photos autographed by personal heroes of Jerry's: Adolph Zukor, Y. Frank Freeman, and Cardinal Spellman.

On a display table in front of the trophy case sat the silver-bound Jewish Bible (in Hebrew) that he'd been given in Ebbets Field, a Christian Bible, and a leather-bound script of *The Ten Commandments* autographed by Cecil B. De-Mille (as near as Hollywood could offer to the Shroud of Turin). Three pieces of art dominated the walls: a painting of Jerry as an Emmett Kelly–style tramp clown (complete with forlorn bandanna full of possessions at the end of a knobby stick), a stained-glass version of the same portrait, and a huge portrait of Jerry, Patti, all the boys, and the family menagerie of dogs and cats painted in the style of one of Picasso's harlequin families. Converted into a theater by lowering a screen from the ceiling, the room could seat twenty comfortably.

Just beyond the glass doors of the living room lay the outdoor recreation area—a collection of pinball machines, Ping-Pong tables, lounge furniture, and telephones beneath a retractable canvas roof. In the garden just past the games stood full-size marble statues in floral niches: Moses and St. Anthony (the latter shipped from Italy). Then came the pool and the remainder of the three-acre grounds.

Throughout the house was strewn an enormous collection of Venetian glass clowns, some as large as three feet tall. There were works of modern American art and a portrait of Jerry by Norman Rockwell. There were also microphones and cameras hidden in the very walls and ceilings, giving Jerry—and the private security force he had hired—a chance to monitor conversations and activity anywhere in the house. This surveillance system was a secret addition to the intercoms that connected the entire house. The boys, who were made to keep their intercoms on at night, thought they could attain some privacy during the day by switching them off; they didn't, however, know about the microphones in the walls. In 1975 Jerry boasted to Tom Synder that he once spanked Gary—who was well into his teens—and repaired to his monitors to hear what Gary had to say about the incident to Patti, who went up to her son's room to console him: "I expected the worst, you know, nasty stuff. You know what he says? He says, 'Daddy's the only one in the world who really loves me.' "

The centerpiece of the first story of the house, for Jerry's purposes, at least, was a soundproofed den he called his stereo room. A large L-shaped wing of the house, it contained the equipment that fed into his radio station, a full-service film-editing room, a recording studio, at least half a dozen professional tape recorders, a sixteen-millimeter movie rig, two thirty-five-millimeter projectors (and a CinemaScope screen that lowered from the ceiling), the control panels for the microphones and cameras hidden throughout the house, and an enormous color-coded library of audiotapes, kinescopes, and films of his life's work (along with a copy of *Modern Times* given to him by Chaplin himself).

There were dozens of cameras, lenses, flash attachments, and tripods. An encyclopedia sat near a TV set so Jerry could look up anything he saw on television that piqued his interest. A desk was lined with telephones and an electric typewriter. There were drawings and writings by the Lewis boys. There were collections of memorabilia and photos of Jerry with his sports heroes. Scattered all over the room, taped to consoles and windowsills and the walls, were apothegms of the sort that filled his "creed book": "The only gift is a portion of thyself"; "The things you keep you lose. The things you give away you keep forever"; "When I'm right, no one remembers. When I'm wrong, no one forgets." The room was positively choked, a dizzying environment for anyone who entered it save its owner and his home secretary, Helene Stebbins, who had served in the same capacity for Louis Mayer.

Journalistic visitors weren't granted access to the upstairs of the house, so they never got a glimpse of his massive wardrobe, which included eighty-eight tuxedoes. At least one room on the upper floor was extraordinary. Jerry had a private bathroom built for himself off the master suite, complete with sofa, full bar, another control system for the surveillance equipment, a television, two telephones, and a stocked refrigerator. It was a self-enclosed apartment within the house, and he spent hours secluded in it, often talking on the phone with girlfriends while his wife and sons listened to him through the door (Chris occupied a bedroom that shared a door with Jerry's retreat and overheard such conversations throughout his childhood).

Patti indulged Jerry's need for a sanctuary, though she was well aware all the while of what he did while he was ensconced in it. "He perceived his bathroom as a haven," she recalled. "I asked for and was granted—for a short time—an extension of the bathroom phone line by our bed. But he soon cut the line and had another, different number installed in the bathroom, and I had to endure overhearing his conversations with other women, and then conceal my frustration and hurt. I still haven't determined if I mentally and emotionally repressed those times to protect myself or the children."

Even with such painful events transpiring within its walls, it was, by any standards, a regal home, staffed with maids, a cook, a butler, nannies, and groundskeepers. But Patti had grown up in poverty and was a frugal mistress. She rose early to shop at sales, she saved trading stamps, she cooked dinners herself. Jerry preferred simple cuisine—Italian and Jewish dishes cooked according to traditional recipes, and grilled steaks and chops—but the Lewises frequently ordered take-out dinners from Chasen's, the posh Hollywood hangout that served caviar appetizers that the boys especially liked.

Jerry teased Patti about her skimpy ways with money—she was even embarrassed by the constant gifts of jewelry he lavished on her—but whenever he was gone, she would return to her habitual manner. On a few occasions, she and the boys took vacations without Jerry and stayed in cheap motels and ate fast food. The boys loved these illicit adventures—trips their father would never abide.

They had a small vacation villa in Palm Springs, and Jerry had the yacht in San Diego, of course. By late 1964 the radio station and the restaurant were sold off—they'd begun bleeding too much of their owner's time and money—but there was no end in sight to the Lewises' splendid lifestyle. Even with the embarrassing disaster of "The Jerry Lewis Show" so fresh in the public mind, he was still the premier comic entertainer in the world, and he lived as grandly as one might expect of someone who had achieved that title.

The Patsy finished shooting on the last day of February 1964, three days late and $131,000 over its original $2.1 million budget. Even then, sporadic reshooting went on until as late as May 12. Jerry and John Woodcock took their footage down to the *Pussycat* to edit a rough version of the film, which was shown to a preview audience on May 19. An August release was scheduled, but it would not be the occasion of another insane personal appearance tour by Jerry and his entourage. The country may or may not have seen a bit too much of him in the last twelve months, but he, in any case, had certainly seen too much of it. He devoted the summer to performing in yet another film, *The Disorderly Orderly*, the last movie he would make with Frank Tashlin.

It wasn't that he and Tashlin were weary of one another or that Tashlin had grown too old for the sort of films he and Jerry made. The truth was that Paramount was learning the same lesson that ABC had learned, although not at a similar cost or to a similar degree of public ridicule: Jerry's commercial potential had leveled out, if it hadn't actually begun to drop. Even before *The Patsy* went into production, Barney Balaban told a reporter from the *Saturday Evening Post* that *Cinderfella* and *The Ladies' Man* "did not necessarily show a profit." The facts were simply economic, of course—they were the two most expensive films that Jerry had made. But the damning thing was that Balaban—he of the match with which Jerry could burn down the studio—was speaking in such a way to the press at all. Jerry had been signed just five years earlier as a kind of savior for an ailing Paramount; now he was being spoken of, however diplomatically, as something of a burden.

When *The Patsy* was released, it made for yet one more blemish on Jerry's record. The critics weren't enthusiastic about it: "It could have been built up through stronger plotting and editing," wrote "Whit." in *Variety*, while Bosley Crowther of *The New York Times*, after confessing he hadn't seen any of Jerry's previous films as a director, announced that he was "gratified to discover that he's no better as a comedian than he used to be." Wiping his hands of the film, he categorized it as "just another moronic mishmash in which Mr. Lewis falls all over himself."

There *was* a lot of stumbling and flailing in the film, but aside from Jerry's physical technique, *The Patsy* was genuinely unlike anything Jerry had done before. A combination of a sequel to *The Bellboy* (it had even been called, early on, "Son of the Bellboy") and a cynical remake of *Pygmalion*, it's rather like Jerry's version of *The Circus* or *Limelight*, a black comic exploration of the nature of comedy as constructed by the Hollywood flesh machine.

After comedy star Wally Brandford dies in a plane crash, his publicist (Keenan Wynn), writer (Phil Harris), director (Peter Lorre), valet (John Carradine), producer (Everett Sloan), and secretary (ingenue Ina Balin) decide to create another star whose coattails they can ride to financial gain. As soon as they have formulated their plan, inept bellboy Stanley Belt (Jerry) barges into their suite dropping ice cubes and glasses. Despite his extremely unpromising mien, they are so convinced of their powers that they decide to cast their Svengalian spell over him.

There are several transformation scenes—Stanley is outfitted, given singing lessons (his deft destruction of vocal tutor Hans Conried's home is among Jerry's career highlights), taught comic timing, brought into the studio to cut a record, broken in at nightclubs, and introduced to the Hollywood press (Hedda Hopper, UPI's Vernon Scott, and Jerry's biographer Richard Gehman all play themselves in the scene). In each regard, he is an abject failure, yet the people behind him push him on, convinced their skills in packaging the star will make up for Stanley's inabilities. (Only the secretary, inexplicably charmed by his stumbling, has a soft spot for him.)

Finally, Stanley is booked on Ed Sullivan's show and abandoned by his handlers, who are convinced that there is no transforming this particular patsy into a star. But Stanley turns the tables on them; improvising an elaborate comedy scene, he is a tremendous hit. He calls them all back to the hotel suite under false pretenses and hires them to support him now that he has a real career.

It's worth rehearsing so much of this plot because it is obviously meant to mirror Jerry's own experience of Hollywood while touching on his favorite narrative themes—the cynical handlers, the clown who comes through with sincerity when his act fails, the women who want to burp him, the lying sycophants and journalists, the absurd means by which nobodies become stars. The film features several Hollywood stars playing themselves—Rhonda Fleming, George Raft, Mel Tormé, Ed Wynn—yet the script asks them all to play phonies. Hedda Hopper is exemplary in this regard; she appears at a cocktail party with an absurdly oversized hat, and only Stanley has the effrontery to laugh at it; when everyone else is appalled at his cheek, however, she praises him for his honesty and predicts big things for him.

The routine on the Sullivan show is truly bizarre. Stanley, trained as a stand-up comic, is so bad that crickets can be heard chirping in the background at one of his club dates, but suddenly he's able to pull off a long silent comedy routine with no rehearsal. It's a nice, well-timed bit, but it doesn't fit logically into the narrative framework of the film—Jerry's handlers have never seen the elaborate sketch before, so how on earth would the Sullivan show have been prepared to present it? Even in the logically unstable world of Jerry Lewis (which more than one critic has compared to that of Lewis Carroll), this is hard to rationalize.

But questions like these seem beside the point. *The Patsy* opens with an impossible stunt out of Tashlin: Stanley falls from a hotel balcony, hits a canopy below, and vaults right back up into the suite. And it ends with an even stranger reprise of the bit: When Stanley apparently tumbles over the balcony again, and a concerned Ina Balin rushes over to see if he's okay, Jerry stands up, out of character, to point out that it's just a movie with a fake set and a crew filming it all. He calls her "Miss Balin"; she calls him "Mr. Lewis"; they walk out of the studio along with the actual crew and go off for lunch.

Thus *The Patsy*, in its maker's eyes, is just another duplicitous instance of Hollywood hype and performance. That the postmodern ending doesn't quite come off—that Jerry's "aspiration . . . exceeds his ability," in the judgment of Andrew Sarris, is almost irrelevant. As a technical accomplishment, *The Patsy* may not equal Buster Keaton's *Sherlock Jr.*, but as a personal testament—the confession of a cold-eyed Hollywood star who knows that his own career is at least partially assembled with the same inauthentic materials as Stanley Belt's— it's frankly self-lacerating. "Jerry Lewis as *The Patsy*," read the opening titles, and the audience can make that identification on several levels. This was not just a simple reappearance of the Kid in a new setting; this was a mature man coming to grips with the fact that his career was built on ephemera and boosted by liars. It's no wonder the film's box office was among the softest yet for a Jerry Lewis picture; there was about *The Patsy* an air of nastiness and self-deprecation that none of his other projects had.

Jerry looked around for other venues, and there was television staring right at him. He couldn't resist it, though he was still smarting from the ABC debacle. He was mentioned as a candidate for a one-shot performance as Billy the Kid on CBS's "Rawhide" series. He spoke about starting a slate of series for children to air on an early pay-per-view system. Neither of these panned out, but he went ahead with another of his notions—directing, acting in, and coscripting an episode of NBC's "Ben Casey" series, starring his old Gar-Ron actor (and Abbey Greshler's client) Vince Edwards. The original title of the hour-long episode was "Of Impoverished Frolic and Earnest Tears," but it finally aired as "A Little Bit of Fun to Match the Sorrow."

He made as personal a project as he could of it, given that it was someone else's show (Bing Crosby's actually—it was one of several prime-time series his company produced). Jerry played a brilliant neurosurgeon driven by inner anxieties to act like a clown. The autobiographical dimension of the project was obvious, as were the resemblances to *The Disorderly Orderly*, which he had just finished filming and which was a kind of comic version of the same material. (As a director, he was all business; when Edwards insisted that a script girl read his lines to cue another actor, Jerry demanded that he do it himself; Edwards refused, then left the set, and Jerry ordered him banned from the stage, the set, and finally the lot until he apologized.) But the show also gave Jerry a chance to express his scientific interests; his years consulting with MDA researchers and physicians had given him a kind of crash course in medicine. As he had learned to direct films by osmosis—asking questions of crew members and hanging around editing rooms and such—so he had, chameleonlike, learned a fair bit about doctors and hospitals and health care. It was only the second dramatic role he had ever played (though, like the other one in "The Jazz Singer," it included elements of comedy), and it went almost wholly unnoted by the critics.

Even if he still looked and acted like a big star, down deep he could feel it starting to fade. He was sliding from the acme.

Something else had begun to happen that made Jerry feel old and passé even at thirty-eight. His eighteen-year-old son Gary had enrolled at a theater arts college in Pasadena in the fall of 1963 and, under the spell of near neighbors such as the Beach Boys and Jan and Dean, and imported acts such as the Beatles, the Dave Clark Five, and the Rolling Stones, he'd started playing rock 'n' roll with some of his classmates.

He had, of course, been hovering around show business all of his life. He had been on many of Jerry's TV shows, going back to his 1957 appearance with Jerry and Danny on NBC. He'd sung in *Rock-a-Bye Baby*—as the childhood incarnation of Jerry's character, Clayton Poole—and he'd appeared in brief roles in other films of his father's. He'd even been on television by himself, appearing on "The George Burns Show" as a solo in January 1959. He'd always liked comedy—he would write comic sketches and run them by his father for critiques. And he'd always had a musical bent, playing the clarinet in the marching band at Black Foxe Military Academy and learning drums from such friends of Jerry's as Buddy Rich when he was as young as eight. He'd bought himself his own drum kit with money he'd earned performing on one of his dad's NBC specials.

Besides all of this exposure to the world of entertainment, Gary may have had even deeper reasons for pointing himself toward performing. Like his own father, Gary was brought up by an entertainer whose attention he could rarely keep for very long. He wasn't abandoned as Jerry had been—Patti stayed at home, largely in capitulation to Jerry's will—but he felt similar longings and pressures to grab attention. The main difference between their two upbringings was in the way their parents treated their ambitions: Jerry was raised by parents who didn't notice him and then shrugged off his desire to perform when he announced it. Gary's father, in contrast, had coddled him and even encouraged his steps toward show business—then often slapped him away when he was close to achieving his goal.

For instance, as a boy, Gary was frequently photographed mugging alongside his dad. He was dragged into photo shoots and TV shows and movies—but then told he wouldn't be allowed to become an entertainer. "It's not only that I don't like most professional child performers," Jerry told Joe Hyams during the filming of *Rock-a-Bye Baby*, "it's that Gary's going to have the advantages of the education I didn't have. I had to quit in the second grade of high school, not because I needed the money but because I couldn't be happy unless I was in show business. I've lived to regret it. I've had to adjust to situations I could have coped with more easily if I had gone on in school."

Still, when it came to including Gary in one of his film or TV projects, Jerry never hesitated at yanking him out of classes. Gary's was a childhood riven with mixed messages. He was encouraged to clown, but he was chastised for cutting up at the dinner table. He was told to keep his mind on school and not on performing, but he was excused from school to act in movies or appear on TV.

Jerry knew he was exerting a potentially harmful influence on his oldest son. "At age eleven," he recalled years later, "Gary developed a nervous tic. He said to me, 'Everybody . . . all my friends . . . are always laughing at you. You're always jumping around like a nut . . . like an idiot.' I told him, 'Getting attention is my business. My whole life is predicated on, "Hey, look at me!"'" Patti found it harder to dismiss Gary's anxieties. "He always walked in his father's shadow," she observed. "He felt he had to measure up to him. I felt this was sad."

Jerry saw talent in his son, but he was protective of his own career, and he frequently stifled his child. He was a producer; like so many of his Hollywood predecessors, he could have taught Gary the business during summers or school holidays. Instead, he got him a job as a car valet at a Sunset Strip restaurant— not even his own, but a place called the Picadilly. Although his father earned between $5 million and $12 million most years, Gary had to save up toward his own college tuition. "He had saved six hundred dollars," Jerry explained to a reporter, "when he fell in love with a nice seventeen-year-old girl from Chicago. Last year he bit into his savings to visit her and wound up with less than he would need for his tuition. . . . I've worked out a deal with him—from earnings he'll pay me four dollars a week—to complete his tuition savings."

Over the years, Jerry had alternated such puritanical lessons in self-sufficiency with grandiose moments of largesse, such as having the boys invite their entire school classes to private birthday parties at Disneyland. Gary, living in a luxurious mansion and working for tips, had lost all perspective on the value of a dollar, according to his own father: "One night at dinner he asked me, 'Dad, do you manage to clear five hundred dollars a week?' Five hundred dollars, to him, you see, is a lot of money because it took him two years to put that aside. I think he's got a very level head about it all and a lot of that comes from his mother. Patti kept me from blowing my steam when he asked about that five hundred dollars. She was right, you know, because he had gotten the point that there were a lot of people to be paid before Dad got his."

It's no wonder that some journalists who met Gary in Jerry's presence got the impression that the son was older than the father; the indulgence Jerry demanded from those around him had kept him, in many ways, from growing up, while Gary's confusions had caused him to mature quicker than he might have liked.

Of course, there were undeniable advantages to being the son of a movie star. When Gary and bandmates Dave Walker, Dave Costell, Al Ramsey, and John West decided they were serious about becoming musicians, they got to perform at Disneyland. And when they approached Jerry's longtime bandleader Lou Brown for advice, Brown introduced them to Liberty Records producer Thomas "Snuff" Garrett. Garrett, born in 1939, had made a specialty of light pop, transforming rockabilly singer Johnny Burnette into a million-seller with "You're Sixteen," and scoring such hits as "Take Good Care of My Baby" and "Run to Him" with lightweight singer Bobby Vee. Along with songwriter and super-session man Leon Russell, Garrett came out to a Paramount rehearsal hall Jerry had hired for the band to practice in, listened with interest to the group, and asked them to come to his office to hear a few songs he thought might suit them.

At the Liberty studios, Garrett tested the band out, cutting a pair of instrumentals with them. Then he turned them on to a song keyboard player Al Kooper had written, which had recently been released as a rhythm-and-blues record by Sammy Ambrose: "This Diamond Ring." The Playboys liked what they heard, an arrangement was worked out, and on November 19, 1964, they recorded it. In the next few weeks, Garrett wound up overdubbing most of the instrumentation with studio players' work: "They let the Playboys feel like they were really a part of it," Gary recalled later, "but in the final mixdown, they kind of buried them." A version of "This Diamond Ring" based on the Playboys' tenth take was released on December 3, 1964.

Three days later, Jerry and Gary appeared on "The Ed Sullivan Show" together. Making the appearance even more epochal for Jerry was the booking of Sophie Tucker, his old supporter from Atlantic City, on the bill; Tucker was introduced as Gary's godmother (a stretch; he was a year old when the singer caught his father's act for the first time). Then Jerry and Sullivan introduced Gary and his band, who lip-synched "This Diamond Ring." Afterward, Jerry and Gary did a bit of shtick together and the band reprised their lip-synching, this time with Jerry pretending to play the violin with them and yowling along.

The appearance on the Sullivan show with an icon of old-time trouperdom and his own son wasn't the only big event for Jerry that night. Soon after the broadcast, he walked a few blocks to the Winter Garden Theater, where the American Guild of Variety Artists fêted him in a benefit for its Youth Fund, raising $148,000 in ticket sales and donations. It was Jerry's first Broadway appearance since playing the Palace almost eight years earlier, and he was determined to make an experience of it. He spent $17,000 of his own money to fly a twenty-three-piece band to the engagement, to jet the Hollywood press out and put them up at the Regency Hotel, to have Al Jolson's old runway reinstalled in the orchestra. "I don't know how to play Charlie Humble," he told his audience that night, "but I'm humble in my own way. I make noise." He did Jolson songs, of course, and in honor of *Funny Girl*, which was the attraction at the theater at the time, sang Barbra Streisand's signature tune, "People." He was warmly received. It was a sweet night.

But it was Gary who was making headlines. In a rise even more astonishing than Jerry's record of "Rock-a-Bye Your Baby," "This Diamond Ring" reached Number One on the *Billboard* charts on January 23, 1965, holding the spot for two weeks and staying in the Top Forty for eleven. With the third track he ever recorded—and his first-ever release—nineteen-year-old Gary Lewis had the greatest success of his life.

It's a hell of a catchy record, with a polish that makes it seem like a dozen singers were singing Gary's part in perfect harmony and a simple melody that's doubled on organ and guitar and backed up by timpani and tambourines. There was no worldliness in Gary's vocal—indeed, it was an awfully upbeat song given the subject matter (rejection, of course). But the thing was pure sugar, an instant pop classic, the type of guilty pleasure that audiences turned their radios up for three decades later.

Garrett knew he had better jump on the Playboys quickly, and he had them back in the studio the week after "This Diamond Ring" topped the charts. He gave them another hot new song, this one written by Glen D. Hardin of the Shindogs, the house band on the TV series "Shindig." "Count Me In" was recorded on February 13 and hit Number Two in *Billboard* in April. The Playboys themselves were even further suppressed on this track, however, with the addition of a trio of backup singers, the Eligibles. In fact, Gary sang not with the band, but to a tape of backing material assembled by Garrett and Russell in the studio with the help of session musicians and singers.

The Playboys probably didn't mind, however. They were like Motown bands, Phil Spector's elaborately produced singing acts, and so many other pop groups that were put together factory-style: fresh-faced kids fronting for arrangers and more skilled, but less photogenic, musicians. Besides, the money was great. Each Playboy was making five hundred dollars a week, whether they played or not, and Gary decided to split all royalties exactly evenly, against his father's advice: "I think you're the worst businessman I ever met," Jerry told him, "but you'll do what your heart tells you." They were in the studio constantly throughout 1965, recording three albums' worth of material and putting a total of five songs in the *Billboard* Top Ten.

None of these hits ever had the lasting power of "This Diamond Ring," though "Sure Gonna Miss Her" had a powerful groove and "She's Just My Style" was an authentically catchy middle-period Beach Boys knockoff. Because they were merely a front for a studio band (Gary, the last instrumentalist among the original players, had turned the drumming duties over to ace session man Jim Keltner), the Playboys were subject to some truly bizarre experiments. On "Time Stands Still," a creepy, almost psychedelically overproduced ballad, Gary sang a chorus in his father's famous mongoloid voice; "Everybody Loves a Clown," another broken-heart song, had a carnival feel to it. There's a freshness and occasional vigor to many of the Playboys' early records, but the sound is so preciously contrived that there's no feel of rock or roll to it; you know it's a studio production, and you can't imagine any of the principals sweating or getting excited about anything they were doing. Still, Garrett was one of the craftsmen of the hour—not an innovator like Phil Spector or an empire builder like Berry Gordy, but a man with his finger briefly on the nation's pulse nonetheless. During the Playboys' heydey, he made a thoroughly respectable collection of records with them, and if their songs lacked the musicality of songs by Lennon and McCartney or Brian Wilson, they were still palatable pop fun.

The children of Hollywood royalty had always tried to cash in on their famous names and on the novelty of a new generation of a renowned family entering show biz. Not long after the Playboys hit the charts, in fact, a truly terrible group was formed by Dean Paul Martin, Jr., and Desi Arnaz, Jr., with the name Dino, Desi, and Billy (third wheel Billy Hinsche had no famous parents). Nevertheless, only Ricky Nelson enjoyed more popular success than Gary did. For a few months, if you squinted just right, you might have thought that just as Jerry had eclipsed Danny, Gary actually had the potential to make a bigger career than his father.

Jerry was still working, though, even if the opportunities were becoming sparser. In January 1965 he began production on *The Family Jewels*, the tenth picture in his fourteen-film deal with Paramount. Once again he would produce and direct a script he'd written with Bill Richmond. This time, though, he would attempt a more ambitious acting chore than he'd ever tried before. Just as the Svengalis in *The Patsy* had tried to make an adult-style performer of Stanley Belt, Jerry would recast himself in *The Family Jewels* by playing seven different roles, some similar to characters he'd played in other films, but most new to his movie audience. It was a comic trick that had been performed by such precursors as Alec Guinness (*Kind Hearts and Coronets*), Peter Sellers (*Dr. Strangelove*), and even Tony Randall (*The Seven Faces of Dr. Lao*), the last two of which were in release when Jerry and Richmond were writing *The Family Jewels*. With its swiveling between the various characters and disguises of its star, the script they developed had a more episodic quality than either of Jerry's last two directorial projects, *The Nutty Professor* and *The Patsy*, but it also had a coherent plotline that distinguished it from his very first films. Jerry had never directed a film without trying to do something he'd never done before, and he had allotted himself more time to make this one than he'd ever taken; he had no specific commitments until April 8, when he would begin shooting *Boeing Boeing*, a Hal Wallis comedy, in Paris.

It was a good thing he'd allowed himself such a cushion of time. On Friday, March 5, he took time off from *The Family Jewels* to drive up to Burbank for a taping of "The Andy Williams Show." He was exhausted from the long hours he'd been putting in on his film, so he suggested to producer Bob Finkel that they tape the dress rehearsal, just in case he was too tired to do another run-through of the act. "I might blow it another time," he said.

They set to taping the show, Jerry came on stage to do his bit, and he slipped in a puddle of water, landing with a bang on the base of his skull. In terrific pain, he wrapped up his number—people must have taken it for just another Jerry Lewis pratfall. "I finished the last three minutes of that show unconscious," he told Hedda Hopper two weeks later. "I don't remember anything for about forty minutes after the show, when I woke up in the hospital."

He had suffered a serious injury; radiologists at Mount Sinai Hospital detected a "fine linear skull fracture," according to wire reports of the incident. For the next few days, he was subject to nausea, double vision, and disequilibrium. After two days of bed rest, he tried to return to the set of *The Family Jewels*, but he had a severe dizzy spell and returned home for another week of recuperation. Still, even a week after he was finally able to get back to work, he was feeling ill effects of the fall: "I'm still having difficulty with one eye," he told Hopper. "I'm told it'll take about six months before it will clear up entirely. I have to turn somewhat to see clearly. This evidently happens no matter who has this type of accident, but it's pretty scary when it happens. I've taken falls for thirty years, but this one I didn't take."

Hal Wallis was concerned that Jerry's accident would threaten the start-up of *Boeing Boeing*. He had Joe Hazen contact Dr. Marvin Levy, Jerry's longtime physician, and Marvin Meyer, one of Jerry's attorneys. Hazen asked Meyer if it would be better for Jerry to skip the picture altogether, but he was told that "just the opposite was the case, that Dr. Levy felt that the best thing in the world for Jerry would be to go to Paris for a couple of weeks." When Hazen asked Meyer if Wallis could call Jerry, he was told there would be no problem.

Two weeks later, on March 24, Dr. Levy filed a report with Wallis for insurance purposes stating that Jerry was in excellent physical health except for a tear of the medial lateral ligaments of his left knee (an old injury he'd suffered horsing around with Dean) and the skull fracture he'd sustained on March 5.

It's worth tracing this episode so exactly for two important reasons. The first is that Jerry has long contended that he had his severe accident fifteen days later, on March 20, 1965, while taking a pratfall off a piano during his closing show at the Sands Hotel in Las Vegas. He gave this date in an interview in the *National Enquirer* in 1974, wrote about it in his autobiography in 1982, and discussed it in an interview in *Penthouse* in 1983. (Patti Lewis repeated the story along Jerry's lines in her own autobiography.) In all these cases, he was specific about the place and time of his injury, and in all these cases he further claimed that he suffered a chip off his spinal column at the base of his skull.

The account in *Jerry Lewis in Person* is the most thorough: "When you take a fall, you have to commit yourself. No rearranging things in midair, no hesitation or you can get hurt. Well, I committed, saw the microphone cable, twisted out of control and landed on my back—165 pounds slamming against this little plug attached to the cable. I was numb, but got up and finished the act. . . . Next morning, I put in thirty minutes trying to get off the bed. The pain was horrendous, almost paralyzing, and it wouldn't stop. I stood for two hours, then went to Dr. Bill Stein, an orthopedic man in Los Angeles."

According to Jerry, Stein fitted him with a metal neck brace and prescribed codeine and Emprin to relieve his pain. He hated the brace and took it off whenever he could, but "the longer I remained free of that accursed contraption, the more my poor aching body cries out for it."

It's completely plausible that Jerry damaged his spinal column as well as his skull when he fell in Burbank. But that he fell onstage at the Sands just two weeks after hurting himself so severely on "The Andy Williams Show" is less likely. There was no second disruption of filming on *The Family Jewels*, and there was no mention of a second fall in Dr. Levy's report to Hal Wallis. Although he might have been at the Sands on Saturday, March 20, it's unlikely, given that he was still in production on *The Family Jewels* and had to be off to Paris in two weeks for *Boeing Boeing*. More impossibly, we are asked to believe that within two weeks of fracturing his skull on "The Andy Williams Show" he was imprudent enough to be performing flips and pratfalls off a piano in Las Vegas. If Jerry ever did take a severe fall at the Sands, it wasn't that spring.

Why, then, his insistence on March 20? Is it that "The Andy Williams Show" is a less impressive-sounding venue than the Sands? Or is it that, as with many specific details, Jerry's memory is simply flawed?

The last explanation is surely the best, especially given the second reason that it's so important to get these dates settled. According to Jerry, the aftermath of the accident was a nightmare of pain and incapacitation. He sought help from neurologists and orthopedists for a year, but the prognosis was always pessimistic: A knot of fibrous tissue had developed along the nerves where his spinal column had cracked. Not even surgery could help him; he would have been luckier, in a sense, if he had broken his back. The pain was grueling and persistent, and to alleviate it, all the doctors could offer him was a regimen of heat, massage, rest, and medication.

The codeine and Emprin were, finally, not enough to numb him. One of his doctors prescribed Percodan for him. It was the first time he'd felt relief since he'd fallen. "Imagine taking your top lip and lifting it all the way over your head," he said, trying to describe his pain. "My left eye goes almost totally out of focus. Both of my legs feel like I'm walking and yet I'm not getting anywhere, the pain is so severe. Yet when I was put on Percodan I would take one and in about twenty minutes I would be able to relax."

A small dose of oxycodone (a synthetic drug similar in effect to morphine)—four or five milligrams—and a cringing cripple would find himself transformed into a functioning person once again.

One magic yellow pill, maybe two, in the course of a day.

And little by little, in due time, he was addicted.

With its star and director injured, *The Family Jewels* took until April 2 to wrap—nearly three months, all told, to produce a film that should have been shot in perhaps eight weeks. Part of it was due to Jerry's injury, but part to his choices as director and producer: "I tried to shoot the picture in continuity," he recalled. "I found, after it was over, that we would have been better off 'blocking' that production"—that is, shooting all scenes involving one of his guises at a time and editing the film into the proper chronology later on. A misjudgment of this sort was made possible by the departure of Ernie Glucksman from the Lewis organization; after the embarrassment of the ABC series, Glucksman, who had more authority over the show than anyone except Jerry, had been shown the door. To the Paramount brass, the failure to replace Glucksman with a similarly capable producer created concern that Jerry was wearing too many creative hats and hurting the studio both during production—by slowing things up and hence making them more expensive—and at the box office, where his self-directed films were doing less and less well. They were pleased that he would be working strictly as an actor on *Boeing Boeing*, and hopeful that the experience would help convince Jerry he was a performer first and foremost.

The stress of his injury, his rush to finish *The Family Jewels*, and the new pressures from Paramount all created an atmosphere of dread around him whenever he was at home. Patti was beginning to develop symptoms of her own. The affairs had been bad enough—"as each new evidence of Jerry's unfaithfulness surfaced, I became more distanced from reality," she realized—but now he was frankly brutal, hollering and slamming doors as if his pain gave him the right to inflict pain on his family. Finally, Patti succumbed: "The stresses caught up with me and I became very ill, with severe pain. Jerry agreed to take me to the hospital, where I immediately underwent intensive testing. That night, Jerry came by in a rush. He handed me a crucifix, and said he had to dash off to Paris since he had promised Hal Wallis he would do a film there. They had shaken hands on a deal, and Jerry would never break a handshake promise. So saying, he disappeared into the night, and I dissolved into tears."

Patti had developed an adrenal malfunction, and she spent much of the time Jerry was making *Boeing Boeing* in the hospital and under nurses' care at home, where she had plenty of time to meditate on the state of her marriage.

■   ■   ■

Whatever he had told Patti at the hospital about the value of a handshake agreement, Jerry had tried to wriggle out of his commitment to Wallis, or at least delay it, almost until the day he left for France. It's not at all clear that his desire to forestall his trip to Europe had anything to do with the state of his marriage; he hadn't yet finished *The Family Jewels*, after all. But he would have to be in Paris for only a week of shooting, and so he went.

In truth, he had to be as pleased as Paramount was to be working on this particular Hal Wallis film. It was a totally new direction for him, one that, if successful, would reinvent his wobbly career. *Boeing Boeing* was based on a French play of the same name that had been a huge hit at the Comédie Caumartin theater in Paris and in an English-language version in London. It was a classic farce à la Feydeau about a writer living in Paris and enjoying the favors of three girlfriends who work as stewardesses on three different airlines; his delicately balanced schedule, according to which only one girl at a time is in town with him, begins to fall apart when a fast new Boeing aircraft becomes the international standard. Things are further complicated by the arrival in Paris of his old American chum who, ignorant of the rules of his friend's ménage, develops romantic designs on the stewardesses himself.

Wallis first became acquainted with the material as early as January 1961, when his East Coast representative, Irene Lee, saw the play in Paris. He bought it right away and had it translated as a vehicle for Dean Martin. When Dean didn't bite at the role, Wallis peddled the script to various comic actors—Peter O'Toole, Peter Sellers, David Niven, Jean-Paul Belmondo, Jack Lemmon, Bob Hope, Frank Sinatra. No one wanted it. Wallis considered moving the setting to Rome and casting Vittorio Gassman; he even considered rewriting it as an Elvis Presley vehicle. Finally, in the spring of 1964, Tony Curtis expressed interest in the film. Once again, Wallis shopped the script in search of a big-name actor to play the visiting American alongside Curtis's Paris-based writer. He finally ran out of options and, after consulting with Paramount, brought the script to Jerry.

Wallis and Jerry hadn't worked together since *Visit to a Small Planet* wrapped in the summer of 1959. Since then, Jerry's star had risen dramatically and then begun to wane, and Wallis's career had slowly but surely ebbed. He was sixty-seven; he had lost his wife, Louise Fazenda, who passed away in 1962; he had seen his output drop to a single film a year. As always, *Boeing Boeing* was a commercial project for him, not an artistic statement. But it was the only iron he had in the fire in early 1965, so he couldn't have been delighted to enlist his old nemesis in it, no matter what his box-office power. As for Jerry, the film was an opportunity to spread his wings and try a new style of comedy—grown-up, sophisticated farce. He would act like an adult, play off actresses, team up with a new sidekick (and old friend). And it would calm Paramount's worries about his taking on too many roles while he planned his next film. He first heard about the script in December 1964, and he signed on within a month, at twenty-five-thousand dollars a week for twelve weeks (plus a hundred thousand dollars to Jerry Lewis Productions for loan of the star and two thousand dollars in living expenses, beyond his hotel bill, for a week in Paris).

Jerry was actually thrilled at the chance to work in Europe. He told Jack Keller that he hoped to do some sight-seeing with Patti while he was there (early plans for the film called for some location work in Rome), and he wanted to use the trip as a means of promoting his own films overseas. He even had a sentimental yen to find Patti's Italian relatives, the families her mother and father had left behind almost fifty years earlier—a scheme scuttled by Patti's illness. None of this fit into Wallis's plans; the cast and crew were to spend a week in Paris, maybe a day or two in Rome, and then return immediately to Hollywood and shoot until mid-June. Wallis and his assistant Paul Nathan knew Jerry well enough, however, that they made no mention to him, Keller, or Keller's assistant Jim Flood about their tight schedule; it would only have agitated him.

They also didn't tell Jerry or anyone in the Lewis organization about Tony Curtis's reluctance to work with Jerry. Although Jerry had been his best man and their mutual participation in the film was stipulated in their contracts, Curtis had been confiding to Paul Nathan that he had no desire to be the next Dean Martin. He used Jerry's presence in the film to make all kinds of absurd demands of Wallis: He would be transported only in a Rolls Royce, he wouldn't share a wardrobe assistant with anyone. Nathan was Wallis's liaison with Marvin Meyer, who was attorney to both Curtis and Jerry, and two weeks before shooting started, Nathan finally told Meyer to rein in his client. As he wrote to Wallis, "I had a half-hour talk with Marvin Meyer today and it was strictly personal, off-the-record, friendly. I told him, now that it was all over, what a shit he has been and the workings of Mr. Tony Curtis. I also told him all the secrets I have been keeping for Tony, whereby Tony refused to work with Jerry and made us the heavies which we weren't."

When Wallis finally got his spoiled stars off to Paris, he found that things proceeded no more smoothly. Jerry arrived at the Hôtel Madeleine Palace with his full entourage (dresser, publicity man, barber, and stand-in/double) and a lobby-choking seventy-five pieces of luggage. He had just left his wife severely ill in a hospital in Los Angeles and had only one thing on his mind: deli sandwiches. When he discovered that the hotel couldn't provide salami or corned beef, he threw a temper tantrum and, even though it was past midnight, took his entourage and luggage to the Ritz. He settled into another suite there, but his second attempt to order Jewish soul food was also rebuffed, though this time, as Wallis recollected, "he decided to stay put and sent one of his people to comb Paris for the salami."

Back in Los Angeles the next month, Curtis began a pattern of disappearing from the set for hours, arguing with his director, and throwing himself into snits over anything he took as a breach of his star status. Wallis wound up closing the set to the press, to which Curtis responded by taking out ads in the trade papers indicating that the barring of reporters wasn't his doing. Wallis wrote furiously to Joe Hazen, threatening to shut the set and hold Curtis responsible for the cost of the delay: "I am pretty tired of all this nonsense in dealing with these sick people and I do not intend to indulge him in any way."

Soon enough, it was Jerry who was drawing the producer's ire with a holdout of his own. On June 10, when Wallis had some four dozen extras sitting around a restaurant set waiting to shoot, Jerry left the studio three hours early with neither warning nor explanation. The next day he didn't show up at all. No one in his office claimed to know where he was. Finally, he turned up in San Diego on his yacht.

He hadn't left to annoy Wallis (though he surely felt no qualms about doing so); he was sitting out the most elaborate and expensive days of the production to protest Paramount's increasing pressure on him to give up directing and producing his own films. He had a new story lined up to shoot in the fall—a romantic farce—and he was planning to shoot it just as he had his previous films. But the studio wanted him to concentrate on acting and leave the directing to someone else. Jerry wouldn't budge, and neither would they. It was shaping up into something bad.

Boeing Boeing finally wrapped on June 22—five days late, quite a bit of it due to Jerry, at an additional cost to Wallis of one hundred thousand dollars. Jerry continued to fight the studio about his power to serve as his own director and about its habit of rereleasing his films in theaters or on TV when his new projects were in the early stages of their initial runs. Finally, Paramount elected not to fight him anymore. In July, after seventeen years, studio executives chose to shake hands with Jerry and let him seek a new home for his production company.

In his autobiography Jerry said he left Paramount voluntarily because he objected to costs charged to his films. He had hired Joe Stabile as his manager and asked him to investigate expenses the studio was levying against his productions. When Stabile reported back about various expenditures such as office furniture and personal entertainment costs that, as standard Hollywood procedure, had been tacked onto his budgets, Jerry said he felt the studio's charges were inappropriate: "Joey's discovery overrode my loyalties to Paramount."

Later still, he declared that it was Paramount's new corporate culture that drove him away. He'd always done business with a handshake, he said, but "When Gulf and Western took over the studio, they didn't know from handshakes. So they sent me papers, and laywers, and meetings, and I said fuck you, and you, and you. Go make your belt buckles, and shove 'em up your ass, I'm outta here!"

But industry speculation was that Paramount (which wasn't officially acquired by Gulf and Western until October 1966) had decided he wasn't worth banking any longer. They had been giving him between $1.8 million and $2 million per picture, and as long as those films made over $3 million or so on their initial release, they didn't mind indulging Jerry's desire to be completely autonomous. But when the receipts for his films began to thin out and their cost increased, Paramount executives grew balky. And when Jerry refused to let someone else direct him and started creating brouhahas on other people's sets, they chose to wash their hands of him altogether.

Back in 1948 Hal Wallis had signed a hot young comedy team. They were cutting-edge, hip, and sexy. Their nightclub shows in New York and Los Angeles drew a tony crowd of celebrities, gangsters, and swingers. But in the two decades that followed, Jerry Lewis had become a family act, and then finally a kiddie act.

He didn't see this as a diminution of his stature. In fact, he bragged about it to Peter Bogdanovich: "The kids, they're smilin' 'cause The Idiot's on his can. They built me a house in Bel Air, I ain't gonna forget that. When they come up to the box office and their little hands reach up to the window with their little money and they say, 'One child, please,' they can't go inside and be disappointed. I mean that. . . . I got a lot of loyal people. There's three-year-olds that grew up and now they bring their three-year-olds to see my pictures. There's this seven-year-old kid and his mother called me up this morning—he's deaf, but he reads me and he laughs. How can I take that away from him?"

He had resigned himself to a narrow niche in the market. It's possible, in fact, to read his many self-righteous pronouncements about the dangerous trend toward realism and adult subjects in films as his way of reminding the industry of the economic power of the juvenile audience, which was now his bread and butter.

Almost immediately after he left Paramount, Jerry was able to place his next film—*Three on a Couch*—at Columbia. But where he'd wind up after that, neither he nor the trade press could be certain; he entered into talks with United Artists, Fox, MGM, Warner Brothers, and Columbia.

For their part, Paramount was publicly sorry to see him go, but they had a replacement act lined up already: a hot new comedy team, in fact, right out of the nightclubs. Even their names had a golden ring to them—Martin and Rossi.

16.

Frogs' Legs and Pratfalls

Homer Simpson, troglodyte daddy to an animated TV family, sits watching the Super Bowl on television as the announcer boasts that the game is being broadcast all over the world. In sequence, a pagoda, an African straw hut, the Kremlin, and a tent in the Sahara flash before us, all with the same sounds of NFL hype emerging from them. Finally, we see two men in striped pullovers and berets sitting on a couch, an open window behind them revealing the Eiffel Tower. Though we can't see the TV they're watching, we hear emanating from it the same game sounds we've heard all along. One of the men mutters a complaint under his breath and aims a remote control at the set. Now the men are smiling broadly. From the unseen TV we hear a holler—"Hey Laaay-deeee!!"—and one of the men announces, contentedly, "Formidable!"

The host of the "Weekend Update" news segment on "Saturday Night Live" reports on the opening of the Euro Disney theme park in a suburb of Paris. "Later that day," he announces, "Goofy was declared a genius."

A New Yorker cartoon: Middle-aged white-collar husband and wife at breakfast. Wife looks glum. Husband says, "I love you the way the French love Jerry Lewis."

Paramount no longer wanted him, TV networks no longer wanted him, even the loyal audience that had supported him on stage and in movie theaters for nearly twenty years was shrinking. But an audience to which he'd only had a passing connection had blossomed into something neither he nor anybody else quite understood.

In March 1965, when Jerry arrived at Paris's Orly airport to begin work on *Boeing Boeing*, he received a rock star's greeting. Although it was the middle of the night, his airplane was met by what *The New York Times* later called "a swarm of wild-eyed fans, a phalanx of reporters, a rout of photographers and a small but select group of France's leading film critics." The crush was so overwhelming that Jerry was forced to hold an impromptu press conference in an airport lounge. The next day, every major French newspaper covered the event.

The entire French capital seemed swept up in Jerrymania throughout the comedian's week-long visit. Le Passy, a Parisian art cinema, held a three-week-long Jerry Lewis festival to commemorate his arrival, and the world-renowned Cinémathèque Française held a systematic retrospective of his work, complete with seminars about the films. As he did at home whenever he was touring in support of a film, he held a reception for journalists in his hotel suite—a private cocktail party for twenty or so members of the French film press. At the soirée, Jerry was presented with an award from his guests, who'd recently voted *The Nutty Professor* the best film released in France in 1964 (against such competition as *My Fair Lady* and *Zorba the Greek*).

Jerry felt a sense of triumph and personal vindication. "After sixteen years in motion pictures," he recalled later, "having put my heart and soul into it, only to find myself denied the recognition I so desperately wanted from the critics of my own country, here the critics honored me." He considered his receipt of the award "a coronation of [a] sort, and my crown was sweet revenge."

During the next few months, word of Jerry's French reputation spread at home. It's not clear what startled Americans most: that his films were more popularly successful in France than those of other American stars, or that his French admirers included intellectuals and serious film critics, groups that reviled or ignored him at home. Nevertheless, it was true: He was both genuinely popular *and* critically respected in France. As early as 1954, when Martin and Lewis were still on good terms, *Living It Up* was released in France as *Ce n'est pas une vie! C'est pas une vie Jerry!* (or, "This isn't a life. It's a Jerry-life"), suggesting that as far as the French public was concerned, the team was a one-man show. But at the same time, respected *cinéastes* in such journals as *Cahiers du cinéma* and *Positif* began writing about Jerry's work in some critical depth as early as 1956.*

The French writings propounding Jerry's art weren't film reviews, but seri-

---

*There were even earlier pseudo-scholarly examinations of him in English—one in Britain's *Sight and Sound* in 1952, the other the following year in the American journal *Films in Review*—but these isolated treatments had no influence on the reception Jerry's work got in Anglophone countries.

ous theoretical treatises about Lewis's comic technique, the social and psychological dimensions of his humor, and his relationship to such forebears as Chaplin, Keaton, and Laurel and Hardy. To be true, Jerry was not a universal taste even in France. The most famous of the *Cahiers* critics, François Truffaut (who later in life was himself, ironically, more admired as a director abroad—in his case, in America—than at home), kept Jerry at a leery distance throughout the Martin and Lewis years. Reviewing *Sailor Beware*, he wrote, "Jerry Lewis, a new comedian, puts on the face of an American 'avant-gardiste,' very effeminate, with a short hairdo and bangs. It goes without saying that he is also overpowered by all the known signs of degeneracy: a fat chin, thick lips, and the hint of a goiter. He crunches everything put in his mouth—even a thermometer (which he mistakes for a candy cane). His blood is colorless and his extremely acute sense of smell allows him to detect women from a distance of three hundred feet."

What Truffaut saw in Jerry—hipsterism, Borscht Belt mincing, infantilism, and even Jewishness (in Truffaut's couched parlance, "degeneracy" and "thick lips")—struck him not as a parody of American excess but as an instance of it. Yet he was one of the few French critics—and, for that matter, French citizens— to fail to see the humor in Jerry's grotesquerie. In Paris alone, for instance, *Artists and Models* sold forty-six thousand tickets in its first week: a good take in an American city, an astounding one in a foreign country with a thriving film industry of its own.

Even more astounding was the intense critical analysis of Jerry in the film journals. To the American public of the 1950s and '60s, the very notion of a film journal would have been alien. Unlike their French counterparts, American moviegoers still thought of the cinema as a medium composed primarily of actors playing in stories. They went to see "the new John Wayne movie" or "the new Western" rather than "the new John Ford film," which would have been a more typical European designation. Part of the difference is due to the prominent role of intellectuals in European popular culture, as opposed to the relative absence of so-called public intellectuals in America in those decades. But it also has to do with the ways in which French audiences—and the French critics whose relatively dense writings they read—understood the cinema: namely, as a medium of directors, not stars, stories, or studios.

This *auteur* theory of film criticism is almost wholly a French invention, though, like Method acting, it was in wide practice before it was ever codified, labeled, or systematically applied. What the *auteur* theory attempts, baldly, is to identify the stylistic, thematic, and personal habits of film directors under the presumption that they (and not screenwriters, stars, producers, studios, or even genres) have ultimate authorial power over a film's creation. A director is seen, in this light, in much the way a novelist or painter or composer is seen, as an artist expressing a particular sensibility through a medium. What especially characterized the cinema, however, according to the French critics first associated with *auteurisme,* is that directors aren't normally able to control their own destinies as artists, so commercial and industrialized are the means of production in the medium. The most powerful *auteurs,* therefore, are the directors who manage to express their vision despite the pressures of employers, famous actors, and even scripts. Howard Hawks, who made films in every popular genre (Westerns, crime films, musicals, screwball comedies, biblical epics, etc.), was a God-like figure to the first *auteuristes* because of his versatility, on the one hand, and his consistent concern with themes of bravery, loyalty, and honest work, on the other; films of his such as *The Big Sleep, Red River, Scarface, Bringing Up Baby,* and even *Gentlemen Prefer Blondes* were covered with encomia in the pages of the most influential French film journals.

Auteurisme didn't appear in America until 1963, when the francophile film critic Andrew Sarris published an essay describing the theory in *Film Culture.* In the United States it remained a marginal, even academic concern for the few people even aware of it; it enjoyed some scandalous repute, in fact, when screenwriters and their critical allies used it as a cudgel in their perennial war on the Hollywood system, claiming that writers, and not directors, were the medium's true *auteurs.*

But in France the theory was widely known and little contested. Just as they were willing to accept writers of what Americans considered "trashy" literary genres (horror or detective fiction) as true artists, just as they accepted jazz musicians and performers of African-American popular music as geniuses, the French public found it completely plausible that the person responsible for approving the lighting and camera movement, signing off on decor and wardrobe, coaching the actors through their scenes, and assembling at least a rough version of the film in the editing room—in other words, the director—was responsible for whatever was artistic in the cinema.

French critics and audiences of the 1950s didn't admire only such virtuosi as Hawks, who seemed able to do anything well. They were also great fans of screen comedy, domestic and foreign, silent and with sound. The French discovered Buster Keaton before anyone in America thought of him as a master; French adults appreciated Laurel and Hardy and Harry Langdon; Chaplin, of course, was considered a master all around the world, but the French made a home for the great comic writer-director Preston Sturges after Hollywood dismissed him as an eccentric egoist with no good work left in him—his last film, *Les carnets du Major Thompson,* released in the U.S. as *The French They Are a Funny Race,* was filmed entirely on French soil (it flopped here, but hit big there). Jean Renoir, widely considered France's most important director, made comedies all the time, and native comic actors such as Fernandel and Louis de Funès were exceedingly popular, if almost unknown abroad.

In the 1950s France did produce one comic filmmaker whose excellence was recognized the world over: Jacques Tati, a quixotic genius who wrote, directed, edited, and starred in his own films, often taking years to create them. Tati was nominated for an Academy Award for Best Original Screenplay in 1953 for *Les vacances de M. Hulot* (*Mr. Hulot's Holiday*), and he won a Best Foreign Film Oscar in 1958 for *Mon oncle* (on a night on which Jerry emceed the broadcast). A gangly six-foot-five-inch Russian (born Tatischeff) with pinched features, Tati specialized in a unique brand of character comedy derived in part from Chaplin's experiments in sound in *Modern Times* but truly original nonetheless. His principal character, Monsieur Hulot, was a well meaning, almost entirely nonverbal Parisian bourgeois, a Gallic everyman whose manners and interests mirrored those of his countrymen with just a slightly detectable ironic dimension. He was, like Jerry's Kid persona, a complete klutz and schlemiel, capable of reducing a quaint sitting room to a shambles while simply trying to straighten a picture on a wall, but he almost always tried to blend in—unlike the Kid, who was always bent on commanding the scene.

Tati's films were shaggier than Jerry's—less indebted, obviously, to Hollywood notions of story line, but also freer of sentimental trappings while nevertheless boasting a sympathetic core. Though Tati directed a mere handful of pictures in comparison with Jerry's copious output, the two men made similar sorts of films—Hulot's disaster-laden visit to a seaside resort hotel is similar in many respects to *The Bellboy*, and *Mon oncle*, a story about a lonely boy who prefers the company of his odd-duck uncle to the stifling atmosphere of his own house, is—like *The Geisha Boy*—a reworking of some of the themes explored by Chaplin in *The Kid* (*The Geisha Boy* was, in fact, known in France as *Le Kid en kimono*). Tati was, like Jerry, a formal innovator, though he experimented more with sound effects, set design, and camera angles than, as Jerry did, with techniques of production such as lighting, miking, and videotape.

A country capable of producing and appreciating a Tati was obviously a place where the comic film was respected as a style of moviemaking with a heritage and a grammar all its own. It's easy to see, therefore, why the French responded so readily to Jerry even when he was still with Dean. French critics and audiences were, in fact, always on the alert for interesting new developments in Hollywood comedy, and they were quick to notice the work of Frank Tashlin when it appeared on their shores. Of course, Tashlin had the advantage of such splashy, popular performers as Dean, Jerry, and Jayne Mansfield appearing in his first imports, thus assuring that they'd be seen. But his eye for the hyperbolic, the grotesque, and the musically comic was immediately appreciated by French *cinéastes*. He was considered a Swiftian satirist of the American Dream as Bloated Nightmare. At home, even around the studios, Tashlin was considered a competent hack, but to French eyes he was a witty magician, capable even, according to a newly converted Truffaut writing about *Hollywood or Bust*, of turning Jerry into someone "more and more delightful with each picture."

When Martin and Lewis split and Tashlin and Jerry began working together as frequent collaborators, enthusiasm for their films among French audiences was extremely high: Box-office receipts for Tashlin-Lewis films were consistently higher than those for Jerry's films with other directors. Moreover, the Tashlin-Lewis films revealed to discerning audiences just how much Jerry had contributed to the movies he made (either with Dean or solo) with less expressive filmmakers. The French audience became aware that Jerry's films with Norman Taurog, Hal Walker, and George Marshall, for instance, contained elements that were more similar to the Tashlin-Lewis films than to any other movies that those pieceworkers ever made. And although they appropriately credited Tashlin with many innovations in his films with Jerry, they also began to perceive a *Lewisienne* touch, a set of stylistic and thematic tics that recurred throughout the comic's career: the excruciatingly drawn-out scenes of comic embarrassment; an attraction-revulsion relationship with women; a fascination with doubles, role-playing, and disguises; and a love of grotesque distortions of the human body, among many other obsessively repeated motifs. (A brilliant *Cahiers* article in 1967 offered a systematic dictionary of *Lewisienne* terms and themes, ranging from his use of child protagonists to his habit of wearing white socks with black shoes.) Nevertheless, even though they realized that Jerry's habitual ideas were in sync with Tashlin's, the French were biased toward directors and thus heaped most of their praise on Tashlin, whose non-Lewis films they saw as further evidence that the director was bringing at least as much to his films with Jerry as was the star.

To their pleasure, however, they found their critical stance in need of adjustment when *The Bellboy* (*Le dingue du palace*, or "The Nut of the Palace") and *The Ladies' Man* (*Le tombeur de ces dames*, or "Casanova and the Girls") debuted in France. An entirely new face of Jerry's became clear: He had, as they'd suspected, been contributing crucially to his films throughout his Hollywood career, as demonstrated by his assured writing and direction of comic sequences, many of which bore the stamp of his earlier work under different directors. Something they'd sensed all along—that the commonalities they felt in Jerry's films were not necessarily created by his producers, writers, or even directors but by Jerry himself, who had been "directing" key passages in his films for years—had been proven. They felt that he had joined Chaplin, Keaton, and Tati in the ranks of full-blown comic *auteurs*, and they were eager to see him reveal even more of his creativity, inventiveness, and personality.

Jerry had many champions among the fraternity of French film critics, ranging from converts like Truffaut to wild-eyed enthusiasts like Jean-Luc Godard, who wrote, "Jerry Lewis is the only American director who has made progressive films," adding that Jerry "was much better than Chaplin and Keaton." He had imitators in French show business and cinema—the Laurelesque comic Pierre Etaix, who wrote a book-length homage to Jerry in the form of a long poem accompanied by dozens of caricatures, and Louis Malle, whose dizzying early film *Zazie dans le métro*, about a rambunctious young girl's tour of Paris, has many of the hallmarks of Tashlin and Lewis's comic experiments.

But no one worshiped Lewis more zealously than Robert Benayoun, a slim, bespectacled writer with *Positif* whose mousy aspect, swollen nose, and dark, carefully combed hair made him look, unfortunately, rather like one of Jerry's comic creations. Benayoun wrote some of the first serious critiques of Jerry's work in the French film press, and he wrote about Jerry more consistently—and more discerningly—than any other critic the comedian has ever had.

Benayoun related to Jerry strictly as a critic throughout the 1950s, offering startling insights into Jerry's art. In the essay "Simple Simon, ou l'anti-James Dean," for instance, he showed that Jerry's ability to convey adolescent and even childish emotions despite his obvious chronological maturity predated James Dean's widely lauded sensitivity and vulnerability. But whereas other of Jerry's French admirers such as Bernard Davidson, André Labarthe, Serge Daney, and Bertrand Tavernier (later a much-lauded director in his own right) kept themselves at critical removes, Beanyoun sought a more intimate relationship with his subject, contacting Jerry's offices in the early 1960s and making the hajj to Hollywood to visit his idol soon after. Benayoun conducted nearly a dozen interviews with Jerry, starting in 1963 and continuing for nearly a decade. He visited Jerry's film sets, he ate dinner at Jerry's house and met the family, he attended the disastrous premiere of the ABC series at the Jerry Lewis Theater itself (he reported to *Positif*'s readers that the show was filled with "riches and hilarities"), while at the same time remaining an important critic of Jerry's films in the French film press and French newspapers. He was, in short, far more of a fan and an intimate of his subject than Americans consider healthy for a critic or journalist, but he was starstruck by Jerry, who cultivated Benayoun as a chronicler of his life, art, and times just as he had Peter Bogdanovich and Richard Gehman. (In a sense, then, while Jerry didn't invent his French reputation, he encouraged it as both good business and an ego boost.)

Benayoun's solicitude may have seemed slightly odd to the French, who were bona fide Lewis enthusiasts without quite sharing the critic's fanaticism. But to Americans, it was downright perverse. Bad enough that an entire nation was praising this comedian, whom his own countrymen had all but dismissed; that one man should seemingly spearhead the canonization singlehandedly was seen as a near-obscenity. In 1968, for instance, when Andrew Sarris sought to distance his own brand of *auteurisme* from the French brand in part by criticizing Jerry, he described Benayoun—without naming him—as "a *Positif* critic who so resembles Jerry Lewis that hero-worship verges on narcissism." Benayoun responded four years later by dedicating *Bonjour, Monsieur Lewis*, his book-length collection of articles, reviews, photos, and facts, to "Andrew Sarris, le Spiro Agnew de la critique américaine."*

The Sarris-Benayoun imbroglio illustrated the failure of the two nations and their film critics to understand each other's perspective on Jerry and his work. To Americans, the French affection for Jerry was a joke, a license to dismiss both the comic and the country with one snide comment; "The French? What do they know? They like Jerry Lewis." To the French, who discovered Edgar Allan Poe, Sidney Bechet, Josephine Baker, and other indisputable giants who found no appreciative audiences on their native American soil, Jerry was yet another genius neglected in his myopic homeland.

In part, the divergence in opinion stemmed from the American audience's long (contempt-breeding) familiarity with Jerry by the time he had achieved something worthy of critical attention. By the early '60s, when Jerry really had become an important director, he had long since passed from the American public's consciousness as a hot item. "Jerry was never chic in America," reflected Peter Bogdanovich, one of the few American writers who took the comedian seriously at this stage in his career. "I think before he and Dean made pictures, there was a moment when they were at the Copa in the late '40s when they were kind of chic. Orson Welles told me that it was to die. He said you'd piss your pants it was so funny. But when they got into pictures, I don't think they were ever chic."

Sarris, similarly, acknowledged that early on "there was a time when people sort of liked him in an odd way, or he could orchestrate an interesting receptivity." But, he continued, by the time Jerry began to direct films, "the bulk of the intelligentsia had abandoned him and had no interest in that sort of thing. He still had a kind of box-office thing with people who knew what they were getting, his films were still making money, but there was no real dialogue over whether he was good or not. I mean, no one debated whether *The Nutty Professor* or *The Bellboy* or these different stylized things he did were any good. There was no one to talk to about them."

As word of Jerry's French reputation spread in the United States (*The New York Times Sunday Magazine* ran a feature article on the subject in February 1966), the situation became a way to demean both France and Jerry Lewis in one fell swoop. The French—eaters of snails and frogs' legs, unpredictable political al-

---

*Years later still, Sarris shook his head in bewilderment at this gesture: "I was very impressed with that, because writing any kind of book is a hard job. It's a chunk of your life, and a lot of work, pain, sweat, and tears. And to dedicate a book to your enemy! I mean, the love of Jerry Lewis runs very deep." For his part, Benayoun remained frankly bitter about the flare-up decades after it occurred. "American critics never understood why French critics appreciate Jerry Lewis," he said. "American critics are not very *au courant*. Critics like Andrew Sarris are very lazy and jump at conclusions too easily."

lies, a nation of rude waiters and pretentious fops—became more ludicrous than ever in American eyes; and Jerry, his audience at home shrinking in both size and age, became more and more a laughingstock who had to appeal to an obscure foreign cult audience for validation as an entertainer.

At no time, perhaps, was the schism between French and American critics more pronounced than in the release of *The Family Jewels* in the summer of 1965. "Film shapes up as comparatively mild entry," wrote *Variety* in its characteristically terse style, while Bosley Crowther flatly declared, "There isn't a gem in the lot." *France-Soir*, on the contrary, declared the film's sentimental ending proof that Jerry was "a true human being and not merely a marvelous laugh-making machine," and Benayoun, writing several thousand words about the film for *Positif*, described how it "deliberately severs space-time and leaves us a series of nearly interchangeable moments, a technique even more audacious when applied here than in a story with a more dramatic appearance."

As it turns out, both camps were right. There is something incredibly doltish about *The Family Jewels*. The plotting is utterly arbitrary, the basic story ludicrous, and the filmmaking characteristically sloppy; in an apogee of Jerry's studied carelessness, each of seven characters he plays wears the wedding band–pinky ring–fancy watch combo that he refused to doff for the cameras. But it's also a sampler of comic invention, with Jerry creating two hilarious new characters—Captain Eddie, the confidently inept airline pilot, and Bugsy, the ruthless, moronic gangster. Additionally, characters from other films are given fresh life—Buddy Love and Professor Kelp are reworked as a caustic circus clown and a bumbling fashion photographer, respectively.

There are dull stretches, but also pleasant surprises: Gary Lewis and the Playboys make a cameo appearance, and Jerry—whom quick-draw pistol artist Bob Munden claimed had the fastest hands he had ever seen on an amateur—performs several amazing pool tricks. But it's rather an impersonal, sporadically lively film, a let-down from the highly personal work in *The Nutty Professor* and *The Patsy*, and far less fun than such Jerry-amok films as *The Bellboy*, *The Ladies' Man*, and *The Errand Boy*. It combines episodic comedy with a farcical narrative, but fails to see either through fully. While the American critics may have been overly hostile, the French notion that Jerry was somehow evading his own personality with the multiple roles, however intriguing, is equally wrongheaded.

Still, finding an insightful and appreciative audience for his work must have brought some comfort to Jerry in the summer of 1965, when he was a man without a studio or a TV network and only the second most popular entertainer in his own house. Gary, with Patti serving as his manager, continued to sell millions of records; he had released three LPs and five singles (all of which hit *Billboard*'s Top Five) during the first year of his career, with well over three million total units sold.

In September Gary was invited to host "Hullabaloo," the NBC prime-time pop music and dance show modeled on the already venerable "American Bandstand." Gary's "guests" were Paul Revere and the Raiders, Barry "Eve of Destruction" McGuire, and a young singer named Joanie Summers. As a lark, Jerry was brought on to cohost the program, which aired on September 20.

To open the show, Jerry and Gary ran out to sing a duet of the Beatles' "Help!" Jerry, sporting a navy sports coat with a red pocket square, uneasily read the lyrics to the song off cue cards and mugged and screeched to compensate for his patent uneasiness. The two pretended to step on each other's lines and joked about Gary's overweening ambition in a kind of sit-com Freudianism (at one point, Jerry "excused himself" for his poor timing: "It's so long since I worked with somebody").

Later on, after introducing Barry McGuire as someone with "something important to say," Jerry himself took a singing turn. Gary announced that "my mother asked me to introduce a new record," and Jerry came out in utter sincerity to sing a song whose title was never given. It was a kind of bad Dylan pastiche, with vaguely poetic lyrics and a brooding undertone. Though he was playing it straight, the very sight of him in this milieu singing this material was so incongruous that it seemed like a joke.

Jerry did some more singing during the show's "Top of the Pops" segment, during which he was saddled with Roger Miller's "Kansas City Star." In a red V-necked sweater, he embarrassedly walked through a chorus of the song, shrugging dismissively as he concluded, a man completely unconnected to the very scene he was making. The show ended with Gary and Jerry bidding the audience adieu ("My son thanks you" and "My father thanks you") and a performance by Paul Revere and the Raiders during which Jerry grabbed lead singer Mark Lindsay's tricorner hat and a spare (unplugged) guitar and began mugging with the dancers on the "Hullabaloo" malt shop set. If it was a travesty, at least he would inject it with some energy.

The week before "Hullabaloo" aired, Jerry began to work on the film Paramount had refused to let him make with their money, *Three on a Couch*. Most of the crew members whose loyalty he'd cultivated in sixteen years at Paramount were no longer with him, as they were full-time employees of the studio. Cinematographer Wally Kelly was along merely as a consultant, and editorial assistant Rusty Wiles was on board as a full-fledged editor, but it wasn't the typical homemade Jerry Lewis film. The script, for instance, had been written by a committee of four, none of whom were Jerry or Bill Richmond; for the first time, Jerry would be directing someone else's material.

At least one other old friend was on the premises—Janet Leigh, playing the female lead as Jerry's romantic interest, a psychiatrist who specialized in the romantic traumas of young women. Much had changed since the days when Janet

Above Stanley to the rescue: *The Bellboy* (1960).

Right Frank Tashlin in
1962.

As Julius Kelp, dancing with Stella Stevens near the climax of
The Nutty Professor.

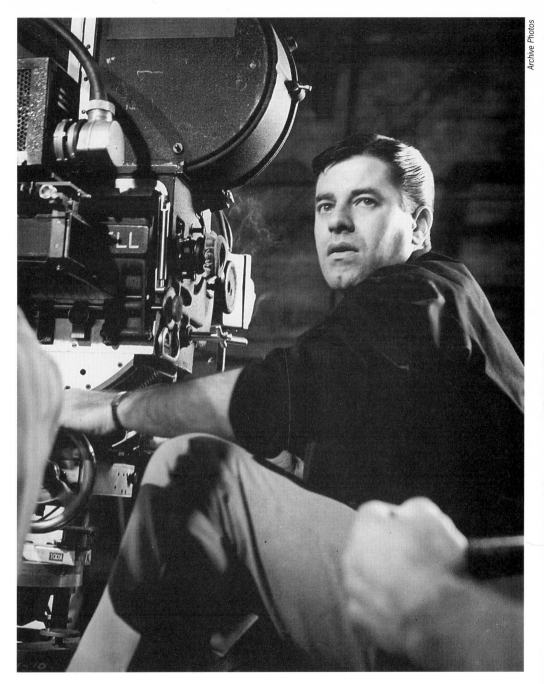

Thicker of body as he nears forty, directing *The Patsy* (1964).

Everybody but the dogs: Ronnie, Jerry, and Gary (top, left to right); Scott, Chris, Joseph, and Patti (middle, left to right), and Anthony (front), probably 1964.

Feelin' groovy, on "Hullabaloo" with Gary, 1965.

March 5, 1965: Being helped to his feet by Andy Williams after the fall that would change his life. Some chorus members are still dancing, thinking it was just another Jerry Lewis bit.

Above "Max no difference!": With Sidney Miller (left) in *Which Way to the Front?*

Left Shouting up some publicity for *The Day the Clown Cried*, 1972.

As Helmut Doork, on the Swedish set of *The Day the Clown Cried*.

The great reunion: With Dean on the telethon, 1976.

Mr. Smooth, late 1970s.

Left Without a net: *Hellzapoppin'* (1976).

Below Prisoner of success: With Robert De Niro in *The King of Comedy* (1983).

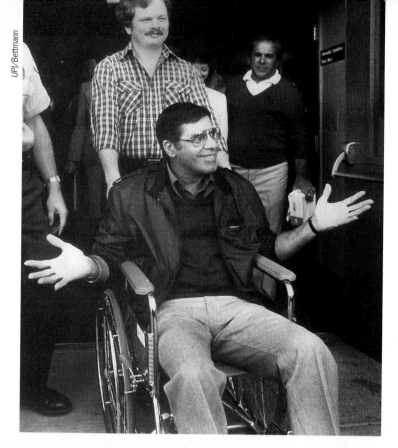

Right Leaving the hospital after triple-bypass surgery, 1983 (Joe Stabile, in sweater, at right; SanDee Pitnick is partly visible behind him).

Below The second wedding: Key Biscayne, February 13, 1983.

Roll over, Dr. Schweitzer: Chevalier of the Legion of Honor, Paris, March 12, 1984.

Mickie Levy

Right Backstage at the Westbury
Music Fair, spring 1993.

Below Visiting the circus with
SanDee and Danielle, 1995.

As George Fawkes, in *Funny Bones*, 1995.

The highest-paid performer in the history of Broadway: As Applegate in *Damn Yankees* (with Charlotte d'Amboise), 1995.

was making silly movies in Jerry's Pacific Palisades backyard: She and Tony Curtis had divorced in 1962, she'd married stockbroker Bob Brandt later that very year, she'd been nominated for a Best Supporting Actress Oscar for her famous brief role in *Psycho*, and, in general, she'd mixed a career as a successful actress with a real-life role as wife and mother. Socially, she hadn't seen much of Jerry since she and Curtis had felt themselves choked out of his circle by the crush of sycophants. In fact, she'd become close with Dean and Jeanne Martin, who had introduced her to her second husband and even stood for them at their wedding (giving Leigh the distinction of having had Dean and Jerry as best men at two different marriages). Still, she was glad to be working with her old friend, and she was particularly impressed at how he had evolved as a filmmaker.

"He had matured and grown so," she recalled. "He was one of the best directors I've ever worked with. I'm not saying *the* best director, but he's definitely at the top. Really, he was wonderful. It was the first time I'd ever seen an instant replay used on the set. And it was wonderful—you didn't get the full scope, but you could see if the scene worked or not, so you would know whether to do it again."

Leigh was taken aback by the relative sobriety of the set, so unlike the atmosphere of high jinks that prevailed when she'd worked with Dean and Jerry on *Living It Up*. Perhaps it was a sign that his childlike exultation in the very process of directing had waned, perhaps he was trying to impress his new bosses at Columbia with his professionalism, but the wild atmosphere that marked the shoot of *The Ladies' Man*, for instance, wasn't in evidence. "There was a sense of gaiety," remembered Leigh. "They'd be throwing the baseball at lunchtime and things like that." But there were no practical jokes of wild outfits or touring groups of foreign dignitaries. It was strictly professional, she said, though not stifling. "You can tell the tone of a set the minute you walk on a stage," she explained, praising the bonhomie on Jerry's set, "and you can tell whether there's harmony or whether everyone's at everyone else's throat. It's tough enough to make movies, you know, and to have that kind of atmosphere is almost intolerable. The people who set the tone are the director and the stars. If somebody's going to be uptight, you can tell right away."

Jerry, she was grateful to remember, wasn't like that. Leigh enjoyed the atmosphere so much, in fact, that she led the crew and extras in a chorus of "For He's a Jolly Good Fellow" when Jerry arrived for lunch.

Not that the shoot was entirely without its troubles. There was the matter of a theme song. Jerry had wanted "I Left My Heart in San Francisco," but was told in a telegram from a Columbia music supervisor that the publisher refused him rights to the song "under any circumstances whatever." (He went instead with a song composed of his own lyrics and Lou Brown's music, "A Now and Later Love.") And, as on *Cinderfella*, a young actress found herself on Jerry's wrong side and was fired from the picture early in production. In this case, it was Jill Donohue, a twenty-six-year-old movie brat (her father, Jack, was a longtime TV director who'd made some light comedy and musical features) making only her second film. On October 4, Louella Parsons reported that Donohue had shown Jerry brash disrespect: "Where are their think-machines when a novice like Jill Donohue, impatient over waiting for her scenes to be shot in 'Three on a Couch,' walks off the set at Columbia? This, after Jerry Lewis, the producer as well as the star, had asked Jill to remain. When he learned she had bolted, Jerry said, 'Fire her. Get someone who will appreciate the break.' Within 24 hours, Kathleen Freeman had taken over."

The contours of the story were essentially true—Donohue had left the picture, Freeman had replaced her. Jerry's office, however, hadn't been caught unawares by Parsons's report. In fact, Jerry's new publicist, Jim Flood,* had planted it. He told his boss that Donohue's press agent had told Parsons that his client had "walked off the picture because she didn't feel the part was good enough for her and the same with the picture, etc." After checking the story with Joe Stabile, Flood fed Parsons the Jerry Lewis Productions version of events, which was the one run in the column. "I don't believe in planting this stuff," Flood told Jerry, "but when they start up it's the only way we can go."

It was only a minor contretemps, and the film—which was shot on Columbia's Burbank lot as well as on locations throughout Los Angeles, in nearby Arcadia, and in San Francisco—concluded principal photography on November 16, just $298,000 over its original $1.8 million budget. One week later, Jerry opened an engagement at the Sands, where, as in the past, he spent his nights on stage and his days sorting through his footage and assembling a rough cut.

There was a final, odd note to 1965, an anonymous, unbilled performance that had a profound effect on Jerry. He had always swiveled ambivalently between the need to be accepted for himself and his work, and the need to be accepted for his fame and fortune. As a kind of experiment with himself, he donned clown makeup and joined the troupe of the Ringling Brothers & Barnum and Bailey circus for a show at L.A.'s Shrine Auditorium. "I played in front of twenty-five thousand people," he recalled, "and not one of them knew who I was."

Some stars like that sort of anonymity, that reminder of life before fame. Not Jerry: "When I left the auditorium," he said, "I pulled off the wig and took off the makeup and I burst into tears. Oh, did I cry! I experienced a shocking revelation—that when a clown is through with a performance, he's nothing, nobody. The people had laughed and wept and applauded. But if I wasn't Jerry

---

*Jack Keller and his wife, Emma, had retired to a cabin they'd built in British Columbia.

Lewis, I could have walked thorugh them afterwards and they wouldn't have known who the hell I was. I trembled so much when I thought about it that I couldn't sleep that night. Next day, I went to a typewriter and wrote a twelve-page screen treatment. 'Two-Faced Clown.' One day I'll make it. When I'm ready."

That day never came.

In December 1965 Paramount released *Boeing Boeing* to disheartening notices in the press; though almost every reviewer praised Jerry for his relative restraint as Tony Curtis's straight man, it didn't matter—nobody was watching. In February 1966, when *Cahiers du cinéma* published a special issue devoted at length to Jerry's work, he was already in production on his thirty-fifth and possibly least worthwhile production, *Way . . . Way Out*, his first-ever film for Twentieth Century–Fox. It was written by William Bowers, who'd been producing screen-plays since the 1940s, sometimes with distinction (he'd been nominated for two writing Oscars, including one for *The Gunfighter*) but more often not. Gordon Douglas, an old-school hack of the sort Jerry hadn't worked with in years, was the director. He was a favorite of Frank Sinatra's, not because he was especially good but because Sinatra could boss him around, ordering the director to shoot with-out him until noon so that his days on the set could be crammed into about four hours.

Still, it wasn't as if the material in *Way . . . Way Out* deserved a better helmsman. Jerry and Connie Stevens were cast as an American couple shot into space to conceive a child before their Russian counterparts, Dick Shawn and Anita Ekberg, could do the same. It was ludicrous—purely a money job (he claimed to have been paid eight hundred thousand dollars)—and Jerry knew it. He was listless on the set—"I'm on the tired side of pratfalls," he told an Associ-ated Press reporter—and he was dreaming of drifting out of the limelight alto-gether, of directing exclusively and making only occasional film and television appearances.

He told Earl Wilson he was almost ready to quit performing: "I'm waiting to find some young idiot to do what I did, and I'll retire behind the camera, which is where I believe my real field lies." He was hoping that Gary, whose band had recorded the title song to *Way . . . Way Out* and who, Jerry told Wilson, had "all that's needed to be our next great comic," might fill the bill; he was eagerly an-ticipating his son's debut in a Kansas City production of *Bye Bye Birdie* that summer.

But he was also having talks with Woody Allen, still a rising young talent with a single screen credit to his name (as actor and writer of *What's New, Pussy-cat?*, 1965's chic sex farce). Allen had a new script to shoot, a parodic crime drama called *Take the Money and Run*—and he wanted Jerry to direct him in it.

He had seen *The Nutty Professor* (in Paris, yet!) and recognized in it a perfect version of the sort of film he wanted to make. He became a big fan of Jerry's work. "He knows how to cinematically film a joke," Allen told *Newsday*. "Even with a long-term joke, he knows how to hold the shot just long enough. The opening scene in *The Patsy*—he comes in as a bellboy juggling the ice cubes— you remember, he held that one just right, just long enough. In my opinion, he's the best comedian's director around."

Allen wasn't just being diplomatic. The fact was, since 1960 (indeed, since the silent era) Jerry was practically the *only* comedian's director around, a man who'd worked on both sides of the comic lens and thus understood comprehensively not only how to come up with a funny performance but how to film one. Knowing that Jerry often made himself available to young comics seeking guidance (he had many conversations with Lenny Bruce over the years, encouraging him even though he was extremely frustrated with Bruce's stubborn insistence on political material and blue language), Allen approached Jerry with the idea of directing the script. As Jerry later remembered, "He came to me to direct *Take the Money and Run*, and I wasn't available. He thought that they'd like to do the picture in eight weeks and it would be so great if I would direct it. I said, 'Woody, I spend twenty-eight weeks in prep. Shooting in eight weeks? We're talking thirty-six weeks.' I said, 'Why don't you do it yourself?' Get a good cameraman, get some good people who will teach you what to do with the lenses, give yourself a good two-three week prelim of learning what it should take you twenty years to learn.' "

Jerry didn't bother to tell Allen about how he'd turned around *The Bellboy* in less than three months, but Allen took the older comic's advice, finally releasing the film in 1969. When he was ready to make his next film, *Bananas*, he once again asked Jerry to direct it and was once again gently rebuffed, but he remained grateful to Jerry for inspiration and encouragement throughout his career.

At around the same time Allen was trying to get Jerry to save him from having to direct himself, another young Jewish comic was finding himself behind a camera for the first time. Mel Brooks, Jerry's reluctant collaborator on *The Ladies' Man*, was shooting *The Producers*, a satire about venal Broadway money men, from his own script. Although neither Brooks's film nor Allen's was the sort of plotless, abstract gag fest that Jerry began his directing career with, and although neither film featured a protagonist as wildly ill suited to life on Earth as Jerry's familiar character, the very fact of these films was a kind of triumphant result of Jerry's insistence on making films of his own.

Whatever Barney Balaban's thoughts in allowing Jerry to direct *The Bellboy*, the establishment of a precedent for other Jewish comics to follow in becoming filmmakers couldn't have been among them. But Jerry had, in fact, formed a bridge connecting early generations of Jewish performing comedians (Danny

Kaye, the Marx Brothers, Milton Berle, Sid Caesar) with a new generation of comics who seized control of the presentation of their material on screen. Moreover, where the Jewish dimension of the older generation's material was almost wholly repressed, Jerry's nebbishy persona, though never explicitly Semitic, paved the way for a comic persona like Allen's to be presented to a larger audience as a frankly Jewish character. Jerry would never play an acknowledgedly Jewish character in a feature film (though several of the characters he played on TV in the 1980s would be explicitly Jewish), but he clearly prepared America for the uncloseting of a wholly Jewish sensibility in Hollywood film comedy in the late 1960s. Surely it was this—not a desire to become another Stanley Belt himself—that drew Allen to Jerry as a mentor. Nevertheless, few other comics or filmmakers were canny enough to realize Jerry's role in their liberation, and Jerry was left to direct himself in films that had no impact on people who weren't already eager to see them.

Television. He couldn't help himself. Like a scab on his knee, it was an irresistible temptation, though every time he played with it he was left bloodied. He did a cameo on an NBC special celebrating the glories of burlesque. He did a cameo on "Batman," sticking his head out a window and having a chat with the Caped Crusader as he climbed a wall. And when Sammy Davis, Jr., fell ill in February 1966, he volunteered to guest-host his NBC variety program for a night.

Sammy had been getting murdered in the ratings by "Hogan's Heroes," the popular concentration-camp sitcom, and he had jokingly "declared war" on his competition. But Hogan himself, actor Bob Crane, didn't care for the tenor of Sammy's remarks. In an interview with *Los Angeles Times* TV critic Hal Humphrey, Crane spoke up about Sammy and about relishing Jerry's appearance opposite his show: "Listen, I know Sammy's a big talent, but people don't like to hear a guy talk about himself that way. Look at what happened to Jerry Lewis after he told everybody how great he'd be with that two-hour show every week. Jerry's a fan of mine, too, and says he watches my show every week. Wonder if he'll be watching this Friday?"

This was just the sort of thing to set Jerry off. He clipped the article and sent it off to Crane with an angry letter. He took pains to prove to Crane that he'd never claimed he'd be "great" on ABC. Jerry was determined to discount the possibility that Crane was misquoted: "Although Humphrey isn't one of my favorite people, I must say, he's one hell of a newspaperman." And he concluded with a bit of advice from an older star to a younger one: "The BIG TIME is a marvelous place to be invited to. Play it BIG and you'll never know the pain of the SMALL TIME again," signing off with the following cryptic note: "cc: Martin Borman [sic], Rudy Hess, E. Braun."

Crane was reduced to groveling by Jerry's letter, hurriedly dashing off an elaborate apology to Jerry. "Never was I so glad to receive a letter as I was yours," he began, claiming that he'd been trying to apologize by telegram ever since Humphrey's article appeared and offering an elaborate explanation of how the columnist had turned Crane's praise of Jerry into ridicule. "Hal extracted what he wanted to hear from me, a rap at Sammy, and God knows why, a rap at you," Crane said, closing on a truly humble note: "Jerry, I hope to hell I haven't bored you with this, but I felt even worse than you about the column."

Feeling that Crane had bowed deeply enough, Jerry wrote a letter absolving the actor of his sins—accepting his explanation "without question"—and reflecting philosophically on the incident: "I wouldn't even guess at the number of people around hating each other because they didn't take the time to check it out."

To Humphrey, however, a writer to whom he'd granted many interviews over the years, he was less forgiving. He sent the columnist copies of all of the correspondence between himself and Crane, along with a caustic cover letter: "I am genuinely sorry the respect I had for you when I wrote Mr. Crane has sadly diminished."

Humphrey, who saved all of the materials Jerry sent him, responded that Jerry had been had by Crane: "I don't recall that you ever accused me of misquoting you in any of the many interviews we have had together, a couple of which, as you recall, you taped." Humphrey declared that he took careful notes of the Crane interview and "was amused to find that Mr. Crane's memory, if you believe him, is more trustworthy." But Jerry didn't answer, content—having slapped a hot TV star and sneered at an important columnist—to let the matter die.

Jerry hadn't stumped for a film since *The Nutty Professor*, so when *Three on a Couch* was released in the summer of 1966, he decided to embark on a fourteen-city tour to promote it. There were other things going on as well—he would spend a week in New York hosting "The Tonight Show" (and get into an ugly spat on his final show with his guest and old friend Jack E. Leonard, who would walk off, leaving Jerry looking dazed and hurt); he would stop in Kansas City to see Gary open in *Bye Bye Birdie*; he would do a lot of camera shopping and spend time at baseball stadiums and race tracks. But the main idea was, as in the past, to sell tickets to a Jerry Lewis production.

This was no Second Jewish Bataan Death March, however. There would be no running to a dozen theaters in each city to perform with a band. He was forty; he didn't need the strain. Instead, he taped appearances for local TV and had sit-downs with local print and broadcast journalists. He even spent time with old friends—he had dinner with Lonnie Brown in Toronto, met with comic Alan Sherman in Boston, and performed a show at Brown's Hotel on the July Fourth weekend.

Still, though he didn't have the old retinue with him, he continued to travel in regal style. The hundred-thousand-dollar tour involved two private airplanes—one for Jerry and his people, one for their luggage. *Variety* got its hands on a copy of a directive the Lewis organization sent Columbia's local press representatives at each of Jerry's stops. The niggling five-page document was eye-opening proof of just how Jerry saw himself. It stipulated that Jerry and his entourage be met at the airport with two "brand new," "meticulously clean" limousines and a bonded truck to carry Jerry's forty pieces of luggage (the recipient was to come to the airport in a taxi). Jerry was to be put up in a two-bedroom suite ("the Presidential Suite whenever possible") with the following amenities: two bottles of Courvoisier Brandy V.S.O.P., a case of beer (Coors where available, Budweiser otherwise), a bowl of fruit, a color TV, and the name of the hotel manager and his apartment phone extension or home telephone number. There were even instructions about autograph requests (they had to be channeled through an aide) and for personal messages: "In almost every city on the tour Mr. Lewis will have friends who will be calling him. You are to direct all such calls to Mr. Lewis' secretary."

Variety also reported that Jerry was to be interviewed in a private hotel room other than his suite, or in the suite itself, if no other room was available, so that he could (openly) record the interview in order "to provide the star with a history of his statements and a record of his changing attitudes in later years." He would thus sit in his black lounging pajamas, complete with brilliant red *JL* monogram (which *Newsday*'s Mike McGrady speculated might glow in the dark, "serving even in the middle of the night as a reminder of identity") speaking forth on such topics as the movie business, the Vietnam War, and civil rights. The tour was over by the second week of July, but it didn't have the impact he had hoped for. Although *Three on a Couch* got positive reviews in some surprising places— Richard Schickel of *Life* declared that the film revealed Jerry "proceeding more intelligently, more funnily than he has in years," and went on to say that "as both director and star he demonstrates admirable economy"—Columbia saw disappointingly modest profits on the film.

It really didn't deserve much more. It's a dreary piece of work, despite giving Jerry another opportunity to play multiple roles. As Christopher Pride, an artist who wins a plum commission from the French government (his own countrymen, tellingly, don't appreciate him), he's dullish, if a full-fledged adult, all Sy DeVore suits, martinis, and haughty demeanor. Pride seduces his psychiatrist girlfriend's patients in three guises—a loud-mouthed Texan, an eager jock, and a nebbishy Southern zoology buff—and even dons drag to play the zoologist's twin sister. Since Pride, out of costume, has almost nothing funny to do (Jerry does handle an early drunken scene well), the film goes painfully without laughs for quite a long time—and even then the caricatures are disappointingly tame (only Rutherford the zoologist allows him to do really broad, funny comedy).

Structurally, the film moves more smoothly and more mindfully of its narra-

tive obligations than anything Jerry had previously made. And the look is striking—modern, clean, and spare, with bold color choices. Price's inner office is entirely white, with a microphone hanging from the ceiling and a theatrical
lighting system that can render the room blue or red at the turn of a rheostat.
But it's not saying very much if the decor is a film's most striking feature. *Three
on a Couch* is certainly a more conventionally mature comedy than anything
Jerry made at Paramount—no surprise, since it's the first film he directed from
somebody else's script. But by the same token, it's flatter, with none of the anarchic flavor of his earlier work. The film evinces the commercial bind in which
Jerry found himself at forty-one—impelled to appeal to an adult audience, yet
best equipped for family comedies and even children's entertainment. Mature
audiences weren't necessarily going to see a new Jerry Lewis movie in the first
place; for the kids, the film had to have been a bore. The conundrum would
haunt Jerry's movies for the rest of his career.

As he did after *The Nutty Professor* tour, he repaired to the sea to recover and
catch up on work. He was writing yet another script with Bill Richmond, and this
one even had a nautical theme. He was on his third boat—*Pussycat* and *Pussycat
II* had given way to *Princess*, a sixty-five-foot cabin cruiser he'd bought the previous year for $200,000 and on which he'd spent an additional $150,000 to update
to his specifications with electronic gizmos, wood paneling, matching armchairs
with "Mr. Captain" and "Mrs. Captain" stenciled on them, and Baccarat crystal.
On July 18 he boarded the boat in San Francisco with a secretary, his stage director Hal Bell, ship's engineer Art Gannon, and skipper Joe Proux. The plan was to
sail to San Diego, where the ship was usually docked, and prepare it for a trip
that he, Patti, and the boys would take to Mexico a week later.

The boat never arrived. At 2:30 A.M. on July 19, just off the coast of Monterey, the hull cracked and the *Princess* began taking on more water than Proux
and Gannon could bail, even with sophisticated pumps. Proux roused Jerry and
advised him of the situation. "The water was rising fast in the engine room,"
Jerry later recalled. "Ten seconds after I got on the radio, raising Maydays. I had
no idea if anyone heard us."

No one had. They began firing flares into the night, but they were far from
any real population on the coast. As dawn approached, with the ship going
down, Jerry had to make a captain's most painful decision: "I watched my children's belongings float across the saloon; toys and things disappearing under
swirling water. The night was fading. Through the mist we saw the dim outline
of land, perhaps a mile away. I gave orders to abandon ship."

The five terrified passengers donned life jackets and climbed into an inflat-
able raft in a desperate effort to make it to shore. The odds were decidedly
against them: The sea was rough, the coastline rocky. After making it most of the
way to the shore, the raft was capsized by a wave. They swam the rest of the way.

As luck had it, a thirteen-year-old boy named Raymond Gould, who lived in the nearby hamlet of Gorda, had seen the flares during the night and alerted his father, who had called the Coast Guard and then made his way to the shoreline to search for survivors. He came upon Jerry and his harrowed party and brought them to town, where they were given coffee, blankets, and dry clothes. Arrangements were made for a rental car so they could drive back home. Before they left, Jerry returned to the beach to watch as his boat, which had been anchored within sight of the shore, slipped under the waves. Eventually, it broke loose and smashed against the rocks. But Jerry was gone by then, driving south in a state of shock.

Some months later, during insurance hearings, it was revealed that the shipyard that built the vessel had used half-inch rivets in some cases where one-inch rivets had been specified. Jerry collected his insurance money—and he boldly bought a new boat with it, the even bigger, more luxurious *Princess II*—but he had been granted an irrefutable glimpse of his own mortality, just the thing to turn a midlife crisis into a dramatic Hollywood potboiler.

Plans were being laid for the new film—known intermittently as *Mind Your Own Business* and *Ready, Set, Die*—to be shot from December 1966 through February 1967. First Jerry would go on a tour of live dates, playing outdoor arenas throughout the country as he had in late summers past. But there was another item on his schedule, something he'd been avoiding for years but that now struck him as an appropriate undertaking.

He hadn't done a telethon for Muscular Dystrophy since 1961. But now he was immersed in the longest hiatus he'd ever taken from feature filmmaking since his arrival in Hollywood, and he'd been merely an occasional guest on TV for the past three years. The telethon wouldn't be a huge media event, by any means, but it would be TV, the medium he could never resist.

The MDA had lured Jerry into a single-station broadcast in the New York area, where the organization's earning power had been decreasing precipitously over the past few years. Bob Ross had been trying to get Jerry to do another telethon since 1964, to no avail. But a new member of the organization's hierarchy—Mucio "Moose" Delgado—had more of an impact on Jerry than Ross and all of his alarming statistics. Delgado was a thickset Arizonan whose family had been touched by neuromuscular disease, and he won Jerry over with his tough-guy-with-a-heart mien (à la Jack Keller) and his refusal to accept any of Jerry's excuses for backing out of charity work. He and Ross called Jerry to a New York meeting and laid out the organization's needs in an effort to change his mind. Jerry, though, was still gun-shy about a real TV project: "I'm not going to stick my neck out and get rapped for doing good stuff," he announced. But Delgado gave him a withering look and he felt cowed.

On Labor Day weekend—the acme of the Borscht Belt summer season, but a graveyard in the TV business (hence the willingness of WNEW-TV in New York to give it over to a show without a sponsor)—Jerry hosted the twenty-hour broadcast. It was a typical charity show lineup, with dozens of guests ranging from Chubby Checker to Joan Crawford to Jackie Vernon to Robert Merrill to Henny Youngman. And when it was over, to Jerry's and the MDA's shock and gratitude, they'd discovered that there was not only an audience for such a program on Labor Day, but it was one with open pockets. The show raised over $1 million in pledges, much more than had been anticipated. In a single day, he had solicited more money for MDA than in the last five years combined.

Maybe there was something to the telethon business after all. . . .

17.

Levitch's Complaint

"I've got to feed my family," Jerry told a reporter that summer, explaining why he always kept himself so busy. "I've had to keep going. I've got to make product."

His latest product—finally dubbed *The Big Mouth* in classic Lewis fashion—took him to Mission Bay, near San Diego, where some years before Joe Stabile had introduced him to the pleasures of boating. Using the newly built Mission Bay Hilton as a location, he shot nearly the whole month of December 1966 in and around San Diego, including sequences at the Sea World theme park. The whole of January and a few days at the outset of February were spent shooting at Columbia and at some coastal locations around Los Angeles. The script was being revised until two weeks into the shoot—always a bad sign—but things went relatively smoothly. Yet another young actress managed to get herself fired before the cameras actually ran. Gail Hunnicutt, who was slated to play the lead opposite Jerry, was replaced by an ingenue named Susan Bay. But other neophyte performers fared better: Rob Reiner, Charlie Callas, Harlan Sanders (the fried-chicken king), and Scotty Lewis all made their film debuts in *The Big Mouth*. Callas, in fact, was Jerry's protégé: Jerry had touted the rubber-faced comic all over Hollywood, doubtless hoping he might be the "young idiot" he'd been looking for.

Gary, it had become clear, would not be the one. He was still releasing records and still touring, but the steam seemed to be leaking ever so slowly from the hit-making engine. The Playboys' five 1966 releases included two that didn't enter the *Billboard* Top Ten and one that didn't crack the Top Twenty—their first records that failed to make a significant impact on the charts. During the summer, after his road version of *Bye Bye Birdie* closed unceremoniously, Gary took the band on a tour of the Philippines (coinciding with a state visit to the island nation by President Lyndon Johnson). And the craziest thing happened to him there: He fell in love.

The object of Gary's affection was Sara Jane Suzara, a Filipino girl he'd originally met in Hollywood and with whom he spent all his free time in Manila. Tall and dark-eyed, with long, black hair, she went by the nickname Jinky. She was a military brat—her father was chief pilot of Manila harbor—and a divorcée, with a six-year-old boy named John. Gary was twenty-one years old, a rock star supporting himself independently of his famous father's considerable wealth. He was quite a catch. They talked about marriage.

And then an even crazier thing happened. In November 1966 he was drafted into the Army. Rich, white, and famous, with a father who knew the President, he might have been the least likely young man in the country to be asked to face action in Vietnam. But he was given an induction date and told to report to Fort Ord, a boot camp just north of the Monterey peninsula, where his father had almost drowned earlier that year.

Jerry wanted to stop it. "I was going to call Bobby Kennedy to spring Gary," he revealed years later. But when he spoke to Gary and discovered that the young man wanted to serve his country, he backed off. Reflecting on his son's maturity, he was proud. He even bragged about Gary's patriotism: "I ran around Hollywood yelling, 'Want to hear what my son said?'"

The Playboys had one last gig together on "The Ed Sullivan Show" in early December, Gary and Jinky spent a few precious weeks together, and on December 28 the whole family drove to the airport to see him off. He came back on weekend passes; basic training seemed not to have any ill effects on him. But the war was escalating, and the unspoken subtext to all of these brief family reunions was the reality that Gary was likely to be called up to active combat. He and Jinky became engaged on January 25, 1967, and decided to get married as quickly as possible. A wedding was planned for March 11 at St. Paul the Apostle Church in Westwood. Patti immersed herself in the plans, shopping with the bride for an eight-hundred-dollar gown, for which she and Jerry paid. Two days later, they celebrated with a huge catered affair. Jerry remembered it as festive, but an undertone of gloom must have resonated throughout the party. Afterward, Gary returned to Fort Ord and an almost certain deployment overseas.

Not that it was any consolation, but the household Gary left behind was becoming less and less hospitable to the Lewis boys. Jerry may have wanted to surround himself with children, he may have been subject to sudden urges to smother them with hugs or gifts, but he didn't care to share his wife with them, and he even seemed to resent having them around, soundproofing their quarters in the house. They satisfied a need in his life to matter to somebody, but he would fly into rages whenever they escaped his control.

Indeed, with the pain in his neck so severe and his dependency on Percodan, Norodan, and Valium increasing, he himself was barely under control. "He did not act himself," said Patti. "He was irritable and impatient—more than we had ever seen. At times, the kids, who used to be excited about making signs to welcome him home, fled when he pulled into the driveway."

It was, in fact, the boys who were most stung by his temper. He was, in his own words, "a very heavy, heavy disciplinarian," bragging to a reporter, "My right hand is heavy but my left hand is caressing." He described his firmness as a reaction to the laxity of his own upbringing: "When I was young, I wasn't disciplined at all. I've raised my boys the old-fashioned way, with spankings, sending them upstairs if they misbehave at parties, the works. I believe discipline is the proof of love. We're very close."

The boys, especially the four youngest, whose memories of home life didn't stretch back to Jerry's best years in show business, remembered growing up in an atmosphere half-nurturing, half-punitive—the punishment meted out by Jerry, the nurturing by Patti. Years later, raising another baby, Jerry admitted as much. "I was a taskmaster of discipline," he confessed. "The only thing that I didn't know about is that when I wasn't around, my ex-wife wasn't a disciplinarian." He would always boast that his sons had turned out well because he had molded them with his firmness. But the boys didn't necessarily see it that way.

Chris, who was nine when Gary went into the Army, remembered that Jerry's very arrival in the home was an emotional coin toss for his sons: Which father had returned to them? "He could be one of two people," he recalled, "the loving father who hugged and kissed us, or an angry stranger to stay away from. If he walked in the front door and whistled to us, we ran and embraced him. If he came in with no whistle, we could hear his huge key ring hit the marble entry table and know it was time to head for the hills."

Dinner was another ritual during which the boys gauged their father's mood. Though Jerry allowed himself to make a mockery of decorum, throwing food at the ceiling or pouring and rubbing it on himself like a baby, the boys were strictly forbidden to horse around in like fashion. "We were to sit quietly, speak only if spoken to, and eat quickly and silently," remembered Joseph. "We had to ask permission to rise. If we happened to ask when Dad was watching television, we were scolded. Many offenses could be committed at the dinner table. By far the worst was walking in front of the television. We were required to go the long way around the large marble table." Jerry would wither his sons when they crossed his line of vision: " 'Damn it, get out of the way!' "

Getting the kids out of the way was a preoccupation with him. "I didn't even say hello when I came home," he reflected later. "I just flopped on the couch, wanting to be left alone. It was always Patti telling the boys to scoot." He was showing the same sort of indifference toward his children that Danny and Rae had demonstrated toward him, and he recognized what he was doing—especially to Patti. "When it came right down to truth," he confessed, "about giving, about spending an extra moment or two with her to discuss the children or some other concerns she may have had over the day-to-day routines of family life—if she got eight minutes from me it was a lot."

Jerry's detachment from the family was clear to everyone, even the youngest boys. They knew that whenever Patti approached their father with a problem, she would be hurried away with the response, "I'll fix it." But, as she recalled, this was most often a simple stalling routine: "He meant to, I hoped he would, and sometimes he did. But often the relationship stayed broken or the dilemma went unresolved."

When he did take action, it could be either wildly inappropriate—when Patti got upset about Gary's having bought a motorcycle, for instance, Jerry resolved the crisis by buying the bike from him—or violent. Almost to a one, the boys have come public with stories about the verbal abuse and physical punishment they received from their father. The boys' responses to and memories of Jerry's punishments were varied in specifics, but the general tenor was uniform. Scotty proudly boasted in later years that he was "the only one of the children [Jerry] never hit." Chris hated Jerry's shouting at him so much he "often wished he would hit us instead of yelling," and Anthony, who always spoke about his father with intelligence and compassion, simply declared that Jerry was "the consummate disciplinarian."

Of course, there was another Jerry—the man who made his children laugh, who kissed them on the lips with every arrival (even into their twenties), who took them deep-sea fishing and to baseball games and to movie sets, who could lavish expensive presents and elaborate attention on them. And sometimes his obsession with orderliness proved comic even to himself: He would try to film Christmas mornings for posterity, but drove himself to absurd distraction trying to get six boys to follow his stage directions while their presents sat waiting for them under the tree. But as his career slipped away from him in the 1960s and '70s, and as his dependence on Percodan and other drugs increased, he became more and more the screaming, profane, withering man whose sons dared not cross in front of the TV set.

He would always speak pointedly in interviews about his fathering skills, about the happiness and intimacy he shared with his boys. When the boys were young, even these orchestrated hugs and pats satisfied them: "I remember telling Anthony once that our father really loved us a lot," said Chris. "I knew this because I always heard him say it on television." But as Jerry's ability to relate humanely with his family deteriorated, and as his sons grew old enough to comprehend the gap between his public pronouncements and his private behavior, they grew more and more alienated from him. As Patti reflected, "Every time I heard Jerry expound upon his treatment of the boys, I knew that, to a certain degree, he *was* there for the older kids, and I always knew he meant what he was saying. However, *doing* what he was saying was another matter."

■ ■ ■

With *The Big Mouth* shot, he took his ritual trip to Las Vegas to perform at the Sands and begin cutting the film, which would be previewed in April. And he began to plot a course for his next projects. He'd been offered a role in Walter Shenson's production of *Don't Raise the Bridge, Lower the River*, a comedy about an American con man who can't manage either his marriage to an English-woman or his outlandish get-rich-quick schemes. As in *Boeing Boeing*, he would be strictly hired talent ("I just went to England to do the picture because it was my financial pleasure to do so," he admitted). Jerry Paris, who had played the next-door neighbor on (and, later, directed) "The Dick Van Dyke Show," would be making his directorial debut with the film; the script would be written by Max Wilk, author of the popular novel on which the film was based. Shooting was scheduled for May through July 1967 in London.

The trip to Europe would allow him a pleasant diversion. At the behest of Robert Benayoun, he would attend the Cannes Film Festival and allow himself to be fêted by the press and the crowds. He was ready for his French fans this time: Walking along the Riviera city's famed Croisette, he greeted starstruck passersby with wild flourishes ("Hello, you bunch of frogs! Here's Zherry Loueee!") and under-his-breath dismissals (Benayoun was charmed to discover that Jerry's universal pet name for new acquaintances, "Pussycat," had evolved into "Cocksucker"). He rented a large yacht so he could cruise to Antibes, Monte Carlo, and Villefranche, and he was delighted to learn that it was cap-tained by an old German seaman who'd served in the war; he quizzed him re-peatedly about his exploits. When he attended the festival debut of Francis Coppola's *You're a Big Boy Now*, he created a gridlock of paparazzi in the theater lobby. Festival officials tried to escort him to a VIP area where Shirley MacLaine and Vincente Minnelli were seated, but he refused to be separated from his en-tourage and sat with the regular festival audience. He held a press conference in the Palais des Festivals, greeting his interlocutors. "This makes me think of the Nuremburg trials." He stayed, however, taking dozens of questions and patiently waiting for Benayoun to translate for him. He was the smash hit of the festival—and he didn't even have a film with him.

He took at least one other trip during the shooting of *Don't Raise the Bridge*, flying to New York to appear on the debut of "The Merv Griffin Show" in prime-time syndication. He did a lot of shtick: playing the trumpet while smoking a cigarette, "rescuing" a lady from the balcony with a wobbly ladder, standing in as straight man for the avant-garde topless cellist Charlotte Moorman (who wore clothes for the show), and performing in a comedy skit.

It wasn't his only TV appearance that year. NBC had done the unthinkable: Within four years of the ABC catastrophe, they had signed Jerry to do an hour-long variety series starting that fall. Bob Finkel, onetime "Colgate Comedy Hour" director and the producer who watched Jerry take his hideous fall on

"The Andy Williams Show," would produce the series through his Teram Company, which would work in partnership with Jerry Lewis Productions.

"You may think we have courage bordering on a desire for self-destruction to present Jerry Lewis," remarked NBC president Don Durgin at the time the series was announced. "But we believe he can be the biggest single hit on television." Durgin, the network reasoned, was in a good position to know. Under his aegis, Dean Martin had become one of the medium's hottest stars, hosting a spectacularly successful Thursday night variety show that consistently ranked in the Nielsen Top Ten. The combination of Jerry's desire to keep up with Dean and Durgin's hunch that Martin and Lewis could be hits independently on his network had prevailed over the overwhelming evidence of Jerry's previous failures in the medium.

The hype was exciting, the money was big. According to Finkel, it was "the most expensive comedy show NBC has ever done. We're spending in the neighborhood of thirty-five to forty thousand dollars for guests and extras alone, and we'll have big sets and comedy props." The whole thing was so intoxicating that even former co-workers of Jerry's—grown men who should have known better—were lured into the fold.

"One day, Pancho Villa came riding down from the hills asking all the peasants to join him," remembered Ed Simmons. "I got a call from Jerry asking if I wanted to be head writer for his show." Simmons had done well since he and Norman Lear had left "The Colgate Comedy Hour" in such a huff, writing for series starring George Gobel, Red Skelton, and other comedy stars. "The money was very attractive," he said of Jerry's offer. "And I went. Like a schmuck."

The series had a much tighter format than the one on which ABC had gambled. By Finkel's edict, there would be five days of rehearsal each week. The show would be taped—without an audience—and then edited into an airable format. In addition to Simmons, a writing staff of five was aboard (along with Jerry and Bill Richmond). Jerry wouldn't be allowed to sit behind a desk and "be himself." There would be an emphasis on guests—Lynn Redgrave, Sonny and Cher, Harold ("Odd Job") Sakata, and the Baja Marimba Band would appear on the debut program—and on skits in which Jerry would reprise beloved characters from his movies and stage act: the Nutty Professor, the Poor Soul, the Mexican Bandit, Captain Eddie. NBC was even affording the program a popular lead-in: "I Dream of Jeannie."

When the series finally debuted on Tuesday, September 12, 1967 (at 8:00 P.M., satisfying Jerry's urge to "play to my kids"), the critics were underwhelmed. True, there had been none of the drumbeating that had boosted expectations for the ABC series, but viewers might have expected a little more than the tepid program they found. "This was a Jerry who didn't provoke strong feelings. Either way," wrote Barbara Delatiner in *Newsday*. *Variety* followed suit. Acknowledging that the star was being grounded in skits and would therefore "rise and sink on his material," reviewer "Pit." announced that the stuff Jerry had to work with was "a very uneven mix." Praising Jerry's pantomime abilities and granting that "Lewis contrived to inject some engaging moments despite the handicaps," the review ended by pronouncing that "more moments of inspired lunacy will be needed if Lewis' Tuesday night lease is to remain in force."

The producers, however, stuck by their guns—it was to be a show driven by sketches and guests—and the series wound on. Jerry made funny with famous guests (Ben Gazarra, Lawrence Harvey, Janet Leigh, Bobby Darin, Martha Raye), he sang ("Beyond the Blue Horizon," "Witchcraft," "Embraceable You," a seventeen-song medley with Mel Tormé), he did painfully forced skits (a "square" trying to fit in with "swingers," a kleptomaniac married to a police-woman, a surfer overloaded with equipment, a thirty-year-old on his first-ever date). There were bits that could have been pulled right out of his films (a door-man who wreaks havoc on a luxury hotel, a bungling bag boy promoted to store manager, a man disrupting a movie set) and one that actually was—the crashing-of-the-Hollywood-premiere pantomime bit from *The Patsy*.

But the show was a wan affair, more embarrassing in its way than the ABC series, which at least crashed with a bang. "Those looking for insightful comedy," opined a *Variety* follow-up review, "will have to look elsewhere." They did. Jerry's show quickly fell victim to CBS's "Red Skelton Hour" in the ratings; even a plug from Dino, who told his vast audience, "Don't forget to watch 'The Jerry Lewis Show'" at the end of his season premiere, didn't help. It wasn't quite a disaster—it regularly beat ABC's *Dirty Dozen* knockoff, "Garrison's Gorillas"—but nobody connected with it was fooled into thinking it was a hit. Before long, Jerry went on automatic pilot, thinking of other projects with which he might busy himself.

Having enjoyed himself so much at Cannes in May, he traveled to Mexico in November, where he was the invited guest of the Acapulco Film Festival. Unlike Cannes, an internationally respected competitive festival and studio trade market, Acapulco was purely a vacation festival, an excuse for hotels to draw film buffs and celebrity-gawkers and a chance for the Mexican film industry to sell itself to its northern neighbors. Jerry was to be put up at the government-owned luxury hotel, El Presidente, but when he got there, his suite wasn't ready. He launched into a temper tantrum, running through the halls of the hotel banging on sleeping guests' doors. Finally, he returned to the airport in a huff, snubbing both Mexican officials and Motion Picture Association of America president Jack Valenti, who was to host a reception to introduce Jerry to Mexican VIPs. When reports of the outburst hit Hollywood, Jim Flood issued a denial, stating that Jerry left Acapulco because he'd been suffering "a twenty-four-hour sickness which occasionally strikes visitors to Mexico." But the Mexico City newspaper *El Heraldo* wasn't convinced, stating that "the famous comic seems to have little

sense of humor in real life," and predicting that Jerry's behavior "makes it probable that his movies will never be exhibited in Mexico again."

Of course, it was becoming less and less probable that many venues would
be *wanting* to exhibit a Jerry Lewis movie again. *The Big Mouth* had opened that
summer to the usual hostile press—calling the film "tired and overdone,"
Howard Thompson of *The New York Times* begrudgingly acknowledged that "the
kids love him, mouth and all"—and a box office that was disappointing for a
Jerry Lewis–directed film. It did manage to earn more, however, than *Boeing Boeing, Way . . . Way Out*, and even *Three on a Couch*, indicating that, directing
himself in a certain type of role, he still could draw a public to watch him.

What they saw was a strange mixture of expertise and amateurishness indeed. *The Big Mouth* was the only film that Jerry both wrote and directed while
at Columbia, yet in ways it seems less like a Jerry Lewis film than anything else
he ever did. For one thing, it parodies a specific movie genre, the spy film, and
has a linear (if shoddily assembled) plot. For another, Jerry's chief character, Gerald Clamson, is almost not comic at all—not, like Christopher Pride in *Three on
a Couch* or Willard the chauffeur in *The Family Jewels*, because he's the starting-
off point for a series of comic characters, but because he's only mildly debili-
tated in contrast to almost every other protagonist in a Jerry Lewis production.

For all the strained plot, *The Big Mouth* is a pretty tepid film. Jerry is so low-
key as to be transparent (though, always, he's funny in a subordinate, Kelpish
role), and the supporting cast just doesn't make up for the star's lack of comic
invention. Jerry allows himself only one truly outrageous comic scene—he dons
whiteface and a white fright wig and masquerades as a kabuki player to escape
from the gangsters. It's a funny bit, but it doesn't make the movie.

Most appalling of all, though, is Susan Bay, who reads her lines as if they
were random strings of words. Indeed, given the lifelessness of her performance,
and Jerry's own torpor in the vaguely comic role of Gerald Clamson, the film
takes on an almost documentary air: Watching the two costars working together
at a hotel in San Diego and calling each other "Gerry" and "Suzie," you get the
macabre sense that you're watching filmed rehearsals, a voyeuristic touch that
enlivens the otherwise moribund movie. Though Jerry himself seems lively, the
film doesn't share any of his intermittent energy.

This failure-on-all-counts wasn't lost on Columbia executives, who were beginning to look at Jerry the way their counterparts at Paramount had: With his
hands in producing, writing, directing, and acting, they felt he was becoming not
only less and less able but less and less marketable. They saw no indication that
he had found his form as an actor; his "grown-up" roles (*Boeing Boeing, Three on
a Couch*, and *Way . . . Way Out*) hadn't clicked with the adult audience to which
they were pitched, and they'd left his usual following of children utterly cold.
Comedy styles had changed. Peter Sellers was now a big star doing some of what
Jerry used to do, but with an even more amazing vocal talent and a frankly de-

generate undertone; he played the sorts of roles that Jerry righteously insisted he'd never take: lechers, perverts, and Nazis. Jerry was struggling to keep up with the metamorphosis without any luck, and his bosses at Columbia and NBC didn't want him to experiment.

They didn't even want him to direct. When Jerry set to work on his next Columbia film, a marital comedy entitled *Hook, Line, and Sinker*, he was forced to hire a director, even though he was producing the film. He so resented the stipulation that he went and hired George Marshall—George Marshall!—the seventy-eight-year-old director of *My Friend Irma* and other Martin and Lewis films that Jerry had hated making. It was absurd: Jerry had written off Marshall as an old hack back in 1949; he had refused to allow him to direct *Three Ring Circus*; he'd had Marshall forced on him in *The Sad Sack*. Now, by hiring him, he was virtually flaunting his intention to supersede his director.

Marshall was still averaging a picture a year well into his sixth decade in the business. Nevertheless, the only explanation for his presence on *Hook, Line, and Sinker* was that Columbia insisted that a real comedy director be behind the camera, and Jerry knew he could have his way with the old man. Knowing Marshall wouldn't interfere while he directed the film himself, Jerry filled the picture with his perennial collaborators: cinematographer Wallace Kelly, editor Rusty Wiles, assistant director Hal Bell, associate producer Joe Stabile, and Stabile's bandleader brother, Dick. *Hook, Line, and Sinker* would be the final film of Marshall's career, and Jerry's last film for Columbia. He waited until he'd shot his last TV show of the season, made the movie quickly—about eight weeks, including location work in San Diego and some foreign exteriors—and left in a huff.

He was, in fact, beginning to talk about the movie business in the sort of contemptuous terms he usually reserved for television or critics who had bad things to say about him. He continued to decry the increase of profanity, nudity, and violence that had characterized the American cinema since the film industry had eased its production code a few years earlier. When he spoke about his distaste for new trends in the film industry with Earl Wilson that summer, he explained it in economic terms, as if to disguise his personal antagonism. Sneering about the presence of sex and violence in films, he argued "it's not really in the hands of the producers. It's in the hands of the public, which is to blame. As long as the public wants to buy it, they're going to make it. I've had a couple of dozen scripts submitted to me that I just wouldn't go near. I got one the other day with a title you wouldn't believe. The funny part is, eventually, they get done! . . . Some freaks are making an awful lot of money and an awful lot of noise in our business. I can't understand some of it; it's like going to a zoo."

On January 22, 1968, ten months after she and Gary were married, Jinky Lewis gave birth to a daughter, the first Lewis girl. She was named Sarah Jane, just like her mother—and, coincidentally, after Jerry's maternal grandmother. Gary and

Jerry were shown in a wire service photo, hugging and grinning with big cigars stuck in their mouths.

Gary still hadn't been sent overseas, so he hadn't yet been required to give up his musical career, which he kept alive with weekend recording sessions. The Playboys were continuing, however, to slide down the charts. Just as Jerry had lost touch with the comedy audience, so Gary had been left behind when the English pop bands he'd emulated turned to more sophisticated musical ideas. On both sides of the Atlantic, bands scrambled to follow the Beatles' lead—few as cluelessly as Gary Lewis and the Playboys, whose peppy, streamlined party sound bore no relation to the Sgt. Pepper–era baroque psychedelia coming out of London.

Liberty had turned Gary over to producer Leon Russell, but the change didn't generate a hit; "The Loser (with a Broken Heart)," the first Playboys record on which Gary's nasal, constricted voice wasn't double-tracked, didn't even crack the Top Forty. The new production team crafted two Gary Lewis albums in 1967 alone—Listen! and New Directions—and a handful of singles, released to moderate success. Gary was actually relieved that the records didn't make it. "Jill" and "Girls in Love" were such elaborate psychedelic productions that all he could think was "If they become big, big hits, how am I going to duplicate these things on stage?"

As the date of Gary's overseas service neared, he and Snuff Garrett reunited to complete as much recording as they possibly could. He was due to be shipped out on March 11—his first wedding anniversary—and two nights earlier he recorded "Sealed with a Kiss," the old Bobby Vinton hit. He was never reckoned an expressive or personal singer, but that particular performance was laden with emotion for him. Within forty-eight hours, he would travel to a war zone, leaving behind a wife and newborn daughter. When he described the recording years later, the wound still seemed fresh: "If I could have been given another chance to sing that," he said, "I would have taken it in a second. That's the only song I will never listen to as long as I live. I cringe every time I hear it."

Almost two months after Gary left Fort Ord for Asia, the song was released at home along with another single, "Rhythm of the Rain," also recorded in a hasty final session. "I remember having the songs out and not being able to go around the country and promote them," he said years later. "I remember thinking, 'Gee, these'll never make it!'" The public, though, recognized the heartfelt pathos in his singing; "Sealed with a Kiss" was his first Top Twenty hit in nearly two years.

Jerry was neither so busy nor so lucky. He had almost nothing to do in the summer of 1968 but prepare for another excruciating year of his NBC series. He had no movies in preparation, he had no studio to release his work, he did no live touring—nothing. Plans were in the works for his third consecutive Labor Day telethon (the success of the 1966 program had convinced him to turn the event into an annual project), but the man who just a few years earlier was putting in twenty-hour days in film, TV, live shows, charity work, and even a privately run radio station was at a near-standstill, terrified that his career had ground to a halt.

Years before, everyone had talked about how badly it seemed Dean would fare after the split, and how wonderfully Jerry would do. And until *The Young Lions* and the Rat Pack days, it seemed Dean was indeed headed toward oblivion. But now the worm had turned: Dean was still making records that sold well, he was still in demand as a film actor, and his TV show was a staple in millions of homes. It was Jerry who was struggling, as much at sea as the night the *Princess* sank out from underneath him.

Dean made repeated pitches for Jerry's show on his own program; it became a running gag, and a painful one for Jerry. Kay Gardella of the New York *Daily News* asked him about it in his Burbank dressing room before his second season on NBC began, and he unburdened himself to her. "Dean was twelve years ago," he told her when she asked if they would appear on one another's shows. "I don't see any reason for exchanging guest spots. This is a subject I could discuss all day with you, if I had time. It's all right for Dean Martin to mention me in kidding on his TV show. He's doing it in character. He can do jokes about his wife, booze, and even me and get away with it. I can't do that. Detrimental jokes of any kind I can't do. While Dean is in character, it's okay. He gets away with it fine. However, if I kidded about Dean on my show, or referred to our old partnership, the hurt and pain would show. You don't live and work with a guy as long as I did without the divorce being painful. How do you tell your audience you loved the guy? To kid what was and still is painful, because it might be saleable today, would be beneath my dignity. I'm still too sensitive about it. Dean can do it because the character he plays lets him do it. I can't."

He launched dispiritedly into the TV season. Producer Bob Finkel had added Nanette Fabray and the Osmond Brothers as regulars, Jerry had developed a new character named Ralph Rotten, and NBC moved him to 7:30, when prime time began in those days. Once again, the show, while not necessarily an artistic disaster, was murdered in the ratings, this time by "The Mod Squad," the interracial, coed, hippie cop show. By the end of the year, Jerry's show was ranked sixty-eighth out of eighty-six series rated by Nielsen.

He'd had enough: If he was going to bomb again, it would be on his own terms. He did away with the tape-and-edit format, choosing instead to do the show in front of a live audience and air a relatively whole version of the performance. "This way, there's a little thing called spontaneity," he told reporters. "It can make good material greater and weak material better."

As with the ABC series, he placed the blame for the show's poor performance on his network: "NBC wanted to do the show in a certain way. I had to do it that way until they got wise to the situation. Now there's going to be more of Jerry Lewis on camera. NBC's strong point was 'Let's forget Jerry Lewis, let's do comedy characters.' I sometimes wondered why they hired Jerry Lewis, but I hopefully went along. Now we'll have fewer characters, more comedy, and no canned laughter."

To Ed Simmons, however, the advent of the new, looser format halfway through the second season signaled the return of the obstinate old Jerry who wouldn't listen to anyone back in the "Colgate Comedy Hour" days. "It got so that finally he was putting such obstacles in your path that you couldn't write anything," he recalled later. Simmons decided he'd rather do without his fifty thousand dollars per year. He walked into Bob Finkel's office one day and announced to Finkel and Jerry, "This is it, fellows. Tear up my contract. I'm not working here anymore. You don't have to pay me what you owe me. Just let me out."

Simmons went on to more success in TV; he produced and served as head writer for "The Carol Burnett Show," which debuted that same season and won him several Emmys, and developed such hits as "Welcome Back, Kotter." But he never forgot how exciting a comedian Jerry had been when they'd met, and how badly, in his view, Jerry had served his own talent and potential. "I used to have fantasies," he said years later, "of grabbing Jerry and really slapping him around, and then, when he's on the floor, I'd say, 'Okay, you had enough? Now, you son of a bitch, you're gonna listen to me and I'm gonna make you the greatest fucking comic there's ever been in this world.' I realize if I ever did that, I couldn't have changed him, because the greatness is not there. I think I was dazzled early on."

In December 1968 all of the Lewises drove out to Los Angeles International Airport to meet Gary's plane. Gary was returning from his nine months of overseas duty in one thankful piece. He was smiling, wearing a light-colored pullover, hugging his wife and daughter and parents and brothers, but he had changed. They couldn't see it at first. He went through the motions of restarting his recording career, he spent time around the house (he and Jinky and their kids lived at the St. Cloud mansion), and he participated in the holidays.

Soon, though, Jerry knew there was some trouble. "I didn't see my son," he remembered later, "I saw an old man." Gary dragged himself around in a daze, sitting and staring as if into his own skull, speaking slowly and quietly, letting his voice drift off and losing track of his own conversation. He told Jerry shocking stories about battles he'd been in, ambushes he'd witnessed, atrocities, inhumanity. He'd seen a friend ripped open by sniper fire while they sat eating lunch. He'd shot the enemy in close combat. And he was unable to repress or forget any of it.

Many, many Vietnam-era veterans bore similar psychological wounds, of course, but few of them had, as Gary did, an Asian wife and Eurasian daughter waiting back home for them even before they went to war. Jerry recalled that this fact gave his son special pain.

"Father," Gary asked him, "Did you ever have your finger on the trigger and as you looked through the sight you see this man coming, who's got a daughter like Sarah Jane, and you have to squeeze the trigger or he's going to get you?"

"You squeezed it, or you wouldn't be here," Jerry responded.

"But she doesn't have him."

"Fuck him. I don't know him. I don't know if he has a daughter. You can help yourself by understanding that you might have got a single guy."

But Gary would have faded out again.

Jerry was frank with reporters about the toll the war had taken on his son: "He came back totally devoid of any feelings or emotions. He just doesn't give a damn about anything anymore. When I sit him down and say, 'You've got to try to get your head back where it was,' he says, 'Why?'"

Gary spent months in his withdrawn state, and Jerry was sick whenever he saw him: "I'd come home from the studio and I'd see Gary sitting, staring out into space. Eight months, nine months, just sitting. I said, 'Talk to me, just talk to me.'" (In later years, he would describe his son's detachment less solicitously, telling a reporter that Gary had been "an absolute fucking zucchini.") Inevitably, thinking back to how he wanted to stop Gary from serving in the first place, Jerry felt it was his fault. "If I had known the facts, when my son said, 'I want to fight for my country,' I'd have ripped his fucking throat open." But nobody suspected in November 1966 that things would have gone so badly.

Now that he knew the price of his own patriotism, however, Jerry began to turn his attention to his other sons. Ronnie was eighteen, and Scotty and Christopher were nearing their teens. He seriously considered moving the family of boys out of the country. "They'll never get another one of mine," he vowed later. "They'll have to come and get me. . . . Now, if I saw the Russkies on the shore of Malibu, I'd stick a gun in my granddaughter's hand. That's different. But don't you go talking draft to me if you're going to go playing in El Salvador. . . . You ain't getting any of my sons. If I have to make cunts out of them, I go chop. I'll castrate them. Do you get the picture?"

But Gary couldn't be fixed so handily. His grief and anomie were coupled with drug use. He smoked pot, took pills, "and this and that," according to Jerry. "He hid them in his shoes, his jackets, in the lampshades—Christ knows where! We got him as much help as we could." Joseph remembered that Jerry initially reacted to Gary's drug use with rage. Patti recalled that Jerry saw Gary's condition somehow as a kind of betrayal: "When Gary turned to drugs, Jerry refused to acknowledge the reasons behind this. He turned our son's pictures against the walls, or jerked them down in anger. There was no outward empathy. As a wife, I had to believe that somewhere within he felt for Gary's situation, but all we saw was the rage."

Eventually, his anger turned into compassion: Where Jerry couldn't relate to Gary's postcombat stress, he could readily comprehend his son's substance dependency. He himself was taking more Percodan than his prescription called for, and he knew how narcotics could genuinely help someone in genuine anguish. "I got him cleaned out," he confessed, "but then I started supplying him with marijuana. He needed it for whatever his pains were."

Gary eventually emerged from his cocoon and recorded a new album for Liberty, a self-produced project abjectly titled *I'm on the Right Road Now*. But he was so far out of the rock mainstream that the album died outright. Liberty released him. As an entertainer, he had fallen even more precipitously than his father, and had even fewer options open to him.

In February 1969, Jerry finally broke off relations with Columbia Pictures. He was frustrated with the studio's insistence that he not take on so many diverse responsibilities on his films; they wanted him as an actor or not at all. But he still felt he could do it all, and truth be told, he was beginning to prefer directing. *Variety* reported that Columbia didn't mind seeing Jerry go, "in view of some recent softening of Lewis' box office performance." Three years earlier, when Paramount suggested he was "unprofitable," he threatened to sue them for slander. Now he merely packed his things and moved to Warner Brothers, where executives had agreed to let him both direct and star in his own films.

He appeared on a TV special honoring Jack Benny's seventy-fifth birthday. The next month, he created a flap while guest-hosting "The Tonight Show." Speaking off-the-cuff about racial segregation, he said that he'd recently fulfilled a lifelong ambition by "using the bathroom while flying over Mississippi." Gulf States Theaters, a large exhibition chain in the South, announced it would henceforth ban his films, yanking *Hook, Line, and Sinker*. Some NBC affiliates in the state followed suit, pulling his show off the air.

The latter certainly didn't bother him. He had given up on television yet again. The revamped format of his show didn't win any new viewers. The last installment, not nearly as heralded as the final episode of the ABC series, aired on April 15. *Hook, Line, and Sinker* costar Peter Lawford was his final guest. Lawford and Jerry played comics trying to impress a stolid show-biz executive, there was a spoof of the Academy Awards, and Jerry sang "Rainbow 'Round My Shoulder" and "Put on a Happy Face."

But he certainly wasn't trying to put a happy face on his experiences in the medium. After more than a decade of struggling to find a voice and an audience on television, he sounded serious about washing his hands of it forever. "Television destroys dreams," he told *The New York Times*. "Television has been one of the most destructive forces in our society. Ask me about violence, and I'll tell you television has caused it. . . . Sirhan Sirhan would never have carried a gun if he had not seen the way Jack Ruby shot Lee Harvey Oswald in a crowded corridor."

As for his own experience in the medium, he was grateful it was over: "I knew I was going to be part of twenty hours of trash that would never be seen again. Psychologically I couldn't put very much into it. The temporary nature of television destroyed me. Essentially, I always have in mind that my great-great-great-grandchildren will see me in my pictures, that I have to be impeccable for *them*. There is no way they can see me on television. Thank God! And I hated the endless hypocrisy, and lying, the crap, the stopwatch. My funny bone has no time for statistics. I couldn't bear the clock dictating when I would start and finish a joke. And the censorship—network censors are stupid, anticreative men. What those stupid morons don't understand is that when you're given freedom, you don't abuse it."

Having given TV the kiss-off, he set out on a brand-new venture. He would direct Lawford and Sammy Davis Jr. in a sequel to their 1968 swinging London comedy *Salt and Pepper*. It was a British film, produced by Milton Ebbins and written by Michael Pertwee. Jerry, a man without a movie studio, was now a man without a country. He grew a beard—in part to hide the weight he had put on his famously skinny frame, which he also camouflaged by wearing athletic warmup clothes in lieu of his natty Sy DeVore yacht wear and suits—and, packing fifty-one pieces of luggage for his three-month trip, he headed off to London, where he could count on a respectful reception from the European press.

It wasn't as if he didn't have *any* opportunities at home. They were simply ones he didn't understand. Richard Zanuck, Darryl's son, had, at age thirty-five, been producing films for ten years and serving as production chief and president at his father's company, Twentieth Century–Fox, for more than five. In 1969 he tried to interest Jerry in appearing in a film adaptation of a hot novel by a Jewish writer from Newark—the naughty best-seller *Portnoy's Complaint*. Jerry absolutely refused to do it.

"The picture business was not doing what I believed they should be doing," he recalled. "I got a whole moral code about that. I turned down discussions with Zanuck at Fox about *Portnoy's Complaint*. I told him he's a fucking lecher. Ha! I said not only wouldn't I participate in *Portnoy's Complaint*, I wouldn't know how to participate in it. I read it because it was the thing to do in Hollywood. I wouldn't know how to fucking make that movie, nor would I know how to appear in it. And Zanuck says to my attorney, 'He can't turn down this kind of money.' And my attorney said, 'You'd be amazed at what he can do. The first thing he can do is tell you that you can't buy him for that project. Not for *any* money.' Zanuck said, 'Everyone's got a price.' My attorney said to him, 'You ain't getting this kid. Try.' Zanuck tried everything he knew. Everything. Came to me through L. B. Mayer. Came to me through other friends. Came to me through even Muscular Dystrophy. He was going to donate five hundred thousand dollars to Muscular Dystrophy. I said, 'My kids don't want your fucking money for what you want me to do for it.' He said, 'This is above and beyond the deal. This is a bonus.' And my attorney said, 'He doesn't want your fucking money.' "

The story isn't quite accurate in its details—Mayer died in 1957, as Jerry should well have known, having bought his house from his widow—but Richard Zanuck never did get Jerry into his film. (Nor, in fact, did he ever make it himself—the following year, his father fired him from Fox, and *Portnoy's Complaint* was eventually adapted into a tepid film starring Richard Benjamin.)

In London no one dared broach such smut with Jerry. He was treated with the respect normally accorded a Chaplin or Welles. He was, after all, a visiting foreign director of high repute. Journalists from all over Europe turned up on the set. A Portuguese entrepreneur put together a charter package flying eighty-five of his cinephile countrymen to London to watch the shoot. Jerry had once again turned his working environment into a carnival: Just as in the Paramount days, the entrance to his sound stage bore a sign reading THIS IS NOT A CLOSED SET. COME ON IN—YOU ARE MOST WELCOME. And he had upped the ante by announcing on British TV that everyone was invited to come watch him work. As a result, in addition to the usual swell of journalists, friends, hangers-on, and idling workers from elsewhere in the studio, Jerry's sound stage was choked with visitors of all ages from all over England, an American nun (who was also a professor of film studies at a stateside university!), and a knot of French writers and critics, among them a contingent from *Positif* that included Robert Benayoun.

Patti and the boys flew over for a visit—the film was begun in July, giving them a chance to spend their summer vacation abroad (Gary, pointedly, did not make the trip). Jerry allowed Ronnie to work for a few days as an unofficial still photographer on the set, giving him instructions on a professional Bell and Howell camera (Benayoun learned that Ronnie, who was nineteen years old and nearly a head taller than his father, wasn't allowed to drink so much as a beer because Jerry felt it might lead him to use marijuana and more harmful substances). The boys were on the set when production moved to Eastnor Castle in Ledbury, and they got to meet horror movie stars Christopher Lee and Peter Cushing, who had cameos in the film. Otherwise, it was a sight-seeing trip for them, Patti's first visit to Europe since 1953; on July 21 she and the boys watched Neil Armstrong step onto the surface of the moon on a gigantic TV screen that had been set up for a throng in Trafalgar Square.

The atmosphere on the set was all back-patting and bonhomie. Sammy and Jerry had long been close; Lawford and Jerry had become friends more recently. There was much hugging and kissing and grinning for press cameras (Jerry didn't appear in the film, scuttling a scene in which he was to make a cameo). Sammy even announced that he would permit the planned film version of his autobiography *Yes I Can!* to be directed only by Jerry.

Working wholly behind the camera, Jerry directed in the old Chaplin style, acting out gestures and routines for his actors and encouraging them to follow his example exactly. The only friction occurred whenever producer Ebbins showed up to see how his film was progressing. Jerry detested Ebbins—"He's not a filmmaker," he confided to Benayoun—but acted like an obsequious schoolboy in the presence of a grumpy dean whenever the producer appeared. As soon as Ebbins had left the set, though, Jerry would begin to take off on the producer's body language and vocal mannerisms in a cruel imitation that cracked up the rest of the crew.

With the British journalists and visiting American writers with whom he spoke on the set, Jerry adopted a sagacious mien. The *Sunday Times* of London sent a team of journalists out to MGM's Boreham Wood studios to interview him, and they wound up running more than a page of Jerry's uninterrupted thoughts on filmmaking, film criticism, comedy, the American racial situation (despite its absurd plot and "groovy" trappings, he saw *One More Time* as a film about brotherhood between blacks and whites), and the struggle for human dignity. One class of humans that, he felt, possessed no dignity whatever—namely, his American critics—came in for a new type of scolding. Compared with their European counterparts, he announced, American critics were not only obtuse but positively fallacious: "I don't expect the critics to say bravo—they can say any goddamn thing they please—but I want them to *look* at my films, not send some kid who works in the copy office and say, 'Tell me what the plot is and I'll fill up a few lines.' We only have about six or seven real critics in America—the rest are ex-copyboys, people who used to write about radio, and when that went out, they wrote about television, and now it's the thing to discuss 'cinema.' "

The sad fact was, despite his thin skin—did he really expect critics to apply themselves to *Hook, Line, and Sinker?*—he was right about the state of American film criticism, which was still in a sort of journalistic infancy, especially compared with European models. Most film critics in the States were merely reporters, telling their readers the plot of a film and briefly commenting on whether or not they enjoyed it. The sort of elaborate lengths to which critics elsewhere in the world went to explain Jerry's talent were utterly beyond the capacity—or, frankly, the desire—of American newspapers to report.

When he wasn't being so testy, though, he spoke cannily to the *Times* about his brand of comedy as it related to the comic styles of some of his most famous precursors: "Comedy is a man in trouble, and comedians react to it in different ways. Chaplin was a ballet dancer—he'd dance through trouble. Keaton became part of a well-oiled machine—he'd slip easily through a small opening. I'd have my arms outstretched and get stuck."

Insights like these no doubt came to him because the respect accorded him by his European interlocutors sharpened his thoughts. But he had, in fact, been expounding publicly on the cinema and on comedy for some time now. In 1966

Arthur Knight, a professor of cinema studies at the University of Southern California, had invited Jerry to lecture to his students.

Jerry had often made himself available to newcomers to the film business. In 1961 he and UCLA drama instructor Ron Carver had conducted a workshop for young comics on the Paramount lot, auditioning more than five hundred applicants to select a pool of forty young men and women to sit at his feet and learn a few tricks of the trade. In 1965, '66, and '67 he directed short films starring actors from the Film Industry Workshops, an institution financed and given work space by Columbia Pictures to develop young talent.

Even with these experiences behind him, Jerry was a bit nervous about lecturing at a university. Knight nevertheless pressed him until Jerry admitted, "Do you realize that I'm a dropout? I have no diploma!" It didn't matter to Knight, and Jerry went ahead with the class, announcing humbly beforehand to the assembled students that "I'm not a qualified lecturer. Anything I say and feel you're going to have to pull out of me, but I'll tell you anything I know."

It went well. In fact, he liked it so much that he had Jim Flood call Knight a few months later to ask if he could return. Finally, Knight offered him a full-fledged weekly class, the title Professor of Film Studies, and ninety-four dollars a month. Jerry's Cinema 501 course met Monday nights on USC's downtown Los Angeles campus, and it quickly became a hot ticket. The standing-room-only crowds included undergraduates, graduate students, and even nonstudents who crashed the lectures with his blessing and crammed the aisles. Jerry positively glowed with the attention, and he did his best to live up to his new responsibilities.

"The homework I used to do before I had a goddamn class was as much as I used to do before I went on the set," he remembered. And his classes, like his workdays, extended way beyond the norm: "On a Monday night, we would meet at seven o'clock, and before you know it, it's three in the morning, two in the morning. I'd wrap up the class at midnight, but like twenty of them would stand around my desk. And I'd say, 'Why didn't you talk to me about that when we talked about that?'"

The experience overwhelmed him. He recorded his lectures, amassing an astounding 480 hours of audiotape. In the second year of his course, he posed for *Esquire* with his paycheck in his hand (delighted with his cost-of-living raise to one hundred dollars a month). He saw his position at the university as the triumph of the poor schlemiel who had been expelled from Irvington High: "I had only two years of high school," he told a reporter. "I want to rub the noses of the people who said, 'You won't amount to nothing. Without an education what will you become?'"

Despite all his success and his power as a producer, he had been only a dilettante in business over the years. The radio station, the restaurant, the dinner theaters

he'd begun buying up years before—they were hobbies, all of them, not elements of any real financial plan for his future or his family's security. But in September 1969 he launched a venture meant to change all of that. He had arranged
with some people doing business as the Network Cinema Corporation to begin
the Jerry Lewis Cinema Corporation, an international chain of franchised automated movie theaters. The company took out ads soliciting interested franchisees not only in Hollywood trade papers and magazines catering to theater
owners but in mainstream publications such as *Life*: "If You Can Press a Button
and Meet Our Investment Requirements," one ad blared, "You Can Own *One or
a Chain* of JERRY LEWIS CINEMAS."

It was an era when national business franchising was all the rage. The Jerry
Lewis Cinema Corporation had two competitors in the United States alone in
its theatrical franchising plans—Automated Theaters of America and McGuire
Cinemas. Fast food operations and car washes were similarly popular as invest-
ments; Jerry's new partners themselves had made their money in automobile
rental and barbecue restaurant chains. Jerry's wasn't the only enterprise fueled
by a celebrity endorsement, either—Minnie Pearl and Joe Namath had lent their
names to chains of restaurants, for instance.

But Jerry Lewis Cinemas would be different from all other movie theaters in
the country, chains or otherwise, by virtue of their highly modern design. The
architecture and decor of Jerry Lewis Cinemas were created by Broadway stage
designer Robin Wagner. Wagner had come up with a spare, modernist look: two-
story glass walls, streamlined concrete columns, and globular chandeliers. Wagner had nothing to do with the logo—the familiar caricature of young Jerry with
his mouth open and eyes shut would appear on all advertising and signage. Nor
did he design the auditoriums. Those adhered strictly to the demands of the automated Italian Cinematographica projection system, in which a single push of
the button controlled lights, speakers, curtains, and film projection.

But the most unusual attribute of the theater chain was its booking policy.
In order to maintain their franchise agreement, theater owners and operators
would be required to exhibit films selected and booked by the chain itself. And
each of those films, the plan maintained, would qualify as family fare. Jerry, once
again on the stump to denounce films that contained nudity, violence, or profanity, declared, "We have all these mimic-morons copying the Swedish films,
and I think they've gone about as far as they can do. I'm not a prude; a lot of that
stuff is marvelous as long as you don't put it on camera. I wonder about the people who make such crap. I wonder if they have children."

In February reporters were invited to Warner Brothers Studios, where Jerry
was shooting his latest film, *Which Way to the Front?*, for a press conference with
the principals of Jerry Lewis Cinemas. On a set bedecked with giant Nazi flags,
reporters were fed a buffet and allowed to mingle with NCC board members
Gerald Entman (who was also president), Jerry Rudolph, James Journigan, and

Charles Beaumont, the newly appointed West Coast marketing director. Jan Murray, who had a feature part in *Which Way*, came out to schmooze with the press and tell everyone that Jerry was running late.

That evening, reporters learned the specific financial details of the corporation's franchise plans. They learned that since the initial offering, more than 140 theaters had been contracted. As a result, the company's original plan to build 750 theaters in five years was expanded to a projected 3,000. Owners of individual theaters would pay franchise fees of ten to fifteen thousand dollars, a cost that did not include property, buildings, or equipment packages—all of which they had to buy or lease on their own. A prospectus issued to potential investors promised, among other perks, the cooperation of Jerry himself in publicizing new theaters. Under the heading "Jerry Lewis: Your Image Maker," the document announced that "Jerry Lewis makes personal appearances as his schedule permits. . . . Jerry Lewis, always major news copy, holds press conferences to enhance the image of your cinema. . . . Jerry Lewis has written, directed and performed in a color movie to introduce your cinema to your audience."

On March 25, 1970, with 354 theaters slated to open in a total of eighteen states, the first Jerry Lewis Cinema opened in the Wayne Shopping Mall in Wayne, New Jersey, eleven miles north of Irvington. Jerry himself arrived for a ribbon-cutting ceremony five days later, flying up from Washington, D.C., where he'd spent the afternoon testifying before the Senate Small Business Subcommittee on Urban and Rural Economic Development. At the request of New Jersey Senator Harrison A. Williams (who would be exposed a decade later in the Abscam sting), Jerry spoke on "The Impact of Franchising on Small Business."

Apart from his celebrity cachet, Jerry could rightfully address the body, because his business was booming. By May there were five hundred units under contract. In January an ad in *Variety* had declared that thirty-one states had licensees (as well as Ontario, St. Croix, the Virgin Islands, and Italy). Surprisingly few of these agreements, though, were translating into actual theaters. In April 1971 there were only twelve operating Jerry Lewis Cinemas in the U.S. (At the grand opening of the one in Basking Ridge, New Jersey, a local mother and her kids buried porno films under the theater's cornerstone.)

The next month, Gerald Entman told *Variety* there would be fifty theaters running by the end of the summer, that 1,720 theaters had been contracted for, expansion was expected into Canada, England, France, West Germany, and Italy, and the company would do $500 million in business in the next five years. But by January 1972 one-third of the regional areas remained unclaimed, even though start-up costs had shrunk. When the company's exhibitors and area directors met at Caesar's Palace that month for their annual national convention (featuring a dinner show on opening night starring Jerry himself), interested investors who attended the event and signed on had their airfare and hotel bills paid for by NCC. It was the first outright financial incentive the company offered, a sign that its projected revenues might be more than just a little optimistic.

Aside from hosting a press conference to promote his theaters on its set, *Which Way to the Front?*, Jerry's fortieth film, was noteworthy for a number of reasons. For one thing, it marked his return to a movie set for the first time since *One More Time* wrapped—a span of nearly fourteen months. For another, it was his third consecutive film for a different studio. Warner Brothers had gone partners with him. Jerry invested his own money in the shoot, and the studio distributed the film and shared revenues, much the same arrangement he'd had with Paramount for *The Bellboy*, but without the security of a long-term deal beneath it. He would produce and direct the new film himself, a task he hadn't attempted since *The Big Mouth*.

In several key ways, *Which Way* would be among his most interesting works. It was a World War II story—his first period film since *Cinderfella*—and another film in which Jerry played a character somewhat like his real-life self: Brendan Byers, a rich, bored, 4-F egoist who cannot abide his rejection from the military. Determined to help his country, Byers capitalizes on his striking resemblance to a Nazi general and forms a private army to kidnap and replace him, sabotage the German military machine, and kill him. Jerry didn't write the material—the script was by Dee Caruso and Gerald Gardner, who'd originated the idea along with Richard Miller—but its clear dependence on Chaplin's antifascist masterpiece *The Great Dictator* held obvious appeal for him.

With the exception of the moderate success of *The Big Mouth*, he hadn't had a hit in years, and this material was further from the commercial mainstream than anything he'd ever done. Warner Brothers might have sensed as much—the company was tuned-in enough to have bought the rights to Michael Wadleigh's documentary *Woodstock*, which was still being edited, and Donald Cammell's Grand Guignol rock film, *Performance*. If they thought they were getting a comedy franchise by signing Jerry, they didn't seem overly concerned that he would be launching it with so anachronistic a project.

Jerry shaved his beard down into a natty goatee that gave his bored millionaire the air of a satyr and his Nazi general that of a devil; he actually looked pretty good. He set to work on November 30, 1969, on Warner's Sound Stage 2. As when he first arrived at Columbia four years earlier, he brought favored crew members along for the picture—Rusty Wiles, Wallace Kelly, Lou Brown, Hal Bell, and Joe Stabile, the core of his organization for the past few years. And he hired performers who had worked with him frequently (Kathleen Freeman, Milton Frome, Fritz Feld) or whom he had known for years, Jan Murray chief among them.

As on other shoots, Jerry spent a fair bit of time distracted by business matters—the start-up of his theater business, in this case. But the overall atmosphere was spirited and genial. "We had such laughs on the set," Murray remembered. "We had so much fun. At night, I would come up with jokes—because I'm a stand-up comedian, that's the way my mind works—and I'd come in the next day, and he'd say, 'Great, Jan, but I was thinking of the scene, too. Let me just run down my idea of the scene and then you can tell me and maybe we can incorporate it.' Well, he would put in such hysterical shtick and we would scream laughing, and he'd say to me, 'What were your things?' And I'd say, 'Forget it. I had two jokes.' I didn't understand the motion picture process the way that he did."

Murray also recalled the pains Jerry took as a director and producer to see that everything in the film came out just right. "We were out on location," he said, "and Jerry yells, 'Cut!' And he says, 'These actors are too damn uncomfortable in these uniforms. They don't fit right, they don't look right.' He shut down for a few hours, and he made a call, and all of a sudden a half-dozen seamstresses and tailors showed up, and they worked feverishly for a few hours to make the costumes look the way he liked it."

The film wrapped in February 1970, and Jerry and Rusty Wiles edited it under the eyes of Warner Brothers executives. When it was released that summer, however, it was to apathy and disappointment. "As a comedy," wrote *Variety*, "*Which Way to the Front?* is a tragedy. . . . The film, which might as well be titled *The Six Stooges Go to War*, is not only unfunny but embarrassing." Howard Thompson of *The New York Times* was far gentler, admitting he found some of it "really hilarious."

There *were* some precious moments in the film, which is surprisingly more coherent than anything Jerry had done in several years—surprising because it was so different from his typical fare. Much of the gagging is less than inspired, in part because Jerry delegated the mugging to Franken, Murray, and Willie Davis (as his black chauffeur, Linc). But once Jerry dons a Nazi uniform and starts screeching inane orders in a thick mock-German accent, the film spins with a new energy altogether. He has good scenes with Kaye Ballard, who plays his Italian mistress, Paul Winchell as his adjutant, and even son Ronnie Lewis—his adopted son, the only blond in the family—who plays a Lieutenant Levitch, whom Jerry pummels in the course of awarding a medal.

The high point is indeed Jerry's tête-à-tête with Hitler (Sidney Miller, a teen actor of the 1930s). When Jerry's character and Hitler first meet, they rush at each other in slow motion like lovers in a bad melodrama—a moment clearly inspired by some of the Hitler-Mussolini takeoffs in *The Great Dictator*. The two characters engage in all kinds of burlesque shtick:

> *Hitler:*　(pointing to a single head in a photo of a huge Nazi rally)
> 　　　　　Who is that?
> (Byers shrugs.)

Hitler: It's Max!
Byers: Max who?
Hitler: Max no difference! (The two men howl.)

When the meeting ends, the energy drains lamentably from the film. Fortunately, there's little left to resolve before it ends.

Two of Jerry's acolytes, Mel Brooks and Woody Allen, had made their debuts as directors in the time since Jerry had made *The Big Mouth*, and in the vitality of *Which Way to the Front?* one can sense Jerry's enthusiasm at a new kind of license in filmmaking. He comes as near to swearing as he ever had in a film— "Damn it!" he yells at one point, and "What the hell is going on here?" a moment later. And if the notion of a comedy about Nazis seems derived from Brooks's classic "Springtime for Hitler" sequence in *The Producers*, recall that Brooks's Hitler character was explicitly theatrical, whereas Jerry's is the real man. It's a full-scale Jewish comedy about Nazism—the first since Ernst Lubitsch's *To Be or Not to Be* nearly thirty years earlier. Jerry wasn't driven to the project by social conscience, but he obviously relished the freedom he felt in the liberal filmmaking environment of the late 1960s. Responding to his lifelong fascination with the Nazis—and his sense of having been persecuted by critics and the Hollywood establishment—he made a film mocking the thing he most feared. It wasn't as personal as *The Nutty Professor* or *The Patsy*, but it was unjustly ignored.

Jerry, however, wasn't too proud of it. "I got a little sloppy," he said a few years later when discussing the film. Murray also thought it could have come off differently. "There's a better movie on the cutting room floor," he said. "What bothered me was that that hysteria, all that marvelous comedy that we ourselves were shrieking at and that we shot—I didn't see a great deal of that on the screen. I thought we had a funnier picture."

While respectful of his friend's talent, Murray came to see that Jerry the editor wasn't quite up to the prospect of putting together a film made by Jerry the actor and Jerry the producer. "I remember saying to him, 'Jerry, why are you cutting this thing?' " he reflected. "I said, 'Why don't you take a month off so you can see it with a new eye—and then don't *you* cut it.' You can't be objective: When I would go to see the dailies, I would see nothing but myself. And when I suggested this to him, he said, 'Jan, when I cut the film I don't see Jerry Lewis, I just see the character.' And he *thinks* so, but I think it's very difficult to do."

The most galling thing about the film from Jerry's point of view, though, was the way Warner Brothers handled the release. As he saw it, the company decided the film was a stinker and cut their losses by releasing it as a B-feature. For years he bitterly complained against his treatment at the hands of his new employers. "*Which Way to the Front?* wasn't even seen in this country," began a typical reminiscence of the events. "Warner Brothers had a picture called

Woodstock, so everything else they had was shoved on the back burner. My children couldn't even see *Which Way to the Front?* in a theater in Los Angeles. I had to show it to them at home. Fortunately for me, it played in Germany in Berlin for sixty-four weeks. I got the negative costs of the film out of this one engagement."

Jerry may not have been right about *Woodstock*, which was released into theaters in April 1970, when *Which Way* was still being edited. But the last detail of his story was more or less true: *Which Way to the Front?* was hugely popular overseas. In France, where *One More Time* hadn't even been released—partly because of its erratic distribution pattern, partly because there wasn't much interest in a Jerry Lewis film without Jerry himself in it—*Which Way*, under the title *Ya, ya, mon général*, was his most popular film since *The Nutty Professor*. But at home, it was barely shown; in July 1970 it got a brief run in Los Angeles, and limited national distribution six months later. According to one Warner Brothers insider of the period, "The picture was dumped, thrown away. . . . See, a Jerry Lewis picture always had a floor. You knew you could probably get your money back. But it also had a ceiling. And about this time investors started looking only for things that had the potential of going way over the top."

More than ever, Jerry was convinced that American journalists—and now the American studios—were engaged in a personal campaign against him. He did almost no publicity for *Front*, even though it was his own production, and when he did show up for a press conference at a New York hotel, he couldn't hide his contempt. "He entered, looked around the now half-filled room, forced a tight, congealed little smile to his lips, and in a voice tinged with heavy irony, began to speak," wrote one reporter who covered the event. "Throughout the hour in which he answered questions, the irony never left and was sometimes expanded to extreme bitterness."

The rest of 1970 was a blur of little projects. Jerry directed an episode of the TV series "The Bold Ones" entitled "In Dreams They Run," dealing with muscular dystrophy. He appeared on "The Englebert Humperdinck Show." He hosted (with Sammy Davis, Jr., and Charlie Callas) a TV special about circus clowns. He and Patti came to New York in the spring, where they had dinner at 21 with Earl Wilson, and Jerry snapped back at the columnist's comment that there was "something marvelous" about Martin and Lewis: "There was something marvelous about the *Hindenburg*, but it burned and you don't keep talking about it."

He had begun appearing as a character in an animated TV series that aired on Saturday mornings on ABC. "Will the Real Jerry Lewis Please Sit Down?!" was a half-hour show in which a cartoon Jerry donned disguises and adopted voices and got in and out of wacky troubles (David L. Lander, who later would play Squiggy on "Laverne and Shirley," did Jerry's voice). It was, in effect, a throwback to the Jerry of old—not the filmmaker, not the would-be romantic comic, not the talk-show host and telethon personality, but Frank Tashlin's favorite cinematic instrument, the rubbery wild man with no fear of embarrassment. This cartoon Jerry—a janitor with the Odd Job Employment Agency—was essentially the same character that had been featured in D.C. comic books during the mid-1960s, when Jerry's star shone brightly enough to support such a strange tie-in. Those comic books—"The Adventures of Jerry Lewis"—had been an adjunct of his career, an additional means of exposure; now Jerry's animated alter ego had more of an audience than he himself did. Despite his efforts, he hadn't found a way to surpass his own past in the minds of the American public; unable to replay the Kid into his mid-forties, he bequeathed the role to a cartoon character.

Only the telethon was working out for him. After the success of the 1966 edition, the public had endorsed the newly annual event by pledging more and more money each year: $1.25 million in 1967, $1.4 million in 1968, $2.039 million in 1969. That year, he inaugurated what he called "The Love Network," a coast-to-coast linkup of stations that carried the broadcast. For a single day, the telethon would be seen on almost as many stations as one of the three big networks. It worked spectacularly: When the 1970 telethon ended, with an exhausted Jerry wringing out a lugubrious rendition of "You'll Never Walk Alone," the tote board read $5.093 million. It was his most successful enterprise of any sort since he'd left Paramount.

The Friars roasted him at the end of 1970; the March of Dimes named him Man of the Year a few months later. He would no longer work with Warner Brothers—someone in its distribution office had allowed *Which Way to the Front?* to go on a double bill with *Deep Throat*, he claimed—and talks with Twentieth Century–Fox for a multipicture deal had ceased. He blamed the times. The scripts were morally repugnant, the audiences willing to settle for depravity. It became a point of pride for him that he wouldn't consent to the kind of projects the studios were asking him to make. "I was waiting for the theaters to be cleaned out," he said some years later. "I had scripts put on my desk: 'The Ant That Sucked Denver,' 'The Homosexual Matricide Case of the Undernourished Faggot Who Loved a Rabbi.' But how many times can you watch two chicks in a motel with some guy with black socks whipping the bejesus out of some S&M?"*

However wild his exaggerations, there was no doubt he was fed up with Hollywood, maybe even with America itself. In April 1971 he played a few dates in

---

*He would tell versions of this story again and again over the years, always with outlandish phony script ideas to give an impression of the state of Hollywood in the early 1970s. And for some reason they would all focus on homosexuality and matricide: "Jerry is a psychopathic homophile who is held on matricide charges," went one such example; "a cross-dresser who's a transvestite accused of matricide," went another; "*Matricide*. Do it as a comedy," went still a third.

Philadelphia and Chicago and then flew to Paris, where he would play at the great music hall l'Olympia. And he mused to an Associated Press reporter that he was seriously considering taking up residence overseas: "There's a great peace of mind in Europe," he said. "I have seen a world of friendliness here the like of which I've never seen before." Of course, he had enjoyed warmth and affection at home, but that was decades ago, when he and Dean were in the flush of their success and he could stop traffic in Times Square by tossing photos of himself out of his dressing room window. Now that he had to travel seven thousand miles from home for a similar feeling of goodwill, he felt spurned. He had won over America with a comic character born of abandonment; now America was abandoning him. And for the first time in his life, he seemed not to have the energy to fight back.

"It's a good feeling to be working live again," he told a reporter in 1971 at the start of what turned into a world tour. "It's rejuvenating." He would begin in Paris, and proceed on to London, Rome, New York, Los Angeles, Honolulu, Fiji, Sydney, Tokyo, Honolulu, and Miami. Then he would do a big tour of outdoor theaters in the eastern United States and Canada. But France was the favored destination. The trip began and ended there, and no single engagement was as long as the one at l'Olympia.

Although he had played the London Palladium with Dean and as a solo, he had never performed live on the Continent. He would spend several weeks in the French capital—rehearsing, performing, taping television interviews (he appeared for ninety minutes on the enormously popular Sunday night talk show "L'invité du dimanche" with a panel composed of Louis Malle, Robert Benayoun, and Pierre Etaix), cementing the presence of Jerry Lewis Cinemas in France, Italy, Germany, and the United Kingdom, appearing on the prestigious broadcast of the "Gala de l'Union des Artistes 1971" (where, in clown garb, he upstaged host Maria Callas), and investigating the possibilities for film and TV projects in Europe.

He arrived with an entourage of perhaps a dozen. Patti had planned to accompany him but stayed instead in California to attend to Joseph, who was beginning to develop a difficult asthmatic condition (she would eventually arrive to catch Jerry's final show in Paris and spend some time traveling with him). Ensconced in a suite at the Hilton, Jerry gave interviews to journalists and spent time reading a book that Patti had lent him: *Your Inner Child of the Past* by pop psychiatrist W. Hugh Missildine.

He opened at l'Olympia on April 15, heralded by preview stories in the major French newsweeklies. The bill opened with a bike act called the New Dollys, the Frank Olivier dancers, and singer Freda Payne (who had just had a hit with "Band of Gold"). After an intermission, Jerry took the stage to the strains of "Rock-a-Bye Your Baby with a Dixie Melody" and launched into his act. He conducted the orchestra, he did a bit of the old record act, he pantomimed a boxer who became a crooner, he danced, he sang. He kept props and bits of costumes tucked into Lou Brown's piano and pulled them out to juggle or to adopt a character. In short, he did the same things he had been doing in American theaters for years and years to an increasingly indifferent public. But the French audience went absolutely wild. According to *The International Herald Tribune*, "He holds an alien audience's delighted attention for 45 minutes, leaving it begging for more." The review noted that though Jerry confessed to being "a poor linguist and a lazy scholar" and thus performed in English, "he has curtailed his customary effusive chatter . . . concentrating on song, imitations, comic pantomime and monkeyshines. . . . There is skill, precision and finesse to all Jerry Lewis does." A dazed Robert Benayoun—who lingered around Jerry's hotel for the whole of the comic's stay in Paris—called the show "an extraordinary lesson in subtle control of comic art."

In September, after the remainder of the tour had been completed, he returned briefly to Paris to create, direct, and star in a half-hour special for Italian TV. Dressed in full clown regalia, he played in some fifteen skits with such generic burlesque titles as "The Prestidigitator," "The Thirsty Man," "The Airplane Passenger," "The Shave." It was a display of the very sort of pantomimicry that his European audience most appreciated from him, and, in fact, the nearest thing he'd done since *The Bellboy* to silent comedy. Shot over four days, it aired that fall under the title "L'uomo d'oro": "The Man of Gold."

18

Shirley Temple in Auschwitz

It had been thirty years since he'd left Irvington High to throw his skinny frame into pantomiming records in burlesque houses. The frame had filled out, and so had the life: He had gotten everything out of show business that he could have possibly wished for. He felt an urge to give something back. The charity work was part of this, no doubt, as was his teaching at USC.

But even when he was making heartfelt gestures of this sort, he liked people to recognize him for it. Hence the title of the telethon—"The Jerry Lewis Telethon for Muscular Dystrophy." And hence the publication in 1971 of a book based on his teaching: not one of his self-styled anas of cribbed philosophy, but an honest-to-goodness organized and edited volume of his thoughts on the film-making process, culled from a half-million feet of audiotape of his USC lectures.

The Total Film-maker, as it was known, was a legitimately remarkable book for its time. Few directors had ever gathered their thoughts on the filmmaking process in a comprehensive volume, and Jerry aspired to just that—a systematic look at the process of filmmaking in chronological order and from the stand-point of every key figure in the creation and marketing of a film. In addition to fourteen chapters of advice, anecdotes, and explanations of the process of film-making, the book included more than thirty pages of Jerry's thoughts on the art of comedy, on film comedy specifically, and on his fellow comedians, pronounc-ing in conclusion that "the great ones, the giants, are Chaplin, Stan Laurel, and Jackie Gleason, in that order."

It's a remarkable volume, choked with the sort of minutiae that bedazzled him. The notion of Jerry Lewis as a director may have puzzled and amused his countrymen, but *The Total Film-maker* made it obvious that he knew what he was doing. He had an obsessive knowledge of budgeting, lenses, heavy equip-ment, the operations of scenic and wardrobe and sound departments, and of course, the business of selling a film to the public. He discussed the way to handle a crew, what to do with temperamental actors, and how the money men in the industry viewed the creative process. The title of the book was no lie—from acting to producing to editing to drumming up business in the sticks, he had done it all.

That his USC students must have benefited from hearing this sort of stuff from him was obvious. They had been the original audience for the material, and the book, while published by Random House and intended, presumably, for a nonacademic audience, still carried a sense of propagandism toward the young. The clearest sign of this was its prologue, a brief introduction that, unlike the remainder of the text, was created expressly for the page and not edited from audiotape.

Where the text proper reveals Jerry's working methods and biases, the prologue is an indication of how he hoped to present himself in the early 1970s—a leader of youth, enthusiastic, empathetic, and hip. He wrote about the world as "our big round put-on," about young people who "want to say their thing," and about "leaving the over-thirties to wallow in their own messes." Then, in a wild riff printed in italics, he let loose:

> Film, baby, powerful tool for love or laughter, fantastic weapon to create violence or ward it off, is in your hands. The only possible chance you've got in our round thing is not to bitch about injustice or break windows, but to make a concerted effort to have a loud voice. The loudest voice known to man is on thousand-foot reels. Campus chants about war are not going to help two peasants in a rice paddy on Tuesday. However, something might be said on emulsion that will stop a soldier from firing into nine children somewhere, sometime.

With its crazed rhythm, skewed slang, strange details, and advice that readers make themselves heard without attempting to specify what they might say, it's like some weird Las Vegas incarnation of Allen Ginsberg.

The prologue gets odder: "I have a confession. Crazy. I have perched in a cutting room and licked emulsion. Maybe I thought more of me would get on to that film."

And odder still: "You have to know all the technical crap as well as how to smell out the intangibles, then go make the birth of a simian under a Jewish gypsy lying in a truck in Fresno during a snowstorm prior to the wheat fields burning while a priest begs a rabbi to hug his foot."

It finally devolves into a chantlike finale:

> More important: *make film, shoot film, run film.*
> Do something.
> Make film. Shoot anything.

It does not have to be sound.
It does not have to be titled.
It does not have to be color.
There is no *have to*. Just *do*.

By the time he got around to writing a conclusion to the book, he had simmered down. "I am moving more behind the camera," he wrote. "I have been
taking pratfalls for thirty-seven years and my ass is sore." He spoke in sage,
prophetic terms about the industry and the future of the director's craft. He saw
a day when new directors would get their starts in television (and indeed, they already had: witness the career of director Arthur Penn, who'd broken in as an assistant director on "The Colgate Comedy Hour"). He predicted that the advent
of "home cassettes"—videotaped movies—would revolutionize film exhibition.
He spoke admiringly of Michelangelo Antonioni and Stanley Kubrick, two of the
industry's reigning artistic geniuses. Most amazingly, he singled out a twenty-
one-year-old director he'd recently met in whom he saw great things: Steven
Spielberg.

Spielberg wasn't a student at USC, but he knew some of the people who attended the school, Francis Ford Coppola and George Lucas among them.
Through the student grapevine, Jerry had heard about Spielberg's twenty-four-
minute homemade movie, *Amblin,* and he invited the young man to show it
during his class. "It rocked me back," he remembered. "He displayed an amazing
knowledge of film-making as well as creative talent." Spielberg would, of course,
get the chance to demonstrate his skills to the world, but not through Jerry's
good offices. Sidney Sheinberg—right-hand man to Lew Wasserman and a high
executive in both MCA (which had left the agenting business in 1962 when it
was declared a monopoly by the courts) and Universal Pictures—gave the young
director his first real break directing episodic TV. Still, Jerry would always claim
some credit for having been the first to notice Spielberg's remarkable talent, and
Spielberg wouldn't deny it.

In fact, several of Jerry's students went on to careers in the industry, and he
saw himself in later years as a kind of foster uncle to them. True, he recognized
that there was a limit to his influence: "What could I teach George Lucas?" he
once asked an interviewer. "He was my student for one semester, and you know
right away he's got it all. One thing George didn't have as far as I was concerned
was the ability to really crack that young 'I'll get that establishment' syndrome.
It was tough to get through. I never knew if I did or I didn't. George's success I
doubt very strongly had anything to do with his being in my classes."

But in time, his notion of himself as a father to the generation of gifted directors who debuted in the late 1960s and early 1970s came to include not only
such reluctant apprentices as Lucas but directors he'd met only in his capacity as
a celebrity being interviewed or others who'd merely read *The Total Film-maker.*

"Randy Kleiser was one of my students at USC," he said of the future director of *Grease* and *The Blue Lagoon.* "Peter Bogdanovich, Steven Spielberg, George Lucas. I had a great group there. I don't think that they came away with anything that I taught them, although Randy still persists with what he learned from my book. Scorsese carries it on the fucking set. It's his bible. Marty'll make no bones about being one of my biggest fans. I make that statement with complete love and affection. Coppola was also a student. In 1961, when I was doing *Ladies' Man,* Coppola was on that set every single fucking day. Every day."

Besides his charity work, and besides passing the benefit of his experience on to a new generation of directors, there was another way Jerry hoped to do something important beyond all the entertainment he'd offered the world over the years. He wanted to make a film on an important theme—and he had had his eyes on a particular project for some years. In 1966, during the production of *Way . . . Way Out,* his longtime sound engineer Jim Wright signed on as coproducer of a film based on a script by publicity flack Joan O'Brien and TV critic Charles Denton. The film, known as *The Day the Clown Cried,* would tell the fictional story of a dislikeable, unsuccessful (and gentile) German circus clown named Karl Schmidt who was sent to Auschwitz for satirizing Hitler and was subsequently used by his Nazi captors to lead unsuspecting Jewish children into the gas chamber. Under the aegis of producer Paul Mart, the film would be directed that spring in Europe by Loel Minardi.

Like many people in Hollywood, Jerry had heard tell of this remarkable story, which O'Brien had conceived about five years earlier when she was thinking and reading about the Holocaust while simultaneously doing publicity work for Emmett Kelly. It had an obvious mix of horror, pathos, and drama, and it drew the attention of several important talents over the years, Milton Berle, Dick Van Dyke, and Joseph Schildkraut among them. But none of these performers had been able to pull a film together, and the thing seemed destined never to be made, a legendary "great unproduced screenplay."

In the spring of 1971, when Jerry was playing at the Olympia Theater, he was visited by Belgian producer Nathan Wachsberger, who had imported European films into the U.S. in the 1930s, been a partner of George Jessel's in a production company, and made many unexceptional films in Europe. Wachsberger had an option on O'Brien's script, and he wanted Jerry to star and direct. "I have made a deal with Joan," Jerry recalled Wachsberger announcing. "We absolutely agree that you are the only one who can play Helmut exactly as she envisioned him." (Significantly, in Jerry's memory, Wachsberger uses not the name O'Brien gave her protagonist—Karl Schmidt—but the name Jerry imposed upon the character when he rewrote the script—Helmut Doork.) Jerry had nothing even in the pipeline back in Hollywood. He agreed to look the material over.

His initial response to the proposal, he recalled, was fear. "The thought of portraying Helmut still scared the hell out of me," he wrote in his autobiography. But Wachsberger laid it out for him as a rare combination of a sweet deal and an important project: French and Swedish financing, the resources of Europa Studios (the very lot where Ingmar Bergman worked), a cast of fine European actors. Jerry finally relented. By August 1, *Variety* was reporting that Jerry Lewis Productions and Wachsberger had agreed to do the film together with a start-up date set for sometime later that year.

It turned out to be an optimistic plan. Jerry wanted to rewrite O'Brien's script, and he still had obligations to Caesar's Palace in Las Vegas to fulfill before the year ran out. (His three-year deal with the casino, calling for him to appear four weeks a year, was winding down, but he renewed it that winter, stipulating that for 1972 he preferred to work his obligation off in a single month to give him time to make the film.)

In February 1972 he and his new publicist, Fred Skidmore, flew to Stockholm to see to preproduction chores. They went to Germany and Poland to visit the sites of concentration camps. And they went to Paris, where Jerry shot some material for the film while performing with the Bouglione Cirque d'Hiver and saw to his theater business (France's first Jerry Lewis Cinema opened in March 1972).

On April 5, shooting of the film proper began in Stockholm. To prepare for his role, Jerry, who'd been putting on weight in the past few years, lost thirty-five pounds on a grapefruit diet. Joining him in the cast were Swedish actors Harriet Andersson (longtime collaborator of the great Bergman), Ulf Palme, and Sven Lindberg, along with Jerry's French admirer, comedian Pierre Etaix. Press releases were distributed. Hollywood trade papers carried announcements.

But something was fishy. Although his $1.5 million film was in production, Nathan Wachsberger was nowhere in sight. After two weeks of filming, Jerry began to get troubling reports of the financial condition of the project. Suppliers hadn't been paid for film and other equipment. Crew members and performers had been issued rubber checks. Wachsberger remained in the south of France, taking Jerry's frantic phone calls and assuring him the money was forthcoming.

Wachsberger had very good reason to keep his distance. He may or may not have had the money, but he definitely didn't have the rights to O'Brien's material. His option on the script had expired. Wachsberger had paid O'Brien a five-thousand-dollar initial fee, but she never received the fifty thousand dollars due her before production began. As a result, Jerry and his company were in Sweden filming something that wasn't legally theirs to make. And O'Brien told a reporter years later that she was certain Jerry was aware of it. "Jerry knew the option had expired," she said, "but he decided to go ahead."

In the face of intransigence from his producer, and with a great deal of time, energy, publicity, and passion already invested in the film, Jerry paid out of his own pocket for expenses that Wachsberger ought to have incurred. It was an abysmal circumstance, and he couldn't hide his anxieties from his colleagues. Lindberg, who played a Nazi in the film, recalled how agitated Jerry was throughout the shoot. "It was clear he was not in good order those months here in Sweden," he said.

And, in fact, Jerry—torn by his anxiety about the state of the production, by the possibility of losing all of the money he was investing in the film, and by the very emotions that the project and his role called up in him—could barely stand the strain. As on his first self-directed films, he pushed himself to his physical limits to see the thing through. "I almost had a heart attack," he told a *New York Times* reporter months later. "Maybe I'd have survived. Just. But if that picture had been left incomplete, it would have very nearly killed me." (Indeed, given his perpetual nerve pain and his drug habits, it might well have.)

At one point, he revealed afterward, he actually closed down the production because of Wachsberger's failure to perform his duties as producer. Nevertheless, he persevered, bleeding his own bank account in the process. As he explained soon afterward, he turned the stress of his situation into a benefit. "The suffering, the hell I went through with Wachsberger had one advantage," he said. "I put all the pain on the screen. If it had been my first picture, the suffering would have destroyed me. But I have the experience to know how to use suffering."

Ultimately, he said, he poured his entire soul into the film in a way he never had before. The experience of shooting the climactic scene struck him as one of the transcendent moments of his life: "I was terrified of directing the last scene. I had been 113 days on the picture, with only three hours of sleep a night. I had been without my family. I was exhausted, beaten. When I thought of doing that scene, I was paralyzed; I couldn't move. I stood there in my clown's costume, with the cameras ready. Suddenly the children were all around me, unasked, undirected, and they clung to my arms and legs, they looked up at me so trustingly. I felt love pouring out of me. I thought, 'This is what my whole life has been leading up to.' I thought what the clown thought. I forgot about trying to direct. I had the cameras turn and I began to walk, with the children clinging to me, singing, into the gas ovens. And the door closed behind us."

In June, when production finally wrapped, Jerry told Swedish reporters that Wachsberger, who he claimed never showed up on the set or made himself available for consultation, had failed to make good on his financial obligations. Wachsberger retaliated by instructing his London lawyers to sue Jerry for breach of contract, claiming that he had all he needed to finish the film without Jerry.

Through the following winter and spring, Jerry edited the movie, taking cans of film on the road with him and working long hours in Los Angeles with Rusty Wiles. He still had no way of knowing if the film would be released, and his frustration and bitterness were obvious. He drank beers in the editing room, and he snapped at Wiles when he said that people who'd seen a rough cut of one sequence felt it was a bit long. "Everybody's an expert," Jerry barked. "There's a fucking genius at every screening. Where were they when the empty pages were in the typewriter? Where were they when we were freezing in fucking Sweden, shooting the film? Too *long*? Jesus Christ! . . . It was the same thing with the dance sequence in *The Patsy*. And I told them then that they should just wait till it was fucking finished before they go telling me what's wrong with it. Just wait till I'm ready. I don't know who the fuck asked for their opinion anyway."

He saved his special wrath, though, for a young Swedish extra who made the mistake of turning her eyes toward the camera during a shot that had been exceedingly difficult to capture. "There she is," he snarled as Wiles showed him the footage. "There's the little cunt. Same little cunt who tried to rape us before. Watch her eyes. There. See it? Following the fucking camera . . . the sneaky little bitch. Vamping for the camera. She pulled that same thing in another sequence, remember? I told her to keep her fucking eyes to the front. That it wasn't a beauty pageant. . . . There's no room for Shirley Temple in a concentration camp."

Increasingly, it seemed that all of the work he was putting into assembling the film would go for naught. Neither he nor Wachsberger had the clout or money to pull the frayed situation together. Europa Studios, claiming it was owed more than six hundred thousand dollars by the production, held on to the negative, although Jerry kept the negatives of the final three scenes (along with duplicates of much of Europa's holdings) as protection against the film's being released without his cooperation. "I took the last three shooting days," he remembered. "I hold those negatives, the last three days. So they have incomplete work there." O'Brien and her co-writer, Denton, for their parts, refused to sell the rights to their property anew to Wachsberger or Jerry in the wake of the production, even after Jerry pleaded with them personally upon his return to the States and showed them scenes from the film.

Much as he may have thought he could win sympathy for his case by showing O'Brien and Denton his footage, the gesture might actually have turned the writers forever against him. "It was a disaster," O'Brien said of the film years later. "Just talking about it makes me very emotional." Jerry had changed more than just the name of her lead character. He had turned him from a mediocre clown into a gifted one, from a gentile to a Jew, and from a bastard into a hero, from "an egoistical clown," according to Jim Wright, who also saw a rough cut of the film, to "an Emmett Kelly, a very sad clown." The original story was a tale of horror, conceit, and finally, enlightenment and self-sacrifice. Jerry had turned it into a sentimental, Chaplinesque representation of his own confused sense of himself, his art, his charity work, and his persecution at the hands of critics. Furthermore, he had used the clown theme as an occasion to work into the film some of the silent routines he had been performing in Europe—clown material like the stuff he did on "L'uomo d'oro." And, to the writers' chagrin, he had a characteristically relaxed attitude toward details: "In one scene," bemoaned Denton, "Jerry is lying in his bunk wearing a pair of brand-new shoes after theoretically having been in a concentration camp for four or five years."

Others to whom Jerry showed his rough cut over the years held similar opinions of what they saw. "I just remember rage," said Joshua White, director of the 1979 MDA telethon. "He played this rage because that's what he was filled with then. He never really commits to the character. He's always just Jerry. He's supposed to be this schlump, but he's got this slicked-back hair."

Comedian Harry Shearer, a longtime Lewis observer and a friend of White's who was allowed by Jerry to view the rough cut, summed up the experience: "The closest I can come to describing the effect is if you flew down to Tijuana and suddenly saw a painting on black velvet of Auschwitz. You'd just think, 'My God, wait a minute! It's not funny, and it's not good, and somebody's trying too hard in the wrong way to convey this strongly held feeling.'"

Despite the webs of financing and litigation that kept the film under wraps, it refused to die completely. In 1980, when Jerry's next film, *Hardly Working*, proved a hit in West Germany and France, Europa Films announced plans to shop the negative of *The Day the Clown Cried* to European concerns who would finish and distribute it. At the time, O'Brien reiterated her claim that the film was made without any legal rights and could never be released. "I'm so sick and tired of stories being circulated regarding the Stockholm fiasco," she said, "that I felt it was time to again state the facts, facts which everyone, including Lewis and the people at Europa Studios, are well aware of."

Later that year, Jim Wright told the Hollywood trade press that he was still developing a script of the story, with Richard Burton in mind for the lead. Nothing happened. In 1991 producers Tex Rudloff (one of Wright's original partners) and Michael Barclay announced they would make a version of *The Day the Clown Cried* in the Soviet Union as a joint production with the Russian company Lenfilm. Again, no film resulted. The following year, yet another plan called for Robin Williams to star and Jeremy Kagan (who'd recently made *The Chosen*) to direct. Yet again, nothing more was heard of the project. In 1994 Barclay was talking about a William Hurt version. But it seemed no likelier than any of his previous efforts.

For his part, Jerry never surrendered the hope that he could see the project through. Writing about the film in 1982, he said, "I'm still hoping to get the litigation cleared away so I can go back to Stockholm and shoot three or four more scenes." In 1984 he spoke of finishing the film—and of making *The Nutty Professor II*.

Eventually, *The Day the Clown Cried* became a sore point with him; interviewers who poked too closely at the topic could find themselves subjected to withering retorts. A pair of *Cahiers du cinéma* interviewers who went to speak with him in 1993 wrote that they'd been cautioned in advance against mentioning the film.

Just as he had sworn to himself that he would someday see a cure for muscular dystrophy, he swore he would live to see the release of *The Day the Clown Cried:* "One way or another, I'll get it done. The picture must be seen, and if by no one else, at least by every kid in the world who's only heard there was such a thing as the Holocaust."

He no doubt meant what he said, even if he was unconsciously paraphrasing the famous malapropism of Samuel Goldwyn: "I don't care if it doesn't make a nickel. I just want every man, woman, and child in America to see it!"

In the spring of 1972 Frank Tashlin died after suffering two heart attacks in a span of three days. He had directed his last film four years earlier, but his career had started to peter out a few years before that, at roughly the time that he and Jerry stopped working together. Hollywood had apparently come to see him as "that Jerry Lewis director" and relegated him to movies with Phyllis Diller and an aging Bob Hope.

In the last years of his life Tashlin had turned to writing children's books, and one in particular captured his resentment at having been abandoned by Hollywood. Peter Bogdanovich described it in an obituary in *The New York Times* as being about "a carefree possum hanging contentedly from a tree. Some people come along and, because he is hanging upside down, they mistake his smile for a frown, and proceed to take him into civilization in order to make him happy. After several days' exposure to the real world, he has been made so miserable by what he has seen that his mouth turns downward sadly—though, because he is still upside down, he finally, to the joy of the people, *appears* to be smiling."

Later that year, when Jerry was performing at a theater in suburban New York City, he got a call backstage from his mother. Danny Lewis had had a stroke. Jerry flew down to Miami, where his parents had moved once Danny had finally thrown in the towel on his career. Danny spent weeks in the hospital, and when he finally came home to his luxurious condominium, he was diminished in both body and mind. He spent his days in bed and in a wheelchair, attended to by his wife and an in-home nurse, singing occasionally in what his son proudly boasted was still perfect pitch, but unable at other times to remember what he'd eaten an hour earlier.

As Jerry's working life now consisted almost solely of live appearances in hotels, casinos, dinner theaters, and in the summer, outdoor amphitheaters, he worked Miami into his schedule more frequently so he could see more of his parents. But he was still in demand for overseas performances, which could be staged as events and were therefore much more lucrative than domestic appearances. In the winter of 1972–73 he toured the world as he had two years before—

Europe, Australia, Africa. In Hobart, Tasmania, he played a round of golf and struck an eleven-year-old boy on the head with an errant tee shot. In South Africa, he and Patti received a traditional Zulu welcome, and a miles-long throng of well-wishers ushered his motorcade into Johannesburg. "I have that welcome on tape," he told friends back home. "Nothing like that would happen here."

In March 1973 he and Milton Berle played a two-week engagement at the Deauville Hotel in Miami. It was a disaster. Berle treated Jerry like hired help: Even though he wrote the routines they were to do together to segue between Berle's opening act and his own closing act, Jerry had to listen while Berle dictated tempos and line readings and bits of stage business as if Jerry were still the same green kid who once guested on "Texaco Star Theater." Worse, the crowds didn't go for Jerry's act. Where Vegas and Tahoe and Catskills audiences brought their own energy to the theater with them, the retired Jewish couples who swelled a Miami crowd seemed to take Jerry's energy as an affront. Plus, the Deauville had booked the show into an enormous room that was only half-full for most of the performances. "We were wrong to come here," Jerry told Patti. "The place is wrong. I don't belong in Miami."

As the engagement wore on, he grew increasingly bitter about his situation. When Jan Murray and his wife, Toni, came backstage one night to share Jerry's birthday with him, Jerry nostalgically spoke of the reception he'd received in foreign cities on his recent tour and pronounced, "Miami's a toilet. The best thing you can do for it is to pull the chain."

Some days later, in his hotel room with his assistant, Bob Harvey, he launched into a drunken tirade. "Miami sucks!" he shouted. "The people here know from nothing. *Nothing* do they know. They know 'shit' and they know 'fuck,' and anything else is out of their league. If you don't open with 'fuck,' you bomb. 'Hickory dickory dock, the mouse ran up the clock: Fuck him, let him stay there.' Then you're a hit."

He slammed a wine bottle against a wall: "I christen this hotel 'Motherfucker'! Pull out the pilings, you sons of bitches!" And then he busied himself setting an ashtray, a toilet bowl, and a tiled bathroom floor on fire with lighter fluid. "That's it," he screamed, as Harvey raced around putting out flames. "Burn! Burn, you motherfucker! Burn down the fucking hotel! Burn down the whole fucking town!"

The ugly finale of the trip came when Jerry was served with a lawsuit in his Deauville Hotel dressing room one night after a show. A group of Jerry Lewis Cinema franchisees led by Karlene Cobb was seeking $3 million in damages for fraud, breach of contract, and antitrust practices. Network Cinema Corporation executives were aware of the pending litigation, which they'd first heard about the previous fall, and they dismissed the incident in Miami as a publicity stunt. But there was no denying that the Jerry Lewis Cinemas were in trouble, even as the chain was expanding in Europe. The hope that there would be 3,000 Jerry

Lewis Cinemas by 1976 was becoming increasingly remote; by February 1973 there were a mere 190 theaters.

And those venues weren't doing very well. It had, in fact, become clear that there simply weren't enough G-rated movies to keep the theaters stocked with the sort of fare they were meant to show. Some franchisees took matters into their own hands in ways that frankly embarrassed the corporation. In December, for instance, a Jerry Lewis Theater in Greenville, South Carolina, had shown such films as A *Clockwork Orange, Oh! Calcutta!*, and *Fritz the Cat*, brazenly violating the chain's family pictures policy.

That failure to judge what sort of product would be available to the marketplace seemed to extend to Jerry's choice of business associates. When the corporation found itself suddenly undercapitalized, and Jerry found himself without the support of the partners who'd lured him into the exhibition business, the Jerry Lewis Cinema Corporation declared bankruptcy, thus encouraging investors to sue for the return of their franchise fees. Nearly a decade of litigation commenced, and Jerry was subjected to lawsuits in several states.

Years later, he would view the collapse of his exhibition enterprise from a philosophical remove: "My dream was to see it say 'Jerry Lewis and Sons Theaters.' And to put product in there that I'd be proud of. But the product was gone ten days after we even started the fucking company. Oh, well."

At the time, however, he was desperate. He had an unreleased film on his hands, he had no offers of any sort for film or TV work ahead of him, his father sat addled in an apartment in a city he detested, his oldest son couldn't shake his drug use or find a way back to a productive civilian life, he himself was taking as many as fifteen Percodans a day—even though he no longer had a prescription for so much as one—and now he was facing a legal cost he couldn't possibly survive if the time ever came that he had to pay it.

He did his ritual tour of summer theaters that year, appeared as a clown on a German TV special (a live appearance in Cologne was canceled by the threat of anti-American student rioting), held his telethon in Vegas for the first time ever. Even then he couldn't get things right. Thinking aloud on the telethon about a divinity who could create a disease that took such a horrible toll on innocent children, he told a national audience, "God goofed," invoking a minor furor in the press ("Not even a militant atheist is as offensive as someone who thinks he is so important he reduces God to a bungling middleman," wrote one critic) and doubtless repelling viewers across the country.

On October 2, 1973, his twenty-ninth wedding anniversary, the pain, the drugs, and the hopeless situation he felt himself to be in finally overwhelmed him. "I felt everything was finished," he confessed years later. "I didn't have the stamina to sustain one more sweep of that red hand on the clock." He retreated to his sanctum sanctorum, his private bathroom, opened the padlock on a drawer, pulled out a .38 revolver, loaded it, and stuck it in his mouth.

"I came as close as you could come," he told a reporter. "I had the thumb in the cocking position. You know how you chew a piece of gum sometimes with a bit of tinfoil still stuck to it, that terrible feeling? Put a fucking .38 barrel in your mouth and see what that tastes like." He sat thinking of the peace and consolation that would follow if he pulled the trigger: "It would be over so fast, and would be such a relief." And then he heard a couple of his sons running through the house, playing and laughing, and he managed to stop himself from crossing an irreversible line. He took the gun from his mouth and rode his anguish out.

It had to have been the drugs.

Yes, his workaholism had been neutered by his lack of career opportunities. Yes, his financial situation was precarious. Yes, he was anguished at having been abandoned by a public that less than a decade earlier overwhelmed him with adoration. Yes, he was in frequent, horrid pain.

But suicide? Even if the melodrama of the scene is exaggerated, the very notion that he would choose to share such an anecdote indicated how seriously wrong things had gone for him. He had lost control of himself. The drugs were in charge.

He was hooked on Percodans not only because of their inherently addictive nature but also because of their effect on his unremitting pain. He needed them just to get out of bed. "When I got up in the morning," he told a reporter, "it would take twenty minutes for me to get out of bed, having slept in a brace all night. When I stayed in hotels, I would give a bellboy twenty-five or thirty dollars every day to knock on my door, open it with a pass key, crush three Percodans with a spoon for me, then dissolve them in hot water from room service so they would get into the bloodstream faster. I'd lie there for twenty fucking minutes until I could move, then get up and pop a Dexedrine."

The addiction had more than just physical and emotional costs. Although his income had greatly diminished in recent years, he was spending more and more money on drugs. He paid a thousand dollars for ten Percodans one night and then five hundred dollars for a single one the very next day. He was buying uppers. And he was buying marijuana, which he had begun to experiment with as both a painkiller and an aphrodisiac. ("Once I came from January 3 to mid-February," he told a reporter about his experiences combining sex and drugs. "It was the longest shoot in the history of America. I mean, it sucked my skin inward and became part of my marrow.")

Yet even though he was in the throes of addiction, he recognized that his drug abuse had been instigated by the need to relieve pain. And in an effort to address his pain medically, he was willing to travel the world and try almost anything. He visited neurosurgeons throughout Europe and Asia in hope that something could be done to repair or relieve the damage in his spine. One physician suggested an operation that could as easily leave him paralyzed as cure him. He demurred. And as his quest for a remedy continued, so did his Percodan habit.

The boys weren't aware of just how severe the problem had become. But they noticed undeniable changes in his behavior. As Anthony recalled it, he had turned from the angry man of a few years earlier to a detached one. "The results of Dad's addiction were mostly passive," he said, "such as his sleeping on the couch all day." He was no longer the heroic father whose return to the house marked a highlight of the day. Indeed, he carried himself like a stranger. "The drugs put great spiritual distance between him and all of us," Anthony reflected. "He was basically in his own world." (Only Gary, who'd had his own drug problems, might've been savvy to just how badly off Jerry was; in March 1972 Gary was subjected to embarrassing publicity when he was arrested in Van Nuys and accused of illegal possession of sleeping pills, charges of which he was subsequently cleared.)

Patti, however, knew more than her sons about the side effects of her husband's spinal injury and drug abuse: bowel irregularities (including what he called "shameful" incidents and "weeks" of constipation), impotence, disequilibrium, numbness, blurred vision. To her, though, the onset of Jerry's drug abuse was related not only to the physical pain he was suffering but to the state of his career. "I felt he was going in circles of diminishing size," she remembered, knowing how desperately he had worked in the past and how desperately he desired to keep on working. She came to see that his loss of himself in drugs had supplanted his former loss of himself in work. "I believe Jerry's work symptoms were precursors to his chemical addictions," she said. "It would have been wonderful if, in some way, we could have personally filled Jerry's empty space with our love for him, and our deep pride in him." But he needed more than his family's support—he wanted the world's. And it was no longer his to summon forth.

Two books about Jerry were published in 1973, and even that honor proved mixed for him. In France, Robert Benayoun published *Bonjour, Monsieur Lewis*, a cornucopia of praise for the great comic star, part scrapbook, part wacky French theoretical treatise, part exacting factual encyclopedia; the handsome work was never translated into English, but Jerry had a case of French copies in his office. At almost the same time, Arthur Marx, Groucho's son, published a scathing and factually dubious dual biography of Dean and Jerry. *Everybody Loves Somebody Sometime (Especially Himself)* painted a portrait of Jerry as a petty, egoistic has-been while depicting Dean as a dignified, talented scallywag. Jerry loathed the book; he claimed never to have read it, but he attacked NBC talk-show host Tom Snyder for asking him about it.

The two books perfectly embodied the chicken-and-egg situation of Jerry's career: Just as he was beloved and loathed at once, he had no work and was in no shape to work. Throughout the mid-1970s, he toured Vegas, the Catskills, the Poconos, Reno and Tahoe, Miami, Europe, and the summer amphitheater circuit. He still traveled in the style he had become accustomed to in his flush days—over one hundred pieces of luggage, limousines, and first-class airline seats. And he still comported himself like a persnickety star if things weren't to his liking. In August 1975 he became furious when his two-night engagement at a twenty-thousand-seat arena in Cleveland was cut back to one night, shouting at the promoters and refusing to meet some locals who'd won a contest by raising money for the MDA (the one-night stand, as it happened, drew only five thousand attendees, even with Pat Boone and Connie Stevens sharing the bill). In September 1976 he stormed off the stage at the Westbury Music Fair, a suburban New York theater that had long been a regular venue for him, when the sound system acted up.

He made a very few TV appearances, mostly as a talk show guest (in 1974 he did some deep-sea fishing on "Celebrity Sportsman"). There was talk that he would appear in a Broadway comedy—entitled, ironically, "Feeling No Pain"— that never came to be. He even turned up with Patti on a couple of televised specials with evangelist Oral Roberts and directed a short film for Roberts's syndicated television network.

This last curiosity resulted in part from Patti's withdrawal from the turmoil of her marriage into a variety of spiritual outlets—Roberts's ministry among them—and from a mutual recognition between Jerry and Roberts that they were, in fact, at the top of the heap in the same business. Roberts had been one of the inventors of televangelism, soliciting money from a worldwide congregation linked electronically by television. And Jerry, of course, had become more and more widely known to the American public as The Man Who Did the Telethon.

The 1970s were the absolute heyday of "The Jerry Lewis Telethon" and of the telethon as a genre. What had begun as a last-gasp version of the vaudeville and burlesque revue in the late 1950s was by the 1970s a practice conducted on a huge scale by a few charities (the United Negro College Fund, the March of Dimes, the Fund for Cerebral Palsy), by religious entrepreneurs like Roberts, and by Jerry Lewis.

Jerry had turned the telethon into his career—indeed, the fight against muscular dystrophy seemed to have become his life's work. And ironically, while his film, TV, and stage projects floundered and even dried up, his philanthropic career burgeoned. In 1972, the last year the telethon originated in New York, he raised $9.2 million in a broadcast that was carried on 140 stations. Moving to Vegas the next year, he raised about 35 percent more ($12.4 million) on almost 10 percent more stations. Every year, the thing grew more lucrative and spread its electronic net wider. In 1975, when $18.8 million was raised, "The Jerry Lewis

Telethon," carried on 195 stations, was the thirteenth most-watched broadcast in the history of the Nielsen TV ratings.

It was a queer sort of triumph for Jerry, who broke down into tears of gratitude at various moments during each annual broadcast—most characteristically during the finale, when he sang "You'll Never Walk Alone," a staggeringly inappropriate song from Rogers and Hammerstein's *Carousel*, to the "kids" for whom he exhausted himself. On the one hand, he was the star of a hit show—a hit for which the nation not only dropped all else on a summer holiday weekend but actually opened its wallets, to staggering results. On the other hand, whereas the success of his films had always seemed to him an obvious personal triumph, he could never be certain with the telethon that it was to him and not his cause that the American public was responding with its support.

Throughout the decade, the telethon came to embody a kind of show-business excess that previous generations had unthinkingly supported but that seemed self-parodic in the age of punk rock and "Saturday Night Live." It regularly featured such performers as Charo, Don Rickles, Tony Orlando and Dawn, Norm Crosby, Steve and Eydie, Sammy Davis, Jr., Vic Damone—exemplars of a waning era of showmanship and entertainment. Jerry was flanked by a cadre of emcees who spelled him for various episodes during the broadcast—David Hartman, Chad Everett, and the omnipresent Ed McMahon, who early in his service with the telethon became famous within the organization for his ability to predict the final tally that the tote board would register.

With time, the telethon would become synonymous with the sort of tackiness and glitz that Americans understood by the words "Las Vegas." Of course, there was more than just Vegas on the screen each Labor Day: The telethon still had a New York adjunct, along with a Los Angeles feed, and viewers would be treated to entertainment segments broadcast from those locations and featuring performers who couldn't be in Vegas in person. And in each of the MDA's satellite cities—the two hundred or so stations across the country that carried the broadcast—local celebrities such as weathermen and disc jockeys spoke directly to their neighbors in an effort to raise money. But the telethon's emphasis on money, gaudiness, broad emotionalism, and lounge-style entertainment all glittered with the vulgarity the casino city represented.

This tacky aura was reinforced by the impression that the telethon had mutated over the years from a charity event into a Jerry Lewis event. It was more than just the elision of the words "muscular dystrophy" from the name of the program, more than just the omnipresent cartoon caricature of Jerry, more even than the streams of celebrities coming on stage and singing Jerry's praises. It was the sense—not just among show people, but among the public at large—that Jerry had come to see the telethon (and the fight against neuromuscular disease) as an extension of himself.

The telethon utterly consumed him. Where in the 1960s he would meet a handful of times per year with MDA officials, film a few public service announcements, and maybe do something as visible as a telethon, by the 1970s he was devoting himself to MDA business more than to his own career affairs. There were frequent meetings (he had an office on the twenty-seventh floor of the MDA's New York headquarters and personalized it with his usual decor of mementoes, gadgets, and photos, though none of his family), there were appearances across the country at events staged by MDA's corporate sponsors, gratis performances at charity events sponsored by various celebrities in exchange for their work on Jerry's telethon, commercial tapings for MDA and for its sponsors, planning sessions and rehearsals for the telethon. . . . It never stopped. Even for a man who could be consumed by his work, it was a harsh routine. And it paradoxically kept him from the work that had made him what he was. As his manager, Joe Stabile, told a reporter in the mid-1970s, "Jerry spends so much of the year on muscular dystrophy that he's not developing film and TV projects like he should be doing."

Spurring him on, inevitably, was the sheer success of the thing: high Nielsen ratings, a wide network of stations, record-breaking donations each and every year. Ever since *Boeing Boeing*, Jerry had tried to find a forum in which the public would allow him into its good graces as an adult. It couldn't have been a coincidence that the telethon began less than a year after that film's failure. Seeking a way out of his screeching Kid character, he tried romantic leads and sophisticated comedies, but only the persona he presented to the public in the telethon seemed to hook an audience. Furthermore, it was a success in television, his old bête noire, on his own terms: no network executives, no censorious sponsors, no week-to-week grind of ratings worries and rehearsals. For a single day, all over the country, he had, in effect, his own TV network and the freedom to do whatever his instincts told him would be right.

To his family, the telethon was both a point of deep pride and another omnipresent obligation that stole him from their company. Patti saw in his dedication to the cause the same sort of all-consuming escape that had driven him into performance and drugs and performances. She was glad to see that the boys were asked to assist their father in the telethons more and more frequently as they grew older. But she recognized that the telethons were a source of pain for her sons—"His work addiction left its mark on the boys"—and that they were especially stung to see their father, who so rarely had time for them, pleading in public for a group of strangers he identified as his "kids."

In fact, this aspect of the MDA fund-raising drives—the use of children to tweak the national conscience—was intimately intertwined in the public consciousness with Jerry's very personality. Other charities—especially the March of Dimes, whose campaigns the MDA imitated in particular—had long used children as symbols of the ravages of disease in an attempt to curry America's guilt and open its wallets. But Jerry and the MDA made a particular point of the tragedy of childhood disease.

To be true, this approach was, for the most part, apropos to muscular dystrophy: Duchenne's muscular dystrophy, the disease that undoubtedly first drew Jerry's attention to the cause, cruelly attacked young boys and rarely allowed its victims to live into their twenties. (There were, of course, many other strains of neuromuscular disease that the MDA was invested in discovering cures for, including amyotrophic lateral sclerosis—better known as ALS, or Lou Gehrig's disease—which most commonly struck down people in their thirties or even older.)

To the end of exploiting the pediatric aspect of neuromuscular disease, the MDA pursued two lines of attack that eventually became identical in the public consciousness with the telethon and with the disease itself: the use of an annual "poster child," a squeaky-clean, photogenic young muscular dystrophy sufferer; and the creation of the slogan "Jerry's Kids." The success of these tactics became evident as references to poster children and "Jerry's Kids" bled into the popular culture as phrases in the national lexicon, as fodder for stand-up comics, even as appropriated by the Grateful Dead (the rock band whose acolytes adopted the name "Jerry's Kids" in honor of guitarist Jerry Garcia). Promoted tirelessly in MDA-related advertising for national products such as breakfast cereal, soda pop, and beer, and on ubiquitous billboards and point-of-purchase ads in convenience stores, fast-food restaurants, and even bowling alleys all over the nation, the notion that Jerry was doing all he could for some otherwise helpless kids became an intrinsic part of the MDA's charity drive.

Of all of the telethons Jerry did for MDA, the archetypical one had to have been the 1976 show. An audience of between 84 million and 100 million viewers tuned in to two hundred stations during the twenty-one-and-a-half-hour broadcast and pledged $21,723,813 in donations. They saw more than 150 acts, ranging from Tony Bennett, the Moiseyev Dancers, and Lola Falana to the University of Kansas cheerleaders and novelty lounge acts right off an antique vaudeville stage. And they got nearly a full day's worth of a fifty-year-old Jerry cajoling, cavorting, pleading, excoriating, singing, dancing, and mugging his heart out at the Sahara Hotel's Space Center convention facility, in an effort to get them to donate, as he put it in his opening remarks, "a dollar more." (Each year, the MDA boasted, the telethon earned more than it did the previous year, and on this eleventh annual broadcast, Jerry kept that record intact; the 1975 broadcast had pulled $18.8 million.)

As in previous years, the MDA hierarchy was in attendance: Bob Ross, Mucio Delgado, and MDA president Pat Weaver, among others. But added to the organizational family was an entire group of technicians and other volunteers who over the years had come to make up the telethon's in-studio "family": director Artie Forrest; his wife, Marcy, the show's talent coordinator; his son, Richard, the associate producer; tote board tabulators Fred Schaefer and Jerry Weinberg; Jerry's manager, Joe Stabile, and his wife, Claudia, also serving in production capacities; even the men of the United States Navy, who for years had served the telethon—in uniform—as ushers and a backup security force. Lou Brown, Jerry's longtime bandleader, was on hand. And five of Jerry's sons (Gary was the sole exception) were listed in the show's credits as production assistants, along with the Forrests' sixteen-month-old daughter, Nicole. (Patti, too, was there for moral support, though she didn't speak on camera or appear in the credits.) The telethon was so big that Bicentennial summer that three journalists for major publications turned up in Las Vegas to chronicle the overnight grind: Harry Shearer (whose story, "Telethon," ran in *Film Comment*), Michael Tolkin (the future author of *The Player*, then writing for the *Village Voice*), and Jerry's old friend Peter Bogdanovich (on assignment for *Esquire*).

The show was fabulously costly: $1 million for lights, video, sound, microphones, sets, and so on, including payments to the stations on the Love Network to compensate for the advertising revenue they would forfeit during the broadcast; $1 million for the elaborate phone system that was the hub of the pledge drive; $750,000 to the Theater Authority for performance waivers that allowed entertainers to donate their appearance time. Jerry had a trailer parked inside the hotel as his private retreat and dressing room; it was outfitted with a milkshake machine, oxygen tanks, kosher salamis, turkey legs, bottled water, and blackberry brandy. A consort of private security guards augmented the Sahara's own force. Every member of the crew wore a custom-made dark blue shirt with an Al Hirschfeld caricature of Jerry crooning into a microphone emblazoned on its back. Jerry had a large red book with "Telethon '76" embossed in gold ink on the cover. Every conceivable inch of space was taken up with Jerry's logo and the title of the show. Just like the Jerry Lewis Theater on Vine Street, the Sahara had been thoroughly rebuilt and refitted to his exacting specifications.

Not only did the schedule call for Jerry to stay up for the entire twenty-one and a half hours of the show (he'd be onstage almost all that time), but he would also be up for a full day before that, rehearsing, revving up his crew and staff, seeing to the sort of last-minute details he characteristically refused to delegate to others.

At 6:00 P.M. Pacific time on Sunday, September 6, the show began. The opening number combined footage of Jerry pensively preparing for the telethon in his trailer with a prerecorded vocal track—a ballad about his mixed feelings at the outset of the huge task before him ("Before the show begins tonight, my life goes flashing by . . ."). As the song wound down, he walked deliberately toward the stage and then through the curtains, where a standing ovation greeted him. He immediately launched into a bossa nova–style rendition of Stevie Wonder's

"You Are the Sunshine of My Life," with special lyrics written for the telethon.
After another ovation, he introduced Ed McMahon ("my pussycat") and began
his first speech of the evening, telling the country about his need to raise that
"dollar more." Then came the first of the myriad of guests, singer Vicki Carr,
who capped her performance with a plea for donations in her native Spanish (off
camera, Jerry mocked her by muttering gibberish to an appreciative group of
sponsors in a down-front box).

Through the following hours, the familiar telethon pattern would be followed—a roundelay of live acts (Perry Como, Tony Bennett, Lainie Kazan, Abbe
Lane, Dionne Warwick, Joe Williams, Jan Murray, Marilyn McCoo and Billy
Davis, and Freda Payne among them), a parade of sponsors bearing huge checks,
a dozen or so songs from Jerry, and educational and inspirational segments featuring MDA researchers and MDA patients and their families.

Breaking up this flow were three taped segments featuring Jerry and an uncredited actress as the parents of a child with neuromuscular disease—played in
clown makeup, in pantomime. In a similarly maudlin vein, Jerry sang live the jin-
gle that had been used by 7-Eleven to advertise its campaign asking America to
let MDA keep its change for Jerry's Kids. "Can I have your love?" it began, a raw
expression of Jerry's defining impulse. Somehow in his heart he had conflated
America's charitable instincts with love for himself as a public figure and even as
one more lonely child. Of course, he could be so shameless about his emotional
neediness only on the telethon—no Vegas or Catskills audience would tolerate
such a plea for pathos. He admitted as much to a reporter soon after the
telethon ended, saying that in those other contexts "people are paying money to
see a man work, whereas here I am begging. There's a big difference. There has
to be." And as a beggar, he seemed to feel, he had the right to emote from a profoundly needy portion of his soul.

The scheduled highlight of the 1976 telethon was certainly the appearance
of Frank Sinatra, who was performing at Caesar's Palace, just down the strip.
Sinatra hadn't appeared live on a muscular dystrophy telethon since Dean and
Jerry's epochal one in 1953, and at the height of the "Ol' Blue Eyes" phase of his
career, he was easily the biggest name on the show. He would do two sets, the
first coming right before his own midnight show at Caesar's. His appearance was
the occasion for yet another layer of security to spring up at the Sahara—thick-
necked, menacing types who unconvincingly sported the identification pins that
marked the hotel's own, less imposing guards. Finally, preceded by Pat Henry
and Sam Butera, the two comedians who were billed under him in his own act,
Sinatra hit the stage. It was just before midnight Pacific time—almost 3 A.M.
back east.

After performing a song, Sinatra called Jerry over, presented him with a
check from a Vegas hotel, and accepted Jerry's hugging and cooing. "This man

meant $2 million to us last year," revealed Jerry, speaking of Sinatra's videotaped 1975 performance.

Then Sinatra began to ad-lib, catching Jerry, who had a page of scripted material in his hand, off guard.

"Listen," he said. "I have a friend who loves what you do every year, and who just wanted to come out." He turned toward the wings: "Would you send out my friend?"

The curtains parted, and a shriek went up in the audience. Jerry couldn't see what was happening at first. And then Sinatra's friend turned the corner and walked toward center stage.

It was Dean.

They hadn't seen each other in more than a dozen years, and now, on live television, in front of millions of people and the godfather of show business, they were together.

Dean, looking lean and sharp, wore a wide, mischievous grin as he paced deliberately toward center stage, a cigarette in his right hand. Jerry, shaking his head at Sinatra with an amazed "how-could-you" demeanor, passed his microphone to Lou Brown and tucked his pages into his jacket. Dean approached him from behind Sinatra, almost timidly, but Jerry reached right out to him. With huge, heartfelt grins, they embraced. Dean was closest to the camera, his eyes locked closed in a swoon.

They held on to each other for a good ten seconds, Jerry mumbling to Sinatra, Dean kissing Jerry on the cheek. They drifted slowly apart, but they couldn't keep from touching one another: Jerry held Dean's lapel, Dean tapped Jerry on the nose.

It was so intimate Sinatra couldn't stand it: "All right, all right, break it up. What is this here?" he barked in mock gruffness, stepping in between them. But he, too, felt the authentic warmth of the moment. "I think it's about time, don't you?" Sinatra asked, to which Dean responded by kissing *him*.

Jerry could only stand staring at his former partner, his mouth churning as he bit his lower lip in an effort to allay the tears that already filled his eyes. He and Dean reached across Sinatra and patted each other on the cheek. Jerry muttered to Sinatra, "You son of a bitch," breaking all three of them up. Sinatra finally backed away: "There they are, folks." All the while a standing ovation washed over them. It was an undeniably historic show-biz moment, electric even for those who had no taste for Jerry or his charity work.

Finally, after almost two minutes of nervous stares and smiles and all that wild applause, Jerry found a way out of it. He slipped into the Kid: "So, are you workin'?" It was a great line, and Dean matched it: "I do a couple of weeks at the MGM Grand." Jerry, encouraged, tried another line, saying he'd heard a rumor that they'd split up, but Dean didn't respond. Sinatra stepped in, shooing Jerry away; Jerry made a big show of dejection as he departed, shuffling his feet and whining, "There he goes again!" Then Sinatra and Dean started to sing, and Dean did something pointedly antic and attention grabbing. While Sinatra sang relatively straight, Dean screwed up the lyrics, wandered around the stage, and broke jokes to the band. *He did Jerry*, and Jerry stood at his dais chewing his lip in amazement. He was thinking of how they could be friends again: "We'd play golf together; we'd talk and reminisce, catch up on the last twenty years, maybe look forward to better times ahead." But Dean's act seemed a redoubt to such a scenario. As Jerry had after the split, he seemed to be expressing his independence by playing both halves of their old act. They embraced one last time and Dean left, waving. "So long, Jer!"

Jerry was floored. The telethon was supposed to be an emotional roller coaster for him, but nothing could compete with what he'd just been through. Sadly, he was almost unsure that it had even happened. He was so addled by his Percodan-and-Dexedrine diet that he would need to be reminded of Dean's appearance. "I didn't have any recollection of it the next day," he later confessed. "I had to run a videotape to see what happened because I was told that Dean and I were on television." Worse, he felt some resentment. Dean had smelled of booze; "Jerry was very hurt by the fact that Dean was drunk," a friend told a reporter soon afterward. Indeed, the next afternoon, when a tape of the reunion was replayed for the national audience—most of whom had been asleep when it occurred—Jerry spoke to the telethon audience in a way that denied his own emotions: "I have some strong principles. That man made a success of me, but I didn't like some of the things he did, and I'm sure he didn't like some of the things I did. And I still wouldn't work with that drunk."

It was, of course, partly a joke, but its grotesquely hectoring tone was consistent with the sort of posture Jerry generally adopted in the later hours of telethons. Early on Monday morning, for instance, after Freda Payne had performed for them, Jerry sensed a lethargy settling in over his in-studio audience and chose to counter it with a lecture. "I think it's very important to make two disclaimers," he began. "I have to do this, because my instinct usually serves me well. One: The early hours of the morning. People that are seated in the studio. It's hardly possible for you to be totally energetic and enthusiastic. But these performers are coming from all parts of the world to help us. They have no way of knowing our appreciation and gratitude. They only know and live and *survive* on an audience's applause. So if you would be kind enough, as you indeed are the audience in the studio, if you could just acknowledge that, it only takes a moment, and I repeat, as any good doctor will tell you, it's good for the system. 'Cause you'll *atrophy* just sitting there. It makes performers feel good, and it then lessens my load of having to let them know you are indeed grateful. Because that's just words. Who says they really believe that? So I would appreciate it if you would consider that, the next time a performer steps on this stage."

He continued with another pointed speech about the need to greet taped appearances by performers such as Kirk Douglas, Mary Tyler Moore, and Peggy Lee with appreciative ovations as well: "I think they're entitled to the same applause as the performer that's here live."

Later in the day, as the tote board showed a number that threatened not to eclipse last year's total, he launched into a tarter tirade: "We've had fun. I guess we've been a little lazy. We really got some work to do. I've been tiptoeing. I've been passive, and I guess that doesn't do the job. I have a reputation for being abrasive, for being an egomaniac. I guess I have to turn some of that on now. You might examine the possibility that I'm a fool, doing what I'm doing up here. I doubt that. I like what I am. Maybe it's time for you to examine what you are."

He then grabbed a white bucket from a stagehand and sallied into the audience to provoke them into emptying their wallets for him, announcing, "End of Mr. Nice Guy." It was a routine as old as the telethon itself: The band played a rousing number and Jerry ran up and down the aisles, whooping and teasing and shouting and practically grabbing money right out of people's hands. When it was over, he returned to the stage and showed off his loot to the camera: "See this? I grabbed a bundle from this little cocking crowd."

The hours ticked down. Oral Roberts came on to endorse the MDA. Jerry sang a rewritten version of Barry Manilow's "Could It Be Magic?" "Help me to help them *now! now!*" Sinatra returned, in a leisure suit, to sing "Bad, Bad, Leroy Brown." Lola Falana, the Moiseyev Dancers, another replay of the Martin-and-Lewis reunion.

Finally, just after 3 P.M., the tote board rang up $20,160,994: a new record, and the first time the tally ever exceeded $20 million. In the remaining half-hour, another $1.5 million would be added. But Jerry was coasting by then, assured of his "dollar more" and then some. He made a final, grateful confessional speech: "My sons can say that I did something with my life, but I want to say that I'm ashamed of myself. Around nine-thirty this morning I almost gave up. Oh, boy, I almost gave up. I was quitting emotionally. Last year's figures had been much higher and I didn't think I could make it, but this is proof that if you hang in there, the man upstairs, he won't let you down." He launched into his obligatory finale, "You'll Never Walk Alone," with the inevitable catch in the throat toward the end. Putting his microphone down, he turned and walked directly off the stage, ignoring the standing ovation he left in his wake.

Most telethons ended right there, with the tote board still tallying pledges (in those pre-computer revolution days, it ran about forty-five minutes behind the actual phoned-in totals; moreover, the MDA always proudly boasted that its actual donation levels perennially exceeded the pledge total by some 5 to 10 percent.) The momentous Martin-and-Lewis reunion, however, provoked a few overtures on Jerry's part toward his old partner; he sent Dean a handwritten note that evening, and, getting no response, sent gold medallions to both Dean and

Sinatra a few days later, engraving messages of thanks and love on them. Sinatra phoned his thanks; once again, Dean remained silent. The following August, Jerry had Joe Stabile visit Dean at the MGM Grand to invite him to that year's telethon and to request a meeting between Dean and Jerry at Dean's convenience. Dean promised to visit Jerry at the Sahara, but never showed up.

Peter Bogdanovich had long looked forward to a reconciliation of the former partners. "A few years before," he remembered, "Harold Hayes at *Esquire* said to me, 'We want to do a Christmas cover. We want to do Jerry and Dean embracing. We want to do "Peace on Earth, goodwill to men."' Jerry was willing to do it, but Dean wouldn't."

The 1976 telethon gave Bogdanovich new hope, however, that the old partners might work together on a movie he was hoping to get off the ground with Sinatra in the lead role. "Frank coordinated it," he recalled. "I was working on Jerry, and Frank was working on Dean. And Frank got Dean to say okay. Or, as Frank quoted him, 'Who gives a fuck?' Which was his way of saying, 'All right, let's do it.' And Jerry said he'd do it, and it just didn't work out for a variety of reasons." The plot sounded irresistible: "The characters never spoke to one another till the very end. Frank was the leader of these guys who were degenerate gamblers and really down on their luck and just scraping by, conning people, stealing. And Dean and Jerry played these two guys who were in the same crowd but never spoke to each other in person. It all went through Frank or one of the other guys in the group. And they didn't actually speak to each other until the very end, and then it was just a look where they kind of both smiled at each other."

But like the hypothetical reunion of the team, it never came to be.

It was during this same period of unprecedented fund-raising success that the telethon first had suspicions cast on it. There were whispers, never substantiated, that Jerry skimmed money off the top—why else would he work so hard at it, right?—and that the organization covered up the profits it diverted to its spokesman with crooked bookkeeping practices (one of the most nefarious theories was that Jerry took for himself all of the monies received beyond the actual pledge total, the famous "extra money"). These charges of fraud were, in part, a manifestation of the public's awareness that Jerry's career had, save for the telethon, all but ended. How, the doubters seemed to ask, could he maintain his famously opulent lifestyle on his meager string of personal appearances? (The answer, as Patti might have told everyone, was "not very well." The Lewises' massive house was, in her words, "falling into disrepair. In fact, the boys often wondered if the house would withstand a good hard wind!" Though she knew about his lavish spending habits—clothes, gifts, absurdly luxurious travel habits—she had no clue how much money he was spending on drugs, amassing, by his own testimony, thousands of pills; besides not working as much as he used to, besides not curtailing his regal ways with money, he had the same financial burden of addiction as any junkie on the street.)

Jerry maintained that conspiracy theories about the telethon reflected not public awareness that his career had slowed but rather the mood of the nation after Watergate. "From 1949 to 1974," he said, "that's twenty-five years—we never heard that Jerry Lewis got paid by the Muscular Dystrophy Association. Never did we receive a piece of mail or a postcard, or hear an innuendo or an assumption. Never, in twenty-five years. You know when it started? Right after August 9, 1974, when Richard Nixon left the White House. The first letter came into my office in New York with that question, then a couple of postcards, then a couple of letters, and then a newspaperman."

The rumors disgusted him, he told a reporter at the time. "I was fucking *beyond* myself to think there are people saying that there was one cocksucker who was saying anything negative." He became physically ill thinking that even in this, the most selfless work he'd ever undertaken, he could be ridiculed. "I would either throw up—literally," he remembered, "or I'd have to stay in bed—twelve, thirteen hours in a dark room—and just lie there." Approached by journalists with charges of malfeasance, he could become hostile and caustic. "Yeah, and every time one of my kids dies, they give me the wheelchair so I can melt it down for an ashtray," was his retort to one. Still, as much as he hated the innuendoes, he knew he couldn't lash out at whispers and shadows.

In August 1977, though, a flesh-and-blood version of his nemesis emerged when he heard that a radio talk-show host in Cleveland had announced on the air that Jerry was pocketing 40 percent of the telethon take. Soon after the telethon, Jerry flew to Cleveland and, along with an MDA lawyer, walked in on the disc jockey unannounced, eliciting an over-the-air apology and a full-page ad in the major Cleveland papers absolving Jerry and the MDA of the charges; the deejay, to cap the episode, was fired.

That same fall, Jerry got another shocking phone call about his charity work. This time, though, it was unbelievably good—an Associated Press reporter calling to get his reaction to the news that Representative Les Aspin of Wisconsin had placed his name in nomination for the Nobel Peace Prize for his efforts in the fight against dystrophy. "Jerry Lewis is a man for all seasons, all people, and all times," announced Aspin. "His name has, in the hearts of millions, become synonymous with peace, love, and brotherhood." The prize, awarded in the fall of 1978, went not to Jerry but to Menachem Begin and Anwar Sadat in the wake of the Camp David accords; but Jerry would boast about his nomination for years, even claiming in an autobiographical 1994 TV special he produced that he was nominated not for his charitable work but "for bringing forty years of laughter to the world."

19.

A Defeated Jew

If the 1976 telethon was a highlight of Jerry's late professional life, it was immediately followed by a disappointment greater in scale and public awareness than even the failure to complete and release *The Day the Clown Cried*. It involved his participation in a revival of *Hellzapoppin'*, the classic Broadway burlesque revue that ran for 1,404 performances when it first opened in 1938.

Under the aegis of Broadway producer Alexander H. Cohen, Jerry would be the focal point of a completely rewritten and restaged version of the very sort of thing he'd grown up admiring and spent his career emulating—"a razzle-dazzle fun house," in the words of Cohen's letter to potential investors. Cohen didn't seem a likely proctor for this sort of stuff—his résumé included such productions as *Ulysses in Nighttown*, *Little Murders*, *Richard Burton's Hamlet*, and long-running performances by the likes of John Gielgud, Marlene Dietrich, Victor Borge, Maurice Chevalier, and Mike Nichols and Elaine May. But he had been a huge fan of the original show in his youth, seeing it some fifteen times, by his reckoning. In fact, he'd mounted a brief revival of *Hellzapoppin'* in 1967 as part of the Montreal Expo, with Soupy Sales in the starring role. With Jerry on board, Cohen felt he could fulfill his longtime dream of bringing the show back to Broadway. Such was his confidence in his star that, aside from Jerry, only Abe Burrows (the writer of *Guys and Dolls*, *How to Succeed in Business Without Really Trying*, and *Cactus Flower*, who'd been hired by Cohen to direct and coauthor the show) was mentioned in the show's prospectus. "With Jerry Lewis," Cohen told Earl Wilson, "you really don't need another star."

By August 1976 financing, schedules and, yes, another star, were in place. Songs had been commissioned from Jule Styne, Hank Beebe, and Cy Coleman; lyrics had been written by Carolyn Leigh and Bill Heyer; choreographer Donald Saddler had been hired. The production was capitalized at $750,000. The largest share of the money came from Cohen's own Brentwood Television corporation, the entity that produced the Tony Awards show. Some came from the Shubert organization. And some came from traditional Broadway angels, private investors whose contributions ranged from one thousand to fifty thousand dollars. The show would begin rehearsals in mid-October in New York, travel for road engagements in Baltimore, Washington, D.C., and Boston, then hold previews in New York leading up to a February 13, 1977, premiere. Costarring with Jerry would be English actress, comedienne, and stage brat Lynn Redgrave.

Just before rehearsals began, Cohen scored the biggest coup of all. He had arranged with NBC to have the New York premiere broadcast live over the network as part of its new weekly series of specials, "The Big Event." Hosted by Flip Wilson, the program would bring viewers backstage to see footage of auditions, rehearsals, out-of-town performances, and finally, ninety minutes of the actual first act of a live Broadway show on opening night. To Cohen, it seemed that "this kind of cross-pollination between the theater and television is long overdue and has enormous potential for the future." To NBC, which invested $350,000 in the show (the costs of which were mounting already), it seemed like a sure-fire ratings hit. To Jerry, the combination of a legitimate Broadway debut and a live national TV event seemed like a living dream: show-business history with him at center stage.

Rehearsals with the cast of forty-eight and a full orchestra began upstairs from Broadway's Minskoff Theater on October 25, and there was trouble almost immediately. Jerry had never taken film direction very docilely, but he had taken it; no one, however, had ever told him what to do on a live stage, not even Dean. He found his instincts continually countered by Abe Burrows, whose ideas as both writer and director of the show were necessarily more defined than Jerry's wild-man tendencies. Furthermore, Jerry was discovering to his frustration that Alexander Cohen wasn't just a money man but an actual hands-on producer with his own ideas of what the show ought to be like. During rehearsals, Cohen—who had invested nearly $800,000 of his own and his company's money in the show, the costs of which were soaring well over $1 million—actually had the effrontery to tell Jerry what was and wasn't funny. When such arguments arose, Jerry would slap a hundred-dollar bill on a table and challenge the producer: "*There!* Now you put a quarter—that's four-hundred-to-one odds, not bad—and we'll see who's right." (Cohen later claimed to have won all the bets: "I hated to take his money so often, and I always gave it to Muscular Dystrophy.")

Such lightheartedness wasn't the rule, however. The frictions between Jerry and those who would supervise him were real, and a mere three weeks into rehearsals, Burrows was squeezed out of the director's chair in favor of Jerry Adler, a Cohen protégé who had been serving as the show's production manager. In effect, went the Broadway buzz, Cohen was having so many problems controlling Jerry that he would essentially direct the show himself with Adler as his assistant.

It was a desperate move—the show was to begin previews in Baltimore three days later.

For the Baltimore premiere, Cohen hired two Amtrak cars to transport more than one hundred Broadway opinion makers south to see both the show and the newly refurbished New Mechanic Theater. What they saw was a show that, even given its revue format, was disjointed and unfinished. *Variety*, while praising Jerry as "once more a man funny in his own time," claimed that the show was "only half the fun it could be" and needed "tons" of work. The show was so un-polished that a local reviewer mistook its inadequacies for disdain toward an out-of-town audience, writing, "How much nicer if Lewis had considered this pre-Broadway presentation as the real thing, before a real live audience, worthy of his ultimate performance."

The biggest problems, it was universally agreed, were in the script. As it stood, the show was, like the original *Hellzapoppin'*, a series of variety acts: a plate spinner, a troupe of jugglers, a dog act, an escape artist, comedy sketches, blackout skits, even faked interruptions from the audience (in one of these, a man in the orchestra seats, hearing that the show consisted of two and a half hours of Jerry Lewis, took out a pistol and shot himself), interspersed with lavish chorus-line numbers. But the once-common taste for this sort of thing had di-minished, or at least mutated into a taste for televised variety shows, which were themselves on the wane: By 1977 only Carol Burnett and Donny and Marie Os-mond were hosting network variety hours.

The closest thing *Hellzapoppin'* had to the sort of story contemporary audi-ences expected was a wisp of a plot about a loud-mouthed usherette who contin-ually interrupted the show only to be invited on stage and perform a production number of her own, "A Miracle Happened." This story was conceived and writ-ten by Jerry, and it was performed by a red-headed ingenue named Jill Choder— the same young actress who had performed with Jerry in the "Mr. and Mrs. Clown" segments that had aired during the 1976 telethon. Everyone involved with the show understood that Jerry had a master-protégée relationship with Choder. As a result, though she struggled with the vocals and the critics ignored or dismissed her, Jerry adamantly insisted that her part not be trimmed or recast.

The box office in Baltimore was a disaster. The show needed to gross $140,000 each week to break even, but it hit that mark in only one of its three weeks. Worse, rumors had begun drifting north to New York about conflicts be-tween Jerry and Redgrave, leading John Clark, the actress's husband, to tell Jerry's long-sympathetic chronicler, gossip columnist Earl Wilson, that "some-body's been circulating false stories that Lynn and Jerry are at each other's throats."

If the stories weren't true in Baltimore, a decidedly different tenor overtook the company by the time it reached Washington's National Theater in Decem-ber. Once again, the critical notices were dismissive. *"Hellzapoppin'* never manages to rise above the level of tired mediocrity," wrote David Richards in *The Washington Star*, adding that Jerry's work consisted of "nothing you haven't seen him do on the small screen." In *The Washington Post*, Richard Coe was moderately kinder, saying that "Act I will do almost as it is. But Act II needs considerable sharpening." The company had arrived in the capital in the midst of a severe, and snowy, deep freeze. The resulting anemic ticket sales meant that the show would lose a record $260,000 during its four-week run.

As soon as the D.C. reviews were in, Jerry called Cohen and Adler to a meeting at his Watergate Hotel suite to discuss serious revisions for the show. Jerry, who was allowed to add his old typewriting pantomime bit and a monologue in the guise of six-year-old "Little Jerry" after Baltimore, had prepared a memo describing the changes he felt were necessary. Chief among these was the dismissal of Redgrave.

Jerry would later claim he never suggested anything of the sort, that it wasn't his costar but the material Cohen had forced on her that he wanted to cut. "I said to Alex, 'How could you demean this artist by giving her shit?'" he said. "'I want her to come off like a class performer. You got her doing chicken shit that chorus girls could do.'" Specifically, he recalled, he was revolted by a production number in which Redgrave played an Eighth Avenue prostitute in hot pants (an easily recognized allusion to her recent film *The Happy Hooker*).

But whatever Jerry's feelings, Cohen and Adler had an agenda of their own. They wanted to keep the hooker number (Cohen infuriated critic-hating Jerry by telling him that he wanted the eminent Boston drama critic Elliot Norton to see the piece before he would consider tossing it), they wanted Choder's role cut substantially, and they wanted Jerry and Redgrave, who were on stage together only for a few brief comic sketches, to perform a duet. A rehearsal of this new song, "Butterflies," was held against Jerry's vehement protest. When he finally acceded, it was with amazingly ill grace, demanding that the rehearsal be held on Christmas morning and lying flat on the floor of the rehearsal space throughout the number. When he was through upstaging his costar, he stood up, announced of the number, "It's cute, like the second stanza of the national anthem," and walked out, refusing to perform it ever again.

The ensuing battle between Jerry and Cohen infected the already sagging morale of he entire troupe. Each man had courted the company with extravagant Christmas gifts—Jerry gave Gucci key rings to chorus and orchestra members and Vivitar cameras to the featured players, along with handwritten notes to everyone. But, as Adler recalled, "Every time I scheduled a 'Butterflies' rehearsal, Jerry said, 'We're not going to do it, no way.'" Actually, Jerry told Adler, there was one way he might change his mind, a way that he knew Cohen would never accept: "He was willing to do the number with Jill, but not Lynn. He just went too far for Jill. Finally it became the burning issue. It went beyond 'Butterflies,' beyond the show. It got into the area of discipline. Was *he* going to run the show or were we?"

Complicating things even more for Jerry was the presence of Patti and some of the boys, who had come to Washington to share the holidays with him. Jerry felt unable to let his family get too close to the show. Although she spent several days back east, Patti saw *Hellzapoppin'* only once, never went backstage, met none of the cast or crew, and wasn't even introduced to Cohen. And though she had witnessed the disasters of the ABC series and *The Day the Clown Cried*, she was amazed at Jerry's total inability to right the situation. "Jerry has a well within himself from which he draws on all sorts of needed solutions. I have seen him draw on that reservoir, successfully, many times," she remembered. "This time, no pails full of wit emerged."

As bad as things were in Washington, Boston was worse. The weather, for one, was more severe. When *Hellzapoppin'* arrived in town, there were twenty-five inches of snow on the ground and the streets were impassable with ice. On January 6, they gave their first performance at the Colonial Theater and waited for Elliot Norton's review to rescue them.

It didn't. "There is some fun in this addled revue," wrote the dean of American drama critics in *The Boston Herald American*, "but the pace is slow and laggard much of the time and the stars don't really have enough fine first rate material." He found the choreography "less than inspired," the sets "gaudy but rarely ever beautiful." Of the variety acts, he noted, "They are all fine, but they are fillers, aren't they?" He castigated Jerry for his Little Jerry bit ("He pulls up his pantlegs, sucks at a lollipop and imitates a five-year-old boy in a number that is geared for the enjoyment of six-year-old boys") and ended with a magisterial note of dismissal: "Shall we say *Hellzapoppin'* needs work? We shall. We must."

Norton's review was actually the kindest the show got in town. *Boston Globe* critic Kevin Kelly absolutely raked Jerry over the coals, referring to his "long-since questionable talents" and his "black patent leather hair," and declaring that "he can't sing (even within an off-key comedic style), can't dance, can't ad lib convincingly." Of the show, he said, "The evening's beckoning, wide open, gap tooth smile finally is revealed as a mock tic paralyzed in place."

It was devastating. Cohen took matters into his hands with ruthless purpose. He cut Choder's "Miracle" number; he cut Redgrave's hooker number. He called his many contacts in New York for a show doctor and finally settled on Tommy Tune, who was in Boston within the week. Along with Cathy Rice, a chorus girl who'd become romantically involved with Adler (and would eventually marry him), Tune created a new opening for the show, a tap dance number. The second act got a new opening as well, a routine in which Jerry would try to emcee but be continually heckled by shills in the audience. These revisions were presented so brusquely to the demoralized cast that one chorus member ran offstage in tears.

On Saturday, January 15, Cohen met with four of Jerry's representatives: manager Joe Stabile, an attorney, and two agents from the William Morris Agency. Cohen was trying to convince them to force Jerry to rehearse "Butterflies" with Redgrave when a call came from the theater, where a matinee performance was in progress. It was Jerry. Having heard of plans to cut more of Choder's part, he was refusing to take the stage for Act 2. Moreover, should Cohen consider coming to the theater to resolve the situation, Jerry declared he had a loaded gun in his dressing room.

The next day, Jerry, Cohen, and three of Jerry's representatives met in a suite at the Copley Plaza Hotel. Over the course of two and a half hours, Jerry announced that he would rehearse the number with anyone but Redgrave; according to a published account, he said that all he was willing to do with his costar was "take out his cock and piss on her." But Cohen had convinced the business minds to persuade Jerry that he would have to do whatever the producer asked. And whether he liked it or not, Choder was going to be fired. Jerry began to cry (according to one account, "backstagers estimated that he wept openly at least fifty times" through the course of the show), then asked to be allowed to break the news to the actress.

Things had reached a complete meltdown. The box office in Boston was the worst yet: $69,000 the first week, $87,000 the second. Despite nine months of publicity in New York, only $500,000 in tickets had been sold for a theater that was capable of selling $250,000 a week. NBC executives who saw the revised show felt there was a long way to go before they would be happy airing it.

Yet another show doctor was called in, Jerry's old staff writer Dick Cavett. "I didn't think the show was so bad," he recalled. "Lynn was splendid. And I thought Jerry was funny. And it would've probably been slaughtered by the critics and found an audience. I went backstage and saw Jerry, who was not at all happy. He said, 'This is my big problem right now,' and he rattled a bottle of Percodan."

But Cohen felt Jerry himself was the big problem. He had long suspected that the only way to salvage his show was to get Jerry out of it, but now he saw that the only way to get Jerry out of it was to shut it down altogether. On Wednesday, January 19, his office issued this statement: "*Hellzapoppin'* is being withdrawn for recasting and other repairs after Saturday night's performance in Boston because in the opinion of the producer, Alexander H. Cohen, it is not ready for Broadway and cannot be made so in the three weeks remaining before its scheduled opening."

Jerry was beside himself. He spoke with Earl Wilson, claiming that he had always been willing to rehearse with Redgrave but that the material didn't warrant the effort. He blamed Cohen for overextending the budget; he blamed the critics; he blamed the unions; he refused even to discuss Adler. "I didn't wait forty-five years to get killed in Boston," he groused. During that day's matinee performance he appeared "red-eyed and puffy," according to one press account. And despite all the kind words he had for her in the papers, when a skit in the first act called for him to react to something Redgrave said by spritzing out a sip of water, he aimed the spray at her.

Behind the scenes, Jerry was working for a miracle. When he'd announced the close of the show, Cohen had said, "*Hellzapoppin'* is for sale to anyone who wants to buy." Jerry, in conference with impresarios and theater owners Jerome and Maggie Minskoff, hoped to take him up on the offer. But money would be a sticking point. Cohen and his investors were nearly $1.3 million in the hole, and neither Jerry nor the Minskoffs had that kind of capital to invest in the project.

Just after the show's final performance, Jerry stepped in front of the curtain to make an announcement. "I plan desperately in the next few days," he said, "to keep the show together and bring it to New York. I think it's terribly important to be uningenuous [*sic*] at moments like this." Backstage he told the cast, "The show isn't good enough for the critics, but we have a show that is terrific for the people. I'm not making any promises. I'm only telling you I'm going to give it one hell of a try." But back in New York, he had no luck raising the money. Talk of his saving the show tapered off and died.

He was bitterly stung by his experience with the theater. "I have never been in this position where the work you do will be judged by one critic and that will have an effect on the continuation of said performing," he told Cliff Jahr in an interview published in *New York* magazine. The interview, conducted in Lewis's MDA office, began on a note of rancor that indicated just how far Jerry had sunk into paranoia and blame casting. "I will have lawyers bust you in the mouth if you get me to say anything," he growled. "You want the story that will give me a lawsuit. I don't need your fucking story that badly."

Jahr was astonished: "Are you pissed off at me or something?" he asked.

"No." Jerry shrugged. "I'm pissed off with life."

Actually, he was most pissed off at Cohen, whom he called "the Hitler of the theater. . . . He doesn't want a hit! He wants to hang out with Richard Burton and ride around in his fucking Cadillac. Sick man. He's a star fucker." He especially resented Cohen's presumption in telling him what he could and couldn't do onstage. "He gave my attorneys an ultimatum," he said. " 'Jerry will do what I tell him! He will sing what I tell him! Stand where I tell him'—I sent my people back to tell him to stick the show up his ass. . . . He's a fraud. A *con man*. You think Hitler wanted to rule the world? Shit, he was a fucking pygmy."

Back in California a few days later, his final efforts at reviving the show fruitless, he adopted a more humble posture. "You're looking at a defeated Jew," he told UPI's Vernon Scott. "I invested eight months of my life in that show. It cost me three-quarters of a million bucks in lost club dates, concert tours, and out-of-pocket money. The financial losses don't bother me. The disillusionment is what

I can't cope with. My lifelong dream has been to play Broadway. And now it's over. This is the lowest point of my show-business career."

But there would be a coda that would dig just a little deeper into the quick. In the wake of the show's failure, Cohen had been left not only with his personal losses but the ire of a group of limited partners who wanted to sue him for failing to bring the show to Broadway. Maryland real estate man Charles Walsh led a group of twenty or so backers who, like Jerry, felt that the show would have been a hit even if critics and out-of-town audiences hadn't liked it. "The William Morris Agency believes *Hellzapoppin'* could have run at least nine months at the Minskoff Theater," Walsh told columnist Liz Smith. "The show had tremendous ongoing publicity. All it needed was fine tuning. Cohen just closed it without consulting his partners, Jerry Lewis or anyone." But Walsh—whose $1,000 loss paled in comparison with the $770,000 lost by Cohen and Brentwood Television—went unsatisfied.

Another angry investor, Maggie Minskoff, avenged herself against Cohen with more success, banning his limousine from its usual parking space in Shubert Alley, the private thoroughfare that she owned jointly with the Shubert Organization. One day, when Minskoff found a limousine idling in the alley, she inquired whose car it was and was told "Mr. Cohen's." She ordered it to move on, only to find out that it was owned by lawyer Roy Cohn.

Another time, Cohen left his car in the disputed spot and returned to find it with four slashed tires, although, according to *Variety,* "Nobody had been seen behaving suspiciously thereabouts and no accusations were made."

But if Cohen was rankled by such matters, Jerry was the one who came out the big loser. Cohen was so bitter about Jerry's demeanor throughout the run of the show—and his ugly statements about him in the wake of the cancellation— that he pursued arbitration against Jerry for breach of contract.

Galled, no doubt, by the new Broadway season's smash hit success, *Sugar Babies,* a burlesque revue starring Mickey Rooney and Ann Miller that was obviously cast from the same mold as *Hellzapoppin',* Cohen began a vendetta against Jerry, forcing hearings that began that autumn and continued through December 1979, when the arbitrator who'd been hearing the case died. Undeterred, Cohen demanded that testimony and other procedures recommence with a new arbitrator. This second round of hearings dragged on for more than a year before Jerry and his lawyers finally threw in the towel. They paid Cohen $39,000 as a settlement, bringing the matter to a close. The sum didn't hurt as much as what it represented. Although Jerry didn't admit to any breach of contract or any liability for the fate of the show, the settlement itself was, according to *Variety* and *The New York Times,* the first such financial payment from a performer to a show of any kind. In the history of Broadway, a history peopled with more temperamental egos than could be found in any other field, no other performer had ever been made to tender a financial settlement to producers for gumming up rehearsals. Jerry may not have made it to Broadway, but he never-theless made theater history.

When *Hellzapoppin'* closed, Jerry was fifty years old and for all intents and pur-poses finished: no movies, no TV appearances, no shows built around him. Through 1977 and 1978, he did his circuit of live stage performances at home and abroad, and he made a sole TV appearance, guesting on "Donny and Marie." The telethon had become the stuff of camp legend—magazine articles started appearing written by journalists who'd stayed up all night with Jerry, some not even in Vegas but in their homes. Other articles cruelly underscored his utterly diminished stature: "Jerry Lewis Is Not a Schmuck," read a *Village Voice* headline; "Hellzafloppin! Is This the End of Jerry Lewis?" asked a *New York* magazine cover.

He still had a movie star's ego. He was often accompanied by a double, who would enter buildings or leave limousines before him to divert a crowd and pro-vide safe access in and out of buildings (his associates would always say that he received death threats on opening nights or at telethons, just as he had claimed years earlier that the births of all of his sons after Scotty had to be attended by armed guards because of kidnapping threats).

And he could still be petulant about working conditions, even on the set of a commercial for the telethon. After much planning, the advertising company handling the MDA's account had been shocked to discover in the summer of 1977 that Jerry would agree to produce a commercial for the charity only if vari-ous demands of his were met: There would be only one take, and the studio would have to be outfitted with a working soda fountain and a freezer full of ice cream. When he showed up at the set—a mock-up of Dr. Frankenstein's labora-tory—he treated the crew with diffidence and ignored the expensive dessert cart he had insisted on. Ever the tinkerer, he approached a panel of switches and threw one of them, shorting out the entire set. Told it would take hours to get everything up and running, he left altogether, sticking the MDA with an expen-sive tab for ads that were never even shot and leaving the advertising agency scurrying at the last minute for a way to promote the telethon.

But even though his career seemed over, Jerry's financial needs and his pure, sim-ple thirst to be noticed wouldn't let him relax. So he took his Percodan to keep his spinal pains at bay, he took his Dexedrine to keep himself awake, and he tried to keep working.

The drugs were beginning to take more of a toll than ever before. He was having accidents: a broken wrist, a fainting spell in a shower stall, a complete loss of consciousness at a charity event in Chicago. By the time of the 1978 telethon, he was receiving injections of Xylocaine in his spine and hiding his Percodan ad-diction from his doctors. His intimacy with his own drug habits, coupled with his frequent contact with MDA's scientific advisors, turned him into something of a maven on medical matters. Thus, when his friend Jack Eglash of the Sarah Hotel complained about severe migraine headaches, he agreed to accompany him to Houston, where the heart surgeon Michael DeBakey, with whom Jerry had become friendly through the MDA, had recommended a specialist.

Walking through the hospital with Eglash soon after the telethon, Jerry collapsed. DeBakey thought he'd had a heart attack. But a cardiac checkup showed Jerry's heart was fine. When they x-rayed his abdomen, though, the doctors found that he'd been bleeding from a fist-sized ulcer, the symptoms of which the drugs had masked even from Jerry. DeBakey pried the story of his Percodan abuse out of him and called Patti to Houston. They put Jerry under sedation and gave him steroid injections for his spine. The vigil lasted nearly two weeks; Patti spent her time knitting and visiting Bishop Fulton Sheen, who was convalescing in the room next to Jerry's.

When Jerry was taken off sedation and the ulcer had healed, DeBakey lectured him about the Percodan and tried to make him see what he'd done to himself. When he returned home to California, he "flushed, crushed, discarded, and threw away," by his reckoning, "about seven or eight thousand Percodans." (Patti, however, would recall that his Percodan use persisted at least into the next year.)

The siren song of the screen was calling him again. He hadn't been on a movie set since Sweden in 1972, and no one in Hollywood wanted to do business with him. He claimed, like Norma Desmond, that the movies had changed, not him, and that he would make his comeback when the medium proved itself worthy once again. In 1978 he began to suspect that maybe the time had come. The rage for meaningful films with adult themes and bleak tones—the trend that had driven him from the screen—had died. In the wake of the new escapist blockbusters—disaster movies and space operas—came an audience for raucous comedy. John Landis's *Animal House*, a physical comedy with youthful appeal, was a big hit that summer, and in its grosses Jerry saw a place where films of his might thrive. "I waited until the circle turned," he told a reporter who asked why he was making a new film. "I was very depressed by what I saw happening, and I wouldn't play the game." Indeed, given his mental and physical state during the 1970s—"I don't have any recollections of doing telethons '73, '74, '75, '76, '77," he told a reporter. "I don't remember those five years. Those five years are a blank"—he really couldn't have played the game.

To accomplish a comeback, though, he would have to call on resources beyond the traditional corridors of Hollywood financing. As with *The Day the Clown Cried*, he found a producer from outside the usual Hollywood circuit; this time it was Joseph Ford Proctor, a thirtyish entrepreneur best known for staging wine-and-cheese tastings at the New York Coliseum.

Proctor initiated talks with Jerry when the two met on some MDA-related business—he had found a script called *Hardly Working* by Michael Janover about an unemployed circus clown that struck him as a perfect Jerry Lewis vehicle. Additionally, Proctor had rounded up $3 million in financing from a group of nine Floridians, none of whom had ever invested in a film before.

Something about Proctor must have struck Jerry as promising. He had many of Jerry's commercial instincts—he explained that with Jerry's name he could presell the film in Europe, and he developed a plan to mount tie-in campaigns with more than two dozen manufacturers. Jerry wanted to rewrite Janover's script, and he wanted control over casting and crew; Proctor was amenable on all counts. To demonstrate his own willingness to see the project through, Jerry put his salary in escrow. There was so much good feeling in the air that he and Proctor were already making plans for other films: "That's Life," described as "a senior citizens' *Animal House*," with Ruth Gordon, Molly Picon, and Red Buttons; and a sequel to *Hardly Working* entitled "*Hardly Working* Attacks *Star Wars*." In this heady atmosphere, production on *Hardly Working* began in and around Fort Lauderdale in the spring of 1979.

The decision to make the movie in Florida was predicated on a number of factors. Proctor's investors were there, of course, and part of the lure he'd used to attract them was a promise of access to Jerry's set. Furthermore, as with *The Bellboy* nineteen years earlier, Jerry felt it would be easier to work out of eyeshot of the Hollywood press and with the assistance of crews and performers less jaded than those in Los Angeles.

And there were personal reasons. In Miami he could be alone. His parents had moved to Vegas, in part so that Danny could be closer to his son in case his diminished condition worsened. And Patti remained at home, where Joseph was still in high school. Indeed, given what he later told reporters about the state of his marriage at this time, the need to be away from home might have been what attracted him most about the *Hardly Working* shoot. Perhaps kicking drugs had cleared his mind, perhaps it was merely the midlife crisis of a fifty-three-year-old who'd never stopped to evaluate his situation before, but he seemed to see suddenly the sort of marriage he was in: "Bored. Locked in routine. No fun. This crazy man who makes people laugh walks into his house and it becomes a somber place of discomfort and displeasure."

In his mind, the decision to go to Florida was a decision to leave his old life behind. But it was also an opportunity to let loose on impulses he'd entertained intermittently throughout his adult life. "I guess I realized, 'Hey, you only go around once. I'm at the three-quarter turn. I haven't had a lot of fucking laughs,'" he said a few years later. "I went to Florida to make *Hardly Working* and felt a distinct difference in how happy I was, with all of those responsibilities left behind in California. I was literally playing bachelor for the first time, and I really enjoyed it. I finally let Patti know that I wasn't making my children happy,

I wasn't making her happy, and maybe I needed to be a bachelor. . . . I was going to do such swinging, with plenty of playing. 'Let's get a yacht, fuck three-
quarters of Brazil.'"

Thus determined to turn his life into a *Satyricon*, but earnest nevertheless
to bring in, under budget, a film that would relaunch his career, Jerry began work
that spring. In some regards, it was a typical Jerry Lewis shoot: He doled out
Tootsie Pops to visitors (he charged a dollar apiece for autographs, with proceeds
going to the MDA), tickled the bare feet of crew members, and gave relatively
unlimited access to the press (though he refused to discuss *The Day the Clown
Cried*, the financial conditions of Jerry Lewis Cinemas, or *Hellzapoppin'*). With
the budget-minded Proctor signing off on his decisions, he was allowed to improvise somewhat—altering a static shot into a tracking one, for instance. Although none of his old crew members would be connected with the film either
during principal photography or in postproduction, he filled key roles with familiar faces: Susan Oliver (onetime ingenue of *The Disorderly Orderly*), Buddy
Lester, Steve Franken, and such old comic hands as Roger C. Carmel, Harold J.
Stone, and Billy Barty. Even thirty-three-year-old Gary was on hand, playing
disco music with a revamped Playboys.

And there was somebody new in his life. Partly in his eagerness to fulfill his
bachelor fantasy, partly in a sincere effort to pull off a parody of *Saturday Night
Fever*, he had auditioned a hundred or so dancers to find someone to cut a rug
with him in a fantasy sequence. Among the auditioners was Sandra (or SanDee,
or Sam, by all of which names she went) Pitnick, a divorced, twenty-nine-year-
old former airline stewardess and dancer originally from North Carolina. Not
only did Pitnick get the part, but she got a dinner invitation from Jerry—a married man with two sons older than her.

"I didn't know she was turning me on," Jerry said later. "The first night was
pretty boring for her. I didn't make a move. It was disgusting. Which tells me I
wasn't getting turned on per se. I just wanted someone to have dinner with."

They saw each other again, and Jerry's manner toward her changed. She
found the experience disconcerting. "I idolized him. I adored him before I ever
met him. I was so frightened of him," she recalled. "One of the most precious
things he ever gave me came within the first week, when I confronted him with,
'Wait a minute! What are your motives? What do you see in me?' He said, 'You
have no self-confidence. If I can just be your friend and give you self-confidence,
I want to try to do that.'" Whether she was simply starstruck or he had really
told her something truthful about herself, it worked. Before long, they were en-
meshed in a full-blown affair.

He had had many liaisons over the years, of course, but this one had a tenor
of its own. Combined with his determination to embark on a new life, it was the
most substantial threat yet to his marriage. Compounding the guilt he must certainly have felt was the presence of his twenty-three-year-old son Scott on the

set as an assistant to the director. To Patti, the thought was abominable. "It has always grieved me that the presence of his own son . . . did not deter him from conducting an affair with the woman he is married to now," she said later. (Scott saw his father's dissolute behavior for what it was. "Dad looks awful in the film," he remembered. "His face is drawn and ashen, his eyes are red." But he found himself imitating it to some degree; while his father was courting SanDee Pitnick, Scott met a young woman of his own during the shoot, married her, then later divorced her.)

When Patti brought Anthony, Christopher, and Joseph to Florida to spend some time with their father, Jerry stiff-armed them. "He appeared to be in a world of his own," she recalled, "tolerating us to some degree but never spending time with us. It bothered me, mostly for the boys." She suspected he was still using drugs, and she knew about his affair. But she had always been determined to protect the boys, and she was more hurt for them than for herself, such as when Joseph begged his father to play golf with him and Jerry refused. Jerry tried to make a show of his love for his family, but his heart wasn't in it. They returned to California.

In Florida Jerry had more than the unraveling of his marriage to contend with. With production so smooth that he finished two days ahead of his eight-week schedule, Proctor and his money—whatever money he had, at any rate—vanished. Like almost all films, *Hardly Working* had inched slightly over its budget—not a hemorrhaging, exactly, but enough to bring postproduction to its knees before Jerry could see it through. He needed completion money to pay some of the film's creditors and to cover the costs of editing, scoring, and distributing the film.

He tried to find financing through the usual routes—banks, movie studios and distributors, completion bond companies that periodically bankrolled stalled film productions—and through less usual ones. When news of his financial troubles spread, he later told an interviewer, the dark forces he had come to know back in his days with Dean surfaced to lend a hand. "A dear friend," he said, "brought me $4 million in a Samsonite briefcase. He put it down and said, 'You're all straight.' I said, 'Sweetheart, I can't touch that. My life is not just as a film director or an actor. I have a whole muscular-dystrophy life. Do you understand?' 'Shit,' he said, 'there's got to be a way.' I said, 'Not in your lifetime.' And I was hurtin' bad. That would have straightened me out."

Fortunately, there were less sinister methods of financing the film. Even though Proctor had vanished, the snowbirds and Palm Beach millionaires whom he'd lured into investing in the film were still around. Two especially—Jan and Rosie Smith, old vaudevillians who had made a fortune in Florida real estate after quitting the stage—were sympathetic to Jerry's cause, and encouraged James McNamara, a young investment broker from Palm Beach, to arrange financing for postproduction and distribution. Under the banner HWC, Inc., Mc-

Namara and nine investors provided a $15 million bank that would help see *Hardly Working* through and, it was hoped, initiate other film projects in Florida. Jerry and *Hardly Working* got $1.5 million from HWC; McNamara, who was delighted to be working with "a mature Jerry Lewis, a comedian who will go down in history as one of the great clowns of all time," was named as producer on the finished film, which nowhere in its credits mentions Proctor.

There was one last brouhaha in Florida, one of the sort that had become requisite for him. For months he'd been planning to do a live one-nighter in Daytona Beach on March 25, during the *Hardly Working* shoot, like in the old busy days. The only room in town that was big enough, however, was the local jai alai fronton—a long, shallow stage with a wide auditorium in front of it. When Hal Bell, Jerry's longtime road manager, arrived at the building to rig up his set, however, he discovered that it was in no shape to be remade into a concert hall; indeed, Jerry claimed, the specifications that Bell had forwarded to promoter W. James Bridges weeks earlier had been utterly ignored.

Three hours before the concert was to begin, Jerry refused to perform and headed back to his condominium. He also refused to return the advance he'd received—fifteen thousand dollars in two equal payments (only the second of which was actually due back the promoters). He claimed that the William Morris Agency was holding the money in escrow pending discussions with Bridges, but Bridges wanted blood. He sued Jerry for thirty thousand dollars. Jerry countersued for losses of his own. Like the conflicts with Nathan Wachsberger, Alexander Cohen, and the Jerry Lewis Cinema franchisees, the bickering between Jerry and Bridges would drag on into obscurity.

Jerry, meanwhile, busied himself with the editing of *Hardly Working*, taking time off in May to go to France, in part to sell the foreign rights to the film, in part to serve on the jury at the Cannes Film Festival. That year's top prize at the festival was split between Volker Schlöndorff's *The Tin Drum* and Francis Ford Coppola's *Apocalypse Now*—a movie about a child in Nazi Germany who refuses to grow up, and a war epic by a former USC student about an irrational general who sets himself up as a god in the outer reaches of the Vietnam War.

Jerry must have felt right at home.

Jerry's string of embarrassing small roles on TV continued in 1979 when he played the ringmaster on a "Circus of the Stars" installment. He really had become more welcome overseas than at home. In March 1980, for instance, *Hardly Working* opened in Germany, the unlikely site of the massive success of *Which Way to the Front?* a decade earlier. Once again, Jerry's name on the marquee was the charm: The film did $768,000 in its first three days, $2.5 million in its first seventeen. In France the reception was even greater. On April 8 Jerry appeared on TV with Princess Grace in a tribute to the great movie clowns. The next day, which had been proclaimed national "Jerry Lewis Day," the film opened in theaters throughout the country. In Paris alone, nearly 140,000 tickets were sold; only *The Nutty Professor* and *Which Way to the Front?* had been bigger hits for him there. But he was still unable to find a distributor at home. It was a galling situation: The film was a certifiable hit, it had more than paid for itself overseas, but no one in America wanted to show it.

Indeed, it seemed no one in America wanted him at all. When he played Atlantic City on Memorial Day weekend, the newspapers reported that he was getting half as much for tickets as the casinos were asking for bigger stars. Worse, he was forced to deny, with the support of MDA telethon executive producer George Schlatter, rumors that he was being stripped of his traditional Labor Day position.

He acted as if he had no recourse but to spit at the world. He used to express his ego in his work, but with his expressive avenues shutting down in front of him, he increasingly vented himself in pure spleen. He was still lashing out at film critics—"I think most critics are whores," he told an interviewer that spring—but he had resumed his attacks on Hollywood itself as well. Lamenting the passing of the great producers and studio bosses who had ruled the industry when he was young, he derided the "unbathed, hip, presumably sophisticated coke-sniffing putzes doing our business." He mocked the box-office stars of the day: "You can mention whoever you like, including Redford, Newman, Travolta, whoever, they've got to go twenty more years before any of them can get the response that I get anywhere in the world."

He was able to be frank about his own volatility. "You aren't ever going to meet anybody who loves his sons better than I love mine," he told a writer, "but they cross me in my game plans and my ground rules and I'd turn them off like *that.* 'Cause I love very hard and you can't fuck with that, it's very fragile. I love too hard and too deeply and I can turn from total love to infinite indifference in a microsecond. . . . The important thing is that I haven't the slightest understanding of why I am like that. I'm basically a selfish person. I think of myself first in most instances."

But let anyone else criticize him, and he would unleash his venom with especial relish. When asked about his detractors at the time *Hellzapoppin'* fell apart, he answered, "The people you're talking about wouldn't like to know Jerry Lewis in person either because then they'd lose somebody to rap. They need that to get through their fucking little timid lives."

When Merrill Schindler of *Los Angeles* magazine pushed him on this point, when he asked Jerry several times why he inspired hostility, he got a frightening glimpse of Jerry's self-image: "I'm a multi-faceted, talented, wealthy, internationally famous genius. I have an IQ of 190, that's supposed to be genius. People don't like that. People really don't want waves made. 'Why can't Jerry Lewis be like I am?' Just show up, stand on the marks and say the words. That's to be singularly [*sic*] faceted. Why does he have to write, direct, produce, et cetera?

Why? That's no one's fucking business. The single-faceted human being takes it
as a personal affront. . . . Ten years ago, if you had shown that quote to me, I'd
be vomiting all over the couch. The interview would be over and I'd be screaming and kicking my feet. I have the greatest antidote for that sort of statement,
and I hope you print it. The answer to all my critics is simple. I like me. I like
what I've become. I'm proud of what I've achieved. And I don't really believe I've
scratched the surface yet. I'm an egomaniac. I may have an ego that's bigger
than others', but thank God if that's brought me to where I am. And that's my
answer."

When he gave this interview, Jerry was living in a rented condominium in Las
Vegas. Although Schindler saw no evidence of her, SanDee Pitnick was living
there as well. She had been traveling with Jerry through Europe in support of
Hardly Working and had taken a vacation with him in Hawaii. They had actually
hit the papers in the islands when they were stopped by authorities in some sort
of mix-up when out for a jog.

Patti had endured a lot over the years, but this was more than she was willing to take. "Jerry was blatantly waltzing a girlfriend around the world," she recalled. "I'd lived through his various affairs and quick infatuations, but this was
just too much!"

"It reached the point that Patti just couldn't stand the humiliation any
more," a friend of hers told gossip columnist Marilyn Beck. "She's bitter. She's
also hurt." She had always looked the other way when she became aware of her
husband's dalliances, but now she'd been practically abandoned: Jerry had spent
a sole week at home with her in Bel Air during the past year.

By midsummer she was considering splitting up with him altogether. "It was
becoming apparent that I no longer had any security to hold on to," she remembered, "and no category in which I could file my long-term marriage grievances.
For years, I had been trying to hang on to a marriage that had ceased to possess
mutuality. I was torn between the two contradictory choices: to hang on or to let
go."

Then, out shopping in the supermarket one day, she had her mind made up
for her. The cashiers and clerks, all of whom knew her well, were scurrying in
front of her, pulling tabloid newspapers out of their racks. Out of curiosity, Patti
picked up one of the papers. On the cover was a headline that nearly knocked
her down: "AFTER 36 YEARS I NEED TO GET OUT AND PLAY—Jerry Lewis: Why I
Dumped My Wife." It was as if he was willing to speak to her only through the
media, confessing his sins against Patti, announcing, "I'm the heavy in this
piece."

The media went on a field day, following Jerry and SanDee's trail around the
world. "I believe she and Jerry are now in London," one of SanDee's Florida
friends told the *New York Post*, while another refused to talk at all: "SanDee is

not here, and I wouldn't tell you where she is if I knew. I know exactly what you're after and she wouldn't answer your questions. Neither will I."

Those close to Patti counseled her to divorce Jerry and make him pay for what he was putting her through. But she had so dissolved her identity in his that she didn't feel capable of making so complete a break. Taking into account her religious scruples, she wouldn't divorce him at first but merely sought a legal separation. In time, however, the fact that she was married to a man who was living with another woman disturbed her more than the prospect of violating a Catholic taboo. In September 1980, thirty-six years after they first met in Detroit, she filed for divorce in California Superior Court, asking for $450,000 a year in alimony, custody of and support for sixteen-year-old Joseph, and half of their community property, which she judged to be worth in excess of $7 million.

These demands would have been hard enough for Jerry to meet, but he was also facing a mid-October trial date in Los Angeles Federal Court stemming from the bankruptcy of Jerry Lewis Cinemas. The litigation had dragged on through seven years of disclosures and depositions, and he was now the last remaining target for a group of angry franchisees who'd refused to back down. His entire life's earnings were in jeopardy. He had only one way to hang on: On October 13, he filed for bankruptcy in Federal Court in Las Vegas, seeking to readjust his debts under Chapter 13 of the Bankruptcy Reform Act and staying all legal proceedings against him.

It wasn't, according to attorney Alan L. Isaacman, a classic bankruptcy filing. There would be no liquidation of Jerry's assets, but rather a request for a court-ordered settlement of debts. In papers filed over the next few weeks to disclose his financial status, he revealed that he made approximately $1 million per year, netting $600,000 after taxes; his checking account contained $140,000; he hoped to make $2 million in 1981. He was willing to pay Patti $108,000 annually (less than one-quarter of what she'd sought), and he estimated that he could live on $16,000 to $24,000 per month.

Patti, uncertain whether the bankruptcy was "real or contrived," nevertheless "continued to believe and trust his word that he would do what was right." She had always abdicated financial responsibility to him, signing whatever he put in front of her. "It was usually preceded by some song and dance about his just needing my signature and asking if I trusted him," she remembered. "Once in court a judge asked me if I knew I was being stonewalled. I was so naïve, I did not even know what 'stonewalled' meant. (At that time Jerry was taking out a loan on our house for drugs.)" She scoffed at the settlement figures bandied about in the newspapers. "If I had received half of some of the mentioned sums," she said, "I would be rich. I am not. Like many 'gray' divorcées, I have never been schooled in the art of settlements."

When the settlement finally did arrive, she felt manipulated once again. "I was at the mercy of the attorneys," she recalled. "Many who observed the final proceedings related that the judge was very partial to Jerry. He gave him the most attention and showed him compassion." (Her description would be the only account of the divorce proceedings publicly available; all relevant transcripts, disclosures, and filings were sealed as part of the settlement.) When Jerry finally fetched the last of his belongings from St. Cloud Drive in mid-December 1981, a grieving Patti consoled herself with a Bing Crosby Christmas special and readings from the Bible.

For the boys, the divorce was equally traumatic. Their relationships with Jerry had suffered through the previous years. Proud of the ways the boys had grown up without any trace of jaded movie brat manners—"each had a girlfriend from a very middle-class background," she bragged to an interviewer—Patti nevertheless recognized that they all had some sort of aversion to their father. Other than Ron, who worked in television as a set supervisor, "the other children do not want to be involved professionally with Jerry." She laid the blame squarely at her husband's feet. "It seems they were more toys to him than people," she said, "to be played with when young, and then put aside. When they grew up, Jerry just could not handle the competition."

His relations with his sons were strained more than ever during the months of tabloid headlines, divorce, and separation. Patti and Joseph were living alone in the big house in Bel Air, and Scott moved back in with them, only to find himself overwhelmed by the depressing atmosphere: Patti was taking tranquilizers; Joseph was jittery and asthmatic. Chris, twenty-three years old at the time, worked up the nerve to confront his father ("I told my dad what I thought of him," he recalled), and it was almost two years before they would speak again. (One son, Anthony, gravitated toward Jerry after the divorce; Gary—whose ex-wife, Jinky, and daughter, Sarah Jane, lived in the Philippines—and Ron, who was married, were both in their thirties and seem to have viewed the events with more equanimity.)

Besides Patti, the one who suffered the most was Joseph, who, five years younger than his closest sibling, never knew his father during the flush years of his life and career. Joseph was the one who had spent the most time with Patti when Jerry was off with other women or suffering the effects of his drug addiction. He was the one likeliest to be ignored by a father inching toward middle age with little concern for anything but his ego needs and his failing career. When Joseph was a frightened young kid, Jerry would show up at his Little League games with a sixteen-millimeter movie camera and scare the life out of him; he would freeze on the field in his father's presence. But he desperately wanted his father's attention. Patti recalled a time when Joseph had wanted to talk with Jerry in person about some matter and Jerry would speak to his son only over the phone; a few nights later, Joseph sat in anguish watching the TV as Jerry told Mike Douglas and Jonas Salk that "I never put my children on hold. I'm always there for them."

When Jerry was finally out of the house, Joseph took the boldest, most antagonistic action he could think of. With his mother and his brother Chris by his side, he busted into Jerry's private bathroom. Wielding a pair of bolt cutters, the boys approached a drawer that was sealed with a padlock. "If anyone plays with this lock" read a sign on the drawer, "it would create serious trouble for the party involved." They broke the lock and opened the drawer. "It contained several ounces of marijuana and many prescription drugs," Joseph remembered. They found pills and two loaded pistols. "My God in heaven!" Patti screamed. "I almost vomited," Joseph recalled. "That was what he had been doing—not lying on the marble floor to soothe his aching back, as he had said! It was a cheap alibi from a cheap father. I lost what little respect I had for the man."

One morning in November, Jerry went golfing near his home in Vegas and then stopped by the hospital to see Danny, whose health had been failing. He found his mother in tears. Danny was gone.

Jerry went inside to sit with the body for a few minutes, staring mutely, unable to express gratitude, rage, or anything else. In less than two months he had lost everything—his family, his financial security, and now his first hero. His life had spun wildly away from him. Even if he had been able to speak to Danny, what shadow of it all could he have possibly conveyed?

Danny had never been easy on him; even a few years before his death, he had caught a show of Jerry's and spitefully told him, "You were okay—for an amateur." Perhaps it was a joke, but Jerry took it to heart. Danny had always seemed to him the very embodiment of manhood and show-biz savvy—"He knew everything— *everything*—about the racket," Jerry avowed—and with his passing, Jerry sensed the passing of a way of life both on and off the stage. The trouble for him was that he didn't know any other ways to comport himself. He buried his father in Las Vegas, but he would never be able to bury his dependency on him—or the hurt his father had inflicted on him and which he had inevitably passed on to his own sons.

20

"Why Am I a Criminal?"

In the spring of 1981, almost two years after *Hardly Working* was shot, Jerry had the last laugh. Twentieth Century–Fox had picked up the domestic distribution rights to the picture—and found itself, to its utter astonishment, with a hit on its hands. For one dizzying week in April, *Hardly Working* was the Number One film on *Variety*'s weekly box-office chart; the returns were so high the first weekend that Fox actually had some regional exhibitors count their receipts again, unable to comprehend how a Jerry Lewis movie could gross $4.16 million in only three days in only seven hundred theaters.

The critics hadn't done anything to help it. Typical was Alan Stern's notice in *The Boston Phoenix*, which went after Jerry personally ("the only emotion he arouses is pity") and only then began to eviscerate the film. *Time* wondered aloud "why Jerry Lewis would choose to run around, fall down, go cross-eyed or winsome in one more movie comedy," while *Newsweek* declared, "If 'Hardly Working' fails to break you up, it may well leave you in a state of terminal depression."

But other reviews indicated that a younger generation of American critics, raised on French New Wave cinema and the *auteur* theory, had learned how to appreciate what Jerry was doing. In the *Soho Weekly News*, the estimable critic Jonathan Rosenbaum called *Hardly Working* "the most politically honest film I've seen this year . . . a key document of the Reagan era . . . unbearable, terrible, wonderful, stupid, brilliant, awful, shocking, inept, and even very funny." He compared it to late films by Preston Sturges and Charlie Chaplin (*Mad Wednesday* and *A King in New York*, respectively) and concluded by saying that "Jerry Lewis *is* America, and both are hardly working. So it's hardly surprising that this is a movie that tells more truth than any of us is entirely ready to bear." Jerry had never had a review like that in English in his life.

To be fair to its admirers, the very shape and idea of *Hardly Working* indeed promised a kind of fascinating satire, a meditation on both the economy of the era and the status of its star—a clown without a job or, for that matter, a home. But the actual execution is an awful botch: choppily edited, poorly photographed, shot with none of the visual verve of Jerry's first few films. Jerry blamed the script—"the worst thing I've ever put pen to paper," he called it— but the final result betrays even the creaky story.

Despite the episodic plot—which followed an out-of-work clown through a series of job and costume changes, the film really doesn't contain a single memorable sequence. It had been more than a decade since Jerry had made a film of this sort, but it was as if he had stored up absolutely no material in all that time. He looks pudgy, slow, out of it: His hair is long and greasy, he wears geeky sweater vests, he is red-eyed, gray-faced, and sluggish; you can see his health isn't what it once was.

Among the lifeless scenes in the film, one stands out for obvious reasons— the parody of *Saturday Night Fever*. Putting aside the fact that the original was four years old when the long-delayed *Hardly Working* finally appeared, the scene is shocking in its lifelessness. A quarter-century earlier, Jerry ripped apart *Living It Up* when he danced like an amphetamine-riddled chimp with Sheree North; a decade after that, he drew comedy and pathos by dancing alone in *The Nutty Professor*. But in *Hardly Working* his reflexes and agility are gone; there's not a funny moment in the bit. Worse, he looks not like a parody of a suave dancer but like a depraved old man *trying* to parody a suave dancer. And SanDee Pitnick, dancing along with him, is photographed flatly and unflatteringly and nearly out of focus. Her face, pretty in real life, doesn't photograph well; her features flatten out, and her eyes seem dim. Jerry never had bothered to learn how to film an actress glamorously. They dance very closely together—alas, Jerry doesn't even try to make a joke of the scene—and you realize that with its curious production history and its unusual Fort Lauderdale setting, *Hardly Working* is a vanity film, a project made by its creator simply for the sake of making it. Fox couldn't help scratching its corporate head at the box-office returns; why would anyone pay money to see this?

The domestic success of *Hardly Working* reinvigorated Jerry spiritually, if not financially—no portion of its profits came directly to him. He began looking for another opportunity to write and direct; along with longtime co-writer Bill Richmond, he was working on a new script, but there was no production deal in sight. He'd also begun, along with a writer named Herb Gluck, who'd previously co-written an autobiography by football-great-turned-sitcom-actor Alex Karras, to work on his memoirs for Atheneum, a New York publishing house. Maybe he was right; maybe the circle had turned back to comedy. Maybe he could re-create himself for a whole new audience—the kids of the kids he and Dean had enthralled all those years ago.

His newest film project didn't seem a likely vehicle for a beloved clown's comeback, though. Not that it wasn't a worthwhile project: He had been signed to costar in Martin Scorsese's *The King of Comedy*, in which he would play a Johnny Carson–inspired late-night talk show host named Jerry Langford. In the course of the script by former *Newsweek* film critic Paul Zimmerman, Langford is harassed, stalked, and eventually kidnapped by two autograph hounds: Rupert Pupkin, a vaguely psychotic misfit who wants to perform a comedy act on Langford's show, and Masha, a loony young Park Avenue girl who has developed a sexual obsession with Langford.

Scorsese, whose previous film was the masterful boxing picture *Raging Bull*, wouldn't seem a natural for this sort of black comic material. But his 1976 film *Taxi Driver* had recently been used as evidence in the trial of would-be Presidential assassin John Hinckley, who had developed a psychotic fixation on Jodie Foster (one of its costars) and meant to win her affection by killing Ronald Reagan. Zimmerman's story about an obsessed fan who can't recognize the difference between his own life and life on the TV screen therefore had a personal resonance for Scorsese, a onetime Roman Catholic seminarian whose films often dealt with themes of guilt and purgation.

Jerry wasn't Scorsese's first choice for the role of Jerry Langford. Carson himself, an obvious candidate, refused the job, telling the director—famous for encouraging his actors to create their own roles through extensive improvisations and retakes—"You know one take's enough for me." Frank Sinatra was the next actor who came to Scorsese's mind, and when he proved unavailable, Scorsese thought about casting someone from among the whole roster of Rat Pack entertainers, Joey Bishop and Sammy Davis Jr. included. He considered Orson Welles, but dismissed the thought because "he wasn't 'show business' enough." He thought of Dean Martin. And inevitably, after he thought of Dean, he thought of Jerry.

Scorsese contacted Jerry, whom he found working in Lake Tahoe. "Jerry has done nearly everything in show business," Scorsese recalled. "He has a lot to draw on and he was eager to play the part. I had two meetings with Jerry over the course of a year and a half. I could see the man was *ripe* for it." But the matter of deciding whether Jerry was suited to the role was in the hands of Scorsese's long-time collaborator, actor Robert De Niro, who had first brought the project to the director's attention and who felt the need to develop a deep rapport with the actor who'd be playing Langford. "What we went through before we decided that we were gonna do it!" Jerry remembered years later. "Bobby and I had five meetings, five separate meetings in six months." It was all at the younger actor's behest. "Bobby has to know the people that he's gonna work with," Jerry explained. "What he needs from them, I can't tell you—whether he has to know that they're genuine, whether he has to know that they're just goddamn good actors, that they'll commit—I'm not too sure, but he needs to know some stuff."

At their meetings, De Niro grilled Jerry extensively about his past—his years with Dean, his personal life, his thoughts on the filmmaking process, his relationship with his parents. In retrospect, it's clear he'd already settled on Jerry as his costar and was trying to develop the fanatical relationship with Jerry Lewis that Rupert Pupkin had with Jerry Langford. When he felt that he'd delved into his subject sufficiently, De Niro returned to New York and approved the casting. Then, after the papers were signed, he gave Jerry a call. " 'Jer—I need you to know that I really want to kill you in this picture,' " Jerry recalled De Niro telling him. " 'We can't socialize, we can't have dinner, we can't go out.' I said, 'Bobby, whatever turns you on, sweetheart. . . . Are there any ground rules about saying good morning?' "

It was counterintuitive casting, to say the least. Except for the ill-fated remake of *The Jazz Singer* and the 1965 episode of "Ben Casey," Jerry had never played a wholly dramatic role (presumably, *The Day the Clown Cried* would have been another exception). Moreover, he hadn't ever really succeeded on screen in an adult persona, despite all his efforts to reinvent himself since *Boeing Boeing*. Scorsese, though, knew just what he wanted from Jerry; he'd seen it on TV every Labor Day for years. In the telethon host the director saw the embodiment of High American Show Business of the Late Twentieth Century. He was especially struck by the telethon's "combination of money pouring in for charity and its Vegas sensibility," and the way it "seems at times to verge on nervous breakdown." Seeing the Labor Day broadcast as a kind of raw psychological performance, Scorsese said, "The thin line between reality and drama seems to be shattered constantly during this telethon. Anyone who could conjure up and sustain this atmosphere is quite extraordinary."

Prior to production, the filmmakers asked Jerry to help create the role he would play. He dove into the chore. He met with De Niro, Scorsese, and Zimmerman to share with them some of his expertise on the matter of celebrity. After nearly four decades in the limelight, he was the only one among them who had lived through the unfathomable experience of being a globally known face; De Niro, even on the heels of his Best Actor Academy Award for *Raging Bull*, was the sort of chameleonic personality who could slip in and out of rooms without disturbing the air.

"They don't know celebrity," he bragged afterward. "They only know anonymity. You could walk by Bobby De Niro today, you wouldn't know him. It's just the way he is. And for many of the films—*Taxi Driver, Mean Streets, Bang the Drum Slowly, Raging Bull, The Deer Hunter*—who the fuck knows who that is? They needed me to tell them about celebrity. And we wrote together. Paul Zimmerman and Marty and myself, we wrote the things that they had never heard about." The most memorable such inclusion was based on a lady who bumped into Jerry one night in Las Vegas and switched from praising him to the heavens to cursing him when he refused to talk to her husband on the phone.

" 'You should get cancer,' " she shouted after Jerry as he walked away. "It's a true story," he recalled.

With De Niro cast against his usual volatile, animalistic, ethnic type as Rupert Pupkin and avant-garde comedienne Sandra Bernhard cast as the ragged Masha, filming began in Manhattan and on Long Island in the spring of 1982. It was Jerry's forty-sixth film, but the first he'd ever shot in New York.

Even though he'd been consulted on the creation of his character, Jerry had determined to adopt the appropriate respect for Scorsese's dominion over the set. "I went in with a very simple philosophy," he said. "If what they do got *Raging Bull* up on the screen, then I'm prepared to do whatever's necessary. Bobby and Marty have eccentricities that I as a filmmaker had to adjust to because I wasn't there as a filmmaker."

When filming began, he approached Scorsese, who had just recovered from a bout of pneumonia and had been forced to stick to an early starting date by producer Arnon Milchan, to tell him that he would cooperate to the fullest. " 'I know I'm number two in this picture,' " Scorsese recalled Jerry saying. " 'I won't give you any difficulty and I'll do what you want. I'm a consummate professional. I know where I stand. If you want me to wait around, you're paying for my time, I'll do that.' "

Scorsese helped make Jerry comfortable on the set through the sort of naturalistic strategies he liked to use with his actors. Jerry was allowed to wear his own clothes, for instance, and in a scene in Langford's apartment, Jerry's shih tzu, Angel, was seen as Langford's dog. Scorsese encouraged Jerry to relax in the role, to play Langford by being himself: "The less Jerry does, the better he is," he told a visitor to the set. He recalled that Jerry helped to keep the pressurized atmosphere of the shoot light and lively. "He was very funny between takes," said Scorsese. "And when he started cracking jokes I'd get asthma attacks from laughing. It got to the point of being maniacal, you had to shake him to stop it."

But there was much in the making of the film that Jerry found unnerving. There was the matter of professional discipline. On his own sets, Jerry may have cavorted and clowned, but he never failed to put in at least a sixteen-hour day; he did so much homework and preparation that his antics were almost a necessary countermeasure to the exacting control he exerted. Above all, he was a crewman's director, starting work early in the morning and striving to wrap production on schedule almost as if he himself were a union worker making an hourly wage. After all, he had produced many of the films he directed; it was his own money he'd be wasting if he wasn't strict about time. But his sense of discipline was also part of his personal code of professionalism, the trouper's credo he had learned from his father and during his own days in burlesque dives along the eastern seaboard.

In contrast to Jerry's Studio Era notions of responsible filmmaking, however, the Stanislavskian improvisational techniques of Scorsese and De Niro seemed chaotic. Jerry would arrive at the set at 9 A.M., only to cool his heels for hours before his director and his costar arrived; he would prepare to do certain scenes only to discover that Scorsese had judged De Niro's mood inappropriate for that material and had decided to shoot another sequence entirely; he would watch in astonishment as the director and his star shot take after take after take of scenes that he himself would have got in one or two tries.

"If they had hired me as a part of the filmmaking team," he reflected, "I'd have killed them both, because it was against everything I was taught." But he kept his mouth shut. "When I am a passenger on the other captain's ship," he said, "I'm just a passenger. And it means if I see this ship going down because this fucker's pulling the cork out, he ain't gonna hear anything from me."

He was appalled at the amount of time Scorsese was willing to give De Niro to get into each scene. "When I saw Take 29 for a scene with no words—just walking from a theater mob to a limo—I said, 'We're in a mess,' " he recalled. "I never saw the number 29 before in my career! When I saw we had four pages of dialogue the next day, I said to one of the crew, 'If this doesn't go 138 takes, I'll buy you a car.' "

Eventually, he was able to decipher the order beneath the apparent chaos and appreciate what Scorsese and De Niro were up to. "In order to work with Bobby you have to make a deal with the Devil," he explained. "Bobby is no fool. He knows his craft. And that his craft needs his time, it needs his gut to go for it. Marty would tell him from now until next Tuesday that Take 5 was super. But De Niro knows fucking well that if he goes into Take 12 and 14 and 15 he'll find an 'if' and an 'and.' If he does Take 20, he'll pick up a quick turn, and on Take 28 he's got lips tightening, which he never had through the first 27 takes. I watched him feign poor retention just to work a scene. I watched him literally look like he couldn't remember the dialogue. He knew the fucking dialogue. It was masterful. There's nothing he did that didn't stagger me."

But De Niro didn't deploy his arsenal of Method acting tricks only on his own performance. He coaxed Jerry into improvisations in some of their scenes together, never more vividly than in an emotional encounter between Pupkin and Langford at Langford's country estate. During the scene, Pupkin insists that his fantasy relationship with Langford is real, until the talk show host turns violently on him, bellowing and chasing him from the house.

According to Scorsese, the scene took two weeks to shoot: "It was just so painful because the scene itself is so excruciating." But some of that pain was imposed on Jerry by his colleagues. De Niro knew he would achieve the verisimilitude he hoped for, but he wanted to make certain that Jerry's rage was genuine. As the crew prepared to film the climactic moments of the scene, De Niro began baiting Jerry with anti-Semitic epithets, announcing that Jews had " 'turned this world into garbage for five thousand years.' "

"I said, 'You cocksucker, you're lucky you're alive. I'll rip your fucking head off,' " Jerry remembered. "I didn't know he and Marty had met already, to go for it. 'Do you realize you are close to my ripping your fucking head off?' And the cameras are rolling. I know Marty is getting what he wants. I know Bobby is feeding me. But for me not to be aware of two cameras and an entire crew, and Bobby De Niro, throwing dialogue at me, 'Maybe the Jews were motherfuckers in the first place.' That didn't. . . . But 'If Hitler had lived, he'd have gotten all of you cocksuckers' was the fucking trigger. He knew—the son of a bitch knew. And he's doing this to me because he's just off camera. I pulled him into the scene by three feet, and I was on my way. Whew! He came into the dressing room. 'Are you okay?' 'Yes, I'm fine. I never want to work with you again.' "

He had a similarly unsettling experience filming a long scene in which Sandra Bernhard's character, Masha, delivered an improvised monologue about her psychotic passion for Langford while he sat tied to a chair with medical tape like a mummy. For all of the embarrassments he had put himself through at Dean's side or in his self-directed sagas about the lives of the world's most abject misfits, he had never gone through anything like this—complete physical incapacitation at the hands of an odd-looking, pistol-packing young woman in a bra and panties. As with De Niro, Scorsese allowed Bernhard to improvise in the scene—through which Jerry, gagged, has no lines whatever. She employed various bits from her bizarre stage act, equal parts performance art, psychological confessional, and parody of the High Show Biz that Jerry embodied.

Scorsese recalled that Jerry tried to be magnanimous about the sequence at first. "The sexual threat to Jerry was very important," he said, "but he used to crack up laughing. Then it became difficult to deal with, and his comments and jokes became edgier."

Bernhard, making her first film, had been nervous about working with Jerry from the start. She remembered him as "the most intimidating factor in the whole situation." Jerry was already signed to the film when Scorsese was still auditioning, and she, of course, knew who he was and had heard what he was like: "Jerry Lewis was a large, looming figure. So I was scared to meet him, and he lived up to his reputation. He's one of the only show-biz people I met who really has an aura. We kind of worked together a little bit when I auditioned. But there wasn't any big meeting of the minds. He came in right when they were making their final decision about me."

While she found working with Scorsese rewarding, she didn't feel any warmth coming from Jerry, even before their big scene together. "He didn't have anything to do with making things easier," she recalled. "I was just who I was, and that's who he was stuck with. I think he would've felt the same way about any actress who he had to play that role with." And the several days over which the scene was shot were nightmarish. "It wasn't a smooth thing at all," she recalled. "It was a very uncomfortable thing. And I don't think he felt comfortable at all in the situation. Being intimidated by a young woman isn't really Jerry's forte. I don't think it would've worked if it had been this nice, sweet off-screen relationship. All the dynamic off camera served the parts."

After the scene was over, Bernhard was actually invited on to the telethon—and slotted at a 4 A.M. spot. It was emblematic of her experience with her costar. "The movie was it," she said. "We didn't bond. He wasn't particularly nice to me. At the time I took it personally, but shortly after I realized that there was no reason to take it personally. He was from a different generation—why should he relate to me? And that's where we left it. He's too crazy. He's too out there. He's not a pleasant person. He just isn't. He would just say mean things and snap at me."

Whether or not he felt he had been manipulated into his performance by Scorsese and his costars, Jerry was extremely proud of his work on the film, and in his memories the discomforts of the shoot dissolved. "It was the easiest job I ever had in my life," he remembered more than a decade later. "I didn't have to do a fucking thing but show up. All I had to do was play the character, read the dialogue."

But Scorsese understood just how difficult it was for Jerry to play in a straight role and to work under such alien conditions. "Jerry is totally surreal," he told a reporter. "But he was very easy to direct. The role was difficult. He had to look as if nothing were going on—as if he were just walking along the street. He wasn't used to acting that way, and he had to keep his face less than elastic. That's very hard to do."

Moreover, Scorsese had gotten Jerry involved in the improvising, and one of the results of the experiment—Langford's heartfelt confession to his kidnappers that his life was unenviable—stood as one of the highlights of Jerry's performance. "He really got into the dramatic stuff," Scorsese said. "I think he's a wonderful actor."

There were limits to the contributions the director was willing to accept from Jerry, however. When he got wind that Zimmerman and Scorsese differed on how the film should end, Jerry called the writer and the director together to offer an ending of his own devising—Rupert shouldn't, he felt, be able to pull off his dream and become a star; rather, Langford should escape from Masha and arrive at the studio in time to see Rupert gunned down. Zimmerman didn't even want to hear Jerry out; he shook his head "no" even as Jerry was speaking. But Scorsese kept his actor happy by listening carefully to his suggestions and chastising Zimmerman for failing to respect Jerry's opinion. By such diplomatic, respectful gestures, he won Jerry over for the duration of the filming and beyond: When *The King of Comedy* opened in February 1983, Jerry did everything he could to promote the film.

Now, while his career blossomed in midlife springtime, and while he entertained offers from other filmmakers who were interested in casting him now that he had proven his box-office mettle, Jerry found himself confronted with a strange new sort of antagonism toward his charity work. The telethon was still coaxing at least a dollar more out of America each year—more than $31 million in 1981. But now the old whispers that Jerry was somehow profiting from his work had transmuted into attacks on the way he conducted it. In particular, there was criticism of the telethon as a kind of freak show that preyed on the handicapped by projecting images of them as helpless, pitiful children.

In a September 3, 1981, *New York Times* op-ed piece entitled "Aiding the Disabled: No Pity, Please," Evan J. Kemp Jr., executive director of the Disability Rights Center, declared that the Labor Day telethon had bred "vast frustration and anger" among the nation's disabled population. Zeroing in on the equation of all handicapped people with "poster children" and "Jerry's kids," Kemp called the telethon "a television show that reinforces a stigma against disabled people."

It was a thorough, point-by-point attack. By focusing only on handicapped children, Kemp wrote, the MDA "seems to proclaim that the only socially acceptable status for disabled people is their early childhood." A further result of the stereotype of disabled people as helpless children, Kemp said, was that "it intensifies the awkward embarrassment that the able-bodied feel around disabled people." Finally, he declared that "the telethon's critical stress on the need to find cures supports the damaging and common prejudice that handicapped people are 'sick.'"

Kemp, who'd lived his whole life with neuromuscular disease, spoke about the MDA and its methods from a knowledgeable point of view. His parents were themselves handicapped by neuromuscular disease, and they helped found the Cleveland chapter of the MDA years earlier. Furthermore, he was a nephew of Drew Pearson, the influential newspaper columnist who had been an early advocate of the MDA and whose persecution at the hands of McCarthyites in the early 1950s had caused the organization to seek new spokespeople in the entertainment world, Jerry Lewis among them.

Kemp's article wasn't the only unkind murmur about the telethon in the media. Just two weeks before the piece ran, Jerry had appeared on a taping of "The Phil Donahue Show" during which Donahue called into question the MDA's use of poster children and the organization's intimate ties with corporations. In particular, he objected to the way many of the MDA's corporate sponsors tied their donations to consumer purchases—for every box of cereal the public bought, for instance, Kellogg's would donate a fixed sum to the MDA. The popular talk show host decried "all this pompous, self-righteous 'my kids' and put-your-dimes-and-pennies-in-here" and summarized the new charges against the MDA's fund-raising strategies: "The charity enterprise and structure in this country is a competitive, rancor-filled, inefficient system that does not speak equitably to the various difficulties that afflict not only young people but older people as well. To make it worse, we have a bunch of greedy, bottom-line companies coming in here, and their motive has more to do with selling merchandise than with helping the kids."

Jerry, visibly shaken by these arguments, which he seemed to take as personal attacks, adamantly defended both his fund-raising techniques and his corporate sponsors. "The corporate structure is not all that heartless," he argued. "We never, ever exploit my kids in any way. We let the people know that a child has been given a dirty deal—not pity. We do not pity them. Many of them will say to you, 'I'm not crippled, I'm inconvenienced.' That's courageous. That's stunning. That's exquisite as far as I'm concerned." And, in case anyone was wondering, he added, "They want me to sing 'You'll Never Walk Alone.' That's meaningful to them."

Donahue's audience, however, felt the MDA should reform its attitudes toward the disabled and enter into less obviously commercial relationships with its sponsors. A woman stood up to announce that she found the MDA's approach, specifically in the telethon, unbearable. "I find telethons kind of repulsive," she said. "I hate them! I will not turn them on. I turn them on and it looks like a zoo." Jerry shot back an ugly retort: "I've got to get you an autographed photograph of Eva Braun."

As the show wore on, Jerry more and more responded to criticisms of MDA and its fund-raising techniques as if they were attacks on himself. He seemed to be seeking pity not for the kids but for Jerry, the put-upon angel struggling to perform noble acts in a hostile world. "There's nothing wrong with a do-gooder," he stated. "And there's nothing wrong with the charity gain. There's nothing wrong with corny. I've lived an entire life on corn—crying, spreading my emotions through comedy and through seriousness. We need more people in this world to say what they feel from the heart rather than the head."

But after fifteen years of telethons, the novelty had worn off for a great many people, and the MDA had its leanest fund-raising season in the early 1980s. In 1982, for the first time in the history of "The Jerry Lewis Telethon," the tote board tally at the close of the show was *lower* than it had been the previous year. Jerry evinced his desperation in an angry monologue delivered toward the end of the broadcast. "Why am I a criminal?" he asked the audience. "What we are doing here is great work. . . . We've only been at peace 557 days in the last seventeen thousand years. Had they had telethons, we'd have had peace, I'm sure. Is that idealistic? Is that old-fashioned, mid-Victorian? Is that stupid? Is that rhetoric? No! That's what I believe."

In the aftermath of the disappointing returns, an MDA spokesperson blamed "the economic situation and the high rate of unemployment" for the declining donations. But it would take another three years before the 1981 total was topped. The frightening thing from the organization's standpoint was the possibility that Jerry himself may have been turning people away. But, as they well knew, Jerry would never give up his position as front man for the MDA without a fight that would be uglier than anything he might blurt out on TV out of sheer exhaustion.

Ironically, the telethon troubles were surfacing at a time when Jerry seemed actually to have revived his movie career. Even before *The King of Comedy* would be released to critical acclaim, his stock was already rising. Not only had he found producers to finance the new film he wanted to make, but he'd been signed to yet another plum role in a film by a young director. This time, he agreed to play two parts in a film version of Kurt Vonnegut's science-fiction satire *Slapstick*, to be written, directed, and produced by a twenty-two-year-old *auteur* named Steven Paul. Young as he was, Paul had significant experience behind him. Two years earlier, in 1980, he had performed the same Lewisian hat trick of creativity in making *Falling in Love Again* (aka *In Love*), a Jew-from-the-Bronx-falls-for-WASP-princess story starring Elliot Gould, a debuting Michelle Pfeiffer, and Paul himself in a small role.

Slapstick (of Another Kind), as the Vonnegut adaptation was known, must have seemed terribly exciting. The project had attracted an enormous variety of performers, from costars Madeline Kahn and Marty Feldman to an oddball variety of personalities who performed roles ranging from a few lines of narration (Orson Welles) to cameo appearances (Virginia Graham, Merv Griffin) to feature parts (Jim Backus, Pat Morita).

Jerry was dazzled by Paul's youthful enthusiasm and versatility; "He reminds me of me," he remarked soon after shooting began. He was so happy to have the job that he deferred his salary in exchange for participation in the profits of the film, which even without paying Jerry cost $4.5 million. But at least one aspect of the film disturbed him. On the day the shoot began, Jerry learned it was a nonunion production. Jerry had always valued the contributions of his crew members down to the lowliest gofer, and he understood and respected their need to unionize. He was mollified when Paul sat down with representatives of the Teamsters and other unions to reach an understanding, namely, that because of the film's relatively low budget, the unions would not boycott the production.

Otherwise, Jerry watched patiently as his young director worked out Vonnegut's cartoonish story. He played both Caleb Swain, a wealthy "beautiful person," and Wilbur, one of his deformed teenaged twins who was actually a brilliant space alien (Kahn played both Jerry's wife and the other twin). He took no part in the actual directing, however much he joked about Paul's youth with reporters. "I helped him a couple of times and gave him the wrong angles," he told Army Archerd of *Variety*. "But I never let him film them."

When it was all over, though, he was distressed with what he saw. The film was disjointed, truly unreleaseable. Jerry wanted to help Paul cut the film into something more presentable, in particular into something that his fans would recognize. "You cannot just slap Jerry Lewis's name on the marquee without explaining what's going on here," he recalled telling Paul. "Or else we're misrepresenting the movie." But he was rebuffed. The film would remain in limbo a year, only to emerge in 1984 to anemic box office. By then, Jerry was doing everything he could to distance himself from the debacle. "This is either going to be a cult movie or you'll never hear of it," he said. "I hated the script. It didn't make any sense. It *still* doesn't." It didn't matter—nobody came to see the film, and Paul's career went into a swoon. He didn't receive another credit of any sort until his name appeared on the script of *Never Too Young to Die*, a 1986 spy movie spoof cast with offbeat rock 'n' roll stars.

In early September 1982, in time to catch the annual wave of telethon publicity, Atheneum released *Jerry Lewis in Person*, an autobiographical account of his fifty-six years. As a historical document, the book perpetuated and even initiated as many inaccuracies about his life as it dispelled; chronologies were inexact, accounts of unpleasant episodes in his life were manipulated to his advantage, tragedies and failures such as the Jerry Lewis Cinema story were ignored altogether.

All this, of course, made it a standard celebrity autobiography. But there were moments of genuine frankness in the book as well—confessions, for instance, about his drug addiction and the dissolution of his marriage. Particularly unusual was the number of instances the book recorded of his breaking down and sobbing, painting a portrait of a man frequently overcome by his emotions. And astounding by its relative absence was an account of the family he had with Patti—most of the boys weren't even named in the text. If his sons had been estranged from by him by the divorce, this snub did nothing to help forge a reconciliation.

The book wasn't the first time Jerry had bared himself to the public. He'd been forthright about his Percodan use and his divorce in magazine interviews. But the level of detail with which he treated these matters in his autobiography opened a new question: What would the book have been like if he'd decided to be entirely truthful throughout?

Indeed, he was to hint years later that he had originally intended to produce a much less saccharine account of his life. He had started out with some thirteen hundred pages of manuscript, he claimed: "Brutally honest stuff." His publisher had taken a look at this volatile material and dubbed it "a monster book," a potential blockbuster. But, claiming to be overcome with concern for the dignity of others, Jerry excised almost everything inflammatory he had written.

It wasn't that he thought too highly of himself to reveal his own transgressions and failings. "I can be pretty objective and look at Jerry Lewis from a distance," he claimed. "You'd be amazed at what I'd write about him. Because it wouldn't be flowers and fucking gifts and candy. It would be an interesting exercise. Because I got some news for you: The negative would outweigh the posi-

tive. If you're gonna be really honest. Now, whether I could write where the negatives have come from or justify them, I don't know."

But he claimed to be unable to publish such things under his name. The
final version of the "monster" manuscript was a three-hundred-page tour of his
life's highlights as he saw them from a breezy, ellipsis-laden remove. The world
greeted it for what it was—marzipan. It received only fleeting attention in the
book-reviewing press: Such traditional review venues as *The New York Times*, *The
Washington Post*, and the weekly newsmagazines didn't bother with it at all. Like
The Total Film-Maker, it never saw a second edition. Jerry kept cartons of the
book on hand at his office; whenever charities contacted him for donations for
auctions, he would autograph a copy and send it out. "It served its purpose," he
reflected.

The last time Jerry had made as many as two films in a single year was 1967, but
in June 1982 he was on his third movie set in twelve months. He had finally
found financing for a new film of his own. Peter Nelson, who'd produced two
made-for-TV films, and Arnold Orgolini, a novice producer, had recently formed
a production company and hit upon Jerry's script as their first project. The story,
know as *Smorgasbord*, centered on Warren Nefron, a misfit so inept he can't even
kill himself when he's overwhelmed by his screwed-up life. Under the guidance
of a psychiatrist, he essays a number of therapeutic cures for his depression, each
one leading to disaster. Like *Hardly Working*, it was an episodic film, but it was,
in an elliptical way, even more personal. If the earlier film was an embodiment of
Jerry's career crises throughout the 1970s, this one was as frank about his inner
turmoil as his autobiography had tried to be. Even through its prism of gags and
shtick it emerged an unmistakable revelation of his long-term feelings of loneliness and inadequacy.

Smorgasbord was shot in Los Angeles throughout the fall of 1982. Jerry kept
an office in Scarlett O'Hara's old Tara mansion, now an office building on the
former Selznick International lot in Culver City. Though Jerry later announced
with pride that he'd "like to get as many of [his] old crew together as possible,"
most of the principal creative collaborators—editor Gene Fowler, cinematographer Gerald-Perry Finnerman, and composer Morton Stevens among them—
were joining him for the first time. The cast, on the other hand, was filled with
old Lewis friends. Milton Berle and Sammy Davis, Jr., had small roles; Herb
Edelman, costar of the ill-fated *Hellzapoppin'*, played the psychiatrist; and longtime Lewis bit player Buddy Lester was on hand, as was John Abbott, an English
comic actor Jerry had met on *Who's Minding the Store?* and with whom he was
reunited on *Slapstick (of Another Kind)*.

Scott Lewis, the only one of the boys then pursuing a professional relationship with his father, served as associate producer, and he made a gushing show of
his reverence for his dad's comic gifts to reporters who visited the set. After

laughing deeply for nearly two hours as Jerry shot a scene of physical business in a bar, Scott told Lynn Hirschberg of *Rolling Stone,* "My God, I just hope I've inherited some of his amazing ability. We're both Pisceans, so maybe . . ."

The success Fox had enjoyed with *Hardly Working,* coupled with strong advance word about Jerry's work on *The King of Comedy,* had drawn interest in *Smorgasbord* from domestic distributors. Warner Brothers had bought domestic rights from Nelson and Orgolini, but they wanted to test the film before they made any formal plans to exhibit it. Late in 1982 Jerry and Gene Fowler set to work editing a rough version of the film in Las Vegas, where Jerry was living openly with SanDee Pitnick in a condominium at the Las Vegas Country Club. In mid-December he took a quick publicity trip to Europe to do some bush-beating for the film, which would open there in a cut not subject to Warner Brothers approval, and then returned to his condo to finish work on the domestic version.

On Sunday, December 20, he felt a pain in his chest while working in his editing room. Assuming it was indigestion, he knocked off work, took an antacid, had a light supper, and went to bed. The next morning, when he woke with the same pain, he became alarmed. "This is no indigestion," he told SanDee. "I'm having a heart attack."

They drove to Desert Springs Hospital, where Jerry, walking in under his own power, told doctors he felt he was on the verge of a traumatic cardiac episode. The doctors administered a series of tests and began consultations with Dr. Michael DeBakey, Jerry's adored personal physician (he carried his picture in his wallet) in Houston. They kept Jerry in the hospital overnight, with SanDee sitting by his side.

At around midnight, he had the heart attack he had felt brewing. "Suddenly my eyes rolled," he remembered soon afterward. "The pain was a son of a bitch." The hospital staff went into immediate action, administering nitroglycerine and pounding on Jerry's chest. For something like seventeen seconds his heart stopped beating completely. He was, for a brief moment, clinically dead. "My kind of attack is the worst," he remembered. "It's like a TV going off at night when they say, 'That concludes our programming for today.' I felt my body freeze."

The previous day's tests had revealed to Dr. Harold Freikes that an artery leading to Jerry's heart was 90 percent occluded. At 5:45 A.M. on Tuesday, a three-doctor surgical team, attended by ten assistants, began to perform a double bypass surgery on him. Jerry, who'd awakened in the hospital's intensive care ward after his heart attack, was terrified. He knew all about heart surgery from his experiences alongside DeBakey, who had allowed him to photograph operations in Houston. He knew they would use a retractor to pry apart his ribs, that they would remove his beating heart from his thorax. The surgery lasted more than two hours, with doctors removing a healthy vein from his calf to replace the blocked artery in his chest. He was returned to the intensive care unit afterward so that his recovery could be monitored.

He spent eight days recovering in the hospital before he was permitted to go home. It was a traumatic period. "I had devastating nightmares afterwards," he recalled. "The tears poured like a faucet." He wept over the fact that his dog, Angel, couldn't visit him in the hospital; SanDee was so moved by Jerry's grief that she smuggled the dog in for a visit. Four of his sons also came to visit him there, including the estranged Chris, who woke up on the day Jerry entered the hospital with a premonition that his father was ill.

The pain he suffered through the first stages of his recuperation was intense, Jerry remembered, but the single most traumatizing thing had been the glimpse he felt he'd been given of the afterlife. "I was gone and they brought me back," he remembered a few years later. "I saw the other side. And there was nothing. You know how at the end of a day your TV tube goes *psssh* and goes black? That was it. I was looking for a billboard that said, 'Jerry Lewis loves Brown's Hotel.' I should give people hope by telling them there's a yellow brick road and all that, but I saw nothing." Later still, he was even more decisively certain about the experience. "Judy Garland isn't there," he said. "It isn't beautiful. It's bleak."

Returning home, he accepted the reality that he would have to change many of his lifelong habits if he was going to stay alive. He gave up smoking—a four-packs-a-day habit. He began eating more carefully, eliminating salt and sugar from his diet. And he began to respect his body more by making sure he got at least eight hours of sleep each night and avoiding stressful situations. "I allow myself only five minutes of stress at a time, maximum," he explained. "I can't stand incompetence, and I used to be wildly impatient. Now if a clerk in a store is goofing up, instead of blowing my stack, I say, 'What the hell, so it's another ten minutes.' We were having a staff meeting the other day and we got into an argument. After a while, Joe Stabile, my manager, looked at his watch and said, 'Hey, Jer, it's five minutes.' I said, 'Right, let's move on.' If I've got an ugly situation, I face it right away and then dismiss it. I don't hold it."

A Hollywood publicist who knew Jerry for years confirmed that the near-death experience mellowed the comic. "Jerry was an absolute pussycat after his heart attack," he told *Esquire*. "Before that, I dreaded working with him. Look in his mouth. He's got three rows of teeth."

Encouraging him toward recovery was the slate of work he had ahead. In January, just three weeks after surgery, he attended a sneak preview of *Smorgasbord* at a theater in Vegas. It went badly: Warner Brothers declared the film unreleasable and wouldn't even consent to reconsider the decision after further editing. They determined after some time to premiere the film on one of their cable TV stations, where it made its appearance in 1984 as *Cracking Up*. Overseas, however, the film more than paid for itself, with 160,000 paid admissions in Paris alone upon its April 1983 release.

It didn't really deserve much more attention than it got—although plenty of worse films found their way into distribution. An episodic comedy without as much connecting material as even the very loose *Hardly Working, Smorgasbord* (as it should be known, for the word is a key element in the film, as well the name of a Jerry Lewis film within the film) gives Jerry the opportunity to put together a few very funny gags, but it's hardly the sort of coherent narrative that contemporary film audiences might have hoped to see. It's just a sequence of comic set pieces; some of them are splendid, but they pop up and disappear without explanation or coherence.

Yet again, Jerry plays a complete and total failure (how he can afford his tailor-made suits and jewelry is, of course, never explained—though this is the only film in his entire career in which, divorced and not yet remarried, he doesn't wear a wedding band). With the help of an indulgent psychiatrist (Edelman), he explores his family history, his own biography, and some of the nagging manifestations of his mental condition. Finally, his doctor cures him with posthypnotic suggestion, but winds up inheriting his defects and deficiencies.

Within this framework, Jerry includes some of his traditional trademarks— modernist decor (sleek patent leather sofas, monochromatic rooms, absurd kinetic art), an art gallery come to life, Jerry himself playing multiple roles, and a blurring of lines between the world of the film and the off-camera world. The first motif is hilariously explored in the psychiatrist's office, whose floor is so heavily waxed that Jerry can't cross the room without destroying it in bravura physical (and almost totally silent) fashion. Jerry is remarkably limber for a man in his mid-fifties, and when he ends the bit by spilling an entire bag of peanut M&M's all over the roan-colored floor, the sequence achieves a tactility exceedingly rare in the cinema. But it's a level of comedy the rest of the film never reaches.

In *Variety* (which reviewed it upon its Parisian debut), Leonard Klady astutely observed, "It would be a genuine surprise if *Smorgasbord* repeated the North American success of *Hardly Working*. There is a genuine Lewis audience still, but it is certain to tire of this rehash." Still, as with *Hardly Working*, some respected critics used *Smorgasbord* as an attempt to revive esteem for Jerry as a filmmaking talent. When a two-day run of one of the test prints of the film was held in New York in 1985, Jim Hoberman of the *Village Voice* wrote " 'Smorgasbord' has the ascetic, abstract quality that one associates with auteurs in the moody twilight of their obsessions." Undeniably true, but the film is still a weak entry on even Jerry's checkered résumé, and Warner Brothers' decision not to distribute it—whether, as Jerry suspected, a sign of personal malice ("Warner Brothers did it to me a second time," he reckoned) or a simple function of market analysis—probably spared Jerry another barrage of ugly reviews.

■ ■ ■

The King of Comedy, on the other hand, was almost certain to win a public and a following among critics. In advance of the film's opening, Jerry gave interviews to *People*, *Rolling Stone*, and even *McCall's* (where he spoke about "The Joys of Being a Grandfather"). He appeared on "Late Night with David Letterman" and hoped to pull off a stunt involving his autobiography—he wanted to provide all 550 audience members with a copy of *Jerry Lewis in Person* but not have one for the host (when he couldn't drum up enough copies in time for the taping, he called the prank off). And he hosted NBC's "Saturday Night Live," performing in a few sparkling skits with young comics (and obvious Lewis fans) Eddie Murphy and Joe Piscopo. In one routine, Jerry was wheeled in for open-heart surgery and given anesthesia, only to dream in his ether swoon that a drunken Dean Martin (Piscopo) was his surgeon, and a swinging Sammy Davis Jr. (Murphy) his anesthetist; in another, he was escorted into a Parisian film studio to watch Tim Kazurinsky dub The King of Comedy into French, only to hear all of Jerry Langford's dramatic lines delivered in the familiar wheedle of the Kid.

If he was supposed to have mellowed, he didn't sound it in an interview he gave the New York *Daily News* during the week he spent in town. He could still get exercised on the subject of the press, for instance. "I will not allow injustice," he announced. "I will not allow inaccuracy, and I am not a subject of ridicule. I was not put on this earth to please those who would be happiest if I went on my ass and/or their sadness if I score well. I'm not here for them. I'm here for *me*. And if I can contribute something for all of you when I'm doing what I need to do for me, I've lived a life. If you've got what I got—I was living with it for seven, eight, maybe nine years anticipating that finally I would read the press off."

If that didn't sound sufficiently like the tantrum-prone, presurgery Jerry, he continued: "I live in a selfish, selfless kind of a cocoon. You cannot get by in this world, apparently, if you are a courageous, honest crusader and/or stand-up, straight-ahead man who will not take shit. I'll sit in the corner and let you pound me if I've got it coming. If I don't have it coming, you'd better know what you're doing, because you're tangling with a goddamn son of a bitch."

Anyone who was surprised by this sort of talk coming from a funnyman-philanthropist only needed to see *The King of Comedy* to know for certain that there was an ebon side to Jerry's character. With the exception of Buddy Love, Jerry Langford was absolutely the closest thing he'd played to himself on screen. Cocky, aloof, a sometime dandy, yet lonely, sarcastic, and capable of venomous outbursts, Langford was the quintessential Great American Star.

For the first time in his life, Jerry was almost universally heaped with praise. Vincent Canby of *The New York Times* spoke of Jerry's "brilliant solemnity," while his colleague Janet Maslin called Jerry's work "one of the best things" in the film. In *The New Yorker*, Pauline Kael was even more specific: "Jerry Lewis is the only real thing here," she wrote, adding that "Lewis doesn't try to make the off-camera Langford likeable; the performance says that what the off-camera star feels is his own damn business." "A shrewdly disciplined performance," wrote Richard Schickel in *Time*, while Jack Kroll of *Newsweek* called Jerry's work "extraordinary." Indeed, when *The King of Comedy* was named one of the decade's ten best films by a group of critics polled in *American Film* magazine in 1989, Jerry's contribution was clearly one of the elements people remembered most vividly.

Of course, Jerry felt the praise was his due—failing, it seemed, to recognize a difference between his work for Scorsese and his work for himself and other directors. "Those reviews—and I read every single one of them—were incredible," he said a decade later. "And I just laughed. They all wrote about what a good actor I am. I've been doing it for fifty-five years! Where have these people been? Just because I don't take a pratfall in a motion picture, I'm now a great actor? For those of you who study comedy, you have to remember this expression: 'He *acts* like a fool.' " He insisted, despite his earlier testimony of the emotional toll that Scorsese and De Niro exacted from him, that he did nothing for the duration of the film but show up on the set.

But—for once—he was being modest about what he accomplished. Of all of the work he ever did, only *The Nutty Professor* comes as close as *The King of Comedy* to indicating just what the man was like beneath the skin. And where the former film only revealed the real Jerry as a pair of counterposed tropes, the latter has an almost documentary feel. Contributing to the effect was Scorsese's methodology: Wearing his own clothes, sitting with his own dog, with a picture of his adolescent self on his mantle, Jerry Langford is very, very nearly Jerry Lewis. He has a caricature of himself as the logo of his show and his company; he plays golf; he lives in a pristine, modernistic environment; he has an explosive, caustic temper; he feels compelled to display himself to his public (despite his celebrity, he walks the streets of Manhattan to go to work) yet simultaneously loathes it (he tells Rupert that if he becomes famous, "then you're gonna have idiots like you plaguing your life"). Buddy Love should have given America all the insight it would ever want into the black side of Jerry's nature, but America took *The Nutty Professor* for a fairy tale, not a confession. Nobody who saw *The King of Comedy*, on the other hand, came away thinking that Jerry Lewis was a genial, breezy guy.

He's all over Scorsese's film, appearing in eighteen scenes. He plays the haughty celebrity, the lonely successful man, a joshing chum (in Rupert's fantasies), the consummately professional talk show host, a pleading prisoner, an immobilized victim. He walks confidently in the sunlight (where he meets the lady who tells him in one breath that he's "a joy to the world" and in the next that he "should only get cancer") and races desperately through the night after escaping Masha's clutches. Most memorably, he belittles Rupert in the venomous outpouring of rage that De Niro coaxed from him with his off-camera anti-Semitic remarks.

It's a chilling scene. Rupert and his date (played by De Niro's ex-wife, Diahnne Abbott) have come to Langford's country house and have made themselves at home in Jerry's absence. After a hilarious phone call from his Asian butler, Jerry arrives at home carrying a golf club and simmering with rage. At first he patiently sizes up the scene, saying as little as he can as Rupert attempts to reconcile his fantasy life (in which his good pal Jerry has invited him for the weekend) and the colder reality.

Finally, Langford sees that no amount of gentle coaxing will rid him of this pest. "Did anyone ever tell you you're a moron?" he asks. "Do you understand English? Take your things and go!"

Rupert desperately attempts to bridge the gap between himself and his idol by appealing to their common humanity, but Langford doesn't feel obliged to see the intruder as his equal. When Rupert begs for just ten minutes of attention, Langford refuses: "I have a life, okay?" "So do I," says Rupert, to which Jerry responds, "That's not my responsibility!"

Finally, Langford shatters all Rupert's fantasies. "I told you to call to *get rid of you!*" he shouts, and it's clear that the character's anger is also the actor's. "If I didn't tell you that, we'd still be standing on the steps of my apartment!" Beaten, Rupert admits, "Well, all right, I made a mistake." "So did Hitler!" shouts Jerry, red-faced, snarling, and leaning forward with menace.

It's stunning, as if the bile of a lifetime has spewed out without Jerry's knowing it. Astonishingly, Scorsese gets two other such moments out of him: the look of horror and revulsion on his face as he sits tied to a chair in a room full of candles while Bernhard cavorts in her brilliant monologue, and the improvised confession with which Langford hopes to achieve his release from his captors. Speaking reasonably, like an adult with another adult, with some of his natural haste but with a genuine sense of groping beneath his words, he describes his life to Rupert and Masha: "I'm sure you can understand, doing the kind of show that I'm doing, it's mind-boggling. There's so much stuff that comes down, you can't keep your head clear. And if that's the case, I'm wrong. You're right, I'm wrong. If I'm wrong, I apologize. I'm just a human being, with all of the foibles, all of the traps, the show, the pressure, the groupies, the autograph hounds, the crew, the incompetence, those behind the scenes you think are your friends and you're not too sure if you're gonna be there tomorrow because of their incompetence. There are wonderful pressures that make every day a glowing, radiant day in your life. It's terrific. Okay. If all of that means nothing, if I'm wrong, despite all of that, I apologize. I'm sorry. If you accept my apology, I think we should shake hands and we'll forget the whole thing." This patient explanation of the hell of celebrity life is just as convincing as his volcanic tirade, another remarkable glimpse into the mind of Jerry himself.

■　■　■

One week before *The King of Comedy*'s nationwide opening, Jerry and SanDee flew to the Sonesta Beach Hotel in Key Biscayne to be married. It was supposed to be a small, private ceremony, with MDA executive director Bob Ross serving as best man and Claudia Stabile, wife of Joe, standing as the matron of honor. But unbeknownst to the bridal party, ABC-TV was using the hotel's facilities that weekend to tape an athletic competition show, "The Superstars." Nevertheless, the couple was wed by a rabbi on Sunday, February 13, 1983, exchanging rings and standing for a UPI photograph showing the groom attempting to swallow his bride's face the way he'd so often wrapped his mouth around an entire water glass.

Afterward, Jerry confessed that he was nervous during the ceremony, a condition he ascribed to his recent brush with death. "There wasn't another marriage in my life," he said. "The first was so long ago. I felt like a young stud starting out all over again." Indeed, the wedding in Key Biscayne rather echoed his secret elopement to Connecticut with Patti: Danny was gone, Rae was sick at home in Las Vegas, none of his six sons were present.

He had, in fact, failed to reconcile with most of the boys since the divorce. Scott was willing to work for him, but Jerry kept him at a distance. During the shoot of *Smorgasbord*, for instance, Jerry told him, "I love you, but I didn't work my fingers to the bone for you or your mother. I did it all for me. All of you got in the way, and so I'm releasing myself from those obstacles to see if I can enjoy my life totally."

Chris, who had remained almost entirely estranged from his father from the time he had seen the contents of Jerry's bathroom drawer, made some overtures to Jerry after the heart surgery. He came to Las Vegas along with his fiancée to have dinner, but he was so uncomfortable in Jerry's presence that he couldn't look him in the eye. Jerry didn't make it easy on him. "I'm almost resentful the boys weren't quicker in coming around to me," he said soon afterward.

Only one son remained by Jerry's side without pause from the divorce onward. Anthony, Patti's most exacting, together son, was considering a wedding of his own when his parents' marriage dissolved. He was in his early twenties, he remembered, and he and his fiancée, Sharon, "found ourselves being dragged into a political undertow which was not only forcing us to choose sides, but was also overshadowing any and all notions of our getting married." Patti, in fact, asked the couple to put their wedding plans on hold until her own marital situation was settled, but they wouldn't; Sharon's parents even called Patti to ask if she could help pay for the big wedding the young couple hoped to have. Patti, with nothing of her own to spend, told Anthony to ask his father for money.

Jerry leapt at the chance; he promised the couple a big Las Vegas wedding, as his treat. Told about these new arrangements—which she knew involved SanDee—Patti refused to attend the wedding, and the rest of the boys announced they would sit it out with her. "Sharon and I were unable to make a logical, collected decision as to how to handle the whole issue," Anthony recalled. In their confusion, he and Sharon decided to keep themselves virtually incommunicado from Patti and the other boys.

When the wedding was celebrated, Jerry stood as his son's best man, but Rae was the only other family member in attendance. At the precise hour that the service was being held in Las Vegas, Patti and the other boys went to dinner at Chasen's in Beverly Hills and toasted the absent newlyweds with champagne. Afterward, the Hollywood rumor mill viciously reported that the estranged Lewis boys and their mother had spent Anthony's wedding night celebrating their solidarity in rebuffing Jerry, but as Patti admitted later, "the truth is, I was crying."

In the aftermath of this calamity, Anthony and Sharon became favorites of Jerry's. "Sharon and I were always with Dad and had a very good time together," Anthony remembered. They had their first child, Kimberly, in March 1982, and she appeared with her grandfather in magazine and newspaper photographs and articles. But Patti was denied access to the child altogether. For at least a year after the baby was born, Patti was so thoroughly spurned by Anthony and Sharon that she became active in lobbying Congress for federal legislation to mandate visitation rights for grandparents. Democratic Congressman Mario Biaggi of New York was trying to introduce federal legislation of a type that already existed in forty-two states, and Patti contacted him to support his efforts.

As it turned out, Biaggi was glad for Patti's help because, among other things, she had become something of a nationally recognized figure since her divorce. As a visible member of a group known as LADIES ("Life After Divorce Is Eventually Sane"), she spent her days making public the plight of late-life divorcées such as herself. The group had been founded in the early 1980s by Michael Landon's former wife, and it ranks had swelled over the years to include ex-wives of such performers as Ken Berry, George Segal, Buddy Ebsen, Erik Estrada, Leonard Nimoy, Flip Wilson, Don Knotts, and Glen Campbell. That these women had been party to high-profile marriages no doubt made their cause attractive to the media; Patti made several appearances on daytime talk shows, including one taped the very afternoon she and Jerry signed their final divorce papers. But it was also true that in a culture that was aging demographically and more prone than ever to divorce, her cause was of interest to millions. The group dedicated itself to easing the burden of older divorcées by recommending attorneys who were supportive of women's needs, by directing people to counseling and therapy, and by forming a network among organizations that offered older divorcées assistance. They even provided for a novel kind of buddy system: When a member of the organization appeared in court as part of her divorce proceedings, someone else from the group would show up as well. They counseled one another through such pains as their ex-husbands' highly publicized new marriages and helped each other deal with their greatly diminished financial resources.

Despite its obvious potential to be a conduit for feelings of antagonism or even revenge, LADIES was more like a spiritual organization dedicated to mutual support, the rebuilding of members' self-esteem, and the setting of an example for women undergoing divorces from less famous men. Patti spoke on live and televised religious programs and in front of such national organizations as Displaced Homemakers. Although she had always been spiritually inclined, her work with LADIES brought her closer than ever to the sources of her faith.

She certainly needed it—she had very little in the way of material recompense to show for her thirty-six-year marriage. In 1983 she was forced to put the Bel Air house on the market. Asking $7.5 million for a house in something less than pristine condition, she had to wait nearly three years before she sold it, afterward buying a smaller home in nearby Westwood and filling it with the mementoes she and Jerry had accumulated on St. Cloud Drive.

She wasn't the only Lewis displaced after Jerry's heart attack and remarriage, however. When their father's ill health pulled most of the boys back toward him, Anthony found himself shunted aside. "Since then," he reflected, "things have been generally amenable but sporadic." He and his wife reconciled with Patti, who was finally given the chance to meet her grandchildren. "All three of us have crossed that line between love and contempt," Anthony explained, "and realized how distasteful it is on the other side."

There was one last family postscript to Jerry's second wedding. On the very weekend that Jerry and SanDee went to Key Biscayne, Rae Lewis entered a hospital in Las Vegas complaining of chest pains. Her heart was failing. She held on for two weeks, then finally lost her struggle on February 25. Danny had been gone for two years. Just as she'd spent her life sticking by him even when it meant leaving her only child behind, she was buried by his side in the desert.

21.

Commander

Jerry resumed live performances in April 1983, a mere dozen weeks after his heart surgery. "His doctors think it's a good idea, getting back into the swing of things," Joe Stabile told the *New York Post*. "He won't be doing pratfalls, but Jerry's a spontaneous performer." In fact, his schedule was curtailed to ensure his recovery was complete. After the previous year's flurry of movie activity and the commotion of publicity surrounding the release of *The King of Comedy*, 1983 was a very quiet year. His work on the telethon, for example, was cut back by the inclusion of more and more pretaped segments, many without him at all. Indeed, he'd never again go without sleep for the duration of an entire telethon; guest hosts covered the early-morning hours for him while he got his quota of rest.

He did find the energy to make a film that year, albeit under unusual circumstances. He had long spoken of making a film in France with his admirers there such as comedian Pierre Etaix, but none of those plans had ever come to fruition. In the summer of 1983, however, after introducing *The King of Comedy* at the Cannes Film Festival along with Scorsese and De Niro, he set to work on a movie directed by Michel Gerard, a maker of broad French comedies that never showed in the U.S., and starring Michel Blanc, the slight, bald actor best known to American audiences for his portrayal of the title role in Patrice Leconte's *Monsieur Hire*. In the film, entitled *Retenez-moi . . . ou je fais un malheur* ("Hold me back or I'll have an accident"), Jerry played a Las Vegas policeman visiting France and staying with his ex-wife (Charlotte de Turckheim), who has remarried a stereotypically dapper Frenchman (Blanc); a farcical roundelay follows, with the two men combining forces to crack an art-smuggling ring and the wife having to choose which man she wants to end up with.

It was an extremely low-key affair for Jerry, who seemed almost not to want his countrymen to know that he was working abroad. Spotted by a New York reporter while buying a vase and glasses at Baccarat's Paris showroom, he snapped, "We don't pose for pictures! You're not going to stand there all day, are you?" (He had put on weight, the reporter noticed, and was sucking on an empty pipe, presumably as part of his no-cigarette routine.)

The film opened in Paris on January 13, 1984, to generally receptive reviews ("The recipe is good and the mayonnaise well set," said *France-Soir*) and a healthy box office—not quite as strong as for *Smorgasbord* or *Which Way to the Front?*, but significantly better than *The King of Comedy*, which had just as much trouble finding a commercial niche overseas as at home. Americans wouldn't even get a chance to decide whether they were interested in *Retenez-moi*, however. Though French viewers heard Jerry's voice dubbed, an English-language version, *To Catch a Cop*, was also prepared—but neither Jerry nor the producers could ever find an American distributor for it.

It wasn't surprising that Jerry's debut in a French film was well received. But some observers were taken aback on the day it opened to learn that Jerry would be given a state honor by the French government. In a ceremony at the Eiffel Tower attended by more than two hundred journalists and photographers, Jack Lang, France's Minister of Culture, made Jerry a commander in his nation's Order of Arts and Letters, the nation's highest cultural honor. The presentation made for some smirking headlines back home, but the fact was that many artists from around the world were honored in this fashion by the French government: Musicians, painters, and poets far less connected to the French people than Jerry belonged to the Order (a few years later, for instance, Sylvester Stallone would join its ranks).

More startlingly, however, Jerry returned to France two months later to receive a higher honor. On March 12, 1984, during a gala performance by Rudolph Nureyev at the Paris Opera to benefit the Pasteur and Wiezman institutes, Jerry was given the French Legion of Honor for his charity work. While the Order of Arts and Letters was an acknowledgment of Jerry's unique artistry, the Legion of Honor was another sort of recognition altogether, one normally reserved for foreign heads of state, military heroes, beneficiaries of humanity, and the most absolutely revered artists. It was the most exceptional honor the French government could award, and President François Mitterand pinned it onto sad little Joey Levitch.

Jerry was so proud of this distinction that he wore the ribbon commemorating it when he returned to the States later that month. He showed up at the offices of the New York *Daily News* ostensibly to promote *Slapstick (of Another Kind)*, but wearing his Legion ribbon on his black sweater and talking about it eagerly. "Anyone who receives the medal gets to wear this ribbon," he explained. "And every Frenchman recognizes it. Look at the company I'm in. There's a guy named Pasteur, and there's Albert Schweitzer, John F. Kennedy, Emile Zola, Charles de Gaulle, Dwight Eisenhower, General Pershing, and Alfred Hitchcock.

Not bad, huh? When they gave me the medal I couldn't speak. It was as if I had cotton in my mouth. It was the biggest thrill of my life, and now, when I go to France, I get two bodyguards. I told President Mitterand I didn't need them. He told me that they need them. They consider us some sort of national treasures. I'm so proud it's unbelievable."

It helped to ease the pain he must have felt at being denied a Best Supporting Actor nomination from the Motion Picture Academy for *The King of Comedy* (Jack Nicholson and John Lithgow were cited for *Terms of Endearment,* Charles Durning for *To Be or Not to Be,* Sam Shepard for *The Right Stuff,* and Rip Torn for *Cross Creek,* with Nicholson the eventual winner). The fact that Jerry had been castigating the academy in the press for some years no doubt played a role in his being neglected. He had pointedly never received the Jean Hersholt Humanitarian Award, for instance, even though the prize had gone to people who'd committed themselves to charitable causes for a year or two or who raised minuscule percentages of what he'd raised for the MDA.

He stubbornly denied harboring any resentment about the academy: "I never even think about such a thing," he said. "I've never thought about it until this second that you've mentioned it." But in fact, he had been complaining about the academy for years. In particular, he saw a bias in the voting toward drama, which he repeatedly told interviewers was an easier art than comedy. "There's no category for comedy at the Academy Awards," he groused in 1982. "There's a category for the guy who puts a new bulb in the toilet of the movie house. They also have a category for magnetic-strip systems that are utilized by the extension of perspiration from a yak's ass. They have categories for *everything,* but not for comedy."

The lack of such a category hurt such performers as Charlie Chaplin, Stan Laurel, Danny Kaye, and Peter Sellers as much as it did him, but Jerry took it as a personal affront. "I have a simple philosophy," he explained. "Don't say no swell stuff over my grave. I'm opening up a chain of eulogy stands where anyone can go in, and for twenty bucks they read to you all the swell stuff they're going to say when you croak. I want to hear it *now.* Tell me *now.* That's all I ever say to the academy, but every year the Irving Thalberg Award [for life achievement] goes to this wonderful conglomerate from Pittsburgh Ball Bearing Paints because it put up enough money to make a two-reeler out of *The Great Gatsby,* which is a porno film in Tokyo."

In conjunction with the release of *Slapstick,* Jerry appeared on the cover of *Parade* magazine, the nationally distributed Sunday newspaper supplement. It was his first appearance on the cover of the magazine in years, and it marked the beginning of a long relationship between Jerry and its editors. On Labor Day weekends henceforth, Jerry would be shown on the cover of the magazine with an MDA poster child; an article would appear inside under his own byline.

The April 1984 story, however, was a visit-with-a-celebrity piece by journalist Dotson Radar. It told the story of Jerry's heart surgery, described his wedding to SanDee, and recounted Jerry's life with all the old stories. Two odd little revelations in the story stood out, however: a statement about the origins of *Jerry Lewis in Person*—"I think I really wanted to write my biography more to be able to mention that Jack Kennedy and I were friends than anything else"—and a revelation that he had authorized the MDA to continue using his name in its fundraising efforts even after his death. "It was one of those nights when you can't sleep and have to get something off your chest," he said of a memo he'd written to the organization. "I wrote, 'Turn my death into paydirt. Anybody who's honest and cares can replace Jerry Lewis, but beg the people to give in his memory. Look at how much he gave; it probably killed him. Turn me into a theatrical martyr, use my death positively. Don't waste it. *Use it.*' That letter was the most devastating thing I ever did in my life." It might well have been, but for someone who didn't care to have any sweet words spoken over his grave that were denied him in life, he was pretty specific about the contents of his own eulogy.

"A lot of people who do talk shows are nothing but conversationalists. You need a cuckoo bird, a nut, a man with a point of view and deep concerns. People with the guts to say what they mean."

It was April 1984, and he was talking to *TV Guide*. There was a new scheme in the works. Jerry Lewis Films and Metromedia Video Productions had signed an agreement to create and market a week's worth of talk-variety shows as a pilot for a potential syndicated series with Jerry as the host.

Metromedia president Robert Bennett had come up with the idea when he'd seen *The King of Comedy* on video and realized, as he put it, "that this man should be on TV in the U.S." Bennett contacted Jerry in Paris and proposed a course of action, and Jerry happily agreed. "I can't think of anyone better equipped to perform the role of talk show host than Lewis," Bennett said. "His close associates tell me this show has him more excited than anything else in the past twenty years."

They spent two months preparing. Joe Stabile and Bill Richmond were slotted as executive producers, with Richmond also picking up writing duties. Artie Forrest, the man behind the telethons, would produce and direct. Lou Brown would provide the house band. Charlie Callas would be the sidekick and announcer. It was filmed at Metromedia Square in Hollywood, and if it proved a hit in syndication in the spring, a year's worth would be made that fall.

On June 11, the premiere telecast of "The Jerry Lewis Show" appeared on independent stations across the nation. Jerry greeted his audience with open arms: "I just wish the best wish I could ever wish for you—to have people in show business as your friends." The first guest was Frank Sinatra, followed by Suzanne Somers. On the second show, Norm Crosby and William Shatner showed up. Mel Tormé and Tony Orlando made it later in the week. No one watched. And, according to Kay Gardella of the New York *Daily News*, they didn't miss anything: "There's just too much backslapping on the program. It's embarrassing. Just get on with it." *Variety* was a touch gentler, calling the show "a mixed bag" and pointing out that Jerry "talked a good deal, more than his guests." But Metromedia wasn't encouraged by either the product or the ratings. Poof: Another TV show dead.

Jerry went overseas again to make another French comedy, this time set in Paris and Tunisia. *Par ou t 'es rentre? On t 'a pas vue sortir* ("How Did You Get In? No One Saw You Leave") was written and directed by Phillipe Clair, a veteran practitioner of low-budget comedies that had more than a whiff of *Lewisienne* grotesquerie about them, and produced by Tarak Ben Ammar, a Tunisian money man who'd been trying for some time to promote his homeland as a filmmaking mecca. Like his previous French film, this one was a farce, with Jerry as a private eye hired to catch a rich man (Clair) with his mistress so his wife could reap a handsome divorce settlement. When the detective and the rich man become friends, they flee to Tunisia, where they find themselves embroiled in a dispute among Italian, Arab, and American interests in a war of fast-food chains. Jerry's voice was dubbed, as in his earlier French film, but this time in a comically moronic Algerian accent—rather as if Jacques Tati were to make a Hollywood film and have his voice dubbed as a hillbilly.

When the film opened in Paris that November, it received the worst reviews Jerry had ever had in France. The journal *Cinéma*, long supportive of Jerry's career, pronounced it, "incomprehensible, abnormal, absurd, and calamitous," adding, "You can count the gags on the fingers of a single hand. You smile two or three times . . . before slipping into a lethal ennui. His previous French film was ominously entitled 'Hold Me Back or I'll Have an Accident.' The accident has happened." Parisian audiences seemed undeterred by such notices—the new French film was even more popular than his previous one. But once again, no American distributor could be found to touch it.

Jerry himself dismissed his two ventures into French comedy as failures. "These are not very good movies," he admitted. "As long as I've got control, you'll never see them in this country." Although he was quick to point out they weren't his films ("I had no input because I trusted the directors"), he was frank about the work he did: "I gave little energy and that's what's on the fucking screen." How revved up could he have been, after all, at the thought of having to cross an ocean to get a picture made?

He bided his time in Las Vegas golfing, playing racquetball, and riding his bike. He and SanDee went to Italian restaurants. They kept a boat in San Diego and a condo in Miami. He was nearing sixty, and though he felt and looked youthful, he was living as though he were retired. And it was not by his own choice. He still did live appearances, and he had more time than ever to devote to the MDA, but he was itching to do more. When he came to Brown's Hotel in the late summer of 1985, a reporter asked him about his inactivity and the critics who claimed he was finished. "There's an element of envy here," he shot back. "Are they one of the ten most recognizable people in the world? Do they know the royal family in England or the king of Sweden? Do they wear the Legion of Honor on their lapel?"

But protests of this sort sounded hollow. He was more and more becoming an elder statesman, whether he cared to see himself that way or not. Of course, he was always glad to accept the appreciation and respect of younger talents. He gloried in the fact that Steven Spielberg recognized him from the dais after screening *E.T.* at Cannes in 1982, for instance, explaining to a reporter that the celebrated young director *"always* knew about respect." He was supportive of younger comics such as Steve Martin, Chevy Chase, Martin Short, and Howie Mandel, whose work often seemed derived from his own best material. In March 1986 he was invited to the very first "Comic Relief" show, an all-star comedy revue held to raise money for the homeless and hosted by Billy Crystal, Whoopi Goldberg, and Robin Williams. The air was thick with famous comedians, but when Jerry was introduced to the wall-to-wall show-business audience at the Universal Amphitheater and strolled onto the stage, he got the only standing ovation of the night. "When I saw that audience stand up, and all of my peers backstage," Jerry reflected, "what they were saying was, 'Thanks for your body of work.' They're the ones that are all my little road companies, who have learned just as I learned from whoever I learned from. What a night. I was dumbfounded. One of the few times I've stood on a stage and was, 'Duh . . . duh . . . duh . . . duh . . .' "

In the summer of 1986 he performed at the Just for Laughs Festival in Montreal. In that city, which he'd long believed was lucky for him, he received something less than the adulation he got at "Comic Relief." In particular, he got what *Variety* described as "a mildly negative review" from Lucina Chodan in the city's English-language daily, *The Montreal Gazette.* He made the mistake of discussing his reaction to the review with reporters: "You can't accept one individual's [opinion], particularly if it's a female, and you know, God willing—I hope for her sake, it's not the case—but when they get a period it's really difficult for them to function as normal human beings."

Challenged for these remarks by *Variety*'s reporter, who happened to be female, he put his other foot in his mouth, bullying his questioner with double entendres. "I wasn't attacking the female gender by any means," he said. "Not with the type of sex drive I have, honey. I have nothing against women. As a matter of fact, there's something about them that I love, but I just can't put my finger on it."

Local women's groups, pointing out that Chodan's review was one of the more positive notices that Jerry's performance received, were outraged. Sylvia

Gold, chair of the Canadian Advisory Council on the Status of Women, told *Variety*, "It's a message to the MDA that it's time to find a chief fund-raiser who is more attuned to the values of the day." Radio talk shows crackled with the voices of women disgusted with Jerry's attitudes. Back in Hollywood, he released a statement to the press hoping to put an end to the matter: "I really lost my temper and let my anger at one woman put words in my mouth that could easily have been construed to defame all women. That's the essence of prejudice and I'm guilty. . . . I didn't make a movie called *The Big Mouth* for nothing."

He had an easier time of it that fall, when he was roasted by the Friars at a luncheon in New York, an event where ribald talk was encouraged. He'd been fêted by the club some sixteen years earlier, but it was the Friars' eightieth anniversary, and they were pulling out all the old-timers for a new round of lucrative fund-raisers; they'd even roasted Dean a few months earlier. Friars prior Jack L. Green presented Jerry with a watch commemorating the occasion, along with a check for the MDA in the sum of ten thousand dollars, a cost allayed by the hundred-dollar-per-person fee the twenty-six hundred attendees paid for their tickets.

If Jerry had begun to absent himself slightly from the telethon in 1983 in part to save wear and tear on his mending heart, by 1986 he had reoriented himself toward the show entirely. He had taken over the producing reins, dedicating himself to planning the show earlier in the year than he ever had, and spending significant blocks of time backstage during the broadcast itself making sure the show ran properly. Of all the telethons he'd done, it was the one that featured him on screen the least.

In December of the following year, he brought the telethon to France. It was a forty-eight-hour event with Jerry participating in advance publicity and as an on-air performer. Technicians and equipment were donated by unions; the Lions' Club gathered twelve thousand volunteers to answer the phones and provide other nontechnical support. During the broadcast, a live feed came in from a train traveling throughout the country and collecting money from regional donation centers. The in-studio talent lineup was decidedly more European than the Vegas telethon ever boasted—Marcel Marceau, chanteuse Nana Mouskouri, Paul McCartney, the Bee Gees, a jazz trio led by Michel Legrand. The MDA had never tried anything like it, and they had hoped to raise maybe $10 million over the course of the weekend; they did three times that, garnering $30.2 million altogether. Even though his strongest European box office was in Germany, he always could rake it in in France, and his telethon there became a regular event.

In May 1987 Wilbert J. LeMelle, president of Mercy College in Dobbs Ferry, New York, awarded Jerry an honorary doctorate of Humane Letters, declaring that Jerry was "a shining example for people everywhere that one person can have an impact on society and change the world."

It was a decade of honors for him. A few years earlier, he'd won Boston University Law School's N. Neal Pike Award for service to the handicapped. John R. Silber, the infamously caustic one-armed president of the university, made the presentation to Jerry at the Helmsley Palace Hotel in New York. Earlier still, he'd won the Department of Defense Medal for Distinguished Public Service and the Hubert H. Humphrey Humanitarian Award from the Touchdown Club of Washington, D.C.

But what he wanted most—to work again in front of big audiences—seemed finally beyond his grasp. He scaled back his expectations and found new kinds of work. In March 1987, along with longtime MDA colleague Patty Duke, he starred in NBC's made-for-TV movie called *Fight for Life*, the based-on-truth story of Bernie Abrams, an optometrist from Columbus, Ohio, whose adopted daughter has fallen prey to a rare and virulent form of epilepsy. When he discovered that a drug used to combat the effects of the disease in Europe had not yet been cleared for use in the U.S. by the Food and Drug Administration, Abrams went on TV to plead his case tearfully before the public.

Variety didn't care for the film, declaring that it was "loaded with sincere good intentions, but the pacing and the action weigh the drama down." Nevertheless, the film gave Jerry the first opportunity in his life to play an explicitly Jewish role; he wears a yarmulke, quotes the Talmud, coaches his son through the haftarah reading for his bar mitzvah, hosts a traditional Shabbat dinner, describes his desire to fight the FDA as a mitzvah, and speaks aloud to God like Tevye. He also got the autobiographical opportunity to play a man going on TV with tears in his eyes to plead with the public for assistance in his fight against pediatric disease: "I don't apologize for crying," he blubbers in surprisingly unconvincing fashion for a man to whom tears come so easily in public. "I'm crying for the children of America."

Patty Duke wasn't the only old chum he worked with that year. He teamed with Sammy Davis, Jr., in the fall and winter for a series of live performances. The two had worked together before on a one-shot comedy special for the HBO cable network, but their debut in Atlantic City marked their first real effort at a joint act. They opened their shows together, then alternated back and forth for about two hours, leaving room for improvised bits and mutual joshing. "We try to do things that are commercial," Sammy told the press, "the things that people expect from us, plus a few surprises." But the audience response wasn't enough to warrant taking the act to another level.

A few months later, Sammy teamed with Sinatra and Dean for a national tour of large arenas. "We're happy to be doing this thing," Dean told reporters at the big press conference that announced the tour. "What the hell." He couldn't hide his contempt for the enterprise, though, or for its self-satisfied opulence.

During the opening performance at the Oakland Coliseum, he flicked a lit cigarette into the crowd. A few nights later, he argued with Sinatra and quit the tour, announcing ill health as the cause (belying this bit of PR whitewash, he opened a run in Vegas soon afterward). Jerry would have killed to have filled the slot, but Liza Minnelli was selected as Dean's replacement.

Another era passed the following summer. He had still been making occasional appearances at Brown's Hotel, but the Brown family had fallen on hard times. The old Catskills had died in the 1960s with cheap air travel, the demise of traditional Eastern Jewish mores, and the advent of American youth culture. Many of the hotels had hung on by catering to a new clientele, business conventions instead of families. With the rise of casino gambling in Atlantic City, however, even that business dried up. Some hotels were torn down, their acreage converted to condominium grounds. Grossinger's, the Ritz of the mountains, was sold to a faceless corporation in 1986. And Brown's Hotel, which had advertised with Jerry's youthful caricature for three decades, declared bankruptcy in July 1988.

During the proceedings, it became known that Lillian Brown had given Jerry a fifty-thousand-dollar check for recent appearances at the hotel but told him frankly that it wouldn't clear her bank. Naturally, he sympathized. "This is one of the few times in anyone's life where they don't mind waiting for the money," he told reporters. "When Lillian gave me the check, she asked if I would mind waiting until she told me to deposit it, in light of Brown's difficulties. Of course I didn't mind. I have nothing but love and respect for her and the Brown's resort. We all look forward to performing there again in the future." But the Brown family sold the hotel, and the skinny, lonely kid they greeted there so warmly more than forty years earlier never returned. "I haven't been to the Borscht Belt in three or four years," he said in 1993. "Since my Aunt Lil and the hotel severed, I haven't been there."

That November, the American Museum of the Moving Image in Astoria, Queens, presented a month-long program entitled "Jerry Lewis: A Film and Television Retrospective." Scott Bukatman, an instructor at the School of Visual Arts, organized the program along with the museum's David Schwartz. Together, they selected some two dozen films for screening, from *My Friend Irma* to *Smorgasbord*. They contacted Jerry to find out if he could supply them with other materials—TV shows, blooper reels, and so forth—and if he'd be willing to make a personal appearance. "He was obviously suspicious of us," said Schwartz. "He seemed surprised, first of all, that we wanted to do the retrospective at all. He was even less receptive when we told him we wanted to include some of the television work."

Eventually, Jerry agreed to provide some items. Archivist Bob Furmanek, who'd been organizing Jerry's warehouses of memorabilia, film footage, and audiotape since 1984 ("We literally started at one end of the room and worked our way through," Furmanek said of his ongoing organizational project), gave the museum such items as old episodes of "The Colgate Comedy Hour," Jerry's NBC solo specials from the late 1950s, the episode of "Ben Casey" that Jerry directed and acted in, appearances of Martin and Lewis on Milton Berle's "Texaco Star Theater" and on "Welcome Aboard," a variety show from 1948. He supplied bloopers and films about the making of films. Most amazingly, he discovered footage of the 1952 Olympic Committee Telethon, when Dean and Jerry ran Hope and Crosby off the stage, and a complete 1954 Copacabana performance, filmed secretly by a member of the audience and then sold to Jerry for his collection.

In addition to being so generous with his archives, Jerry agreed to appear one evening to present and discuss film and television clips. Another night of the month-long program consisted of Bukatman lecturing on "The Film and TV Work of Jerry Lewis." Despite the outstanding curatorial effort, however, the retrospective was met with snickers in the press. Jerry's career had been moribund for so long, and the French jokes had become so common, that the very notion of such an undertaking was seen as funny. Some critics, to be fair, knew what a major event the retrospective was—J. Hoberman of the *Village Voice* wrote appreciatively about Jerry and Frank Tashlin in describing the program—but it wasn't the career-reviving shot in the arm Jerry had long hoped for.

A few months later, though, a small, enthusiastic TV audience got a chance to see Jerry in a way no one had before, and he went over very well. Stephen J. Cannell, creator of blockbuster TV action series such as "The Rockford Files" and "Hunter," had admired Jerry's work in *The King of Comedy* and approached Jerry with a proposal to guest-star in a multi-episode storyline on his "Wiseguy" series.

A critically acclaimed program with an extremely loyal following, "Wiseguy" was a modern mob drama whose plots, unusually dense for a prime-time series, unfolded over the course of four- to six-week "arcs" that demanded close attention. As a result, the series was never popular enough to secure a definite spot on CBS's roster; it moved time slots each season, sometimes more than once. Furthermore, frictions between Cannell and lead actor Ken Wahl led to the development of long arcs focusing on different undercover agents so the series could continue without its ostensible star.

In this tenuous atmosphere, Jerry agreed to appear in a five-part story as Eli Sternberg, a Manhattan garment district executive so besieged by mob extortionists that his son hires a bodyguard. Among the players was the fine stage actor Ron Silver, cast as David, Eli's son and presumable heir. Exteriors for the episodes were shot in New York, but most of Jerry's work was done in Vancouver, British Columbia, where producer Cannell made all of his series.

When the "Rag Trade Arc," as the episodes were know, aired in early 1989, reaction to Jerry's performance was extremely positive. Though it was unusual for critics to review installments of established series, Hank Gallo of the New York *Daily News* broke with standard practice to tell readers that "Lewis really shines." Cannell was delighted with Jerry's work, announcing to the press, "This guy has some great acting strokes that he really hasn't shown."

Indeed, of all the roles he'd had since *The King of Comedy*—and maybe even more than the role of Jerry Langford—Eli Sternberg brought out something of the beast that inhabited the real Jerry. In part it's because the role allowed him to play the bully. As a comic actor and as a writer of comedy, he had often created scenes in which a blowhard withered an underling, but Jerry had always played the mouse suffering the lion's roar. In his "Wiseguy" episodes, however, he played a boorish, insinuating, brusque, egoistic, driven, foul-mouthed son of a bitch who yelled at mobsters, employees, picketers, bodyguards, his cousin, his wife, his son. And while in a good many of these tirades Jerry's diction betrayed an unconvincing shallowness—a sense that he really hadn't tapped his natural store of anger—some of them were hair-raisingly deep. As the episodes wore on, and Eli's inevitable financial and emotional ruin became apparent, he achieved a weary, caustic air wholly in character with some of his off-camera attitudes.

Lord knows the script afforded him many opportunities to see himself in it. Whether the "Wiseguy" writing staff knew it or not, they were handing Jerry lines he could have lifted from his own recent life: "It's cheaper than another heart attack." "I'm gonna end up in court till the end of the century. If I live that long. And in all probability, I'm gonna lose my house. And my future earnings, assuming there are any." "I was thinking of my father and how ashamed of him I was. Of his accent, his clothes. He was married to my mother for fifty-eight years." "For forty years I told myself I was building a business for others. But that was a lie so I could delude myself into thinking that the accomplishments were justified. I lied to the only person who believed it."

Some of this dialogue must have been shattering for him to utter (and surely Jerry contributed to it: His parents had been married exactly fifty-eight years at the time of Danny's death). And the notion of a once-successful father whose business lies in ashes and whose son is unable to inherit anything from him must have struck an equally deep chord. There are other attributes of Eli that mark him as Jerry—a fetish for guns, a weepiness that seems based in genuine exhaustion and grief. But the bluster and self-analysis were exceedingly personal for him, and even though he worked with five different directors on the episodes, he walked away with dramatic scenes consistently.

Advance word about his work on "Wiseguy" was so strong that Jerry found himself cast as a gangster in director Susan Seidelman's feminized Mafia comedy *Cookie*. Co-written by novelist Nora Ephron and Alice Arlen, the film told the story of Dino Capisco (Peter Falk), a mobster recently paroled from a thirteen-year prison term and reunited with his illegitimate daughter,

Cookie (Emily Lloyd). Jerry was cast as Arnold Ross, a higher-up in the organization.

The film's potential for broad comedy was never quite realized—the plot was preciously overcomplicated in faux screwball fashion, and perhaps Seidelman wasn't quite close enough in sensibility to her mobsters to bring their coarse humor to life. There were undeniably tasty scenes of mob-family reuniting and quarreling, and the sight of Jerry bedecked in his characteristic jewelry and slick suits and talking about his sex life or his desire for revenge against a character named Dino was charming. But the film opened in the summer of 1989 to tepid reviews and like box office, and despite Jerry's winning presence in it, no new projects for him arose.

In the spring he was working with Sammy again in Vegas, this time at Bally's Hotel. On Wednesday, June 7, a night when he wasn't playing there, he showed up anyway, shouting from the wings, "How the hell long are you gonna stay on?" and wheeling a giant birthday cake out to Dean, who was in the middle of his act. "You surprised me," Dean said honestly—his birthday wasn't for another ten days—and he added, "I love you and I mean it." Jerry saluted his old partner: "Here's to seventy-two years of joy you've given the world. Why we broke up, I'll never know."

They had actually rekindled their friendship two years earlier, when Dean suffered the sort of calamity that never failed to stir Jerry's heart. Dean Paul Martin, Jr., the oldest of Dean's children from his second marriage, died in a plane crash when the jet he was flying as a member of the California Air National Guard crashed into a snow-covered mountain. Jerry called with his condolences, and in the ensuing conversation the resentments between them began to look trivial.

They began to talk now and again. Jerry would have preferred a more intimate relationship, but Dean, always reserved, had become markedly reclusive. So his former partner settled for periodic contact by phone. In ensuing years, whenever he was asked by interviewers about Dean, he would always claim that he had just recently spoken to him. "I talked to him like ten days ago," went one such account. "He's very happy: 'How you doing, pallie?' I said, 'You still don't remember my fucking name?' 'Aw, come on, you know what I mean.' 'Are you okay?' 'Aw, I'm fine, having a ball.' He's not having a ball, but he wants me to think he is."

Jerry, of course, had never lost a child, but he suffered such a massive affront at the hands of one of his sons that year that he must have felt as if the loss of a son would have been a relief. In May 1989 Joseph, his bitter youngest son, appeared as the primary source of a three-page cover story in the *National Enquirer* describing Jerry's violent outbursts, his indifference toward his children, his philandering, and his drug abuse. It was a resounding slap in the face. No matter what he had done over the years, he'd always thought of himself as a good father. But here was a rebuke he couldn't hide or deny.

Jerry was already suspicious of Joseph's behavior because of the trouble the twenty-six-year-old had been giving Patti, and he suspected that his son had been paid twenty-five thousand dollars by the tabloid newspaper for his story. Still and all, the piece was shocking in its details and virulent in tone.

"All my life I've been asked what it's like being Jerry Lewis's kid," Joseph said. "And all my life I told the same lie: 'It's great, he's great.' It wasn't great. It was pure hell. There were always whippings, and he was always yelling. My older brothers got chased around the house and slapped and punched. Even today we're all afraid of him. But I'm finally speaking out because I feel people need to know that the clown they see on the screen is not the same man who raised six terrified sons. My dad is a mean-spirited, self-centered jerk. Thank God for my mother. She was a saint." He concluded his revelations with a caustic comparison of himself and the muscular dystrophy patients for whom Jerry campaigned. "There are two sets of Jerry's Kids," he said. "Those physically crippled by a dreadful disease and those emotionally crippled by a dreadful father."

In the article, Joseph recounted his version of Jerry's violence toward his sons. The most hideous of these, recalled by Joseph as the worst beating in family history, was a punishment administered on Anthony with a wide leather belt that Jerry had dubbed "The Strap." According to Joseph, the incident began when he and Anthony were playing grocery store in the kitchen and a can fell on the younger boy's foot, eliciting a wailing cry. "Dad came charging in, grabbed Anthony—who was about nine—and dragged him to where The Strap was kept," remembered Joseph. " 'I'll teach you!' he yelled at Anthony. He pulled down Anthony's pants and whipped him a good twenty times with The Strap. Then he screamed at Anthony: 'How many more do you want?' Anthony's poor, scared reply will stay with me forever: 'Not many more, Daddy.' My father proceeded to beat him another ten times. I was so scared I almost wet my pants."

When Joseph's claims were printed in the *Enquirer*, Jerry's office explicitly denied that Jerry had ever beaten his sons.* But the article was a public embarrassment Jerry couldn't countenance. He developed a pure hatred for Joseph, writing him out of his official press biography (which henceforth spoke of his "five sons") and speaking about him as if he were dead. "He's in Forest Lawn," he said. "I buried him. I wish I could tell you that I close the door at night and cry my heart out, but I don't. Someone who lives by a code of loyalty as I do, and to do that to someone close to you for money, I could never forgive. Love hard, hate hard."

---

*Chris also recalled seeing Anthony receive a whipping—"It was very educational," he said, although he provided no details—and Patti indirectly supported these stories by allowing the boys to write about Jerry's corporal punishment of them in her 1993 autobiography.

He would grow visibly upset as he described his feelings of betrayal, but he would soften as he spoke about the way Joseph's story caused his other sons to rally around him. "Five sons came to Las Vegas to say they were ready to go to Florida [where the *Enquirer* is published] and tell about the father *they* knew," he revealed. "And I loved them for their naïveté in thinking it would be something they could do." (Later accounts by some of Joseph's brothers would talk of violence by their father, but none was as specific or venomous.)

The article came at a particularly unfortunate moment for Jerry and SanDee, who were trying to start a family. SanDee, in her late thirties, had never had a child of her own. Jerry, already the grandfather of six, was still longing for the daughter he and Patti had spent so many years Thinking Pink for. When SanDee finally did conceive, Jerry was so delighted he announced to an audience in Paris that he was going to be a father again. Joseph greeted his father's news by declaring, "I pity that poor baby. Jerry Lewis doesn't know how to be a human being, much less a father. . . . That child will be held up and hugged in front of the camera, and it will raise millions for a wonderful cause. But it will never know the love of a real father." The dire prediction turned out to be moot: SanDee miscarried.

In 1990 Jerry fulfilled his long-held wish to direct a film abroad. As part of *How Are the Children?*, a UNICEF-sponsored anthology film exploring the rights of children worldwide, he made an eight-minute segment called "Boy." It was an almost completely silent film about an eleven-year-old white boy living in an all-black world and being subjected to quiet, insidious racism and outright racist bullying. In an ironic final twist, it was revealed that the boy's mother, father, and sibling were black as well. There was a delicacy to the film that was neither sentimental or mawkish—two obvious traps for this sort of material. The camera work, along with a score by the great French film composer Georges Delarue, was subtle and assured. The acting was somewhat wooden, but at least the youngster wasn't some sort of anguished Joey Levitch fighting his fate with tears or tomfoolery. Alongside short films by Filipino director Lino Broca, Nigerian director Euzhan Palcy, and the Franco-Swiss team of Jean-Luc Godard and Anne-Marie Melville, it held its own as a sober, assured work and indicated, more than anything else he'd made, what he might do as the director of a real drama.

But not all of his late-life meditations on the plight of the less fortunate were so felicitously realized. On September 2, 1990, to mark the twenty-fifth anniversary of the telethon (which for that one year originated from Los Angeles), he wrote his annual cover story in *Parade*. This time, he had a novel idea: Rather than tell the story of a poster child, boast about the MDA's research gains, or try to find a new way of pleading for donations, he would write a work of fiction. He would write about what his life would be like if he had muscular dystrophy.

"What if . . . the twist of fate that we hear so much about really happened?

What if . . . when the gifts and the pains were being handed out, I was in the wrong line?" he began. "I decided, after forty-one years of battling this curse that attacks children of all ages . . . I would put myself in that chair . . . that steel imprisonment that long has been deemed the dystrophic child's plight."

What followed was one of the most tone-deaf appeals in the history of charity fund-raising. He began by imagining trying to use the bathroom: "It's still only the early hours of the day, and already I am beginning to feel trapped and suffocated trying to visit that bathroom." He imagined himself having to be pushed to get places, being abused by students at school (whom he suspected of "spilling oil in my path when I'm going it alone"), having able-bodied people fill the handicapped parking spaces with their vehicles, being manipulated into a photogenic posture for a family snapshot, having poor access to restaurants, airplanes, hotels, and sports arenas, finding himself at the mercy of intrusive therapists, whispered about and pointed at in public.

After refiguring his own life, he pushed toward a finale. "I know the courage it takes to get on the court with the other cripples and play wheelchair basketball," he wrote.

> But I'm not as fortunate as they are, and I'd bet I'm in the majority. I'd like to play basketball like normal, healthy, vital and energetic people. I really don't want the substitute. I just can't half-do anything—either it's all the way or forget it. That's a rough way to think in my position. When I sit back and think a little more rationally, I realize my life is half, so I must learn to do things halfway. I just have to learn to try to be good at being half a person . . . and get on with my life.
>
> I may be a full human being in my heart and soul, yet I am still half a person, and I know I'll do well if I keep my priorities in order. You really cannot expect the outside world to assist you in more ways than they already do, and I'm most grateful for the help I receive. But I always have the feeling in the pit of my stomach that I want to scream out: "Help!" Or: "See what has happened to me!" Or: "Is anybody watching?" But those screams are usually muffled by the inner voice that tells me what to do and when, and tells me softly and strongly, "Be still . . . Hush . . . Drive quietly . . . Try to make as few waves as possible."

It was an appalling performance. Not only did he explicitly invoke the notion that muscular dystrophy sufferers were "half" people, but he underscored their plight by making himself the focus of it. The editors of the magazine did him no favors by letting it run, but it was surely a precise reflection of his thoughts. Worse, it was exactly the sort of thing that people had begun grumbling about a decade earlier, when he found himself confronted on "Donahue" by a host and audience who mistrusted his tactics as a fund-raiser. Not only had he not renounced the pity approach, but he was willing to extend it shamelessly to himself to draw attention to his cause. It was in his bones—the Book of Job laced in schmaltz—and he saw absolutely nothing wrong with it.

Attitudes toward the disabled had changed elsewhere, even if Jerry, the nation's most visible champion of those suffering from crippling disease, hadn't seemed to notice. Just weeks earlier, George Bush had signed into law the Americans With Disabilities Act, the most sweeping body of civil rights legislation since Lyndon Johnson's Great Society. Henceforth, those who discriminated against the disabled could face the same sort of legal prosecution to which practitioners of racial and sexual prejudice were subject. And sitting by Bush's side as he signed the ADA into law was the man whom he'd appointed to oversee the Equal Employment Opportunity Commission, the administrative body charged with enforcing right-to-work laws: Evan J. Kemp, Jr., the same Nader's Raider who'd first spoken out against Jerry a decade ago.

Kemp was first named an EEOC commissioner by Ronald Reagan in 1987, and he advanced to the agency's chair when Clarence Thomas was named to the federal bench by Bush. Now, as the nation's most powerful opponent of discrimination against minorities and the disabled, he was prepared to use the full force of the government to quash the sort of bigots who'd made his own life so hellish. And here was the most visible and arrogant of them, making more of a spectacle of his insensitivity than ever. In effect, Jerry was telling the world that the disabled were pitiful children unable to fend for themselves at a time when even a Republican administration was making equal opportunity for the disabled the law of the land.

With his New York Times piece, Kemp had already succeeded in getting the campaigns for Easter Seals and cerebral palsy to reconsider the use of pity and the exploitation of children in their fund-raising. "Other telethons called me and wanted to know what problems I had with the pity approach and what other methods they could use," he recalled. But now he had the power to go after the MDA, which had thus far assiduously ignored his arguments. Not that they had ignored *him*, exactly: According to Kemp, the MDA actually hired an adult with neuromuscular disease to get close to him at the Disability Rights Center and report back to them on his activities. Eventually, this "spy" confessed to Kemp. "He told me they wanted to know what I would do," Kemp says.*

Less deviously, the MDA made the magnanimous gesture of inviting Kemp, then their only public critic, to appear on the 1982 telethon, where he gave a ninety-second speech about living independently with a disability. "The MDA

---

*Leslie Bennetts of *Vanity Fair* spoke to this alleged "spy," who confirmed Kemp's account. "They told me they felt Evan had cost them $4 million in contributions, and they wanted to discredit him," he said, speaking on condition of anonymity, because, he added, "I'm not prepared to take on Jerry and the boys. They would try to destroy me. What little I have, they would try to take it away." The MDA absolutely denied the story.

seemed to feel if I'd be quiet, all their problems would go away," Kemp said. But given the bully pulpit of EEOC chairmanship, he was determined to speak his mind. In 1991, at a fund-raiser for Pennsylvania Governor Richard Thornburgh, Kemp released a statement to the press contrasting political fund-raising with the Jerry Lewis telethon. "The MDA got ahold of it and they hit the roof," Kemp recalled.

Actually, the MDA was of two minds about such criticism. One group within the organization was already working to alter its image so that the very beneficiaries of MDA's work wouldn't feel belittled by it. In 1991 these people put together a task force within the MDA to get feedback on the telethon, and MDA advertising and activities, from sufferers of neuromuscular disease. Jerry, on the other hand, was among the hard-liners who refused to acknowledge that there was any validity whatever to the criticism. In his mind, Kemp was like the film critics or the TV critics or the Nazi bullies of Irvington—someone who disliked him personally, someone before whom he would not bend.

Kemp wasn't the only pebble in the MDA's shoe. Dianne B. Piastro, a nationally syndicated columnist based in Long Beach, California, responded to Jerry's *Parade* piece with shock and anger. "In a single two-page article," she wrote in "Living with a Disability," a column distributed to more than seven hundred newspapers through the Newspaper Enterprise Association wire service, "he managed to violate every tenet of the disability rights movement, and to send 'his kids' the message that disabled people have been working for years to erase: Your life is not worth anything if you have a disability. . . . Jerry Lewis is so terrified and repelled by disability and wheelchairs that he gets people to cry and feel pity to prove his fears are justified. But in doing so, he robs kids of dignity and pride. His efforts seem to have nothing to do with understanding or caring about their full participation in society. Many believe Lewis' form of benign oppression has finally gone too far."

Piastro, an investigative journalist with ties throughout the disabled community, began to write regularly about the actual dispersal of funds by the organization among researchers and sufferers of neuromuscular disease. She requested income tax forms from the organization, cited examples of waste, inconsistency, and futility in MDA's expenditures, and became a vocal critic of the lavish salaries received by such MDA officers as executive director Bob Ross, who took home the third-largest salary of any charity executive in the nation even though MDA was a funding organization and not a patient-care or research entity.

Piastro's columns drew the ire of the MDA: Ross threatened to sue both her and the NEA syndicate (a threat he never saw through), and the organization launched a letter-writing campaign against Piastro, giving its loyalists not only the addresses of newspapers that carried her column but her home address as well (that she was a grandmother confined to a wheelchair had no tempering effect on their response). And, in time, various newspapers that regularly carried

"Living with a Disability" began to kill columns that dealt with the MDA's financial affairs.

A new film project came along, a strange hybrid of foreign art film and American screwball comedy. A French producer, Claudie Ossard, and a Yugoslavian director, Emir Kusturica, hired Jerry to play Leo Sweetie, an Arizona Cadillac dealer engaged to a woman half his age (supermodel Paulina Porizkova). When Leo summons his nephew Axel (Johnny Depp), a daydreaming New York State fish and game warden, to Arizona for the wedding and offers him a new life as a car salesman, the young man finds himself involved with a flighty widow (Faye Dunaway) and her unstable stepdaughter (Lili Taylor). A would-be actor cum Casanova (Vincent Gallo) working at Leo's car dealership rounded out the principal cast. This most improbable of stories—written, according to Jerry, by Kusturica at more than twice the length of the average screenplay—was known as *The Arrowtooth Waltz*.

Kusturica was a brilliant young director widely respected in critical circles both in Europe and the United States for his ability to combine dreamily poetic imagery with coarse, earthy humor and political themes. His 1981 film *Do You Remember Dolly Bell?* had won a prize for the best first film at the Venice Film Festival. Four years later, his second film, *When Father Was Away on Business*, won the Palme d'Or at Cannes and was nominated for an Academy Award for Best Foreign Film. His third, *Time of the Gypsies*, was produced by Columbia Pictures and won him a Best Director prize at Cannes. Six months after its premiere, he was awarded the Roberto Rossellini Prize for life achievement in film by a group of European critics. He was thirty-four years old.

In 1988 Kusturica had been lured to the U.S. by Czech émigré Milos Forman to teach cinema at Columbia University, and he had begun conceiving of projects to make in America, among them an adaptation of *Crime and Punishment* set among Russian immigrants in contemporary Brooklyn. But the financing for *The Arrowtooth Waltz* had come together first, so in April 1991 he set off for Douglas, Arizona, to make it.

Right away, Kusturica had trouble. Like many European directors, he was used to working with small budgets, nonunion crews, and producers who respected the authority of the director the way impresarios respect the egos of opera stars. In the States, however, even with European money and fellow Yugoslavs as principal crew members, he was under much more pressure to perform. Besides which, the script was overlong and incomplete. The producers were so intent on meeting a schedule and cutting the script to fit their budget that they literally drove Kusturica off the set six weeks into the production. When they looked for him the next day, they found him not in his Arizona hotel, not in his New York apartment or in his Paris apartment, but in Sarajevo.

Production was shut down while Kusturica regrouped and worked on the script (the press was told that the director, who "had trouble adjusting to the fast-paced working style of the American crew and felt overburdened with pressures from completion bond parties to wrap up shooting," had suffered "a nervous collapse"). Jerry sat and watched, an innocent bystander.

"I like Emir so goddamn much," he recalled. "He's such a sweet man— thirty-five years old, energetic, enthusiastic, wonderful man. He got fucked and refucked. Oh, what they did to him. He had a script that was 265 pages. They said 'Go away, shut the picture down, take a rest.' But 265. 'We can't put up any more money,' they said. 'Cut the script.' He went away for two weeks, we all sat in Arizona, he came back, it was 294. It was then, I suspect, they realized there was no fucking way. . . . He started out with a $19 million budget and it swelled to about $32 million."

Actually, the hiatus was more like three months—in part, said some observers, because Kusturica, according to news reports, "was said to be 'reluctant' to resume the film or deal with his difficult stars," namely Jerry and Dunaway. Eventually, enough of the script was shot so that production could cease, but Kusturica lost control of the film in the editing process, and any trace of his original conception was lost as well.

"They took it from him," Jerry said. "And they just indiscriminately cut it. It makes no sense. I did it because it was off the wall. There ain't no fuckin' wall left with what they've done to it. . . . His first cut was nine hours. Then he said he would give them a break and bring it down to two-forty. They said, 'We can't sell a movie over two hours.' He cut it to two-twenty. But after they had taken it from him and cut it, he had nothing to cut."

The film languished for the better part of a year while Ossard tried to convince Warner Brothers, which owned the American distribution rights, to release it. Newly retitled *Arizona Dreams*, it opened to enthusiastic box office and moderately positive reviews in Paris in January 1993. The next month, it was shown at the Berlin Film Festival, where critics in the Hollywood trade press took it as a failed but worthy effort on Kusturica's part; strangely, none of their reviews had a word to say about Jerry's performance.

Jerry himself didn't know what to make of it. "I saw the film in Paris," he said. "And the lines were around the block. No one understands it. And the journalists wrote, 'Jerry Lewis's name is on the film, why should there not be people around the block?' The film makes no sense. . . . What they have on the screen changed from what I read in the script to something that doesn't make any sense. But I mean, *any sense.* . . . It's the worst piece of shit you'll ever see in your life. It will never be seen by American eyes as far as I'm concerned. If the picture takes off, it'll take off for like a minute and a half until word gets around."

Warner Brothers, the same company that wouldn't release *Smorgasbord* in theaters a decade earlier, agreed with him. They showed it at film festivals in North America in 1994, and released it on video the following spring. (A longer director's cut saw a limited release in 1995.)

It was rather a shame that the film was so cursorily distributed: *Arizona Dreams* was no artistic triumph, but plenty of inferior films were given more sporting chances. Like Kusturica's other films, it was filled with audacious cinematic inventions—flying ambulances; fish swimming through the desert air; Eskimos; bizarre nightmares, sets, and, situations. In its two-hour video version, it hardly holds together and rarely gives the impression that it ever had a chance to be coherent, but it's got plenty of charm and vitality.

As Leo, Jerry does some interesting things with a relatively small part. At first he's extremely sympathetic, courting his nephew and his own young fiancée with a patient, even patronizing tone, smiling through his frustrations and seemingly shrinking back from his urge to dominate the screen. But in scenes where he tries to sell a car to a balky customer or loses his temper with his nephew's older lover, traditional Jerryisms emerge: the wheedling voice, the mercurial body language, the angry gravity (he actually uses the word "fuck" with Dunaway, a career first). In his last two scenes, he's quite affecting. In the first, he dies in an ambulance, weakly muttering a stream of hallucinatory phrases; in the second, he appears in his nephew's dream as an Eskimo, chattering away lovingly in a cryptic tongue presumably of his own invention (the scene is subtitled in English). The love in Depp's face at these moments seems real both within the film and without, as the regard a young, physically limber actor might hold for an old master of his craft.

For all that didn't work in *Arizona Dreams*—and there was a lot of it—there was plenty that did, and Jerry's work was indisputably among the positives. He was pushing toward a stage in his life when he could truly play a living legend, adding grace and weight to projects without the onus of carrying them on his back. But nevertheless, his career seemed finally to have petered out. He was welcome in America's homes for twenty-one and a half hours a year, but otherwise they didn't seem interested. He had set out to become Charlie Chaplin—and he almost had—but now he was treated more like Charlie Callas.

22.

New Mirrors

After SanDee's 1989 miscarriage, she and Jerry refused to give up hope of ever having a child together. They began investigating adoption. In the summer of 1991 they found a young pregnant woman willing to give them her child—a baby they'd chosen because it had been confirmed through amniocentesis to be a girl. On March 23, 1992, almost forty-seven years after Gary was born, Jerry and SanDee were at the hospital for the birth of their daughter. They named her Danielle Sarah, after Jerry's departed father and grandmother. "The tears streamed down my cheeks from complete joy," Jerry remembered. "I've cried before out of sheer happiness, but never out of ecstasy. I'd wanted her for so long."

He was a born-again father. There was never enough time for Gary and the other boys when he was out conquering the world, but for Danielle he was always available. A few weeks after she was born, Jerry and SanDee showed her off to neighbors at their condominium in the Turnberry Isle development near Ft. Lauderdale. And on May 12, when he appeared on "The Arsenio Hall Show," he brought along her picture and showed it off to the fawning host. Predictably, the audience cooed; also predictably, Patti and the boys, who hadn't even known that Jerry was planning to adopt a child, were affronted. It was worse than his annual fawning over strangers' children on the telethon; he spoke about Danielle as if she were the only child he'd ever raised—as if she were the girl he and Patti had tried to have for years. "I'm having the time of my life with her," he boasted. "She's an incredible baby, she's a miracle baby. I tell everybody, 'All other children prior to this birth are inauthentic children. They're not real children. This is a real child.'"

Whereas the boys were fobbed off on Patti and a variety of nannies and housekeepers, Danielle got her father's attention from the time she opened her eyes. By the time she was a year or so old, they had a complete routine together. "I'm up at seven-thirty every morning," he said. "And it's her time with me. I start by opening the door, and that face, when she sees me—and it's now 'Daddy.' She's very bright: She walked at eleven months old and had a vocabulary of fifty words at eleven months. So I go in and I get her. I change her britches and I clean her and I put her in new britches and put her little shoes on. I take her into the salon, we turn on 'Barney,' and she and I have cereal together. We have Sugar Frosted Flakes. She loves them. So does Daddy. We get through with that. We watch 'Sesame Street.' Then I warm her bottle, give her her bottle, she lies here with me, and the fucking world could just fall off somewhere. And she finishes her bottle and we talk. She loves my pens and my papers and my stuff on my desk. We write notes. And before you know it, I've had two and a half hours of bonding time with her."

Danielle was taken everywhere her father went; when she was two years and nine months old, he would claim to have spent a mere eleven days apart from her during her whole life. She came aboard the cruise ships where he had begun performing during the summers, toured Europe and Vegas and Atlantic City, came to the telethon. When she was eighteen months old, she even appeared on his annual *Parade* cover with him in the place usually reserved for that year's poster child.

It was a telling substitution, if only because his off-camera attitude toward the MDA's smiling young dystrophics could be so distinct from the way he behaved with them when America was watching. At a photo session with 1993 poster child Lance Fallon, Jerry reacted to the boy's excitement at seeing him by asking out loud, "What did he get for breakfast? A little Ritalin never hurt any kid." When, during a lull in the shoot, Lance and another child began playing noisily with one another, Jerry pounced on them: "We can't have that, children, or you'll be out of the show so quick you'll never know what happened."

And in fact, not all of the news involving his own children was especially sweet. The twice-divorced, thirty-five-year-old Christopher was arrested in 1990 for burglary and grand theft in the disappearance from a suburban Los Angeles warehouse of 168 limited-edition prints by Erté and other artists worth two hundred thousand dollars. In March 1992 he changed his not-guilty plea to one of no contest to one count and faced a possible prison term of up to five years, eight months.

Jerry did a quickie cameo bit in Billy Crystal's 1992 film *Mr. Saturday Night*, a three-hour shoot at the New York Friars' Club done as a favor to the younger comic. He produced three one-hour specials about the Martin and Lewis years that aired on cable TV's Disney Channel. He taped an appearance on Whoopi Goldberg's syndicated talk show. It was all the exposure the public and the industry seemed to want of him.

He hated being left out of the business, and he let his hatred be known in interviews. "There's nothing I want to do more than film," he told one interviewer. "But I won't do what somebody believes is filmmaking if it isn't close. I'd just as soon do the dinner show in Akron. I won't hide it. They pay a lot of money—*a lot of money*. I'm happy to work with anybody who brings the same commitment that I do. I've seen people who believe in film just as I do, and we're gonna mesh and get together and do it. I used to sleep overnight at Paramount in my cutting room. Such excitement . . . I didn't know where the months and years went, I had such fun. And everything was done with a handshake. Now if I have a meeting with someone who's the head of a motion picture company, I have to stop by Toys R Us first. I'm talking to a guy about a $12 to 15 million project, and he looks like he has to go *caccy*."

Still, he would reveal himself to be frankly jealous of the opportunities available to filmmakers of the 1990s: "I'd give my balls to be able to remake a couple of films with today's technology. DAT recording, Steadycams, Lumicranes, digital graphics. . . . The gags that I had to create with practical actual materials because that's the way it was . . . I couldn't wait eight weeks for a process house to show me a little mouse sitting on a window. I'd shoot the joke myself. I'd have the art department build me a mouse, put a battery up his ass and move it. . . . To this day I wish I had one film left in me where I had this crazy son of a bitch, the twenty-year-old Jerry. If I coulda had him . . . my Christ! I probably would've destroyed him."

In 1992 the telethon received the most negative publicity it had ever experienced. Piastro and Kemp had laid the groundwork for a public rejection of the MDA, the telethon, and Jerry by disabled rights activists all over the country. Prior to the 1991 telethon, the Alliance for Research Accountability, a charity watchdog group, announced, "We don't like Jerry's attitude. We don't like his use of slick sentimentality to raise money. He portrays those kids as worthless lumps of flesh unless they can find a cure. At the same time, the MDA is making millions of dollars and they haven't found anything in all their years of research."

Simultaneously, the American Coalition of Citizens with Disabilities chimed in with a similarly antagonistic assessment. In a statement from its director, Judge Reese Robrahn, the group said, "We feel that this emphasis on 'Jerry's Kids'—pale, wan, brave but probably doomed—has helped create a stereotype of disabled persons which has in turn led to the wrong public policies."

Jerry's response that year was to plea even more fervently for people to give to the telethon. At the very opening of the 1991 show, he addressed the protests that had preceded it. "I've never used the terms 'disabled' and 'handicapped,' " he claimed. "Please, I'm begging for survival. I want my kids to live. I don't ask you to pity them. I'm asking you to keep them alive." America responded as it almost always had—with at least a dollar more: $45.07 million altogether.

Still, Jerry wasn't satisfied to let Evan Kemp and those like him have their say. On February 6, 1992, Jerry wrote to George Bush asking that Kemp be fired.

Describing himself as "a point of light," Jerry wrote that Kemp was "misusing the power of his governmental office" in attacking him and the telethon. Indeed, he could only explain Kemp's feelings as rooted in revenge, telling Bush that Kemp began speaking out against the MDA when he was refused a grant for his Disability Rights Center.

But really, the thing that hurt Jerry the most about Kemp's criticism was the personal dimension. As he confessed to Bush, Kemp's attacks had taken an emotional toll on him. "The blitzkrieg of critical abuse we at MDA have had to withstand over the past several months has had a severely demoralizing effect on me," he wrote. "If this undeserved vicious attack has the blessing of the nation's highest office, I don't see how I'm going to be able to do the telethon."

For about a week, Jerry didn't hear back from the President, and he got so angry that he wrote White House chief of staff Samuel Skinner to complain about his treatment and reiterate his objections to Kemp's behavior. Kemp wanted to meet Jerry face-to-face to discuss their differences, but Skinner and his staff preferred to handle Jerry themselves with a public statement indicating that the White House had "no position" on the MDA or the telethon. When Kemp asked to read the letter before it went out, he was refused. That summer, he spoke out in *The Washingtonian* magazine about the telethon and how he'd been frozen out of the White House's reaction to Jerry's letters. This indiscretion evoked yet more protests from the MDA and earned Kemp a public rebuke by Skinner, who wrote to the MDA to assure it that "we have talked further with Mr. Kemp, reiterating the President's full and enthusiastic support for the MDA and the Labor Day Telethon, and our expectation is that he will refrain from attacking the organization and the event in the future."

But the White House couldn't stifle all of Jerry's critics. And at least one particular group of them was irresistible to the media. Mike Ervin and Chris Matthews were a brother and sister from Chicago in their mid-thirties. They had both spent their lives coping with neuromuscular disease, and they had both been, many years earlier, MDA poster children. In reaction to Jerry's insensitive *Parade* article and his apparent hostility to critics of the telethon, they and some other former poster children formed an organization called Jerry's Orphans and made plans to picket the facilities that were hosting local telethon hookups in various cities.

"Our goal is not to put the MDA out of business," said Ervin. "Our goal is to put Jerry Lewis out of the disability business. He has no business being there. He doesn't understand in any way, nor does he wish to, the majority of the [disabled] population."

Matthews agreed that theirs was almost a personal crusade against the very figure of Jerry. "They have a spokesperson who thinks he's the god of disability," she said. "And he just totally misrepresented what we've spent our lives fighting for. . . . He painted the worst picture of disability he could paint."

In 1991 Jerry's Orphans organized pickets against the telethon in Los Angeles and two other cities. No one had ever seen anything like it—people in wheelchairs carrying placards and chanting against a charity event they had once been instrumental in promoting. But Jerry's Orphans were representative of a burgeoning movement among disabled Americans, a grass-roots civil rights movement that could be as radical and provocative as the African-American, gay, and women's movements. The movement had voices that spoke toward national consensus such as *Mainstream,* a magazine with a circulation of more than fifteen thousand that called the telethon a form of "high-tech begging." And it had saucier voices such as those heard in *The Disability Rag,* a made-on-the-fly publication with a circulation of two thousand that referred to disabled people as "crips," had lifestyle pages that defined "disability cool," and castigated consensus builders in the disabled community as "Uncle Tiny Tims."

Jerry's Orphans alerted the media that they and similar organizations such as Disabled in Action and the Tune Out Jerry Coalition would be picketing the 1992 telethon in more than twenty cities across the country, and they got a great deal of attention in the press, which reported that the group now boasted a mailing list of three thousand names. When the Associated Press called Evan Kemp to get his reaction to the protesters' activities, he seemed to side with them, saying, "I have always had problems with the pity approach to raising money." This evoked a furious response from MDA executive director Bob Ross, who wrote to George Bush that "Evan Kemp's continued disregard for your express wish that he cease his criticism of our Labor Day Telethon . . . is not only grievously . . . damaging to the association . . . but represents in a very real sense an outright rebuke of your authority."

In the face of such opposition—in the face of his 'kids' grown into angry young men and women—Jerry was completely flustered. Twice in the week before the 1992 telethon the Associated Press tried to get him to comment on the activities and opinions of the protesters, and twice he claimed not to be able to find the time to speak to the news organization—"the first time in more than a decade," the AP reported, that he didn't speak out when asked to. He showed up on Larry King's television show to defend himself, and appeared on ABC's "Prime Time Live" broadcast in a similar role. At all times, he spoke about the good work that MDA did, but he never failed to get his shots in at the protesters personally, just as he suspected that they were rejecting him personally.

"You have to remember they're sitting in chairs I bought them," he told *Vanity Fair* soon after the 1992 telethon. "This one kid in Chicago [Ervin] would have passed through this life and never had the opportunity to be acknowledged by anybody, but he found out that by being a dissident he gets picked up in a limo by a television station. What do they want me to do? They want me to not raise $120 million Labor Day? They want me to stop work in the labs? There's nineteen of them that are telling me not to raise $120 million. I don't give a good goddamn what they call it; I am giving doctors money so that your new baby and my new baby never have to deal with this. I must be doing something right; I've raised one billion three hundred million dollars. These nineteen people don't want me to do that. They want me to stop now? Fuck them. Do it in caps, FUCK THEM."

Others connected to the MDA defended the telethon, the organization's fund-raising tactics, and Jerry himself in calmer, less inflammatory fashion. Various adults with neuromuscular disease, some of them MDA board members and familiar faces to longtime telethon watchers, said they felt no indignity in being referred to as "kids." Others pointed out that the most pernicious strain of muscular dystrophy did indeed strike only children—and kept them from ever becoming adults. And for many people, Jerry and the telethon were a symbol of American charity that no protesters could discredit, however intimately they were connected with the struggle themselves. Still, it was a confusing spectacle: disabled people boycotting an event intended to help them and hosted by a man who had risen to fame with an act many viewers took to be a caricature of disability.

For the MDA, the stakes of this battle were monumental. In addition to the more than $45 million it expected to raise each Labor Day through phoned pledges, it took in another $50 million or more in corporate donations and combined donations from groups like firefighters and postal workers during the telethon. Indeed, about 90 percent of the organization's total income for the year was generated by the telethon. It could not let the event be sunk. Rumors circulated that Jerry was under pressure from the organization to give up his prominent position. And the MDA ignored his refusal to hear out the protesters by constructing a more balanced telethon. The show was reconfigured to include lengthy informational spots about adults with neuromuscular disease who had families and careers; more time was spent discussing the MDA's work with people stricken by nonpediatric strains of the disease. Watching this newly sensitized telethon, even Evan Kemp announced that he was "extraordinarily impressed" by the progress the MDA had made.

All the controversy surrounding the telethon inevitably invited reporters to investigate the MDA's financial affairs. There had been inquiries by journalists ever since the suspicions about Jerry skimming money from the telethon first arose, but no such exposé turned up anything. The general impression these investigations left was that while MDA might not have been a saintly organization—its executives made handsome salaries, and it functioned out of a lavish headquarters—neither was it crooked. In 1993 *Money* magazine, in an article devoted to telling its readers which charities were on the up-and-up, rated the MDA fourteenth in its survey of large charities (with incomes over $100 million annually), as judged by the percentage of overall income spent on patient, research, and education programs.

But Dianne Piastro and *Memphis Business Journal* reporter Scott Shepard dug deeper, investigating the particular nature of these programs, and came away with a more unsettling view. One thing that Piastro discovered was that the MDA didn't care to share its financial information, even though required, as an untaxed, not-for-profit group, to submit financial statements each year to the IRS. And when she did uncover the MDA's tax filing, she discovered some information that ran contrary to the image that the organization tried to project.

The MDA told the IRS that it raised $109.7 million in 1990 and earned another $9 million in dividends, interest, rental income, and the like. The organization also reported that it owned a $101.9 million portfolio of stocks, treasury notes, and money market fund shares. "It could look," wrote Shepard of these assets, "like MDA was settling in for the long haul." And, indeed, the organization wrote off $14 million as a loss when it gave up its New York headquarters and relocated to Tucson, Arizona, where it hoped to build a new facility—a strange gesture indeed for a body that was working to put itself out of business by curing a disease.

MDA executives, Piastro learned, were paid handsome salaries even by big-time charity organization standards: Bob Ross was paid more than $288,000 per year, despite the fact that MDA was a funnel, a middleman, and not an actual research organization. Several other key MDA officials earned near-six-figure paychecks, and salaries for MDA employees rose 11 percent in 1990, a year during which much of the country felt the pinches of recession.

Most damningly, Piastro demonstrated that the MDA didn't so much pour its research and patient service dollars into the scientific and dystrophic communities as sprinkle them. In 1990 MDA gave $20 million to 459 researchers, or an average of $43,000 per donation; similarly, $20.2 million was spent on 315,530 donations to patients, averaging about $64 a head. (Both of these total figures were lower than the $22.2 million that MDA spent on fund-raising, and they looked lower still when stacked against such figures as the $6.9 million for unspecified travel expenses that the MDA incurred for itself.)

In effect, despite a high ranking from *Money* magazine, which reckoned that the MDA spent 76.7 percent of its income on such "good works" as research, patient services, and public education (much of which was itself a form of solicitation and fund-raising), the organization's actual expenditures were a bit more limited in scope and, in many cases, more internal than you would think if the telethon were your only source of information. Furthermore, despite the high profile that Jerry's work had afforded the MDA, it barely qualified for *Money's* list of charities with annual budgets of $100 million or more—all the more reason to question the way the organization chose to manage the relatively small amount of money that the public gave it.

Ironically, the public feuding between the MDA and its critics and the resulting investigations into the MDA's financial affairs all took attention away from the fact that the organization had actually sponsored some groundbreaking work in combatting Duchenne's muscular dystrophy, the strain of neuromuscular disease that so tragically affected young boys. In 1986 geneticists at Children's Hospital in Boston identified the gene that, when defective, caused Duchenne's to occur. The gene provided the blueprint for a protein called dystrophin, which was essential to the proper development of nerves and muscles; in its deformed version, it produced a defective form of dystrophin that kept the host's muscles from developing appropriately.

As heartening as this discovery was, the chance to perform therapy on the dystrophin gene was considered slim, for the gene was too large to be manipulated. For several years, neuromuscular research was stopped at this chasm between recognizing the problem and developing a solution to it. (An ironic sidelight, and one the MDA didn't advertise, was that the identification of the culpable gene would allow parents to screen their unborn children for neuromuscular disease and terminate pregnancies if they discovered that their child was subject to Duchenne's.)

In 1992, however, Jeffrey Chamberlain, a thirty-four-year-old geneticist at the University of Michigan whose research was partially funded by the MDA, announced that he and his colleagues had developed a "minigene" to correct the flawed dystrophin-producing gene and had successfully inserted it in the fertile eggs of mice carrying the flawed gene. In effect, the mice—which were only single-celled embryos at the time of the gene therapy—were bred to carry Duchenne's and were then cured by the insertion of the minigene. The next step, the insertion of the minigene into a human specimen, was a long way off, but Chamberlain's research proved that gene therapy could solve the problem and that the potential for a cure to Duchenne's (and, by extrapolation, other genetically determined diseases) was very real.

And this was only one avenue of research, albeit the one closest to Jerry's heart: MDA-financed scientists had, in fact, isolated the genes that, when flawed, were responsible for fourteen other neuromuscular diseases. All of a sudden, it seemed, a new world of potential cures was opening in front of them.

For Jerry, this was the miracle he'd been awaiting for four decades. "I'm gonna beat this cocksucker, that I promise you," he said when asked how research was progressing. The MDA's scientific advisors were optimistic that he might be right. At a 1993 meeting in Tucson, they told him, " 'For your seventieth birthday you're gonna have the cure.' "

Prior to the 1992 telethon, however, he got a scare that made him wonder whether he'd ever see his seventieth birthday. Every August, before production on the telethon began, he would fly to Houston for a complete physical and a consultation with Michael DeBakey. In the summer of 1992, after all the tests were completed, Jerry and SanDee were informed by DeBakey that Jerry had prostate cancer.

He was given a choice of treatments—a two-month regimen of radiation and chemotherapy, or surgery, which, given the early detection of the condition, was likely to be successful. He chose the surgery, but asked the doctors if they could wait until after the telethon. They agreed. Then he stalled them some more, pointing out that he would be in Houston in mid-October to address a convention of ALS researchers. The doctors pinned him down to a date: They would perform their surgery on October 19.

The telethon went on as planned, with Jerry revealing his condition only to Joe and Claudia Stabile, his closest friends and business associates. He was so guarded about his condition that he kept it a secret even from his sons. Gary spoke to his father within a week of the operation and knew nothing about it. "He didn't tell me he was having surgery for cancer," he told the press. Anthony, too, was in the dark: "He hasn't said anything to me." Jerry's office went so far as to issue a phony press release saying that he was in Houston to have back surgery.

On October 18, Jerry, SanDee, and Danielle arrived at Methodist Hospital in Houston. Jerry had arranged for the room next to his to be set up as a nursery for the baby, and he arranged with DeBakey to have the anesthesia administered in his own room so he wouldn't have to be conscious when he was separated from his wife and daughter. The doctor agreed, Jerry was put under, and the four-hour operation was carried out successfully. At sixty-six, he had dodged another bullet.

It was, as a result, a slow winter. In the spring of 1993, he performed in Europe, where he was appearing more frequently as opportunities at home grew more scarce. Later on, he was invited by his old friend Alan King to participate in a comedy festival he was putting together in New York—not as a performer, but as the emcee of a night of Catskills comics at Avery Fisher Hall. He hadn't played Manhattan in more than a decade. Prior to the show, he performed a sold-out concert at the Westbury Music Fair. Soon after these New York dates, he played a few concerts in the midwest at conventions of MDA sponsor corporations. The shows so invigorated him that he began to formulate plans to do a national tour after the telethon.

When the telethon rolled around, however, he had a small brushfire on his hands. The cover of that week's *National Enquirer* bore the headline, "BLOCK-BUSTER NEW BOOK: My Nightmare Life with Jerry Lewis . . . by his wife of 36 years." Patti had written an autobiography, and she spared him little embarrassment in the process. *I Laffed Till I Cried: Thirty-Six Years of Marriage to Jerry Lewis* was a strange volume indeed. Coauthored by "non-disclosure writer" Sara Anne Coleman, it told Patti's life story in a choppy style that revealed its probable origins as a series of taped interviews. It relied for many of its facts on Jerry's autobiography or on press releases from his office. It included passages written by each of the couple's six sons (including Joseph, back in his mother's graces despite having permanently alienated his father). Its three appendixes described the contents of Patti's Westwood house, some favorite recipes of the Lewis clan, and Jerry's films, with annotation and analysis by Scott. And it was released by WRS Publishing, a religious book publisher in Waco, Texas, that included in its books' back pages an 800 number that readers could call to suggest new book ideas.

For all that, however, the book was an extremely candid portrait of life around Jerry and his many moods. It spoke about—without explicitly describing—incidents of infidelity, drug abuse, hostility, financial mismanagement, even violence against the boys (including some of Joseph's long-public accusations, which were borne out by his brothers' testimony and by the very fact that his mother included them in her memoir). Patti claimed she had written the book to help support herself; that Jerry's alimony payments were insufficient was evinced by her need to give up her Westwood house in 1993 and move into a small West Los Angeles apartment. But there was clearly a measure of revenge involved; the book may even have begun after Patti heard the news that Jerry and SanDee had adopted a baby girl. Jerry never said a word about the book in public. And Patti determinedly tried to maintain an air of dignity. "She's too much of a lady to let the whole story come out," her coauthor said. Indeed, approached with requests for interviews about her marriage, Patti would let Jerry know that someone had been asking questions about him.

Jerry still worked extremely closely with the MDA and its sponsors, virtually on a daily basis. He toured the country fulfilling commitments to sponsors—showing up at cocktail parties, emceeing banquets, even giving full-fledged performances. He met with scientific advisors to the MDA, and he was proud of the unique way he could forge working relationships among laboratories. "You should hear some of the fucking speeches I give to them," he boasted. "One day I said, 'Do you realize that you might have 40 percent of the answer and he's got 60 and I don't see the two of you talking? How would you like that I don't see that you're funded this fucking year?' "

Perhaps his proudest point, though, was the Love Network itself, the national chain of independent stations he organized each year to carry the telethon. Even though the MDA paid stations a fee for the commercial-free use of their airwaves for the duration of the broadcast, it was still incumbent upon Jerry and the organization to make sure the station managers were disposed toward carrying the show each year. His old Catskills instincts kicked in. "I organized the general managers' meeting where we bring them all to the national headquarters in Tucson," he explained. "We had 185 of them this year. I get the Loews Hotel in Tucson to give me housing and food for all of them. I then get United Airlines to fly them to me. I then get 7-Up to do the dinner, then I get Budweiser to pick up all their golf, all of their extras. I'm talking about hitting Budweiser for $450,000. Between Budweiser, 7-Up, United Airlines, we're talking about $1.6 million. It doesn't cost MDA a nickel, and we really put it on.

"This year, I did a concert for them with the Tucson Symphony. Wynton Marsalis, Maureen McGovern, and myself performed with the Tucson Symphony, and all these general managers with their wives and friends, and we did it at the university, a two-thousand-seat house. We were getting three thousand dollars a ticket for outsiders. We filled the house. And I made nice with the general managers. We had a cocktail party, reception, big dinner, prizes, golf, tennis. And my greeting to them every year is the same thing: 'Good morning, gentlemen. Welcome to Tucson. You are here for our obsequious drill. We hope that you know you're gonna be brown-nosed from now until the time you leave. We will suck around and do whatever is necessary to give you pleasure.' I do it every year. I tell 'em the truth. And they love it. They fuckin' love it."

The telethon itself had mutated over the years. Though it still epitomized the Vegas exemplar, it had skewed its talent roster toward a more Middle American palette than during its 1970s heyday. By the early 1990s the principal entertainment came not from New York or Los Angeles but from Branson, Missouri, the Ozarks tourist trap where many older country and pop stars had opened theaters to perform for folks too moral or budget-conscious to visit Vegas, Atlantic City, or Florida. From the Osmond Brothers (without Donny or Marie) to Tony Orlando to Mel Tillis to Yakov Smirnoff, the town was rotten with acts on the downslide.

The infusion of Branson performers in the telethon marked not only a shift away from Jerry's once cosmopolitan, ethnic, and coastal audience to a Bible Belt crowd—the same folks that televangelists hit up for money—but also a general diminution of the stature of the telethon itself. Where it used to host the biggest names in traditional show business, it had become a refuge for old friends of Jerry's (Steve and Eydie, Norm Crosby, even Gary, still singing "This Diamond Ring" at forty-nine) and young acts who'd passed Jerry's auditions. The parade of sponsors—7-Eleven, Kellogg's, Budweiser, Harley Davidson, Brunswick Bowling Centers—seemed tawdrier in this light, the spectacle of tuxedo-clad Jerry accepting checks from strangers creepier than ever. If the 1970s telethon was a kind of acme of postwar American show business, the 1990s telethon was a parade of lowest-common-denominator signifiers of postcapitalist America. Jerry didn't even cry at the end any longer, even though his final tallies inched closer and closer to $50 million every year.

Jerry put together a national tour in the fall and winter of 1993. It was to be a true career-summing act, a two-hour, one-man show (with musical accompaniment) reviewing everything he'd ever done in show business. There would be film clips of him and Dean onstage and in movies, clips from the films he made with Frank Tashlin and on his own, clips from telethons. He would sing, dance, tell jokes, do impressions and pantomime, conduct the band, perform sleight-of-hand tricks with cigarettes and canes and audience members' handkerchiefs, even take questions from the audience and greet them in a reception area after the show. As a capper, he would bring Danielle out onstage and sing to her, a touch the audiences in New York had really enjoyed in the spring (apart from the baby, longtime fans had seen the whole act before). Entitled "Jerry Lewis . . . Unlimited," the tour was mounted by Columbia Artists Management, a booking agency primarily involved in developing tours for classical artists such as symphonies, dance troupes, and instrumentalists. The company had, however, scored well with recent tours built around such performers as Steve Allen, Sid Caesar, and Mel Tormé, and took that as an indication that it could promote Jerry successfully as well.

The "Unlimited" tour had two halves—a midwest, southwest, and Pacific coast tour in October, and an Atlantic coast tour in February and March. It would take him, by a customized touring bus, to seventeen states, Canada, and Puerto Rico, though not necessarily to the biggest or likeliest sites. It kicked off in Ohio, but in Toledo, not Cincinnati, Cleveland, or Columbus; in Southern California, he would play Azusa and Cerritos, not L.A.; in the Bay Area, San Raphael and Cupertino, not San Francisco or Oakland; in New York, Queens College and Brooklyn College, but not Manhattan. In effect, he was booked like a specialty act into college auditoriums and performing arts centers, not the large downtown theaters where popular acts usually performed. With stops like Peoria, Sarasota, Elmira, Schenectady, Kalamazoo, and Hershey on the itinerary, it sounded like one of Danny's burlesque circuit tours or the sort of thing Jerry himself was doing forty years earlier when Abbey Greshler turned him into an emcee.

Jerry promoted the tour with appearances on "The Late Show with David Letterman," "Later with Bob Costas," and "Sally Jesse Raphael" (this last appearance was so filled with praise for Jerry from friends and son Gary that it seemed a pointed rejoinder to Patti's book and the negative publicity the telethon had been getting). Despite all the publicity, however, the tour had troubles from the start. In Toledo, the first stop, ticket sales were so sluggish that the promoters offered two-for-one pricing in the final few days before the performance; even then, only a two-thirds house turned up. His performance at the University of Illinois in Champagne-Urbana was similarly undersold. In Amarillo it was weaker still—less than half the house. "It's not that we're dealing with a financial bonanza here," admitted Bob Kay of Columbia Artists.

By the time he got to the West Coast, disaster struck. Bill Graham Presents, the booker for two dates in the Bay Area and two in the northwest, found itself sitting with virtually empty theaters after the first week of sales. "We're used to

seeing 50 percent of the house sold after the first weekend of sales," said the organization's Lee Smith, "not the eighty or one hundred tickets that it actually
was." Smith was so appalled by the initial advance sale that he wrote Kay to warn
him that Jerry was in for a major disappointment if these shows went on as
scheduled. "We were so stunned by the sales that we told them that these dates
shouldn't play," he recalled, "and they said, 'Tough.' They were going to play
these dates if there were one hundred people in the house. They gave us absolutely no indication that they would allow the dates to be canceled." It was
shaping up as a major embarrassment—after nearly six weeks of sales in Portland, Oregon, for example, some 250 tickets were sold for a 2,700-seat auditorium.

Finally, the Graham organization convinced Kay to spike all four shows and
bought out the contract. On the night he closed in Cerritos, Jerry got the news
from Kay—they would not be heading north. Jerry would get paid by Columbia
Artists regardless—he had a guaranteed contract with the agency—but he was
crestfallen. "It was very difficult for him," remembered Kay. "He was majorly depressed in his dressing room. He had tears in his eyes."

There was, of course, some finger-pointing afterward. Kay blamed the Graham organization: "They didn't do any promotion." But Smith saw it as a matter
of Jerry's audience having changed its habits since the last time he'd tried anything as large as the "Unlimited" tour. "The demographic that goes to these
shows is declining in size and in the desire to go out to live performances," he
reasoned. Indeed, only in places where he could count on a large vestige of Jerry
Lewis fans from the old days did he play before the sort of houses he'd hoped to:
Southern California, New York City, South Florida.

And if those audiences had read the trade reviews, they might have stayed
home, too. *Variety*'s Jim Farber called "Jerry Lewis . . . Unlimited" "a show
that thrives on saccharine sentimentality and sarcastic abuse." While he acknowledged that the audience "seems to love it all," he complained that "every
element of the show seems unlimited: The length (especially without an intermission); the stream of corny, abusive, racially tinged jokes; the song-and-dance
numbers; even the grainy film clips."

In the *Los Angeles Times* Lawrence Christon, the paper's regular reviewer of
comedians, wrote that "Jerry Lewis is far from tired. Would that were true of his
act." Like Farber, Christon found the show overlong, but he was more analytical
in explaining his distaste: The rap on Lewis by his knowledgeable peers is that
he was never able to metamorphose his Idiot persona beyond postadolescence,
"and you can see here how he shored up his incapacity for change by taking
refuge, like so many other stalled performers, in Las Vegas, where time never registers."

Farber and Christon were both particularly appalled at the way Jerry turned
the show's question-and-answer session into a chance to ridicule his audience.

Both writers mentioned an overweight woman who stood up to announce that she considered him the second most important man in her life after her father and that she'd been waiting forty-two years to see him in person. His response? "I'm in room 134 at the Sheraton. Come up after the show and we'll make it true." Then he turned to the band and said, "That's the broad I've been telling you about. There's enough for everyone!" When a young couple stood up to express their admiration for him in noticeably tongue-tied fashion, Jerry told them that they looked "like two perfect schmucks." Nevertheless, when he left the stage that night, as on most nights throughout the truncated tour, he received a warm standing ovation. He could prove it; at his request, one of the Cerritos performances was videotaped so that his daughter could see it when she was older.

Though he'd passed Social Security age, he kept pursuing ways to reemerge as a significant presence in the business. In 1993 he had appeared on an episode of the NBC sitcom "Mad About You" as an eccentric billionaire who wanted to hire someone to make a film about his life. Playing alongside popular young stand-up comics Paul Reiser and Steven Wright (a droll, deadpan wit and Jerry's perfect opposite), he made a winning elder statesman—tan, full of energy, and surprisingly generous with the spotlight. Brandon Tartikoff, the former NBC and Paramount chief who had set up his own production company, liked Jerry's appearance so much he was inspired to begin talks with the comic about a sitcom pilot—Jerry would play a foul-tempered attorney—but nothing material emerged from the discussions.

The following year, Jerry found himself cast in a feature film role that would take advantage of those very qualities that Tartikoff responded to, in addition to the darker side he'd shown in *The King of Comedy* and "Wiseguy." *Funny Bones* is the story of Tommy Fawkes, a struggling young comic whose father, George, is a famously successful comedian. After flopping hideously on a Vegas stage in his father's presence, the young comic flees to England, his father's birthplace, an Eden less golden than he has been led to expect.

Jerry, of course, played the dad, and Tommy was played by the American actor (and remarkable late-Jerry lookalike) Oliver Platt; Leslie Caron played a character from out of Jerry's past (a sly reference to Jerry's famous French following). Peter Chelsum, the English writer-director of *Hear My Song*, a film about a legendary Irish tenor and the larcenous young theater owner who tries to book him, wrote and directed. Chelsum set the film in the British seaside resort of Blackpool—his own birthplace, a sort of cross between Atlantic City and the Borscht Belt, a once-popular tourist spot now gone to seed but still famous for the variety of show-business acts it birthed in its heyday.

With his affection for old-time show biz and physical comedy, Chelsum wrote the script with Jerry in mind, and sent it to the comic without thinking of who else might have played the role. Reading this paean to entertainers with "funny bones," Jerry responded immediately. He called Chelsum to accept and then asked him, "How do you know all this stuff?" Chelsum responded that he didn't know how—he just knew it.

"Are you Jewish?" Jerry asked.

"No."

"Well, you sell like a fucking Jew!"

Jerry put on some twenty-five pounds to play George Fawkes and went off to spend two months in England shooting the film. Chelsum and his producer, Simon Fields, were a bit jittery about the star's arrival. "You hear stories, and you do worry," Chelsum admitted. "But Simon had to deal with all that." When Jerry and his scores of suitcases turned up, Chelsum found that the star was a perfect gentleman on the set. Like Martin Scorsese, who'd directed Jerry through his last really worthy film role a decade earlier, Chelsum declared that he and Jerry "got on terribly well."

He recalled that on the comedian's last day on the set, he received a call from his agent at William Morris, who asked him point-blank "how Jerry had been." Afterward, Chelsum told Jerry—another Morris client—about the conversation: " 'And how did they ask that?' Jerry wanted to know, and I told him that I'd laughed and said that he'd been impeccably directable." Indeed, on Jerry's last day on the film, Chelsum revealed that he was surprised at just how cooperative Jerry had been. "I told him, 'You know, Jerry, you saw me scratching my head some days, and you never said anything, as you might've done,' " he recalled.

Chelsum appreciated not only Jerry's cooperativeness but the inimitable aura he brought to his role and even his modest improvisatory touches. Entering Tommy's dressing room in Vegas, for instance, Jerry was told by the director to lay claim to the place. He created his own bits of business, pacing the room as he spoke to his son, helping himself to the grapes in the congratulatory fruit basket on the coffee table, gesturing toward the wall with his chin and murmuring, "Hmm—new mirrors." Later on, he upstages his son's debut by stepping up to the mike before him and doing shtick, feigning humility but grinning broadly at the ovation. It's a moment so Lewisian as to feel documentary.

Chelsum claimed not to know much about Jerry's life, but parts of his script would be impossible for anyone else to have played. In addition to the show biz–starved son whom he forever eclipses, George Fawkes has another son, a bastard child who lives in England and works as a comedian—a pantomimist with a dummy act! Lee Evans, the brilliant English comic playing the role, is as close a simulacrum of the chimplike young Jerry as Platt is for the barrel-chested older man. Indeed, while the film is most explicitly concerned with the two brothers and the vexing question of what makes for real comic inspiration, it is also a kind of tribute to Jerry Lewis and the strains of comic performance that have emanated from him: the young-wild-man comedy practiced by entertainers like

Evans, Jim Carrey, and Pauly Shore, and the slick Vegas act embodied by Tommy Fawkes and the thousands of faceless stand-up comics who have passed through the Labor Day telethon.

Funny Bones had its world premiere at the Sundance Film Festival in Park City, Utah, in the winter of 1995, and advance word on the film was very strong. Jerry made the trip to drum up interest in the picture, and Chelsum gave an interview to *The New York Times* in which he revealed that Disney was at sea as to how to release the film: "Your stars make it look like a B-picture," he was told. *Variety* loved the film, calling it "a tour de force," while acknowledging that its "commercial prospects are . . . likely to be erratic." Jerry and Leslie Caron, reviewer Leonard Klady noted, "are magical in roles that blur the boundaries of their real and screen personae."

Chelsum, of course, wasn't the first director to add weight to a film by hiring Jerry to appear in it. But Martin Scorsese's casting of Jerry in *The King of Comedy*, had a different effect, revealing the sobriety, loneliness, and anger inside the telethon host. The role might have served as a restorative to Jerry's waning career, but it left the creepy suspicion that Scorsese had captured his actor's ugliness a bit too accurately. Chelsum's Jerry, however, is closer to the public image of the man: Jerry the Vegas guy, Jerry the French guy, Jerry whose son was a big pop star, Jerry who was once a force of nature as a physical comic. If he doesn't have the ferocity of Jerry Langford, George Fawkes is instead a perfect embodiment of what is best about the actor. He is the Jerry of the charming surface, of the legend, the guy who gave David Letterman such pleasure as a guest on his show—the Tony Bennett of physical comedy, dug by youngsters who had no prior association with him but who ate up both Jim Carrey and Harry Connick, Jr.

Very few people who saw *Funny Bones* weren't favorably impressed—only Terrence Rafferty of *The New Yorker*, among nationally read critics, didn't like it—but very few people saw the film. Disney never quite figured out how to release it—"They don't know whether to make fifty prints or five hundred," said one regional publicist for the company—and the hesitant, low-key distribution and advertising pattern resulted in a weak box office. Jerry had made a favorable impression, but it wasn't widely felt.

Disney also played a large part in another project of Jerry's, the ongoing dream that he would be able to make a sequel to *The Nutty Professor*. There'd been talk about such a film for a decade. In 1984 there was a script co-written by Jerry and Bill Richmond to be produced in part by Jerry's son Chris for Triad Productions. Two years later, Warner Brothers was said to be producing a version of *The Nutty Professor* with Jerry merely acting in it and Joe Piscopo playing his son. In 1988 Jerry told the press he had $9 million raised for a *Nutty* film of his own, with Patti, of all people, as his coproducer. Three years later, during the break in filming *Arizona Dreams*, he was back to discussing the movie with Warner Brothers, hoping to film it before touring the nation in a revival of *Sugar Babies* (the successful knockoff of *Hellzapoppin'*); neither project materialized. Finally, appearing on Sally Jesse Raphael's syndicated talk show in the fall of 1993, he announced to great enthusiasm from the audience that "The Nutty Professor 2" was going to be made by Disney.

Not quite. Early in 1994 it was announced that Eddie Murphy, himself a onetime king of comedy fallen on leaner years, would be acting in a remake of— not a sequel to—*The Nutty Professor*, with Lewis fan John Landis directing and Ron Howard's Imagine Entertainment producing for Universal. Murphy would play Julius Kelp not as a clod and a swinger, as Jerry had, but as a fat man and a normal-bodied man, a choice that all but removed the pathos from the material (*USA Today* even ran a photo of Murphy in his fat-guy makeup). But there were creative differences among the filmmakers; Landis left, making way for Tom Shadyac (who directed faux-Jerry Jim Carrey in the wildly popular *Ace Ventura, Pet Detective*), and playwright and "M*A*S*H" TV series creator Larry Gelbart was called in to rewrite the script. After several months Gelbart, too, left the project, declaring, "I'm sorry, but it became two different pictures." Jerry, for his part, objected to the way the project was proceeding without his input. According to Brian Grazer, the film's producer, Jerry was "Machiavellian" in negotiating away the right to make the film. "Jerry was very nice at first, then he hardened his stance," Grazer explained. Eventually, Jerry was assured an executive producer credit and a chance to appear in a small role, and the film began shooting in May 1995.

Jerry had problems closer to home to contend with. In the late 1980s he and his family were being stalked by Gary Benson, a middle-aged Navy veteran who had apparently gone from admiring the comedian to wanting to harm him: Rupert Pupkin come to life. Benson continually called Jerry's house, visited Jerry's offices, and had gone so far as to date a woman who worked as a housekeeper for Jerry and SanDee and thereby gain entry to their home. Another time, he arrived at the office and told one of Jerry's secretaries he was armed with a gun and wanted to get Jerry. Jerry's lawyers were successful in getting a judge to issue a restraining order against Benson, but the man was clearly beyond reason. In February 1994 he got too close to Jerry again and was arrested by Las Vegas police; a judge ordered him held on $1 million bail. A year later, Benson pled guilty to a felony charge of aggravated stalking and was released on his own recognizance pending enrollment in a psychiatric care program.

Late in 1994 news of another project materialized. Jerry would tour the country in the road production of *Damn Yankees*, the classical musical that had debuted while he and Dean were still together. It had been revived on Broadway to brilliant reviews and solid box office in 1992. Jerry was slated to play the Devil, known in the play as Mr. Applegate, a figure who transforms a baseball fan into a brilliant player and the lowly Washington Senators into a pennant-contending team.

In December the show's producer, Mitchell Maxwell, announced a radical plan. He had already announced that the Broadway production would close at the end of the year—it had enjoyed a healthy run, but it was winding down, and he wanted it to bow before the usual midwinter box-office lull. Now, however, with Jerry's name available for the marquee, he would reopen the show on Broadway at the end of February, hold it there for a few months, and then take it out on the road. They would do nine shows a week; it would be the busiest Jerry had been in decades.

There was an air of uncertainty about the enterprise; no such hiatus had ever been pulled off on Broadway before. Unions, performers, theater owners, investors were all asked to let the red ink pour for a few months. Yet Maxwell was confident that he could swing it. "I'll lose money going on hiatus," he said, "but it's an exposure that doesn't cripple the show in the long run." He was so confident, in fact, that he made his nonbilled actors, whose contracts expired at the end of the regular run, an informal promise to rehire them all. "I don't think I'm going to see any attrition," he announced.

Jerry could afford to sit back and see what happened. He was already cast in the touring company, and he had no qualms at all with Maxwell's ambitious plans. If the producer felt he could reopen *Damn Yankees* in New York with Jerry Lewis as the Devil, then Jerry Lewis would do nothing to stop him. In January 1995 he held a press conference in a room above Sardi's, boasting to reporters that he would bring "brilliance" to the hit play. He tap-danced for the cameras, he did shtick ("There's no humility in my family. I got it all"), and he even lost his temper, albeit with a smile on his face: Asked if he'd done enough singing in his career to handle the musical portions of his role, he snapped at the questioner: "What do you do, live in a cave? Did you know Lindbergh landed in Paris?"

He was beaming, thrilled at the prospect of doing the one thing he'd never done before professionally, of performing just the way Jolson had, as Danny Lewis had always longed to. It seemed possible: People spent more than $100 million *three times* in 1994 to watch Jim Carrey do Jerry's shtick in movies. Why wouldn't they show up to watch the real thing in person? At sixty-eight, he stood poised to make his Broadway debut—in a role for which, he joshingly admitted, he'd inadvertently been rehearsing all of his life.

The thing sold tickets.

The New York area had always been good for him, but the presales for *Damn Yankees* surprised everyone. The deal had been structured so that Jerry would directly profit from ticket sales, and the public thirst to see him in the show was so great that he would earn a reported forty thousand dollars a week—the highest salary ever paid a performer on Broadway according to a variety of reports (but, astoundingly, the same sum he commanded as a live solo performer in the late 1950s). It was such a huge bonanza that it wiped away all other memories: Approached by a reporter who wanted to know about the *Hellzapoppin'* debacle, he shot back, "You want to talk about Auschwitz? Is that interesting to you? I don't talk about anything negative," and walked away.

About positives, however, he was downright effusive. In the weeks leading up to previews of the show, which began on February 28, he was everywhere in the media: all the New York newspapers, TV talk shows (he did his second "Late Show with David Letterman" in a year and a half), magazines. Ensconced in a suite at the Waldorf Towers, he did tons of press, all of it fluff: He joked about being the devil, he bragged about losing the twenty-five pounds he'd put on for *Funny Bones* ("What I'd do for a knish," he wailed; "I'd have an affair with a lesbian"), he showed off his little girl Dani (the only one of his children or grandchildren whose photos he hung in his dressing room), and he talked—almost obsessively at times—about his father. In every single interview he gave, he paused at some moment to announce that his appearance on Broadway was the fulfillment not only of his own lifelong ambition but the greatest ambition that Danny Lewis ever held for himself or his son. "It was a dream of my dad's that I'd make it here," went one such passage. "My dad is looking up over a cloud giggling," went another. During still another, he merely looked heavenward and muttered, "Dad . . . Dad . . ."*

When the play finally opened officially—on March 12, 1995, just four days before his sixty-ninth birthday—it was received resoundingly well. "Jerry Lewis is legitimate at last," wrote Vincent Canby in *The New York Times*. Remarking the "surprisingly self-effacing" quality of Jerry's performance ("he seems to have acquired that laid-back Las Vegas body language"), Canby actually did something no other American critic had ever done: He asked Jerry to do more. "On those few occasions when he seems on the verge of mugging, that is, when his eyes discreetly cross or his voice takes on the idiot edge, the fans scream with pleasure. . . . At this point in its run, *Damn Yankees* looks as if it could use a little more of the anarchic Lewis spirit. . . . It will be interesting to see what *Damn*

---

*In several of these interviews, he spoke sentimentally about his Grandma Sarah as well, but there was a curious postscript to these reminiscences. Yetta Litwack, one of Sam Rothberg's daughters from his first marriage, revealed to gossip columnist Liz Smith that she had approached Jerry to ask him to contribute to the upkeep of his grandmother's grave and had been rebuffed. In a similar vein, after Jerry told the producers of the Tony Awards broadcast that he couldn't participate in the show because of family commitments (he wasn't eligible for nomination, as *Damn Yankees* had been revived the season prior to his joining the cast), Smith revealed that Jerry's strong sense of family didn't stop him from ignoring an invitation to his youngest son Joseph's wedding some two weeks earlier or, on another recent occasion, refusing to see family members who tried to visit him at his Florida condominium. "To use his family as an excuse to get out of the Tonys doesn't wash," said an unnamed cousin.

Yankees is like in several months, especially if (as seems possible) Mr. Lewis has his own Applegate whispering in his ear, 'Go on, Jer, let her rip.' "

"How did the Bar Mitzvah boy do?" asked Clive Barnes in the *New York Post.* "Just dandy. . . . Although he keeps outrageousness delicately at bay, he occasionally indulges in a devilish double-take or fiendish grimace, just sufficient to indicate to the faithful the divine lunacy that still lurks round the corner."

The new, subdued Jerry didn't sit well with everyone. "If Jerry's going to be in a show, why shouldn't he be Jerry?" wondered Howard Kissel in the *Daily News.* And there were some outright negative comments: "He dwelleth in the uneasy limbo of overacting and underdoing," wrote Linda Winer in *New York Newsday.*

But in all it was a smashing debut, especially considering the sort of treatment he'd received over the years. The opening night crowd was star-studded: Douglas Fairbanks, Jr., Matthew Broderick, Molly Ringwald, John Turturro, Mayor Rudolph Giuliani, and Penelope Ann Miller were in attendance (though there were some reports of tickets being sold outside the theater for less than face value). Frank and Barbara Sinatra sent a card, Leonard Nimoy (husband to Jerry's *Big Mouth* leading lady, Susan Bay) sent a bouquet, Jerry's son Chris sent a jar of caviar. Afterward, still more celebrities (Tatum O'Neal, Barbara Walters, Patricia Kennedy Lawford, Ben Vereen) showed up at Tavern on the Green to sip Dom Perignon with Jerry and pore over the early editions of the papers; Jerry was so pleased with Canby's notice that he read it aloud to the room.

In fact, Jerry Lewis as Applegate *was* a bit of all right. Though *Damn Yankees* was, like all the revivals dotting Broadway during the Nineties, a bit of a shell game—familiar books and scores gussied up with new sets and sold to tourists at outrageous (but presumably New York–style) prices—there was an undeniable appropriateness to Jerry's playing the part of Beelzebub ("The devil is a role made in heaven, for Chrissakes," he told an interviewer), and there was a genuine buzz about the appearance of such a storied star in a live show.

Knowing that they were there to see him, Jerry played to the crowd. He smiled at his own funny lines, he joshingly urged applause from the audience with hand gestures, he stopped to bathe in the thrilled responses that followed on his slipping into The Kid's voice or his squeal of "La-a-a-a-a-dy." For the most part, he wasn't really acting: Very few of his line readings had any dramatic weight to them; he rarely sounded as if he was playing a role at all. But he did some truly terrific physical bits (being dressed down by the temptress Lola, he sat in comic stupefaction à la Stanley from *The Bellboy*), and he absolutely brought down the house with his one-man number, "Those Were the Good Old Days," showing some fancy footwork and a dazzling ability with a cane and top hat.

It was an entirely apt song: Traipsing a stage in the very Times Square that he and Dean had drifted through anonymously fifty years earlier, performing in a show that had originally appeared on Broadway at around the time he and Dean had begun to feud, he had found a kind of time warp that seemed to preserve only the best aspects of his talent. He had always loved to work live, and the audiences were literally exultant in the familiar bits he threw at them. Never mind that some of his shtick was in questionable taste (he did some nance stuff; he closed the first act by lying on his back and spreading his legs with his hands while yelling "Make a wish!"), never mind that some of it was the very stuff America had grown so tired of in the Seventies and Eighties. *Damn Yankees* fed upon its audiences' love for a bygone era, and it wasn't too hard for people to remember how ubiquitous Jerry was in those greener days. Of course, he was having the time of his life.

The next weeks were his most jubilant in decades. He was the subject of a long segment on NBC's "Dateline" in which Bob Costas practically canonized him. He appeared live on CBS's "Late Late Show with Tom Snyder" after a day in which he gave two performances, and was up at the crack of dawn the next day, his birthday, to sit in for Regis Philbin on "Live with Regis and Kathie Lee." As the spring wore on, plans were made for a film of *Damn Yankees*, and for a year-plus of European touring with the show; if it all held together, he'd play Applegate until the millennium.

There were more print interviews; the epitome was an invitation to speak to the National Press Club in Washington, D.C. In a yellow shirt open at the neck and a dark jacket, he declared, "My war with the press is over," defended "polack" jokes, claimed to have spoken at "seventeen hundred universities" and to "five thousand film and acting classes," declared that he was utterly indifferent to groups that protested his fund-raising techniques, and answered questions from the audience with the self-satisfied air of a precocious little boy who knows the adults approve of him.

It was a truly remarkable Indian summer—a late-life embrace from a public many believed had recoiled from him forever. Jerry himself, though, never lost the hope that the people loved him.

"They have put me right where I am," he declared, "giving me glowing affection and support. I'm an American icon."

And he was.

Epilogue: J & I

You know what kills me more than anything? I don't give a shit what they write. The thing that kills me is that they come with a disguise. That's what kills me. Why don't you just come and tell me you wanna do a rip piece? I'll give you all the material you want. You wanna rip me? I'll give you shit that's real. That I'm guilty of. That'll make great reading. Why the fuck would you have to make up anything? Putz: Ask me! I'll give you shit that you won't believe, that no one's ever written. As long as it's real, and it's true, it's okay with me. I don't care how I come off as long as it's the truth.

—Jerry Lewis to the author, 1993

It began in the winter of 1992, soon after I'd begun research on this book.

A friend suggested I contact Suzanne Pleshette, who'd made her film debut beside Jerry, and I wrote her to request an interview. She responded by saying that she'd be happy to oblige me, but that she would never participate in such a project without Jerry's knowledge and had therefore written him for his okay.

I hadn't yet made contact with Jerry, though I had spoken to his manager, Joe Stabile, during the writing of the proposal for this book. Stabile told me he suspected Jerry would be only marginally interested in a biography, that a book on Jerry's film career was in the works,* and that I was welcome to approach the office again once I had a contract in hand.

When I had, in fact, secured a contract, I was a bit reluctant to announce

---

*That book, *The Jerry Lewis Films* by James L. Neibaur and Ted Okuda, was released by Mc-Farland late in 1994.

the fact to Jerry immediately. I felt I ought to do some research first in order to make my contact with him as productive as possible. I didn't want to get canned, press release–style answers to serious questions, and I felt that by eliminating certain lines of inquiry altogether—by concentrating on specific facts and not generalities, for instance—I would reap the most from any potential contact with him. I remember telling an audience at a writing seminar that I would want either twenty hours with Jerry or one truthful answer to one pointed question; anything else, it seemed, would be diluted or superficial.

But, having been outed by Suzanne Pleshette, I wrote a careful letter to Jerry introducing myself, my work (I sent clips), and my intentions. I wrote with a mixture of impersonality and familiarity, I thought—making it clear that I knew a good deal about him, indicating that I respected his privacy and would understand his not wanting to participate in the project, but hoping to hear from him.

In mid-January 1993 I was on the phone with a local editor of mine when the call-waiting beep sounded and I switched lines.

"Hello?"

"I'd like to speak to Shawn Levy."

"This is Shawn."

"Shawn, this is Jerry Lewis."

My heart pounded. "Jerry . . ." I groped for something to say, hoping to sound casual. "Thanks for getting back to me."

I don't recall much of the ensuing conversation. Jerry described his general reluctance to involve himself in such inquiries ("I'm an easy target," he confessed), but he felt that my letter allowed him to "open [his] heart" on a "new day." He would be happy to meet with me whenever we could work it out.

And there was one last thing: He'd heard from Suzanne Pleshette; had I been carrying on an investigation behind his back? I assured him that I had approached Pleshette so early in my work simply because she and I had a mutual friend and I was traveling to Los Angeles at that time on other business. He seemed satisfied, and we said good-bye, planning to compare our schedules soon and arrange a time to meet.

Within a few weeks, we had scheduled an April appointment on his yacht in San Diego. I planned a few other research activities, scheduled a few other interviews, sought out an appropriate gift (I settled on a three-volume 1904 edition of Boswell's *Life of Johnson*—the language's great biography by a man who actually knew his subject), and flew south for the appointment.

Early one April morning, I arrived at the Marriott Hotel, where Jerry's boat was docked, about twenty minutes early, and scoped the place out. From across the marina, I could see an especially handsome yacht among the very large vessels in the gate-protected berths: *Sam's Place*, it was called, and its home port was identified as Las Vegas. Satisfied that I'd found him, I parked, killed a few minutes looking at the gift shops in a nearby tourist complex, and went into the marina office to call the boat. At the stroke of 10:00 A.M., I walked down to the gate, where Jerry was to meet me.

"I call that timing!" he announced as he saw me, clearly—with my long black pants and black briefcase—the only writer in the vicinity.

"I try to be prompt," I replied.

He looked great. He was sixty-seven years old and extremely fit. He was barrel-chested (just like, as I was to learn later on, his father late in life) and strode spryly on skinny legs. He wore very short white shorts, a synthetic red athletic pullover (rather like a softball jersey, but with no writing or markings), Reebok court shoes, high white sweat socks, and a fair amount of jewelry: a pricey watch, rings, a gold bracelet, a gold necklace.

We shook hands, talked about the weather, and walked down to the boat. Alongside his sixty-eight-foot Grebe motor yacht—"The last size boat for one person to handle," he explained—was a sporty red motorboat emblazoned with the name *Jerry's Place*. I stepped over a red welcome mat bearing the familiar young-Jerry cartoon logo, put down my bag, presented my gift, met the ship's captain, and sat down opposite Jerry in the main cabin with a Sprite he offered me.

The furnishing was sparse, just like his film sets: baby gear (a stroller, a playpen with toys, diapers and wipes), a small TV with a VCR and a portable cassette player beside it (the sole tape in evidence was a Gary Lewis and the Playboys greatest hits collection), tasteful pale rattan furniture. The decor was largely nautical—brass-and-teak barometers and the like—with one pointed exception: On the glass coffee table was a large, colorful clay statue of Jerry as a clown walking a half-dozen dogs.

The talk turned to my project. Jerry was eager to learn how I'd settled on him as a subject, and I explained that his life had touched so many fascinating subjects—Dean Martin, the *auteur* theory, charity telethons, slapstick comedy, vaudeville, Las Vegas, and so on—that it was irresistible. I indicated that I thought he'd been neglected as an artist, and that one symptom of that neglect was the lack of a real biography of him.

He took this all in with a pleased look. He told me about run-ins he'd had with the press. He singled out an article that had appeared in *Esquire* two years earlier and that was filled with shocking, profanity-laced quotations from him. He had called the writer after the article appeared, he said, to declare his displeasure (I had already heard about this incident from a friend of the writer's). The story was meant to symbolize his principled attitude toward journalism as a craft and his wariness as a subject; as he spoke he grew visibly angry.

Soon enough, the mood passed and we got down to work. I took out my tape recorder and placed it on the table between us, and I began asking questions. At first we spoke of little things—his home in Las Vegas, life with six sons versus life with the new baby (Danielle, asleep below deck, was just over a year old).

Then I broached more important matters. I had wanted to demonstrate to him that I'd done my homework, and I asked him about three specific and relatively obscure incidents: the jewelry heist when he hosted "The Tonight Show" in New York, the night he kept an intruder at bay at his Pacific Palisades house, and the murder of his cousin Judy. He was surprised and, I think, impressed that I knew about these events, and he spoke freely about them—though not, as I knew even then, entirely accurately.

I chose not to challenge anything he said. Indeed, my attitude was one of extreme caution. I was trying to be as forthright as I could, but as I sat with him I knew that I would, at some point in the research or the writing or the release of the book, become in his mind, like the *Esquire* writer, just another Judas in the press. There was no way to tell this story without telling the negatives, and whenever the negatives were mentioned, I knew, Jerry flew into rages.

But that first day on the boat was cordial and tranquil. He introduced me to SanDee and the baby (when SanDee was headed out to do some shopping, she asked Jerry for cash; he pulled out a roll of bills—ones on the outside, larger denominations within—and handed her "a C-note"), he sat very close to me, eyeing my watch and fiddling with the baggage tag on my briefcase, which sat on the floor by my feet.

We talked for more than three hours, covering a variety of what I thought would be the most innocuous topics: his comic influences, his comic descendants, his teaching, his ensemble of actors, the Academy Awards, emerging film technologies, hired-gun projects he'd made during the 1980s and '90s. He spoke about muscular dystrophy, and he related the stories of a few afflicted families so honestly and tearfully that I thought I might cry myself. I told him I'd seen a copy of the Paramount camera department report about his use of the video assist on *The Bellboy*, and he was overjoyed; he asked if I could have it sent to him, and I told him I thought I might—there were several copies of it in the archive I'd been working with, and it would be easy enough, I reckoned, to have the curator at the USC archive send a copy of the report to Jerry Lewis, the very donor of the papers.*

Finally, we parted with promises to keep in touch with each other. Jerry invited me to plan further interview sessions, to do some traveling with him (he wanted me to see his home and office in Las Vegas and to visit MDA headquarters in Tucson), and to think of him, in effect, as a collaborator. It seemed to me he saw in the appearance of an interested young writer a means to resurrect his lot in the public eye.

He did *not* want to authorize the book in the sense of reading it prior to

---

*I did finally arrange for the curator to send one of these documents to Jerry, and Jerry thoughtfully sent the original along to me; after our final conversations, however, he also gave a copy to Neibaur and Okuda, who published it as an appendix to their book.

publication. He spoke at length about the disappointment he had suffered at the meager sales of *Jerry Lewis in Person*, his 1982 autobiography, and he understood that my entering into a relationship with him would necessarily preclude any editorial authority on his part. He asked if the book would be called "the unauthorized biography," and I told him that such a title was generally meant to signal a more salacious book than I intended to write. But he agreed that we'd both be best served if I were to remain strictly independent. He would speak with me, show me things, provide me with materials, and give the okay to any friends of his who sought clearance from him before speaking with me. He seemed to bless the project wholeheartedly when he told me that the book he'd written in 1982 had been a "nice" book but hadn't sold, adding that "nice sucks" and that I could only "take care" of myself and my family by doing the job right.

In the following weeks, Jerry positively effused over me. He called my home several times, once catching my wife in my absence and telling her about all my fine qualities. He sent me a few items he thought I'd appreciate. When I told him my mother would be attending an upcoming performance of his at the Westbury Music Fair, he insisted that I find out for him exactly where she would be sitting so he could "give her the thrill of a lifetime." (As it turned out, on the night of the show Jerry wasn't able to reach her seat, but afterward she found her way to the dressing room and identified herself. "Shawn Levy's mother has been found," an assistant declared, and my mom and her friends were invited backstage, where Jerry greeted them in a kimono and posed for photos. Again, Jerry told my mother about all the wonderful things he'd discovered in her son; he was extremely excited to work with me, he said, to which my mom responded, "It'll be good for you.")

Throughout this honeymoon, I kept lapsing into uneasiness. I couldn't forswear my obligation to write a truthful book—a book that would be filled, I knew, with episodes that would be painful and upsetting to Jerry. But I also couldn't cut the line between us and deny myself the access he was promising me. It was clearer to me as time went on that I would have to do something to make a break between us—that I couldn't hypocritically smile and hug him, on the one hand, and write honestly about his personal and professional traumas, on the other. But I didn't know how to do it.

It didn't matter.

The second time I met with Jerry on his yacht was in early July 1993, and it was as distinct from our first meeting as could be.

Driving to San Diego that morning, I took a curve in the highway too fast and spilled hot coffee all over myself. I stripped to my underwear and tried to dry my clothes out with the air-conditioning, then raced to a shopping mall to buy a new shirt and a new pair of shorts and make it to the boat on time.

When I arrived, I was immediately struck by a change in the air. Jerry arrived to meet me at the marina gate in the company of a young deckhand and, for the only time in our two meetings and ten or so phone calls, used the Idiot voice: "It's Shawn Levy, and he's getting dangerously close to me!"

That was a strange way to say hello, I thought. Then he added, "I've got a lot to do today so I wanna get you out of my hair." Although I was the Golden Biographer and had flown a thousand miles, I was now officially a nuisance.

We began our talk pretty quickly (I hadn't brought a gift). We spoke generally about anti-Semitism—he showed me the charm he'd designed for his necklace: a cross and a Star of David combined—and then we got into specific questions.

I had used up a lot of my softball questions last visit, and I'd decided to speak more directly with him and ask him about specific predecessors whose work his act resembled, about the split of Martin and Lewis, about Abbey Greshler, Hal Wallis, the Arthur Marx book, his inactivity in the 1970s, *The Day the Clown Cried*. It was a risk, I knew, but in broaching these subjects, I would give him a chance to define our relationship once and for all: Were we going to be honest collaborators, or was I just a bright youngster who'd be told and allowed to say only good things?

I got my answer quick enough. I used the word "spastic" to characterize his onstage body language.* It provoked the first outburst of the morning: "The word 'spastic' is terrible. Some fucking writer who didn't take the time to watch the work titled my work." Okay.

I asked about the comics who'd charged that Jerry had borrowed bits from them. One in particular, Catskills stand-up Gene Baylos, drew a lengthy, hostile response. "He's the biggest joke in show business. His name is a joke. Gene Baylos had every chance to be a big comic if he would've used his head, but he didn't. I wouldn't take anything from Gene Baylos. Unless I was in biology class. No unkindness meant."

Fortunately, this discussion led us into a discussion of comic styles, the sort of generic Grand Old Man of Comedy topic that he loved to talk about. And that led us to a discussion of the mechanics of mounting the telethon, and of other sorts of MDA business that he oversaw. For a long time, we spoke placidly.

And then I asked about Dean. At first he talked in familiar terms about how the partnership was "a love affair" and about specific things they did in the act

---

*It might better describe his offstage body language. In person, he can't sit in repose. His face churns, his hands gyrate at the wrist, his fingers rub against each other, his neck bobs left and right, causing his whole head to pivot on his chin. It's not quite a palsy, but it's unsettling, and it gives him the air of someone always on the verge of upset, of somebody waiting for the other person to finish speaking so he can jump down their throat. It's as if years of contorting his body has finally stretched it to uncontrollable limpness—like a rubber band that has lost its elasticity from overuse.

that the critics and audience never caught on to: the difference in the thickness of their heels, the way they subtly shifted into acting as each other's straight man.

He became more somber as talk of Martin and Lewis wore on, and he got up to get himself a beer—at about eleven o'clock in the morning.

In the next minutes, he spoke bitterly about Hal Wallis, he described the painful experience of making *Hollywood or Bust*, he talked about the psychic toll of the feud between him and Dean, about the trouble he'd had at home with Patti as a result of his struggles with his partner, about the trauma of finally separating himself from Dean and heading out on his own.

In ways, it was a remarkably frank talk. "If you sat with Dean, you'd never have this discussion because he was never really that within," he said. But it seemed to drive him deeper and deeper into the funk he'd been in ever since I arrived. "Let's talk about something else," he said. "I'm starting to get depressed."

I can't say that I was conscious of the decision, but I must have known by the tenor of the discussion that we wouldn't be talking at this sort of depth very much more, if ever. I told him I wanted to discuss the demise of Martin and Lewis just a bit more.

He didn't like it. "What do you wanna do, a Kitty Kelley book? Just be careful, 'cause I'll come after you. I still have a picture of your letter to me, what brought us together. I respected what you put in your letter. You better just be that."

Satisfied at having delivered this warning, though, he answered my next question, but it wasn't long before he wanted me to know exactly what he thought of my kind. Reflecting on contemporary accounts of his split with Dean, he suddenly launched a tirade against reporters in general. "The press, of course, are cunts, like they've always been and they always will be. They're getting worse. They're not getting better, they're getting worse. They're just absolutely fucking scum."

He had a specific instance in mind. "I just did a fourteen-page layout for *Vanity Fair* and I have the worst hunch in my life, I have the worst hunch. I took her into my home, took her here on my boat, had her at my child's birthday. I mean, we really did an in-depth piece for *Vanity Fair*, and now I'm starting to get some vibes. I have a feeling I'm gonna get fucking shot down. And it's not like they got a virgin, but my instinct is too fucking good. I just fell in love with this dame. She's a very heavy nice wonderful lady, a good journalist. Something's telling me I'm in for it. I have no idea why I feel that. Nothing has happened. Haven't heard from her. She's well and happy with her husband and her children and she's a contributing editor to *Vanity Fair*. I did the photographs. We did a great layout with my daughter and my wife and did all the things you do for a big layout. Yesterday, I got up and I said to Sam, 'I have a feeling that I'm gonna get fucked. Royally. But not easy. I have a feeling I'm really gonna get *zetzed*.' She says, 'Oh, my God.' Because she knows when I get that instinct it's usually right. We finished it like six, eight weeks ago. Something told me yesterday morning. It just hit me like that. Why do I feel this? I'm just hoping I'm wrong."*

He had a pet theory about why the press had such an ambivalent relationship with him: "See, they will pursue anything that will smell or that they can infer smells. They've been that way all their lives. That's why I have such a wonderful feeling about the press. I use them like they use me. I want their space. And I want it before the telethon. If that's my contribution to my kids, that's my business. But to think for one minute that they're noble or that they have any integrity or morality . . . you're a fool to think that. And I give of myself totally. I spew out my emotions. Nobody gives interviews like I give. 'Cause I have nothing to hide. I just pour out. But some of the shit that I pour out, if it's misconstrued or it's written poorly, it sounds strange. Well, that's the chance you take in our business."

But he was only prepared, he announced, to take such chances for so much longer. "One day I'm gonna do what Frank [Sinatra] did. One day. I'm just gonna say nobody, ever again, about anything, before anything, at any time, until I die. Which I'm getting very close to. Frank and I have talked about it a number of times. He said, 'Listen, my life is better, my peace of mind is better, my stomach is better, and I'm a better person because of it. I feel self-esteem that I won't let this scum into my life.' And you can't argue with it. You can't. He said, 'They get into my life in spite of what position I've taken, because when I appear somewhere they're in my life. But they can't come close to me. They can be in my life from a fucking distance.' He said, 'And that's what you should do if you wanna survive.' I said, 'I'll do it, Frank, the day that I decide I don't need them anymore, I'll do it.'"

The tension as he launched into these attacks was palpable and sickening. The phone rang—someone calling about MDA business—and I was grateful for the chance to consult my notes and change the subject. Unfortunately, I had prepared to discuss only topics that weren't likely to dispel his ugly mood.

After a few more questions, and feeling like the air was draining from the cabin, I turned the conversation to *The Day the Clown Cried* and the period of inactivity that followed the dissolution of the incomplete project. How did it feel, I asked, to be left without something significant to work on?

"What do you think? What do you think?"

He was shouting.

*He wasn't. The piece by Leslie Bennetts, "Jerry vs. the Kids," appeared in the magazine's September 1993 issue. It was no butter-up job: The most thoroughgoing and intensely researched account yet of the controversy over the MDA's fund-raising tactics, it presented Jerry as a thin-skinned, angry, fading man lashing out at any note of discord in the world. Moreover, where he had waited until the 1991 *Esquire* piece ran before shouting at the reporter, he called Bennetts at home one night to register his disgust before her story ran, giving her yet another instance of his ugliness to write about.

"How can you ask a question like that?" He pointed to my tape recorder on the coffee table. "You should hear what you just asked me. You're an insensitive prick, you know that? What the hell is wrong with you? What sort of sick childhood did you have, or what's missing in your life that you can sit there and ask me things like that?"

I was absolutely stunned to be hearing this sort of thing. I knew that he was in a twisted mood from the time I'd arrived, and the conversation of the preceding hour had been extremely uncomfortable for me, but until this moment I thought we'd been speaking as grown men with a common interest and purpose.

I was apparently alone in that impression.

"I had a sense of this the last time we spoke," he continued, "but I didn't say anything because I figured, 'He's young.' But you need to hear this. Frank Tashlin once gave me a talking-to like this, and I learned from it. We could've done good work together, but now you're just gonna get bits and pieces and it won't be any good."

I did the only thing I could do. I listened, red-eared, and tried to keep looking him in the face, and then, when he'd petered out, I apologized, saying that if I'd in any way stepped beyond the bounds of decency I was truly sorry. Groping for a way to explain any impropriety, I said that perhaps my hours of isolated research on him had numbed me, that I was perhaps guilty of seeing him more as a subject than as a person, that I never meant to offend him with my questions.

He took this as an occasion for a second salvo, misconstruing what I'd said as a confession that I was awed to be in his presence and suggesting that I ought to choose another line of work if I found myself overwhelmed by "a hero."

The tape recorder had clicked audibly to a stop during my apology, and I had to resist the impulse to throw a new tape in it. In part, I was honestly afraid he would have restrained me or resorted to some other physical means of bringing the conversation to an end.

I apologized again—I can't even recall what I said—and he launched into a third assault, which I've also repressed (there was something about my book's being "buried in the cinema section at Waldenbooks").

Finally, he seemed to accept my apologies, saying something like "If you tell me that's what you meant, then I believe you, and I believe you're sorry."

Before I realized what was happening, he grabbed my tape recorder: "I've never talked to anyone like that before, and I have to have this."

"That's mine," I said, "and it's got an hour and a half of my work on it."

"I'm just going to erase that part of it," he replied, "and I'll send it back to you."

I could have taken the tape from him, but I was shell-shocked. I chose to take him at his word and give him a chance to erase his outburst (which I wrote down on paper immediately after we parted).

I then stood up, told him I was leaving, and gathered the rest of my things. He said we'd talk again, he shook my hand, and he had the young deckhand walk me to the gate.

For the next few weeks, I absolutely could not work; indeed, I could barely *sleep*. The thought of spending another year or so researching and writing about Jerry Lewis positively shook me with nausea. The tape arrived in the mail—with no note attached—and was uncorrupted save for the sudden silence after my final question. I called his Las Vegas office to leave the message that I'd received it.

About a month later, Jerry wrote to me. An "Author's Query" I'd sent to *The New York Times Book Review*—a month or so before I'd ever written Jerry—had finally appeared in print. Jerry, obviously not familiar with the format of these open requests for interviews, reminiscences, letters or photos, declared it, "highly unusual to say the least." I called him up, still holding on to the illusion that we were going to continue speaking to one another, to assure him that such queries were a standard practice. He shrugged it off.

Finally, in mid-August, I sent him a fax requesting the opportunity to attend the telethon. He called the next day, telling me that there was "a problem with the ticketing" and he didn't know what he could do. Besides, he said, he'd be too busy to talk with me. I didn't want to take any of his time, I assured him; I just wanted to observe the telethon as a fly on the wall, as it were. He said he'd see if that was possible and that he'd get back to me.

Not twenty minutes later, the phone rang again. It was Jerry calling to say that he hadn't been honest with me and that he "didn't want [me] there," that he was only interested in "surrounding [himself] with people that supported [him]."

I told him I wasn't antagonistic to him or his work and that I was truly puzzled as to how he got such a negative impression of me.

"I'm not your therapist," he snarled.

Fine.

"Good luck with the telethon," I said.

"Thank you."

"Good-bye."

"Good-bye."

And that, I figured, was that.

A few months later, there was a strange denouement to it all. In December 1993 I wrote a letter to Patti Lewis after reading her book, requesting an interview and letting her know that I had spoken with Jerry and that he had chosen not to participate in my research. I didn't hear back from her.

The following January, I was visiting Los Angeles and woke up at five-thirty in the morning, shaken from my sleep by the Northridge earthquake. My host's home was far enough from the epicenter that we still had power, and I spent the early morning watching TV accounts of the disaster. I called my wife when I knew she'd be awake and told her what had happened. About an hour later, she called back.

"Someone just called here looking for you, and I think it was Jerry Lewis, but he hung up without leaving a message."

It didn't make any sense to me. I *was* speaking to a lot of old friends and acquaintances of his in Los Angeles, but I had been doing as much all along, and I'd always taken care to let people know that Jerry knew about the project and wasn't involved with it.*

The next day, it all became clear. He had followed his call to my house with a call to my editor at St. Martin's. Patti had sent the letter I'd written her, and he was calling to denounce me and my work. I was "doing a *National Enquirer* job," he said, and I "needed a personality transplant." He didn't care if I spoke to Patti, he said, but he wanted St. Martin's to know what they were getting into by working with me.

My editor assured Jerry that he'd seen several hundred pages of the manuscript and that the writing was respectful and fair. Jerry seemed calmed by this and by the editor's respectful tone, but before he ended his call there was a warning: "The ball's in your court now, I can't do anything until the book comes out, and when it is [out], I'll take whatever action is necessary."

And that really was that.

Jerry went on to make his so-called rapprochement with the press during the season of *Damn Yankees*.

And I went on to write this book—conscious that many of the awful things I heard about him were true.

It was an extremely difficult task, as each day of work revived in my mind the hostility I'd encountered on that boat in San Diego. But, ironically, I think Jerry and I were both well served by his outburst and subsequent rejection of me and my work.

He was able to avoid what I'm sure he now takes to be a gross betrayal and distortion.

And I was able to write the most truthful account of his life that I could.

---

*At least one interview subject certainly asked Jerry for the go-ahead to speak to me after our falling out and was given the okay.

Filmography

AS ACTOR (1 = also as producer; 2 = also as writer)

Martin and Lewis Films

My Friend Irma (1949, Paramount) d: George Marshall; with Marie Wilson, Diana Lynn, John Lund

My Friend Irma Goes West (1950, Paramount) d: Hal Walker; with Marie Wilson, Diana Lynn, John Lund, Corinne Calvet

At War with the Army (1950, Paramount) d: Hal Walker; with Polly Bergen, William Medrek, Dan Dayton

That's My Boy (1951, Paramount) d: Hal Walker; with Eddie Mayehoff, Polly Bergen, Ruth Hussey, Marion Marshall

Sailor Beware (1951, Paramount) d: Hal Walker; with Robert Strauss, Marion Marshall, Corinne Calvet

Jumping Jacks (1952, Paramount) d: Norman Taurog; with Mona Freeman, Robert Strauss, Don DeFore

The Road to Bali (1952, Paramount) d: Hal Walker; cameo

The Stooge (1953, Paramount) d: Norman Taurog; with Eddie Mayehoff, Polly Bergen, Marion Marshall

Scared Stiff (1953, Paramount) d: George Marshall; with Lizabeth Scott, Carmen Miranda, Leonard Strong, George Dolenz

The Caddy (1953, Paramount) d: Norman Taurog; with Donna Reed, Barbara Bates, Romo Vincent, Joseph Calleia

Money From Home (1953, Paramount) d: George Marshall; with Marjie Millar, Pat Crowley, Sheldon Leonard

Living It Up (1954, Paramount) d: Norman Taurog; with Janet Leigh, Sheree North, Fred Clark, Edward Arnold

Three Ring Circus (1954, Paramount) d: Joseph Pevney; with Joanne Dru, Zsa Zsa Gabor, Gene Sheldon, Elsa Lanchester

You're Never Too Young (1955, Paramount) d: Norman Taurog; with Nina Foch, Diana Lynn, Raymond Burr

Artists and Models (1955, Paramount) d: Frank Tashlin; with Dorothy Malone, Shirley MacLaine, Eddie Mayehoff, Eva Gabor

Pardners (1956, Paramount) d: Norman Taurog; with Lori Nelson, Jeff Morrow, Agnes Moorehead

Hollywood or Bust (1956, Paramount) d: Frank Tashlin; with Pat Crowley, Anita Ekberg, Maxie Rosenbloom

Solo Films

The Delicate Delinquent (1957, Paramount) (1) d: Don McGuire; with Darren McGavin, Martha Hyer, Milton Frome

The Sad Sack (1957, Paramount) d: George Marshall; with David Wayne, Phyllis Kirk, Peter Lorre

Rock-a-bye Baby (1958, Paramount) (1) d: Frank Tashlin; with Connie Stevens, Marilyn Maxwell, Reginald Gardiner

The Geisha Boy (1958, Paramount) (1) d: Frank Tashlin; with Suzanne Pleshette, Robert Hirano, Sessue Hayakawa, Marie McDonald

L'il Abner (1959, Paramount) d: Melvin Frank; cameo

Don't Give Up the Ship (1959, Paramount) d: Norman Taurog; with Dina Merrill, Diana Spencer, Mickey Shaughnessy

Raymie (1960, Allied Artists) d: Frank McDonald; sings title song

Visit to a Small Planet (1960, Paramount) d: Norman Taurog; with Joan Blackman, Earl Holliman, Fred Clark

The Bellboy (1960, Paramount) (1, 2) d: Jerry Lewis; with Bob Clayton, Bill Richmond, Milton Berle

Cinderfella (1960, Paramount) (1) d: Frank Tashlin; with Ed Wynn, Judith Anderson, Anna Maria Alberghetti, Henry Silva

The Ladies' Man (1961, Paramount) (1, 2) d: Jerry Lewis; with Kathleen Freeman, Buddy Lester, Helen Traubel, Pat Stanley

The Errand Boy (1961, Paramount) (1, 2) d: Jerry Lewis; with Brian Donlevy, Howard McNear, Fritz Feld, Sig Ruman

It's Only Money (1962, Paramount) d: Frank Tashlin; with Zachary Scott, Joan O'Brien, Jesse White

It's a Mad Mad Mad Mad World (1963, United Artists) d: Stanley Kramer; cameo

The Nutty Professor (1963, Paramount) (1, 2) d: Jerry Lewis; with Stella Stevens, Del Moore, Buddy Lester, Kathleen Freeman

Who's Minding the Store? (1963, Paramount) d: Frank Tashlin; with Jill St. John, Agnes Moorehead, John McGiver, Ray Walston

The Patsy (1964, Paramount) (1, 2) d: Jerry Lewis; with Ina Balin, Phil Harris, Peter Lorre, John Carradine, Keenan Wynn

The Disorderly Orderly (1964, Paramount); d: Frank Tashlin; with Susan Oliver, Glenda Farrell, Everett Sloane

The Family Jewels (1, 2) (1965, Paramount) d: Jerry Lewis; with Sebastian Cabot, Donna Butterworth, Neil Hamilton

Boeing Boeing (1965, Paramount) d: John Rich; with Tony Curtis, Suzanna Leigh, Dany Saval, Christiane Schmidtmer

Three on a Couch (1966, Columbia) (1) d: Jerry Lewis; with Janet Leigh, Mary Ann Mobley, Gila Golan, Leslie Parrish

Way . . . Way Out (1966, 20th Century-Fox) d: Gordon Douglas; with Dick Shawn, Connie Stevens, Anita Ekberg

The Big Mouth (1967, Columbia) (1, 2) d: Jerry Lewis; with Susan Bay, Harold Stone, Charlie Callas, Buddy Lester, Del Moore

Don't Raise the Bridge, Lower the River (1968, Columbia) d: Jerry Paris; with Terry-Thomas, Jacqueline Pearce, Patricia Routledge

Hook, Line & Sinker (1969, Columbia) (1) d: George Marshall; Peter Lawford, Anne Frances, Kathleen Freeman

Which Way to the Front? (1970, Warner Brothers) (1) d: Jerry Lewis; with Jan Murray, Sidney Miller, John Wood, Steve Franken

Hardly Working (1981, 20th Century-Fox) (2) d: Jerry Lewis; with Susan Oliver, Deanna Lund, Roger C. Carmel, Harold Stone

The King of Comedy (1982, 20th Century-Fox) d: Martin Scorsese; with Robert De Niro, Sandra Bernhard, Diahnne Abbott

Smorgasbord (a.k.a. Cracking Up) (1983, Warner Brothers) (2) d: Jerry Lewis; with Herb Edelman, Sammy Davis Jr., Milton Berle

Slapstick (Of Another Kind) (1984, Serendipity) d: Steven Paul; with Madeline Kahn, Marty Feldman, Pat Morita, Jim Backus

Retenez Moi . . . ou je fais un malheur (1984, Imacite-Coline) d: Michel Gerard; with Michel Blanc, Charlotte de Turckheim

Par ou t'es rentre? On t'as vu Sortir (1984, Carthago) d: Philippe Clair; with Philippe Clair, Marthe Villalonga

Cookie (1989, Warner Brothers) d: Susan Seidelman; cameo

Mr. Saturday Night (1992, Columbia) d: Billy Crystal; cameo

Arizona Dreams (1995, Warner Brothers) d: Emir Kusturica; with Johnny Depp, Faye Dunaway, Lili Taylor

Funny Bones (1995, Hollywood) d: Peter Chelsum; with Oliver Platt, Lee Evans, Leslie Caron

As Director Only

One More Time (1970, United Artists) with Peter Lawford, Sammy Davis Jr., Maggie Wright, John Wood

Boy (1990, C91 Communications), short, with Isaac Lidsky

A Note on Sources

In trying to account for the seven decades of Jerry Lewis's life—public and private—I relied as frequently on the work of other writers as I did on original research. In a very real sense, this book would have been impossible to write were it not for the writing that went before it. The following citations should be taken as the most cursory of acknowledgments of my deep debts to my journalistic predecessors and peers.

Libraries and Archives

Four libraries provided materials that were absolutely essential to my work.

The Cinema-Television Library at the University of Southern California is home to the papers of Jerry Lewis Productions, a vast collection presided over by the genial and resourceful Ned Comstock, who also directed me toward valuable materials in the Hal Humphrey Collection that I would not have otherwise found.

The Margaret Herrick Library of the Academy of Motion Picture Arts and Sciences houses the Hal Wallis papers, a Sargasso Sea of documents I never could have navigated without the selfless help of Sam Gill and Howard Prouty. Additionally, I availed myself of the library's excellent clippings files, its defensive sets of periodicals, and diverse materials from the Hedda Hopper collection.

The New York Public Library for the Performing Arts is home to the most astoundingly complete collection of clippings, photos, and publicity materials I've ever seen. I literally gave myself cramps transcribing all the crucial information I gathered there.

And if it weren't for the equally amazing resources of the Museum of Television and Radio in New York, I would have written this book without the benefit of having seen some truly crucial performances and occasions.

Additionally, I depended upon the resources of some less specialized libraries. I'd especially like to mention the Irvington Public Library in New Jersey; the Millar Library at Portland State University; the Multnomah County Library, the Washington County Library, and the Astoria Public Library, all in Oregon; and the library at the University of California, Irvine. Powell's City of Books in Portland might not be a library, but it's bigger than many, and it's bailed me out of more than one jam.

Books

Three books proved invaluable for obvious reasons: *The Total Film-Maker* (Random House, 1971) and *Jerry Lewis in Person* (Atheneum, 1982), both by Jerry himself, and *I Laffed Till I Cried: Thirty-Six Years of Marriage to Jerry Lewis* (WRS Publishing, 1993) by Patti Lewis.

I repeatedly consulted the troika of earlier Jerry Lewis biographies: *That Kid* (Avon, 1964) by Richard Gehman, *Everybody Loves Somebody Sometime (Especially Himself)* (Hawthorn, 1973) by Arthur Marx, and, from among several French books, *Bonjour, Monsieur Lewis* (Eric Losfeld, 1972) by Robert Benayoun.

Two books stood out as being especially useful for specific periods of Jerry's life: *Pieces of Time: Peter Bogdanovich on the Movies* (Arbor House, 1973) and the magnificent *Dino: Living High in the Dirty Business of Dreams* (Doubleday, 1992) by Nick Tosches, without reference to which no one can say a sensible word about Dean Martin. A lengthy and sensitive interview with Patti Lewis appears in *Are You Anybody? Conversations with Wives of Celebrities* (Dial Press, 1979) by Marilyn Funt. I learned almost everything I know about Abbey Greshler from *The Deal Makers: The Men Who Took Over Hollywood,* an unpublished manuscript by Mark Christensen and Cameron Stauth.

Another set of books contained briefer but equally important passages on Jerry's life or work. These include *More Funny People* (Stein and Day, 1982) by Steve Allen; *Has Corinne Been a Good Girl?* (St. Martin's Press, 1983) by Corinne Calvet; *Cavett* (Harcourt Brace Jovanovich, 1974) by Dick Cavett and Christopher Porterfield; *American Directors,* Volume II (McGraw-Hill, 1983) by Jean-Pierre Coursodon with Pierre Sauvage; *The Early Film Criticism of Francois Truffaut* (Indiana University Press, 1993) by Wheeler Winston Dixon; *My Story* (Grove Press, 1977) by Judith Exner with Ovid Demaris; *Vulgar Modernism: Writing on Movies and Other Media* (Temple University Press, 1991) by J. Hoberman; *Martin Scorsese: A Journey* (Thunder's Mouth Press, 1991) by Mary Pat Kelly; *There Really Was a Hollywood* (Doubleday, 1984) by Janet Leigh; *Boxed In* (third edition, Northwestern University Press, 1989) by Mark Crispin Miller; *The Jerry Lewis Films* (McFarland, 1995) by James L. Neibaur and Ted Okuda; *Heartland* (Harcourt Brace Jovanovich, 1976) by Mort Sahl; *The American Cinema: Directors and Directions, 1929–1968* (E. P. Dutton & Company, 1968) by Andrew Sarris; *Comedian Comedy: A Tradition in Hollywood Film* (UMI Research Press, 1981) by Steve Seidman; *The Cinematic Body* (University of Minnesota Press, 1993) by Steven Shaviro; *The Palace* (Atheneum, 1969) by Marian Spitzer; *Scorsese on Scorsese* (Faber and Faber, 1989), edited by David Thompson and Ian Christie; *World Film Directors, Volume II (1945–1985)* (H. W. Wilson & Company, 1988), edited by John Wakeman; *Starmaker* (Macmillan, 1980) by Hal Wallis with Charles Higham; *The Great Comedians Talk About Comedy* (Citadel, 1968) by Larry Wilde; and *The Show Business Nobody Knows* (Cowles Book Company, 1971) by Earl Wilson.

From another set of books, I gleaned a great deal of information about the cultural background of Jerry's life and art. They include *American Humor in France* (Iowa State University Press, 1978) by James C. Austin; *What's the Joke?: A Study of Jewish Humor Through the Ages* (Weidenfeld and Nicolson, 1986) by Chaim

Bermant; *Farce: A History from Aristophenes to Woody Allen* (Simon and Schuster, 1982) by Albert Bermel; *A Thousand Sundays: The Story of the Ed Sullivan Show* (Putnum, 1980) by Jerry Bowles; *A Clinician's View of Neuromuscular Diseases* (Williams and Wilkins, 1977) by Michael H. Brooke, M.D.; *The Crazy Mirror: Hollywood Comedy and the American Image* (Horizon Press, 1969) by Raymond Durgnat; *Jolson: The Legend Come to Life* (Oxford University Press, 1988) by Herbert G. Goldman; *World of Our Fathers* (Harcourt Brace Jovanovich, 1976) by Irving Howe; *What Made Pistachio Nuts? Early Sound Comedy and the Vaudeville Aesthetic* (Columbia University Press, 1992) by Henry Jenkins; *A Summer World: The Attempt to Build a Jewish Eden in the Catskills. . . .* (Farrar, Straus & Giroux, 1989) by Stefan Kanfer; *Give! Who Gets Your Charity Dollar?* (Doubleday, 1974) by Harvey Katz; *The Charity Racket* (Thomas Nelson, Inc., 1977) by Robert A. Liston; *The Comic Mind: Comedy and the Movies* (second edition, University of Chicago Press, 1979) by Gerald Mast; *The Joys of Yiddish* (Pocket, 1968) by Leo Rosten; and *The American Burlesque Show* (Hawthorn, 1967) by Irving Zeidman.

Finally, from among the literally dozens of film, television, popular music, and show-business reference works I consulted, these half-dozen essentials: *The Paramount Story* (Crown, 1985) by John Douglas Eames; *The Film Encyclopedia* (all-new edition, Harper Perennial, 1994) by Ephraim Katz; *Leonard Maltin's Movie and Video Guide, 1994* (Signet, 1994), edited by Leonard Maltin; *Motion Picture Players' Credits: Worldwide Performers of 1967 Through 1980 with Filmographies. . . .* (McFarland and Company, 1991) by Jeffrey Oliviero; *A Biographical Dictionary of Film* (second edition, William Morrow & Co., 1981) by David Thompson; and *Halliwell's Film Guide* (eighth edition, Harper Collins, 1991) edited by John Walker.

Articles

If I relied upon hundreds of books in researching this book, I used literally thousands of articles. Many of these were used strictly to confirm minute—but vital—details. Others gave more general, but equally valuable insights into the way in which Jerry was perceived by his public at various stages of his career. Still others were useful simply because they gave me a feeling of confidence in summing up such a busy man's life.

I have chosen to cite the following articles as especially useful because I found myself compelled to turn to them again and again while thinking and writing about Jerry's life and work. They tend to be long and wide-reaching, and they stand, in my mind, as true milestones in Jerry's lifelong love-hate relationship with the press.

By citing these articles alone, I don't mean to slight the authors of the great many others that I found invaluable. Film reviews, spot news reports, uncredited items from Associated Press, United Press International, *Variety,* and *The Hollywood Reporter,* obituaries, opinion columns, even passing mentions in articles about other subjects were crucial to shaping my understanding of Jerry Lewis. To the writers of those stories, my thanks; I literally could not have done it without you.

Alpert, Hollis, "'Le Roi du Crazy,'" *The New York Times Magazine,* February 27, 1966.

Alpert, Hollis, "Dialogue on Film," *American Film,* September 1977.

Angeli, Michael, "God's Biggest Goof," *Esquire,* February 1991.

Bennetts, Leslie, "Jerry Vs. the Kids," *Vanity Fair,* September 1993.

Bogdanovich, Peter, "Sinatra and Company," *Esquire,* February 1977.

Davidson, Bill (with Jerry Lewis), "I've Always Been Scared," *Look,* February 5, 1957.

Delson, James, "Penthouse Interview: Jerry Lewis," *Penthouse,* May 1984.

Driscoll, O'Connell, "Jerry Lewis, Birthday Boy," *Playboy,* January 1974.

Gehman, Richard, "The Zany Thinker," *The American Weekly,* May 20, 1962.

Handy, Bruce, "Jerry Goes to Death Camp!" *Spy,* May 1992.

Higham, Charles, "Jerry Isn't Just Clowning Around Now," *The New York Times,* July 30, 1972.

Hirschberg, Lynn, "What's So Funny About Jerry Lewis?" *Rolling Stone,* October 28, 1982.

Jahr, Cliff, "Hellzafloppin: Is This the End of Jerry Lewis?" *New York,* February 7, 1977.

Jackson, Nancy Beth, "Jerry Lewis Tries a Comeback Film," *The New York Times,* April 29, 1979.

Jerome, Jim (with Doris Klein Bacon), "After Open-Heart Surgery, King of Comedy Jerry Lewis Bounces Back with a Bride-to-Be," *People,* February 7, 1983.

Krutnik, Frank, "Jerry Lewis: The Deformation of the Comic," *Film Quarterly,* Fall 1994.

Linn, Edward, "The Search for Jerry Lewis," *The Saturday Evening Post,* October 12, 1963.

Madsen, Axel, "America's Uncle," *Cahiers du Cinema* #4 (U.S.), 1968.

McGilligan, Patrick, "Recycling Jerry Lewis," *American Film,* September 1979.

Peploe, Mark, and Hercules Bellville, "Comedy Is a Man in Trouble," *Sunday Times* (London), November 16, 1969.

Rader, Dotson, "And Sometimes He Cries," *Parade,* April 22, 1984.

Rutt, Todd, "Duke Mitchell and Sammy Petrillo: Those Two Fireballs of Fun," *Psychotronic Film and Video,* Fall 1991.

Shindler, Merrill, "Jerry's Revenge," *Los Angeles,* August 1980.

Shearer, Harry, "Telethon," *Film Comment,* May/June 1979.

Taves, Isabella, "Always in a Crowd—Always Alone," *Look,* December 23, 1958.

Tolkin, Michael, "Jerry Lewis Is a 50-Year-Old Kid," *The Village Voice,* September 27, 1976.

Williams, Brian, and Neal Hitchens, "Jerry Lewis Beat and Viciously Whipped His Kids," *National Enquirer,* May 9, 1989.

Acknowledgments

So many people were so inordinately kind to me as I set about writing this book that I don't quite know by what right I can call the finished product mine. Again and again I was amazed as people opened their homes, hearts, attics, and libraries to a total stranger on a curious mission. I can't thank them enough for their generosity. So much of what is best about this book came from them; judgment for what I did with it falls on me alone.

For reminisces, materials, referrals, and other invaluable resources, I'm grateful to Robert Benayoun, Leslie Bennetts, Sandra Bernhard, Peter Bogdanovich, Judy Cannon, Tim Casebeer, Dick Cavett, Leon Charash, Peter Chelsum, Fran Cohen, Ann Colgrove, Richard Connolly, Judy Englander, David Fantle, Larry Fine, Russell Fornwalt, Kathleen Freeman, Brian Gari, Jody Geiger, Eydie Gorme, Richard Grudens, Olga Hill, Florence Horn, Stan Horton, James Jacobs, Lee Jecman, Bob Kay, Evan Kemp, Julius La Rosa, Steve Lawrence, Norman Lear, Janet Leigh, Marlena Libman, Alan Lowenstein, Ed Margulies, Ben Mattlin, Jan Murray, Roger Paulson, Dale Pearce, Diane Piastro, Alison Poole, Tom Ranieri, Teresa Redburn, Sister Rose William of the Daughters of St. Paul, Jonathan Rosenbaum, Andrew Sarris, Ron Schenkenberger, Lawrence Shapiro, Ed Simmons, Irv Slikovsky, Lee Smith, Timothy Springfield, Ada Tesar, Scott Townsend, Ben Urish, Hilde Waring, Art Zigouras, the editors of *The New York Times Book Review* for printing my Author's Query, and the residents of 396 Union Avenue in Irvington, New Jersey, for not dismissing me as nuts when I showed up asking questions.

Among these many benefactors, Jeff Abraham, Dale Bonifant, and Barbara Sender stand out as being exceedingly generous with materials that turned out to be vital to my work—and exceedingly patient in waiting for their return. And without Marshall Katz and his memories and photos, this book would be infinitely poorer.

In Newark, Paul Carvelli greased the wheels of bureaucracy and uncovered an essential document. In Paris, Catherine Hoffman and Bertrand Lorel assembled an authoritative collection of clippings and statistics. Doug Holm turned up a trove of goodies and read an unwieldy manuscript with a canny—and foster—eye. Julia Wotipka, who blithely said, "Call me if you need anything," and never dreamed I would do just that, was an awesome research machine. Lenny Popky, Paul Harris, and Gabrielle Schwab provided beds, meals, and camaraderie.

Early in my writing career, I was encouraged—and, more important, hired—by Bill Krohn, Harley Lond, and Wolf Schneider, and I hope they find in this book some of the promise they were so kind to think they saw in me back then. Similar thanks go to Cameron Stauth, who served as father confessor to this project from the get-go.

Several editors kept me working and eating during the years I put this book together. I'd especially like to thank Richard Jameson of *Film Comment*, David Higdon of *Rip City*, Suzanne Mikesell and Babs Baker of *Pulse!*, Bill Redden of *PDXS*, Constance Rosenbloom of *The New York Times*, and Mark Wiggington of *The Oregonian*. Thanks as well to Bill Flood of the School of Extended Studies at Portland State University. As for Karen Brooks of *The Oregonian*, no freelancer could imagine a more supportive or collegial friend.

Ruth Nathan, who took a chance on an unknown, was instrumental in finding this book a home, as was Bill Thomas, the first person to get it. Alan Borrud expertly reproduced many of the photos, Larry Hamberlin kept me from going out in the world with prepositions stuck between my teeth, and Paul Sleven helped keep me in legal check. And Chris Koseluk is the best damn photo researcher in the world.

Without Cal Morgan—friend, coach, and editor par excellence—this book might be an uncollected pile of musings, jottings, and Xeroxed pages. It's almost as much his as mine.

To Paul Bartholemy and Lucretia Thornton, I'm inexpressably grateful for shelter, support, and love. No one could wish for more from his family.

Similarly, John and Theresa Carvelli, Dominic and Lucille Vecchiarelli, and Thomas Shand have been in my corner all along, as have been their children.

My sister, Jennifer Levy, is the most encouraging person I know, and I can only hope to someday return her enthusiasm for me and my work.

My mother, Mickie Levy, would have written the whole book for me if she could have. The very fact that I did it is the merest down payment on the lifetime of selflessness she's shown.

My father, Jerome Levy, taught me with unerring taste what was funny and with unfaltering humanity what was valuable. He didn't live to see this book finished, but that won't necessarily stop him from enjoying it.

The amazing brothers Vincent Bartholemy Levy and Anthony Augustine Levy provided intermittent peace and quiet and a constant reminder that no work is more important than the life that goes on around it.

And my debt to Mary Bartholemy—editor, partner, cook, nanny, analyst, booster, my irreplaceable you—cannot ever be erased.

Index